Armenia & Azerbaijan

John Noble

Michael Kohn, Danielle Systermans

RUSSIA

Mineralnye Vody

Pyatigorsk

SVANETI (p94)
Mysterious mountain enclave
with wonderful walks and
175 tall defensive towers

KAZBEGI (p100)
High Caucasus town surrounded
by magnificent mountains and the
iconic hilltop Tsminda Sameba Church

Mt Elbrus
(5642m) ▲

C A U C A S U S

Nalchik

Gagra

Gudauta

M1

ABKHAZIA

Sukhumi

Mt Shkara
(3200m) ▲

Mestia

Vladikavkaz

Mt Kazbek
(5047m) ▲

Tkvarcheli

SVANETI

Mamisoni
Pass

Kazbegi

Ochamchire

Jvari

Gali

IMERETI

Oni

RACHA

Barisakho

Zugdidi

M1

SAMEGRELO

Ambrolauri

SOUTH
OSSETIA

M3

PSHAVI

BLACK
SEA

Senaki

GEORGIA

Sachkhere

Tbilisi

Tskhinvali

BATUMI (p89)
The charming, fun-loving jewel of
Georgia's Black Sea holiday coast

Poti

Kutaisi

Tqibuli

Chiatura

Samtredia

Zestaponi

M1

Khashuri

Kareli

Gori

M1

Kaspi

Mtskheta

Kobuleti

M2

Ozurgeti

GURIA

Borjomi

M8

TBILISI

M9

ADJARA

Akhaltsikhe

Batumi

A306

Rustavi

Sarpi

Vale

SAMTSKHE-JAVAKHETI

M6

Marneuli

M4

Sarp

M11

Bolnisi

KVEMO
KARTLI

M7

Hopa

Posof

Akhalkalaki

Guguti

Krasny Most

Sadakhlo

Rize

TBILISI (p47)
The prettiest Caucasus city,
an age-old Eurasian melting
pot with a 21st-century attitude

Ardahan

Bavra

A306

Alaverdi

Tashir

Haghpat

Sanahin

Ijevan

SHIRAK

LORI

M24

**HAGHPAT & SANAHIN
MONASTERIES (p201)**
World Heritage–listed medieval
churches among the forests and
canyons of the lush Lori region

Gyumri

Vanadzor

Dilijan

ARMENIA

Kars

Mt Aragats
(4090m) ▲

Hrazdan

Sevan

KOTAYK

TURKEY

Talin

ARAGATSOTN

Ashtarak

Gavar

M1

YEREVAN

Erzurum

Armavir

Echmiadzin

ARARAT

ARMAVIR

Igdir

Ararat

Erzurum

Ağrı

Mt Ararat
(5165m) ▲

Sadarak

YEREVAN (p145)
Cafés, concerts, museums, galleries
and late-living nightlife, with
Noah's Mt Ararat as a backdrop

Doğubayazıt

Bazargan

DILIJAN (p190)
Mountain town with gingerbread
houses and great hikes to hidden
monasteries, Goshavank and Haghartsin

ELEVATION

3000m
2500m
1500m
1000m
500m
0
Below Sea
Level

Qareh
Ziyā Eddin

Tatvan

Lake Van

Van

Khoy

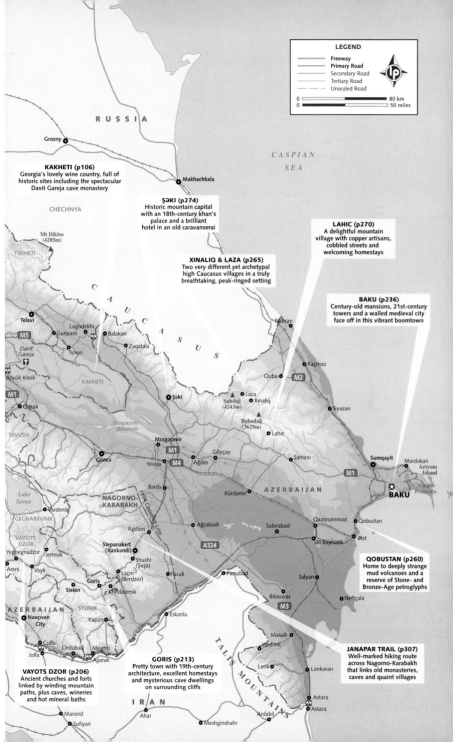

LEGEND

Freeway
Primary Road
Secondary Road
Tertiary Road
Unsealed Road

0 _____ 80 km
0 _____ 50 miles

KAKHETI (p106)
Georgia's lovely wine country, full of historic sites including the spectacular Davit Gareja cave monastery

ŞƏKI (p274)
Historic mountain capital with an 18th-century khan's palace and a brilliant hotel in an old caravanserai

LAHIC (p270)
A delightful mountain village with copper artisans, cobbled streets and welcoming homestays

XINALIQ & LAZA (p265)
Two very different yet archetypal high Caucasus villages in a truly breathtaking, peak-ringed setting

BAKU (p236)
Century-old mansions, 21st-century towers and a walled medieval city face off in this vibrant boomtown

QOBUSTAN (p260)
Home to deeply strange mud volcanoes and a reserve of Stone- and Bronze-Age petroglyphs

JANAPAR TRAIL (p307)
Well-marked hiking route across Nagorno-Karabakh that links old monasteries, caves and quaint villages

GORIS (p213)
Pretty town with 19th-century architecture, excellent homestays and mysterious cave dwellings on surrounding cliffs

VAYOTS DZOR (p206)
Ancient churches and forts linked by winding mountain paths, plus caves, wineries and hot mineral baths

On the Road

JOHN NOBLE Coordinating Author
I never cease to be amazed at the skill, love and time that medieval stone carvers must have put into their work, and Georgia is an absolute wonderland for any lover of beautiful old architecture. This church doorway is at Ananuri.

DANIELLE SYSTERMANS An incredible wonder of Azerbaijan is its sheer variety of landscapes. On this day I'd hiked in the bucolic oak woods of Altı Agaç, found dozens of curious little fossils in the pink-striped Candycane Mountains, and now here I was staring out across Arizona-style badlands. All within 40km.

MICHAEL KOHN On this particular day, hitching through the Debed Canyon, I was picked up by an extended family that was transporting a convoy of cars to Yerevan from Tbilisi. After about 20 minutes of driving we stopped at a roadside *khoravats* joint and ordered up a feast of grilled meats and vegetables, plus vodka shots. Just another day on the road!

See full author bios p343

Georgia, Armenia & Azerbaijan Highlights

Snow-capped mountains and sunny seashores, buzzing cities and secluded villages, hospitable peoples and an incredible depth of history – there are a lot of attractions in Georgia, Armenia and Azerbaijan. We asked our authors, staff and travellers what they love most about the region. Share your highlights at www.lonelyplanet.com/bluelist.

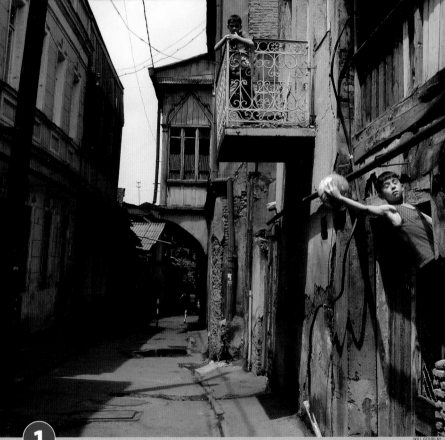

WILL GOURLAY

1 TBILISI'S ELEGANCE & BUSTLE

Tbilisi (p47) is fantastic to wander around. Off the main drag, the architecture of Tbilisi is reminiscent of Miss Havisham's manor in *Great Expectations*, all cracked plaster and creaking parquet floors. It was elegant once but the grounds staff have been away for a while! Rustavelis gamziri, on the other hand, is all bustle. A walk along here opens your eyes to the modern city while reminding you of the rich heritage the Georgians are so proud of.

Jess Birkett-Rees, Traveller, Australia

PAUL CARSTAIRS/ALAMY

PALACE OF THE SHIRVANSHAHS

One of my favourite books is *Ali and Nino*, so visiting the Palace of the Shirvanshahs (p244) was a highlight of my trip to Azerbaijan.

Marie-Claire Gaston, Traveller, Canada

3

MARK ELLIOTT

2

MT ARARAT FRAMING KHOR VIRAP

Khor Virap (p176) has very beautiful scenery, with Mt Ararat in the background. The view was amazing when I was there. It was a Sunday, and it was very crowded at the church. One goat and two chickens were sacrificed and everybody was happy. I walked around to the nearby cemetery, where the gravestones were so interesting.

Mario Kempf, Traveller, Germany

JOHN NOBLE

4

A CANINE WALKING COMPANION IN KAZBEGI

I did some fantastic day walks around Kazbegi (p102). Before I started my trip to the Caucasus, I read on the Lonely Planet Thorn Tree forum that there is a dog in Kazbegi that sometimes guides travellers to the top. I started to walk to Tsminda Sameba and this little dog came when I was walking through Gergeti. He sniffed me and wagged his tail, and from there on I had a friend. The dog ran ahead of me maybe 100m and then waited. When I reached him, he wagged his tail and then ran ahead and waited for me again. This was a very special experience.

Mario Kempf, Traveller, Germany

SIGHTS & SOUNDS OF YEREVAN

Yerevan (p145) has some beautiful parts and amazing architecture (if you're into Soviet patterns). From the opera to the history of its script, the city has a lot to offer. There's even a bar where you can hear mostly Metallica and Led Zeppelin!

Diana_dale, Bluelist Contributor

STEPHANE VICTOR

ROAD TRIPPING IN SVANETI

Waiting for the Svaneti (p94) marshrutka to get going. 'Twenty minutes,' said the driver, Guran (centre), at 8am. 'About an hour, no more,' he said encouragingly at 10am, when no other passengers had shown up. 'Half an hour,' he said at 12. By 2.45 the vehicle was packed to the gunwales with building materials and fizzy drinks, and we rumbled off. First stop, picking up a consignment of floor tiles. Second stop, lunch: *kubdari* and vodka, three rounds of it, with toasts. Every time we halted on the long, bumpy road, more vodka, toasts and snacks. No way was I permitted to refuse a shot, or to pay for anything. We rolled into Mestia well after dark and Guran dropped me at the door of my homestay (whose owner was Guran's cousin, of course). And his driving was impeccable the whole way.

John Noble, Lonely Planet Author, Spain

JOHN NOBLE

ROBERT HARDING PICTURE LIBRARY LTD/ALAMY

7 HIKE FROM GARNI TO HAVUTS TAR MONASTERY

Garni (p169), the Armenian Acropolis, lies on a high cliffy promontory. In addition to the views and the scenery, the wildlife alone is worth it: I saw my first dung beetles and some rather large-ish spiders. Okay, so 'wildlife' is a stretch. You can, at your own risk, try to make it to Geghard Monastery. We lost the trail and ended up in a friendly village instead.

Pcperrinjan, Bluelist Contributor

JOHN NOBLE

8 THE VIEW FROM JVARI

Jvari (p72) is really special, for the classic early Christian Georgian architecture, its central place in Georgian spirituality, the views overlooking the confluence of the Mtkvari and Aragvi Rivers and along the steep river valleys, and the perspective it provides on the ancient capital of Mtskheta, below, and the modern capital of Tbilisi, away beside the Mtkvari to the south. This place gives a real impression of the strategic significance of Mtskheta, positioned between the Caucasus foothills to the north and the open flood plains to the south.

Jess Birkett-Rees, Traveller, Australia

AN ARMENIAN WELCOME

The hospitality in Armenia was just as I had been told it would be: spontaneous and genuine. In Haghpat (p201) I got into a conversation about Sayat Nova with two young guys and it was all I could do to fend off their invitations for dinner. Later, in the market in Vanadzor (p195), a toothless old man bustled out from behind his market stall to present me with three apples then wave me on my way.

Will Gourlay, Lonely Planet Staff Member, UK

9

WILL GOURLAY

STUNNING, YET OBSCURE: BAKU

One of the most obscure yet stunning cities in the world, Baku (p236) was the backdrop for some scenes in the James Bond oil-terrorism-fest, *The World Is Not Enough*.

Fwoggie, Bluelist Contributor

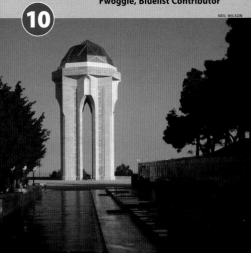

10

NEIL WILSON

11

THE CASPIAN SEASHORE

The Caspian Sea (p258) is strange and compelling: the combination of completely blue skies, heat, opal water and rusting industry are like something out of this world.

John Melzak, Traveller, USA

NEIL WILSON

DAY-TRIPPING TO QOBUSTAN

The trip to Qobustan (p260) was very nice: first along the sea and then to the mud volcanoes, with their views of the Caspian Sea. The semidesert scenery with the smaller mountains was also beautiful. The rock paintings in Qobustan were interesting, although I liked the scenery more. The museum here was small, but made with love – it's worth a visit.

Mario Kempf, Traveller, Germany

NEIL WILSON

12

NIKOLAI IGNATIEV/ALAMY

13 **A GOOD SCRUB**

The bathhouse (p53) I went to in Tbilisi was a genuine local place, full of old men who went there every day. Spending a couple of hours soaking in the hot water with a bunch of naked, toothless and bald yet hairy old guys was the ultimate way to remove traveller grime.

Simon Davis, Traveller, Indonesia

TONY WHEELER

14 **REMOTE OMALO**

'You don't have to make your presentation until tomorrow afternoon,' pointed out the tourism minister at the Tbilisi conference. 'We'll borrow a helicopter from the air force and have a look around the country tomorrow morning.' Well yes, exactly what I was hoping to do! So, soon after breakfast, we dropped in to Upper Omalo (p105), a beautifully remote mountain village dominated by five solid stone watchtowers. It's a prime target for hikers in the country's stunning mountains.

Tony Wheeler, Lonely Planet Founder, Australia

ROCKY MOUNTAIN HIGHS AT AMBERD

If you like to throw rocks and see them tumble for thousands of feet down steep slopes, Amberd (p174) is the place for you. If you don't like heights, this is not for you. Heights galore and rocks galore. Make sure you walk past the fortress to see the foundations of a small medieval town.

Pcperrinjan, Bluelist Contributor

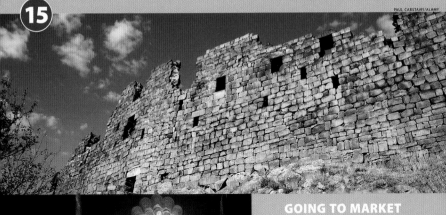

PAUL CARSTAIRS/ALAMY

15

KIM KARPELES/ALAMY

16

ECHOES IN GEGHARD

The *khatchkar*s and churches in Geghard (p169) were really fantastic and we could hear our voices echo through the halls of the cave monastery.

Gianfranco Vicente, Traveller, Italy

GOING TO MARKET IN ŞƏKI

The market at Şəki (p274) is the best in the Caucasus.

Gungajim, Bluelist Contributor

SYLVIA CORDALY PHOTO LIBRARY LTD/ALAMY

17

NORAVANK

Noravank (New Monastery, p207) consists of two buildings in a valley of red caves, some of which are converted into bars and cafés! Both churches have beautiful carvings and graves, and one of them is Armenia's only two-level church.

Diana_dale, Bluelist Contributor

18

MOTHS TO THE FLAME

The Ateşgah Fire Temple (p258) is a must for those with an imagination and an appreciation of history. At first glance it's nothing special but take the time to wander around and read the Sanskrit carvings – it's not hard to feel the ghosts of people who travelled from half a world away to worship the fire that sprung naturally from the earth.

Simon Davis, Traveller, Indonesia

19

20 ANANURI

This 17th-century fortress (p98) is just 45km from Tbilisi. With turrets, towers, huge fortified walls and two fine churches, it's a great site to explore. Georgian early Christian churches typically have simple interiors, adorned with clusters of candles and icons of the saints. At Ananuri you can view original frescoes and visit the graves of Georgian dukes.

Jess Birkett-Rees, Traveller, Australia

Contents

Regional Map Contents

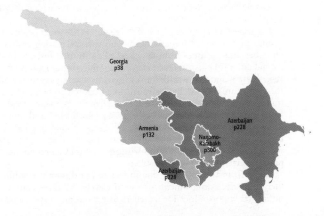

Destination Georgia, Armenia & Azerbaijan

Sitting at one of the earth's great crossroads, Georgia, Armenia and Azerbaijan occupy a mountainous zone on the southern flank of the mighty Caucasus mountains. Here two continents meet between two seas and many worlds commingle at a frontier between Islam and Christendom – all under the watchful gaze of three bigger, much more powerful neighbours: Russia, Turkey and Iran.

Such has been the to and fro of empires and conquerors across these lands – from Roman legions to Mongol hordes, the Red Army to the Ottoman Turks – that it's a wonder they exist as independent nations. Indeed, for much of their past they didn't, and when they did, they often had very different borders from the ones they have now. But through all their tribulations their peoples have forged very different, and proud, identities. All three countries share a recent past as republics of the Soviet Union. Today, while their fates remain as intermingled as ever, post-post-Soviet Georgia, Armenia and Azerbaijan present three distinct faces to the world.

Islamic Azerbaijan, now ruled by Ilham Əliyev (son of its long-time president Heydar Əliyev), is riding the crest of an oil boom. But while skyscrapers sprout in its Caspian-side capital, Baku, life goes on much as before in the timeless villages of the Caucasus mountains. Armenia and Georgia are the two oldest Christian nations on earth. Today Armenia is dubbed the Caucasian Tiger for its economic growth rates, and manages to remain friendly with Russia, the USA and Iran all at the same time. It is however at loggerheads with neighbouring Turkey over the almost-intractable WWI genocide issue. This has some farcical results, such as when trucks carrying goods between the two countries have to travel a very long way round through Georgia because the Armenia–Turkey border is closed. Georgia got a later start in the economic recovery business but is now making strides; its problem is its fraught relations with giant northern neighbour Russia. And while Georgia rubs along fine with Armenia and Azerbaijan, the latter pair are tensely stalemated over Nagorno-Karabakh, a now de facto–independent area of Azerbaijan for which they fought a very bitter war in the 1990s.

'These are three of the most welcoming and hospitable peoples in the world'

For travellers a profound joy of the region is the sheer beauty of its gorgeous, untrammelled scenery, decorated with fascinating castles, palaces, churches and mosques from an extraordinarily rich history. In the three capital cities – Tbilisi, Yerevan and Baku – the contradictions of economic rebirth are plain: vast wealth for some coexists with poverty for others. All three cities are very old, but leafy, balconied, church-strewn Tbilisi is the one that most retains the atmosphere of an ancient Eurasian crossroads. Yerevan is the most relaxed and arguably the most sophisticated, and competes with Baku for the title of most expensive. All three abound in good accommodation, food, shops, cafés and entertainment, and they are the places that will feel most familiar to Western visitors – yet they all retain their strange, part-Eastern, part-Soviet atmosphere.

Away from the big cities, life moves to the different rhythm of rural life, the perfect complement for varied travels. All three countries afford unlimited opportunities for travellers to get out amid spectacular nature, from the snowy Caucasus to the verdant valleys of Armenia or semi-tropical southern Azerbaijan. Modern tourism is still in its infancy in all three countries, but is more developed in Armenia and Georgia. Travel in Azerbaijan is definitely more challenging (though no less rewarding). But you don't have to scratch far beneath the skin of any of the three countries to find one thing they all have in common. These are three of the most welcoming and hospitable peoples in the world – something you'll probably remember longer than anything else from your travels here.

Getting Started

The Georgian, Armenian and Azeri languages are largely unfamiliar to the wider world, so preparing with a few key phrases in the local language or in Russian pays off quickly. Locals will love you if you come out with a couple of phrases in their own tongue, and failing that they'll be happy if they can communicate with you in a bit of Russian. Many professionals in the tourism business speak some English or German, but your average citizen doesn't.

Medical care in the Caucasus countries is pretty basic, so get decent insurance and, of course, be in good health when you set off. The most common form of public transport is marshrutkas (minivans), with limited room for luggage, so you'll thank yourself for packing light.

Most Western passport-holders don't need visas for Georgia (Australians and New Zealanders being among the honourable exceptions), but everybody needs one for Armenia or Azerbaijan. You can obtain a visa at any Armenian entry point, most of Georgia's, and, for now at least, at Baku airport (see this book's country directories for details) but, if you prefer, you can get one from an embassy or online before you go.

Travellers entering Azerbaijan should note that the previous edition of this book was sometimes confiscated by Azerbaijan border officials. We hope these problems will not continue with the current edition, but it's worth noting that some travellers disguised their books or placed them in inconspicuous places in their luggage, to avoid losing them.

The first few days in the Caucasus are always the most disorienting; kick off by exploring one of the capitals, which have far more Western-style facilities than other places. These countries are a curious combination of the First World and the Third, with high levels of culture and education but economies still recovering from post-Soviet collapse. An ability to deal with the unexpected and plans going awry is very useful to bring with you!

WHEN TO GO

See the climate charts (p312) for more information.

Early summer (May, June) and autumn (September, October) are the most delightful seasons to travel in the Caucasus. Spring can arrive rather late in the high mountains of the greater Caucasus and Armenia, but May and June see meadows bursting with wildflowers. A slight drawback is that sudden downpours and cloudy days can beset April and May (the wettest months of the year) and even early June. July and August, when the biggest numbers of visitors make their way to the Caucasus countries, can be stinking hot for days on end in the capitals, but fortunately cooler mountain retreats are never far away. The summer holidays in July and August see seaside action on the Georgian coast, beach life on Lake Sevan, and picnickers fleeing for the mountains from Baku, but even then there's room for everybody.

September is ideal: warm, calm weather and harvests everywhere. Rich autumn colours cover the hornbeam forests of the mountains in October. Winter is wet and slushy in Tbilisi, cold and windy in Baku and downright icy up on the plateau in Yerevan. Many mountain villages become virtually dormant from November to April, with accommodation shutting up shop.

COSTS & MONEY

Budget travellers can get by on around US$40 a day for the basics of accommodation, food, transport and a few drinks and admission charges. If you have US$60 a day you'll be able to afford the occasional trip with a car and driver or a long-distance taxi, use the services of a guide or two, down a few

---

DON'T LEAVE HOME WITHOUT...

- A mobile phone to put local SIM cards into
- A towel
- A torch
- Sturdy shoes – for city pavements as well as mountain trails
- A rainproof jacket
- In summer, your favourite sunglasses and hat
- A long skirt and long-sleeved shirts for women; dark pants and a dark jacket or jumper for men (Caucasus people are pretty conservative dressers)
- Top-quality batteries for your camera, torch and any other gadget that needs them
- Some good reading material (p20)
- Comprehensive insurance
- Two debit or credit cards, one MasterCard and one Visa – some towns only serve one or the other
- Checking your government's travel information site (p313)
- A reserve of patience and flexibility
- Tolerance for smoke – local men chain-smoke with reckless abandon

---

slap-up meals and slumber the odd night in a comfortable hotel. With US$100 to US$150 a day you can enjoy those pleasures for most of your trip.

Accommodation is always the main expense, and like everything else it's at its most expensive in the three capital cities. A comfortable midrange double room costs between US$50 and US$150 in Tbilisi, but more like US$100 to US$150 in Yerevan, and anywhere from US$60 to US$200 in Baku. Budget lodgings are offered by assorted homestays, hostels and cheap hotels, costing between US$5 and US$30 per person. Outside the capitals US$35 to US$70 gets you a double room in a decent hotel, and village homestays and B&Bs rarely charge more than US$25 per person, even with meals included.

Eating is deliciously inexpensive. You might pay US$20 for a big dinner in some of the fancier restaurants in the capitals, but you'd be hard pushed to break US$10 elsewhere and in cheap local eateries US$5 will easily buy dinner with a carafe of wine thrown in.

Public transport is cheap indeed. Travelling from one end of a country to the other costs around US$15 on marshrutkas, which are the quickest, most frequent (and most crowded) option. Buses and trains are generally cheaper but also slower. It's a common practice among locals and visitors – and surprisingly economical – to take a taxi for intercity trips. The three- to four-hour trip between Tbilisi and Kazbegi, for example, costs around US$40, which can be shared between three or four people. Some off-the-beaten-track spots can only be reached with the help of a 4WD vehicle and driver; costs can add up a bit here but are not prohibitive if shared with other travellers.

Bring your money in the form of credit and ATM cards with some cash US dollars or euros as a backup. There are ATMs in all towns but few villages. A credit card is also handy for splurging at one of the better hotels, and maybe buying a carpet, a beaten copper *plov* plate or a precious metal icon of St George in dragon-slaying mode. Dollars and euros can be exchanged in many smaller places as well as numerous money-changers in the cities and towns. Travellers cheques are a real hassle to change outside a few big city banks.

'If you stay in guest-houses or homestays, your cash is going directly to your host family'

Tipping isn't expected but given the low wages of waiters and staff it sure is appreciated. Something approaching 10% or a generous round-up applies in Western-style restaurants. At local restaurants the equivalent of US$1 or US$0.50 is usually plenty. With taxi drivers you should settle on a fee before setting off, and there's no need to top it up when you get out unless you feel like it.

Exchange rates are given inside the front cover of this book, but be aware that rates do fluctuate.

READING UP

The Caucasus has inspired brilliant creative and travel writing for two centuries. See Books in country directories for further recommendations.

'The Caucasus has inspired brilliant creative and travel writing for two centuries'

Adventures in the Caucasus Alexander Dumas travelled through the region in 1858, just as the Russians were subduing Imam Shamil's revolt, and wrote a colourful, amusing account of his journeys.

Ali and Nino Kurban Said's wonderful story of a love affair between an Azeri Muslim and a Georgian Christian a century ago, full of the atmosphere of oil-boom Baku and fascinating in its observations of the Europe-Asia dichotomy.

Azerbaijan Diary and **Georgia Diary** Reporter Thomas Goltz conveys the bizarre atmosphere of the post-Soviet period in these two countries, with some very shrewd political analysis.

Black Garden: Armenia and Azerbaijan through Peace and War Thomas De Waal, a long-time journalist covering the former USSR, gives a highly detailed, rather dry account of the brutal Karabakh war, which ruined Armenia and Azerbaijan in the early 1990s.

Bread and Ashes Tony Davidson walks the Caucasus from Azerbaijan to Georgia, and explores countless fascinating cultural and historical angles along the way.

The Crossing Place: A Journey among the Armenians A stunning evocation of the 20th-century Armenian catastrophe and survival by Philip Marsden.

A Hero of Our Time Mikhail Lermontov's 1840 masterpiece about a bored, cynical Russian officer in the Caucasus was the first, and shortest, great Russian novel. An indirect comment on the stifling climate of the times, it's also strangely relevant today.

The New Great Game: Blood and Oil in Central Asia Lutz Kleveman details the Machiavellian power plays between the US, Russia, local barons and Big Oil in the Caspian Sea oil and gas bonanza.

INTERNET RESOURCES

Armeniapedia (www.armeniapedia.org) Encyclopedic resource on Armenia.

Azerbaijan International (www.azer.com) Great Azerbaijan cultural archive.

Central Asia-Caucasus Institute Analyst (www.cacianalyst.org) News and analysis of Caucasus and Central Asian issues.

Civil.ge (www.civil.ge) Comprehensive, even-handed source of Georgia news from disparate sources.

Eurasianet (www.eurasianet.org) News analysis and cultural features, with resource pages for each country.

Georgia Today (www.georgiatoday.ge) Bright, breezy English-language newspaper.

Lonely Planet (www.lonelyplanet.com) Country information, bookings and the Thorn Tree message board – one of the best Caucasus travel-information resources around.

Tour Armenia (www.tacentral.com) Good culture and tourist information site.

See country directories in this book for further recommended sites.

TRAVELLING SUSTAINABLY

Since our inception in 1973, Lonely Planet has encouraged our readers to tread lightly, travel responsibly and enjoy the serendipitous magic independent travel affords. International travel is growing at a jaw-dropping rate, and we still firmly believe in the benefits it can bring – but, as always, we encourage you to consider the impact your visit will have on both the global environment and the local economies, cultures and ecosystems.

The Caucasus countries present the strange contrast of a region that is fairly lightly populated (15 million people in an area almost the size of England and Scotland combined) and mostly fertile and verdant, yet scarred and scratched by the environmental insouciance of its Soviet past. Even though many smokestack industries have closed down, the region is still struggling with the legacy of chemical poisoning around the Azerbaijan town of Sumqayıt, pollution of the Caspian and Black Seas, untreated sewage running into rivers, and the incredible industrial wasteland that constitutes parts of Azerbaijan's Abşeron Peninsula. Ageing vehicles running on low-grade fuel make air quality in the three capitals pretty poor at times. Yet much of the environment remains pristine, with great expanses of forest and woodland and villages that subsist on mostly small-scale, low-tech agriculture (though they may be raiding the forests for firewood).

Getting There & Around

Most visitors inevitably fly into the region. With several borders closed, the only ways in by land are from Turkey to Georgia or the Azeri enclave of Naxçivan, and from Iran to Armenia and Azerbaijan. And the only way through these borders is by motor vehicle (unless you're on a bicycle). Once inside Georgia, Armenia or Azerbaijan, marshrutkas will whisk you quickly, if not very cleanly, almost anywhere you want to go for minimal cost. There are also some generally slower buses and reasonably widespread train networks, though these too are slow and not so frequent. Once you're based in a place for a few days, you can leave the internal-combustion engine behind and get out on your own feet or maybe horseback, or ride the metro systems in the capital cities.

'You'll be helping these countries' economies just by being there'

Tourism in the Caucasus Countries

Georgia and Armenia are working hard to promote tourism as an engine of economic revival (and Azerbaijan is just waking up to its potential). You'll be helping these countries' economies just by being there. Most development so far is refreshingly small-scale and locally owned. If you stay in guesthouses or homestays, your cash is going directly to your host family, while most of the region's midrange hotels belong to companies that are at most medium-sized. Such businesses have a way of spreading the tourism income out around their communities, by putting visitors in contact with local guides, drivers and the like. Most of the food you'll eat will be locally grown and quite likely organic, because that's how most food is in the Caucasus – grown in gardens or on small farms, and sold at local markets. Watch out for the meat of rare species like bears turning up as a treat at barbecues, though.

Tourism in these three countries today (distinct from Soviet-era organised group tourism) is such a young industry that the concept of ecotourism rarely extends beyond getting out and about in nature. But most of the travel companies and guides who lead people to the mountains, forests and villages have a deeply protective attitude toward their lands. Whether that will remain so if tourism really takes off is a moot point – there are already concerns about uncontrolled development at Georgia's ski resorts (with heliskiing from Gudauri and snowmobiling around Bakuriani raising specific worries), hunting tourism in Azerbaijan and Georgia, and off-road Jeep tours anywhere.

Bear in mind that, especially outside the cities, these are still traditional and mainly poor people, conservative in dress and often religious. You'll feel more comfortable if you dress modestly, and this is essential when visiting churches as well as mosques. If you want to visit a monastery or convent, respect the privacy and peace of the inhabitants.

The staggering hospitality offered so often in the Caucasus is hard to refuse but shouldn't be taken advantage of. If you stay overnight and wolf down a feast, it's thoughtful to give a gift in return (if your gift is money, present it tactfully to avoid causing offence).

'The staggering hospitality offered so often in the Caucasus is hard to refuse'

Sustainable-Tourism Programmes

Of the three countries, environmental awareness is most developed in Georgia, and some national parks there, such as Borjomi-Kharagauli (p118) and Kolkheti (p84) have set up genuine sustainable-tourism programmes to help spread the benefits of tourism around local communities. Similar projects are underway elsewhere in Georgia in Svaneti (p96) and the Vardzia area (p121).

Responsibletravel.com (www.responsibletravel.com) has listings of socially and environmentally sustainable holidays in the Caucasus countries. **WWF** (www .panda.org) is working to develop ecotourism in the Caucasus. Georgia's biological farming association, **Elkana** (www.elkana.org.ge), is starting a rural tourism programme with accommodation, food and activities at wineries and farms.

Itineraries
CLASSIC ROUTES

CITY TO CITY
Two to Three Weeks / Yerevan to Baku

The Armenian capital **Yerevan** (p145) is a laid-back mecca for café-goers and a hub of cultural activity, with the backdrop of legendary Mt Ararat. The core treasures of the ancient Armenian church are close by: **Khor Virap Monastery** (p176) sits beneath Ararat's snowy peaks; **Geghard Monastery** (p169) once protected the holy lance that pierced Christ's side; and **Echmiadzin** (p171) is the Armenian equivalent of the Vatican. **Tbilisi** (p47) is the most attractive city in the Caucasus, with tree-lined boulevards, charming old churches and the style of a city moving forward in the 21st century. Take excursions to the old Georgian capital **Mtskheta** (p70) and up to **Kazbegi** (p100) for a taste of Caucasus mountain majesty. En route to Baku, detour to the extraordinary cave monasteries of **Davit Gareja** (p113) and the mountain town of **Şəki** (p274), with its 18th-century khan's palace. Vibrant **Baku** (p236) combines the architecture of two oil booms – one 100 years ago and the other right now – with a medieval walled city at its core. From Baku, venture out to the raw, primordial landscape of petroglyphs and mud volcanoes at **Qobustan** (p260).

A trip centring on the three capitals, with their quality accommodation, restaurants and services, plus excursions to some of the cultural and natural wonders around them.

COAST TO COAST
One Month to Six Weeks / Batumi to Baku

Get a relaxed and easy introduction to the region at **Batumi** (p89), Georgia's fun-loving Black Sea resort. Head on to pretty **Kutaisi** (p77), with the beautiful Bagrati Cathedral and Gelati monastery, then experience the surreal side of Stalinism in the old dictator's home town, **Gori** (p73). Enjoy the quirky buzz of **Tbilisi** (p47), where Europe embraces Asia and the present coexists with the past, and take in the splendours of the nearby old Georgian capital, **Mtskheta** (p70). Veer south into mountainous Armenia, visiting the World Heritage monasteries of **Haghpat** (p201) and **Sanahin** (p201) en route to **Yerevan** (p145), packed with cafés, galleries and museums. From Yerevan take easy day trips to **Khor Virap Monastery** (p176), with its great view of Mt Ararat, and the rock-hewn **Geghard Monastery** (p169). Admire turquoise **Lake Sevan** (p177) and stay in forested **Dilijan** (p190).

Return to Tbilisi and venture up into the magnificent high Caucasus at **Kazbegi** (p100). Moving east, enjoy the amazing cave monasteries at **Davit Gareja** (p113) and the welcome of Georgia's wine-growing region, **Kakheti** (p106). Cross into beautiful northern Azerbaijan with its nut-tree forests, poppy-filled fields and mountain vistas. Old **Şəki** (p274), with its khan's palace, and **Lahıc** (p270), a unique Persian-speaking coppersmith village, are the best places to get an insight into provincial Azeri life. The landscape mutates into harsh semidesert as you approach **Baku** (p236) with its big-city boomtown buzz; explore the Old Town and enjoy the vibrant nightlife. Venture along the **Abşeron Peninsula** (p258), where unusual Islamo-animist beliefs, a fire temple and a collection of medieval fortress-towers await beneath a Mad Max facade of oil-industry degradation.

A trip from end to end of Trans-caucasia, visiting the three national capitals and most of the region's best-known sights.

ROADS LESS TRAVELLED

DISTANT MOUNTAINS, HIDDEN VALLEYS   Two Months

Deep in the south of Azerbaijan, Talysh is a region of spectacular scenery, remote villages and sleepy towns such as **Lerik** (p287), and **Lənkəran** (p285). Swing through Baku and to the carpet-weaving town of **Quba** (p263), then to **Laza** (p266) for the hike to the mountain-top village of **Xınalıq** (p265) and (if it's summer and you're fit) on over the 2915m Salavat Pass to **Vəndam** (p273), near Qəbələ. Continue to historic **Şəki** (p274) and either **İlisu** (p279) or **Zaqatala** (p279), both great bases for mountain walks. Crossing into Georgia you immediately come upon the remote **Lagodekhi Nature Reserve** (p115), with its beautiful woodlands and glacial lakes. Continue north to astonishingly beautiful **Tusheti** (p104; only accessible in summer). From Tbilisi, swing down to southern Armenia, with the ancient churches and forts of the **Yeghegis Valley** (p209), the stalactite-filled caves near **Areni** (p207), and **Tatev monastery** (p216) perched above the Vorotan Canyon. Venture into Nagorno-Karabakh, where the ruined Azeri ghost city of **Agdam** (p301) is possibly the most striking place in the Caucasus. **Gandzasar Monastery** (p306) is both a living religious centre and ravishingly beautiful. Head back to Georgia for the long ride to the region's ultimate mountain retreat – the remote valleys and stone towers of **Svaneti** (p94), at the feet of 5000m-plus giants like Ushba and Shkhara. **Mestia** (p96) makes a good base. The mountains of southern Georgia hold Queen Tamar's cave-monastery complex at **Vardzia** (p121), and a back door into Turkey via Posof.

A thorough exploration of some of the region's lesser-known but most intriguing corners, for people with a sense of adventure, more time than money, and some basic language skills. Accommodation outside the capital cities might not be up to Best Western standards, but local hospitality more than compensates.

TAILORED TRIPS

CASTLES, TOWERS, CHURCHES, MOSQUES & CAVES

Much of Transcaucasia's architectural heritage is set in impossibly beautiful locations. Start with Tbilisi's **Metekhi Church** (p55) and **Narikala Fortress** (p55), then move out to the old churches of **Mtskheta** (p70) and to the sublime **Tsminda Sameba Church** (p102). Enjoy Kutaisi's **Bagrati Cathedral** (p79) and **Gelati monastery** (p81) before you head up to the towers of **Svaneti** (p94). Don't miss the cave monasteries of **Vardzia** (p121) and **Davit Gareja** (p113).

Within a day trip of Yerevan are **Echmiadzin** (p171), with its 15th-century Mayr Tachar cathedral, and rock-hewn **Geghard Monastery** (p169). Magnificent

Amberd fortress (p174) sits on the slopes of Mt Aragats. Northern Armenia's Debed Canyon is home to the monasteries of **Haghpat** (p201) and **Sanahin** (p201). Down south there's masterly monastic architecture at **Noravank** (p207) and **Tatev** (p216). Nagorno-Karabakh too has monastic gems, at **Gandzasar** (p306) and **Dadivank** (p307).

Baku's **İçəri Şəhər** (p243) is home to both the 15th-century Palace of the Shirvanshahs and the 7th-century Maiden's Tower. The fire temple at **Suraxanı** (p258) is the only one of its type. The best historic mosque in Azerbaijan is the **Cümə Mosque** (p268) at Şamaxı, while the decorated **Mömina Xatun mausoleum** (p289) in Naxçıvan is Azerbaijan's most impressive tower.

TAKE A WALK

With its beautiful valleys and high, spectacular yet accessible mountains, the Caucasus is a walker's paradise.

The main mountain range provides much of the best country. The peaks, valleys, passes and glaciers of Georgia's **Svaneti** (p94) are the natural counterpart to the architectural drama of its ancient defensive towers. The **Kazbegi area** (p102) offers walks to glaciers and beautifully sited churches. **Tusheti** (p104) is a remote region of steep valleys, sharp black crags and dramatically perched villages. An exciting long trek (10 days to two weeks) connects Kazbegi to Tusheti via intriguing **Khevsureti** (p103).

In Azerbaijan the villages of **Xınalıq** (p265) and **Laza** (p266) are the top choices for hiking, including the trek from one to the other. The **Lahıc area** (p270) is lovely too.

Armenia, especially its hilly north, is particularly good for day hikes, through the valleys between **Haghartsin Monastery** (p192) and **Dilijan** (p190) or the mountain forests around **Goshavank Monastery** (p192), or in the **Yenokavan Canyon** (p194). Closer to Yerevan you can hike the country's highest mountain, **Mt Aragats** (p175), or explore the beautiful area around **Garni** (p169) or the Khosrov Nature Reserve (p176).

The best way of all to explore Nagorno-Karabakh is on the well-marked, 190km **Janapar Trail** (p307), which links old monasteries, caves and quaint villages.

Georgia's **Borjomi-Kharagauli National Park** (p118) and the **upper Mtkvari valley** (p121) near Vardzia cave monastery both have excellent networks of marked trails.

Snapshots

CURRENT EVENTS

The three Caucasus countries have staged a remarkable economic turn-around since the dark days of the 1990s. By 2006 they were posting some of the best economic growth rates in the world. The most spectacular numbers were those of Azerbaijan, with an astounding growth rate of 34%, thanks in large measure to the new Baku-Tbilisi-Ceyhan (BTC) pipeline, pumping Azerbaijan's Caspian oil to the Turkish Mediterranean port of Ceyhan. Even Georgia, the slowest off the mark in economic recovery, could claim a healthy 9% growth rate. Critics point out that the wealth is spread unevenly, that most of the new wealth in all three countries is controlled by a small number of 'oligarchs' and that little of it trickles down to the general populace (this is probably least true in Armenia). While the city centres and wealthy suburbs of Baku, Yerevan and Tbilisi are full of people in expensive clothes parking expensive cars outside expensive cafés, life has certainly improved a lot less in the working-class suburbs and the countryside, and for professionals in non-commercial fields like health and education. Still, the general direction is up, thanks in Armenia and Georgia to energetic free-market reforms which began in the late 1990s in Armenia but only after the 2003 Rose Revolution in Georgia.

Armenia receives over US$1 billion per year in remittances. Three fourths of that comes from Russia.

For many people outside the region, the only exposure they've had to Caucasus culture was Georgia's and Armenia's entries in the Eurovision Song Contest. But arts too are thriving here – Yerevan and Tbilisi boast very active theatre and gallery scenes, and both Baku and Tbilisi stage top-drawer annual jazz festivals.

Less promising is the story on corruption: Georgia, with its avowedly anticorruption government, was ranked only 79th out of 180 countries on the Corruption Perceptions Index of Transparency International in 2007. Armenia was 99th, and Azerbaijan came a dismal 150th (equal with Zimbabwe and the Congo Republic).

Armenia has made steady progress on democratic standards, and its 2007 parliamentary elections were judged largely fair by international observers. Rarely have impartial observers been moved to commend Azerbaijan's Əliyev dynasty for holding free and fair elections or encouraging free speech.

Georgia seems to have good democratic credentials, with a government that was carried to power by protests against the flawed elections of 2003. Yet President Mikheil Saakashvili's track record took a knock with the bizarre events of late 2007, beginning when opposition parties mounted exactly the same kind of Tbilisi street protests against poverty, corruption and authoritarianism that Saakashvili himself led against his predecessor, Eduard Shevardnadze. The protests were dispersed with some violence, and Saakashvili declared a temporary state of emergency, making it known he believed the protests were part of a coup attempt backed by Russia and the Georgian media magnate Badri Patarkatsishvili. Saakashvili then called a snap presidential election for January 2008, which he won, with international observers declaring the vote democratic despite some irregularities.

Attempted coup or not, relations with Russia were pro-Western Saakashvili's biggest ongoing problem. Spooked by Georgia's desire to join NATO and the EU, Russia has subjected its small neighbour to all manner of bullying including a boycott on imports of Georgian wine and mineral water from 2006.

Armenia meanwhile manages to pull off the incredible juggling feat of remaining on friendly terms with Russia, the USA and Iran all at once, and reaps the rewards in terms of investment and aid. It is however deeply at odds with Azerbaijan and Turkey over Nagorno-Karabakh and with Turkey over the WWI genocide issue, although there have been faint hopeful signs of the beginnings of a thaw in Armenian-Turkish relations.

Any solutions to the region's bitter territorial and ethnic quarrels – which caused so much loss of life in the 1990s and still leave hundreds of thousands of people refugees in their own lands – are still very far away. Georgia has ambitions of bringing South Ossetia back into the fold by negotiating with Ossetians who oppose separatist leader Eduard Kokoity and favour a federal status for South Ossetia within Georgia. But there is no inkling of rapprochement between Georgia and the breakaway region of Abkhazia, nor between Armenia and Azerbaijan in the bitter territorial dispute over Nagorno-Karabakh. At least there has been no serious fighting since 1994.

> Armenia has had recent success in raising the water levels of Lake Sevan. The level has gone up 2m since 2003.

HISTORY

This mountainous isthmus between the Black and Caspian Seas, today at the frontiers of Europe and Asia, Islam and Christendom, has been one of the great melting pots of history. Innumerable waves of conquerors and colonists washing into and over the region from all directions make its story one of the most complicated, and most fascinating, in the world – and have left one the world's trickiest ethnic jigsaws. The three Caucasus nations today are just the latest of scores of republics, kingdoms, principalities, emirates, khanates and satrapies that have blossomed and died here down the centuries.

It is essential to look beyond current national boundaries to gain an understanding of Caucasus history. Georgia first came together when a number of small principalities were united in the 11th century. By the 15th century, this united Georgian kingdom disintegrated and only began to reunify in the 18th century. The current Republic of Azerbaijan is less than half the size of historic Azerbaijan, the rest of which, with perhaps two-thirds of the Azeri people, lies in Iran. Modern Armenia is just a tiny part of ancient Armenia, which at one time held sway from the Caspian Sea to Lebanon. Over the centuries large parts of the region have been incorporated into Macedonian, Roman, Persian, Byzantine, Arab, Mongol, Ottoman, Russian and other empires. Georgians, Armenians and Azeris see themselves as inheritors of ancient national traditions and they look to the past to define themselves in the present. Such has been the ebb and flow of rulers and boundaries down the centuries that almost any territorial argument can be backed up by pointing to some period of history.

> Sergei Paradjanov's great 1968 film *The Colour of Pomegranates* recreates the world of Sayat-Nova, Erekle II's Armenian court poet, who died defending Tbilisi from the Persians.

Early Empires

Some aver that the history of the Caucasus region began in the unspecified time when Noah's Ark grounded on Mt Ararat (in modern day Turkey, just west of the border) in the biblical flood. What is known is that Stone Age tribes inhabited the region at least 100,000 years ago. The Caucasus' first significant influence on the outside world, many millennia later, may have been such basics of civilisation as astronomy and astral timekeeping, which some historians believe emerged from here rather than from Babylonia or Sumer, Iraq. Astronomical complexes at Zorats Karer and Metsamor in Armenia date from around 3000 BC. Perhaps 4000 years ago, the Aryans swept east from the region to create Vedic India, and it may have also been from the Caucasus that the founders of the Hittite empire reached Anatolia (central Turkey) around the same time.

Greeks, Persians and Romans brought the classical pagan faiths and philosophies to the Caucasus in the 1000 years before Christianity took hold, helping to create rich local cultures. The Greeks established colonies in Colchis (western Georgia) perhaps as early as the 8th century BC. The Armenians originated as a group of Anatolians (from central Turkey) who took over the decayed Urartu kingdom at Van in eastern Turkey in the 6th century BC. They were incorporated successively into the Persian Achaemenian Empire, the Macedonian Empire and the Seleucid Empire. When the Romans defeated the Seleucids in 189 BC, they allowed two former Seleucid satraps (provincial governors) to set up independent Armenian states. These were united by Tigranes the Great (r 95–55 BC), who built an empire 10 times the size of modern Armenia with its capital at Tigranakert, west of Lake Van.

To find out more about the Caucasus region's special ecological value, check www.biodiversity hotspots.org or www .panda.org/caucasus

Tigranes made the mistake of allying with Mithradates of Pontus (in northern Turkey) in opposition to Rome. General Pompey arrived in 66 BC to crush the resistance, and Rome took control of Armenia and Georgia. Armenia ended up as a buffer between the Romans and the Persians, who fought long wars for control of the region.

First Christian Kingdoms

The Armenian church records that two apostles visited their country and won followers in the decades after the death of Jesus. In 301 King Trdat III was converted to Christianity and Armenia became the first nation officially to embrace the religion. The eastern Georgian kingdom of Kartli (or Iveria), and the state of Albania in what's now Azerbaijan (no relation to Balkan Albania), followed suit within the next 30 years or so.

As the Christian Byzantine Empire expanded towards the east from Constantinople, western Armenia and western Georgia fell under its sway, while their eastern areas came under Persian control. But Armenia successfully resisted Persia's efforts to impose the Zoroastrian religion.

The Arrival of Islam

Muslim Arabs arrived in Azerbaijan in 642, set up an emirate in Tbilisi in 654 and gained control of Armenia in 661. Opposition to Muslim conversion saw many Armenians leave for Byzantine territory, the beginning of the vast Armenian diaspora which is now spread worldwide. In the 9th century the Arabs recognised a local prince of the Bagratid family, Ashot I, as king of Armenia, while another branch of the family had managed to install itself in the Tao-Klarjeti region, straddling the border of modern Georgia and Turkey. By the 11th century the latter branch controlled most of Georgia.

The Seljuk Turks, originating from Central Asia, brought death, plunder and destruction to much of the Caucasus region in the 11th and 12th centuries, but Georgian king Davit Aghmashenebeli (David the Builder, 1089–1125) managed to drive the Seljuks out of Georgia, establishing its medieval golden age. David's great-granddaughter Queen Tamar (1184–1213) controlled territory from western Azerbaijan to eastern Turkey, including many Armenian regions. The 12th century was also a time of material and cultural progress in Muslim Şirvan, as modern Azerbaijan was by then known.

The whole region was floored by the next great wave from the east, the Mongols, who invaded in the 1230s, soon followed by the Black Death and then in the late 14th century by another ruthless Asian conqueror, Timur (Tamerlane). The Şirvan khanate did manage to retain some autonomy and by the 15th century Baku was a prospering trade-route centre. In 1501 Şirvan was conquered by fellow Azeris from what's now northern Iran, who converted it from Sunni to Shia Islam.

The next pair to fight over the Caucasus region were the Persia-based Azeri Safavid dynasty and the Ottoman Turks, who had taken Constantinople and swept away the Byzantine Empire in 1453. Georgia came to be divided between the two in the 16th century; in 1514–16 the Ottomans took over all of Armenia – and kept most of it for nearly 400 years. After the Safavid collapse in 1722, a new Persian conqueror, Nader Shah, installed Bagratid princes in eastern Georgia.

Russia Arrives...& Stays

Peter the Great began the great Russian push south in the 1720s, capturing the Caspian coast as far as Baku before being pushed back by the Persians. The east Georgian king Erekle II accepted Christian Russian control at the Treaty of Georgievsk in 1783 in exchange for protection from his Muslim foes, and Russia went on to annex the Georgian princedoms one by one through the 19th century. Russia wrested the khanates then comprising modern Azerbaijan, as well as Yerevan and Naxçıvan, from Persia in the early 19th century, and took the Batumi area (southwest Georgia) and Kars and Ardahan (northeast Turkey) from the Turks in the 1870s.

Winston Churchill had a taste for Armenian brandy, which Stalin obliged in some quantity.

Russia's involvement in the Caucasus opened up a whole new cultural frontier for it, as well as a territorial one. The region inspired much romantic art and writing about flashing spurs and mountain guerrillas, with Pushkin, Tolstoy, Lermontov and others bringing the Caucasus into Western literature. At the same time, incorporation into the tsarist empire introduced new dimensions to life in the Caucasus. Improved education brought with it new ideologies such as nationalism and socialism. The latter was encouraged by the oil boom at Baku in the late 19th century, where appalling working conditions reminiscent of the Californian and Australian goldfields coexisted with the wealth garnered by the investing classes.

A good half of historic Armenia and perhaps 2.5 million Armenians were left in the Ottoman Empire after the end of the Russo-Turkish War in the 1870s. Many Armenians emigrated to the Russian-held corner of their traditional homeland, but unrest among those who stayed led to a series of massacres of Armenians in the 1890s, and in 1915 the Young Turk government in Istanbul ordered the killing or deportation of virtually all the Armenian population within the Ottoman Empire. Deportation meant walking into the Syrian deserts. In all, well over a million are thought to have died.

Following the Russian Revolution, Transcaucasia declared itself a federation independent of Moscow on 22 April 1918, but national and religious differences saw it split quickly into three separate independent republics: Georgia, Armenia and Azerbaijan. A resurgent Turkish army under Mustafa Kemal pushed into the region, before the Red Army came south to reclaim it 1920–21; Turkey still managed to emerge with eastern and northeastern areas that had been in Armenia and Georgia.

Stalin's mother believed her son should have stayed at the seminary and become a priest.

Georgia, Armenia and Azerbaijan were thrown together in the Transcaucasian Soviet Federated Socialist Republic, one of the founding republics of the Soviet Union in 1922. Antinationalist repression, led by Georgian Bolsheviks Stalin, Beria and Ordzhonikidze, and the Great Terror of the 1930s saw hundreds of thousands of people from the region executed or banished to the Gulag. It was also Stalin, as Commissar for Nationalities, who placed Karabakh, with its mainly Armenian population, within Azerbaijan. The Transcaucasian Republic was split into separate Georgian, Armenian and Azerbaijani Republics in 1936.

The later Soviet period, after Stalin's death in 1953, was relatively calm, despite worsening corruption. Today this is looked back on with some nostalgia by many older people as a time of stability and jobs. But the wider

Soviet economy stagnated, and Mikhail Gorbachev's efforts to deal with this through *glasnost* (openness) and *perestroika* (restructuring) unlocked latent nationalist tensions that would tear both the Caucasus region and the whole Soviet Union apart.

Independence

The late 1980s saw violence and upheaval flare in the Caucasus. In 1988 Karabakh declared its wish for unification with Armenia, Armenians were massacred in the Azerbaijan town of Sumqayıt, violence spiralled in both republics, and the large numbers of Azeris in Armenia and Armenians in Azerbaijan started to flee. By 1990 Armenian and Azerbaijani militias were battling each other in and around Karabakh; Soviet troops had to fight their way into Baku to maintain Soviet control there. The Georgian independence movement became an unstoppable force after Soviet troops massacred 20 peaceful demonstrators in Tbilisi in April 1989. The Azeri region of Naxçıvan was actually the first part of the Soviet Union to declare independence (beating Lithuania by a few weeks) in January 1990, but soon rejoined Azerbaijan. Georgia, Armenia and Azerbaijan all declared independence in 1991, and the Soviet Union formally split into 15 different nations in December that year.

The Caucasus region was immediately plunged into savage internal strife. Independent Georgia's first president, Zviad Gamsakhurdia, was driven out in a civil war in 1991–92, and bloody fighting in South Ossetia (1991–92) and Abkhazia (1992–93) left both these regions effectively independent of Tbilisi. The entire 250,000 ethnic-Georgian population of Abkhazia was driven out. In Karabakh, several years of vicious fighting ended with a 1994 ceasefire and a victory for the Armenian and Karabakhtsi forces over the Azeri army. The war resulted in the loss of an estimated 30,000 lives and hundreds of thousands of refugees were forced to flee. Karabakh has been a de facto independent state ever since.

The economies of all three countries nosedived with the wars, the refugee problems and the ending of Soviet state support for industry and agriculture. In Georgia, former Soviet foreign minister Eduard Shevardnadze managed to stabilise the political situation but without much economic progress and with ever-growing corruption. In Azerbaijan, another ex-Communist boss, Heydar Əliyev, returned to power in 1993 and managed to restore stability, overseeing the Karabakh ceasefire and negotiating a lucrative deal with Western oil companies over Azerbaijan's Caspian oil reserves. In Armenia, President Levon Ter-Petrossian weathered several years of instability before resigning in 1998, to be replaced Robert Kocharian, who oversaw the beginnings of an economic revival.

PEOPLE

It's interesting to consider each nationality's view of its neighbours. The Armenians may have fought a war with the Azeris, but person to person they prefer them to the Georgians, whom they see as proud, wilful and only superficially Christian. The Georgians don't like the Armenians very much either, especially their country's friendly relations with Russia. They regard the Armenians and the Azeris as less sophisticated and less European than they are. The Azeris, with 800,000-odd refugees among them, are bitterly opposed to the Armenian occupation of Karabakh and its surrounding territories. An Armenian joke sums it up well: a boy asks his grandfather why the Armenians haven't sent a man into space. The old man replies, 'If the Armenians sent a cosmonaut into space, the Georgians would die of envy. If the Georgians die of envy, the Armenians will die of pleasure. And if the Georgians and Armenians die, the Azeris will be left with all the land.' Add

The 2003 documentary *Power Trip*, directed by Paul Devlin, reveals much about the tribulations of the transition as it chronicles an American company's attempts to bring paid-for electricity to Tbilisi.

Ezster Spat's *Yezidis* is the fruit of several years of close contact with these enigmatic mountain people.

in some other feisty nationalities – notably the Abkhaz, the Ossetians, the Chechens, the Lezgins and the Talysh – and the Caucasus is like Asia and Europe in miniature.

The only Armenians still living in Azerbaijan tend to be those married to Azeris and their children; likewise the only Azeris still in Armenia are those in mixed marriages. Otherwise the ethnic cleansing of Azeris from Armenia and Armenians from Azerbaijan during the late 1980s and early 1990s was extremely thorough, as was that of Georgians from Abkhazia. Georgia has around 300,000 Azeris and 300,000 Armenians in its 4.7 million population today, chiefly in areas near the Azerbaijan and Armenian borders, and there's some discontent among the Armenians, with calls for local autonomy in Javakheti, the region where they're most heavily concentrated. A few Georgians live in northwest Azerbaijan, especially around Qax, but almost no Georgians live in Armenia.

The Russian and Ukrainian minorities have largely departed the region, unless they too are in mixed marriages. Baku, the biggest city in the region, has the largest remaining Slavic community.

While the total population of Azerbaijan has been growing at a steady 50,000 or so per year, both Georgia and Armenia have seen their population shrink by about 15% since independence, chiefly through emigration. In Armenia at least, economic recovery is slowing the decline, and Armenia's population is expected to start growing again by about 2010.

RELIGION

The religions of the Caucasus have enjoyed a big revival since the end of Soviet suppression. New churches and mosques are being built, old ones are being restored, and attendance at services is high. Most Georgians adhere to the Georgian Orthodox Church, one of the Eastern Orthodox churches (which include the Greek and Russian Orthodox Churches). Georgian liturgical music is particularly beautiful and the church's strong traditions of monasticism and fresco and icon art have also revived during the modern era. The church is a conservative and nationalist force in Georgian life.

The Armenian Apostolic Church was the first legal Christian church in the world, dating back to AD 301. It has followed a lonely, independent path separate from the Eastern Orthodox and Catholic churches. It belongs to the Oriental Orthodox churches, along with the Coptic Egyptian and Ethiopian churches. The Armenians have always been mobile as well as pious, and they have held onto a quarter of Old Jerusalem beside the Jews, the Muslims and other Christians since at least 1000 years ago.

Azerbaijan is the only Turkic country to follow Shia Islam, established there in the 16th century by the Safavid dynasty, but in contrast to its Shia neighbour Iran there is little fundamentalism in Azerbaijan. Shia Muslims consider the descendants of the Prophet Mohammed's son-in-law Ali to be the true bearers of Mohammed's message.

Some Abkhaz, Lezgins (in Azerbaijan) and Adjarans (in Georgia) follow mainstream Sunni Islam. The Yezidi Kurds living on the highlands around Mt Aragats in Armenia are among the last followers of the independent Yezidi religion in the Middle East, following an ancient mix of Gnosticism, mystic Islam and hints of the old Persian religion Zoroastrianism. Yezidis have leaders named sheiks who keep their holy books secret.

There have been Jewish communities living peacefully in Georgia and in the mountains of Azerbaijan for millennia, though many have emigrated to Israel since the end of the USSR.

It's hard to beat Kurban Said's *Ali and Nino* for a fictional look at the Caucasian dichotomies of nationality, religion and continent.

People in the Caucasus tend to identify with their religion, even if they don't attend churches or mosques. The old traditions of tying bits of cloth to wishing trees, visiting shrines and graves, and spending lavishly on funerals is pretty common everywhere, more so among rural Georgians than the urban sophisticates of Baku.

ENVIRONMENT

The different habitats of the Caucasus countries embrace deserts, glaciers, alpine, deciduous and semitropical forests, steppes, coastal wetlands and hundreds of endemic plant species. The region is considered a biodiversity hotspot, although many of its species (including 80 animals) are endangered.

Harsh Soviet industrialisation left scars all over the Caucasus; the post-industrial desolation of Azerbaijan's Abşeron Peninsula shows it clearly enough. Deforestation has been going on for millennia – the stark plains around Georgia's Davit Gareja monastic complex were once covered in woodlands – but was stepped up with the energy shortages of the 1990s. Throughout the region, fuel-wood collection and poaching are among the biggest threats to wildlife, along with illegal logging of the thick belts of beech, oak and hornbeam on the lower mountain slopes and larch, pine and spruce higher up. Armenia's Metsamor nuclear power station, which generates 40% of the country's energy, is to be decommissioned because it does not meet international safety standards, but it is to be replaced by a new nuclear plant built with Russian aid. For the future, it's perhaps not so encouraging that Azeri oil is by far the region's biggest global export.

Conservation movements were some of the first civic organisations to appear as a result of Gorbachev's 1980s *glasnost* reforms. In some ways the pressure has eased on the environment since the fall of the USSR – pesticides aren't used with such giddy abandon and some of the nastier polluters such as chemical plants have shut down.

The region has a growing network of national parks, nature reserves and other protected areas, now covering about 12% of Armenia, 8% of Azerbaijan and 6.6% of Georgia. Visitor infrastructure has been developed in some parks, especially in Georgia, with the aim of using tourism to help preserve these areas. Other reserves and parks are still only functioning at a skeletal level.

The reserves protect some rare and spectacular animal species, including the endangered Persian leopard, about 25 of which remain in places like Azerbaijan's Hirkan National Park and Armenia's Shikahogh and Khosrov Natures Reserves (one has also been spotted in Georgia's Vashlovani National Park). Numbers of the two threatened species of Caucasian tur (large mountain goats) are down to about 4000 for the eastern species and 6000 to 10,000 for the western one. Azerbaijan's Şirvan National Park protects the last significant population of the elegant little goitred gazelle (also called the Persian gazelle or ceyran) in Eurasia or Europe. The striped hyena is probably close to extinction in the Caucasus, although Tony Davidson reports seeing one not too far from Kazbegi in his great book *Bread and Ashes*.

The mountain areas are home to majestic birds such as the lammergeier (or bearded vulture) with its 2.5m wingspan, plus brown bears (600 of these remain in Georgia), wolves, lynx, deer, chamois and more. The Black Sea and Caspian coastlines are key summer and autumn migration corridors for many birds. Altogether over 370 birds have been identified in the region, including the endemic Caucasian snowcock.

The Caucasus Environmental NGO Network (www.cenn.org) is a good source of information and contacts on environmentalist activity in the region.

Many Caucasus drivers now convert their cars to run on natural gas. It burns cleaner than petrol, and is half the price.

Georgia

STEPHANE VICTOR

Georgia
საქართველო

With sublimely perched old churches, watchtowers and castles dotting its fantastic mountain scenery, Georgia has to be one of the most beautiful countries on earth. This is a place where (except in the drabber, Soviet-built sectors of some towns) the human hand has much enhanced that of nature. Finally putting post-Soviet internal strife and economic stagnation behind it, Georgia is now developing its tourism potential and making the full range of its attractions safely and readily accessible to travellers. Appealing accommodation for all budgets is becoming available across the country and opportunities for exploring by foot, horse or vehicle are expanding fast.

From the snow-capped Caucasus mountains to its semitropical Black Sea coastline, Georgia abounds in natural variety. Tbilisi, the capital and by far the biggest city, has the atmosphere of an age-old Eurasian crossroads, yet it's also a 21st-century city with European-style nightclubs and eye-catching new architecture. Georgia's deeply complicated history has given it a fascinating cocktail of influences from Turkey, Russia, Persia, Central Asia and beyond, with a wonderful heritage of architecture and art. But today Georgia looks to Europe for its future and is the most Western in atmosphere of the three Caucasus countries.

Perhaps its greatest treasure is the Georgians themselves: warm, proud, high-spirited, cultured, obsessively hospitable and expert at enjoying life. This is a country where guests are considered a blessing. The abundant local wine flows freely, tables are laden with fine food and you'll never cease to be delighted by the warmth of your welcome.

FAST FACTS

- **Area** 69,700 sq km
- **Capital** Tbilisi
- **Famous for** The Golden Fleece, possibly inventing wine, Stalin, hospitality, mountains and dancing
- **Official name** Sakartvelo
- **Phrases** *Gamarjoba* (hello), *Gmadlobt* (thanks)
- **Population** 4.7 million, including an estimated 250,000 Internally Displaced Persons
- **Patron saint** St George

> **GEORGIA INDEX**
>
> - Litre of petrol 1.60 GEL
> - Litre of bottled water 1.25 GEL
> - Bottle of beer 1.50 GEL
> - Souvenir T-shirt 12 GEL
> - Street treat – *khachapuri* (cheese pie) 0.80 GEL, *chebureki* (meat pie) 1 GEL

HIGHLIGHTS

- **Tbilisi** (p47) The delightful Old Town, tree-lined avenues, the Mtkvari River, fine restaurants and fun bars; Tbilisi is the most charming Caucasian capital.
- **Kazbegi** (p100) Superb hiking; Tsminda Sameba Church silhouetted against mythical Mt Kazbek is a truly breathtaking sight.
- **Davit Gareja** (p113) and **Vardzia** (p121) Visit at least one of these extraordinary ancient cave monasteries.
- **Batumi** (p89) Georgia's enchanting Black Sea 'summer capital', with a party atmosphere against a backdrop of green, mist-wrapped hills.
- **Svaneti** (p94) The unique Svan culture, ancient defensive towers and the best alpine scenery in the Georgian Caucasus.

ITINERARIES

- **Three Days** Focus on Tbilisi, the fascinating capital, but take a half-day trip to Mtskheta and a day trip to Davit Gareja.
- **One Week** Starting in Tbilisi, you have time to visit the mountains as well as Mtskheta and Davit Gareja. Try a two-night stay in Kazbegi.
- **Two Weeks** See all the places listed above, before continuing to Gori, Kutaisi, then either the magical mountain stronghold of Svaneti or fun-loving Batumi on the Black Sea.

CLIMATE & WHEN TO GO

The best times to visit Georgia are in May, June and September, when it is warm and sunny but not overly hot. July and particularly August are uncomfortably humid in many parts, and temperatures regularly reach 40°C. However, this is an excellent time to be in the mountains, where it is sunny and cool. This is also the peak season on the Black Sea. Winter can be grim everywhere, although thanks to the buffer of the Caucasus Mountains which protects the country from the icy northern winds, Georgia rarely freezes. There is a surprising amount of rain year-round. See p312 for climate charts.

CURRENT EVENTS

Georgia enjoyed four years of relative stability following the Rose Revolution of 2003, which swept pro-Western Mikheil Saakashvili and his Georgian National Movement to power. But a new political crisis erupted in late 2007 as assorted opposition parties staged big street protests in Tbilisi against poverty, rising prices, and alleged corruption and authoritarianism in the Sgaakashvili government. Claiming that a coup d'état was threatened, President Saakashvili sent in riot police with water cannons and tear gas to clear the protests, declared a temporary state of emergency, and shut down the Imedi TV station, part-owned by his political opponent, tycoon Badri Patarkatsishvili.

The level of force used against the protests horrified Georgians and alarmed Saakashvili's friends in the West, but the president stood by his justification and called a snap presidential election for January 2008. Saakashvili won this with 53% of the vote over an opposition which had been caught unprepared. International observers adjudged the election to be democratic despite some irregularities, but large opposition protests in Tbilisi over alleged electoral fraud continued even after Saakashvili's inauguration for his new term.

Parliamentary elections due in spring 2008 were likely to have a big influence on the course of events. A good showing by the opposition could lead to further protests and instability. It seems many Georgians still view mass public action, rather than elections, as the way to change a government.

The crisis should at least have a sobering effect on the Saakashvili regime, which in its enthusiasm for free-market reforms is seen by many Georgians as insensitive, inflexible and uncaring. Georgia has won international praise for its business-friendly reforms, and a new breed of young, stylish, relatively wealthy Georgians are enjoying life as never before, shopping in glitzy new commercial centres, quaffing cocktails in fashionable bars and dancing to minimal techno in the nightclubs of Tbilisi and Batumi. But with a national

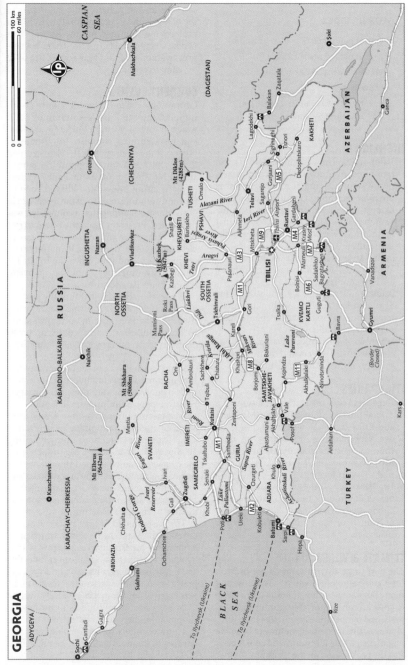

average monthly income of just 107 GEL (US$61) by 2007, it's still a battle for most Georgian families to make ends meet, and Georgians still have scant faith in the integrity of their court system or politicians. Following his inauguration in 2008, Saakashvili promised to reduce unemployment, raise pensions and introduce new social welfare measures.

Domestic troubles aside, Georgia's biggest headache is its fraught relations with Russia. Georgia's pro-Western stance and desire to join NATO has given Russia the heebie-jeebies, and Russia is generally believed to support the separatist regimes in Abkhazia and South Ossetia. In 2006 the Kremlin banned imports of Georgian wine and mineral water, suspended flights, shipping and money transfers between the two countries, and closed the last remaining border crossing.

Meanwhile Georgia is trying to resolve the South Ossetia issue by supporting those in the enclave who favour a federal status within Georgia, rather than incorporation within Russia. In Abkhazia Georgia has installed what it considers to be the legitimate regional government in the one small area it controls, the upper Kodori valley. Georgia offers Abkhazia broad autonomy on the condition that the estimated 250,000 Georgian refugees, driven out in the 1992–93 war, can return. But Abkhazia says it won't even talk until Georgia withdraws from the Kodori valley.

HISTORY

Georgians live and breathe their history as a vital key to their national and regional identities today.

Early Kingdoms

The Georgians know themselves as Kartvelebi, tracing their origins to Noah's great-great-grandson Kartlos. In classical times the two principal kingdoms were Colchis in the west (legendary home of the Golden Fleece and site of Greek colonies) and Kartli (also known as Iveria or Iberia) in the east and south, including some areas in modern Turkey and Armenia.

When King Mirian and Queen Nana of Kartli were converted to Christianity by St Nino in the early 4th century, Georgia became the second country to adopt the Christian faith, a quarter of a century after Armenia. In the 5th century AD, western Georgia became tied to the expanding Byzantine Empire,

while Kartli fell under Persian control. King Vakhtang Gorgasali (447–502), considered the father of the Georgian nation, briefly drove the Persians out and moved his capital from Mtskheta to the current seat of government, Tbilisi. But the Persians were back soon, to be followed in 654 by the Arabs, who set up an emirate at Tbilisi.

The Golden Age

Resistance to the Arabs came to be spearheaded by the Bagrationi dynasty of Tao-Klarjeti, a collection of principalities straddling the modern Georgian–Turkish border. They later added Kartli to their possessions, and when in 1001 these were inherited by King Bagrat III of Abkhazia (northwest Georgia), most of Georgia became united under one rule. The Seljuk Turk invasion in the 11th century set things back, but the Seljuks were gradually driven out by the young Bagrationi king Davit Aghmashenebeli (David the Builder; 1089–1125), who defeated them at Didgori in 1122 and recaptured nearby Tbilisi and made it his capital.

Davit made Georgia the major Caucasian power and a centre of Christian culture and learning. Georgia reached its zenith under his great-granddaughter Queen Tamar (1184–1213), whose writ extended over much of present-day Azerbaijan and Armenia, plus parts of Turkey and southern Russia. Tamar is still so revered that Georgians today call her, without irony, King Tamar!

Death, Destruction & Division

The golden age ended violently with the arrival of the Mongols in the 1220s. King Giorgi the Brilliant (1314–46) did shake off the Mongol yoke, but then came the Black Death, followed by the Central Asian destroyer Timur (Tamerlane), who attacked eight times between 1386 and 1403.

A devastated Georgia split into four main kingdoms: Kartli and Kakheti in the east, Imereti in the northwest and Samtskhe in the southwest. By the early 16th century the Ottoman Turks (who had overrun Christian Constantinople in 1453) and the Persian Safavid Empire were vying for control of Transcaucasia. They continued to do so for over two centuries, with western Georgian statelets generally falling under Turkish control and eastern ones under the Persians. The Safavid Shah Abbas' campaigns in eastern

Georgia in the early 17th century were particularly savage. In 1744 a new Persian conqueror, Nader Shah, installed local Bagratid princes as kings of Kartli and Kakheti. One of them, Erekle II, ruled both kingdoms as a semi-independent state from 1762.

Russian Rule

Russian troops crossed the Caucasus for the first time in 1770 to assist Imereti's liberation from the Turks. At the Treaty of Georgievsk in 1783, Erekle II accepted Christian Russian suzerainty in return for protection against his Muslim enemies. Russia went on to annex all the Georgian kingdoms and princedoms one by one during the 19th century, replacing the local or Turkish rulers with its own military governors.

In the wake of the Russian Revolution, Georgia was briefly independent from 1918 to 1921, but it was invaded by the Red Army and incorporated into the Soviet Union in 1922. During the 1930s, like everywhere else in the USSR, Georgia suffered from the Great Terror unleashed by Joseph Stalin, a cobbler's son from the Georgian town of Gori who had ingeniously taken control of the largest country on earth.

Following Stalin's death in 1953, Georgia began to enjoy a good quality of life – the 1960s and '70s are looked back upon with nostalgia by older Georgians as a time of public order, peace and high living standards. Yet by the mid-1980s Mikhail Gorbachev began his policies of reform and the USSR disintegrated in just seven years.

Independence: From Dream to Nightmare

Georgia's bubbling independence movement became an unstoppable force after Soviet troops massacred 20 hunger strikers outside a government building in Tbilisi on 9 April 1989. Georgia's now anti-Communist government, led by the nationalist intellectual Zviad Gamsakhurdia, declared Georgia independent of the USSR on 9 April 1991. Almost immediately the country descended into chaos. Heavy street fighting overtook Tbilisi in December 1991 as rebel paramilitary forces battled in the city centre to overthrow Gamsakhurdia. He fled to Chechnya and was replaced by a military council, which gained an international respectability when Eduard Shevardnadze agreed to lead it. Shevardnadze had been First

Secretary of the Georgian Communist Party from 1972 to 1985, and Soviet Foreign Minister under Mikhail Gorbachev from 1985 to 1991. He was elected chairman of the parliament and head of state on 11 October 1992.

Shevardnadze's presence did wonders for Georgia's reputation abroad, but at home, devastating internal conflicts continued to worsen. A truce in June 1992 halted the conflict that had beset the region of South Ossetia since it had declared its unification with North Ossetia (in Russia) in 1989. But in August 1992 an even more serious conflict erupted in Abkhazia. For more details about this bitter ethnic war, see p87.

In September 1993 Georgia suffered a comprehensive defeat in Abkhazia, and Gamsakhurdia tried to recapture power from Shevardnadze. A short but bloody civil war in western Georgia was only ended by Shevardnadze's quick negotiation of support from Russian troops already in the country. Gamsakhurdia died on 31 December 1993, possibly by his own hand. The second major consequence of the defeat in Abkhazia was the enforced displacement of approximately 250,000 Georgians from their homes there – a desperate humanitarian and economic burden for a country whose economy was already on the brink of collapse.

The Rose Revolution

For a decade after the Abkhazia debacle, Georgia oscillated between periods of relative peace and security and terrible crime waves, gang warfare, kidnappings, infrastructure collapse and rampant corruption. Shevardnadze at least staved off a total collapse into anarchy, but by the early years of the 21st century, with corruption rampant and economic progress slow, Georgians had lost all faith in him.

Badly flawed parliamentary elections in November 2003 were the focus for a mass protest movement that turned into a bloodless coup, named the Rose Revolution after the flowers carried by the demonstrators. As the highly suspect election results were announced, protestors outside parliament in Tbilisi vowed to remain there until Shevardnadze resigned. Led by former Shevardnadze protégé Mikheil Saakashvili, a US-educated lawyer who now headed the opposition Georgian National Movement, the unarmed throng finally invaded parliament on 22 November. Humiliatingly bundled out of the back door by his body-guards, Shevardnadze announced his resignation the next morning.

The 36-year-old Saakashvili won presidential elections in January 2004 by a landslide, and set the tone for his presidency by appointing a team of young, energetic, outward-looking ministers and announcing campaigns against the plague of corruption. He scored an early triumph within months of taking power when he faced down the semisepa-ratist strongman of Georgia's southwestern region of Adjara, Aslan Abashidze. Just when it seemed Georgia might be plunged into another civil war, Abashidze backed down and left for exile in Russia.

PEOPLE

The Georgian people are one of the chief attractions of this country – their traditions of hospitality and kindness extend to everyone they meet, and until you experience a full Georgian meal with endless courses of sublime local cooking and lengthy toasting ceremonies (see p46), you can't claim to have seen the real Georgia.

The National Psyche

Georgians are irreverent, individualistic, enterprising, good humoured and generally high spirited – pretty much the opposite of the Russian neighbours who dominated them for two centuries. For a good demonstration of the Georgian character, stay in a Georgian home, where you'll be treated like a monarch and fed and watered until you can take no more. Most Georgians are only too delighted to talk with foreign visitors and will go out of their way to help you and make you feel welcome. In fact, few things make Georgians happier than having guests to look after.

Georgians are proud of their culture and their country, but they identify with their own regions as much as with Georgia as a whole, which is something of a mishmash of nationalities.

While some dislike the influence Russia had over the country for two centuries, many Georgians (especially those over 30) speak good, often fluent Russian, are perfectly happy to talk Russian with foreigners, and find it hard to totally dismiss their northern neighbour, having absorbed so much of her culture.

Daily Life

With their agricultural wealth and capitalist instincts, Georgians lived better than anyone else in the USSR. Despite difficulties since independence, most Georgians still manage to live relatively well (and a few live extremely well). City dwellers retain roots in distant villages and will return from visits laden with home-grown produce. Fewer Georgians live in the drab apartment blocks widespread in other ex-Soviet countries; many city homes replicate rural ones, with a variety of small dwellings set around a courtyard.

Most Georgians outside Tbilisi live in big traditional homesteads, often housing three or more generations of a family. Friends and family are of vital importance and Georgians spend copious amounts of time simply enjoying each other's company.

Georgian women generally enjoy a good deal of freedom, holding prominent positions in government and having a large presence in the workplace. But this is hardly a feminist culture – most women are also still expected to be cleaners and cooks in the home.

Population & Multiculturalism

Georgia is a cobbling together of different nationalities and regional identities – some more successfully integrated than others. In the worst cases this has led to secession and war (in Abkhazia and South Ossetia – both areas with languages that are unrelated to Georgian and whose peoples would not consider themselves Georgian). Some 250,000 ethnic Georgians were driven out of Abkhazia during the 1992–93 conflict there and the great majority of them remain internally displaced persons today. Other areas with languages that are part of the Georgian linguistic family, such as Samegrelo (Mingrelia) and Svaneti, have managed to maintain their cultural identity without separation or conflict.

Georgia is also home to around 300,000 Azeris and 300,000 Armenians, mainly near the Azerbaijani and Armenian borders. There is discontent among some members of these groups, especially Armenians, over a perceived lack of attention to their interests on the part of the government in Tbilisi. Some Armenians in the Javakheti area of southern Georgia call for regional autonomy, but these issues have not escalated into conflict.

There is still a small Russian population of around 60,000, mainly in Tbilisi. Anti-Russian feeling was most pronounced immediately after independence but has surfaced again with the recent worsening of Georgia–Russia relations.

RELIGION

The Georgian Orthodox Church has enjoyed a big revival since the end of the Soviet era, with old churches restored, new ones built, and monasteries and convents repopulated by monks and nuns. You will often notice Georgians crossing themselves three times when a church comes into sight. As a Christian nation often threatened in the past by Muslim foes, Georgians' sense of nationhood is intimately bound up with their church.

A small number of Georgians (chiefly in Adjara, which was under Turkish rule until the 19th century) are Muslim, as is the country's Azeri population, while the Armenians are mostly Armenian Apostolic Christians. Many of the country's age-old Jewish population emigrated after Georgian independence, but there are still working synagogues in Tbilisi and Kutaisi.

ARTS

Georgians are an incredibly expressive people. Music, dance, song and poetry all play big parts in their lives.

Literature

For a little known language with only a few million speakers, Georgian has produced an extraordinarily rich body of literature. The national bard, Shota Rustaveli, wrote *The Knight in the Tiger Skin,* a work which every Georgian can quote from. Written in the 12th century, this classic was not translated into English until 1912 (by Marjory Wardrop, who learned Georgian by comparing a Georgian bible to an English one).

Under the Russians from the start of the 19th century, Georgian literature began to develop with many Western influences, particularly romanticism, as personified by Nikoloz Baratashvili (1817–45). One notable 19th-century movement was known as the Tergdaleulebi, literally meaning 'those who have drunk from the Tergi River', which flows from Georgia into Russia – the reference being to Georgians who had studied in Russia and imbibed liberal ideas there. This group promoted public, educational and political reform in Georgia, and

its leading lights were Ilia Chavchavadze and Akaki Tsereteli.

Some Georgian writers in the second half of the 19th century turned to their country's mountains for inspiration. The most prominent were Alexander Kazbegi, novelist and dramatist, and Vazha Pshavela, whom many consider the greatest Georgian poet after Rustaveli.

The principal poetic movement of the early 20th century was the symbolist Blue Horn group, whose most famous members, Titsian Tabidze and Paolo Iashvili, both met tragic ends. Tabidze was arrested and shot in the purges of 1937, and Iashvili killed himself at a Union of Writers meeting when he heard the news of Tabidze's death. Perhaps the best-loved poet of the 20th century was Titsian Tabidze's cousin Galaktion Tabidze (1892–1959), a superbly lyrical writer who also committed suicide.

Leading contemporary authors writing in Georgian include novelist Aka Morchiladze and novelist, playwright and travel writer David Turashvili. Fasil Iskander (b 1929) is an acclaimed Abkhaz author writing in Russia (and Russian). His novels *Sandro of Chegem* and *The House Under the Cypress Tree* are set in western Georgia and Abkhazia.

Cinema

Georgia was one of the first provinces of the old Russian Empire where a film studio was established, and cinema production is still a strong feature of Georgia's cultural life. Tbilisi stages a big annual international film festival (see p60).

Many Georgians consider Sergo Zakariadze (1909–71) to have been their country's greatest film actor, especially for his famous role as an ageing peasant searching for his soldier son in *Father of a Soldier* (1964). Tengiz Abuladze's *Monanieba (Repentance)* was ground-breaking in opening up the Soviet past – a black portrait of a dictator clearly based on Stalin's Georgian henchman Lavrenty Beria, it won the Grand Prix at Cannes in 1987.

The Georgian directors with most international recognition today tend to be expats based in France. Otar Iosseliani, who has lived in France since 1982, had international success with *Favourites of the Moon* in the 1980s. *Monday Morning* (2002) and *Farewell, Home Sweet Home* (1999) were both filmed in France, although they retain a strong Georgian identity. Julie Bertucelli's *Since Otar Left* (2003) is a clever tale of three generations of women sharing a Tbilisi flat, while Gela Babluani directed the scary thriller *Legacy* (2007), focused on a blood feud in the Georgian countryside.

One of the best recent films spawned by Georgia (albeit not Georgian-made) is Paul Devlin's 2003 documentary *Power Trip*, about an American company's struggle to provide paid-for electricity in post-Soviet Tbilisi, with all the culture clashes this involves.

Music & Dance

Live music is always close at hand in Georgia. Many homes have a piano and someone ready to play on request, and dinners are often extended by polyphonic singing round the table. Georgian three-voiced polyphonic folk music was mentioned by the Greek historian Xenophon as long ago as 400 BC. It used to accompany every aspect of daily life, and the songs have survived in various genres: *supruli* (songs for the table, the most famous being 'Mravalzhamier', which means 'Many Years'), *mushuri* (working songs), *satrpialo* (love songs) and *sagmiro* (epic songs). Georgian folk festivals, such as Tbilisi's Art Gene Festival (p60) and Svaneti's Kviroba festival in July, are great opportunities to hear the best rural singers, as is the October grape harvest season in Kakheti.

Sagalobeli (beautiful church chants) have been part of Georgian music for at least 1500 years and are enjoying a revival and renewal today. Excellent choirs accompany many church services around Tbilisi, usually at 4pm on Saturday and 9am on Sunday, including at the Anchiskhati Basilica (p53), Sioni Cathedral (p53) and Mamadaviti Church (p58).

Georgia's exciting traditions of folk dance range from lyrical love stories to dramatic, leaping demonstrations of male agility, usually with beautiful costumes and to the accompaniment of string and wind instruments and drums. Top professional groups such as Erisioni and the Sukhishvili Georgian National Ballet are often touring overseas, but don't miss them if they happen to be performing at home.

Jazz too is highly popular in Georgia (Tbilisi and Batumi host annual festivals), while minimal techno is the optimal beat for many Tbilisi clubbers. The most beloved rock artist is still Irakli Charkviani, even though he died in 2006. Georgia's first major classical composer was the opera writer Zakaria Paliashvili, famous for *Abesalom and Eteri* (1919) and *Daisi* (1923). The most famed contemporary composer is Gia Kancheli, born in 1935 and now living in Antwerp. His works are informed by his devout Orthodox faith, and he has been described as 'turning the sounds of silence into music'.

Theatre

Tbilisi boasts an amazingly lively theatrical scene for a city of its size.

Four directors have dominated Georgian theatre since the early 20th century: Kote Marjanishvili and Sandro Akhmeteli in the 1920s and '30s, and Misha Tumanishvili and Robert Sturua since the 1970s. Marjanishvili and Akhmeteli were both denounced for 'anti-Soviet activities,' and while Marjanishvili died of natural causes in 1933, Akhmeteli was shot in 1937 by the Soviet regime.

With these two men began Georgia's love affair with Shakespeare, continued by Tumanishvili and Sturua. Sturua's *Richard III* (1980) and *The Caucasian Chalk Circle* (1975) daringly burlesqued dictatorial regimes and won critical acclaim throughout the world, as did his 1986 London production of *Hamlet* starring Alan Rickman. He is still director of Tbilisi's Rustaveli National Theatre, where he has staged 17 different Shakespeare plays.

Visual Arts

Many Georgian churches are adorned with wonderful old frescoes. The golden age of religious art in Georgia was the 11th to 13th centuries, when Georgian painters employed the fully developed Byzantine iconographic system and also portrayed local subjects such as Georgian monarchs and saints. There were two main fresco schools: one at Davit Gareja cave monastery and the other at the monasteries of Tao-Klarjeti (now in Turkey). During the same period artists and metalsmiths were creating beautiful icons from jewels and precious metals that remain among the country's greatest treasures today.

Perhaps the last major artist in the tradition of fresco painting was one who painted not religious images in churches but scenes of everyday life in restaurants and bars in Tbilisi. Self-taught, and in his lifetime largely unrecognised, Niko Pirosmani (1862–1918) expressed the essential spirit of Georgian life in a direct and enchanting way. After his death in poverty and obscurity, his work was acclaimed by the modernists, foremost among whom were Davit Kakabadze, Lado Gudiashvili and Shalva Kikodze. All three lived for a time in Paris in the early 20th century, influenced by the radical artistic ideas they encountered there. Their associate Elene Akhvlediani (1901–76) painted colourful scenes of old Tbilisi and Georgian historic sites that still have a lot of appeal. Today Tbilisi has a burgeoning gallery scene with much colourful though not fantastically original art.

Architecture

Georgian church architecture is one of the most distinctive features of the landscape and a highlight of the country – not least because of Georgians' talent for placing their sacred buildings in the most scenically sublime locations.

Early churches took two main forms: the basilica and the central-domed church. Roman-influenced basilicas were rectangular in plan and divided into three parallel sections. In three-aisled basilicas (such as the 6th-century Anchiskhati in Tbilisi) the three parts were separated by arcades. In triple-church basilicas, such as the two at Nekresi, the three parts were divided by solid walls and each had its own barrel vault.

Most central-domed churches had an equal-armed, cross-shaped ground plan, with the dome sitting on a cylindrical stone drum rising above the central space. In the 'tetraconch' variety, each arm of the cross has an apse (semicircular end), and the cross may have its angles filled with corner rooms to result in a square building. The Jvari Church near Mtskheta, built about 600, is a classic tetraconch, and served as the model for Ateni Sioni, Dzveli Shuamta and other early churches.

A fusion of the basilical and central-domed forms yielded the elongated-cross church of Georgia's golden age from the 11th to 13th centuries, with a drum and pointed dome rising above the meeting of the cross's arms. Such are the beautiful tall Alaverdi, Svetitskhoveli (Mtskheta) and Bagrati (Kutaisi) cathedrals.

Invasions put a stop to much monumental building from the 13th to 18th centuries, although the frequent danger of attack did inspire the picturesque, tall defensive towers that characterise Svaneti and other high Caucasus valleys. Some Persian style is evident in the many balconies and galleries that still adorn houses in the Old Town of Tbilisi and elsewhere.

The 19th and early 20th centuries saw Georgia putting its own quirky twist on styles brought by the Russians, including neoclassicism in Tbilisi and Art Nouveau in Batumi. Contemporary architecture since the fall of Soviet power has focused partly on the building of new churches – in modern materials but traditional forms, most notably Tbilisi's mammoth Tsminda Sameba Cathedral – but also on Western-influenced prestige projects like new luxury hotels and shopping centres, and Tbilisi's eye-catching new presidential palace.

ENVIRONMENT

From the snowy heights and alpine meadows of the Caucasus to the semitropical coast of Adjara and the semidesert border with Azerbaijan, Georgia has a fantastically diverse ecological make-up and is a nature lover's delight. Flora and fauna are particularly diverse in the Caucasus, where wildlife includes bears, wolves, boars, deer, lynx and the two species of Caucasian tur (ibex). Jackals occur all over the lower-lying parts of the country. Georgia also supports 360 recorded bird species, including 11 types of eagle and four vultures, and over 4000 plant species (300 endemic to Georgia).

The Caucasus is connected to the 'Lesser Caucasus' ranges of southern Georgia by the Likhi Range, which you'll cross between Khashuri and Kutaisi on the M1 highway. This forms a barrier between wetter, more lushly vegetated western Georgia and the drier east. Georgia's main river, the Mtkvari (or Kura), rises in northeast Turkey and flows through Borjomi, Gori and Tbilisi and on into Azerbaijan, where it enters the Caspian Sea.

Environmental protection has moved forward since Georgia passed its 1996 Law on the System of Protected Areas, and 6.6% of national territory is now under protection of varying levels, including five national parks. Sustainable tourism is seen as an important support for protected areas, and well-organised visitor facilities are in place at places such as Borjomi-Kharagauli National Park (p118), Kolkheti National Park (p84) and the

---

KNOW YOUR KHACHAPURI

An excess of these is not the thing for slimmers, but Georgia's ubiquitous cheese pies are the perfect keep-me-going small meal, as well as playing a part in many a feast. Different regions have their own varieties, but you'll find many of them all around the country:

- *khachapuri Acharuli* The Adjaran variety is a large, boat-shaped calorie injection, overflowing with melted cheese and topped with butter and a runny egg.
- *khachapuri Imeruli* Relatively sedate, these round, flat pies have melted cheese inside only.
- *khachapuri Megruli* Round, with cheese in the middle and more cheese melted on top.
- *khachapuri penovani* Square and neatly folded into four quarters, with the cheese inside the lightish crust – particularly tasty!
- *khachapuri achma* This large variety arranges its bread and cheese in layers, lasagne-style.
- *kubdari* Not really a *khachapuri*, since it has a minced-meat filling, but it looks like one and does the same job!
- *lobiani* Same story but this time with beans inside.

Lagodekhi Nature Reserve (p115). There's useful information about protected areas on the website of the **Department of Protected Areas** (www.dpa.gov.ge).

FOOD & DRINK

One of the best reasons to visit Georgia is for its food – diverse, fresh, imaginative and filling, it's a joy and, to Georgians, one of the most important aspects of the national culture.

Staples & Specialities

The great staple for everybody, travellers and locals, is the *khachapuri,* essentially a cheese pie (see above).

The second most common dish in Georgia is *khinkali* (meat dumplings). These are usually served without any accompaniment, but they are delicious. You are not supposed to eat the doughy nexus at the top of the dumpling, though this being Georgia, a few people do. It's virtually impossible to order fewer than five of these at a time, even though they are quite substantial.

More substantial Georgian dishes typically involve lamb, chicken, beef or turkey in various spicy, herby sauces or stews – see our Menu Decoder (p46) for an explanation of the most popular dishes.

Drinks

More than anything, Georgians love to drink, and wine is a passion, particularly in Kakheti, where you will no doubt taste the unique homemade white wine made by fermenting the grape on the grape skin – a process used only for red wine in the West. The pinkish result is a fine drop that tastes nothing like normal white wine. Most commercially marketed Georgian wine tends to be sweet to Western taste buds, although the Saperavi grape is reliably crisp and plummy.

Vodka is a common drink throughout the country, but trying the national firewater, *chacha,* is a real experience.

The two commonest Georgian beers are Kazbegi and Natakhtari. Natakhtari is smoother and creamier than the slightly acidic Kazbegi.

Georgia's favourite nonalcoholic drink is Borjomi, a salty mineral water which was the beverage of choice for every Soviet leader from Lenin on. It polarises opinion, and is certainly an acquired taste. Nabeghlavi is a less salty alternative. Georgians often claim that tap water is safe to drink throughout the country, a boast that is hard to verify. If you prefer bottled water, Borjomi Springs is a fine thirst-quencher: it's neither carbonated nor salty, although it can be hard to find outside big towns.

Where to Eat & Drink

Georgians eat and drink at all times of the day, and restaurants tend to keep suitably long hours, typically noon to midnight (exceptions to this are noted in individual reviews). Breakfast can be the trickiest meal to get outside your accommodation. While some places may serve up eggs, bread and tea early in the morning, others will offer only *khachapuri.*

Outside Tbilisi, restaurants are almost universally cheap – it is rare for a Georgian dish to cost more than 5 GEL or 6 GEL, while a full slap-up feast will rarely be more than 20 GEL per person.

Tbilisi has the best selection and variety of restaurants, but eateries around the country have improved a lot. The surly Soviet service ethic is dead and buried, and while Russian fare remains a popular alternative to Georgian dishes, more restaurants now display an openness to other foreign cuisines. For Georgian regional food, some of the best you'll eat will be offered in homestays and guesthouses.

At the bottom of the Georgian food chain are the *sakhachapure* and the *sakhinkle,* cheap workers cafés where *khachapuri* or *khinkali* are literally the only thing served. Cafés tend to serve sweet dishes – Georgians make some excellent pastries and cakes for those with a sweet tooth.

Some better-quality Georgian restaurants are really party places, where people go for loud music, dancing and lots of drinking as well as eating. These can be lots of fun if you're in company, but not very pleasant for the single traveller or even some couples. Staff will do their best to make everybody feel at ease, but if places like this are your only option, it's a good idea to eat early, before the place fills up with revellers.

Vegetarians & Vegans
Vegetarians will fare well in Georgia. *Khachapuri, badrijani nigvzit* (aubergine with walnut paste), *pkhali* (crushed walnuts and garlic with spinach or beetroot paste) and *lobio* (bean paste or stew with herbs and spices) are all standard fare, and breakfast will often provide *matsoni* (Georgian sour yogurt drink) or perhaps bread with cheese or honey. Vegans will find things harder, as much Georgian food involves some sort of milk product.

Habits & Customs
If you are lucky enough to be invited to a *supra* (feast – literally 'tablecloth'), you'll need to understand the basic etiquette of these festive events. While strictly speaking the word *supra* applies to any meeting where food and drink are consumed, it's likely that foreign guests will experience the full works, which usually means staggering amounts to eat and drink. A selection of cold dishes will be followed by two or three hot courses as well as some kind of dessert. Make sure you try everything, as much to temper the onslaught of concomitant alcohol as to keep your hosts happy.

Bear in mind that Georgians toast only their enemies with beer – wine or spirits are the only drinks to toast your friends with. However, you should only drink when someone proposes a toast. This can be a surprisingly serious, lengthy and poetic matter, even at small gatherings of three or four friends. Larger gatherings will have a designated *tamada* (toastmaster), and some complex *supras* will involve an *alaverdi,* a second man whose role it is to elaborate on the toast, while a *merikipe* is there to pour the wine. If you are toasted, do not reply immediately but wait for others to add their wishes before simply thanking them – you should wait some time and then ask the *tamada* if you can make a toast in reply.

Eat Your Words
Georgian menus often look daunting, even if there's an English translation available, but you'll find that the following list explains a large proportion of most menus.

MENU DECODER
ajapsandali – spicy vegetable mixture
ajika – chilli sauce
apkhazura – spicy meatballs
asetrina – sturgeon
badrijani – aubergine (usually with walnuts and garlic)
bazhe – walnut sauce
chakapuli – lamb with tarragon and plums
chakhokhbili – chicken or turkey in tomato sauce
chanakhi – lamb with potatoes, aubergine and tomatoes
chebureki – triangular pies stuffed with minced meat
chikhirtma – chicken broth with a leg of chicken floating in it
churchkhela – string of nuts coated in a sort of caramel made from grape juice and flour
ghomi – maize porridge
kababi – doner kebabs
khachapuri – cheese pie
kharcho – soup with rice, beef and spices
khashi – tripe and garlic soup
khinkali – spicy meat dumplings
kuchmachi – chopped, seasoned and simmered offal (of chicken, calf or lamb)
kupati – sausage
lobio – bean paste or stew with herbs and spices
matsnis supi – yogurt soup
matsoni – sour yogurt drink usually consumed at breakfast

mchadi – corn-flour bread
mtsvadi ghoris/khbos – pork/beef shashlyk
mzhavi – pickled vegetables
ojakhuri – meat with potatoes, onion and garlic
pkhali – beetroot, spinach or cabbage paste with crushed walnuts and garlic
plovi – rice with meat, mushrooms or fruit
satsivi – cold turkey or chicken in a spicy walnut sauce, traditionally a New Year dish
shkmeruli – chicken in garlic sauce
sulguni – smoked cheese
tqemali – plum sauce
tskhotskali – boiled river fish, served cold
tvini – brains, usually beef

TBILISI თბილისი

☎ 32 (international), ☎ 22 (domestic) / pop 1.7 million

Almost 10 times the size of any other city in Georgia, Tbilisi is where it all happens. Politically, culturally, economically and socially, this is the hub of the country and the place to which Georgians gravitate for action and excitement. Capital of Georgia (in its various incarnations) almost continually since the 5th century, Tbilisi brims with history and has a dramatic setting on hillsides either side of the swift Mtkvari River. Its Old Town, at the narrowest part of the valley, is still redolent of an ancient Eurasian crossroads, with narrow, winding alleys, handsome religious buildings, and old balconied houses and caravanserais (travellers inns).

Tbilisi is also a modern city moving forward in the 21st century after the strife and stagnation of the late 20th. There is a wide and growing array of good accommodation

---

GEORGIAN STREET NAMES

The spelling of Georgian street names varies slightly, depending on whether words such as qucha (street), gamziri (avenue), moedani (square) or chikhi (lane) are present. In Georgian, Sioni Street is Sionis qucha (Street of Sioni). To simplify matters, we use noninflected names alone in addresses – for example Sioni 23 rather than Sionis qucha 23. Only when there is more than one street with the same name (for example Chavchavadzis qucha and Chavchavadzis gamziri) have we included the full name for clarity.

---

and places to eat, and a busy cultural scene and nightlife. Prestigious new building projects – from a new presidential palace to five-star hotels, shopping malls and leisure facilities – are giving Tbilisi a new dimension, although little money is steered towards the working-class neighbourhoods (or the chaotic and dirty bus stations). The most attractive of the three Caucasian capitals, Tbilisi is still the beating heart of the Caucasus and should not be missed by any visitor.

HISTORY

Despite evidence of settlement in the area stretching back to the 4th century BC, Georgians prefer the legend that King Vakhtang Gorgasali of Kartli founded Tbilisi in the 5th century. The story runs that when the king was hunting, a pheasant fell into a hot sulphur spring and was conveniently cooked for dinner. Another version has it that a wounded deer fell into the hot sulphur spring and was miraculously healed. Either way, Tbilisi takes its name from the Georgian *tbili* (warm), and there seems little doubt that the magnificent hot springs, which still lure visitors today, attracted the king to the spot.

In fact Gorgasali won the town back from the Persians, who had invaded in 368, and moved his capital here from Mtskheta in the late 5th century. His son King Dachi completed its construction after his father's death. But in 645 the Arabs captured Tbilisi and kept it as an emirate for four centuries.

In 1122 the Georgian King David the Builder (Davit Aghmashenebeli) took Tbilisi and made it capital of a united Georgia, building a palace near the Metekhi Church. Under David and his descendant Queen Tamar, Georgia enjoyed its medieval golden age and Tbilisi developed into a multiethnic city of 80,000 people, known for its production of weapons, jewellery, leather and silk clothing. The golden age was ended with a vengeance by the arrival of the Mongols in 1235, followed in turn by the Black Death, then conqueror Timur (Tamerlane), who destroyed the city in 1386, and the Persians, who captured Tbilisi twice in the 1540s.

Tbilisi made some cultural progress under the Persians during the 17th and 18th centuries, and in 1762, as Persian control waned, the city became capital of a united eastern Georgia under King Erekle II. Erekle's protector Russia, however, withdrew its troops

GEORGIA

GEORGIA

CENTRAL TBILISI

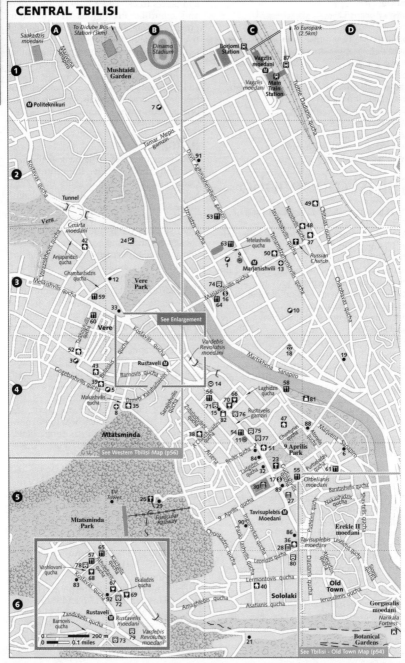

to fight the Turks, allowing Agha Mohamed Khan to inflict Persia's last and most devastating assault on Tbilisi in 1795. His army killed tens of thousands and burnt the city to the ground; few buildings today predate 1795 in any substantial form. Russia annexed Georgia in 1800 and proceeded to recreate Tbilisi in the imperial mould, laying out wide streets and squares such as Rustavelis gamziri and Tavisuplebis moedani, and building libraries, schools and theatres. By the late 19th century, Tbilisi had a population of 159,000, the majority of them Russian or Armenian.

While the Soviet era saw huge growth and relative prosperity (the city's population passed one million in the 1970s), Tbilisi became a centre of resistance to the late Soviet regime, culminating in troops killing 20 hunger strikers outside the government building on Rustaveli on 9 April 1989. Georgia's parliament declared Georgian independence from the USSR in the same building exactly two years later. Rebellion against the government of Zviad Gamsakhurdia then erupted in fierce fighting on the city's streets in December 1991, destroying several central landmark buildings.

The following years were dark ones. Although gun-toting gangsters ceased to rule the roost, the economy nosedived, and in 1993 Tbilisi had to find room for thousands of Georgian refugees fleeing from Abkhazia. While a few people got very rich in the 1990s, general living standards sank, corruption and crime were endemic, and frequent power cuts blacked out the city.

In the Rose Revolution of November 2003, protesting crowds again filled central Tbilisi and finally poured into the parliament building to drive out President Eduard Shevardnadze. Since then, corruption has been reduced, Tbilisi has enjoyed a new flood of foreign aid and investment, the city centre is being refurbished, and tourism is bouncing back. Though prosperity has yet to trickle down to many of the general populace, Tbilisi has more confidence, energy and optimism than for many a year.

ORIENTATION

Tbilisi is centred on the Mtkvari River, which runs through the middle of it roughly northwest to southeast. The old city lies on the right (west) bank where the valley narrows to a gorge, below Narikala Fortress. Tavisuplebis

GEORGIA

INFORMATION
Armenian Embassy......................1 C3
Beeline..2 C5
British Embassy.....................(see 36)
Chinese Embassy.........................3 A4
Dutch Embassy......................(see 85)
Fedex..4 F6
French Embassy...........................5 A4
Geoland......................................6 D5
German Consulate.......................7 B1
German Embassy...................(see 85)
IMSS...8 B4
Internet Café...............................9 C3
Israeli Embassy..........................10 C3
Java Cyber Café.........................11 C4
Magti..12 B3
PMG Pharmacy..........................13 C3
Post Office & Call Centre..........14 C4
Prospero's Books......................15 C4
TBC Bank & ATM......................16 C3
TBC Bank ATM....................(see 51)
TBC Bank ATM.........................17 C5
Telephone Centre.....................18 C4
Wild Georgia............................19 D4

SIGHTS & ACTIVITIES
Abanotubani............................20 E6
Business Centre........................21 C6
Echmiadzin Cathedral..............22 E6
Kashveti Church.......................23 C5
King Vakhtang statue.........(see 26)
Laguna Vere Pool.....................24 B3
Mamadaviti Church..................25 B5
Metekhi Church........................26 E6
Museum of Georgia..................27 C5
Museum of Money....................28 C5
National Pantheon....................29 B5
Parliament................................30 C5
Presidential palace...................31 E5
School No 1..............................32 C5
State Concert Hall
   (Philharmonia).....................33 B3

Tsminda Sameba
   Cathedral.............................34 E5

SLEEPING
Betsy's Hotel.............................35 B4
Courtyard by Marriott...............36 C5
Dodo's Homestay.....................37 D3
Hotel Beaumonde.....................38 B4
Hotel British House...................39 A4
Hotel David..............................40 C6
Hotel GTM................................41 E6
Hotel Iliani...............................42 A3
Hotel Kartli..............................43 A4
Hotel Kopala............................44 E6
Hotel Lile.................................45 E6
Hotel Old Metekhi...................46 E6
Hotel Tori.................................47 C4
Irine Japaridze's Boarding
   House...................................48 C3
Khatuna's Homestay.................49 D2
Nasi Gvetadze's
   Homestay.............................50 C3
Tbilisi Marriott Hotel................51 C5
Vere Inn...................................52 A4

EATING
Ankara......................................53 C2
Cafe Nikala...............................54 C4
Caravan....................................55 C5
Chocolate.................................56 C4
Csaba's Jazz-Rock Café.............57 A6
Dzveli Metekhi...................(see 46)
Dzveli Sakhli............................58 C4
El Depo.....................................59 A3
Hotel Kopala.......................(see 44)
Kafe Literaturuli.......................60 A3
La Brasserie........................(see 36)
Populi.......................................61 D5
Puris Sakhli..............................62 E6
Sachashnike.............................63 C3
Shemoikhede Genatsvale..........64 C3
Tokyo.......................................65 A6

DRINKING
Acid Bar...................................66 C4
Dublin......................................67 B6
Le Café.....................................68 A6
Nali..69 B6
Near Opera...............................70 C4

ENTERTAINMENT
Blues Brothers..........................71 C4
Jazz Club Non Stop...................72 B6
Kino Sakhli...............................73 B6
Marjanishvili Theatre................74 C3
Nabadi Theatre.........................75 C4
Paliashvili Opera & Ballet
   Theatre.................................76 C4
Rustaveli National Theatre........77 C4
Success....................................78 A6
Switch......................................79 B6
Traffic......................................80 C6

SHOPPING
Dry Bridge market....................81 D4
Gallery Artgasm...................(see 15)
Georgian Souvenirs.............(see 11)
Old Carpets & Kilims................82 C4

TRANSPORT
Air Baltic..................................83 A6
Airzena Georgian
   Airways................................84 C5
Austrian Airlines.......................85 F6
Avis..86 C5
BMI.....................................(see 36)
Badagoni Tour.....................(see 36)
Bus & Marshrutka Station.........87 C1
Cosmo Group...........................88 D4
Georgian National
   Airlines................................89 C5
SCAT..90 C5
Turkish Airlines........................91 B2
Ukraine International
   Airlines................................92 B6

moedani (Freedom Sq) marks the northwest edge of the Old Town. Rustavelis gamziri (Rustaveli Avenue), the main artery of modern central Tbilisi, runs 1.5km northwest from Tavisuplebis moedani to Rustavelis moedani (Rustaveli Sq).

Outside these central areas, the main districts of interest to travellers are Vere and Vake to the northwest, with their hotels, restaurants and some sights; and the area with budget accommodation on the east bank between the river and the main Tbilisi train station (which is 2km northeast of Rustavelis moedani).

The airport is 15km east of the centre, to which it's connected by train, buses and taxis.

The two main bus stations are Didube, 4km north of the train station, and Ortachala (for mainly international departures), 2.5km southeast of the Old Town. A metro system links the northern and western suburbs (including Didube and the train station) with the centre.

Three very obvious landmarks, visible from far and wide, are the massive new Tsminda Sameba Cathedral high on the east side of the city, and the silver-coloured statue of Kartlis Deda (Mother Georgia) and the city's TV tower, both atop hills on the western side.

INFORMATION
Bookshops
Geoland (Map pp48-9; ☎ 922553, 921494; www .geoland.ge; Telegrapis chikhi 3; ✆ 10am-7pm or later) Georgia's best map supplier, Geoland sells Soviet military 1:50,000 sheets (the best available topographic and hiking maps) at 5 GEL per A3 sheet, plus its own excellent 1:250,000 maps covering Georgia in six sheets (30 GEL each), and a 1:650,000 country road map (30 GEL). You can buy these maps at the office or order by email. Geoland also plans to

bring out its own updated 1:50,000 trekking maps and a Tbilisi city map, and it's opening a travellers' café on site.
Prospero's Books (Map pp48-9; ☎ 923592; Rustaveli 34; ⏰ 10am-9pm) This English-language bookshop and café has a terrific if expensive selection including lots of titles on Georgia and the Caucasus region.

Emergency

Emergency services are contactable on the following numbers, but operators are likely to speak only Georgian or Russian. For petty theft or muggings it is best to find a local police station, which should at least provide you with a report.

If you speak no Georgian or Russian and have no local friends who can help you, contact your embassy.

Ambulance (☎ 03)
Fire (☎ 01)
Police (☎ 022)

Internet Access

There are internet cafés in most neighbourhoods of Tbilisi. Recommended central ones include these:

Internet Café (Map pp48-9; Davit Aghmashenebeli 108; internet per hr 1 GEL; ⏰ 10am-10pm) Inexpensive basement establishment.

Java Cyber Café (Map pp48-9; ☎ 424789; Rustaveli 18; internet per hr 2 GEL; ⏰ 10am-10pm; ✗) Clean, up-to-date, English-speaking, nonsmoking facility.

Prospero's Books (Map pp48-9; ☎ 923592; Rustaveli 34; internet per hr 4 GEL; ⏰ 10am-9pm) Two computers in Tbilisi's English-language bookshop; agreeable atmosphere and café service too.

Internet Resources

etbilisi.com Good listings for museums, galleries, theatres, bars and nightclubs.
www.info-tbilisi.com Restaurant, bar, hotel and some entertainment listings.

Laundry

Laundry (Map p56; Chavchavadzis gamziri 33a; ⏰ 9am-6pm Mon-Fri, to 1pm Sat) A traditional laundry, charging around 20 GEL for a full load. It's a tiny yellow building opposite Big Ben supermarket.

Tbisi Laundry (Map p56; ☎ 292992; Mtskheta 8; ⏰ 10am-7pm Mon-Fri, to 1pm Sat) Also does dry cleaning.

Medical Services

Private Western-standard medical facilities, all with 24-hour emergency service, include these:

Curatio (Map p56; ☎ 921592, emergency 901; www.curatio.com; Vazha Pshavela 27B) Has English-speaking GPs and provides home visits, in-person consultations and free telephone consultations round the clock.

IMSS (Map pp48-9; ☎ 920928; www.imss.ge; fax 920928; Makashvili 31) Consultations (US$80, follow-up US$40) and 24-hour Western-standard inpatient care available with UK- or US-trained doctors. All staff speak English.

MediClubGeorgia (Map p56; ☎ 251991, emergency 899581991; www.mcg.com.ge; Chavchavadzis gamziri 5) All doctors speak English.

Medicines are widely available at pharmacies (*aptiaqi* in Georgian, but often signed 'Apotheka'). Even if your Western brand name is not stocked, they will usually have a chemically identical local version. Twenty-four-hour pharmacies include these:

Aversi (Map p54; Pushkin 11)
Aversi (Map p56; Chavchavadzis gamziri 54)
PMG (Map pp48-9; Marjanishvili 33)

Money

Tbilisi is full of ATMs issuing lari on MasterCard, Visa, Cirrus and Maestro cards. There are also plenty of exchange offices where you can buy lari for cash euros, US dollars and often roubles or British pounds. At the airport there are several ATMs and at least two 24-hour bank branches offering currency exchange.

Some ATMs, including those of **TBC Bank** (☎ 272727; www.tbcbank.com.ge) Marjanishvili (Map pp48-9; Marjanishvili 7); Rustaveli cinema (Map pp48-9; Rustaveli 5); Tbilisi Marriott Hotel (Map pp48-9; Rustaveli 13); Airport (Tbilisi airport), will dispense US dollars as well as lari.

Post

Fedex (Map pp48-9; ☎ 911940; www.fedex.com; Ketevan Tsamebulis gamziri 39)
Post Office (Map pp48-9; Rustaveli 31; ⏰ 9am-6pm Mon-Sat, to 3pm Sun) Useful city-centre office where you can also make photocopies and phone calls.
TNT (Map p56; ☎ 250328; www.tnt.com; Melikishvili 41)

Telephone & Fax

Telephone Centre Rustaveli (Map pp48-9; Post Office, Rustaveli 31; ⏰ 8am-2am) Aghmashenebeli (Map pp48-9; Post Office, Davit Aghmashenebeli 44; ⏰ 9am-8pm Mon-Sat, to 5pm Sun) Pay at the counter for national and international calls from booths. Fax service available too.

You can buy Georgian SIM cards at many outlets (take your passport with you). Here are the main outlets of the three principal mobile networks:

Beeline (Map pp48-9; ☎ 200611; www.georgia.beeline
.net; Rustaveli 14) In the centre.
Geocell (Map p56; ☎ 770177; www.geocell.ge; Pekin
24) In Saburtalo.
Magti (www.magti.com.ge) Centre (Map pp48-9;
☎ 921310; Kostava 47) Vake (Map p56; ☎ 253385;
Chavchavadzis gamziri 21)

Tourist Information

A city-centre **tourist information office** (Map p54;
Tavisuplebis moedani) should be open in front of
the city hall by the time you reach Tbilisi. The
airport information office (☎ 433141; ⏰ 24 hr) can
give you basic information, such as how to
get into the city.

Travel Agencies

Good local agents can take the organisational
hassle out of any kind of activity, from a city
tour to a hiking expedition, and good guides
can open your eyes to things you'd otherwise
never know.

A half-day Tbilisi city tour for up to five
people with a good agency and a guide
speaking English, German, French, Italian
or Spanish costs around US$40 to US$70
per person. Day trips out of the city can cost
from US$50 to US$120, while a four-day
guided Caucasus trip with at least some hiking is typically between US$350 and US$650
per person.
Badagoni Tour (Map pp48-9; ☎ 936243; www.badagni
tour.com; Tavisuplebis moedani 4) Badagoni specialises in
wine and food tours but also offers a range of other trips in
Georgia, Azerbaijan and Turkey.
Caucasus Travel (Map p54; ☎ 987400; www.cau
casustravel.com; Leselidze 44) Long-established Caucasus
Travel can set up just about any group or individual trip,
from half-day city tours to climbing awesome Ushba. It's a
very professional outfit which also books accommodation
and rents cars (it's the local Hertz agent).
Explore Georgia (Map p54; ☎ 921911; www.explore
georgia.com; Chakhrukhadze 6) This young company,
headed by highly experienced mountain guide Nick
Erkomaishvili, focuses on activity-based travel, including
climbing, hiking, horse riding, bird-watching and
archaeological tours.
GeorgiCa Travel (Map p56; ☎ 252199; www.georgi
catravel.ge; Shanidze 22) Well-established, professional
GeorgiCa offers a full range of cultural and adventure
trips, and will happily construct tailor-made itineraries.
Also offers trips combining Georgia with Armenia and/or
Azerbaijan.
Levon Travel (Map p56; ☎ 250010; www.levontravel
.ge; Chavchavadzis gamziri 20) A US-based outfit, Levon

runs tours in Georgia and offers good deals on air tickets,
especially to and from North America.
Wild Georgia (Map pp48-9; ☎ 899941320; www.wild
georgia.ge; Tsinamdzghvrishvili 17) Enthusiastic agency
specialising in hiking and horse riding in Tusheti, home
town of its director, fluent-English-speaking Eka Chvritidze.

DANGERS & ANNOYANCES

Tbilisi has shaken off the very bad reputation
it once had for muggings and street violence.
We never felt endangered nor heard of any
crimes affecting foreigners while researching
this edition.

However, Western governments do warn
that travellers may still be subject to petty theft
and even assaults, urging care on the metro,
in marshrutkas (minibuses), and off the main
streets in the city centre and the Vake, Vere
and Saburtalo districts, especially after dark.
Taxis are inexpensive, so don't hesitate to take
one if you're uneasy about walking or taking
public transport.

SIGHTS

The Old Town, where Tbilisi began, is the
most fascinating area for exploring. There's
also plenty to see in the Avlabari area, on the
left bank of the Mtkvari; the 19th-century
city focused on Rustaveli; and the western
suburb of Vake. Most of the many churches
that are among Tbilisi's most beautiful and
interesting sights are open during daylight
hours every day.

Old Town ქალა

Tbilisi grew up below the walls of the Narikala
Fortress, which stands on the Sololaki ridge
above the west side of the Mtkvari gorge.
Today the twisting alleys of the Old Town,
which is known locally as Kala, are still full of
hidden courtyards and carved wooden balconies leaning at rakish angles. Though almost
no buildings here survived the destruction by
the Persians in 1795, many of those standing
today date from soon after that and still have
the Eurasian character of earlier times.

AROUND GORGASALIS MOEDANI

A good place to get your initial bearings
is **Gorgasalis moedani**, now a rather bland,
traffic-infested junction but once the setting of Tbilisi's bustling bazaar. From here
the Metekhi Bridge crosses the river to the
Metekhi Church (p55), busy Gorgasalis qucha
heads off southeast along the riverbank, and

Leselidze and Sharden dive into the maze of streets to the north. **Sharden** and parallel **Bambis rigi**, along with Erekle II a little further north, are narrow pedestrian streets lined with fashionable galleries and cafés.

Just above Gorgasalis moedani is the large **Armenian Cathedral of St George** (Map pp48-9; Samghebro), founded in 1251 (although the current structure dates mainly from the 18th century). Its interior is surprisingly small but it has interesting frescoes. King Erekle II's Armenian court poet Sayat Nova was killed here during the Persian invasion of 1795 and his tomb is in front of the main door.

The social hub of the area is further south – Tbilisi's famed sulphur baths, the **Abanotubani** (Map pp48-9; Abano). Alexanders Dumas and Pushkin both bathed here, the latter describing it as the best bath he'd ever had. Abano (Bath St) is full of subterranean bathhouses with beehive domes rising at ground level, most dating back to the 17th century. The most impressive, the above-ground **Orbeliani Baths** (Map p54; 8am-10pm), has a Central Asian feel to its blue-tile mosaic façade. Entry to the male or female communal pools here costs 2 GEL, while a very invigorating massage is 5 GEL; small private rooms are 10 GEL.

A short distance uphill behind the baths is the **mosque** (Map p54; Botanikuri), built in 1895 and the only mosque in Tbilisi that survived Lavrenty Beria's antireligious purges of the 1930s. Unusually, Shiite and Sunni Muslims pray together here. The interior is prettily frescoed and visitors are welcome to enter (after removing shoes). At the top of this street are Tbilisi's **Botanical Gardens** (Map 000; Botanikuri; admission 1 GEL; 9am-7.30pm). It's easy to wander for two or three enjoyable hours in these extensive, waterfall-dotted gardens, which were opened in 1845 on what had earlier been the royal gardens.

The main thoroughfare of the Old Town today (though sometimes traffic-clogged) is **Leselidze**. Tbilisi's main **synagogue** (Map p54; Leselidze 47) is a very welcoming place built in 1904. A short walk further up the street is the **Jvaris Mama Church** (Map p54; Ierusalimi 8), where there has been a church since the 5th century. The current structure dates from the 16th century; its frescoes were recently restored in striking reds and blues, and the atmosphere is exquisitely pious and calm. Next door is the disused Armenian **Norasheni Church** (Map p54), dating from 1793.

SIONI & SHAVTELI

In times past the Old Town's main thoroughfares and merchants areas were Sionis and Shavtelis quchas, both now quiet pedestrian streets, pleasant for strolling. The **Tbilisi History Museum** (Map p54; 982281; www.museum.ge; Sioni 8; admission 3 GEL; 11am-5pm Tue-Sun), housed in an old caravanserai, includes some wonderfully evocative photographs of pre-Soviet Tbilisi and montages of old artisans' workshops.

Next door is the **Sioni Cathedral** (Map p54; Sioni 6). The cathedral was originally built in the 6th and 7th centuries, but it has been destroyed and rebuilt so many times that it is difficult to say which part comes from when, although the south portico is undeniably the work of a shabby 1990s contractor. What you see is mainly 13th-century, though the southern chapel was built and the cupola restored in 1657. The most important sacred object here is the cross of St Nino which, according to legend, is made from vine branches bound with the saint's own hair. A replica of this is displayed to the left of the altar, with the real thing kept safe inside. On the opposite side of the street is a tall bell tower built in 1812, the first example of Russian classicism in Tbilisi.

North of the Sioni Cathedral, Sionis qucha becomes Erekle II qucha, which leads to **Erekle II moedani**, site of the walled **residence of the Catholicos-Patriarch** (Map p54; head of the Georgian church) and of a leafy little park. The large Church of the Archangels here was destroyed by the Mongols in the 13th century. Later, three smaller churches were built from the ruins, one of which is the **Karis Eklesia**, at the north end of the park.

From here Shavteli, once the throbbing medieval hub of the Old Town, continues north. Here you'll find the **Anchiskhati Basilica** (Map p54), the oldest surviving church in Tbilisi, built by King Gorgasali's son Dachi in the 6th century. The name comes from the icon of Anchi Cathedral in Klarjeti (now in Turkey), brought here in the 17th century and now in the Fine Arts Museum (p57). The church is a three-nave basilica that has been restored several times, most notably in the 17th century, when the brick pillars and upper walls were made. In 1958 restorers found the remains of 17th-century frescoes under the 19th-century ones. Just west of the church is a brick bell tower and gatehouse, typical of late-medieval eastern Georgian style. Beyond here Shavteli leads out to busy **Baratashvilis**

GEORGIA

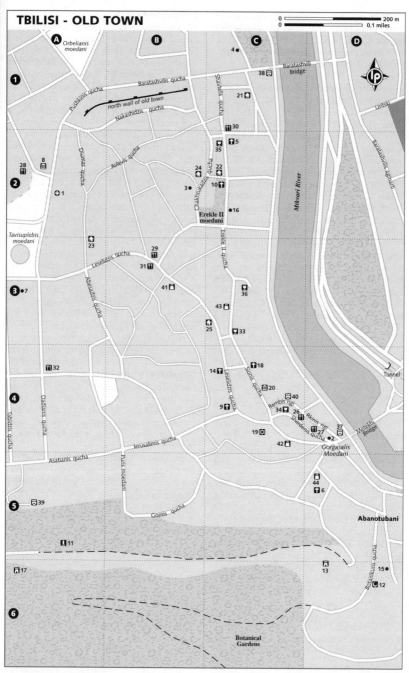

TBILISI - OLD TOWN

GEORGIA

qucha, running alongside the north wall of the Old Town.

Narikala Fortress & Around

Dominating the city skyline (until the TV tower came along, anyway), **Narikala Fortress** (Map p54; Chidini; admission free; ☽ 9am-9pm) is an ancient symbol of Tbilisi's defensive brilliance. The most direct way up to it is to follow the street beside the Armenian Cathedral of St George (p53). The fortress walls date from various periods, the earliest from the 4th century, when it was a Persian citadel. The foundations of the towers and most of the present walls were built in the 8th century by the Arab emirs, whose palace was inside the fortress. Subsequently Georgians, Turks and Persians captured and patched up Narikala, but in 1827 a huge explosion of the Russian munitions stored here ruined not only the fortress but also the **Church of St Nicholas** inside it. The church was rebuilt in the 1990s with the help of funding from a police chief. There are superb views over Tbilisi from the top of the fortress.

From outside the fortress entrance, you can follow a path west in front of the walls along to the statue of **Kartlis Deda** (Mother Georgia; map p54). As attractive as a 20m aluminium woman can be, this symbol of the city holds a sword in one hand and a cup of wine in the other – a perfect metaphor for the Georgian character, warmly welcoming guests and passionately fighting off enemies. Beyond Mother Georgia you pass the ruins of the **Shahtakhti (Shah's Throne) fortress** (Map p54), which housed an Arab observatory, and then a modernistic complex that looks like

a space station but is actually a new **business centre** (Map pp48–9) built by the Georgian-Russian multi-billionaire Boris Ivanishvili. Beyond here the road loops down to the Sololaki neighbourhood.

Avlabari & the Left Bank

Avlabari is the dramatically located slice of Tbilisi above the cliffs on the left (east) bank of the Mtkvari, across the Metekhi Bridge from the Old Town.

At least twice foreign conquerors (Jalaledin in 1226 and the Persians in 1522) used the bridge for forcible conversion of the Georgian population to Islam (many resisted and were tossed into the river). The bridge was controlled by a fortification on the rocky outcrop above it, where you can now see the **Metekhi Church** (Map pp48-9; Metekhis aghmarti) and a 1960s equestrian **statue of King Vakhtang Gorgasali** (Map pp48–9). This is where Gorgasali built his palace, and the site's original church, when he made Tbilisi his capital in the 5th century. King David the Builder had his palace here too, and it was here that Queen Tamar married her second husband, David Soslan. That palace and its accompanying church were destroyed by the Mongols in 1235. The palace too passed through several incarnations until its final destruction in the Persian sacking of 1795.

The church we see today was built by King Demetre Tavdadebuli (the Self-Sacrificing) between 1278 and 1289, and has been reconstructed many times since. An old-fashioned design for the 13th century, it is thought to be a deliberate copy of its predecessor. The church was converted into a theatre in 1974,

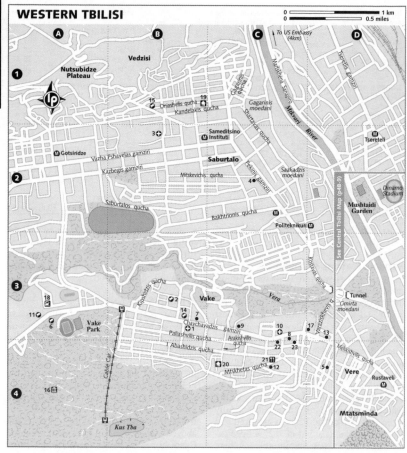

finally being reconsecrated in the 1980s. The tomb of early Christian martyr St Shushanik – tortured by her husband in 544 for refusing to convert to Zoroastrianism – is to the left of the altar.

Historically the Avlabari area housed Tbilisi's large Armenian population, one that has traditionally been focused around the **Echmiadzin Cathedral** (Map pp48-9; Ketevan Tsamebulis moedani), which is currently closed for restoration.

High on Elia Hill above Avlabari rises the biggest symbol of Georgia's post-Soviet religious revival, the **Tsminda Sameba (Holy Trinity) Cathedral** (Map pp48–9); (an unmissable landmark by night and day), consecrated in 2004 after a decade of building work. A massive

expression of traditional Georgian architectural forms in concrete, brick, granite and marble, it rises 84m to the top of the gold-covered cross above its central dome. The main entrance to the cathedral's extensive grounds is on Uritski, reached via Meskhishvili up the hill from Ketevan Tsamebulis moedani. The cathedral is five-aisles wide but its emphasis is on verticality, with a result like one single, many-bulwarked tower. The huge dome creates a larger and much brighter central space than you'll find in most Georgian churches. A big new illuminated manuscript of the New Testament, in a jewel-studded silver cover, stands in a glass case to the right of the altar. There's a whole large second church beneath the main one, down 81 steps from the west end. Designed by Archil Mindiashvili, the building was paid for mostly by donations from anonymous businesspeople and citizens. Some controversy surrounded its construction on the site of an old Armenian cemetery.

Not far below the cathedral, Georgia's large new **presidential palace** (Map pp48–9) is under construction between Tsutskiridze and Abdushelishvili. It's an equally unmissable landmark given that it's topped by a large, egg-shaped glass dome equipped with neon lights of constantly changing colour.

Rustaveli & the New Town

Tbilisi's main artery is **Rustavelis gamziri**, running 1.5km north from Tavisuplebis moedani. Laid out by the Russians in the 19th century and strung with elegant and important buildings, it tends to be the place in Tbilisi you always find yourself walking. A refurbishment programme has spruced up Rustaveli: façades have been restored, flower beds planted and new pavements (on which cars can no longer park) laid . Several new top-end hotels are also being added to its landscape.

Tavisuplebis moedani (Freedom Sq), with the city hall on its south side and a Marriott hotel on the west, was Lenin Sq in Soviet times.

Georgia's last Lenin statue, toppled in 1990, stood where a golden St George now spears his dragon.

Just off the northeast corner of Tavisuplebis moedani is the **Fine Arts Museum** (Map p54; ☎ 999909; Gudiashvili 1; admission 1.50 GEL; ☼ 11am-4pm Tue-Sun), a comprehensive if underwhelmingly presented storehouse of Georgian art and artisanry from several centuries BC up to the late 20th century. Sections may be closed because of air-conditioning problems, and at the time of research the museum was due for renovation, which may put it out of action altogether for a while. The major highlight is the treasury section, which can only be entered with a guide (no extra charge). This contains a great wealth of icons, crosses and jewellery in precious metals and stones from all over Georgia and old Georgian churches and monasteries on what is now Turkish territory. Many of Georgia's most sacred and revered objects are here. Don't miss the beautiful little pectoral cross of Queen Tamar, set with four emeralds, five rubies and six pearls – the only known personal relic of the great 12th-century monarch. The museum also has sections devoted to the wonderful paintings of Niko Pirosmani; 19th-century Persian and Azerbaijani art and crafts; and Georgian, European and Russian paintings of the 18th to 20th centuries. The building was once a seminary: Stalin studied for the priesthood here from 1894 to 1898 until expelled for revolutionary activities.

Off the opposite corner of Tavisuplebis moedani is the well-presented **Museum of Money** (Map pp48-9; ☼ 923806; Leonidze 10; admission free; ☼ 10am-1pm & 2-4pm Mon-Fri), set up by the National Bank of Georgia next door. You can see Georgian money from the 6th century BC to the present day, including the Monopoly-style coupons used in 1993–94 before the lari was introduced.

North along Rustaveli from Tavisuplebis Moedani, almost opposite Tavisuplebis Moedani metro station, is the **Museum of Georgia** (Map pp48-9; ☎ 998022; Rustaveli 3; admission 3 GEL, tour 10 GEL; ☼ 11am-4pm Tue-Sun). This is Georgia's top museum, though in 2007 the whole place was shut for renovations of unspecified duration. The main rooms cover Georgia's history, including a section on the Soviet occupation and an exhibit on the 1.75-million-year-old skulls found at Dmanisi, 80km southwest of Tbilisi, which may be the oldest human remains found outside Africa. Most stunning of

TBILISI IN ONE DAY

Begin with a coffee and *khachapuri* at one of the cafés on **Rustaveli** (p64), before wandering the atmospheric alleyways of the **Old Town** (p52), dropping into some of the fascinating old churches on the way, and crossing the river to the **Metekhi Church** (p55) with its panoramic views. A walk up to the **Narikala Fortress** (p55) and **Kartlis Deda** (p55) above the city will give you great views and help to work up an appetite for lunch at one of the popular Old Town eateries. Visit the **Museum of Georgia** (p57) – or, if it's not open, the nearby **Fine Arts Museum** (p57) – and then wander back into the Old Town or along Rustaveli for some **shopping** (p67). In the evening head out to a traditional Georgian restaurant (p63) with as many people as possible for some serious feasting. For a nightcap and a spot of live music head to the crowded bar and restaurant strip on **Akhvlediani** (p64, p65 and p65).

all is the basement treasury (guide obligatory) with an outstanding collection of archaeological finds including gold artefacts and jewellery from pre-Christian Georgia.

Back on the west side of the street, the high-arched Georgian **Parliament** (Map pp48–9) was constructed as the Soviet government building between 1938 and 1953 and finished off by German POWs. Momentous events in Georgia's recent history have taken place here: the Soviet massacre of 20 Georgian hunger strikers on 9 April 1989; Georgia's independence declaration on 9 April 1991; on 6 January 1992 President Gamsakhurdia fled the building after being besieged in it for two weeks; and the Rose Revolution on 22 November 2003. A small monument in front of the Parliament commemorates the dead of 1989. The next building, **School Number 1** (Map pp48–9), was gutted in the 1991–92 fighting, but was reconstructed soon after. It was founded in 1802 to prepare sons of the Georgian nobility for the Russian Civil Service. In front of the school are statues of the 19th-century writers and reformers Ilia Chavchavadze and Akaki Tsereteli.

Opposite School No 1 stands the **Kashveti Church** (Map pp48–9), on a spot where it is said pagan rituals used to take place. The first church here is supposed to have been built in the 6th century by Davit Gareja, one of the ascetic 'Syrian fathers' who returned from the Middle East to spread Christianity in Georgia. According to legend, a nun accused him of impregnating her. He replied that if this were true, she'd give birth to a baby, and if not, to a stone, which duly happened. Kashveti means 'Stone Birth'. The existing 1910 building was designed by architect Leopold Bielfeld as a copy of the 11th-century Samtavisi Church, 60km northwest of Tbilisi.

On the same side of the road, past the Tbilisi Marriott Hotel, is the elegant **Rustaveli National Theatre** (Map pp48–9), built between 1899 and 1901 in a baroque-cum-rococo style. A little further on is the **Paliashvili Opera & Ballet Theatre** (Map pp48–9), created only slightly earlier (1896) in a fantastic Moorish style.

Just after the post office building made from glass and yellow stone comes **Vardebis Revolutsis moedani** (Rose Revolution Sq; formerly Republic Sq), which has views towards the Caucasus mountains. Rustaveli branches left just before this square towards **Rustavelis moedani**, easily identified by a 1937 statue of the poet himself (and a McDonald's restaurant).

North from Rustavelis moedani, Kostava leads up to the **State Concert Hall** (Philharmonia; map pp48–9) and **Vere Park**. The musical fountains outside the concert hall are a favourite with Tbilisi kids wanting to cavort and cool off in the heat of summer.

Mt Mtatsminda

Mtatsminda is the hill topped by the 210m-high TV mast looming over central Tbilisi from the west. You can get up there by a steep funicular railway from Chonkadze. At the funicular's halfway stop is the **Mamadaviti Church** (Map pp48–9), an 1850s construction on the site of a hermitage of St Davit Gareja. Just below the church, the national **Pantheon** (Map pp48–9) contains graves of writers and public figures including Ilia Chavchavadze and Zviad Gamsakhurdia.

At the top of the hill, **Mtatsminda Park** (Map pp48–9) spreads over more than 1 sq km, with wonderful views and a new amusement park that includes what Georgians consider Europe's highest roller coaster (60m high).

Vake ვაკე

Considered Tbilisi's most prestigious neighbourhood, home to many nouveaux riches and expatriates, Vake is said to have been built over the graves of the victims of the 1930s purges. It's a pleasant neighbourhood of apartment blocks and houses, with a good sprinkling of bars, cafés and shops. Bus 55 from Tavisuplebis moedani runs along Rustaveli, up Kostava then along the length of Vake's main avenue, Chavchavadzis gamziri.

Vake's main claim to fame is **Tbilisi State University** (Map p56), near the start of Chavchavadzis gamziri. The main university building, circa 1906, is elegant, white and neoclassical. It was originally a school for the nobility.

Attractive **Vake Park** is about 2km beyond the university. A sporadically operating **cable car** (0.40 GEL one-way; ⏰ 10am-8pm) sails up to **Kus Tba** (Turtle Lake; map p56), a popular summer spot for sunbathing, swimming, boating and strolling. The **Open-Air Museum of Ethnography** (Map p56; ☎ 230960; Kus Tba 1; admission 1.50 GEL, tour 10 GEL; ⏰ 10.30am-9pm Jun-Sep, to 4pm Oct-May) is about 3km beyond, and uphill from, the park. This collection of nearly 70 traditional, mostly wooden houses from around Georgia is spread over a wooded hillside with good views, and makes an enjoyable visit. The most interesting exhibits are in the lower section of the museum (near the entrance), where the buildings are kitted out with fine traditional furnishings, rugs and utensils. There's also an archaeological section, which includes a basilica from the 6th and 7th centuries. You can reach the open-air museum by walking up from Vake Park, or down the road from Kus Tba (about 2km). Or take bus 59 from opposite Marjanishvili metro station or along Kostava or Chavchavadzis gamziri to its last stop, then walk or take a taxi 2km up the road between the concrete pillars opposite.

ACTIVITIES

In the searing heat of the Tbilisi summer, a cooling splash can be just the thing. The open-air **Laguna Vere Pool** (Map pp48-9; ☎ 998231; Kostava 34; admission 15 GEL; ⏰ 7am-1pm & 2-9pm Mon-Sat, 8am-1pm & 2-8pm Sun) is popular with locals. It's a mite antiquated but has a clean 50m by 25m pool. First-time visitors need to pay 5 GEL extra for a cursory medical inspection.

Much more luxurious and modern (and expensive) is the beautiful 50m indoor pool at **Vake Swimming Pool & Fitness Club** (Map p56; ☎ 252575; www.vakefitness.ge; men/women 90/54 GEL; Chavchavadzis gamziri 49B; ⏰ 7am-11pm Mon-Fri, 9am-10pm Sat, 9am-9pm Sun). The pool is heated to a constant 28°C. Admission includes use of a state-of-the-art fitness club.

For water-slide excitement, there's **Europark** (☎ 690181; Trikotazhi 3; admission 50 GEL; ⏰ 10am-8pm; Ⓜ Elektrodepo), an aquapark opened in 2007 in the Nadzaladevi district, offering 12 slides, four pools, palm trees and several cafés.

Any time of year is good for a traditional bath and massage experience at Tbilisi's famed sulphur baths, the **Abanotubani** (p53).

WALKING TOUR

This walk takes you through the heart of Tbilisi's New Town and the narrow streets of the Old Town, then across to the dramatically located left bank of the Mtkvari.

Start outside Rustaveli metro station, one of the city's main hubs and home to the grotesquely large main branch of McDonald's. More interesting are the **monument (1)** to the national bard Shota Rustaveli and the pleasantly Stalinist **Academy of Sciences (2**; Rustaveli 52), with its landmark tower and spire. Walk along Rustaveli to soak up the bustling, cosmopolitan atmosphere of Tbilisi's main artery, strung with handsome and important buildings such as the **Opera House (3**; opposite), the **Rustaveli Theatre (4**; opposite), the **Kashveti Church (5**; opposite), the **Parliament (6**; opposite) and the **Museum of Georgia (7**; p57).

From **Tavisuplebis moedani (8**; p57) at the end of Rustaveli, head down Leselidze at the far left corner of the square, then along Diumas, the first left off Leselidze. Take the first short lane to the right after the Hotel Dzveli Ubani and then follow Avlevi down to the left through an area of quaint Old Town houses. Avlevi emerges on pedestrianised Shavteli; turn right here, passing the **Anchiskhati Basilica (9**; p53) and **Erekle II moedani (10**; p53) and into Erekle II qucha with its cafés. Continue along Sionis qucha, past the **Sioni Cathedral (11**; p53) and the **Tbilisi History Museum (12**; p53), and then duck into Bambis rigi or Shardenis qucha, both lined with smart cafés. Either of these narrow pedestrian streets brings you out on **Gorgasalis moedani (13**; p52), with Narikala Fortress rising on the hill above.

Take the small street (Samghebro) in front of the lovely **Armenian Cathedral of St George (14**; p53) down to the **Abanotubani (15**; p53),

GEORGIA

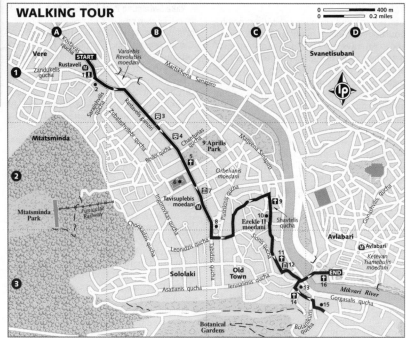

WALK FACTS

Start Rustaveli monument
Finish Metekhi Church
Distance 4km
Time two hours

Tbilisi's traditional sulphur baths. Head back to Gorgasalis moedani and across the Metekhi Bridge and up the hill to finish your walk at the emblematic **Metekhi Church** (16; p55).

FESTIVALS & EVENTS

The highlight of the year is **Tbilisoba**, the festival of new wine and the city's founding, on the last weekend in October.

This is a wonderful time to visit – the whole city comes out to party, and plenty of entertainment and fun take place on and off the streets.

Tbilisi is also big on arts festivals:

Art Gene Festival (www.artgeni.ge) This Georgian folklore festival tours the country and culminates with several days of music, dance, poetry, cooking and crafts in Tbilisi, in June or July.

Tbilisi International Film Festival (www.tbilisifilm festival.ge) Showcases recent Georgian and international movies; held in the last quarter of the year (dates vary). Season tickets for all showings are as little as 25 GEL.
Tbilisi Jazz Festival (www.easternpromotion.com) International artists fly in for 10 days of jazz in late June; ticket prices for headline acts can be astronomical.
Tumanishvili Georgian International Festival of Arts (GIFT) Mainly international drama performances, around the second half of October.

SLEEPING

Places to stay are located mainly in the Old Town and the New Town in the centre, and in the suburbs of Vere and Saburtalo further north. Prices given here include the tax that is often left out of hotel publicity. Most midrange and top-end establishments accept credit cards; note that they also quote their prices in dollars, not lari.

Budget

Home from home for backpackers in Tbilisi is Marjanishvili, a leafy street that's full of local life, east of the Mtkvari River but only one metro stop from Rustaveli. Several homestays of varying character offer inexpensive accommodation here. They don't serve food but there are plenty of economical eateries and food shops nearby.

Khatuna's Homestay (Map pp48-9; ☎ 566281, 899 173609; Chitaia 12; per person 8 GEL) This small apartment between Marjanishvili and the train station offers supercheap beds crowded into its couple of rooms, plus a bathroom with a shower and hot water. It's fine and friendly, and Khatuna and her young daughter speak some English.

Nasi Gvetadze's Homestay (Map pp48-9; ☎ 950894; Marjanishvili 30/92; per person 20 GEL) Retired teacher Nasi Gvetadze has the longest-running Marjanishvili homestay in her homey old apartment. It's still an inexpensive and well-kept place to stay if you don't mind paying for showers (2 GEL for hot, 1 GEL for cold) and that she likes to lock the door at midnight. Nasi speaks fluent German and rudimentary English. Hers is the last entrance on the right in the courtyard.

Irine Japaridze's Boarding House (Map pp48-9; ☎ 954716; www.iverieli.narod.ru; Ninoshvili 19 B3; per person 20-25 GEL; 🔀 💻) Artist Irine's two-storey apartment is the hub of Tbilisi's backpacker social scene. She delights in the international atmosphere and has stacked her six rooms with beds and bunks to squeeze in as many travellers as possible. If you like a crowd and don't mind waiting for the shower, this is a great place. Guests can use the kitchen, and a load of laundry costs 5 GEL. Go in the entrance with two headless stone lions and up to the top of the stairs. Bicycles welcome!

ourpick **Dodo's Homestay** (Map pp48-9; ☎ 954213, 893327010; dodogeorgia@gmail.com; Marjanishvili 38; dm/ private room per person 25/30 GEL) Dodo's is the choice pick for budget travellers who like a slightly more spacious, less hectic atmosphere. The single-storey house has five large guest rooms and a shady courtyard for sitting out. Members of the extremely helpful family speak excellent English, German and Italian. Cooking facilities and washing machine are free.

Hotel Lile (Map pp48-9; ☎ 773856; Ghvinis aghmarti 19; r 70-90 GEL; 🔀) The friendly Lile is a short walk across the river from the Old Town, close to Avlabari metro station. Rooms are good value and comfortable, all with good bathrooms and air-con, though the street is busy with loud traffic.

Midrange

There are many good midrange choices in the centre and in nearby leafy Vere.

Hotel Dzveli Ubani (Map p54; ☎ 922404; www .dzveliubani.com.ge; Diumas 5; r incl breakfast US$40-80; 🔀) This small hotel has a great location, just off Leselidze in the Old Town. Cosy, well-equipped rooms with good modern bathrooms are available at reasonable prices. Staff speak English, and it's one of the best deals in its range.

Hotel Kartli (Map pp48-9; ☎ 982982; hot_kartli@gol .ge; Barnov 32; s/d incl breakfast US$40/50; 🔀) Good-value Kartli, in a fairly tranquil uphill part of Vere, makes guests feel at home with 12 cosy, rustically furnished rooms, four of which have air-con. The helpful staff speak English and German and the terrace restaurant (mains 6 GEL to 15 GEL) is a popular lunch spot.

VIP Hotel (Map p54; ☎ 920040; hotel@vipmail.ge; Leselidze 31; s/d US$50/60; 🔀) The VIP stands in a quiet courtyard off Leselidze in the thick of the Old Town. Rooms are spacious, with quality dark-wood furniture; those on the top floor are air-conditioned and enjoy great views across to the east bank of the Mtkvari.

Hotel Charm (Map p54; ☎ 986348; www.hotel charm.ge; Chakhrukhadze 11; r incl breakfast US$40-80; 🔀) The atmospheric, centrally located Charm is a small, family-run hotel boasting a superb collection of antique furniture. The lounge includes a white Steinway, while the breakfast bar is rich with taxidermy. Three rooms on the 1st floor (each with a private bathroom) are extremely comfortable in 19th-century Georgian style, while the three on the 2nd floor share a very clean bathroom and toilet. There's billiards downstairs.

Hotel David (Map pp48-9; ☎ 935006; www.david hotel.ge; Paolo Iashvili 16A; s/d incl breakfast US$50/60; 🔀) A smart and comfortable small hotel not far from Tavisuplebis moedani. Rooms are equipped with attractive wooden furniture and satellite TV. You pay extra to use the small gym and sauna.

Vere Inn (Map pp48-9; ☎ 294733; www.hotels-tbilisi .com; Barnov 53; r US$50-90; 🔀 🍴) A very pleasant and reasonably priced option, this hideaway in Vere has four good-sized, quirkily but tastefully decorated rooms and is exceptionally friendly. The English-speaking owners are full of useful information and breakfast is included with all but the US$50 room.

Hotel GTM (Map pp48-9; ☎ 273348; www.gtmkapan .ltd.ge; Metekhis aghmarti 4; r incl breakfast US$59-95; 🔀)

GEORGIA

With good prices and a great location opposite the Metekhi Church, the medium-sized GTM is understandably busy and popular. The more expensive rooms tend to be exterior, often with balcony; the cheaper rooms are interior or smaller.

Hotel Lago (Map p56; ☎ 380517, 899742433; hotel lago@hotmail.com; Kandelaki 27; s/d incl breakfast US$60/75) Despite its off-centre location in Saburtalo, it's well worth considering this unique hotel, which is furnished from top to bottom with French antique furniture. Friendly, cosy and elegant, it's unmarked outside except for the street number; ring to enter. Rooms 7 and 8 share an enormous walk-out balcony.

ourpick Hotel British House (Map pp48-9; ☎ 988783; www.british-house.ge; Belinski 32; s/d incl breakfast US$80/100; ❄ ☐) British owned but Georgian run, this little hotel is elegant, exceptionally welcoming, and located in a quiet, leafy part of Vere. The rooms are traditional in style but offer modern comforts.

Hotel Old Metekhi (Map pp48-9; ☎ 747431; www .oldmetekhi.ge; Metekhi 3; incl breakfast s US$80-110, d US$130; ❄) Perched on a rocky cliff above the Mtkvari, Old Metekhi is a traditional establishment favouring individual attention over visitor numbers: despite its size, it only has 15 rooms. Rooms are comfortable rather than luxurious, but most have attractive marquetry floors and balconies with fabulous views. Overall, one of the most pleasant places to put up in Tbilisi. The popular Dzveli Metekhi restaurant is attached.

Villa Mtiebi (Map p54; ☎ 920340; www.hotelmtiebi .ge; Chakhrukhadze 10; s/d incl breakfast US$85/100; ❄) A small Old Town hotel that provides modern conveniences while maintaining its original late-19th-century elegance. At the centre of the hotel features a lovely skylit, plant-draped atrium, where continental breakfast is served. Rooms are soundproofed and have excellent up-to-date bathrooms, and service is personal and attentive.

Hotel Beaumonde (Map pp48-9; ☎ 986003; bali103@ hotmail.com; A Chavchavadzis qucha 11; r incl half board & alcohol US$90-120; ☐) The Giorgadze family will make you feel very welcome in their charming small hotel. The rooms are large and comfortable, and the hotel has good extra touches such as a library and a roof terrace with paddling pool.

Hotel Kopala (Map pp48-9; ☎ 775520; www.kopala .ge; Chekhov 8/10; s/d US$90/105, ste US$120/135; ❄ ☐) Classy Kopala has one of the loveliest positions in the city, above the Metekhi Church. Many of its spacious rooms have large balconies overlooking the Old Town, and the staff are amiable and efficient. The excellent restaurant enjoys the same great views, and the hotel also boasts a bizarre meeting hall in the style of an 18th-century Metekhian mansion – definitely the place for a surreal corporate retreat.

Hotel Iliani (Map pp48-9; ☎ 335710; www.iliani.com; Anjaparidze 1; s $90, d US$100-120; ❄ ☐) On the so-called 'Hill of Dreams', the recently renovated Iliani is one of the most pleasant midrange hotels in Tbilisi, with good service. Most of the well-designed, individually furnished rooms have balconies overlooking a leafy garden. It's on a quiet residential street, a short walk from Kostava and the centre of town, and has its own good restaurant.

Hotel Tori (Map pp48-9; ☎ 923765; web.sanet.ge/tori; Chanturia 10; s/d incl breakfast US$95/118; ❄ ☐) This friendly and comfortable place has a highly central location near Rustaveli, along with neat, clean rooms that boast great bathrooms. There's a restaurant and an exchange office, plus a fitness room, billiards, a sauna and a Turkish bath for your spare moments.

ourpick Hotel VIP Victoria (Map p56; ☎ 291877; www.victoria.com.ge; Arakishvili 1 chikhi 3; r incl breakfast US$118-142; ❄ ☐) A fine place to unwind, this charming small hotel in Vake is popular with international agency staff and businessfolk. It's modern, tasteful and very comfortable, with parquet floors, spacious and quiet sitting areas, interesting original art and even fur-covered toilet seats!

Top End

At least six more top-end international chain hotels – Radisson, InterContinental, Kempinski, Hilton, Hyatt and yet another Marriott – are due to open in Tbilisi in the next few years.

ourpick Hotel Ambasadori (Map p54; ☎ 920403; www.ambasadori.ge; Shavteli 13; incl breakfast s US$115, d US$135-170; ❄ ☐ ☕) An elegant hotel in a great location overlooking the Mtkvari, the Ambasadori is an excellent alternative to the bigger, pricier establishments. Almost new but in attractive fin-de-siècle-style, it features well-equipped rooms with very comfortable beds, plus a rooftop pool overlooking the Anchiskhati Basilica. Service is friendly and polished, and the sepia-tint photos of old Tbilisi add character.

GEORGIA

Betsy's Hotel (Map pp48-9; ☎ 931404; www.betsyshotel
.com; Makashvili 32-34; s/d incl breakfast & dinner US$165/195;
❄ ☎) A favourite with Georgia's numerous
international-agency workers, this oasis of
American-run efficiency is understandably
popular. The rooms are bright and very comfortable and some boast great views over the
city. The cocktail bar and restaurant are both
highly recommended, and there's a bookshop
and a small outdoor pool (don't expect to be
able to work off the *khachapuri*).

Courtyard by Marriott (Map pp48-9; ☎ 779100;
www.courtyard.com/TBSCY; Tavisuplebis moedani 4; r from
US$277; ❄ ☐ ☒ ☎) The less expensive and
less formal of Tbilisi's two Marriotts, the
Courtyard is another little island of Western
comfort, with amiable staff. Rooms are typical
international business class, brightened by
colourful art and offering 54-channel satellite
TV. The good indoor pool and fitness club are
included in room prices.

Tbilisi Marriott Hotel (Map pp48-9; ☎ 779200; www
.marriott.com/TBSMC; Rustaveli 13; r incl breakfast from
US$325; ❄ ☐ ☒) This palace of excellent
service and facilities is aimed at a business
and international-organisation crowd, so is
rather formal and quiet. The rooms are spacious, with supercomfortable beds, and the
bathrooms are huge. The hotel also houses the
Majestic Restaurant (with Italian food), as well
as a ballroom and a very good fitness centre.
Originally built in 1914–15, the hotel was reduced to a burnt-out shell during the 1991–92
fighting. Marriott restored it to more than its
former splendour and reopened it in 2002.

EATING

Tbilisi restaurants span a broad range from
traditional-style feasts of superb Georgian
fare to less boisterous eateries serving all
sorts of other cuisines. There's also a great
café culture.

Old Town

At the heart of the Old Town are the three
pedestrian streets Erekle II, Sharden and
Bambis rigi, all lined with fashionable cafés,
bars, restaurants and galleries. Other eateries
are scattered around the Old Town and in the
Metekhi area just across the river.

Teremok (Map p54; ☎ 877454414; Dadiani 18; dishes
2.50-11 GEL; ❂ 10am-11pm) This cosy little restaurant in the style of an old Russian cottage specialises in scrumptious bliny, little
round pancakes beloved of Russians and

indeed most people who have ever tried them.
You can enjoy them with mushrooms, meat,
cream, jam, cheese, fruit or many other options. Other Russian and Ukrainian dishes
are served too.

Prestige (Map p54; Leselidze 40; dishes 3-6 GEL; ❂ 9am-
1pm) This fairly standard beer bar has a leafy
back garden where it's nice to sit out over
a *mtsvadi* (shashlyk) or a *khachapuri* on a
summer evening.

Puris Sakhli (Map pp48-9; ☎ 999537; Gorgasali 7; mains
4-10 GEL; ❂ noon-11pm) A short walk from the
sulphur baths, Puris Sakhli (Bread House) is
one of Tbilisi's most popular and lively spots
for a meal. The menu is in English as well as
Georgian, and a huge feast for two is unlikely
to be more than 40 GEL.

Sans Souci (Map p54; ☎ 986594; Shavteli 13; mains
5-10 GEL; ❂ 10am-12.30am) This quirkily attractive little restaurant makes a great place for
lunch or dinner. It offers friendly service and a
view of both the Anchiskhati Basilica and the
Hangar sports bar. The food is Georgian with
original twists – try the leek hors d'oeuvre
for starters.

China Town (Map p54; ☎ 754114; Sharden; mains 5-15
GEL; ⓥ) Colourful and consistently popular,
China Town serves authentic Chinese dishes
including tofu combinations and plenty of
other options for vegetarians. There are meat
dishes on offer too.

Dzveli Metekhi (Map pp48-9; ☎ 747407; Metekhi 3;
mains 7-15 GEL; ❂ noon-10pm) Across the Metekhi
Bridge from the Old Town proper, this understandably popular place attached to the
Hotel Old Metekhi (opposite) has sought-after
balcony tables with superb views over the Old
Town. The food is excellent Georgian and
international fare, plus there's a good wine
list. Live music most nights.

Hotel Kopala (Map pp48-9; ☎ 775520; Chekhov 8/10;
mains 7-17 GEL) Also on the Metekhi side of the
river, the restaurant of the Hotel Kopala has
one of the best views in the city (across the
river to the Old Town) and a fairly tranquil
ambience. It serves some of the best Georgian
food and a good range of wines too.

12 Rue Chardin (Map p54; ☎ 923238; Sharden 12; mains
8-25 GEL) The best place for a proper meal on the
Sharpen strip, with a mainly European menu
and ambience, and French wine.

Shemoikhede Genatsvale (Map p54; ☎ 439646;
Leselidze 25; 2-course meal incl drinks 15-30 GEL; ❂ 8am-
11pm) Neat, modern and less atmospheric than
the other Shemoikhede Genatsvale (p64), but

with the same excellent Georgian food and efficient service. Easiest identified by the Pirosmani painting on the street frontage of a dog and three men eating.

Rustaveli & Around

Caravan (Map pp48-9; ☎ 996691; Purtseladze 10; mains 6-30 GEL; ☒ noon-3am) Interesting lounge-style restaurant-café with an East-meets-West literary ambience. Eclectic and well-prepared food – from Uzbek *plov* to French steak or Norwegian salmon – is served at low tables with cushioned benches in a relaxed space amid kilims, hookahs and assorted prints and posters of writers.

ourpick Dzveli Sakhli (Map pp48-9; ☎ 923497; Marjvena Sanapiro 3; mains 8-25 GEL) Down by the river, the expansive 'Old House' is one of the best places in town, serving authentic dishes – with a twist – from all over Georgia. There's often excellent Georgian music and dancing in the main dining hall, which has long banquet tables, ideal for small groups with time to enjoy a full evening. If you fancy a quieter meal, choose the partly open-air riverside hall. Service isn't rapid but the food is worth a wait. You can order wine by the jug.

Csaba's Jazz-Rock Café (Map pp48-9; ☎ 923192; Vashlovani 3; mains 10-15 GEL; ☒ noon-4am) Anyone curious about what to expect from a Hungarian-Georgian restaurant will be pleasantly surprised by the excellent salads and meat dishes in this friendly little establishment with a wooden interior. Most nights live jazz or rock is an enjoyable accompaniment from 8.30pm to 10pm.

Tokyo (Map pp48-9; ☎ 995632; Akhvlediani 17; mains 15-40 GEL) This sleek Japanese place is one of Tbilisi's most stylish restaurants. The superb sushi is all prepared authentically, although it is pricey.

La Brasserie (Map pp48-9; ☎ 779100; Courtyard by Marriott, Tavisuplebis moedani 4; continental/full breakfast 21/32 GEL; ☒ 6.30-11am Mon-Fri, to noon Sat & Sun) The Marriott Courtyard's not-too-formal restaurant is just the place if you feel like a truly enormous buffet breakfast. Wi-fi available too.

CAFÉS & CHEAP EATS

Chocolate (Map pp48-9; Rustaveli 36; snacks 1-2 GEL; ☒ 24 hr) Excellent little café serving baklava and other Turkish sweets, *khachapuri* and good coffee.

Kafe Lotus (Map p54; ☎ 877469197; Tavisuplebis moedani 7; mains 1.50-2.50 GEL; ☒ 10am-8pm Mon-Sat; Ⓥ)

This vegetarian canteen is one of the best places for lunch on the run in Tbilisi. It's cheap, cheerful and delicious, and the menu includes vegetarian versions of traditional Georgian meat dishes and oriental fare.

Cafe Nikala (Map pp48-9; ☎ 998283; Rustaveli 22; mains 3-5 GEL; ☒ 9am-11pm) A bright self-service place with dependable salads, rice and meat dishes, *khachapuri* and cakes – a far cry from the dreary self-service canteens of Soviet times.

SELF-CATERING

Plenty of supermarkets offer a large range of foodstuffs. One of the best in the centre is **Populi** (Map pp48-9; Georgian Trade Centre, Vekua 3; ☒ 8am-11pm).

Marjanishvili & Around

Ankara (Map pp48-9; ☎ 957281; Davit Aghmashenebeli 128; mains 4-8 GEL; ☒ 8am-10pm) A short stretch of this busy street looks like it has been transplanted from Turkey, with Turkish restaurants, Turkish businesses and even a Turkish hotel. The Ankara is a modern, clean, air-conditioned restaurant done out in pink and white, where you can get plenty of good salad and sweets as well as kebabs and other meaty dishes.

ourpick Shemoikhede Genatsvale (Map pp48-9; ☎ 910005; Marjanishvili 5; 2-course meal incl drinks 15-30 GEL; ☒ 8am-11pm) The name means 'Drop in, Love' and this restaurant enacts that invitation with terrific Georgian food in a fun, old-fashioned, but not overwhelming tavern ambience, with good service. Spot it by the Pirosmani painting of three men and a dog displayed outside. The house speciality is the excellent *khinkali* (with potato- or mushroom-stuffed varieties as well as meat) but there are very good *mtsvadi* (meat kebabs) and *chkmeruli* (sizzling chicken in garlic sauce). Wash it all down with draft beer or good house wine. The menu is in Georgian only, but some staff speak English.

CAFÉS & CHEAP EATS

Sachashnike (Map pp48-9; Davit Aghmashenebeli 114; mains 3-4 GEL; ☒ 7am-9pm) Straightforward and excellent-value place convenient for the Marjanishvili homestays. You can get *khinkali* for 0.40 GEL each, pork *mtsvadi* for 4 GEL and a carafe of Georgian wine for 3 GEL.

Vere & Vake

El Depo (Map pp48-9; Ghambashidze 10; khinkali 0.40-0.50 GEL; 24 hr) One of the most central branches of the popular *khinkali* chain – a good place to enjoy this Georgian staple, with rustic wooden tables and other traditional decor. Does good *lobio* too.

Il Garage (Map p56; ☎ 877780090; Mtskheta 1; mains 10-17 GEL; noon-10pm Mon-Sat, closed Aug) Sardinian chefs whip up yummy concoctions of fresh pasta at this minimalist haunt facing the so-called Mrgvani Baghi (Circle Garden). Eat inside or surrounded by greenery on the patio.

CAFÉS & CHEAP EATS

Kafe Literaturuli (Map pp48-9; ☎ 444546; Tarkhnishvili 2; cakes & pastries 2-5 GEL; 10am-1pm) The Literary Café is a great stop near the Philharmonia for tea, coffee and sweet snacks. One branch of a small chain, it's calm and informal, with neat modern design and a mildly trendy, artsy atmosphere.

DRINKING

The Old Town, especially the pedestrianised streets with their strings of designer bars and pavement cafés, is Tbilisi's fashionable place to drink and socialise. The longer-established strip of bars and restaurants around Akhvlediani is a less-sceney alternative with less-inflated prices. Most bars serve meals as well, and stay open until at least 1am.

Old Town

On Erekle II, Sharden and Bambis rigi it's a case of wandering along and seeing which bar grabs your fancy.

Café Kala (Map p54; ☎ 899799737; Erekle II 8/10; noon-2am) The bar that got the Erekle II scene going back in 2004, Kala is still consistently the most popular. There's a comfortable, arty atmosphere, free wi-fi and the city's best live jazz from 9pm to midnight. The food is pretty average.

Moulin Electrique (Map p54; ☎ 899359264; Erekle II 4/10; noon-2am) This funky two-level nook attracts a cool 20s crowd. The décor is a collection of random small objects that might have been assembled at the Dry Bridge market (p67).

Chardin Bar (Map p54; ☎ 752044; Sharden 4; noon-2am) Gilt, velvet plush and photos of fashion models pull in the beautiful people to chatter over cocktails and cakes to a techno and ambient background.

Hangar Bar (Map p54; ☎ 931080; Shavteli 20; 11am-last customer Mon-Fri, noon-last customer Sat & Sun) Focus for the expat community's testosterone tendency, this Irish-American bar proclaims itself the 'home of live rugby', shows TV sport and serves Tex-Mex and Italian food. It's always bustling and the welcoming staff speak perfect English.

Rustaveli & Around

Running off the north end of Vardebis Revolutsis moedani, Akhvlediani (formerly Perovskoy and still widely known by that name), along with neighbouring Kiacheli and Vashlovani, is home to a cosmopolitan variety of bars and eateries, several of which offer live music. You can always find somewhere lively to drop into here.

Laghidze, running down off Rustaveli beside the Opera House, is home to a small clutch of interesting bars.

Dublin (Map pp48-9; ☎ 984467; Akhvlediani 8; 10am-3am) The tight rock bands at this popular and convivial Irish bar usually get at least a few people dancing. The music may not be original, but the musicians sure know how to play it.

Nali (Map pp48-9; ☎ 986859; Kiacheli 4/1; 1pm-2am) It's always worth checking out this other Irish pub, bigger than Dublin, for its live rock music and atmosphere.

Le Café (Map pp48-9; ☎ 934913; Vashlovani 4; noon-4am) A slick little bar with French ambience, Le Café is enjoyable to drop into for relatively quiet conversation.

Near Opera (Map pp48-9; ☎ 899681166; Laghidze 2; 11.30am-2am) This concisely named bar, popular with all ages, is a multichambered affair with décor seemingly inspired by Aubrey Beardsley. An excellent jazz trio plays from 9pm most nights.

Acid Bar (Map pp48-9; ☎ 899101238; Laghidze 2; 10am-2am) Hip little two-level bar with studenty ambience and a Cuban theme.

ENTERTAINMENT

Tbilisi has a fairly busy after-dark scene. You'll find listings in *Georgia Today* (www .georgiatoday.ge) and *The Messenger* (www .messenger.com.ge) and online at etbilisi.com and www.info-t bilisi.com.

Live Music

Many Georgians seem to think music is best heard while eating, so while a lot of restaurants provide musical entertainment (heaven or hell depending on quality and volume), venues where you can just go for the music and a drink are comparatively rare.

To hear traditional Georgian music, you need to eat at a restaurant with this kind of entertainment.

Two good bets are **Dzveli Sakhli** (p64) and the smart **Two-Side** (Map p54; ☎ 439038; Bambis rigi 7; ☽ noon-2am).

Some city-centre bars put on live jazz, rock or blues, starting about 9pm. The best include the jazz at **Café Kala** (p65) and **Near Opera** (p65), and the rock at **Dublin** (p65). The small, smoky **Jazz Club Non Stop** (Map pp48-9; ☎ 921664; Akhvlediani 6; admission free-10 GEL) and the larger, purpose-built **Blues Brothers** (Map pp48-9; ☎ 931226; www.bluesbrothers.ge; Rustaveli 38; admission free-10 GEL) are both dedicated to live jazz and blues (from 9pm most nights), but atmosphere and musical quality are hit or miss.

Nightclubs

There's now a handful of good DJ clubs, though most of them shut up shop during July and August, when the scene migrates to Batumi.

ourpick Night Office (Map p54; ☎ 923016; admission 15-35 GEL; ☽ from 10pm Fri & Sat) This hi-tech, laser-illuminated space under the Baratashvili Bridge, with three bars and room for 1000 clubbers, is the top party spot in town. International guest DJs fly in many weekends. You can dance to almost any electronic beat here, including breakbeat, house and the locally popular minimal.

Traffic (Map pp48-9; ☎ 999858; Leonidzis chikhi 1; ☽ 7pm-last customer) Down an alley near Tavisuplebis moedani, this LA-style lounge is popular with locals and expats. DJs spin electronic music till very late.

Tunnel Club (Map p54; ☎ 898177715; Asatiani 30; admission 15 GEL; ☽ from 10pm) Popular club set inside a former nuclear shelter in the hill below Mother Georgia. The setting is certainly unique and the dance floor must be one of the longest and thinnest in the world.

Switch (Map pp48-9; ☎ 899119655; Rustaveli 37; admission 20-30 GEL; ☽ from 11.30pm Fri & Sat) Another top club, with minimal and other techno beats and occasional headline guest DJs.

Maidan's Club (Map p54; ☎ 751188; Rkinis rigi 6; ☽ 7pm-5am) Convenient if you don't want to move far from the Old Town bars, this place offers cocktails and DJs in a long space

with two dance areas and ample outdoor loungers too.

Theatre & Dance

Georgia's great drama tradition continues to thrive, and Tbilisi has far more active theatres than most cities its size. Foreign plays, including Shakespeare's, are as popular as ever – nearly always in Georgian, though the Rustaveli Theatre offers simultaneous English translation for some shows.

Most theatres close during July and August.

Georgia's top folk song and dance groups, such as **Erisioni** and the **Sukhishvili Georgian National Ballet**, spend much of their time touring overseas, but if they happen to be performing in Tbilisi their spectacular shows are well worth the money.

Rustaveli National Theatre (Map pp48-9; ☎ 936583; www.rustavelitheatre.ge; Rustaveli 17; admission 5-25 GEL) The biggest theatre, headed by Robert Sturua, internationally famous for his interpretations of Shakespeare and Brecht.

Paliashvili Opera & Ballet Theatre (Map pp48-9; ☎ 206040; www.opera.ge; Rustaveli 25; admission 10-50 GEL) Opera, ballet and classical concerts regularly play to full houses here.

Nabadi Theatre (Map pp48-9; ☎ 989991; Rustaveli 19; admission 35-68 GEL) Doubtless with tourists in mind, Nabadi presents a show of music, dance and song about Georgian legends and culture, with some food and wine thrown in. Not bad.

Marjanishvili Theatre (Map pp48-9; ☎ 953582; Marjanishvili 8; admission 7-10 GEL) Another of the top drama theatres, recently refurbished.

Cinema

In general-release cinemas nearly all films are dubbed into Russian. **Kino Sakhli** (Kolga; Map pp48-9; ☎ 988326; kolga.geoweb.ge; Dzmebi Kakabadzeebi 2; admission 5 GEL) shows foreign films in their original language (usually English), or Georgian or Russian films with English subtitles, at 8pm on Monday, Wednesday and Friday.

Gay & Lesbian Venues

The one acknowledgedly gay (or gay/mixed) bar is **Success** (Map pp48-9; ☎ 998230; Vashlovani 3; spirits & cocktails 5-10 GEL; ☽ noon-5am), which is less stylish than it was. But several other bars and cafés are gay-friendly, including Le Café (p65), opposite Success, and Café Kala (p65) in the Old Town.

SHOPPING

Tbilisi doesn't rank with Paris or Milan as a shopping destination, but you'll find a selection of distinctive products – from dolls to artworks, carpets to wine – that will serve as great mementos. Interesting shops are dotted along Rustaveli and in the Old Town.

Dry Bridge market (Map pp48-9; 9 March Park; 8am-1pm Sat & Sun) is the most interesting market. You'll find all kinds of knick-knacks and charming miscellanea from art, accordions, samovars and electrical gadgets to china, glass and silver being sold off by impoverished old folk.

Old Carpets & Kilims (Map pp48-9; Rustaveli 32; 10am-6pm) Come here for a variety of rugs from Georgia and around, and Central Asian suzani textiles. Be prepared to haggle.

Gallery Artgasm (Map pp48-9; Rustaveli 34; 11am-9pm) In the courtyard next to Prospero's Books, this gallery offers a range of funky items, from copper sculptures and enamelled jewellery to embroidered bags. All created by Tbilisi designers.

Georgian Souvenirs (Map pp48-9; Rustaveli 18; 10am-7pm) Some of the stock here veers towards the kitsch, but the icons, dolls and puppets are eye-catching, and the decorative wine bottles are full! It's the spot if you're hankering for a Caucasian sword.

Carpet Shop (Map p54; Leselidze 27; 11am-8pm) This unnamed shop halfway down the hill on Leselidze boasts 'carpet nice; price nice', and has an array of rugs from across the region. Locals shop here, so it must be good.

Meidan 91 (Map p54; 723546; Gorgasalis moedani; www.meidan91.wanex.net; 10am-7pm) Touted as the oldest carpet shop in the Caucasus, Meidan 91 is an Aladdin's cave of carpets, samovars, pewter and antique regional dress from across Georgia.

Green Sun Souvenirs (Map p54; Erekle II 11; greensun .etbilisi.com; 11am-11pm) This place offers a range of interesting knick-knacks, from figurines to embroidered scarves.

Dom Vina (Map p54; Leselidze 55; 10am-7pm) A bountiful wine cellar offering up tipples from across Georgia.

GETTING THERE & AWAY
Air

Tbilisi airport (433121/41), 15km east of the centre, has a modern terminal opened in 2007 and a growing range of international flights (see p320 for more information).

There were no domestic flights at research time, though Batumi and Mestia flights are constantly talked about.

Airline offices in Tbilisi include the following:

Air Baltic (Map pp48-9; 932829; www.airbaltic.com; Berika Travel Agency, Kostava 14)

Airzena Georgian Airways (Map pp48-9; 485560; www.georgian-airways.com; Rustaveli 12)

Austrian Airlines (Map pp48-9; 774506; www.aua .com; Sheraton Metechi Palace Hotel, Telavi 20)

AZAL (Azerbaijan Airlines; Map p56; 251669; www .azal.az; Chavchavadzis gamziri 28)

BMI (Map pp48-9; 940719; www.flybmi.com; Tavisuplebis moedani 4)

Georgian National Airlines (Map pp48-9; www .national-avia.com; 922020; Rustaveli 5)

Lufthansa (Map p56; 243324; www.lufthansa.com; Paliashvili 16)

SCAT (Map pp48-9; 921800; www.scat.kz; Contact Travel Agency, Ingorokva 12)

Turkish Airlines (Map pp48-9; 959022; www .turkishairlines.com; Davit Aghmashenebeli 147)

Ukraine International Airlines (Map pp48-9; www .flyuia.com; 433555; Ekaladze 3)

Bus & Marshrutka

Tbilisi has three long-distance bus and marshrutka stations: Didube (the main hub for national transport), Ortachala (for Kakheti, Armenia, Turkey and Greece) and the main train station (for western Georgia and further Yerevan services). See destination sections later in this chapter for further schedule details – and remember it's all subject to change!

Didube bus station (347239; Tsereteli; M Didube) is a sprawling chaos outside Didube metro station. In the first yard you reach, just outside the exit tunnel from the metro, you'll find marshrutkas to Gardabani, Borjomi, Bakuriani and Akhaltsikhe. A second yard, straight ahead from the metro tunnel, then across a small road and behind a line of buildings, is the departure point for marshrutkas to Mtskheta and Kazbegi, and the bus to Barisakho. For further services walk 300m to the right along the above-mentioned small road. Here you'll find the Okriba bus station on your left, with buses to Kutaisi, and two chaotic yards on your right, with marshrutkas to Gori, Kutaisi and Batumi and further marshrutkas to Borjomi and Akhaltsikhe. Buses to Gori leave from the back of the first of these yards.

Ortachala bus station (☎ 753433; Gulia 1) is something of a backwater, about 2.5km southeast of the Old Town. From here marshrutkas depart for Yerevan (30 GEL, six hours) via the Sadakhlo border point, Vanadzor and Sevan, hourly from 7am to noon. Note that if you want to get off before Yerevan, you still have to pay the full 30 GEL fare. Marshutkas leave for Qax, Azerbaijan (10 GEL, five to six hours), via the Lagodekhi border crossing, at 8am, 11am and 1pm. A minifleet of four or five buses run by different companies departs at noon for Istanbul (US$40, 27 hours) via the border at Sarpi, Hopa, Rize, Trabzon (US$25, 11 hours) and Samsun. There's also a minibus to Trabzon (US$25, 11 hours) at 8pm by **Golden Travel** (☎ 877457680), and a 6am bus by **Özlem Ardahan** (☎ 899919958) to Istanbul (US$50, 27 hours) via the Posof border point, Kars, Erzurum and Ankara. For the truly hardy, several companies run buses to Thessaloniki and Athens (€100) from Ortachala. You can reach Ortachala on marshrutka 94 from in front of Tbilisi's Borjomi train station via Marjanishvili metro station, Vardebis Revolutsis moedani (lower level), Tavisuplebis moedani and Gorgasalis moedani. Bus 55 runs to Ortachala from Vake via Rustaveli (it stops opposite the Opera House) and Tavisuplebis moedani, and marshrutka 150 runs between Didube and Ortachala bus stations.

Further marshrutkas to Yerevan (30 GEL, six hours) go from the front of the main train station (Map pp48–9), on Vagzlis moedani, at 8am, 10am, 1pm and 5pm.

Further marshrutkas and buses to Kutaisi, Batumi, Zugdidi and Poti depart from a yard at the back of the main train station (Map pp48–9) on Tsotne Dadiani.

There is no bus or marshrutka service from Tbilisi crossing into Azerbaijan via the Krasny Most border crossing. If you don't want to take the train, fly or go via Lagodekhi, you have various choices.

- Take a marshrutka from the main train station to Krasny Most (4 GEL, one hour); buses and marshrutkas run from there to Gəncə and Baku.
- Get a bus from Lilo market, near Tbilisi airport, to Krasny Most or beyond.
- Get a marshrutka from Tbilisi train station to Marneuli (2 GEL, 45 minutes), 30km south of Tbilisi, where buses depart for Baku.

Car

Taking a taxi for an intercity trip can be surprisingly inexpensive, especially if shared between three or four people. Your accommodation can usually organise this for you, or you can go to one of the bus stations or the train station, where drivers wait. Typical one-way fares are 80 GEL to Kazbegi or 100 GEL to Yerevan. A return trip to Davit Gareja is also around 100 GEL.

If you fancy your chances driving yourself on Georgian roads, car rental is easy enough to arrange, though not necessarily cheaper than taking a car with a driver.

Avis (Map pp48-9; ☎ 923594; www.avis.com; Tavisuplebis moedani 4) Also at the airport.

Cosmo Group (Map pp48-9; ☎ 920960; cosmo@gol.ge; Atoneli 31)

Hertz (Map p54; ☎ 987400; www.caucasustravel.com; Caucasus Travel, Leselidze 44)

Train

Tbilisi's **main train station** (Map pp48-9; ☎ 566253, 993253; Vagzlis moedani) is the railway hub of Georgia. Trains from Tbilisi are generally slower, less frequent, more comfortable and a bit cheaper than marshrutkas and buses.

The station is due for rebuilding but meanwhile remains a slightly confusing place. Schedule information is currently available at the left-hand end of the line of ticket windows. Some is also given in English on www.info-tbilisi.com and (in Georgian) on the Georgian Railway site (www.rail way.ge).

The only international trains are the overnight sleepers to Baku and Yerevan. The train to Baku (2nd/1st-class 40/78 GEL, 14 hours) leaves at 5.15pm daily. Given the shortage of road transport from Tbilisi to Azerbaijan, this is the most convenient way to get to Baku and to stops en route such as Gəncə. The train to Yerevan (4th/3rd/2nd/1st-class 12/16/24/45 GEL, 15 hours) however takes a painfully slow, roundabout route via Vanadzor and Gyumri, and only runs every two days (on odd dates from Tbilisi to Yerevan and on even dates from Yerevan to Tbilisi) . It leaves Tbilisi at 3.40pm.

Tickets for the Baku and Yerevan trains are sold at window 7 in the main train station. It's advisable to book a day or two ahead, though at busy times (eg the summer holiday season) you might be told the train is fully booked.

Within Georgia, the most useful trains include the night train to Zugdidi (3rd/2nd-class

5.50/11 GEL, eight hours, 9.30pm) and the night train to Batumi (3rd/2nd/1st-class 15/23/40 GEL, eight hours, 10pm). This Batumi sleeper, with air-conditioned 1st- and 2nd-class compartments, is another train for which it's advisable to book ahead. Note that Batumi appears as Makhinjauri (the exact location of its station) on some timetables.

Day trains include the 8.50am to Batumi (20 GEL, eight hours), the 2.45pm to Poti (8 GEL, six hours), both with 3rd-class seating only, and the 9.15am to Kutaisi (3rd/2nd-class 5/10.50 GEL, 5½ hours) and Zugdidi (3rd/2nd-class 6/11.50 GEL, eight hours). There's also an 11.40pm departure to Poti.

Elektrichky (electric trains with seating only) run from Tbilisi's Borjomi station, next door to the main station, to Borjomi (2 GEL, 4¼ hours) at 7.15am and 4.55pm, and to Kutaisi (3.50 GEL, 5½ hours) at 4.10pm. For these you pay on the train.

All the above domestic trains stop at Gori, and most at Mtskheta.

See p327 for general information on train travel in Georgia, Armenia and Azerbaijan.

GETTING AROUND
To/From the Airport
Bus 37 (0.40 GEL, half-hourly, 7am to 7pm) runs between the airport and the train station. The route into town is via Ketevan Tsamebulis gamziri on the east side of the Mtkvari, then Tavisuplebis moedani, Rustaveli and Melikishvili in the city centre.

Going out to the airport, one of its stops is at Rustaveli 26, opposite the Opera House. From 7pm to 8.30pm there are a few services just between the airport and Samgori metro station.

A new rail link between the airport and Tbilisi's main train station was almost ready as this book went to press. The ride to the city will take 20 minutes, with trains running about every 40 minutes.

The official taxi fare from the airport to the city centre or vice versa is 25 GEL (30 GEL at night), but going from the city to the airport, a taxi hailed on the street will probably charge 20 GEL.

Public Transport
BUS & MARSHRUTKA
Buses (0.40 GEL) and marshrutkas (0.50 GEL) provide an effective above-ground complement to the metro, though their route boards are in Georgian only. Useful services are mentioned where appropriate elsewhere in this section.

While buses only stop at predetermined stops, you can get on and off marshrutkas anywhere along their route. Pay when you get off. To get the driver to stop, yell out *'gaacheret!'* ('stop!').

METRO
The deep, dank Tbilisi metro is the standard fast, efficient Soviet system seen all over the ex-USSR.

It operates from 6am to midnight with a flat fare of 0.40 GEL, and the two lines connect you to most important parts of the city, meeting at Vagzlis Moedani station. A third line appears on the official maps, but a shortage of funds makes its construction highly improbable for now.

The stations of most use to visitors are Tavisuplebis Moedani (Freedom Sq, for the Old Town), Rustaveli (city centre), Marjanishvili, Vagzlis Moedani (main train station) and Didube (main bus station).

TBILISI METRO

GEORGIA

Signs are only in Georgian but the station name is announced at each stop, and just before the doors shut the name of the next station is also announced.

TAXI
Taxis are plentiful and almost always unmetered. Agree on the fare before getting in unless you are so familiar with the city that you know what your ride will cost. A shortish ride of a couple of kilometres in central areas costs 2 to 3 GEL; longer rides may be up to 10 GEL.

AROUND TBILISI

A cradle of Georgian culture, the region west, northwest and south of the capital is known as Kartli, after the mythical father of the Georgian people, Kartlos, whose progeny made their home at Mtskheta. Two towns in particular reflect contrasting sides of the Georgian story. Nobody can understand Georgian spirituality without visiting the ancient royal and religious capital of Mtskheta, just outside Tbilisi. Here St Nino converted the Iverian kingdom to Christianity in the 4th century. In Gori, Joseph Stalin was born Iosif Jughashvili in 1878; his influence on the modern world has been variously calculated in terms of the tens of millions of deaths in his notorious Gulags, or as victory against Nazi Germany in WWII.

MTSKHETA მცხეთა
☎ 37 (international), ☎ 27 (domestic) / pop 8000
To a non-Georgian, Mtskheta's near-mystical importance in Georgian culture is hard to describe. Containing some of the oldest and most important churches in the country, Mtskheta has been Georgia's spiritual heart since Christianity was established here in about AD 327. It was capital of most of eastern Georgia from about the 3rd century BC to the 5th century AD, when King Vakhtang Gorgasali switched his base to Tbilisi. It remained a spiritual capital, however, and Mtskheta's Svetitskhoveli Cathedral is still the setting for important ceremonies of the Georgian Orthodox Church. With an alluring setting where the Mtkvari and Aragvi Rivers meet, less than 25km from the centre of Tbilisi, Mtskheta makes a very easy and enjoyable day trip from the capital.

Orientation & Information
The main Gori highway from Tbilisi bypasses Mtskheta to the east. Coming from Tbilisi to Mtskheta, you'll turn off the highway well before it passes the town, then drive along the right bank of the Mtkvari River, before crossing a bridge into Mtskheta. If you are in a marshrutka or bus, get off once you draw level with the large Svetitskhoveli Cathedral to your right.

The **Tourism Information Centre** (☎ 322128; Arsukidze 3; ☽ 8am-8pm), with helpful, English-speaking staff, stands opposite the main gate of Svetitskhoveli. Staff can provide guides in several languages for Mtskheta's sights at 25 GEL per hour – best to contact them in advance for this.

Sights
Dominating the low-rise town is the grand **Svetitskhoveli Cathedral** (Arsukidze; ☽ 8am-10pm). It's a large (for its time, enormous) building from the 11th century, early in the golden age of Georgian church architecture, with an elongated cross plan, adorned with beautiful stone carving outside and in.

According to tradition, Christ's robe lies buried beneath the cathedral. Apparently a Mtskheta Jew, Elioz, was in Jerusalem at the time of the crucifixion and returned with the robe to Mtskheta. His sister Sidonia took it from him and immediately died in a passion of faith. No-one could prise the robe from her grasp, so it was buried with her. As years passed people forgot the exact site of the burial. When King Mirian decided to build the first church at Mtskheta after his conversion, the wooden column designed to stand in the centre of the church could not be raised from the ground. St Nino, in an all-night prayer vigil, had a vision of a young man imbued with fire who raised the column. Miraculously, the column slowly moved of its own accord to the burial site of Sidonia and the robe. The column subsequently worked many miracles and Svetitskhoveli means 'Life-Giving Column'.

In the 5th century King Vakhtang Gorgasali replaced King Mirian's original church with a stone church, whose modest remains are visible to the left of the cathedral today. The present building was constructed between 1010 and 1029 under Patriarch Melkisedek, and, despite being damaged in the 14th century by Timur, it's still one of the most beautiful

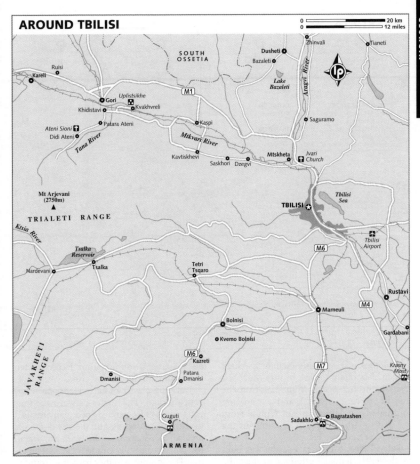

AROUND TBILISI

churches in the country. The defensive wall around it was built in 1787.

Inside, Christ's robe is believed to lie in the nave beneath the square, tower-like pillar, which is decorated with colourful frescoes of the conversion of Kartli. The tomb of Erekle II, king of Kartli and Kakheti from 1762 to 1798, lies directly in front of the altar. Vakhtang Gorgasali's tomb is behind this, cordoned off and with a raised flagstone. The frescoes in the main nave and south aisle date from the 16th to the 18th centuries.

Two other churches in Mtskheta are well worth visiting. The tiny but charming **Antioki Church**, in the grounds of a nunnery near the riverbank behind the cathedral, dates from St Nino's time. Renovated in 2000, it manages

to retain its modest charm despite the recently painted frescoes. The large **Samtavro Church** (Davit Aghmashenebelis qucha; ☽ 9am-7pm) is also now part of a nunnery. Once the palace church of the lords of Mtskheta, it was built in the 1130s. King Mirian and his wife, Queen Nana, are buried in the southwest corner, under tombstones from the early 20th century. The little church in the Samtavro grounds, Tsminda Nino, dates from the 4th century and stands on a spot where St Nino is said to have prayed.

Mtskheta Museum (☎ 899223181; Davit Aghmashenebelis qucha 54; admission 0.50 GEL; ☽ 10am-5pm Tue-Sat) has an interesting collection of finds from archaeological excavations in the Mtskheta area, labelled in both English

GEORGIA

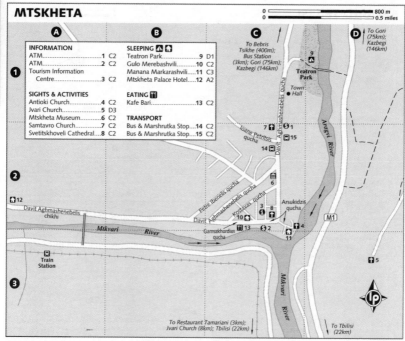

MTSKHETA

0 ___ 800 m
0 ___ 0.5 miles

INFORMATION
ATM...........................1 C2
ATM...........................2 C2
Tourism Information
Centre........................3 C2

SIGHTS & ACTIVITIES
Antioki Church.............4 C2
Jvari Church................5 D3
Mtskheta Museum.........6 C2
Samtavro Church..........7 C2
Svetitskhoveli Cathedral...8 C2

SLEEPING
Teatron Park.................9 D1
Gulo Merebashvili.........10 C2
Manana Markarashvili....11 C3
Mtskheta Palace Hotel....12 A2

EATING
Kafe Bari....................13 C2

TRANSPORT
Bus & Marshrutka Stop....14 C2
Bus & Marshrutka Stop....15 C2

and Georgian. Highlights include jewellery and an elaborately worked bronze ritual belt from the Bronze Age, perfume vials from the 2nd to 5th centuries AD, and a miniature mother-of-pearl Iranian sun temple from the 3rd or 4th century AD, found in the Samtavro cemetery.

Bebris Tsikhe, Mtskheta's castle, was built in the early feudal period to protect the town's northern approaches. It's a romantic ruin situated at the north end of Davit Aghmashenebeli, about 1.2km past Samtavro Church.

JVARI CHURCH
Visible for miles around on its hilltop overlooking Mtskheta from the east, **Jvari Church** (☉ 9am-10pm) is to many Georgians the holiest of holies, the country's spiritual heart. Jvari, or the Holy Cross Church, stands where a sacred wooden cross was erected in the 4th century (either by St Nino before she converted Mtskheta, or by King Mirian soon afterwards). In the 6th century Guaram, the *eristavi* (duke) of Kartli, built a small, simple church beside the cross. Between 585 and

604 Guaram's son Stepanoz I constructed the main church over the cross.

Jvari is a classic of early Georgian tetra-conch design. The angles between the four equal arms of its cross-shaped plan are filled in with corner rooms, and the low dome sits on a squat, octagonal drum, with the overall result of a beautifully symmetrical little building. The interior is rather bare, but from the church site there are spectacular views over Mtskheta and the convergence of the Aragvi and Mtkvari Rivers. The road up to the church from Mtskheta takes a highly circuitous route; the easiest way to get there is by taxi (15 to 20 GEL round trip, including waiting time). If you're feeling fit, you can walk up there from Mtskheta in about one hour by crossing the footbridge from Teatron Park, then following a path from the far (east) side of the busy highway, which winds up to the road behind the church.

Sleeping
Mtskheta is an easy day trip from Tbilisi, but there are several accommodation options. You can camp for free (without any facilities

or supervision) in **Teatron Park**, off Davit Aghmashenebeli towards Bebris Tsikhe.

The tourist office offers details of about 15 homestays, for which it can arrange bookings. Two good ones are the houses of **Manana Markarashvili** (☎ 899116862; Arsukidze 85; per person incl dinner 20 GEL, breakfast 5 GEL), 300m from Svetitskhoveli, and **Gulo Merebashvili** (☎ 322636; Arsukidze 15; per person 20-25 GEL), facing Svetitskhoveli. The modern **Mtskheta Palace Hotel** (☎ 32-910202; fax 32-911717; Davit Aghmashenebelis chikhi; r incl breakfast 150-200 GEL; ❄ ❑) is quite palatial but rather devoid of atmosphere.

Eating

Mtskheta is famous for its *lobio*, which can be found in any local restaurant, served in a traditional clay pot. Mtskheta is a popular spot for Tbilisi folk to come for a meal, especially at weekends, and several establishments cater to them, though most are several kilometres out of town, requiring a taxi or marshrutka ride from central Mtskheta.

Kafe Bari (Gamsakhurdia 17; dishes 2-5 GEL; ☺ 10am-midnight) Easily the best of the central options, this smart little place is a stone's throw from Svetitskhoveli and serves up appetising *lobio, mtsvadi, khinkali, khachapuri* and more. The menu is in Georgian but staff speak a little English.

Restaurant Tamariani (☎ 32-544412; mains 7-15 GEL; ☺ 10am-11pm) About 6km from the centre on the Tbilisi road, the Tamariani has a lovely setting on a terrace right by the Mtkvari and serves a good range of Georgian favourites. Live music frequently heightens the party mood of its customers.

Getting There & Away

Marshrutkas to Mtskheta (1 GEL, 30 minutes) leave Tbilisi's Didube bus station every 15 to 20 minutes from about 8am to 8pm. The last marshrutka to Tbilisi leaves Mtskheta at about 9pm. *Elektrichka* trains to Gori also stop at Mtskheta station, although it's a 15-minute walk from there to the centre.

GORI გორი

☎ 370 (international), ☎ 270 (domestic) / pop 50,000

To all Georgians, Gori is synonymous with just one man: this is the town where Iosif Jughashvili – later Joseph Stalin – was born and went to school. Place of pilgrimage or macabre monument to Stalin's enduring popularity in his homeland, Gori is an intriguing place. There's an abundance of older historical attractions within easy striking distance, making an overnight stay a good idea, though it can also be done in a day trip from Tbilisi.

Orientation & Information

The town is dominated by various paeans to its best-known son: the main street is broad Stalinis gamziri (Stalin Ave), running south towards the Mtkvari River. The large Stalinis moedani (Stalin Sq), with its tall Stalin statue, opens out at the junction with Chavchavadze,

---

ST NINO & THE CONVERSION OF GEORGIA

While some of the legends that have grown up around St Nino are ridiculously far-fetched, there is no doubt that Nino is the historical figure to whom the 4th-century Christian conversion of Iveria (eastern Georgia) can be attributed. Nino is generally believed to have hailed from Cappadocia in eastern Turkey and a widespread version has it that she was the daughter of a Roman general, Zabulon, and was also related to St George. Other accounts aver that she was a slave girl. The most common account of her youth has it that she was brought up in Jerusalem under the eye of an uncle who was Patriarch of Jerusalem, and at the age of 14 experienced a vision of the Virgin Mary telling her that her destiny was to convert the Iverians to Christianity.

Coming to Iveria in the 320s, Nino won respect from the people by her good deeds and the miracles she performed. But it was only at Mtskheta, when her prayers managed to save Queen Nana of Iveria from serious illness, that she won a royal convert. King Mirian was harder to convince, until he was struck blind while hunting, only for his sight to be miraculously restored after he prayed to the Christian God – leading to mass baptism in the Aragvi River for the townsfolk of Mtskheta. Mirian made Christianity the official religion of Iveria in about AD 327. The vine-leaf cross that the Virgin allegedly gave Nino (and which Nino later bound with her own hair) is still kept at the Sioni Cathedral in Tbilisi. She remains Georgia's most venerated saint, and is buried at Bodbe Convent in Kakheti (p113).

and the large Stalin Museum complex and park are a short trot further north. The bus station is at the west end of Chavchavadze, 500m from Stalinis moedani; the train station is across the Mtkvari from the south end of Stalinis gamziri. You'll find a few ATMs along Stalinis gamziri.

Sights

STALIN MUSEUM

Possibly the most interesting museum in Georgia, the **Stalin Museum** (☎ 75215; www.stalin museum.ge; Stalinis gamziri 32; admission incl photo permission and guide in English, German or French 15 GEL, video permit 400 GEL; ☒ 10am-6pm) is an impressive 1957 building that exudes a faintly religious air. The visit includes the tiny wood-and-mud-brick house where Stalin's parents rented the single room in which they lived for the first four years of his life. This stands in front of the main museum building, perfectly preserved and with its own temple-like protective superstructure. The rest of the poor neighbourhood in which it stood was demolished in the 1930s as Gori was redesigned to glorify its famous son.

The museum charts Stalin's journey from the Gori church school to the Yalta Conference at the end of WWII and his death in 1953. What's missing is any attempt at a balanced portrayal of Stalin's career. This is a purely selective exhibition telling the glorious tale of a brave local lad who rose to the highest office in the land and defeated Hitler. No mention of the purges, the Gulag, the Ukraine famine or Stalin's 1939 pact with Hitler.

The first hall details Stalin's childhood and adolescence, including his rather cringeworthy pastoral poetry. The emphasis quickly shifts to his political work and revolutionary activities in the Caucasus, organising unions in Tbilisi and setting up an illegal workers' press in Batumi at the end of the 19th century.

Stalin's involvement with Lenin is then thoroughly detailed, taking us through the revolution of 1905, Stalin's Siberian exile, the revolution of 1917, the Civil War and Lenin's death in 1924. The first hall does display the text of Lenin's 1922 political testament that described Stalin as too coarse and power-hungry and advised Communist Party members to remove Stalin from the post of General Secretary, but your guide is unlikely to draw this to your attention. Two other key players in Stalin's life – Trotsky and Khrushchev – remain unsurprisingly absent from the displays.

One room is devoted to Stalin's eerie death mask, lying in state, while the next one is full of tributes and gifts to Stalin from world leaders and other senior Bolsheviks. Off the staircase leading downstairs, another room contains more gifts presented to Stalin and a reconstruction of his first office in the Kremlin (which he occupied from 1918 to 1922).

To one side of the museum (and included in the tour) is **Stalin's train carriage**, in which he

---

JOSEPH STALIN & GEORGIA

Few people's historical legacy is simultaneously greater and more uncertain than that of Iosif Jughashvili, the Gori cobbler's son who went on to rule the largest country on earth for a quarter of a century. Few would question his achievements: were it not for the Soviet role in WWII, Nazi Germany would probably have won, and in the space of a decade he turned the Soviet Union from a peasant economy into a vast industrial powerhouse – 'taking it with the plough and leaving it with nuclear weapons', as Churchill observed.

Yet the suffering of millions cannot be forgotten. Stalin's Gulags were responsible for the deaths of many millions, and his ruthless Cheka and NKVD (both secret police) terrorised the population from the late 1920s until Stalin's death in 1953. Nor did Stalin's Georgian origins translate into mercy for his own people – the purges in Tbilisi left mass graves in what is now the bourgeois suburb of Vake.

In a country that is still recovering from post-Soviet chaos, and where many still do not reap much material benefit from capitalism, it's perhaps not surprising that some still say they would like to see another Stalin in charge. While they don't seem blind to his faults, people simply prefer to focus on his achievements and the fact that here was a Georgian who, for better or worse, ruled a great power and was one of the key figures of 20th-century history. Portraits, busts and statues of Stalin can be found in all corners of Georgia, and while few are new or even in good condition, there is no sign of them disappearing yet.

travelled to the Yalta Conference in 1945 (he didn't like flying). Apparently bulletproof, it has an elegant interior that includes a bathtub and a primitive air-conditioning system.

GORI FORTRESS

The heart of Gori is the ancient **fortress** (admission free; ⊙ 24 hr), an oval citadel atop the big hill west of the Stalin Museum. The walk to the top is easy; from the Hotel Intourist, cross the square and keep going until you reach the foot of the hill, from where a newly cobbled path leads up to the gate. There are fine views from up here and it's particularly attractive late in the day when the sun is setting.

A fortification existed here in ancient times and it is believed to have been besieged by Pompey in 65 BC. Most of the present building dates from the Middle Ages, with additions from the 17th century.

Sleeping

Homestay (Kristeporek Kasteli 8; per person 10 GEL) Those on a tight budget can try this basic homestay option just below the fortress. To get there from the bus station, take the first street to the left off Chavchavadze as you head towards Stalinis moedani, then the first right, then the first left, and turn left at the end. The house is at the far end of this street, where the asphalt turns to sand. It's no luxury option; no food is available and no-one in the family speaks English, but that shouldn't be a major obstacle.

Hotel Intourist (☎ 72676; Stalinis gamziri 26; r 50 GEL) Most travellers stay at the Intourist, a large building near the museum. Only one floor of rooms is open, but the available rooms are quite palatial, with marble pillars, parquet floors and comfortable-enough rooms. The plumbing needs work, though: water (hot or cold) is only available for five (separate) hours each day.

Hotel Victoria (☎ 75586; fax 70050; Tamar Mepi 76; s/d/tr 65/65/90 GEL, ste 120-140 GEL; ❄) The best hotel in the town, 200m off southern Stalinis gamziri, is a modern place offering large rooms with sitting areas, TV and air-con, and is decent value for money. Breakfast is available for 7 GEL.

Gori Hotel (☎ 70818; Gori-Tbilisi Hwy, 3rd km; r/ste incl breakfast 80/140 GEL; ❄) Set just back from the Tbilisi highway about 4km from town, this is worth considering as it has modern, carpeted rooms and the area's best restaurant.

A taxi from the centre costs 4 or 5 GEL. When leaving you can flag down a Tbilisi marshrutka at the end of the driveway.

Eating

Cake House (Stalinis gamziri 22; pizzas 4.50 GEL; ⊙ 9am-10pm) A pine-panelled café serving *khachapuri* and reasonable pizza. It's between the museum and Stalinis moedani.

Restaurant Intourist (☎ 74433; Stalinis gamziri 26; dishes 2-5 GEL; ⊙ 9am-midnight) Attached to the Hotel Intourist, facing the park in front of the museum, this offers all the Georgian standards in a calm environment.

Nikala (☎ 70824; Stalinis gamziri 4; dishes 2-6 GEL; ⊙ 24 hr) Spacious Nikala, 400m south of Stalinis moedani, serves up tasty Georgian salads, cheeses, fowl (including quail) and meat dishes at very good prices. The *khbosostri* (veal stew with sour plums) is superb. It has an English-language menu and helpful staff.

Gori Restaurant (☎ 70818; Gori-Tbilisi Hwy, 3rd km; mains 4-10 GEL; ⊙ 8am-midnight) The restaurant at this modern hotel 4km from town (4 or 5 GEL by taxi) is the best around Gori, with satisfying, well-prepared Georgian dishes, and a nice outdoor terrace if you prefer to steer clear of the live music inside.

Getting There & Away

Marshrutkas to Gori (4 GEL, 1½ hours) leave from Tbilisi's Didube station about every 40 minutes, from 7.30am to 4.30pm. Buses (3.50 GEL, two hours) go as late as midnight. All westbound trains from Tbilisi's main station or the Borjomi station next door stop at Gori, taking 1½ to two hours.

Gori's bus station is at the end of Chavchavadze, 500m west of Stalinis moedani. Marshrutkas (4 GEL, 1½ hours) and buses (3.50 GEL, two hours) to Tbilisi leave Gori about every 40 minutes until 6pm; marshrutkas to Kutaisi (8 GEL, three hours) go at 7.30am and 9.30am.

AROUND GORI
Uplistsikhe უფლისციხე

This impressive and once enormous **cave city** (admission 10 GEL, guide in English 10 GEL; ⊙ 9am-6pm), on the north bank of the Mtkvari, 10km east of Gori, is one of the oldest places of settlement in the Caucasus. Uplistsikhe was founded in the late Bronze Age, around 1000 BC, but developed mainly from the 6th century BC to the 1st century AD. This was one of the principal political and religious centres of pre-Christian Kartli, with temples dedicated principally to the sun goddess. Archaeological findings from the 4th to 6th centuries AD speak of an ongoing struggle between Christians and adherents of the old religion.

After the Arabs occupied Tbilisi, Uplistsikhe became the residence of the kings of Kartli. A main caravan road from Asia to Europe ran just north of the city, which became an important trade centre with 20,000 people at its peak. Uplistsikhe's importance declined after King David the Builder retook Tbilisi in 1122 and it was irrevocably destroyed by the Mongols in 1240, along with its natural surroundings – there used to be forests here. What you visit today is the 40,000-sq-metre Shida Kalaki, or Inner City, constituting less than half of the original whole. Almost everything here has been uncovered by archaeologists since 1957, when only the tops of a few caves were visible.

Uplistsikhe is strategically located, with a deep valley to the east and cliffs to the west. Entering the main part of the site, you pass through what was the **main gate**, at the head of a small ravine, then wind your way up the main street. Over to the left, on the southwest edge of the site overlooking the river, you'll see a cave with a pointed arch carved in the rock above it. Inside, the ceiling is carved with octagonal designs in a similar style to Caracalla's Baths in Rome. Known as the **Theatre**, this is probably a temple dating from the 1st or 2nd century AD, where religious mystery plays may have been performed.

Further up the street and down to its right is the large pre-Christian **Temple of Makvliani**, with an inner recess behind an arched portico. The open hall in front of the portico has stone seats for priests, and two rounded holes in the floor for the blood of sacrificial animals.

A little further up on the left is the big hall known as **Tamaris Darbazi** (Hall of Queen Tamar). Here there are two columns built into the cliff and a stone seat dating from antiquity. The stone ceiling is cut to look like wooden beams, and there is a hole to let smoke out and light in. This was almost certainly a pagan temple originally, though the great Christian Queen Tamar may have occupied it later. To its left is an open area with stone niches along one side, thought to have once been a **pharmacy**. On the other side of Tamaris Darbazi is a large cave building with the remains of four

columns – probably originally a **sun temple**, used for animal sacrifices, and later converted into a Christian basilica.

The 10th-century church near the top of the hill is the **Uplistsulis Eklesia** (Prince's Church). This triple-church basilica was also built over a pagan temple, probably the most important one.

On your way back down, don't miss the long **tunnel** running down to the Mtkvari River – an emergency escape route that could also have been used for carrying water up to the city. Its entrance is by a short flight of narrow metal steps, behind a reconstructed wall southeast of the Theatre.

GETTING THERE & AWAY

The easiest way to visit Uplistsikhe is by taxi from Gori – the return trip including waiting time normally costs 30 GEL. Marshrutkas leave Gori bus station a few times a day for Kvakhvreli (1 GEL, 20 minutes), the village across the Mtkvari River from Uplistsikhe. It's about a 2km walk from village to site, as you have to go downriver to a bridge then back along the other side. Gori-bound *elektrichka* trains, currently leaving Tbilisi's Borjomi station at 7.15am, 4.10pm and 4.55pm, take 1¾ hours to reach Kvakhvreli (2 GEL).

Ateni Sioni ატენის სიონი

This impressively ancient church has a beautiful setting, above a bend of the wonderfully lush Tana valley and surrounded by high hills and cliffs, 12km south of Gori. The entry to the church itself is through an orchard.

Architecturally, Ateni Sioni is modelled on the Jvari Church at Mtskheta (p72) and was built in the 7th century. Appealing reliefs of stags, a hunting scene and a knight were carved onto the exterior walls later. Inside, the 11th-century frescoes, depicting biblical scenes and Georgian rulers, are among the finest medieval art in the country. They have been painstakingly preserved to prevent further fading, although there are no plans to restore them to their full former glory, as it is precisely their ancient nature that makes them interesting.

A taxi from Gori to the church and back should cost about 30 GEL, or 50 GEL if combined with Uplistsikhe. Alternatively, take a bus from Gori bus station (0.70 GEL, 30 minutes, hourly from 7am to 6pm).

WESTERN GEORGIA

Site of the ancient kingdom of Colchis, and famous as the destination of Jason and the Argonauts in their search for the Golden Fleece, western Georgia has always acted as a conduit for influences from the west into the Caucasus, from the Greeks to St Nino to the Ottoman Turks.

For long periods ruled separately from eastern Georgia, this region was also where the great united Georgian kingdom of the 11th and 12th centuries got its start. Georgia's two largest cities after Tbilisi – Kutaisi and Batumi – are here, and the country's lovely semitropical Black Sea coast and the border with Turkey

ensure a steady stream of visitors. The coast, especially vibrant, charming Batumi, has become a dynamic holiday and commercial area since Georgian independence. There's still a standoff in Abkhazia, where civil war and secession have caused enormous tragedy and suffering.

KUTAISI ქუთაისი

☎ 331 (international), ☎ 231 (domestic) / pop 180,000

Georgia's second city is one of the most ancient in the world. Capital at various times of several different kingdoms and groups of kingdoms within Georgia, Kutaisi has a rich and fascinating history, and much of this is

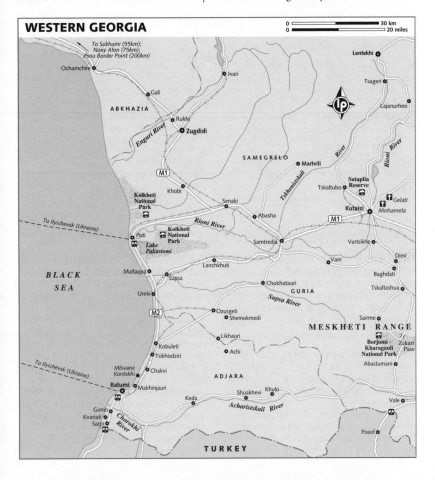

WESTERN GEORGIA

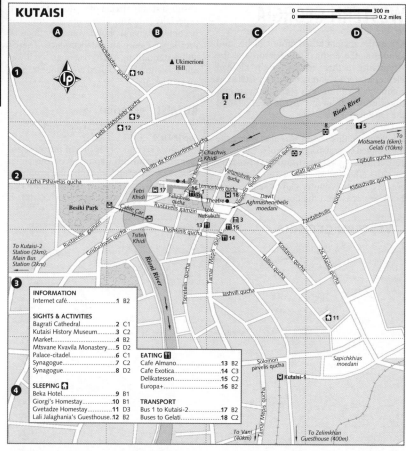

KUTAISI

apparent to visitors. The town is attractive and not without things to see and do, although most people come to Kutaisi to see the surrounding attractions. Modern Kutaisi is still struggling economically, however, and is noticeably less lively than Batumi or Tbilisi.

History

Kutaisi is a very ancient city that has played several key roles in the Georgian drama. It was one of the main cities of ancient Colchis, and a settlement has existed here for nearly 4000 years.

In the 3rd century BC Apollonius of Rhodes referred to 'Kutaia' in a poem about the Argonauts, and some scholars believe this was the city of King Aeëtes, father of Medea.

At the end of the 8th century AD Leon II, Duke of Abkhazia, renounced Byzantine suzerainty and declared himself king of Abkhazia, transferring his capital from Anakopia (in modern Abkhazia) to Kutaisi. In 1001 Abkhazia's King Bagrat III inherited the eastern Georgian kingdom of Kartli, effectively uniting western and eastern Georgia under one rule for the first time in many centuries. It was in Kutaisi that David the Builder was crowned Georgian king in 1089. These two famous rulers left great architectural monuments in the shape of the Bagrati and Gelati cathedrals. Kutaisi was the political, economic and cultural centre of Georgia until 1122, when Tbilisi took over after David liberated it from Arab rule.

Kutaisi resumed its role as capital of the western region when Georgia was again divided in the 15th century after the invasions of the Mongols and Timur.

In the early 17th century Giorgi III of Imereti developed the left bank of the Rioni, but the city suffered a 101-year Ottoman occupation from 1669, during which Bagrati Cathedral was blown up. In 1770 the city was recaptured by Georgian and Russian forces.

Under the Soviet regime Kutaisi became Georgia's second most important industrial centre, and its population grew significantly, only to shrink again with the decline of its industries after Georgian independence.

Orientation

Kutaisi is built around the Rioni River. The city centre is on the left bank, focused on Davit Aghmasheneblis moedani and the adjacent central park. The modern city spreads mainly to the south and west (across the river) from the centre. To its north, the right bank rises up to an older area where the landmark Bagrati Cathedral overlooks the city.

The main bus station is 3km west of the centre, beside Kutaisi-2 train station. The other train station, Kutaisi-1, is 1km south of the centre.

Information

ATMs are plentiful around the central park, especially on Tsereteli to its south, and there are lots of money changers around the market area just northwest of the park.

Internet café (Lolo Nutsubizhi 1; per hr 2.40 GEL; ✆ 9am-10pm)

Sights

Every visitor to Kutaisi will want to see Bagrati Cathedral, while those with more time will enjoy visiting the History Museum, wandering the busy **market area** around Lermontov, and exploring the attractive central streets and the old Jewish district.

BAGRATI CATHEDRAL

If you cross the Chachvis Khidi you can walk up cobbled streets lined with attractive houses and gardens to the magnificent ruins of the 11th-century **Bagrati Cathedral** (Kazbegi; admission free; ✆ 9am-8pm) on Ukimerioni Hill.

Bagrati was built by King Bagrat III, the uniter of western and eastern Georgia. An Arabic inscription (no longer visible) on the north wall recorded that the floor was completed in 'Chronicon 223' (1003). Stone porches on the western and southern sides were added later in the 11th and 12th centuries. A great cupola rose over the centre of the cathedral, but in 1692 a Turkish explosion brought down both cupola and ceiling to leave the cathedral in a ruined state. The western porch and the cathedral's eastern, northern and southern arms have recently been repaired and the cathedral is again used for some religious observances.

There are plans to rebuild it fully, but even in its roofless, part-ruined condition it has a stately beauty matched by few churches in Georgia.

The ruined **palace-citadel** immediately east of the cathedral dates from the 6th century and in the 17th century was still reported by French and Russian travellers to be massively impressive. In 1769 King Solomon I of Imereti and the Russian General Todtleben bombarded the castle (which was then occupied by the Turks) from Mtsvane Kvavila hill across the river, reducing it to a ruin. What remains is still of interest: you can see wine cellars at the west end of the palace, a church in the middle, and parts of the medieval walls.

KUTAISI HISTORY MUSEUM

This **museum** (✆ 45691; www.histmuseum.ge; Tbilisi 1; general exhibition/treasury 2/3 GEL, tour in English or German 5/10 GEL; ✆ 11am-4pm Tue-Sat Sep-Jul, to 4pm Sat & Sun Aug), facing Davit Aghmasheneblis moedani, has superb collections from all around western Georgia and is well worth your time.

A guided tour is a good idea as labelling is very poor. The highlight is the Treasury section, with a marvellous exhibition of icons and crosses in precious metals and jewels including a large, reputedly miracle-working icon from the Bagrati Cathedral.

The rest of the collection ranges from archaeological finds (including figurines of fertility gods from the 8th to 6th centuries BC, one of them famously androgynous), to medieval weaponry, historical art, manuscripts going back to the 10th century, costumes, musical instruments and even the first telephone used in Kutaisi.

MTSVANE KVAVILA

Kutaisi used to have one of Georgia's largest Jewish communities but since independence most of the 1000 or so families have emigrated to Israel. A handsome 1880s **synagogue** (Gaponov 12) in the old Jewish district is still in use, but the smaller **synagogue** (Gaponov 49) further up the street is now disused. The street leads on up the hill to the **Mtsvane Kvavila (Green Flower) Monastery**, with three churches and the Pantheon where famous Kutaislebi (denizens of Kutaisi) are buried.

Sleeping

The selection of hotels is poor, but a slew of homestays fills the gap.

Gvetadze Homestay (☎ 43007; Tbilisi 3rd Lane No 6; per person 10 GEL) Suliko and Mediko Gvetadze provide a friendly welcome at their house, 700m east of Davit Aghmasheneblis moedani, in the third lane off Tbilisi. Meals are available at a modest extra charge, and the wine flows freely! But the bathroom needs an overhaul and water is sometimes in short supply. The house is in the side street opposite Tbilisi 100.

Giorgi's Homestay (☎ 43720, 895591511; giorgihomestay@mail.ru, giorgihomestay14@yahoo.com; Chanchibadze 14; per person 15 GEL, half board 30 GEL; 🖳) Hospitable, English-speaking Giorgi Giorgadze and his family provide clean, plain rooms in their ample house on Ukimerioni Hill, a short walk from the Bagrati Cathedral. They'll make you feel at home, and Giorgi is full of helpful travel and sightseeing tips. The shared bathrooms are sparkling clean and have hot water. The food is very good.

Beka Hotel (☎ 46923; Debi Ishkhnelebi 26; half board per person 40 GEL) An impressive white mansion on Ukimerioni Hill with superb views from the large terrace, the Beka is more guesthouse than hotel. Run by a friendly Russian- and Georgian-speaking couple, it has eight excellent, spick-and-span rooms with comfy beds.

Lali Jalaghania's Guesthouse (☎ 48395, 899376525; Debi Ishkhnelebi 18; half board per person 40 GEL) A couple of doors from the Beka, the Jalaghania house has similarly spacious and comfortable accommodation. Neighbour Marina speaks some English.

Zelimkhan Guesthouse (☎ 22441; Vakhushti Bagrationi 67; per person incl breakfast 55 GEL) A 15-minute walk from the Kutaisi-1 station, this tall, three-storey, vaguely Art Deco house has bright rooms and good breakfasts. It's pricier than other options but still highly recommended.

Eating

Kutaisi lacks superb restaurants, but there's still plenty of opportunity to eat well.

Café Exotica (Tamar Mepi 15; dishes 2-4 GEL; 🕑 9am-9pm) A popular spot for Georgian fast food, including some of the best Adjaran *khachapuri* this side of Batumi. The prices are unbelievably cheap.

Europa+ (Paliashvili; mains 4-5 GEL) The best restaurant in the centre, with neatly set tables and colourful murals. Go elsewhere, though, if you want to avoid live music with your dinner. It's in the corner of a courtyard set back from the street, and a cocktail bar and a beer bar are part of the same establishment.

Delikatessen (Tamar Mepi 3; dishes 3-6 GEL; 🕑 9am-10pm) This bright, new, brick-arched place just off Davit Aghmasheneblis moedani specialises in good *khachapuri* and there are large photos to help you decide which variety you fancy. It also does cakes, desserts and Georgian pastries.

Club Almano (Tsereteli; dishes 3-7 GEL) A smarter, modestly kitsch place just off Davit Aghmasheneblis moedani. It's a restaurant-cum-bar with a blue-lit mezzanine and tasty Georgian dishes. For a solid main dish, the *ojakhuri* (made from roasted meat and potatoes) is a good bet.

Getting There & Around

Both buses (10 GEL, four to five hours, about twice hourly from 8am to 7pm) and marshrutkas (10 GEL, four to 4½ hours, at least hourly, 7am to 8pm) to Kutaisi leave from Tbilisi Didube. Further marshrutkas leave from the rear of Tbilisi train station hourly from 8am to 6pm.

Buses and marshrutkas from Kutaisi's main **bus station** (Chavchavadzis gamziri), next to Kutaisi-2 train station, go to Tbilisi (10 GEL, four to five hours, hourly from 7am to 7pm), Zugdidi (6 GEL, two hours, half-hourly, 6am to 5.30pm), Batumi (8 GEL, 2½ hours, every 30 or 40 minutes, 6.30am to 5pm), Poti (5 GEL, 2½ hours, hourly, 7am to 6pm) and Borjomi (8 GEL, three hours, five daily, 8am to 1.30pm).

Of Kutaisi's two train stations, **Kutaisi-1** (Tamar Mepe) has trains to Tbilisi (five to 5½ hours) at 12.30pm (3rd-/2nd-class 5/10.50 GEL) and 12.40am (3rd-class, 4.50 GEL), and to Zugdidi (four hours) at 12.30pm. From **Kutaisi-2** (Chavchavadzis gamziri) there's an *elektrichka* to Tbilisi at 4.55am and a train to Batumi (four hours) at 5.45pm.

Kutaisi-2 is also the best place to look for long-distance taxis.

Bus 1 (0.20 GEL) runs a useful circular route (in both directions) between Kutaisi-2, Kutaisi-1 and the city centre (west end of Paliashvili). At Kutaisi-2 or the bus station, catch it on the far side of the road (Chavchavadze), going to the left, for the quicker route to the centre.

City taxis generally charge 0.60 GEL per kilometre.

AROUND KUTAISI
Motsameta მოწამეთა

Motsameta monastery is 6km out of Kutaisi, off the Gelati road. Take the turning marked by a photo of the church and follow this track for a couple of kilometres. This little monastery has a spectacular setting on a cliff-top promontory above a bend of the Tskhaltsitela River. The river's name, meaning 'Red Water', derives from an 8th-century Arab massacre. Among the victims were the brothers Davit and Konstantin Mkheidze, dukes of Argveti. Their bodies were thrown in the river, but the story goes that lions brought them up to the church where their bones were subsequently kept. In 1923 the local Cheka (secret police) took the relics to a Kutaisi museum, with such unfortunate consequences for the Cheka men that the bones were soon returned to the church. It is said that if you crawl three times under the side altar where the bones are, your wish will be granted.

See the Gelati section (right) for transport information.

Gelati გელათი

Georgians have always had a knack for choosing the most superb locations for their churches and this monastery complex, on a wooded hillside 10km northeast of Kutaisi, is no exception.

Gelati was founded by King David the Builder in 1106 as a centre for both Christian culture and Neo-Platonist learning. King David invited scholars such as Iaone Petritsi and Arsen Ikaltoeli to teach here and the Gelati Academy became, according to medieval chroniclers, 'a second Jerusalem' and 'another Athos, albeit superior to it'. Many Georgian rulers were buried here, including David the Builder himself, Queen Tamar (according to her chronicler, although this is disputed) and Bagrat III of Imereti. In 1510

the Ottoman Turks set fire to the complex, but Bagrat III subsequently restored the monastery, and it was made the seat of a bishop and the residence of the West Georgian patriarch. The monks were cast out by the communist authorities in 1922, but the churches were reconsecrated in 1988. President Saakashvili chose Gelati as the site of his inauguration in 2004.

The interior of the main **Cathedral of the Virgin** is among the brightest and most colourful in Georgia. Among the frescoes, painted at various times between the 12th and 18th centuries, note especially the line of eight noble figures in the north transept: these include David the Builder (holding the church) and Bagrat III (with a cross over his left shoulder). Across the corner to the right of David are the Byzantine emperor Constantine and his wife, Helena. The apse holds a famous 1130s mosaic of the Virgin and Child, with Archangels Michael and Gabriel to the left and right respectively. The lower part of this was restored in the Soviet era by painting.

Outside the cathedral's west door is the smaller **Church of St Nicholas**, built on top of an unusual arcaded base, and beyond that, the roofless remains of the **Academy**, where philosophy, theology, sciences and painting were studied and important chronicles and translations written. To the left of these, inside the **South Gate**, lies David the Builder's grave. David gave orders that he be buried here so that all who entered the monastery would step on his huge 3m tomb, a notably humble gesture for such a powerful man.

GETTING THERE & AWAY
Buses to Gelati (0.50 GEL, 30 minutes) leave from Lermontov behind the big theatre in central Kutaisi at 11am, 2pm and 5pm, starting back from Gelati at 11.30am, 2.30pm and 5.30pm. These buses pass the Motsameta turn-off. If you're visiting both places, it's a mostly downhill walk of about one hour from Gelati to Motsameta, should the bus schedules not suit. Buses to Tqibuli from Kutaisi-1 station (8am, 11am, 1pm, 2pm, 3pm, 4pm and 4.30pm) also pass the Motsameta turning and the turning for Gelati (from which it's an uphill walk of a little over 2km to the monastery).

A taxi from Kutaisi to Gelati and back should cost 12 GEL to 15 GEL, slightly more if you visit Motsameta too.

GEORGIA

Vani ვანი
☎ 232

The site of this ancient city is 40km southwest of Kutaisi. Though there's not much to see at the ruins, the modern museum here, all labelled in English as well as Georgian, has spectacular exhibits. The first excavations here took place in the 1890s, after locals had reported gold ornaments being washed down the hill after heavy rains.

Vani (☎ 21602; admission 1.50 GEL; 🕙 10am-4pm) was one of the main centres of ancient Colchis, flourishing from the 8th century BC until it was razed to the ground in the 1st century BC. Some speculate that this could have been the city of King Aeëtes, where Jason came in search of the Golden Fleece.

Archaeologists have found remains of monumental architecture and opulent burials from the 8th to 1st centuries BC. Strong brick and mud walls with towers were built towards the end of this period, when archaeologists think Vani may have become a kind of temple-city, dedicated principally to the goddess Levcoteia. From this latter era the ground floor of the museum displays the spear point of a battering ram, a bronze vessel depicting Greek gods, and large animal-head temple carvings. The most remarkable treasures, however, are on the museum's upper floor,

where you can see fine bronze casts including a statue of a youth, and copies of fabulous gold adornments with animal designs, whose originals are in the Museum of Georgia. The inner upstairs room contains original finds, including a pair of diadem pendants with incredibly fine bird decorations.

The site itself has not been developed for visitors but you can make out some temple areas, defensive walls and a deep ritual well, as well as a small city gate and a section of paved street beside the road below the museum.

Buses and marshrutkas to Vani (2 GEL, 1½ hours) leave the bus station next to Kutaisi-2 train station about hourly from 8am to noon, then every two hours until 6pm. From the Vani bus station, it's about a 15-minute walk to the large concrete museum building. A taxi from Kutaisi is 50 GEL return.

POTI ფოთი
☎ 393 (international), ☎ 293 (domestic) / pop 50,000

Poti, Georgia's main port, is one of the most ancient towns in the country, founded as the Greek trading colony of Pazisi or Phasis in the 6th or 5th century BC, although there is little evidence of this now. It's a pleasant enough town, visited by travellers for two main reasons: the ferry to Ukraine, and the

---

JASON & THE GOLDEN FLEECE

The Ancient Greek myth of the Golden Fleece is known worldwide: Jason, a prince of Thessaly, responded to his uncle Pelias' challenge to go to the land of Colchis, on the eastern shores of the Black Sea, to find the Golden Fleece. Few realise that the myth relates to real places and events. Colchis was a historical kingdom occupying most of western Georgia in antiquity. The Greeks set up trading colonies at places like Phasis (now Poti) and Dioskuria (Sukhumi) in the 6th and 5th centuries BC.

The legend tells that Jason had a special ship, the Argo, built to carry him and 49 other adventurous young Greek rowers, thenceforth known as the Argonauts. After various tribulations, they reached the kingdom of Colchis and sailed up the Phasis River (the present-day Rioni), where they were received by King Aeëtes in his capital (possibly Vani or Kutaisi). Aeëtes agreed to give up the fleece if Jason could yoke two fire-breathing bulls to a plough, and then sow the teeth of a dragon from which a crop of armed men would spring. Jason accepted the challenge but secretly promised marriage to Aeëtes' daughter Medea, who had conceived a violent passion for him, if she would agree to help him. Medea, who was skilled with magic and potions, gave Jason a charm which enabled him to survive Aeëtes' tests and to take the fleece from the dragon that guarded it.

The Golden Fleece itself is related to real mountain traditions: in Svaneti and Racha people sifted for gold in mountain rivers by placing a sheepskin across the rocks, in which tiny nuggets of gold would collect. Amazingly, this technique still exists today in the Caucasus.

If the Golden Fleece story grabs your fancy, dig out Tim Severin's The Jason Voyage (1986), about a modern-day row from Greece to Georgia in a smaller replica of the Argo.

nearby Kolkheti National Park with its wetlands and bird life.

A centre of the slave trade under Ottoman occupation in the 18th century, Poti was absorbed into the Russian Empire in 1828. It developed rapidly after acquiring port status 30 years later: Georgia's first railway was opened in 1871 between Poti and Shorapani, 35km southeast of Kutaisi. The town centre was laid out with an unusual radial plan centred on its cathedral, modelled on Istanbul's Hagia Sofia and completed in 1907. Today Poti has a Georgian navy base as well as a busy container port.

Orientation & Information

The centre of Poti is Rustavelis rkali (Rustaveli Circle), a very large roundabout surrounding the cathedral, with 10 streets radiating from it. Davit Aghmashenebeli, the main street, runs northwest across a river to reach a junction after 1.5km. Here Gegidze, with the Hotel Anchor and the best selection of places to eat, heads to the right (east), while the port is 400m to the west. Kostava runs 600m eastward from Rustavelis rkali to a square which is the terminus for some marshrutkas and has the *bazari* (market) off one corner. The train station is just north of this square, across a bridge.

You'll find ATMs scattered on Davit Aghmashenebeli, Gegidze and Rustavelis rkali. There's an **internet café** (Davit Aghmashenebeli; per hr 2 GEL; ☑ 10am-9m) opposite Aversi pharmacy, 1km from Rustavelis rkali.

Sleeping

If none of the options in town appeals, there are further possibilities a few kilometres south at Maltaqva (p84).

Hotel Kolkheti (Kostava 2; per person 10 GEL) This hotel facing Rustavelis rkali is very, very shabby and occupied by refugees from Abkhazia, but one room with four beds is usually available for budget travellers. Ask in room 218, where Julia speaks English. The only water is stored in the bath, which gets filled every two or three days.

Apartment (☎ 899777692; Room 12, Gegidze 20; r 30 GEL) Nona Topuria rents out this one-bedroom apartment for one or two people next to the Malibu bar. Call her or ask for her at the Türk Lokantasi restaurant across the street. Make sure you understand exactly how the wiring works before you take a shower!

Hotel Anchor (☎ 26000; fax 24600; Gegidze 90; s/d incl breakfast 90/100 GEL; ☒) The best option is this modern hotel near the port, with good, clean, sizable rooms and a decent restaurant. Desk staff speak a little English.

Eating

Easily the best selection of eateries and bars is on Gegidze, within stumbling distance of the port. Most serve food from 9am or 10am to about midnight. **Shore** (mains 4-6 GEL), next door to the Hotel Anchor, with Georgian food served at indoor and outdoor tables, and **Türk Lokantasi** (kebab & salad 15 GEL), with Turkish fare a bit further along on the opposite side, are both good bets.

Getting There & Away

In Tbilisi, marshrutkas and buses to Poti (15 GEL, six to seven hours) leave the rear of the main train station at 9am, 10am, 11am, 12.30pm, 1pm, 5pm and midnight.

Poti has two marshrutka terminals. From the square next to the market, there are departures to Batumi (5 GEL, 1½ hours) every hour or half-hour from 8am to 9pm, plus some to Zugdidi.

The other terminal, about 300m west from the train station along Navsadbuli, has departures to Zugdidi (5 GEL, 1½ hours, about hourly from 10am to 3.30pm), Kutaisi (5 GEL, 2½ hours, about hourly, 7am to 4pm) and Tbilisi (15 GEL, six to seven hours, at 9am, 1pm and 4pm). **Grup Georgia** (☎ 895225445) has buses to Tbilisi (15 GEL, six hours) from its office just across the bridge north of the market, at 1.30am, 10.30am and 1.30pm.

Trains from Tbilisi to Poti take six hours, are 3rd-class only, and leave at 2.45pm (seating only, 8 GEL) and 11.40pm (12 GEL). Departures from Poti to Tbilisi are at 8.45am and 11.40pm.

The Ukrainian shipping company UkrFerry operates two passenger ferries a week each way between Poti and Ilyichevsk, near Odessa, Ukraine. Its agent in Poti is **Instra** (☎ 21998, 21060, 899915696; Gegidze 20; ☑ 10am-1pm, 3-5.30pm), 50m from the Hotel Anchor. See p323 for further information on this service. The Bulgarian company **Intershipping** (www .intershipping.net) operates a weekly passenger-carrying vehicle ferry from Burgas to Poti and back (one-way per passenger/car €150/300, three days).

GEORGIA

KOLKHETI NATIONAL PARK
კოლხეთის ეროვნული პარკი

☎ 393 (international), ☎ 293 (domestic)

This 285-sq-km **national park** (www.knp.ge) encompasses three separate areas of coastline and wetlands north and southeast of Poti. It's the southeastern area, focused on Lake Paliastomi, which is of most interest to visitors, thanks to its large bird population. More than 190 species have been sighted in the park. The best months to visit are September and October, when large and small raptors can be seen migrating southwards, and January to May, when swans, geese, ducks, other water birds and even rare pelicans, storks and booted eagles gather to winter here. The area is also a paradise for frogs (the cacophony in the mating season can be tremendous). Ancient Greek physician Hippocrates wrote that the people here lived in the bogs, making houses out of the materials found here, travelling in boats, and drinking rainwater. (He also commented that the people were so tall and so fat you couldn't see their faces!)

The park has an excellent **visitors centre** (☎ 23065; Guria 222; ☼ 10am-6pm), 4km south of the centre of Poti on the Batumi road. The main access to Lake Paliastomi is 1.5km further south along the same road. At the visitors centre you can buy an English-language field guide to the park's birds and organise pontoon-boat trips on the lake (a two-hour trip costs between 10 GEL and 40 GEL per person depending on group size; maximum: 16 people).

Sleeping & Eating

Hotel Paliastomi (☎ 20929; Lake Paliastomi; cottage 20-50 GEL, d 70-120 GEL; ✵) Right near the lake, 1.5km south of the visitors centre, this small hotel has nice new pine-panelled or blue-painted rooms in its main building, and older but adequate rooms in brick-and-wood cottages. There's no food, but it's a short walk to Restaurant Iasoni, under the same management, on the corner of the main road.

Visitors centre (☎ 23065; Guria 222; r 50 GEL; ✵) The visitors centre has four pleasant pine-built rooms available upstairs, all with bathroom, air-con and TV. There's a café for guests, too.

Getting There & Away

Marshrutkas 5 and 20 (0.40 GEL) from Poti will stop at the visitors centre or the turning to the lake 1.5km further south. You can pick them up at Akaki heading south off Rustavelis rkali.

STEWARD OF THE WETLANDS

If all Georgia's new generation was like Lasha Nodia, you could be happy that the country was in pretty safe hands. Educated, aware, ambitious but public-spirited, he also shares the typical Georgian's love of his country and of his local roots – in this case the Black Sea port of Poti and its surrounding countryside.

Lasha is deputy director of the Kolkheti National Park, established in 1998 to protect the wetlands and coasts around Poti. In Soviet times, official policy was to drain the wetlands to eliminate malaria, but the consequent ecological damage, to an area that is a vital bird refuge and home to rare semitropical plants, was huge. 'Our aim now is to keep what is left,' says Lasha.

The park faces many challenges, including from villagers whose livelihood depends on its lands. 'The arrival of electricity in villages after the Rose Revolution made a big difference,' Lasha comments. 'This has slowed the rate of wood cutting for fuel in the forests.'

Lasha did not come to environmental work from a scientific background. Born in Poti in 1981 and schooled there, he then studied foreign economic relations at Tbilisi State University. His father has a small printing firm in Poti, and Lasha's education, and admirable command of English, were furthered when he won a place on a training programme with a large printing company in Hayward, California. On return to Georgia in 2003 Lasha began working for the national park, initially as manager of the visitor and education programme. A major achievement has been the completion of the park's handsome new visitors centre, built in 2006 after eight years of planning and preparation. The park now employs 28 rangers.

Wages for park employees are inevitably low, and Lasha foresees that one day he may move to work in the private sector. 'But I'll always continue to work here in a voluntary capacity. This park is too important to leave behind.'

UREKI ურეკი
pop 1600

The only genuine sandy beach on the Georgian coast is at Ureki, 15km south of Poti. Ureki's sand is black because it's rich in magnetic iron; in Soviet times its medicinal properties saw three sanatoria built here. Today it's being developed as a small Western-standard resort, largely thanks to the investment of Georgian tycoon Badri Patarkatsishvili, so it's a good place to kick back for a day or two if this appeals to you.

The coast and the resort are 1.5km off the Poti–Batumi highway and the Tbilisi–Batumi railway. There are now about a dozen mostly midsized and midrange hotels fronting the beach or very near to it. Recommended are **Hotel Albatros** (☎ 899503046; www.hotels-tbilisi.com; Magnetiti; d full board US$65; ☒ ☒), on the seafront; **Hotel Edem** (☎ 899101393; d US$40; ☒), also seafront and with a café; and **Hotel Dzveli Sakhli** (☎ 899560560; ureki2005@yahoo.com; Sanapiro; d full board US$60; ☒ ☒), a block back from the beach, with a playground and mini–aqua park.

Batumi-bound marshrutkas will drop you at the Ureki turn-off.

ZUGDIDI ზუგდიდი
☎ 315 (international), ☎ 215 (domestic) / pop 105,000 (estimated, including internally displaced persons)

The main city of Samegrelo (Mingrelia), Zugdidi is 108km northwest of Kutaisi. As the nearest Georgian city to Abkhazia, it has had to absorb a particularly high number of refugees since the 1990s (by some estimates they have doubled its population) and is a centre for Georgians who favour military action to regain Abkhazia. It was also from Zugdidi that deposed President Zviad Gamsakhurdia, himself a Mingrelian, launched his unsuccessful 1993 rebellion against the Shevardnadze government. Today Gamsakhurdia's statue stands on the town's central boulevard, which is named after him.

Despite this troubled recent past, today Zugdidi is a bustling and (at least outwardly) pleasant town that sees few travellers except for those heading for Svaneti, for which Zugdidi is an essential stepping stone.

Orientation & Information
The central boulevard, Zviad Gamsakhurdias gamziri, runs southwest to northeast with a shady park strip along its centre. Rustaveli runs northwest from the middle of the boulevard to the train and bus station, 1km away. About halfway to the station, just past the busy market and across a river, Gia Guluas qucha heads north towards a replica Svan tower. The main departure point for marshrutkas to Svaneti is on the right of this street, just before the Svan tower.

Bank of Georgia ATM (Kostava) Next to Hotel Samegrelo; Kostava runs south off Rustaveli one block west of Zviad Gamsakhurdia.

Computer Service-Centre (Rustaveli 89; internet per hr 1 GEL; ☒ 9am-6pm) Half a block off Zviad Gamsakhurdia.

Sights
The palace of the Dadiani family (old lords of Samegrelo), a castle-like building from the 17th to 19th centuries in a park 500m beyond the north end of Zviad Gamsakhurdia, is now the **Dadiani Museum** (☎ 26439; admission 2 GEL; ☒ 10am-5pm Tue-Sun). The most unusual exhibit is one of Napoleon Bonaparte's three bronze death masks, acquired via a 19th-century marriage between a Dadiani and a descendant of Napoleon's sister. The wooded botanical gardens beside the park are worth a stroll.

Sleeping & Eating
Hotel Zugdidi (☎ 54242; Kostava; r 40-60 GEL) One block along Rustaveli from Zviad Gamsakhurdia then a few steps south on Kostava, this hotel occupies the top two floors of a four-storey building. The rooms have bathrooms with showers, and are clean and parquet-floored, but the beds can be lumpy. No food available.

Hotel Samegrelo (☎ 50745; Kostava 54; r 50-100 GEL; ☒) Almost opposite the Hotel Zugdidi, the Samegrelo provides cosy rooms in red tones with jolly dolphin-motif shower curtains. Some staff speak English and there's also a decent little restaurant (mains 3 to 4 GEL) with a short but good menu.

our pick **Restaurant Diaroni** (☎ 893517851; Konstantin Gamsakhurdia 9; mains 7-15 GEL) For a satisfying full meal with friendly, efficient service, look no further than this atmospheric cellar-like place. A full range of Georgian and Russian dishes is on offer and there's an English-language menu. To find it, head east off the middle of Zviad Gamsakhurdias gamziri and go 50m to the left along the first cross-street.

GEORGIA

Getting There & Away

In Tbilisi, marshrutkas (15 GEL, six to seven hours, every 1½ hours, 8am to 5pm) and buses (12 GEL, seven hours, at 10am, noon, 1pm and 10pm) to Zugdidi leave from the rear of the main train station. The night train leaving Tbilisi at 9.30pm (3rd-/2nd-class 5.50/11 GEL) gets you into Zugdidi at 5.30am, in time to catch a marshrutka to Svaneti the same morning. The return train departs Zugdidi at 11.20pm. There's also a day train to Tbilisi (3rd-/2nd-class 6/11.50 GEL, eight hours) at 9.50am, and an *elektrichka* just to Kutaisi at 7.30am. From outside Zugdidi's train station, marshrutkas and some buses leave several times daily for Kutaisi (6 GEL, two hours), Poti (5 GEL, 1½ hours), Batumi (10 GEL, three hours) and Tbilisi (12 GEL to 15 GEL, six hours).

Marshrutkas and jeeps to Mestia in Svaneti (15 GEL, five to seven hours) leave from near the Svan tower on Gia Gulua any time from 6am on, once they fill up (which can be with goods as well as people).

It's a good idea to be there by 8am – though if you're unlucky you might still have to wait several hours before you get moving. They'll take your name and passport number at the ticket hut with the 'Mestia' sign. Some vehicles may meet the overnight train from Tbilisi but may still not leave Zugdidi until the driver has garnered a full load.

A jeep taxi from Zugdidi to Mestia typically costs around 20 GEL.

ABKHAZIA აფხაზეთი

The greatest tragedy to befall Georgia since its independence is the secession of Abkhazia and the bloodshed and misery that this has brought about.

Once the jewel of the 'Soviet Riviera' along the Black Sea coast, today this de facto independent republic is still struggling to recover from the devastation of the 1992–93 war, unrecognised by any country and with only about one-third of its prewar population of 535,000.

Russian tourism in Abkhazia, however, has grown fast and by 2007 it was also possible for other travellers to venture into the region, although the British **Foreign Office** (www.fco.gov.uk) and the US **State Department** (travel.state.gov) were still advising against it.

If you're tempted to visit, be aware that tensions, kidnappings and violence have flared up repeatedly over the years, especially in the border region between Zugdidi (Samegrelo) and Gali (Abkhazia). Backpackers have been known to be arrested and interrogated at Sukhumi police headquarters. There is useful Abkhazia travel information on the Thorn Tree message board on the Lonely Planet website (www.lonelyplanet.com).

Information

MONEY

Abkhazia's currency is the Russian rouble (R). You can change cash US dollars, and in many cases euros, to roubles at banks and money changers, but Abkhazia's few ATMs only accept Russian Garantbank cards.

TELEPHONE

Abkhazia has the Georgian country code, ☎ 995. If calling from Georgia, dial ☎ 8 before the area code, as for an internal long-distance call.

VISAS

The first step if you want to go to Abkhazia is to apply for a visa. The best first move is to telephone the English-speaking **Abkhazia Foreign Ministry** (☎ 442-63948/65792/70044; www.mfaabkhazia.org; fax 442-63445/65792; ulitsa Lakoba 21, Sukhumi; 🕙 9.30am-6pm Mon-Fri). At the time of research you could apply for the visa by email or fax using a form available on the ministry's website. Supposedly within five days you will then receive a permit to cross the border on a specific date.

In practice you will probably have to make follow-up phone calls to the Foreign Ministry. If you plan to visit in busy July or August, make first contact a month ahead.

Once inside the country you have to collect your visa (US$20 for 30 days) from the Foreign Ministry in Sukhumi. You will need this when you leave Abkhazia.

If you are entering Abkhazia from Russia (at the Psou border point, considered illegal by Georgia while it is not controlled by Georgia) you will need to have a double-entry Russian visa.

Sukhumi სოხუმი

☎ 442 / pop 45,000 (estimated)

Abkhazia's capital (Sokhumi in Georgian; Sukhum or Akua in Abkhaz) has a gorgeous setting on a bay backed by hills thick with

---

THE ABKHAZIA CONFLICT

The roots of the Abkhazian conflict are extremely complicated. Many Georgians see the provocative hand of Russia behind it all, but it is also true that Abkhazians had sought separation from Georgia well before the Soviet Union broke up.

The Abkhaz are linguistically distinct from the Georgians, their language being one of the northwestern Caucasus group (although Russian is now the most common language in Abkhazia). During the Middle Ages, Abkhazia was one of the most important kingdoms of Christian Georgia, but many Abkhaz converted to Islam under Ottoman occupation between the 16th and 19th centuries. Once Soviet power arrived in 1921, Abkhazia was proclaimed an independent republic within the USSR, but was then incorporated into the Georgian Soviet Republic in 1936. From the 1930s there was official encouragement for the settling of large numbers of Georgians in the region, and by 1989 about 46% of Abkhazia's population was Georgian, and only some 18% Abkhaz.

During Mikhail Gorbachev's reforms in the 1980s the Abkhaz began to demand more autonomy. The Abkhazian Supreme Soviet declared Abkhazia a full union republic (separate from Georgia) in 1990, and real conflict broke out in 1992 when the Georgian National Guard moved into Abkhazia and ended up occupying Sukhumi. Abkhazia was then plunged into a year of fighting, with the civilian population suffering terribly. Georgians claimed persuasively that Russian forces assisted the Abkhaz. In September 1993 the Abkhaz attacked Sukhumi in violation of a truce and drove the Georgian forces, and Abkhazia's entire Georgian population, out of Abkhazia; many civilians died while crossing the mountains to Svaneti and Samegrelo. Today Georgia still has approximately 250,000 refugees, the great majority of them from Abkhazia and most of them living in difficult conditions. Since a ceasefire in 1994, a CIS (in fact Russian) peacekeeping force has been deployed in Abkhazia, but Russia appears to be helping the breakaway regime – not just militarily but also by granting Russian passports to Abkhazians, opening the railway between Sukhumi and Sochi, and loosening controls at the Russian–Abkhaz border.

---

luxuriant semitropical vegetation. Much of Sukhumi is still in ruins, but a lot of restoration is going on.

Ruins of the Greek trading port Dioskuria lie beneath Sukhumi Bay. After periods of Roman, Byzantine, Arab, Abkhazian and Turkish domination, Sukhumi was taken by the Russians in 1810. By 1989 it had a population of 120,000, but the city was badly damaged during the fighting between 1989 and 1993, when its large Georgian population was driven out.

ORIENTATION & INFORMATION

The main street is prospekt Mira, two to three blocks inland from the seafront boulevard, naberezhnaya Makhadzhirov. A useful interactive city map, in Russian, is on the web at vmlmapsh.narod.ru/xvmlmap.htm. There are several cybercafés in the central area, charging around R50 per hour. Travel agencies offering tours and accommodation bookings in Abkhazia include **Abkhazintur** (☎ 61643; www.abkhazintur.moy.su in Russian; ulitsa Abazinskaya 35/11) and **Yug** (☎ 62410; ugturizm.h12 .ru in Russian; prospekt Mira 69).

SIGHTS

Sukhumi Fort, on the seafront just west of ulitsa Sakharova, is a Russian rebuilding of a Turkish fort built on the site of a Roman one.

The **Abkhazian State Museum** (prospekt Leona 22; ⊙ 10am-3pm Mon-Fri), with archaeological, historical and ethnographic collections, and the **Botanical Gardens** (ulitsa D Gulia 22; ⊙ 9am-3pm) are both well worth visiting. **Park Slavy** (Glory Park), between prospekt Mira and ulitsa Lakoba, is the burial site of many Abkhaz who died in the 1992–93 fighting.

Sukhumi Hill, 200m high in the northeast of the city, gives good panoramas and much of it is a woodland park.

SLEEPING & EATING

Numerous families rent rooms to tourists. Staff at the Foreign Ministry, where you must collect your visa, can probably help you to find somewhere.

Homestay (ulitsa Akirtava 55, Turbaza district; per person R200) Travellers have been welcomed here by the Kvitsinia family, whose twin daughters speak good English. Rooms are large, with shared toilet and shower. Coming from Gali, you can get off your marshrutka under the railway bridge 500m after the big UN compound. Walk east along Akirtava, a narrow lane to the left of a dilapidated block of flats.

Holiday Home Abkhazia (Otdykh Abkhazia; ulitsa Akirtava; per person R300-500) The cheapest option after homestays; in the east of town.

Hotel Yasemin (ulitsa Lakoba 100; s/d incl breakfast from R1200/1500) Centrally situated, with 32 rooms and a restaurant.

Hotel Sukhum (☎ 68180; www.otel-sukhum.narod .ru in Russian; r with shared bathroom R1100, with private bathroom & air-con R2900-3500; ❄) Excellent small hotel on the bank of the Basla River towards the east end of town. Prices include breakfast.

Hotel Ritsa (cnr naberezhnaya Makhadzhirov & prospekt Leona; s R1040-2600 Oct-May, R1560-3900 Jun-Sep, d R1560-3900 Oct-May, R2340-5850 Jun-Sep) Now rebuilt after war damage, the landmark Ritsa is the top hotel in town, with fan-cooled rooms. It also houses the fanciest place to eat, Restoran San-Remo, with an international menu.

There are several cafés and restaurants along naberezhnaya Makhadzhirov. Travellers have recommended the **Nartaa** (cnr ulitsa Aidgylara) for its excellent Abkhazian food at minuscule prices.

GETTING THERE & AWAY

Taxis for the 20-minute ride from Zugdidi to Abkhazia's southern border at the Enguri (or Inguri) River cost 10 GEL. At the frontier you pass a Georgian guard post and a Russian peacekeepers' post, before crossing the bridge to the Abkhazian border post on the far side (keep an eye on your belongings here). Most people crossing here are Georgian IDPs returning to tend their properties in the Gali area.

From the border you can take a marshrutka (R10, 20 minutes) or a shared taxi (R40) on to Gali, 15km northwest.

You may also find vehicles going through to Sukhumi (R150). Marshrutkas and buses (both R100, two hours) leave Gali for Sukhumi up to about 11am.

From Sukhumi's **bus station** (ulitsa Dzidzaria), in the northwest of town, buses run northwest to Novy Afon (R20, 45 minutes), Gagra (R100, two hours), and the Psou border crossing (R100, 2½ hours), about every half-hour up to 11am, then hourly. The first bus south to Gali leaves at 10am.

Taxis are easy to find.

Other Destinations

The coast northwest of Sukhumi is beautiful, with the thickly forested lower slopes of the Caucasus reaching right down to the shore in places. The multidomed **Novy Afon Monastery** stands out on a hillside about 20km from Sukhumi. Russian monks came from Mt Athos in Greece to found this monastery in the late 19th century. In Soviet times it was a workers holiday home. Nearby, a small train carries tourists through the impressive **Novy Afon Caves**, and atop Iveriis Hill are the ruins of ancient **Anakopia**, capital of Abkhazia in the 8th century AD. There are a couple of homestays on the main road just before Novy Afon's old railway station.

At Bzyb (or Bzipi), 80km from Sukhumi, a road heads off north to **Lake Ritsa**, created by a Soviet-era dam amid beautiful Caucasus mountain scenery at an elevation of 950m. Stalin had a *dacha* (country cottage) on the far shore. The 41km drive up to the lake, via gorges and waterfalls, is spectacular. You can hire boats on the lake.

Gagra, Abkhazia's main resort and highly popular with Russian tourists, has a long beach below thickly forested mountains, 95km from Sukhumi. The old part of town has some charm. There are many homestays on Shapshugskoe, 1km north of the marshrutka station, and on Sayat-Nova, about 500m south of the marshrutka station, west of the railway. Most charge R150 per person.

ADJARA აჭარა

The southwestern corner of Georgia is a highlight of the country and intriguingly idiosyncratic: it's humid and semitropical and has a sizable Muslim population.

Since the loss of Abkhazia, Adjara (also spelt Achara, Ajara or Ajaria) has taken on the mantle of Georgia's holiday coast. Batumi, the Adjaran capital, is the destination of choice for most Georgians – and many Armenians, Azerbaijanis and Ukrainians – in search of summer fun, with a real party atmosphere, especially in August.

Though Adjara's beaches are mostly stony, the climate is beautiful and the scenery gorgeous, with lush hills rising behind the coast, and peaks topping 3000m in the Lesser Caucasus inland.

GEORGIA

Many travellers enter Georgia at the busy Sarpi border post with Turkey, just south of Batumi. Onward transport to the rest of Georgia is good.

Adjarans are ethnically Georgian and speak the Georgian language. Under Ottoman control from the 16th century to 1878, most of the inhabitants were converted to Islam. The Russian takeover in 1878 presaged an early boom time for Batumi as an export terminal for oil from Azerbaijan. In Soviet times Adjara returned to backwater status (the Turkish border was an absolute no-go area), but since Georgian independence it has again become an important entry point to the Caucasus region.

Adjara has retained its status as an autonomous republic within Georgia and until 2004 was the personal fiefdom of its pro-Russian president, Aslan Abashidze, who kept it out of Georgia's internal conflicts but ran an authoritarian, corrupt regime backed by his own militia. A standoff between Abashidze and President Saakashvili climaxed in 2004 when Abashidze sealed the Adjaran border with the rest of Georgia, raising fears of another Georgian civil war. However, Abashidze lost his crucial support from Russia and days later left for ignominious exile in Moscow, to the delight of Adjarans.

BATUMI ბათუმი
☎ 222 / pop 137,000

Although Kutaisi is Georgia's second city population-wise, the resort and port city of Batumi is in many ways the real counterweight to Tbilisi in terms of atmosphere, setting and appearance. Set on a warm semitropical coast with a backdrop of mist-wrapped hills near the Turkish border, Batumi has become the country's summer holiday capital, pulling in tourists from around Georgia and beyond. Its history is a lot shorter than that of most Georgian cities, and it owes much of its unique charm to the elegant fin-de-siècle architecture of its original boom time a century ago.

For most travellers arriving from Turkey, Batumi will be the first Georgian city they encounter, and it makes a great introduction to the country, with its relaxed atmosphere, lots of hotel space, good restaurants and nightlife.

Batumi developed in the late 19th century as the western terminus of a railway from Baku that then carried one-fifth of the world's oil production. A pipeline and refinery built by Ludwig Nobel, brother of Swedish dynamite inventor Alfred, soon followed. Batumi gained free-port status, over 20 foreign consulates set up here, and the town developed into a fashionable resort at the southern tip of the Russian empire and a crossroads between Europe and Asia.

One of the first decisions of the post-Abashidze administration in 2004 was to make Batumi an attractive place to visit, something in which they are, happily, succeeding. Charming old buildings have been restored, renovated and floodlit, attractive new ones are joining them, and strolling around the leafy, low-rise central streets is a real pleasure.

Orientation & Information

The central, oldest and liveliest part of town sits on a broad arrowhead of land with the harbour to its east and the stony main beach running down the western shore, backed by the Batumis bulvari (Batumi Blvd) park.

Two broad avenues, Chavchavadze and Rustaveli, mark the southern and northern boundaries of the central area, with K Gamsakhurdia and Baratashvili the most important cross-streets in the central grid. The bus station is east of the centre, a 1km walk along Tsereteli from Tbilisis moedani on Chavchavadze. Batumi's train station is 5km north of town in Makhinjauri, on the road to Kobuleti.

Adjara (www.tourismadjara.ge) This regional tourism website is useful and attractive.

Internet Café (Melikishvili 23; per hr 1.50 GEL; ☀ 9am-midnight) The most pleasant spot to do your mail.

Internet Café (Marjanishvili; per hr 2 GEL; ☀ 24 hr) Noisy kids but good connections.

Tourist Information kiosks (☀ 10am-2pm & 4-8pm) Evropas moedani (☎ 877909094; cnr Baratashvili & Memed Abashidze) Boulevard (☎ 877909091; cnr Ninoshvili & K Gamsakhurdia) These helpful places provide good city maps and other material on Adjara in English. At research time they only opened from May to October but this may be extended.

Sights

Everyone soon finds themselves strolling along **Batumis bulvari**, the 1.5km park strip fronting the main beach. With its cafés, paths, trees, beach bars and large **Ferris wheel** (per person 0.50 GEL) at the south end, this is the life and soul of the resort. It was originally laid out in 1884 and contains some unique

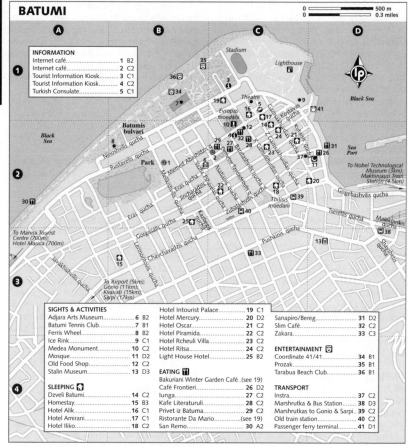

BATUMI

0   500 m
0   0.3 miles

plants and trees. The **beach** itself is fine though stony – extremely busy during the summer months, but kept clean enough. You'll find cleaner waters, and thinner crowds, a short drive south of the city, at Gonio and Kvariati.

The main central square, **Evropas moedani** (Europe Sq), is a broad, attractive space sporting musical fountains which are a magnet for kids on hot summer evenings. Towering over the square is a striking **monument**, unveiled in 2007, to Medea, 'the person who brought Georgia closer to Europe,' according to Batumi's mayor at the time. The Georgian government controversially paid over 1 million GEL for the monument, sculpted by Davit Khmaladze.

The **Adjara Arts Museum** (☎ 73894; Era 8; admission 2 GEL; ⏰ 11am-6pm Tue-Sun) makes a happy break from many of Georgia's more turgid and badly lit museums. The collection covers Georgian art including works by Pirosmani and Elena Akhvlediani, as well as European and Russian painting from the 19th and 20th centuries.

For those who don't make it to Gori, the **Stalin Museum** (☎ 20456; Pushkin 19; admission 2 GEL, guide in English 1 GEL; ⏰ 9am-5pm Mon-Sat) is an interesting and similarly hagiographic establishment. Stalin lived here for just a few months in 1901–02 when he helped organise the bitumen workers and set up an illegal printing press. Rather too amazingly (given that he didn't become famous until almost two decades later), his personal belongings have survived, including a moth-eaten towel and the bed he slept on.

Batumi's last surviving **mosque** (Kutaisi 33), built in the 1860s, is also worth visiting. It's finely painted in pinks, greens and blues, with beautiful Koranic calligraphy on the walls. Friendly men often gather to socialise at the entrance. The nameless **old food shop** (K Gamsakhurdia 12) has very ordinary goods for sale, but its rich gold decoration is a unique memento of pre-revolutionary Batumi.

Batumi's most modern and one of its most interesting museums is the **Nobel Technological Museum** (☎ 54594; Leselidze 3, Tamari district; admission 2 GEL; ☽ 10am-5pm). This takes you back to Batumi's heyday in the late 19th and early 20th century, when it was in the vanguard of the international oil business, with investment from the Nobels and Rothschilds spawning technological innovations here. The museum also looks at the tea industry that grew up at the same time. It's just inland off the road to Makhinjauri train station.

Activities

The good open-air pool at the **Hotel Intourist Palace** (☎ 32123; Ninoshvili 11; admission 30 GEL; ☽ 10am-7pm) is open to nonguests, as is the hotel's excellent **spa** (admission 20 GEL; ☽ 7am-midnight) – see p92.

Batumi Tennis Club (☎ 72258; Batumis bulvari; per hr for 2 incl racquets & balls 20 GEL; ☽ 8am-9pm) has eight good hard courts, and you can ice-skate year round at Batumi's modern **Ice Rink** (Gogebashvili; per hr 5 GEL; ☽ noon-11pm). The gleaming new **Marina Tourist Center** (☎ 76400, 899136565; www .marigroup.ge; Khimshiashvili 10; pool per hr 15 GEL, tennis court per hr outdoor/indoor 10/15 GEL, tennis racquets and balls for 2 15 GEL) has an excellent 25m indoor pool and tennis courts.

Sleeping

Batumi has a large and ever-growing number of hotels, with many attractive new midrange places opening up.

BUDGET

Hotel Iliko (☎ 73892; K Gamsakhurdia 42; r 20-50 GEL; ⚅) This inexpensive little family-run hotel is set around a small courtyard reached through an arch with a 'Sastumro/Gostinitsa' sign (that's 'Hotel' in Georgian and Russian). Room options range from fan-and-shared-bathroom to air-con-with-bath. All are clean and well cared for, if rather small.

Homestay (☎ 898525258, 899797224; Lermontov 24; per person 20 GEL) Kulnasi Miqeladze runs a veritable mini–budget hotel with 18 rooms, most of them newly built, on three floors. They're bare but spotless and good-sized. The shared bathrooms are equally clean and there's a guests' kitchen. Marshrutkas 12, 15 and 15A from the bus station via Tbilisis moedani stop nearby on Chavchavadze.

Hotel Piramida (☎ 32204; Vazha Pshavela 39; r 30 GEL Oct-Jun, 40 GEL Jul-Sep) A good-value, friendly budget option, the Piramida has smallish, well-kept rooms, all with bathrooms and some with balconies. The owner, Almazik, also has a travel agency and can organise city tours and day trips.

Hotel Oscar (☎ 76267; Gorgasali 6; r 40-60 GEL; ⚅) A touch shabby but friendly, the Oscar has ordinary 40 GEL rooms with fans and much brighter 60 GEL rooms with air-con. All have private bathrooms. Not too bad for the price and location.

MIDRANGE

Hotel Mercury (☎ 31401; www.hotelmercurybm.ge; Chavchavadze 10/12; r incl breakfast 60-80 GEL, ste 130 GEL; ⚅) The decent-sized and uncluttered rooms, most with balconies or large windows over the street, plus a raft of extras – roof terrace, 4th-floor bar, basement bistro and sauna – make the Mercury good value. It can fill up during high season.

ourpick Dzveli Batumi (Old Batumi; ☎ 77157; www .davisvenot.ge/dzvelibatumi; batgts@yahoo.com; Kostava 24; s/d 60/80 GEL, ste 150 GEL; ⚅) Friendly and informative hosts Gocha and Irina have converted half a dozen rooms in their old-town home with spot-on contemporary taste, all in various pastel colours, with carpets and satellite TV. A guesthouse with one big difference: flair.

Hotel Ritsa (☎ 73292; www.hotelritsa.com; Z Gamsakhurdia 16; r incl breakfast 70-120 GEL; ⚅) This well situated, 14-room hotel provides comfort and *belle époque* style in a new building, opened in 2006. The cheaper rooms are an especially good deal.

Hotel Marina (☎ 76400, 899136565; www.mari group.ge; Khimshiashvili 10; s 70 GEL, d 90-130 GEL; ⚅ ⛲) Down on the southern seafront, the Marina is a welcoming, English-speaking place in a gleaming new sports-and-tourism facility with a pool, tennis courts, a fitness club, billiards and football pitches – but it's also a fine place to stay if you're not feeling particularly active. Rooms are spacious, modern and pleasant,

GEORGIA

with a wave design theme, and many have balconies. Downstairs are an ATM, a bar, an Asian-theme café and a Mexican restaurant.

Light House Hotel (☎ 33610; www.lighthouse.ge; Kazbegi 4; r incl breakfast 120 GEL) This very stylish new hotel, on a quiet street just out of the busiest part of town, has just 10 rooms in a variety of eye-catching, modish styles and colours. A comfortable and friendly place to stay.

our pick **Hotel Rcheuli Villa** (☎ 70707; rcheuli villa@centerpoint.ge; Jordania 21; r incl breakfast US$50-80, ste US$100-150; ﹡) A lovely pink-painted mansion, newly built in old Batumi style, houses fine rooms with marble floors and elegant imperial-style furnishings. Professional but friendly service helps make this newcomer one of the best bets in Batumi.

Hotel Amirani (☎ 75515; www.hotelamirani.ge; General Mazniashvili 3; r incl breakfast US$60-130; ﹡) This small, central hotel has elegant rooms with parquet floors, thick rugs and classical décor. Reception staff speak excellent English.

Hotel Alik (☎ 75801; hotelalik.gol.ge; Memed Abashidze 12; r incl breakfast US$80-120; ﹡ ﹡) A comfortable, central place where large faux-cactus lamps and gaudy 21st-century bedspreads cohabit with Empire-style chairs. Services and facilities are good, but the sauna and plunge pool are only free to guests until noon.

TOP END

Hotel Intourist Palace (☎ 32123; www.intouristpalace .com; Ninoshvili 11; r incl breakfast US$176-295 Aug; ﹡ ﹡ ﹡) Palace is no exaggeration for this luxuriously revamped large hotel, from its gleaming marble lobby to the large, thickly carpeted rooms, all with balconies. The position facing the Boulevard park is superb, and hotel facilities include two restaurants, a good open-air pool and a spa with sauna, Turkish bath, fitness centre and assorted massages (US$20 to US$80). Room rates vary dramatically with the seasons and can more than halve in winter.

Eating

Batumi is full of lively cafés and restaurants. In addition to those listed here, there are several cafés in the Boulevard park, and from July to September many more open up on the main beach, some making admirable efforts to create a tropical ambience.

Zakara (cnr Pushkin & Vazha Pshavela; khinkali each 0.50 GEL; ﹡ 10am-midnight) This two-level wooden local restaurant is widely reputed to serve the best beef and pork *khinkali* in town (if you aren't sick of them already). It's an animated place with plenty of beer flowing.

Iunga (Era 4; khachapuri 2-3.50 GEL; ﹡ 9am-11pm) There's no better place than Batumi to decide whether you like *khachapuri acharuli*, Adjara's large boat-shaped variety of Georgia's national fast food with a lightly fried egg on top. And there's no better place to try it than this tiny, neat place which specialises in it – if one of its four tables is vacant.

Kafe Literaturuli (☎ 899155443; K Gamsakhurdia 18; cakes & pastries 2-5 GEL; ﹡ 9am-11pm) The Literary Café is a great stop for tea, coffee, cakes and pastries, with a slightly artsy ambience.

Privet iz Batuma (☎ 32217; Memed Abashidze 36; light dishes 2-8 GEL; ﹡ 10am-1am) A fashionable café with a colonial Russian theme and sailor-suited waiters, 'Hi from Batumi' is good for ice cream, cakes, sandwiches, desserts and bliny (pancakes). The interior is air-conditioned and there are outdoor tables too, but you may still have to wait for a table on summer evenings.

Slim Café (☎ 899550065; Memed Abashidze 27; dishes 4-7 GEL) Long and thin (true to its name) and in tasteful style, Slim serves wonderful bliny with fruit and chocolate dripping, plus assorted sandwiches, soups and salads.

Sanapiro/Bereg (☎ 31271; Gogebashvili 9; mains 5-8 GEL; ﹡ 8am-2am) Right on the waterfront facing the harbour, this open-air pavilion is one of Batumi's best places to eat for its location alone. The food (mainly Georgian standards) and the service are fine too.

Café Frontieri (Gogebashvili 28; mains 5-10 GEL) A pleasant open-air spot facing the northern seafront, Frontieri is good for salads, shashlyk, cheese plates, apple pie – and draft Staropramen beer from the Czech Republic.

San Remo (☎ 877950950; Batumis bulvari; mains 5-10 GEL) Another place with sailor-suited waiters, the picture-windowed San Remo serves Georgian and Russian fare on a pier at the southern end of the Boulevard. It's a bit of a party place in the evening, with live music and a small dance floor.

Bakuriani Winter Garden Café (☎ 32123; Hotel Intourist Palace, Ninoshvili 11; cakes & sandwiches 7-9 GEL; ﹡ 8am-4am) The Intourist Palace's large conservatory-style café is the most tranquil and comfortable, and expensive, in town.

Ristorante Da Mario (☎ 32123; Hotel Intourist Palace, Ninoshvili 11; mains 9-25 GEL) Classy service, excellent Italian food and a long wine list make this hotel restaurant overlooking the Blvd a fine dinner spot.

Entertainment

In summer Batumis bulvari is the nightlife capital of Georgia. The main clubs – Tarabua Beach Club, Coordinate 41/41 and Prozak – are all fresh-air venues close to the beach, with stages and large dance spaces where people party till dawn every night. Long lists of guest DJs from around Europe provide high-energy and chill-out beats, helped out some nights by singers or bands. They open their doors around 9pm and start to fill after 11pm, with admission normally 10 GEL to 15 GEL. Plenty of smaller bars along the beach develop their own nocturnal scenes too.

Getting There & Around

As well as marshrutkas, buses and trains to other Georgian destinations, Batumi offers flights and overland transport to Armenia, and flights and ferries to Ukraine.

AIR

The new **airport** (☎ 76649) is 5km south of town on the Sarpi road. Turkish Airlines flies three times weekly to Istanbul and the small Georgian airlines Tbilaviamsheni and Marsi fly to Ukraine (Kiev, Odessa, Kharkov and Donetsk) once or more weekly. Tbilaviamsheni also has three flights a week to Yerevan.

Marshrutkas bound for Gonio or Sarpi from Tbilisis moedani will drop you at the airport.

LAND
Bus, Marshrutka & Taxi

Taxis to or from the Turkish border at Sarpi, 17km south, cost 15 GEL to 20 GEL; marshrutkas cost 1.50 GEL. In Batumi marshrutkas to Sarpi start from Tbilisis moedani. The border is open 24 hours daily and crossing it is normally straightforward, though there can be queues at weekends. Note that 'Hopa' marshrutkas from Batumi go to the Hopa bazaar, a huge market outside Batumi – not Hopa in Turkey!

In Tbilisi, marshrutkas to Batumi (18 GEL, seven hours) leave Didube bus station at least hourly from 8am to 8pm or later. Further marshrutkas and buses (at least every two hours, 9am to 5pm) leave from the back of Tbilisi's main train station.

In Batumi the main **marshrutka and bus station** (☎ 30163; Maiakovski 1) has buses to Tbilisi (about hourly, 7am to midnight), Poti (5 GEL, 1½ hours, eight daily, 8am to 6pm), Kutaisi (8 GEL, 2½ hours, hourly, 7am to 8pm), Zugdidi (10 GEL, three hours, at 11am, noon, 4pm and 6pm) and Akhaltsikhe (18 GEL, six hours, 8.30am and 10.30am) via Khashuri and Borjomi.

From about May to September there's a marshrutka to Akhaltsikhe (15 GEL, six hours, 11am) via Khulo – a route through mountainous interior Adjara which is not passable in winter. Also from here, **Lüks Karadeniz** (☎ 33984) runs buses to Trabzon in Turkey (20 GEL, three hours, every 1½ hours, 11am to 5pm).

Further marshrutkas to Tbilisi go hourly, between 7.30am and 11.30pm, from the **old train station** (cnr Asatiani & Zubalashvili).

Marshrutka 26 runs between the bus station and Tbilisis moedani, which is the terminus for marshrutkas 138 to Gonio (0.90 GEL) and 142 to Sarpi (1.50 GEL), both every 20 to 30 minutes.

Train

Batumi's shiny new **Makhinjauri station** (☎ 54158) is about 5km north of town on the Kobuleti road. Marshrutka 20 (0.40 GEL) runs here from Rustaveli and Gogebashvili, as does marshrutka 1 from Gogebashvili just east of Chavchavadze. The comfortable sleeper train to Tbilisi (3rd-/2nd-/1st-class 15/23/40 GEL, eight hours) departs at 11.25pm; it's best to book ahead for this (and essential in summer). There's also an afternoon train to Tbilisi at 4.45pm (one-class seating only, 20 GEL, seven hours), and an 8am *elektrichka* to Kutaisi (four hours). In July, August and the first half of September a train departs every second morning to Yerevan (3rd-/2nd-/1st-class 30/46/91 GEL, 21 hours).

SEA

Ferries sail about once weekly to Ilyichevsk (Ukraine) from Batumi's sea port. The local ticket agent is **Instra** (☎ 74119; Kutaisi 34). At research time Batumi's **passenger ferry terminal** (☎ 74912; Gogebashvili 3) stood idle – apart from furnishing information about sailings to Sochi in Russia from Hopa in Turkey, 30km from Batumi – after the Batumi–Sochi ferry was suspended in 2007. See p323 for further details on all these services.

AROUND BATUMI

The most interesting sight south of Batumi is the fortress at **Gonio** (admission 2 GEL; ☺ 10am-6pm), 11km from town, past the Chorokhi River. This is a vast and almost totally intact Roman fortress, which now has stunningly luscious gardens and is home to the grave of the Apostle Matthew/Levi. Marshrutkas to Sarpi and Gonio (p93) pass by the fortress, which is by the main road. Until the 12th century Gonio was known as Apsarosi, which may mean 'place with water', or may derive from Apsyrtus who, according to legend, was chopped into pieces and thrown into the sea by his sister Medea.

One of the best examples of Roman-Byzantine military architecture in the world, the fortress covers 47,000 sq metres and has 18 towers, a theatre and a Roman-era bathhouse. From Gonio the road continues for another 6km to **Sarpi** on the Turkish border. The route is lovely, with waterfalls in the lush green hills and mountains, and the sea on the other side.

Both Gonio and Kvariati, 4km to its south (before Sarpi), have pebbly beaches with cleaner water than in Batumi. They are starting to be developed for tourism with a few hotels and beach bars, but still make for a quieter stay than in Batumi. There's a tourist information office at the border at Sarpi.

Batumi's **Botanical Gardens** (admission 6 GEL; ☺ 9am-8pm), 9km north of town at Mtsvane Kontskhi (Green Cape), are well worth a trip. Marshrutka 1 (0.60 GEL) runs there from Gogebashvili just east of Chavchavadze. The lush gardens, with many semitropical and foreign species, cover a hillside rising straight out of the sea, and it takes about 1½ hours to walk the main path at a leisurely pace. A decent, stony beach, much less crowded than Batumi's, is down to the left of the entrance, and there's a handful of cafés and bars around there too.

The main Adjaran town north of here is Kobuleti, 30km from Batumi, a less attractive and more downmarket beach resort, which straggles along the coast for several kilometres.

Sleeping

Gonio and Kvariati have plenty of homestays, many of them right on the beach. Locals let out rooms for between 15 GEL and 50 GEL per person depending whether you need a private bathroom and/or meals. Travellers have recommended Muraba's at Kvariati, next to the big Hotel Neptun.

THE MOUNTAINS

A trip into the Caucasus along Georgia's northern border is a must for anyone who wants to experience the best of the country. Spectacular alpine scenery, wonderful walks and picturesque old villages with strange, tall defensive towers are all part of a trip to the Caucasus. Here traditions are more alive than elsewhere and the hospitality is almost compulsive in its intensity.

Georgia's very identity hinges on this mighty range that rises in Abkhazia, forms the border with Russia and runs the length of the country into Azerbaijan and Dagestan. The Caucasus includes the highest mountain in Europe, Mt Elbrus (5642m), on the Russian side of the border, and remains almost untouched by commercial development in a way the Alps can only dream about.

The most accessible destination is Kazbegi, reached by the dramatic Georgian Military Hwy from Tbilisi, but other areas are more than worth the effort of getting there – including enigmatic Svaneti, a refuge for many things considered essentially Georgian, and beautiful, untouched Tusheti.

It's notably cooler in the mountain villages, which can be a blessed relief in August, and in the hills you should be equipped for bad weather any time. The best walking season in most areas is from June to September. Indeed some areas such as Khevsureti and Tusheti are only accessible for a few summer months.

SVANETI სვანეთი

Impossibly beautiful, wild and mysterious, Svaneti is an ancient land locked in the greater Caucasus, so remote that it has never been tamed by any ruler, and even during the Soviet period it largely retained its traditional way of life. You need a minimum of three days to visit Svaneti (including one getting there and one getting out again), but if you can manage it, Svaneti is a must. Uniquely picturesque villages and snow-covered peaks rising over 4000m above flower-strewn alpine meadows offer marvelous walking opportunities. Svaneti's emblem is the defensive stone tower, designed to house villagers at times of invasion and strife. Around 175 towers, most originally built between the 9th and 13th centuries, survive in Svaneti today.

Until recently Svaneti was rather unsafe, with armed robberies against tourists too common to ignore. It's become a much safer place since 2004, when security forces shot dead the area's leading robber baron and his son, and jailed several other thugs. We did still hear of two attempted armed robberies (one successful) against tourist groups in 2006, but the overall picture is much safer. It's sensible to go with a local guide when you venture out on hikes, or at least get good local information first.

Svaneti's isolation has meant that during the many murderous invasions of Georgia over the centuries, icons, art and other religious artefacts from elsewhere were brought here for safekeeping, and many of them remain in private homes. Svaneti also has a rich church-art heritage of its own, with many of the tiny village churches boasting frescoes 1000 years old. This mountain retreat is regarded by many as the most authentically Georgian part of the country, despite the fact that the Svans speak an unwritten language that broke away from Georgian some four millennia ago and is largely unintelligible to other Georgians.

Svaneti is divided into Upper (Zemo) and Lower (Kvemo) Svaneti. Upper Svaneti offers

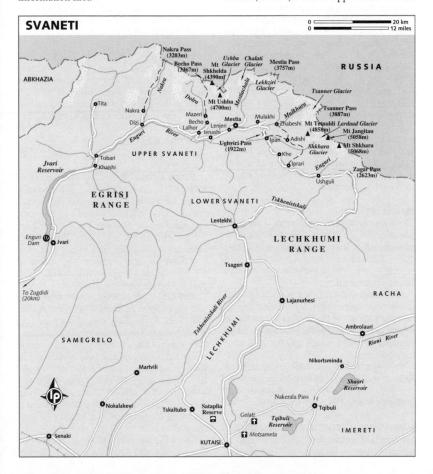

the best walking and climbing as well as the strongest traditions; it is very green, with sub-alpine forests of hornbeam, chestnut, spruce, pine and fir.

There are different species of wild goats, wolves, foxes and bears. The Svans mainly live by farming cattle, though they keep a breed of semiwild pig as well. In recent decades many Svans have moved to Tbilisi and southeast Georgia in search of a less difficult lifestyle. Tourism is one hope the region has for economic improvement.

Svan food tends to be less elaborate than other varieties of Georgian cuisine, but can be delicious.

Typical dishes are *chvishdari* (cheese cooked inside maize bread) and *kubdari* (minced meat in a *khachapuri*-type pie).

The **Svaneti Mountain Tourism Centre** (☎ 895 358049; www.svanetitrekking.ge; Stalin 7, Mestia), an NGO set up to develop locally based tourism in Svaneti, can provide accommodation in Mestia and several other villages (35 GEL per person, full board), plus hiking guides (50 GEL per day), foreign-language guides (30 GEL to 40 GEL per day), horses (20 GEL per day) and vehicle transport within Svaneti.

The office in Mestia is open erratic hours and may only have Russian and Georgian speakers available, so allow a day or two to make any arrangements, or contact the staff in advance. The website is an excellent source of Svaneti information.

Mestia მესტია
☎ 336 (international), ☎ 236 (domestic) / pop 2500

The administrative capital of Svaneti, at an altitude of 1400m, is a conglomeration of at least 10 neighbourhoods, with old buildings and typical Svan towers mixed in among drabber Soviet-era structures.

Mestia has no ATM, but many shops will change cash euros or US dollars. You can access the internet at the **Training & Consultation Centre** (Sgimieri; internet free; ☉ 2-4pm Mon-Fri). Most homestays can arrange guides and jeep transport.

An experienced and well-recommended English-speaking guide here, both for hikes and for visits to Svaneti's churches, is **Eteri Jorjoliani** (☎ 899167121; per day US$25-30).

MUSEUM OF HISTORY & ETHNOGRAPHY
Six hundred metres south from the central square, across two bridges, you'll find Mestia's excellent **Museum of History & Ethnography** (☎ 22158; admission 10 GEL, English-speaking guide 10 GEL; ☉ 10am-5pm Tue-Sun). Despite security problems, the Svans are reluctant to see their amazingly rich treasury of religious items moved from the villages, but this museum's collection is comprehensive, and labelled in English as well as Georgian, so it's the best place to get an overall idea of the glories of Svanetian art.

The exhibit includes a historic collection of 1890s Svaneti photos by Italian Vittorio Sella, and a hall with reproductions of famed Svaneti church murals, but the highlight is the two-room treasury: here you can see a 12th-century Persian silver jug given to Svaneti by Queen Tamar; a number of beautifully illuminated gospels from the 9th to 13th centuries; and golden altar crosses and chased-metal icons of amazingly high quality from the 10th to 14th centuries.

One rare 11th-century icon shows St George spearing the emperor Diocletian instead of his usual dragon. The 12th-century icon of the Forty Martyrs (who died by drowning) has a highly unusual modern quality; this piece is not Svanetian, rather it is thought to be from central Georgia.

SLEEPING & EATING
There are plenty of homestays in Mestia, all offering meals.

Manoni Ratiani (☎ 899568417; Gvaldiri; per person half board 25 GEL, camping per person 5 GEL) Manoni's rooms are a little more basic than the following places but still fine. There's a hot shower, and Manoni also has tents and sleeping bags for camping in her big, grassy garden. Son Irakli speaks English. They're just over 1km east from the central square – up a lane to the right beside a long, white building, 400m past the bridge over the Mestiachala River.

Nino Ratiani (☎ 899183555; ninoratiani@gmail.com; Tamari 1; per person incl breakfast/half board/full board 20/30/35 GEL) Particularly good Svan food (including many vegetarian dishes), a hospitable welcome and clean, comfortable rooms make Nino's one of the best homestays in town. Nino speaks some English and daughter Tamuna is fluent. Their house is the one with the Mini Market shop, 600m along the street towards Zugdidi from the central square. If it's full, they will install you with relatives nearby.

Nino & Eka Japaridze (☎ 899572850, 899389300; per person full board US$25) This excellent home-

WALKS AROUND MESTIA

Some routes are hard to follow without a guide, and much safer with one. Take local advice as you make your plans. You can remove some of the slog from many walks by going partway by jeep, which homestays can help you organise.

A moderately demanding half-day walk that many people do without a guide is up to the **Cross**, visible 900m above Mestia on the north side of the valley (actually just a single pole at research time). The views get better as you go, and from the Cross you can see the spectacular twin peaks of Mt Ushba (4710m), Georgia's toughest and most dangerous mountaineering challenge. From Mestia's central square walk 450m east along the main street then take the lane up to the left. Take the uphill option at all junctions. You pass under an arch after about 350m, and after 150m more the street becomes a footpath: follow this up and after 800m it bends to the right across the hillside, still climbing, eventually to meet a jeep track. You can follow this, shortcutting some bends, all the way to the cross. The round trip from Mestia takes about five hours. If you're feeling fit and energetic, with good weather and enough daylight you can continue to a series of small lakes, about two hours beyond the Cross and some 300m higher.

The walk to the **Chalati Glacier** is another lovely route, taking you out past Mestia's airstrip and up the Mestiachala valley. The last section is up through woods to the foot of the glacier. Watch out for rocks falling off the glacier in summer. This route is a nine- or 10-hour round trip including stops. There is a border-guard checkpoint en route, so take your passport.

You can spend a lovely three days walking to **Ushguli** if you start by taking a jeep as far as Ipari (Nakipari on some maps), about 20km southeast of Mestia. From Ipari the first stage takes you to Adishi, where you can sleep at **Zhora Kaldani's homestay** (☎ 899187359; per person half board 35 GEL). The second day is from Adishi to Iprari, where there are rooms at **Ucha Margvelani's** (☎ 899574783; per person half board 35 GEL). On the third day it's three or four hours' walk from Iprari to Ushguli.

Mazeri village, 1600m high in the Dolra valley, northwest of Mestia, is another fine base for walks. One lovely day route is up to the Ushba Glacier and back. In Mazeri, there's homestay accommodation with mountaineer **Giri Tserediani** (☎ 895563155; per person half board US$25) and **Natia Kvitsiani** (☎ 32-235691, 877411042; per person half board with lunch box US$30), who has a comfortable new guesthouse.

stay, with large, spotless rooms, hot water and creature comforts, is on the north side of the central square. Nino and Eka have six 4WD vehicles and a minibus and can meet groups in Zugdidi or even Tbilisi. Russian and a tiny bit of English spoken.

David Zhorzholiani (☎ 899344948; per person half/full board US$20/25) English-speaking David is a knowledgeable hiking guide. His family's farmstead, just off the east side of the square, has five good clean bedrooms, a hot shower in a good Western-style bathroom – and its own Svan tower!

Tsiuri & Lali Gabliani (☎ 899569358; Gablianis qucha; per person half board US$25) Both of these sisters teach and speak English, and their house has homey rooms, lovely views from the verandah, a hot shower and books on Svaneti in several languages. It's 500m southwest of the main square, near the hospital.

GETTING THERE & AWAY

Getting to Mestia is an adventure in itself. The five- or six-hour marshrutka or jeep trip from Zugdidi (see p86) travels through increasingly spectacular scenery as it runs up the Enguri valley, then the Mulkhura valley. From Tbilisi you can take an overnight train that gets you into Zugdidi at 5.30am, in time to catch a marshrutka to Svaneti the same morning. Alternatively, there's a 6am marshrutka that goes from in front of Tbilisi's main train station all the way to Mestia (25 to 35 GEL, 11 to 12 hours). Get there by 5.30am to ensure a seat.

Returning, a marshrutka leaves Mestia at 5am or 6am daily to Zugdidi and Tbilisi. There may be others later but you can't depend on it.

The jeep roads from Mestia to Ushguli and from Ushguli to Lentekhi in Kvemo Svaneti (via the 2623m Zagar Pass) can be blocked for weeks in December, January and February, but the Zugdidi–Mestia road is normally kept open all year.

Mestia has an airstrip about 1km east of town. Flights have been an on-off affair but may have restarted by the time you go. Agencies and accommodation in Tbilisi or Mestia should know the latest.

Most Tbilisi travel agencies (p52) offer tours with trusted drivers and guides to Svaneti.

Ushguli უშგული

Ushguli, 47km southeast of Mestia and reaching up to 2100m above sea level, is claimed to be the highest permanently inhabited place in Europe, and with more than 20 ancient Svan towers, it was placed on the Unesco World Heritage List in 1996. Actually a conglomeration of four villages (from west to east and lowest to highest: Murqmeli, Chazhashi, Zhibiani and Chvibiani), Ushguli is a highly picturesque and atmospheric spot, set in the highest reaches of the Enguri valley beneath the snow-covered massif of Mt Shkhara (5068m), the highest peak in Georgia and the third highest in the Caucasus. A day trip from Mestia by jeep costs 150 GEL for up to six people.

There's plenty of good walking from Ushguli: it takes about seven hours to walk 8km up the valley to the foot of the Shkhara glacier and back. One tower in Chazhashi houses Ushguli's main **Ethnographic Museum** (admission 10 GEL; 10am-6pm Tue-Sun), with a superb collection of gold, silver and wooden icons and crosses dating back to the 12th century from Ushguli's seven churches. A second **ethnographic museum** (admission 5 GEL), in a barn in Chvibiani, opens erratically and has an assortment of domestic and agricultural artefacts. At the top end of Ushguli, beautifully situated on a hill below Mt Shkhara, is the 12th-century **Church of the Virgin Mary** (Lamaria) with a defensive tower next to it.

SLEEPING

There are several homestays. **Dato Ratiani** (895485622; Zhibiani; per person full board US$30) runs one of the most comfortable, with a hot shower and great meals of Svan food. You can rent horses here for 20 GEL to 25 GEL a day. **Temuraz Nizharadze** (899209719; Chvibiani; per person full board 30-35 GEL) has simpler accommodation just below Lamaria church, with squat

toilets and hot showers when the electricity is working.

SOUTH OSSETIA სამხრეთ ოსეთი

Tensions and occasional outbreaks of violence in and around the borders of the separatist region of South Ossetia rose after the Saakashvili government came to power in Tbilisi in 2003. By 2007, if you did get through the various Georgian, Russian and Ossetian checkpoints around the border of South Ossetia, there was a good chance you would be hauled in for questioning and then expelled. No country recognises South Ossetia as an independent entity and the British and US governments were, at research time, advising their citizens against travel to South Ossetia.

If things ever normalise here, hiking in the Caucasus in northern South Ossetia is likely to be the chief visitor attraction. Marshrutkas run to the South Ossetian capital, Tskhinvali, from Tbilisi's Didube bus station (5 GEL, about three hours). For accommodation in Tskhinvali there's the shabby **Hotel Ireston** (Teatralnaya ploshchad; r with shared toilet R70;), which has an internet café.

GEORGIAN MILITARY HIGHWAY
საქართველოს სამხედრო გზა

This ancient passage from Tbilisi over the Caucasus to Vladikavkaz in Russia is a spectacular adventure. The dirt track through the challenging mountain terrain was only properly engineered as a road in the early 19th century with the Russian annexation of the Caucasus. The scenery is dramatic even before the road gets into the Caucasus itself – the road clings to the side of the turquoise Zhinvali Reservoir and passes the sublime architecture of Ananuri and the ski resort of Gudauri before entering the most remote, eerily deserted mountain regions around its highest point, the Jvari (Cross) Pass. It then descends the Tergi (Terek in Russian) valley with its several settlements as it approaches the Russian border. Unfortunately, due to the continued closure of the Russian–Georgian border, the route is currently a dead end, but Kazbegi, the last town, is a superb base for walking, climbing and bird-watching.

Ananuri ანანური

This fortress with its churches is another example of beautiful Georgian architecture in a beautiful location, even if the surroundings

GEORGIAN MILITARY HIGHWAY

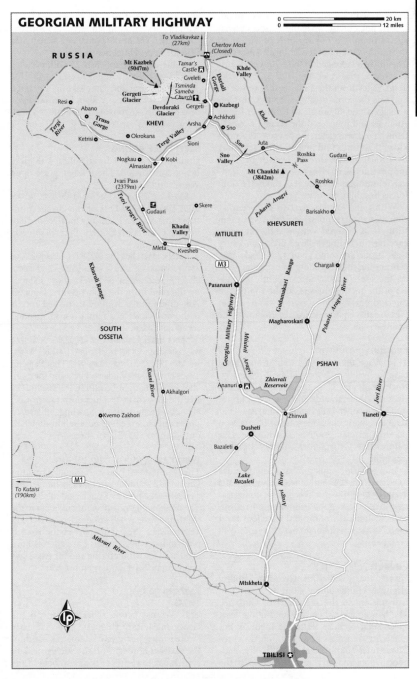

0 _____ 20 km
0 _____ 12 miles

RUSSIA

To Vladikavkaz
(27km)

Chertov Most
(Closed)

Mt Kazbek
(5047m)

Tamar's
Castle

Dariali
Gorge

Khde
Valley

Gveleti

Tsminda
Sameba
Church

Gergeti
Glacier

Devdoraki
Glacier

Gergeti

Kazbegi

Resi

Abano

Truso
Gorge

Tergi
River

KHEVI

Arsha

Achkhoti

Sno

Ketrisi

Okrokana

Tergi Valley

Sioni

Sno

Juta

Roshka
Pass

Gudani

Nogkau

Almasiani

Kobi

Sno
Valley

Mt Chaukhi
(3842m)

Roshka

Jvari Pass
(2379m)

Gudauri

Skere

Khada
Valley

MTIULETI

Pshavis Aragvi

KHEVSURETI

Barisakho

Mleta

Kvesheti

M3

Kharuli Range

Teri Aragvi River

SOUTH
OSSETIA

Pasanauri

Gudamakari Range

Chargali

Georgian Military Highway

Mtiuleti Aragvi

Magharoskari

PSHAVI

Ksani River

Akhalgori

Ananuri

Zhinvali
Reservoir

Pshavis Aragvi River

Jori River

Kvemo Zakhori

Zhinvali

Tianeti

Dusheti

Bazaleti

Aragvi River

M1

To Kutaisi
(190km)

Lake
Bazaleti

Mtkvari River

Mtskheta

TBILISI

are now, with a modern reservoir spread out below, not exactly what the builders envisaged. Ananuri is 66km north of Tbilisi, at the northwest end of the Zhinvali Reservoir. The fortress belonged to the *eristavis* (dukes) of Aragvi, who ruled the land as far as the Tergi Valley from the 13th century onwards, and was the scene of several battles. In 1739 a rival *eristavi,* Shamshe of Ksani, set fire to Ananuri and murdered the Aragvi *eristavi's* family. Four years later, the peasants of Aragvi killed their lords and invited King Teimuraz II of Kartli to rule directly over them. Then the peasants themselves rose up in 1746, leading Teimuraz and Erekle II of Kakheti to join forces to subjugate them.

Within the fortress are two 17th-century churches, the larger of which, the Assumption Church, is covered with wonderful stone carving, including a large cross on every wall. Inside are some vivid 17th- and 18th-century frescoes including a Last Judgement on the south wall. You can climb the tallest of the fortress towers, at the top end of the complex, for fine views: it was here that the last defenders were killed in the fight with the Ksani *eristavi.*

Kvesheti ქვეშეთი

This village 40km beyond Ananuri is a good base for walks or horse rides. A 10km jeep track heads north up the **Khada valley** from Kvesheti, through a dramatic gorge and out into a more open valley with several small villages and many old stone towers. This was on the original main route across the Caucasus before the Georgian Military Highway was built.

In a roadside apple orchard as you enter Kvesheti from the south, the welcoming **Hotel Qvesheti** (☎ 899114377; www.kvesheti.ge; per person half board US$25-30) has good, pine-floored rooms, each with a bathroom, and excellent local food. You can rent horses here for around 40 GEL per day.

Gudauri გუდაური

Shortly after Kvesheti the Georgian Military Highway climbs some 500m by a series of hairpins up to the ski resort of Gudauri. The bare hillsides here are among the least spectacular scenery along the highway but make for Georgia's best downhill ski runs. These total 16km of varied difficulty, with good Doppelmayer chairlifts. Normally the

ski season lasts from December to March, with the best snow in January and February. The only ATM in the Gudauri-Kazbegi area is in the Sport Hotel here.

A one-day lift pass costs 25 GEL per day, and ski-gear rental around 30 GEL to 40 GEL. An added attraction is heliskiing, operated by the Swiss company **Alpin Travel** (www.alpintravel.ch). For ski-touring possibilities check www.caucasus-randonnee.org.

SLEEPING & EATING

Gudauri has about a dozen hotels, with more being constructed. The following are open year-round.

Sno-3 (☎ 899557309; per person half board Dec-Apr US$35, May-Nov US$25) One of the cheapest options, this is a small and cosy four-room place in front of the Sport Hotel, with three showers and free *chacha.*

Hotel Gudauri Hut (☎ 899398123; www.gudaurihut.com; per person half board ski season US$60-65, other times US$40) A medium-sized hotel a short distance up the road from the resort centre, Gudauri Hut offers pleasant, pine-furnished rooms with good views. Ski rental is available and some staff speak English.

Sport Hotel Gudauri (☎ 32-202900, 899559222; www.gudauri.ge; s/d full board from 271/443 GEL ski season, from 174/287 GEL other times; 🏊) This flagship 1980s hotel is still Gudauri's best and the main chairlift starts right behind it. It has a host of free indoor-activity facilities open year-round: clay-court tennis, 10-pin bowling, billiards, a sauna and an excellent pool (all available to outsiders for 50 GEL per three hours).

Jvari Pass ჯვრის უღელტეხილი

The Jvari (Cross) Pass starts about 4km after Gudauri; 2379m high, it takes its name from a cross placed here by King David the Builder. The present red stone cross, about 500m to the right above the road, was erected by General Yermolov in 1824. This part of the road is notorious for avalanches, but galleries have been built for winter traffic and the pass stays open for all but a few days most years.

Kazbegi ყაზბეგი
☎ 245

This is most people's destination on the Georgian Military Highway: a spectacularly located town just a few kilometres south of the Russian border, with the snowy peak of Mt Kazbek towering to the west, behind the famous hill-top silhouette of Tsminda Sameba Church (p102). Kazbegi is the main town of Khevi, the region north of the Jvari Pass.

Now officially named Stepantsminda, but still known as Kazbegi, this is a sleepy mountain town at about 1750m altitude, with mainly Soviet-era buildings. It's a favourite with backpackers for its relatively easy access from Tbilisi (with dramatic scenery along the way), its plentiful homestays and the walking in the area.

ORIENTATION & INFORMATION

The Georgian Military Highway brings you straight into Kazbegi's main square, Stalinis moedani, with its statue of Alexander Kazbegi as well as the marshrutka and taxi stops and the Stepantsminda Hotel. Here Stalinis qucha forks to the right, while the main road leads down to a bridge over the Tergi River, 200m from the square, then continues towards the Dariali Gorge. Immediately after the Tergi bridge a side road turns up to the village of Gergeti on the left (west) bank of the river, almost a suburb of Kazbegi.

The nearest ATM is in the Sport Hotel at Gudauri. You might be able to change euros or US dollars at the Stepantsminda Hotel or at shops or kiosks.

A useful map in English and Georgian of local walking trails is available for 5 GEL from the **Georgian Botanical Institute** (Stepantsmindis qucha; ☺ May-Oct), which is widely known as the WWF Ecostation (a previous incarnation of the building).

ALEXANDER KAZBEGI MUSEUM

Alexander Kazbegi (1848–93) made the unusual decision to become a shepherd after studying in Tbilisi, St Petersburg and Moscow. Later he worked as a journalist and wrote the novels and plays that made him famous. At the end of his life he suffered from insanity. He died in Tbilisi, and his coffin was carried back to Kazbegi. His museum is a five-minute walk north from the main square. You first come to a **church**, dated 1809–11, with a striking relief of two lions with a chain above its door. To its east and west are two structures that look like bell towers but are actually the tombs of Alexander's father and mother. The writer's own grave lies under a large stone sculpture near the fence. He asked to be buried where he could see Mt Kazbek. The **museum**

(admission 1 GEL; Stalinis qucha; ☺ 10am-5pm), in Kazbegi's house, to the left of the church, contains photos, documents and some clothes and original furniture.

SLEEPING & EATING

Kazbegi is very well supplied with homestays (those mentioned here are just a selection), all of which provide meals of basic but tasty Georgian food. Many are closed outside the main season (May to early November).

Nazi Chkareuli (☎ 52480, 895500989; ssujashvili@ yahoo.com; Gergeti; per person 15 GEL, half board 25 GEL) Nazi's house is the backpackers' favourite for its good prices, good meals and sociable atmosphere, with beds squeezed into every available room. Daughter Shorena speaks English. If you walk up towards Gergeti and turn left along the second street, opposite the green *khinkali* hut, Nazi's is the first two-storey house on the right. Many others along this street have rooms too.

Hotel Lomi (☎ 899403264; Stalinis moedani; per person 15 GEL) On the town square, the Lomi is a simple family-run place with agreeable little blue-painted rooms sharing hot-water bathrooms.

Nunu Maisuradze (☎ 52593; per person 15 GEL, half board 30 GEL) A good option with a friendly family and views of Tsminda Sameba and the mountains from the balcony. There's one very nice clean bathroom with a hot bath. Daughter Gvantsa speaks English. The house is 50m up the street opposite Hotel Stepantsminda, with green gates.

Luiza Tsiklauri (☎ 52353; Vazha Pshavela 34; per person half board US$20) Luiza speaks German and has plenty of space for travellers, as well as a hot-water bathroom. Pass Nunu's, then turn right at the top of the street. Luiza's is on the left and has a grey gate.

Kamuna Sujashvili (☎ 52017; Vazha Pshavela 40; per person half board 35 GEL) This new two-storey house, next to Luiza Tsiklauri's, has three good-sized, very clean rooms and an upstairs balcony with mountain views.

Nargiza Alibegashvili (☎ 877415454; makasu75@ yahoo.com; Stepantsmindis qucha; per person full board US$30) Nargiza's modern, three-storey home stands in splendid isolation just to the right of the TV dishes at the top of Kazbegi. There are three big, spotless rooms, the views are fabulous and the food is just as good. Daughter Maka speaks English. It's best to make contact a day ahead.

Hotel Stepantsminda (☎ 899646880; Stalinis moedani; s/d 50/80 GEL, half board 90/140 GEL) This most luxurious, alpine-style option provides good-sized, carpeted rooms with TV, and lovely views of Mt Kazbek from the rooms at the back. Its basement restaurant has a nice terrace but is only open to hotel guests.

The eating-out choices are very limited. The Hotel Lomi restaurant serves good, inexpensive homemade food, and the green khinkali hut on the road up to Gergeti provides *khinkali* and *khachapuri* in summer.

GETTING THERE & AWAY

Marshrutkas to Kazbegi (8 GEL, three hours) leave Didube bus station in Tbilisi every one or two hours from 9am to 5pm. From Kazbegi to Tbilisi, departures are timetabled at 8am, 9am, 10am and 11am, and 1.30pm, 3pm and 5pm.

A taxi to or from Tbilisi can cost anywhere between 50 and 80 GEL.

Around Kazbegi

There are many wonderful walks in the mountains around Kazbegi. For jeep taxis to the start of the more distant ones, ask your accommodation to arrange one or simply find one in the main square. The walking season is from May or June to October or November, depending on the weather.

TSMINDA SAMEBA CHURCH

The 14th-century Holy Trinity Church above Kazbegi at 2200m has become something of a symbol of Georgia – its beauty and piety and the fierce determination to build it on such a lofty, isolated perch are all emblematic of the country and its people. The walk up to the church and the panoramas this affords are a highlight of Georgia. In 1988 the Soviet authorities constructed a cable-car line to the church, with one station in Kazbegi and the other right next to Tsminda Sameba. The people of Kazbegi quite rightly felt this defiled their sacred place and soon destroyed it. You can still see its base in the village, almost behind the Alexander Kazbegi Museum.

It takes about 1½ hours at an average pace to walk to the church from Kazbegi. Head up through Gergeti, turn right at a T-junction towards the top of the village, then go up a narrow path to the left after 20m. This leaves the village behind and reaches a broader vehicle track, with a cemetery to your right. Follow the track up to the left, winding through the woods, and after approximately 30 minutes' walking you will emerge in an open area. Here take a path up to the left through the trees and in five minutes you'll rejoin the track in grassy meadows with the church in view to the left – just five minutes' more walk.

Vakhushti Batonishvili wrote in the 18th century that in times of danger the treasures from Mtskheta, as well as St Nino's cross, were kept here for safety. The beautifully weathered stone of the church and its separate belltower are decorated with some intriguing carvings, one on the belltower appearing to show two dinosaurs. The interior is not particularly unusual, but certainly well worth a look if you get this far!

GERGETI GLACIER

If you're up for another 900m of ascent from Tsminda Sameba, this quite strenuous walk rewards with spectacular views. The path heads straight up the ridge behind the church; an alternative route, more protected on windy days, runs up the left flank of the ridge. The two meet at a cairn at 2960m altitude, from where a path leads on up towards the left side of the Gergeti (Ortsveri) Glacier as it snakes its way down from Mt Kazbek. Head up here for about one hour for views of the glacier, then return. You'll need about nine hours to get up there from Kazbegi and down again the same day.

If you have a day in hand and are experienced on ice or have a good guide, it's possible, with a further 600m of ascent, to cross the glacier and climb to the **Betlemi Hut** (per person US$10), formerly a meteorological station, at 3652m, where you can sleep. The hut has bunks and beds, but bring food, a warm sleeping bag and cooking gear. You can camp for free but the wind can be fierce.

SNO VALLEY

The Sno Valley runs southeast off the Georgian Military Highway 4km south of Kazbegi. About 15km along the unpaved valley road is the small village of Juta (2150m), inhabited by Khevsurs from over the mountains to the east. You can get a jeep from Kazbegi to Juta for around 45 GEL round trip. A beautiful short walk from Juta goes southeast up the Chaukhi valley to the foot of Mt Chaukhi (3842m), a dramatic multipinnacled peak popular with climbers, just 1½ hours from

MT KAZBEK

This 5047m extinct volcano towering west of Kazbegi has much folk history. The Greek Prometheus was supposedly chained up here for stealing fire from the gods, as was the Georgian Amirani, for challenging the omnipotence of God. Amirani's abode was somewhere near the Betlemi (Bethlehem) cave, 4000m above sea level, where resided a hermit and many very sacred objects – Christ's manger, Abraham's tent, a dove-rocked golden cradle whose sight would blind a human being. There were taboos against hunting on the mountain and climbing it. Not surprisingly, the first to conquer this peak were foreigners: Freshfield, Tucker and Moore of the London Alpine Club in 1868.

There is indeed a cave at 4000m, near the Betlemi Hut (opposite), which serves as the base for most Kazbek ascents today. At the hut you may be able to get an experienced local guide (non-English speaking) to lead you up the mountain for €150 to €200 per person – though to ensure guide services it's best to take a (more expensive) package with an experienced agency such as Explore Georgia (p52).

The ascent of the mountain is technically straightforward, though there is some danger in crevasses. The climb generally takes three or four days from Kazbegi.

- **Day 1** Hike from Kazbegi up to the Betlemi Hut at 3652m. It's also possible to camp at 2950m, about 2½ hours short of the hut.

- **Day 2** Spend the day acclimatising by climbing up to the Maili Plateau at 4500m, or to the summit of Ortsveri Peak (4365m) and then back down to the Betlemi Hut.

- **Day 3** Leave in the early hours of the morning and follow the north side of the glacier westward for 4km, passing south of the summit cone, and then up to the broad, snow-covered Maili Plateau at 4500m. Steeper climbing then leads back east to a saddle at 4900m, followed by mixed snow, rock and ice to the summit (six hours). This final section involves about three rope lengths of 35- to 40-degree ice. Descend to the Betlemi Hut for the night (five hours).

- **Day 4** Descend to Kazbegi.

Juta. With more time you can continue up the valley eastward from here towards the 3338m Roshka (Chaukhi) Pass. In one long day from Juta you can get over the pass and down to Roshka village in Khevsureti (p104).

In Juta, **Iago Arabuli** (☎ 899533239) and **Soso Arabuli** (☎ 895545149) have homestays, both charging 25 GEL per person with dinner and breakfast. Iago speaks German and his wife English, and they boast a Western-style toilet.

DARIALI GORGE

North of Kazbegi the Georgian Military Highway follows the Tergi River 11km to the Russian border in the grimly spectacular Dariali Gorge. Here granite cliffs tower over the road, which runs along a narrow shelf above the river. The gorge inspired much awe among 19th-century Russian artists and writers such as Lermontov and Pushkin.

Much of the gorge is across the Russian border, but you can walk or take a taxi (around 20 GEL return) as far as **Tamar's Castle**, on a big rock above the left bank of the Tergi, 10km out of Kazbegi. These ruins are from many different periods. This Tamar, a legendary cruel beauty who chopped off her lovers' heads, is not to be confused with the great 12th-century queen of Georgia.

From Gveleti, 3km before Tamar's Castle, a fine day walk heads up through birch forests and rocky wildernesses to **Devdoraki Glacier** on the east flank of Mt Kazbek. It's 9km from Gveleti to the glacier, with an ascent of 1100m: allow nine or 10 hours there and back. At research time this route was blocked by rock falls, so check beforehand.

KHEVSURETI ხევსურეთი

The mountain region east of Khevi is Khevsureti, a sparsely populated district bordering Chechnya that is home to some fantastic mountain defensive architecture and some unique traditions – including a part-animist religion, the wearing of chain mail well into the 20th century and costumes embroidered with unusual, tiny cross and star patterns – as well as being credited with inventing *khinkali*.

Today Khevsureti's old culture is clinging to life. But its spectacular villages and landscapes of steep, forested valleys and blooming mountain pastures are still there to be enjoyed by determined travellers who don't mind the scarcity of transport and food. Incipient tourism provides some sustenance for a few villagers. Those visitors who come should bring at least some food with them, and some warm clothes as it can get cold at night even in summer. It's also a big help if you're prepared to camp.

The road to Khevsureti turns northeast off the Georgian Military Highway shortly before the Zhinvali Reservoir and runs up the Pshavis Aragvi valley to the villages of Barisakho and Biso, before turning east (now a jeep track) and over the high Datvis-Jvari Pass (open from about June to October), and then northeast down the Argun valley to Shatili, the main village of inner Khevsureti.

Barisakho, about 100km from Tbilisi, is the largest village of the region, with a population of about 200. At **Korsha**, 2km past Barisakho, there's a small but interesting **museum** of Khevsur life, with armour, weapons, agricultural implements and the art of its curator, Shota Arabuli. From Korsha it's about a 7km walk up to **Roshka**, a small, muddy village off the main road, on the route towards the Roshka (Chaukhi) Pass (see p103).

East of Biso, **Gudani** village, about 1km up from the road, is a striking group of tower houses on a rock outcrop. Some 8km past Gudani comes the **Datvis-Jvari Pass** (2876m), from which it's 18km northeast to **Shatili**. Shatili's old town, built between the 7th and 13th centuries, is an agglomeration of tall towers clinging together on a rocky outcrop to form a single fortress-like whole. The old town was abandoned between the 1960s and '80s, and the new village, of about 20 houses, is just around the hill. But several towers have recently been restored and one contains a museum.

From Shatili the track continues 3km northeast to the border of Chechnya. Before the border you'll encounter a 'No Entry' sign, but you can turn south up the Andaki valley to almost-empty **Mutso**, about 8km from Shatili. Mutso's roofless old village on a very steep rock pinnacle across the river is one of the most spectacular in Khevsureti, with large stone tombs in which you can see human skulls. Ardoti is 6km further up the valley beyond Mutso. From **Andaki** (uninhabited), a similar distance beyond Ardoti, begins the very steep route over the 3431m **Atsunta Pass** into Tusheti.

Sleeping

In Korsha, you can stay with **Shota Arabuli** (☎ 32-452099, 895503134; per person half board 20 GEL), artist and curator of the local museum.

In Roshka, photographer **Shota Tsiklauri** (☎ 899399789; per person half board 20 GEL) has rooms in his comfy house at the top of the village.

Shatili has three or four homestays, including **Vazha Chincharauli's** (☎ 877729362), which has hot water and can normally provide meals. The others generally charge 25 GEL per person without food (they may be able to provide potatoes, bread and cheese). There's also a **hotel** (per person US$25, half board US$35).

Getting There & Away

One bus a day leaves Tbilisi's Didube bus station for Barisakho (8 GEL, three to four hours, 5pm) and Korsha, 2km beyond. The bus sets off back for Tbilisi from Korsha at 8.30am. Beyond Korsha, it's a question of walking or trying to get a lift with one of the few passing vehicles, unless you have your own transport or can organise some from Tbilisi.

TUSHETI თუშეთი

Tucked into Georgia's far northeast corner, with Chechnya to its north and Dagestan to its east, Tusheti is an increasingly popular summer hiking area but remains one of the country's remotest and most fascinating and pristine high-mountain regions. The road over the nerve-jangling 2900m Abano (Tseri) Pass was not built until 1978; Tusheti still has no public electricity supply, and evidence of its old animist religion is plentiful in the form of stone shrines known as *khatis,* decked with the horns of sacrificed goats or sheep, which women are not permitted to approach. Tall defensive towers *(koshkis)* still stand in many villages, many of them dating back 600 years or more.

Today most Tusheti folk only go up to Tusheti in summer: to graze their sheep or cattle, attend festivals, cater for tourists and generally reconnect with their roots. Many have winter homes in and around Alvani in Kakheti. The road to Tusheti is only open from about early June to early October, and some of the homestays may not open till July.

Tusheti has two main river valleys – the Pirikiti Alazani and the more southerly

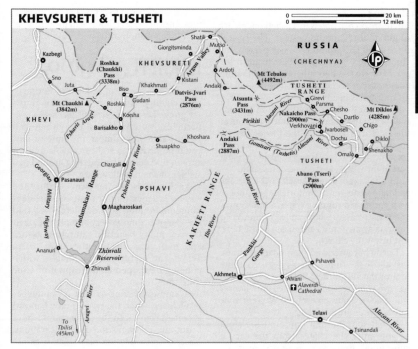

Gomtsari (Tushetis) Alazani – which meet below Omalo, the biggest village, then flow east into Dagestan. The scenery everywhere is a spectacular mix of high, snow-covered, rocky peaks, deep gorges, and steep, grassy hillsides where distant flocks of sheep appear as slowly shifting patterns of white specks.

You can find a reasonable Tusheti map on **Tusheti Protected Areas** (www.tushe tipa.ge).

Sights & Activities

Most of the villages are around 2000m above sea level and have picturesque settings, either sitting above near-sheer hillsides or nestling down by one of the rivers. There's a particularly splendid group of old towers, known as Keseloebi, on top of the crag at **Zemo Omalo**, the upper part of Omalo. **Shenakho**, a few kilometres east of Omalo, is one of the prettiest villages, with its houses of stone, slate and rickety wooden balconies grouped around Tusheti's only functioning church. **Diklo**, 4km northeast of Shenakho, has an old fortress perched on a spectacular rock promontory. **Dartlo**, about 12km northwest of Omalo in the Pirikiti Alazani valley, has another

spectacular tower grouping, overlooked by the single tall lookout tower of **Kvavlo** on the hill 350m above.

Walking routes are innumerable. Omalo to Shenakho and Shenakho to Diklo are two good short walks of a couple of hours each (one way). A good route of about five days starts in Omalo or Shenakho, runs up the Pirikiti Alazani valley to Dartlo and Chesho, then crosses the 2900m Nakaicho Pass over to Verkhovani in the Gomtsari Alazani valley, and returns down the Gomtsari Alazani.

The track up the Pirikiti Alazani valley beyond Chesho, through Parsma and Girevi, eventually leads to the 3431m Atsunta Pass, a very steep and demanding route over into Khevsureti. It's a one-week trek all the way from Shenakho or Omalo to Shatili in Khevsureti.

If you prefer to ride, horses are available in Omalo and Shenakho for between 35 GEL and 70 GEL per day.

Several Tbilisi travel agencies offer tours and treks in Tusheti. A good one run by a Tusheti native, the fluent English-speaking Eka Chvritidze, is Wild Georgia (p52).

Sleeping

There are no real hotels in Tusheti but plenty of guesthouses and homestays. The typical price is 50 GEL to 60 GEL per person, including three meals. It is best to head for places where you know there is a functioning guesthouse or homestay, and if possible make arrangements in advance.

In Omalo, the **Koroichi Guesthouse** (☎ 898156728) is a substantial wood and concrete place near the electricity station at the top of Kvemo (Lower) Omalo. A new guesthouse was under construction in Zemo (Upper) Omalo, the older part of the village, at the time of research.

In Shenakho, **Dato Bukvaidze** (☎ 899616619) and his parents run a comfortable guesthouse with spring-fed running water, a hot shower and three pleasant wood-walled rooms. Wild Georgia agency (p52) also has a house here, just below the church.

Dartlo has several accommodation places. Just above the ruined Russian church at the foot of the village, **Beso Elanidze** (☎ 899118993) has two good, recently converted guesthouses with electric light, showers and Western-style toilets. Meals are available.

In Chesho, the first house on the right as you enter the village from the east, a substantial three-storey wooden construction, is **Eka Abaloidze's Guesthouse** (☎ 855570512, 899618734). Set just above a rushing stream, it has 14 beds, solar-heated showers and 15 horses for rent.

There are also guesthouses or homestays at Verkhovani and Dochu in the Gomtsari Alazani valley.

Getting There & Away

When the Abano Pass is open, Niva 4WDs run daily to Tusheti from Alvani, 22km northwest of Telavi, charging 180 GEL for three or four passengers to Omalo. You can also hire one to pick you up for the return trip. Be at Alvani by 9am – they mostly leave from the central crossroads there. The spectacular drive takes about four hours plus stops.

For a cheaper, less comfortable and even more exciting ride, most days a large Kamaz truck carrying a mix of freight and passengers (20 GEL, standing in the back) lurches its way precariously from Alvani up to Tusheti, taking six or seven hours to Omalo. They leave any time between 6am and noon, when they have a load.

Marshrutkas run to Alvani (2 GEL, 45 minutes, once or twice an hour, 9am to 5pm) from the old bus station in Telavi.

KAKHETI კახეთი

The eastern region of Kakheti is Georgia's wine country. Hundreds of different grapes are grown here, and every village has its own particular variety. Almost everywhere you go in Kakheti, at almost any time of day, you'll be invited to a glass of wine and it's easy to find yourself wandering around in a semipermanent mellow haze.

Kakheti is also an area rich in history and was an independent or semi-independent kingdom for long periods. Here you'll find the incredible monastery complex of Davit Gareja, many beautiful churches, castles and mansions around the main town, Telavi, and picturesque Sighnaghi, which is being developed as the capital of wine tourism.

A very good time to visit is September or October, when the *rtveli* (grape harvest) is being taken in, to the accompaniment of feasts, musical events and other celebrations. Many accommodation places can organise for you to see the harvest in action and join in the partying. The region is famous for its drinking songs, the most famous of all being 'Mravalzhamieri'.

TELAVI თელავი
☎ 350 (international), ☎ 250 (domestic) / pop 22,000

The largest town in Kakheti, Telavi is set in the vineyard-strewn Alazani valley, between the Gombori Mountains and the Caucasus (visible to the northeast). Though of only moderate interest itself, it's the perfect base for exploring the historical, architectural and viticultural riches of Kakheti, and as a jumping-off point for Tusheti in the Caucasus.

History

By the 12th century Telavi was one of the main trade centres in Georgia. In the 13th century Telavi was caught in the onslaught of the Mongol invasion, to revive in the 15th to 16th centuries, and then be twice devastated by the Persia's Shah Abbas I in the early 17th century. In 1672 the Kakhetian King Archil II moved his court back to Telavi from Gremi. In 1744, as the Turks threatened Persian

KAKHETI

hegemony in eastern Georgia, Nader Shah of Persia installed the local prince Erekle II in Telavi as ruler of Kakheti. Erekle and his father, King Teimuraz II of Kartli, managed to establish themselves as de facto independent rulers, and in 1762 Erekle united Kakheti and Kartli as a more or less independent state, ruling with a progressive Westernising policy. Erekle still occupies an honoured place in Kakheti annals today.

Orientation

The centre of Telavi is Erekle II moedani, with the Batonistsikhe Castle on its north side. Erekle meoris (Erekle II) gamziri heads 300m northwest from here to an intersection where Ketevan Tsamebuli runs 250m down-hill (north) to meet another main avenue, Chavchavadze. Telavi's two bus and marshrutka stations are straight on downhill here on Alazanis gamziri – the new bus station on the left and the old one through a short alley to the right after 200m.

Information

You'll find ATMs around the intersection of Chavchavadze and Ketevan Tsamebuli (near the bus stations), and on Erekle meoris gamziri.

1001 Computers (Erekle meoris gamziri 3; internet per hr 2 GEL; ☿ 9am-8pm)
Telephone Office (Erekle meoris gamziri 10; ☿ 24 hr)
Tourism Information Centre (☎ 76338; Erekle II moedani 12; ☿ 10am-6pm) In an attractive verandahed

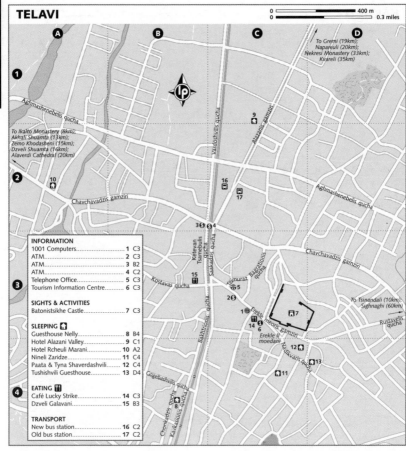

TELAVI

0   400 m
0   0.3 miles

To Gremi (19km);
Napareuli (20km);
Nekresi Monastery (33km);
Kvareli (35km)

Aghmashenebelis qucha

To Ikalto Monastery (8km);
Akhali Shuamta (13km);
Zemo Khodasheni (15km);
Dzveli Shuamta (16km);
Alaverdi Cathedral (20km)

Chavchavadzis gamziri

Aghmashenebelis qucha

Chavchavadzis gamziri

Kostavas qucha

Vazisubnis qucha

Bakhtrionis qucha

To Tsinandali (10km);
Sighnaghi (60km)

Rustavelis qucha

Erekle II
moedani

Gogebashvilis qucha

Nadikvaris qucha

Chonkadzis qucha

Kaklabonis qucha

INFORMATION	
1001 Computers	1 C3
ATM	2 C3
ATM	3 B2
ATM	4 C2
Telephone Office	5 C3
Tourism Information Centre	6 C3

SIGHTS & ACTIVITIES	
Batonistsikhe Castle	7 C3

SLEEPING	
Guesthouse Nelly	8 B4
Hotel Alazani Valley	9 C1
Hotel Rcheuli Marani	10 A2
Nineli Zaridze	11 C4
Paata & Tyna Shaverdashvili	12 C4
Tushishvili Guesthouse	13 D4

EATING	
Café Lucky Strike	14 C3
Dzveli Galavani	15 B3

TRANSPORT	
New bus station	16 C2
Old bus station	17 C2

building on the main square, with English-speaking staff and information on all Kakheti, including accommodation and winery listings.

Batonistsikhe Castle
ბატონის ციხე

The main architectural and historical feature of Telavi, **Batonistsikhe Castle** (admission 5 GEL, English-speaking guide 6 GEL; ☽ 10am-5pm Tue-Sun) was the residence of the Kakhetian kings in the 17th and 18th centuries, built when King Archil II transferred his residence from Gremi to Telavi. Inside the castle yard is a **Persian-style palace** that was constructed in the 1660s, and rebuilt by Erekle II, who was born and died here. The central throne room

holds many historical portraits including one of Erekle himself (above the throne).

The castle precinct contains the remains of two churches: the dilapidated Archil church and a single-naved royal chapel – with holes for firearms in the walls – built by Erekle II in 1758. Included in the admission price are an art museum, with Georgian and western European paintings, and a history museum, in ugly modern buildings behind the palace.

Sleeping

Nineli Zaridze (☎ 71973, 899281144; Akhvlediani 11; per person without/with breakfast 20/25 GEL) Nineli's beautiful house, full of antique furniture, is a two-minute walk from Erekle II moedani. The rooms are large, there's a guest kitchen, and you can have a nice hot soak in the old marble bathtub! Daughter Nino speaks English.

Paata & Tyna Shaverdashvili (☎ 72185; Nadikvari 9; per person 20 GEL) This friendly little homestay has clean, spacious rooms and hot showers, in a quiet house. Nadikvari runs off the southeast corner of Erekle II moedani; at number 9, go through to the back of the street entrance and it's the building in front of you.

Tushishvili Guesthouse (☎ 71909, 877756625; sspiridon@rambler.ru; Nadikvari 15; per person without/with breakfast 25/30 GEL; 🖳) This welcoming homestay is an established travellers' favourite and justly so. Hostess Svetlana speaks some English, cooks fabulous dinners (vegetarian available) and is more than helpful in organising local taxi trips and getting transport information. Nadikvari runs off the southeast corner of Erekle II moedani; the house is numbered.

Guesthouse Nelly (☎ 72594, 99581820; Chonkadze 11; per person half board 35 GEL) The six big, bright, modern rooms here, 500m uphill (south) of the centre, share bathrooms with hot showers. Nelly cooks excellent Georgian meals with fresh, locally grown ingredients, and the wine flows. Nelly and her husband between them speak a little English and German.

Hotel Alazani Valley (☎ 74144; www.elgitour.ge; Alazanis gamziri 75; r incl dinner 50-120 GEL; 🍴) The lobby is spiffy and the rooms comfy enough, but this early-21st-century hotel already has a few cracks, and the atmosphere is rather soulless.

our pick **Hotel Rcheuli Marani** (☎ 73030; rcheuli marani@centerpoint.ge; Chavchavadze 154; r incl breakfast US$50-70, ste US$75-100; 🍴) New in 2007 and definitely the best hotel in town, the Rcheuli Marani is out of the centre, 800m west of the bus stations. Many of the pleasing, carpeted rooms are equipped with big, traditional-style balconies, and prints of paintings by Pirosmani and other top Georgian artists add a welcome arty touch. The hotel also has the best restaurant in town and a nice courtyard garden.

Eating

Restaurant provision is rather bare, but luckily if you are in a homestay you'll usually eat excellently.

Café Lucky Strike (Erekle II moedani; dishes 2-6 GEL) This unexciting café next to the tourist office does average Turkish-style kebabs and pizzas.

Dzveli Galavani (Kostava 4; mains 4-8 GEL; 🕐 noon-8pm) A friendly little Georgian restaurant doing the best meals outside the hotels and homestays. It has an English-language menu, though not much of it may be available.

Hotel Rcheuli Marani (☎ 73030; Chavchavadze 154; mains 10-15 GEL) Telavi's best eatery is this brick-cellar hotel restaurant incorporating an old wine cellar. A good range of Georgian and Russian dishes is on offer.

Getting There & Away

Marshrutkas to Telavi (6 GEL, 2½ hours) leave Tbilisi's Ortachala bus station about every 30 minutes from 7am to 6pm. There are also shared taxis (per person 7 GEL) from Tbilisi's Isani metro station.

Marshrutkas back to Tbilisi go about hourly from 8.30am to 1pm from Telavi's **new bus station** (☎ 72083; Alazanis gamziri), then more frequently until 5pm from another stop below the petrol station down the street. Shared taxis to Tbilisi wait up the street from the new bus station.

The **old bus station** (☎ 71619; Alazanis gamziri) is through a short alley opposite the new bus station. From here marshrutkas and buses leave for Alaverdi Cathedral (1 GEL, about every 20 minutes, 9am to 6pm), Kvareli (2 GEL, one to 1½ hours, about hourly, 9.30am to 5.30pm), Tsinandali (0.50 GEL, at least hourly, 9am to 4pm) and Sighnaghi (4 GEL, 1½ hours, at 3pm). Taxis wait on the corner of Chavchavadze and Ketevan Tsamebuli just up the street from the bus stations.

AROUND TELAVI

The villages and lovely countryside around Telavi are full of fascinating places to visit. Public transport reaches many of them (see above), but you can pack a lot more into your day by taking a taxi tour. Telavi drivers will take you to all or most of the following destinations in one trip for 40 or 50 GEL.

Ikalto Monastery იყალთო

This monastery, beautifully situated in a grove of cypresses 8km northwest of Telavi, was one of two famous medieval Georgian academies, the other being Gelati. Shota Rustaveli, the national poet, is thought to have studied here. The monastery was founded in the 6th century by Zenon, one of the 13 Syrian fathers. Six hundred years later King David the Builder invited the philosopher Arsen Ikaltoeli to establish an academy here, where the doctrines of Neo-Platonism were expounded. In 1616 the complex was devastated by the Persians.

The main **Transfiguration Church** was built in the 8th and 9th centuries, over an earlier church where Zenon was buried, but its appearance was changed in the 19th century by the addition of a brick cupola and the whitewashing of the walls in the Russian style. To the east, the small **Sameba (Trinity) Church** dates back to the 6th century but has been extensively rebuilt over time. There's an interesting small relief of three saints at the top of its façade. The single-naved **Kvelatsminda** (St Mary's Church), to the south, dates from the 12th to 13th centuries. The roofless building behind this was the **Academy**.

Ikalto is 2km uphill from the 'Monastery Ikalto' sign on the Akhmeta road.

Alaverdi Cathedral ალავერდი

At the beginning of the 11th century, when Georgia was entering its cultural and political golden age, King Kvirike of Kakheti had a majestic cathedral built – at 50m high it was the tallest church in Georgia until the recent construction of the Tsminda Sameba Cathedral in Tbilisi. **Alaverdi Cathedral** (⏰ 8am-7pm), 20km northwest of Telavi, is the main spiritual centre in Kakheti and a source of great pride and love for the local people. The exterior is classically proportioned with majestic rounded arches but minimal decoration, typical of Kakhetian churches. Inside, one is struck by the structure's beautiful spacious harmony and the light that streams in from the 16 windows in the cupola. The cathedral has been damaged several times by earthquakes, especially in the 15th and 18th centuries. Whitewashing in the 19th century was yet another form of damage and it was not until 1966 that this was partially rectified and some frescoes uncovered. Note the 16th-century St George and dragon over the west door. The Virgin and Child above the altar is from the 11th century.

A nunnery was added to the monastery here in the 17th century, and some members of the royal family took the veil here. Other buildings include the summer palace of Shah Abbas' governor (the ruins of which have now been restored as the bishop's residence), a bathhouse, a bell tower and a recently renovated *marani* (wine cellar).

The September festivities of Alaverdoba last three weeks, climaxing on 14 September, with people coming from remote mountain areas to celebrate.

Gremi გრემი

This picturesque brick **citadel** (admission to museum & tower 2 GEL; ⏰ 9am-8pm) stands on a small hill by the Telavi–Kvareli road 19km from Telavi, just before the village of Eniseli. Both Eniseli and Gremi are famous for their brandy. Kvareli-bound marshrutkas from Telavi will stop here.

From 1466 to 1672 Gremi was the capital of Kakheti, but all that remains of the market, the baths, the caravanserai, the palace and the houses after the devastation wrought by Shah Abbas in 1616 are some not-very-distinctive ruins. The impressive citadel, however, still stands. Within it, the **Church of the Archangels** was built in 1565 by King Levan of Kakheti (who is buried inside) and contains frescoes painted in 1577. The ground floor of the adjacent **tower-palace**, dating from the 15th century, houses a small museum of local archaeological and historical items. From here you climb up inside the tower: a structure in one of the rooms was thought to be a bread oven, but on examination turned out to be a tunnel, not yet fully excavated but thought to emerge in the yard outside. Another tunnel, which you can enter, leads down from the yard to the foot of the walls where in past centuries the Intsoba River flowed, providing a possible escape route from the citadel in times of danger.

Nekresi Monastery ნეკრესი

Nekresi Monastery is 4km off the Kvareli road from a signed turning 10km past Gremi. You have to walk the last 1.5km uphill through woods to the monastery, but it's well worth the effort as the views across the vineyard-dotted Alazani valley and the early Georgian architecture are marvellous, and you may well have the whole place to yourself!

One of the very first Georgian churches was built at Nekresi in the 4th century. In the 6th century one of the 13 Syrian fathers, Abibos, who converted many of the highland Georgians, founded a monastery here. Abibos was killed after he poured water on a Zoroastrian sacred fire.

The first church you reach at the monastery is a three-church basilica from the 8th and 9th centuries. This triple-church plan is unique to early Georgian churches, the three naves being divided by solid walls into what are effectively three churches. Nekresi's tiny first church, built in the time of King Mirian's grandson Trdati, stands above this in the centre of the complex. It's an extremely small basilica, many times reconstructed. It's thought that its builders had heard about the design of basilicas but not seen any, resulting in a rather idiosyncratic construction with open arches in the walls. Inside, steps lead down to a lower chapel or vault.

East of this basilica is the main Church of the Assumption, another triple-church basilica from the 6th to 7th centuries. Some 17th-century murals adorn the smoke-blackened interior. Beside this is a ruined 9th-century bishop's palace.

Kvareli ყვარელი
☎ 252 / pop 9000

Kvareli, 35km east of Telavi at the foot of the Caucasus, is famous for its semisweet Kindzmarauli wine, and for being the birthplace of the famous Georgian writer, reformer and patriot, Prince Ilia Chavchavadze (1837–1907). Considered by some to be the father of modern Georgia, Chavchavadze was made a saint of the Georgian Orthodox Church in 1987.

Because of the town's proximity to the mountains and their often marauding tribes,

Kvareli's population needed the security of good fortifications. In the 18th century King Erekle II had two sets of walls built, one inside the other. **Ilia Chavchavadze's house & museum** (☎ 20511; Rustaveli 3; admission 2 GEL; tour in Georgian or Russian 5 GEL; ☒ 10am-5pm) contain a defensive tower that was useful on the very day he was born, as Lezgins were at that moment rampaging through the area. This museum has a lot of 19th-century photos and a few personal effects. The house is not very large, but the *marani* is truly impressive.

The importance of wine in Kakheti is demonstrated at the **Kindzmarauli winery**, 3km outside town, by a 2km-long tunnel with 15 side passages (each 500m long) all filled with huge 20,000L metal storage tanks of wine. Kindzmarauli is Georgia's biggest winery and the tunnel is the second biggest wine storage tunnel in the world. The temperature underground is a naturally consistent 14°C, ideal for the preservation of the wines here. Kindzmarauli has no organised visiting programme, but someone will probably show you the tunnel and give you a couple of glasses to taste.

Tsinandali წინანდალი

This village, source of a famous white wine and site of the **Chavchavadze family estate** (☎ 250-71751; Telavi-Gurjaani Rd; admission to gardens free, museum

---

KAKHETI WINERIES

Wine tourism is something Georgia is striving to promote, especially after Russia, the main export market for Georgian wine, banned imports of it in 2006 (Georgia lost US$40 million worth of wine exports that year). Organised winery visits and tastings in Kakheti are still in their infancy, but they will undoubtedly become part of the scene. Meanwhile, it's not hard to organise visits and tastings through your accommodation or travel agencies. Here are five recommended and varied Kakheti wineries to consider visiting:

- **Badagoni** (☎ 32-936243; www.badagoni.ge; Zemo Khodasheni) Based at the village of Zemo Khodasheni, Badagoni is Georgia's biggest winery, producing over two million bottles a year – a modern, hi-tech business with Italian investment.
- **Teliani Valley** (☎ 32-506088, 32-313248; www.telianivalley.com; Tbilisis gzatkesili 3) On the Tbilisi road between Telavi and Tsinandali, Teliani Valley is a recently updated operation with a modern on-site **guest house** (☎ 899363600; per person 90-140 GEL) where wine tours are offered.
- **Shumi** (☎ 250-75333; www.shumi.ge; Tsinandali) A smaller, more typical Georgian winery based in Tsinandali but with 6 sq km of vineyards dotted around the Alazani valley.
- **Napareulis Marani** (☎ 899186414; Napareuli) A family-run operation at Napareuli village, 20km northeast of Telavi.
- **Villa Cinandali** (☎ 250-72500; Tsinandali) The Nikolaishvili family invites visitors to participate in making organic wine at their village home.

5 GEL, museum tour in Georgian, German or Russian 6 GEL; (◷ 10am-6pm) lies 10km southeast of Telavi. Prince Alexander Chavchavadze (1786–1846) was the son of Georgia's first ambassador to Russia and godson of Catherine the Great (but no close relation to Prince Ilia Chavchavadze). Despite his connections, Alexander was three times involved in anti-tsarist activities, for which he was eventually exiled. One of the first Georgian romantic poets, he was visited at Tsinandali by Lermontov and the exiled Decembrist plotters. His daughter Nino married the Russian poet and diplomat Alexander Griboedov in the family chapel here.

In 1854 Lezgin tribesmen from the Dagestan mountains ransacked the Chavchavadze house, kidnapping 23 women and children. Alexander's son David had to mortgage the house to raise the ransom. The hostages were returned, but David was unable to repay the loan and the house passed to Tsar Alexander III. The main room of the house is now a **museum**, with interesting paintings and photos of people and events associated with the house, including the Lezgin raid.

The 200,000-sq-metre park is beautifully laid out in an English style, with fine views, venerable trees and exotic plants such as ginkgo, bamboo, sequoia and yucca. The **Tsinandali Winery**, founded by Alexander's father, Garsevan, is in the northern part. Guides wait at the gate at the top of the estate drive: a two-glass wine tasting will cost you 5 GEL; if combined with a visit to the cellars, which contain wines dating to 1814, plus the gardens and museum, the price is 18 GEL.

Some changes can be expected at Tsinandali as the property has been leased to a Georgia-based company, Silk Road Group, with plans for several million dollars' investment, including one or more small tourist-quality hotels.

Akhali Shuamta & Dzveli Shuamta
ახალი შუამთა და ძველი შუამთა

The convent of Akhali (New) Shuamta and the old monastery of Dzveli (Old) Shuamta stand among beautiful woodlands – a favourite local picnic spot – off the Gombori road west of Telavi. Dzveli Shuamta, dating back to the 5th century, had fallen into disuse when Akhali Shuamta was founded in the 16th century by the Kakhetian Queen Tinatin. The churches at the two sites are fine works of Georgian ecclesiastical architecture.

A 'Monastery 2km' sign, 11km from Telavi, points the way to **Akhali Shuamta**, now a convent again after serving as an orphanage in Soviet times. Wait at the inner gate for one of the nuns to greet you and show you the church (some of them speak English). The brick church has a cruciform design with an unusually high cupola and large crosses inscribed on its extremities. The fine 16th-century frescoes inside portray Queen Tinatin, her husband, King Levan II, and their son Alexander, as well as biblical scenes. Tinatin later became a nun and is buried here. The poet Alexander Chavchavadze (left) is also buried here.

Three kilometres further up the road are the three stone churches of **Dzveli Shuamta**. Nearest to the road is a three-naved 5th- to 6th-century basilica, in a style typical of the earliest period of Georgian Christianity. The next is a 7th-century tetraconch church with a plan derived from the Jvari Church near Mtskheta. Third is another tetraconch church from the same period, but lacking the corner rooms of the otherwise similar middle church.

No public transport comes to Shuamta; a taxi round trip from Telavi is 5 GEL.

SIGHNAGHI სიღნაღი
☎ 255 / pop 2000

Sighnaghi is the most attractive town in Kakheti and has a distinctly Italianate feel to it. Set on a hill 60km southeast of Telavi, the town was developed (over earlier ruins) in the 18th century by King Erekle II, in part as a refuge for the area's populace against Lezgin and Persian attacks. The name Sighnaghi comes from the Turkish word for 'shelter', siǧinak. Each of the six entrances in Erekle's 23 tower walls was named after a local village. Erekle invited Armenian artisans and tradespeople to live here, and by the 19th century Sighnaghi was one of Georgia's leading trading centres. Three-quarters of its houses still date from the 17th, 18th and 19th centuries and a large part of its 4km defensive wall still stands.

Today Sighnaghi is being ambitiously developed into a tourism hub for Kakheti, with an emphasis on wine. It is already the scene of a big wine festival one weekend each October. In 2007 a huge government-sponsored renovation programme turned the town centre into one great building site, making it hard to determine what the place would eventually look like. But the renovation will maintain the town's original style, with its handsome galleried houses built around a series of appealing small squares. In the pipeline are new family-style cellar restaurants, wine-tasting halls, new hotels and other accommodation, a government-run tourist information office, and new museums. All being well it will retain its charm with the addition of new facilities.

Set among wooded hills dotted with cypresses, the town has wonderful views of the Alazani valley and the Caucasus beyond. The main section of the 18th-century **walls** runs along the hilltop on the northeast side of town, where you can enter the tiny **Stepan Tsminda (St Stephen's) Church** inside one of the towers on Chavchavadze. Lower down, on the northeast side of town, is the handsome 19th-century **Tsminda Giorgi (St George's) Church**.

Sleeping & Eating

Sighnaghi is certain to develop many more accommodation and eating options (the tourist offices here and in Telavi will have information). **Hotel Pirosmani** (Davit Aghmashenebeli 6), a new hotel in the excellent small Rcheuli chain (see p109) opened shortly before we went to press. It has a Georgian restaurant and a French café.

David Zandarashvili's (☎ 31029, 899750510; david zandarashvili@yahoo.com; Tsminda Giorgi 11; per person half board 25 GEL) Down near Tsminda Giorgi Church, this very hospitable and helpful family provides good rooms and excellent food, and is a favourite with travellers.

Nana Kokiashvili's (☎ 31829, 899795093; kkshvl@ yahoo.com; Saradzhishvili 2; per person 25 GEL, half board 35 GEL) Nana has four nice big rooms and wide balconies in her fine old house on one of the central squares, and provides good, home-cooked, local food. Her daughter Nino (☎ 893229178) speaks English and her husband can often drive guests to local attractions and even as far as Davit Gareja (right).

Other homestays to try, both up near the old town walls, include **Sergo's** (☎ 899393808; Chavchavadze 16) and the **Bejashvili family** (☎ 31736; Chavchavadze 10).

Pancho Villa (☎ 899192356; Tamar Mepi; dishes 3-10 GEL; ☷ 2pm-10pm Tue-Sun) You can't miss the green and orange paintwork of what is undoubtedly the only Mexican restaurant in Kakheti. Run by Shalva Mindorashvili, who took a liking to burritos and salsa while living in the USA, it serves up simple, tasty and filling versions of Mexican dishes, plus Georgian wine!

Getting There & Away

Marshrutkas to Sighnaghi (6 GEL, 2½ hours) leave every couple of hours from about 7am to 5pm from outside Samgori metro station in Tbilisi, with a similar schedule returning (the first and last from Sighnaghi are at 7am and 6pm). There's a single daily departure from Sighnaghi to Telavi (4 GEL, 1½ hours) at 9.15am. A taxi to or from Telavi should be 30 GEL.

AROUND SIGHNAGHI

Bodbe Convent ბოდბის მონასტერი

Bodbe Convent is 2.5km south of Sighnaghi, an enjoyable walk on country roads, or you could take a cab for 5 GEL or 6 GEL round trip.

The convent, set among tall cypresses, is dedicated to St Nino (see p73), who is buried here. The little church was originally built, over her grave, by King Mirian in the 4th century. It was converted into a triple-church basilica in the 8th or 9th century and has been renovated several times since. Nino's fairly simple tomb, beneath a recently installed marble slab, is in a small chapel in its southeast corner. The murals were painted in 1823 by Bishop John Maqashvili. A convent, founded here in the late 19th century, then turned into a hospital in Soviet times, has functioned again since 1991. Through an opening just northeast of the church, and then down a steep path of 800m, you can reach a small chapel built over St Nino's Spring, which burst forth after she prayed on this spot, where today locals queue up to drink and splash themselves with the holy water.

DAVIT GAREJA დავით გარეჯა

On the border with Azerbaijan, Davit (or David) Gareja is perhaps the most remarkable of all Georgia's ancient sites, and the most interesting easy day trip from Tbilisi. Comprising about 15 old monasteries spread over a large, remote area, its uniqueness is heightened by a lunar, semidesert landscape which turns green and blooms with flowers in early summer. Monstrously neglected during the Soviet era, Davit Gareja has since seen some restoration and is now again inhabited by monks. Two of the key monasteries, and the most visited, are Lavra (the only inhabited one today), and, on the hill above it, Udabno, which has beautiful frescoes (not to be confused with the village Udabno several kilometres north).

Lavra, the first monastery here, was founded by Davit Gareja, one of the 13 ascetic 'Syrian fathers' who returned from the Middle East to spread Christianity in Georgia in the 6th century. The religious complex grew until there were monasteries spread over a wide area. Here manuscripts were translated and copied, and a celebrated Georgian school of fresco painting developed. The monasteries were destroyed by the Mongols in 1265, revived in the early 14th century by Giorgi V the Brilliant, sacked by Timur and then suffered their worst moment of all on Easter night 1615 when Persian Shah Abbas' soldiers killed 6000 monks and destroyed most of their artistic treasures. In 1675 King Archil initiated some restoration and gave stipends to the monks. The monasteries never regained their former importance but remained working until the end of the 19th century.

During the Soviet era the area was used for military exercises, and some of the first demonstrations of the *perestroika* period in Tbilisi were protests against this vandalism. Ironically, the Georgian army then used the area for training in the mid-1990s. These manoeuvres were stopped when protesters camped in the firing range.

Entrance to both Lavra and Udabno is free, but you may want to leave a donation at Lavra. It takes two to three hours to explore both places at a leisurely pace.

The **Lavra** monastery is on three levels, with buildings dating from many different periods. The watchtower and the outer walls are from the 18th century. You enter by a gateway on the middle level which is decorated with reliefs illustrating stories of the monks' harmony with the natural world. From the gateway you go down past the 17th-century Church of St Nicholas to the lower level, where the caves of Davit and his companions are. Davit and his Kakhetian disciples Lukiane and Dodo are buried in the 6th-century cave Peristsvaleba (Church of the Transfiguration) on this lower level. Monks are now living in the monastery again, but you can't enter their quarters (caves in the rock above those of Davit and his companions), and you should refrain from making too much noise. They will also be offended by inappropriate clothing.

To get to **Udabno**, take the uphill path beside the church shop outside Lavra. Watch out for poisonous vipers on this route, including in the caves and especially from April to June.

When you come level with a watchtower overlooking Lavra, take the path leading straight up the hill. In 10 to 15 minutes you will reach a metal railing. Follow this to the left and up to the top of the ridge, then along the far side of the ridge (where the railing deteriorates to a series of posts). The plains and low hills below you now are in Azerbaijan, and the caves alongside and above the path are the Udabno monastery. Some were churches or chapels or rooms, and their inner walls still bear frescoes painted by the renowned fresco school that flourished here between the 10th and 13th centuries. The monastery's refectory, where the monks had to kneel to eat at low stone tables, is decorated with beautiful light-coloured frescoes, the principal one being an 11th-century depiction of the Last Supper. Paintings on the north wall of what was the main church show Davit Gareja and Lukiane surrounded by deer, a reference to the story that deer gave them milk when they were wandering without sustenance in this remote wilderness. Below them are figures of Kakhetian princes.

Finally the path climbs up to a stone chapel on the hilltop, then down past a cave known as Davit's Tears (because of the spring inside) and the top of Lavra monastery, to the watchtower you passed earlier.

Sleeping

Anyone with a particular interest in staying overnight at Davit Gareja can sleep at the **Seismology Centre** (☎ 899536373; per person full board US$35-40) run by David Gotsadze, about 600m back from Lavra monastery along the approach road. There are six clean if basic guest rooms, sharing a bathroom and not-very-powerful solar electricity. You should call ahead.

Getting There & Away

There's no public transport to the remote site, but it's possible to do a day trip from Tbilisi using a marshrutka from Didube to Gardabani (2.50 GEL, one hour, hourly from 9am to 5pm), and then hiring a taxi in Gardabani. Most drivers will do the round trip for around 60 GEL including waiting time.

Many Tbilisi tour agencies (p52) run day trips to Davit Gareja, with the benefit of lunch, comfortable transfers by coach or car, and guides (especially useful at Udabno, where some of the caves are a little tricky to find). Rates are typically around 150 GEL per person for two people or 110 GEL per person for four people.

LAGODEKHI NATURE RESERVE
ლაგოდეხის ნაკრძალი

This remote, 242-sq-km reserve runs up to heights of over 3000m in the Caucasus, above the small town of Lagodekhi in Kakheti's far eastern corner. It's a destination that will appeal to lovers of nature and off-the-beaten-track travel. It's most practicable for those heading into Azerbaijan. The reserve features deep river valleys, glacial lakes and some of Georgia's best-preserved forests, with wildlife including Caucasian turs, wolves, brown bears and lynx. You can make day hikes to waterfalls or to the 11th-century Machistsikhe castle, and there's a three-day, 50km route through the highest parts of the park near the border of Dagestan (Russia).

Accommodation and food are available at the **administration building** (☎ 254-22715, 899385283; vpavliashvili@yahoo.com; Vashlovani 197, Lagodekhi) and a couple of local guesthouses. Some information in English is on the **Department of Protected Areas website** (www.dpa .gov.ge), under 'Services'.

Marshrutkas and slow buses to Lagodekhi (5 GEL, up to three hours) leave the new bus station in Telavi at 7.30am, 8.30am and 1.30pm, and from the old bus station at 3pm. If requested, these may be able to take you on to the Azerbaijan border 4km beyond Lagodekhi. Some buses or marshrutkas run from Lagodekhi across the border to Balakən, Zaqatala or Şəki. Alternatively, take a taxi from Lagodekhi to the border and then a shared taxi to Balakən (AZN1), from which there are marshrutkas, buses and a train to Zaqatala, Şəki and Baku (see p280).

SAMTSKHE-JAVAKHETI
სამცხე-ჯავახეთი

The unpronounceably named southern flank of Georgia is a highly scenic region whose cultural and natural attractions have unfortunately not prevented it from becoming one of the country's most economically backward areas. Its biggest attractions are the spectacular 12th-century cave city of Vardzia and the beautiful Borjomi-Kharagauli National Park. Also here are the popular spa resort of Borjomi and the ski resort of Bakuriani. Landscapes are very varied, from the alpine forests and meadows around Borjomi and Bakuriani to the bare volcanic canyons of the Vardzia area.

Historically known as Meskheti, the region has played an important part in Georgian history. It was part of Tao-Klarjeti, the collection of princedoms from which the Bagrationi dynasty expanded its power in the 9th and 10th centuries, leading to the unification of most of Georgia under their rule in 1008. A cradle of Georgian culture, Tao-Klarjeti extended well into what's now northeast Turkey, where many interesting Georgian churches and monasteries may still be seen. Tao-Klarjeti fell under Ottoman rule from the 1550s to the 1870s. It was briefly part of independent Georgia after the Russian Revolution, but most of it was reoccupied by Turkey when the Red Army attacked Georgia in 1921.

Javakheti is the more elevated southeastern half of Samtskhe-Javakheti. Bordering Armenia, it has a majority Armenian population.

BORJOMI ბორჯომი
☎ 367 (international), ☎ 267 domestic / pop 14,000

Famous throughout the former Soviet Union for its salty-sour, love-it-or-hate-it carbonated mineral water, Borjomi is an attractive resort town clinging to the hills either side of the Mtkvari River, 850m above sea level. The town dates from 1829 when some soldiers discovered the health-giving mineral spring here. A Russian governor of the Caucasus, Count Vorontsov, developed Borjomi as a resort, one that became fashionable with the aristocracy after Duke Mikhail Romanov (brother of Tsar Alexander II) took a liking to it. In the 1890s Duke Mikhail built a summer residence, the Likani Palace, 2km west of the modern centre off the Akhaltsikhe road. It's now a Georgian presidential residence.

During the Soviet era Borjomi attracted enormous numbers of visitors from all over the USSR. After the Soviet collapse, Borjomi's flow of visitors slowed to a trickle, but things are now looking up, with a steady number of new hotels and restaurants opening. Borjomi is a good jumping-off point for Vardzia, and the Borjomi-Kharagauli National Park, right

GEORGIA

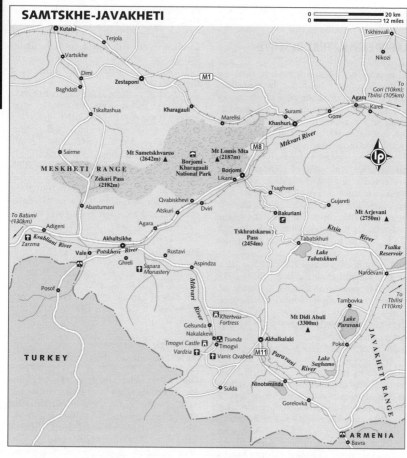

SAMTSKHE-JAVAKHETI

on its doorstep, offers some of the best hiking in Georgia outside the greater Caucasus.

Orientation & Information

The main road through town and also the main commercial street, Rustaveli, runs along the northern bank of the Mtkvari River. Arriving from Tbilisi in the northeast, you'll notice the tourist office in a glass pavilion between Rustaveli and the river. Beside this, a white suspension bridge crosses the river to the southern half of town, where the Borjomi Mineral Water Park is. The sparklingly renovated Stalin-era Borjomi Park train station is on the south bank, just east of this bridge. Rustaveli changes its name to Meskheti 300m west of the bridge, continuing 300m more to

the bus station and then a further 1km to the national park visitors centre. There are places to stay on both sides of the river. A few ATMs are located along Rustaveli.

Borjomi District Tourism Department (www .borjomitourism.ge) This website has maps and descriptions of walking and horse-riding routes in the Borjomi and Bakuriani areas.

Borjomi-Kharagauli National Park (www.national park.ge) The website has information on the main attractions of Samtskhe-Javakheti.

Internet Café (Rustaveli 26; per hr 2 GEL; ⏱ 10am-11pm) Next to the tourist office.

Tourist Information Office (☎ 21397; Rustaveli; ⏱ 10am-9pm Mon-Fri, to 6pm Sat & Sun Jul-Sep) Extremely helpful and informative but unfortunately only open for the summer season at research time.

GEORGIA

Sights

Borjomi's **Mineral Water Park** (9 Aprili; summer admission 0.50 GEL, other times free) dates from 1850 and is a lovely place to walk. This was where the original water spring was discovered, and named Yekaterinsky Spring after the governor's daughter, who was cured here. To reach the park cross the little Borjomula River just east of Borjomi Park station, turn right and go 600m. The park occupies the narrow, wooded Borjomula valley, and its facilities – cafés, kids' attractions and a cinema – have recently been attractively renovated. Mineral water flows from taps in a pavilion straight in front of the entrance, and a modern cable car (down/up 1/2 GEL) carries you above the park to a hilltop Ferris wheel. If you walk about 3km upstream through the park, you'll find a small, natural, spring-fed swimming pool.

The **Borjomi Museum of Local Lore** (Tsminda Nino 5; admission 3 GEL, tour 5 GEL; 10am-5pm Tue-Sun) is housed in the former Romanov offices, in a street off the western end of Rustaveli. The collection includes china, glass and other articles from the Romanov palace, photos and documentation about the Borjomi mineral waters, some exhibits of local flora and fauna, and a papier-mâché map of Borjomi made in 1917.

Sleeping

Borjomi accommodation used to consist mainly of sanatoria of varying degrees of comfort, but there are now some comfortable hotels as well as copious homestays.

Marina Zulmatashvili's Homestay (☎ 22323, 898184550; Shroma 2; per person incl breakfast 20 GEL) One of the best homestays, with a welcoming family in a cosy house. Guests can use cooking facilities here. Son Giga and daughter Maia, usually here in the summer, speak perfect English. From the south side of the suspension bridge, go up the hill on Kostava, then where Kostava bends left downhill, fork right along an unpaved street. Go right at the end of this, then take the first left and the house is at the end on the left. There are several other similarly priced homestays in the same street (at numbers 3, 4, 8 and 9, for example).

Mzia Gogoladze's Homestay (☎ 21552, 895352580; Rustaveli 21; per person 20 GEL) This is another comfortable and friendly place, though less central: it's just before the Bakuriani turning as you head east out of Borjomi, 2km from the tourist office. Breakfast available.

Hotel Victoria (☎ 22631; Kostava 31; r 40 GEL, ste for 3 100 GEL) Has two quite adequate, pine-panelled rooms with shared bath upstairs, and two rather dark but more spacious 'deluxe' affairs downstairs with kitchen and private bathroom. It's 200m up the hill from the south side of the suspension bridge.

Saodzakho Hotel (☎ 20780; Kostava 2; r 60 GEL) A friendly, family-run, small hotel between Borjomi Park station and the suspension bridge. The rooms are cosy and carpeted, with hot showers, and some have balconies. No food, though.

our pick Hotel Borjomi (☎ 22212; Tsminda Nino 3; incl breakfast s 60-80 GEL, d 70-100 GEL; 🞨) A characterful and well-managed place off Rustaveli, next to the museum, this small hotel occupies an attractive tsarist-era mansion and has the most comfortable feel of any hotel in town. The rooms are carpeted and spacious, with private bathrooms.

Borjomis Kheoba (☎ 23072; info@borjomiskheoba .com; Rustaveli 107A; d full board US$85-165; 🞨) Sharing its building with a sanatorium (run separately), this good modern hotel has comfy rooms with top-end touches like toiletries and hair-dryer; some of the more expensive ones are two-level. The pool and the gym are open to hotel guests only. There's also one single room at US$53 with full board.

Eating

You can get *khachapuri, shashlyk,* hot dogs and coffee at the cafés in the Mineral Water Park. In town the main cluster of cafés and restaurants is on Robakidze, just south of the suspension bridge.

Bistro Aguna (Robakidze 2; mains 4-8 GEL; 9am-9pm) A straightforward café, with small booths for private dining, and tasty, if unimaginative, national standards.

Taverna Nia (Robakidze 1A; mains 4-9 GEL) In a two-storey 19th-century house with attractive wooden balconies, the Nia serves very good Georgian cuisine. It's popular with locals and packed on holidays, when it can be very loud – a great Borjomi experience.

Shemoikhede Genatsvale (☎ 23343; Borjomi Park Station; 2-course meal incl drinks 15-30 GEL; 9am-11pm) A big, bright, new place in the train station, serving excellent Georgian food. *Khinkali* are a speciality but there's lots more. This is a branch of the very good Tbilisi restaurant of the same name.

GEORGIA

Getting There & Away

Marshrutkas to Borjomi (7 GEL, 2½ hours) leave Tbilisi's Didube bus station about hourly from 8am to 7pm, with a similar return schedule from Borjomi's **bus station** (☎ 22534; Meskheti 8). Other marshrutkas from Borjomi bus station go to Akhaltsikhe (3 GEL, 1½ hours, about hourly), Gori (4 GEL, 1½ hours, at 7.30am, 10am and 1pm), Kutaisi (7 GEL, three hours, 11.30am and 2.15pm) and Batumi (14 GEL, six hours, 9am). Frequent buses and marshrutkas run between Borjomi and Khashuri (1.50 GEL, 30 minutes), on the main Tbilisi–Kutaisi road, 32km northwest of Borjomi, until early evening.

For those with plenty of time, *elektrichky* from Tbilisi's Borjomi station leave at 7.15am and 4.55pm, taking 4¼ hours to Borjomi Park station. Trains back to Tbilisi leave at 7am and 4.20pm.

A taxi from Borjomi to Tbilisi costs around 80 GEL, while one to Akhaltsikhe costs 30 GEL.

BORJOMI-KHARAGAULI NATIONAL PARK ბორჯომ-ხარაგაულის ეროვნული პარკი

The ranges of the Lesser Caucasus in southern Georgia are less well known and less high than the greater Caucasus along the country's northern border, but they still contain some very beautiful and wild country.

The perfect chance to get out into this landscape is provided by the large Borjomi-Kharagauli National Park, open from April to October, which spreads over more than 850 sq km of forested hills and alpine meadows up to 2642m high, north and west of Borjomi. You might even see one of the park's 60 brown bears.

Nine marked trails of various lengths, some suitable for horses as well as hikers, crisscross different parts of the park, with overnight accommodation available on the longer routes. Trail 7 is a 3km introductory stroll starting from the **park office and visitors centre** (☎ 267-22117, 899233449; www.nationalpark.ge; Meskheti 23, Borjomi; ☯ 9am-6pm Mon-Fri, to 4pm Sat & Sun Apr-Oct), 1km west of central Borjomi. Trail 1 (Likani to Marelisi) is a 40km, three-day route crossing the park from south to north via Mt Lomis Mta (2187m). A popular day route of five or six hours follows Trail 1 up the Likani River valley then turns down Trail 6 to come out on the Akhaltsikhe road

at Qvabiskhevi. You can make this a two-day hike by continuing up Trail 1 to the Lomis Mta tourist shelter, and then returning down Trails 1 and 6. The longest and hardest route is Trail 2 (Atskuri to Marelisi), a north–south route of 50km, taking three or four days.

To visit the park, you need a ticket (free) from the visitors centre, where you can also obtain maps and information, pay for any nights in the park, and arrange for guides or horses. They also have tents (7 GEL per night), sleeping bags (5 GEL per night), backpacks (5 GEL per night) and camping mats (3 GEL per night) for rent.

Though the trails are marked and you're free to hike on your own, the management recommends taking a park guide (33 GEL per day) because some of the paint markers are damaged or missing, and minor trails can be confusing.

Most guides speak at least some English. You can rent horses for 40 GEL per day for rides from Atskuri or Marelisi.

Sleeping

Four basic wooden **tourist shelters** (per person 10 GEL) provide accommodation inside the park. They have spring water but you need to carry a sleeping bag, food and cooking gear. You can also sleep at the ranger shelter near the park's highest point, Mt Sametskhvareo, but there's no water there. There are **campsites** (per person 5 GEL) at the park entrances at Qvabiskhevi, Atskuri and Marelisi.

The park operates small guest houses at the **visitors centre** (r 60 GEL), where the rooms have private bathrooms but there's no food available, and **Marelisi** (per person 20 GEL, breakfast/lunch/dinner 5/6/10 GEL), just outside the park's northern boundary, with four double rooms sharing bathrooms.

Getting There & Away

The visitors centre is a short walk or taxi ride from Borjomi. Marshrutkas running between Borjomi and Akhaltsikhe will drop you off or pick you up at the park's Likani, Qvabiskhevi or Atskuri entry points.

Marelisi is on the Tbilisi–Kutaisi railway, with trains to Tbilisi (three hours) leaving at 4.35am, 5am and 3.15pm. Westbound trains leave Marelisi for Kutaisi and Zugdidi at noon, for Zugdidi at 12.25am and for Batumi at 1.44am.

BAKURIANI ბაკურიანი

☎ 367 (international), ☎ 267 (domestic) / pop 2500

Thirty kilometres up a winding road through pine-clad hills southeast of Borjomi, Bakuriani is the cheaper, and more locally popular, of Georgia's two main ski resorts (the other being Gudauri in the Caucasus, p100). Though new hotels big and small are going up all the time, Bakuriani still has the atmosphere of a mountain village. Developed in Soviet times as a training centre for Olympic skiers, its facilities declined after the Soviet collapse but are now being improved again.

The Bakuriani area is also good for picturesque walks in summer. The climate here is subalpine, with snow usually falling from December to the end of March, but it also has long, warm summers and high ultraviolet radiation.

Approaching the centre of town from Borjomi, you'll turn right (south) up the main street, Tavisupleba. After 500m Tskhakia runs off to the right to the bus station, 120m away, and Tavisupleba becomes Aghmashenebeli. There's a **Tourist Information Centre** (☎ 40037; bakuriani.cenn.ge; Aghmashenebeli 1; ☽ 10am-6pm Mon-Fri) at this corner, where you can find out about good summer walking routes.

The ski season runs from late December to some time in March. The main runs are **Kokhta I**, 1.5km long with a chairlift (per ride 2 GEL), on the eastern edge of town, and **Didveli**, 1.8km with a cable car (3 GEL), to the south. Skiing and snowboarding equipment is available for rent at around 25 GEL a day near the foot of the lifts. You can ice-skate and snowmobile here too.

Sleeping & Eating

Many hotels and guesthouses are scattered around the centre, up Aghmashenebeli towards the Didveli ski run, and along a ring road north and east of the centre which leads to Kokhta-I. In summer most places drop their rates by 10 GEL to 20 GEL.

Sport Hotel (☎ 899537716; Mtis 28; per person 25 GEL, full board 50 GEL) This friendly small hotel is just 200m from the bus station. The bright, pine-fitted rooms have bathrooms and TVs and there's a nice big upstairs sitting area. The hotel can provide a walking or horse-riding guide for 20 GEL per day.

Hotel Apollon (☎ 40288, 899571108; www.welcome .ge/hotel_apollon; Aghmashenebeli 21; per person full board US$40) Another friendly smaller place, with satisfying meals in a cosy dining room, and very comfy, pine-floored rooms with balconies and comfortable wooden beds – 800m up the hill from the centre.

Hotel Villa Park (☎ 40405, 877504747; Rustaveli 25; s/d/tr/q full board from US$90/120/150/200; ☙) This is one of the most luxurious hotels in the centre, with a sizable indoor pool, and buffet meals served in the large restaurant. Rooms are carpeted and attractively furnished. The hotel is up a side street 250m from the bus station.

Restaurants are few, as most visitors eat at their accommodation. For a change try **Natali Restaurant** (Tavisupleba; mains 4-10 GEL).

Getting There & Away

Marshrutkas leave Borjomi bus station for Bakuriani (2.50 GEL, one hour) at least four times daily (7am, 9am, 10.30am and 2.30pm). There are also several marshrutkas and buses daily from Tbilisi Didube (p67; bus/marshrutka 7/10 GEL, three hours). Returning to Tbilisi there are eight departures between 8am and 5pm. A taxi from Borjomi to Bakuriani or vice versa costs 20 GEL to 25 GEL.

Slow but scenic trains run to Bakuriani (2 GEL, two hours) from Borjomi's Chornaya Rechka station (by the Mtkvari River, 2km east of the centre) at 6.50am and 1pm, returning from Bakuriani at 9.30am and 3.40pm.

AKHALTSIKHE ახალციხე

☎ 365 (international), ☎ 265 (domestic) / pop 20,000

The capital and biggest town of Samtskhe-Javakheti, Akhaltsikhe means 'New Castle' in Georgian. In fact, far from being new, the castle that dominates the town dates from the 12th century. The local power in Akhaltsikhe from the 13th to 17th centuries was the Jakeli family, but from 1688 until 1828 it was the centre of a *pashalik* (an Ottoman administrative area governed by a pasha). Little of Akhaltsikhe's Soviet-era industry remains, and unemployment is high, but it's a pleasant enough place, mostly used by travellers as a staging post for the cave city at Vardzia and the beautiful Sapara Monastery.

The bus station is on a square on the north side of the Potskhovi River. Cross the bridge over the river and bear right at two forks and you'll be on the main street, Kostava.

A DRIVING FORCE

Krisha Petrosian is Armenian-Georgian, or a Georgian-Armenian if you prefer. Born of Armenian parents, he has always lived in Akhaltsikhe, a southwestern Georgian town with a sizable Armenian population. Most of his life, Georgia and Armenia were part of the same country, the USSR, and Krisha, while not one to harbour regrets, is one of the many who think life was better back then. 'It's not that we were rich, but everyone had enough,' he avers.

You might meet Krisha, a courteous and friendly man in his mid-60s, outside Akhaltsikhe's bus station, where he regularly waits for customers in his 1990 Soviet-built Volga taxi. Though past retirement age, he continues working to make ends meet. Georgia's old-age pension, 39 GEL a month, is far from enough for Krisha and his wife to live on. He is still happy driving, something he has done for a living all his life.

'I trained as a driver during my military service in the Soviet army. Then I drove buses for years, to and from Yerevan. Later I became a taxi driver.'

After Georgian independence he managed to buy his cab from the government-run taxi organisation he had worked for, and set up as an independent driver. He's happy with his Volga, which still purrs along well and gives a smooth, comfortable ride. 'It's a good worker,' he smiles.

The breakup of the Soviet Union turned Krisha, overnight, into an international kind of guy. He speaks Georgian, Armenian, Russian and Turkish, and two of his three children live in Russia. His son is an officer in the Russian army and his elder daughter is married to a Russian general. Money they send home is a big help in keeping their parents and the second daughter, a young widow, afloat. The second daughter is a qualified pharmacist but is unable to find work.

And the Armenians and Georgians here get along OK with each other? 'A lot of Armenians left Georgia after independence, mainly to Armenia or Russia, but everything is fine now.' You sense Krisha is the kind of guy who'll always make the best of things, whatever potholes the road presents.

Rabati

A wander around Akhaltsikhe's *rabati* (old town), with its multicultural architecture, is well worthwhile. This district is on a hill on the north side of the Potskhovi, just west of the bridge. Rare examples of *darbazebi* (traditional Georgian houses) cluster around the castle, which was built in the 12th century and houses a mosque from 1752 and the ruins of a *medrese* (Islamic school). The castle also houses the fine **Ivane Javakhishvili Samtskhe-Javakheti History Museum** (☎ 21622; admission 3 GEL; Kharischirashvili 1; ☼ 10am-6pm Tue-Sun), whose interesting exhibits include a 16th-century manuscript of Rustaveli's *The Knight in the Tiger Skin* and a large collection of Caucasian carpets. The *rabati* also has a synagogue, an Armenian church and a Catholic church.

Sleeping & Eating

Hotel Meskheti (☎ 20420; Kostava 10; r 25-30 GEL) This superficially renovated ex-Intourist hotel is cheap, central and gloomy. The rooms are survivable, with hot showers.

White House (☎ 20410, 899513595; Aspindza 26; s/d incl breakfast 40/50 GEL, ste 60 GEL) Down a side street off Rustaveli (the Vardzia road), 1km east of the town centre, the White House seems mainly aimed at NGO staff. The rooms are fairly bare but comfy, with good bathrooms and European-channel TVs. The big and rather ornate restaurant (mains 3 to 6 GEL), with gold-ribboned chairs, is probably the best in town.

Hotel Prestizhi (☎ 893937125; Rustaveli 76; s/d 40/50 GEL, incl breakfast 50/60 GEL) A short distance closer to the centre than the White House, the Prestizhi has a very attentive manager and clean, sizable rooms with large paintings in reasonable taste.

There are a few cafés serving *khachapuri*, snacks and meals near the Hotel Meskheti on Kostava, the main street.

Getting There & Away

The **bus station** (Tamarashvili) is busy with marshrutka and bus departures every hour or half-hour, 7am to 7pm, to Borjomi (3 GEL, 1½ hours) and Tbilisi (10 GEL, four hours), as well as to Batumi via Khashuri (18 GEL, six hours, at 8.30 and 11.30am), Batumi via Khulo (15 GEL, six hours, 10am, about May to September only), Kutaisi (10 GEL, 4½ hours, 2.20pm and 3pm), Vardzia (3.50 GEL, two hours, 10.30am, 12.20pm, 4pm and 5.30pm), and to Gyumri (15 GEL, four hours, 7am) and Yerevan (25 GEL, seven hours, 7.10am) in Armenia. A taxi to the Turkish border, 20km southwest of Akhaltsikhe, costs 15 GEL to 20 GEL; taxis and minibuses run between the border and the first Turkish town, Posof (12km from the border). It's a four-hour minibus ride on from Posof to Kars.

VARDZIA ვარძია

The drive into the wilderness from Akhaltsikhe towards Vardzia is as dramatic as any in Georgia outside the greater Caucasus. The road follows the course of the upper Mtkvari, passing through narrow canyons and then veering south at Aspindza along a particularly beautiful valley cutting like a green ribbon between arid, rocky hillsides. Thirty-two kilometres from Akhaltsikhe is the village of Rustavi, from where Georgia's national bard Rustaveli hails. After the unremarkable town of Aspindza, you reach the impressive 10th- to 14th-century **Khertvisi Fortress**, where the road to Akhalkalaki and Turkey diverges from the Varzia road. Inside the impressive walls is a square keep with rounded corners. According to legend, Queen Tamar held a competition to see who could build the best tower. A master stonemason and an apprentice were the contestants. The apprentice outdid his master, who jumped like a bird from the tower and died impaled on the knife in his belt. From the eastern wall two tunnels lead down to the river: one served the castle's inhabitants for water, the other for communication.

Nine kilometres from Khertvisi you come to a stone enclosure beside the road, which is an old **slave market**. Opposite is the turning to

the village of Nakalakevi, whose name means 'a city used to be here'. The city in question was **Tsunda**, which until the 9th century was the capital of Javakheti. Tsunda's remains are just east of the north end of the next village, Tmogvi, 1km further along the road: it's worth stopping to see Tsunda's beautifully ornamented 12th-century Church of St John the Baptist, with, curiously enough, a medieval stone lavatory next to it.

Two kilometres further along the road, but atop a high rocky hill on the other side of the river (which flows far below in the gorge), is the near-impregnable **Tmogvi Castle**, which was already an important fortification by the 10th century. About 1.5km past this, up on the left of the road, are the remains of **Vanis Qvabebi** (Vani Caves), a cave monastery that predated Vardzia by four centuries, with a maze of tunnels inside the rock.

The cave city of **Vardzia** (admission US$3; ☒ 9am-5pm), 16km beyond Khertvisi, is a cultural symbol with a special place in the hearts of Georgians. In the 12th century Giorgi III built a fortification at the site. His daughter, Queen Tamar, established a monastery here, which grew into a virtual holy city housing perhaps 2000 monks, renowned as a spiritual bastion of Georgia and of Christendom's eastern frontier. The story goes that it was Tamar who, as a child, unwittingly gave the place its name: taken hunting by her father, she strayed from her companions and when called to, answered from the caves 'Ak var dzia' (Here I am, uncle).

The remarkable feature of Vardzia as it developed in Tamar's reign was that the inhabitants lived in dwellings carved out of the rock and ranging over 13 floors, with the Church

---

WALKS IN THE UPPER MTKVARI VALLEY

A network of fascinating walking trails has been opened up between Khertvisi and Vardzia, giving access to places like Tmogvi Castle, Vanis Qvabebi and the convent of Zeda (Upper) Vardzia with its 11th-century stone church. You'll notice information boards showing these routes and describing their features in English and Georgian as you travel along the valley. Five routes of up to 8km are marked with yellow-and-black paint stripes and arrows in a project coordinated by the Swiss-based Foundation for Sustainable Development in Mountain Regions. Guesthouses with hot-water bathrooms at Gelsunda, Tmogvi and Vardzia enable you to stay overnight and enjoy exploring this fascinating area: prices including meals range from US$20 to US$30 per person. There are plans for a tourist information centre at Vardzia, guide services and an English-language telephone or email booking facility, but meanwhile for more information you can visit tgmproject .googlepages.com or contact coordinator **Malkhaz Jackelli** (☎ 32-752710, 899555032; mjackelli@gmail .com) or guide **Inga Tkemaladze** (☎ 899114506; tkemaladzeinga@yahoo.fr). Both speak English.

of the Assumption at the centre. To the west of the church, in the area that developed out of the 10th-century cave village of Ananuri, you can see 40 cave groups with a total of 165 rooms, and six smaller churches. On the east side are 79 cave groups, 244 rooms and six more churches. The total includes 25 wine cellars!

Guides are usually available at the ticket office; though none speak English, they can help show you the most interesting caves for a tip of a few lari.

At the heart of the cave complex is the **Church of the Assumption**, with its two-arched portico. The façade of the church has gone, but the inside is beautiful. Frescoes portray many New Testament scenes, and on the north wall depict Tamar before she married (shown by the fact that she is not wearing a wimple) alongside her father, Giorgi III. These were painted between 1184 and 1186, the period of the church's construction. The door to the left of the church door leads into a long tunnel (perhaps 150m) which climbs steps inside the rock and emerges well above the church.

Vardzia suffered a major earthquake in 1283, which shook away the outer walls of many caves. As Georgian power suffered successive waves of invaders, the monastery itself declined. In 1551 the Georgians were defeated by the Persians in a battle in the caves themselves and Vardzia was looted. Today Vardzia is again a working monastery and you may meet some of its inhabitants during your visit.

Sleeping

There's clean, basic accommodation with hot-water bathrooms at **Valodia Zazadze's Guesthouse** (☎ 899116207; per person full board US$20) and a small hotel run by **Gocha Maisuradze** (☎ 898169915, 899543540; per person US$10). They're next to each other, across the river from the cave city; you can ask at the ticket office for directions. The owners live on site. It's advisable to call in advance if you want to ensure places.

Getting There & Away

On current schedules you can just about make it to Vardzia and back in one day by marshrutka from Akhaltsikhe, or even Borjomi. The first marshrutka leaving Akhaltsikhe, at 10.30am, reaches Vardzia around 12.30pm, giving you just about enough time to see the site and catch the last marshrutka back at 3pm (earlier ones are at 8.30am, 9.30am and 1pm). But it's

more comfortable and enjoyable to do it by taxi, which normally costs 50 GEL round trip from Akhaltiskhe or 120 GEL from Borjomi. Drivers will stop at some of the sights on the way, too.

SAPARA MONASTERY
საფარის მონასტერი

Rivalling Vardzia as one of the most beautiful places to visit in the region (and receiving just a fraction of its visitors), Sapara Monastery has a dramatic position clinging to the edge of a cliff. It has existed from at least the 9th century, and has numbered among its monks many important figures in Georgian ecclesiastical history. At the end of the 13th century Sapara became a possession of the Jakeli family, whose leader, Sargis Jakeli, was adept at staying on good terms with the Mongols, which enabled Samtskhe to enjoy a peace unusual for the time. When he grew old, Sargis took monastic orders and changed his name to Saba. His son Beka built the largest of the 12 churches here, **St Saba's Church**, named after the saint whose name his father had adopted, one of the most architecturally important churches of its time. The 14th-century frescoes inside are of high quality.

The first church on the left as you enter the complex is **St Stephen's**. To the south is the earliest surviving structure, the 10th-century **Dormition Church**, which used to house a famous 11th-century stone iconostasis (altar screen), Kankeli. Three of the very fine reliefs from this are now in the Fine Arts Museum in Tbilisi (p57), and two are in the museum in Akhaltsikhe (p120).

Sapara is about 12km southeast of Akhaltsikhe, off the Vardzia road. The drive is beautiful, and you will have great views of the monastery 2km before you reach it. Taxis charge around 15 GEL for the return trip from Alkhaltsikhe.

GEORGIA DIRECTORY

ACCOMMODATION

Georgian accommodation is getting better all the time and very rarely now will you have to stay in a dowdy Soviet-era hotel with flaking paint and cranky plumbing. Tbilisi has dozens of comfortable, modern, midrange hotels charging between US$50 and US$150 per double room, many of them on a refreshingly small, human scale with attentive, friendly service. It also has a fast-growing number of top-end international chain hotels catering to business and official travellers as well as some tourists with particularly generous budgets. Budget travellers can select from a number of homestays or economical guesthouses, usually with dorm rooms. These are definitely not luxurious, but they're usually kept clean and are well run. They're also great places to meet other travellers, and their owners are often very willing to provide travel advice and some help with arrangements.

In the other cities and main regional towns, the choices are similar but cheaper, and usually without the luxury top-end bracket. In the villages in the mountains and elsewhere, the options are usually limited to homestays. These can provide some of your most enjoyable experiences in Georgia, with a warm welcome, and good home-cooked meals usually available, for a typical price of 25 GEL to 40 GEL per person including breakfast and dinner. You may get a private room or you may be sharing. Most of the better homestays now provide hot-water bathrooms. Even in little-visited places where there is no regular homestay, you will still almost always be able to find a bed in someone's home by asking around.

Camping in Georgia is also popular, and a very cheap way to go. There are very few organised campgrounds but equally few restrictions on wild camping. You should be sensible about where you pitch a tent – in the mountains there can be the threat of bears or wolves. If in doubt ask locals. The best place to camp is often in someone's garden, where you'll be enclosed and probably have access to washing facilities.

ACTIVITIES

Walkers, climbers, horse-riders and bird-watchers will be in heaven in Georgia. There are also opportunities for skiing, mountain biking and rafting. The Caucasus mountains stretched along Georgia's northern border provide a vast playground for anyone looking for active travels.

The outstanding hiking regions are Svaneti, Tusheti and the Kazbegi area in the Caucasus, and the Borjomi-Kharagauli National Park in Samtskhe-Javakheti. There are also good walks around Bakuriani in the hills near Borjomi, and a fascinating new network of trails has

been developed in the upper Mtkvari valley near Vardzia, south of Borjomi. On many routes it's fine to go without a guide, though guides are available almost everywhere and recommended for some of the more difficult and remote routes. Serious trekkers will want to do part or all of the route between Kazbegi and Tusheti via the little-known region of Khevsureti. Many walking routes can be done on horseback too, and horses can be rented in many of the same areas.

Give dogs a wide berth everywhere: Georgian mountain dogs are bred for fending off wolves. Peter Nasmyth's *Walking in the Caucasus – Georgia* is an excellent guide to over 40 day routes all around the country. *Under Eagles' Wings* by Katharina Häberli and Andrew Harker covers mountain, horseback and ski touring routes as well as hikes. The **Georgian Speleologists Union** (www.speleo.ge) has a useful website with interactive maps describing walking and horse-riding routes around the country.

The 5047m Mt Kazbek, near Kazbegi, is a classic adventure for climbers, and not too technical. Mt Chaukhi, east of Kazbegi, also presents many exciting routes. Svaneti is another great mountaineering area: twin-peaked Mt Ushba here is the country's hardest climb – potentially dangerous and only for very serious alpinists.

Georgia has two popular ski resorts, with prices much lower than their European counterparts. Bakuriani is Georgia's favourite 'family skiing' destination, while Gudauri, in the high Caucasus, offers longer runs, more developed facilities and the exciting possibility of heliskiing.

Bird-watchers have a huge variety of habitats to head for, from the wetlands of Kolkheti National Park or the mountains of the Caucasus, with their eagles and vultures, to the semi-desert terrain around Davit Gareja. Excellent resources include **Caucasus Birding** (www.birding-georgia.com) and Lexo Gavashelishvili's *Birdwatching Guide to Georgia, Raptors & Owls of Georgia* and *Vultures of Georgia*.

Rafting is growing in popularity on rivers such as the Pshavis Aragvi, Tetri Aragvi, Mtkvari and Rioni. A day's outing from Tbilisi can cost as little as US$20 per person. Two recommended rafting outfits are **Georgian Adventures and Tours** (www.geoadventures.ge) and **Jomardi Club** (www.joma rdi.ge).

Explore Georgia (p52) is a specialist in activity-based tourism, and other good Georgian tour companies, including Caucasus Travel and GeorgiCa Travel, offer a wide range of active trips.

BOOKS

Disappointingly little Georgian writing has been translated into English, though there are at least four versions of Shota Rustaveli's 12th-century national classic, *The Knight in the Tiger Skin*.

Englishman Donald Rayfield has translated some of Georgia's other leading poets, in volumes such as *Aluda Ketelauri* by Vazha Pshavela and *Georgian Poetry: Titsian and Galaktion Tabidze*.

Perhaps the two most widely published of contemporary Georgian writers both write in Russian and live in Russia.

Several of Boris Akunin's highbrow detective and historical novels in the Erast Fandorin and Sister Pelagia series are available in English, as are Abkhazian Fasil Iskander's *Sandro of Chegem* and *The House Under the Cypress Tree*.

British Georgia-phile Peter Nasmyth provides a great introduction to the country in *Georgia: In the Mountains of Poetry* (revised 2006), roaming Georgia in time and space, covering its past and present (including the Rose Revolution) and visiting many of the places you are likely to see.

'Rogue reporter' Thomas Goltz gives a shrewd and colourful account of events since 1992 in *Georgia Diary* (2006), aptly subtitled *A Chronicle of War & Political Chaos in the Post-Soviet Caucasus*.

A great read for anyone interested in Georgia's section of the Caucasus, with a bit of Azerbaijan and Turkey thrown in too, is Tony Davidson's *Bread and Ashes* (2003), filled with the character of the land and its people. The author walks from Tusheti to Svaneti, with a couple of detours and many fascinating digressions.

The Spiritual Treasure of Georgia (Khelovneba Publishers, 2005) is a lovely coffee-table tome covering the architecture, art and history of nearly 100 of the country's churches, monasteries and convents, with text in both English and Georgian. *National Treasures of Georgia*, edited by Ori G Soltes (2001), is a similarly lavish look at the whole spectrum of Georgian arts and crafts. For out-and-out

history there's *The Making of the Georgian Nation* by Ronald Grigor Suny (1994).

For a practical introduction to the Georgian language, try *Survival Georgian* by Patricia Hall and Tatyana Bukia (1996), or *Georgian* by Nicholas Awde and Thea Khitarishvili (1997).

BUSINESS HOURS

Food shops are usually open every day from about 9am to 9pm. Other shops tend to open from 10am to 7pm Monday to Saturday. Banking hours are typically 9.30am to 5.30pm Monday to Friday, with a one- or two-hour break for lunch.

Typical Georgian restaurant hours are from noon to midnight.

Any exceptions to this are listed for individual restaurants.

CUSTOMS REGULATIONS

Valuable works of art or antiques require a licence from the **Ministry of Culture** (Map p54; ☎ 932295; www.mcs.gov.ge; Sanapiro 4, Tbilisi) if you want to take them out of Georgia. Some galleries and shops will provide this, but private vendors are unlikely to. You may have to pay a heavy export duty.

Arriving in Georgia, any medicines you carry should be for personal use and accompanied by a doctor's statement. In theory you may have to pay import duty on any item of goods worth more than 300 GEL. There is no limit on the amount of any currency you can bring into Georgia, but you are supposed to declare it on a customs form, of which you will get a copy to keep.

The currency amounts declared on entry can be exported without making another declaration. Customs rules are posted on the website of the Georgian **border police** (www.gb g.ge).

EMBASSIES & CONSULATES

Foreign embassies and consulates in Georgia include the following (all in Tbilisi unless stated):

Armenia (Map pp48-9; ☎ 959443; armemb@caucasus.net; Tetelashvili 4; ⏱ 10.30am-1pm Mon-Fri)

Azerbaijan (Map p56; ☎ 252639, 253526; fax 250014; Kipshidze II-Bl No 1; ⏱ 10am-noon Mon-Fri, documents distributed 4-5pm)

China (Map pp48-9; ☎ 252286; zhangling@access.sanet .ge; Barnov 52)

France (Map pp48-9; ☎ 934210, 922851; ambafrance@access .sanet.ge; Gogebashvili 15; ⏱ 9am-1pm & 2-6pm Mon-Thu)

Germany Embassy (Map pp48-9; ☎ 447300; www.tiflis.diplo .de; Sheraton Metechi Palace Hotel, Telavi 20) Consulate (Map pp48-9; ☎ 435399; Davit Aghmashenebeli 166)

Iran (Map p56; ☎ 913656; fax 913628; Chavchavadzis gamziri 80; ⏰ 10am-1pm Mon-Fri)

Israel (Map pp48-9; ☎ 964457; tbilisi.mfa.gov.il; Davit Aghmashenebeli 61)

Netherlands (Map pp48-9; ☎ 276200; www.dutchembassy .ge; Sheraton Metechi Palace Hotel, Telavi 20)

Russia Embassy (Map p56; ☎ 912406; www.georgia.mid.ru; Chavchavadzis gamziri 51) Consulate (Map p56; ☎ 912782; Chavchavadzis gamziri 53)

Turkey Embassy (Map p56; ☎ 252072, 252076; fax 220666; Chavchavadzis gamziri 35; ⏰ 10am-12.30pm & 2-4.30pm Mon-Fri) Consulate (Map p90; ☎ 222-74790; Memed Abashidze 8, Batumi)

Ukraine (Map p56; ☎ 311161; emb_ge@mfa.gov.ua; Oniashvili 75)

UK (Map pp48-9; ☎ 274747; www.britishembassy.gov.uk /georgia; GMT Plaza, Tavisuplebis moedani 4; ⏰ 9am-1pm & 2-5pm Mon-Fri)

USA (☎ 277000; georgia.usembassy.gov; George Balanchine 11, Didi Dighomi, Tbilisi; ⏰ 9am-6pm Mon-Fri)

Details of other embassies and consulates in Georgia, as well as Georgian embassies in other countries, are on the website of the **Georgian Foreign Ministry** (www.mfa. gov.ge).

FESTIVALS & EVENTS

Every region of Georgia has its special festivities. Here are some of the main ones:

Mariamoba (28 August) Day of the Assumption of the Virgin Mary, celebrated nationwide.

Alaverdoba (September) Kakheti's main religious celebrations, focusing on Alaverdi Cathedral and lasting three weeks, climaxing on 14 September.

Mtskhetoba (14 October) Mtskheta's significance is underlined by the fact that its annual festival is also a national holiday.

Wine Festival (one weekend in October) In Sighnaghi.

Tbilisoba (last weekend in October) All Tbilisi moves into party mode.

HOLIDAYS

New Year's Day 1 January
Orthodox Christmas Day 7 January
Epiphany 19 January
Mother's Day 3 March
Women's Day 8 March
Orthodox Easter Sunday & Monday April or May; dates vary according to the church calendar
National Unity Day/Independence Restoration Day 9 April
Victory Day 9 May
Independence Day 26 May

Mariamoba (Assumption) 28 August
Svetitskhovloba (Day of Svetitskhoveli Cathedral, Mtskheta) 14 October
Giorgoba (St George's Day) 23 November

INTERNET RESOURCES

georgien.blogspot.com Huge number of links to news sites, blogs etc.

www.aboutgeorgia.net Good for cultural and historical background, with interesting maps.

www.civil.ge An excellent news site, with stories from many different sources.

www.tourism.gov.ge The official tourism site sings Georgia's praises in words and pictures but is short on useful practical detail.

www.tourism-association.ge The developing site of the Georgian Tourism Association covers homestays, active tourism and more.

The websites of some of Georgia's TV stations (p126) and its English-language newspapers (below) are excellent sources of news, features and listings in English.

MAPS

Good topographic maps are important if you are trekking or climbing. The best currently available are Soviet military 1:50,000 sheets produced in the 1970s and '80s. You can buy them by email or in person for 5 GEL per sheet (there are around 260 different sheets for Georgia) from Geoland in Tbilisi, which is also a source of other good Georgia maps (see p50).

MEDIA

The Georgian media is probably the freest in the Caucasus. While scrutiny of the government is generally seen as beneficial for the country's democracy, the standard of journalism is variable and some outlets are owned by business figures with their own agendas to pursue. There are also some complaints of government pressure on independently owned media.

Newspapers

The main daily newspapers in Georgian are *24 Saati* (24 Hours), *Rezonansi* (Resonance) and *Sakartvelos Respublika* (Republic of Georgia). The daily *Svobodnaya Gruzia* (Free Georgia) is the main Russian newspaper.

A surprising number of English-language newspapers is available in Tbilisi. Brightest and breeziest is *Georgia Today* (www.georgia today.ge), which comes out on Friday with a

GEORGIA

mix of straight news, features and the excellent *Tbilisi Life* supplement. The daily *Messenger* (www.messenger.com.ge) is reasonably good on news and entertainment listings. The *Georgian Times* (www.geotimes.ge), published on Monday, is pretty dry, but its website has up-to-date news in English.

Radio

The government-funded **Georgian Public Broadcasting** (www.gpb.ge) has two stations: Sazogadoebrivi Radio (Public Radio; 102.4FM) has a worthy mix of news and talk, while Radio 2 (100.9FM) is mainly music, for a mainly middle-aged and older audience. The independent Radio 105 (105FM) and Radio 1 (106.4FM) play music with a broader appeal.

TV

You'll find around 10 Georgian channels on most TVs, including some regional ones, and usually at least one Russian channel. **Georgian Public Broadcasting** (www.gpb.ge) operates two national channels: the main one, Sazogadoebrivi Televizia (Public TV), includes news, documentaries, debates and sport.

Privately owned channels tend to get bigger audiences, especially **Rustavi 2** (www.rustavi2.com.ge), whose broadcasting played a big part in the Rose Revolution, and **Imedi TV** (www.imedinews.ge), part owned by Georgian tycoon Badri Patarkatsishvili and Rupert Murdoch's News Corporation, which became a thorn in the flesh of the Saakashvili government.

MONEY

The currency of Georgia is the lari (GEL). It's relatively steady, and was valued at 1.76 to the US dollar in 2007. One lari is made up of 100 tetri (still referred to by many people as kopecks!). Bank notes come in denominations of one, two, five, 10, 20, 50, 100, 200 and 500 lari; coins are one, two, five, 10, 20 and 50 tetri, and one and two lari.

ATMs, generally accepting MasterCard, Visa, Cirrus and Maestro cards, are plentiful in cities and most towns.

They all issue lari and a few will dispense US dollars as well. There are also plenty of small money-exchange offices in most towns and cities; they usually take US dollars, euros or Russian roubles.

It's useful to have some of these currencies in cash for times when there isn't a convenient ATM nearby. You can make purchases with credit cards at the better hotels, restaurants and some shops in Tbilisi, but much less frequently outside the capital. Travellers cheques can be exchanged only in some banks.

TELEPHONE

The Georgian landline network is ancient, and almost everyone has a mobile phone. You can make calls to landlines within a town from antiquated street phones using a 10-tetri coin. To call a mobile phone or outside the city you'll need to find a call centre.

Mobile Phones

Anyone with a mobile phone can easily get a SIM card for a Georgian phone network. If you're spending a couple of weeks in the country, this is well worthwhile. SIM cards usually cost just 5 GEL, and the three main networks are **Magti** (www.magticom.ge), **Geocell** (www.geocell.ge) and **Beeline** (www.georgia.beeline.net) – see p52 for their principal outlets in Tbilisi. Geocell has the widest coverage, with Magti close behind.

Once you have a Georgian SIM card you can add credit by buying cards with scratch-off codes for units of 5 GEL or more from many shops and kiosks.

Most mobile calls within Georgia, to mobile or fixed phones, cost around 0.28 GEL per minute.

Phone Codes
CALLING GEORGIAN FIXED PHONES

Most Georgian cities have two area codes: one for when you are calling from other countries (usually starting with 3), and another for calls from inside Georgia (usually starting with 2). The Tbilisi city codes are ☎ 32 (international) and ☎ 22 (domestic). Tbilisi fixed phones have six-digit numbers. All other places have five-digit numbers (and three-digit city or area codes).

To call a Georgian fixed phone from outside Georgia, dial the country code (☎ 995), followed by the city or town's international area code, then the number.

To call a fixed phone from another fixed phone in the same Georgian town, just dial the five- or six-digit local number. To call a fixed phone from another fixed phone in a different Georgian town, or from a mobile, dial the long-distance access code (☎ 8), then the town's domestic area code, then the local number.

CALLING GEORGIAN MOBILE NUMBERS

Georgian mobile-phone numbers have nine digits, starting with 8. To call from outside Georgia, dial the country code (☎ 995), followed by the last eight digits of the mobile number (omit the initial 8). To call a Georgian mobile from within Georgia (from a landline or another mobile), just dial the full nine-digit mobile number.

INTERNATIONAL CALLS FROM GEORGIA

To call internationally from a Georgian fixed phone, dial ☎ 8, then ☎ 10, then the country code, the area code and the number. International calls from Georgian mobiles may require varying prefixes: from Geocell phones it's ☎ + followed by the country code, the area code and the number. Service providers can give you further information.

VISAS

Citizens of EU countries, the USA, Canada, Japan, Israel, Switzerland, Norway, Iceland, Liechtenstein, Andorra, San Marino, Turkey, Kuwait, Qatar, Bahrain, the United Arab Emirates, Oman, South Korea and CIS nations (except Russia) need no visa to visit Georgia for up to 90 days.

If you're not from one of the above countries, you can get a visa from a Georgian embassy or consulate.

Visas are also issued at the official road and air (but not rail or sea) entry points into Georgia.

The standard fee for a 90-day, single-entry 'ordinary' visa, which covers tourism, is 60 GEL or its equivalent. Double-entry 90-day visas (only available at consulates) are 90 GEL.

Visa-issuing procedures are pretty straightforward and can normally be completed in a matter of minutes at entry points to Georgia, although consulates require a few days for processing.

Border Crossings

Georgia's international entry and exit points are as follows. Visas, for those who need them, are available at the road and air entry points only.

Batumi International airport (visas available) and Black Sea port (visas not available).

Böyük Kəsik Rail border with Azerbaijan – visas not available here.

Guguti/Tashir Road border with Armenia.

Krasny Most (Red Bridge, Tsiteli Khidi, Qırmızı Körpü) Road border with Azerbaijan.

Ninotsminda/Bavra Road border with Armenia.

Poti Black Sea port – visas not available here.

Sadakhlo/Bagratashen Road and rail border with Armenia – visas available for road travellers only.

Sarpi/Sarp Road border with Turkey.

Tbilisi International airport.

Tsodna (Postbina) Road border with Azerbaijan, between Lagodekhi and Balakən.

Vale/Posof Road border with Turkey, reached via Akhaltsikhe.

The border with Russia at Zemo Larsi/Chertov Most, north of Kazbegi, was only open to Georgians and Russians for several years until 2006, when Russia closed it ('temporarily') to everybody.

The crossings from Russia into South Ossetia (the Roki Tunnel) and Abkhazia (Psou River between Gantiadi and Adler) are considered illegal by Georgia. Some travellers who continued on into Georgia after entering South Ossetia or Abkhazia from Russia have been fined or jailed. Others have got away without problems.

Visas for Onward Travel

Twenty-one-day tourist visas for Armenia are issued in a few minutes at land entry points into Armenia for US$30.

The same visa from the Armenian embassy in Tbilisi costs US$51 and takes two working days.

Azerbaijan visas (€60 for many nationalities, US$100 for US citizens and US$101 for British citizens) are issued on arrival at Baku airport, but if you are going by land you need to arrange a visa in advance. The Azerbaijan embassy in Tbilisi issues them in three working days.

None of the Central Asian countries has embassies in Tbilisi, so it's best to get their visas before you come, though you can apply in Baku for Kazakhstan and Uzbekistan visas (you'll need an invitation letter or tourist voucher for Uzbekistan, and sometimes for Kazakhstan).

Iranian visas are most easily obtained with the help of agencies such as **Persian voyages** (www.persianvoyages.com) – allow at least two weeks for preparation before you actually apply. For

GEORGIA

Turkey, most Westerners either need no visa or can obtain it quickly at the border.

WORK

Many foreign businesses and international organisations, including NGOs and charities, operate in Georgia and run their Caucasus operations from Tbilisi. If you want to look for work with them in Georgia, you should contact their offices outside the country.

There are few direct employment opportunities for foreigners in Georgia, save teaching English. Organisations with large presences in Georgia include the UN, the Organization for Security and Co-operation in Europe (OSCE) and the International Red Cross.

Armenia

MICHAEL KOHN

Armenia ՀԱՅԱՍՏԱՆ

Although Armenians carry a lot of psychological baggage from a traumatic 20th century, you'd hardly notice it from a quick tour around the country. The rapidly modernizing capital, the boutique tourism industry and the warm welcome you'll receive everywhere seems to belie the country's reputation for tragedy. Rather than letting past woes weigh it down, Armenia has built its memorials, dusted itself off and moved on. Politicians have set their sights on EU membership, while businessmen are enjoying a booming economy dubbed the 'Caucasian Tiger'.

For travellers, easily visited highlights include ancient monasteries, candle-lit churches and high-walled forts – but lasting impressions lie more with the Armenians themselves. You'll easily find friends among these gracious, humble and easygoing people, even without a common language. Ties are best forged around a dinner table, where endless rounds of toasting accompany a meal bursting with fresh vegetables and grilled meats.

Delving deeper into the country reveals a nation with a complex dichotomy. Despite its robust economy and liberalism (for this part of the world), it's simultaneously held back by oligarch attitudes and old feuds with neighbouring countries. It's a tough neighbourhood but Armenia seems to have made the best of it, thanks in part to a supportive diaspora stretching from Sydney to LA.

Much of the current tourist traffic comprises diaspora Armenians seeking a slice of their homeland. Their high standards enticed some international hotel chains and caused over-development in places like Sevan. Yet it's still easy to escape to some hidden gems, including stalactite-filled caves and summer villages inhabited by Yezidi Kurds and Armenian shepherds. As most travellers whiz through on a brief side trip between other places, serious explorers will have the best sights to themselves.

FAST FACTS

- **Area** 29,800 sq km
- **Capital** Yerevan
- **Famous for** Cognac, turbulent history, being the first Christian nation
- **Official name** Hayastan, Hayastani Hanrapetutyan (Republic of Armenia)
- **Phrases** *Barev dzez* (Hello), *Genats!* (Cheers!)
- **Population** 3,215,800

HIGHLIGHTS

■ **Yerevan** (p145) – A lively cultural life, buzzing late-night café scene and some fine museums smooth out some of the Soviet stylings of the Armenian capital.

■ **Lori** (p195)– This northern region offers spectacular scenery at every turn; forests, canyons (such as the incredible Debed Canyon; p199), and a stunning string of medieval monasteries, including Sanahin (p201) and Haghpat (p201).

■ **Goris** (p213) – Armenia's prettiest rural town, with 19th century architecture, hidden leafy lanes and ancient cave dwellings on its outskirts. The incredible Tatev Monastery is a short drive away.

■ **Dilijan** (p190) – Forested mountain retreat town with pleasant accommodation, burgeoning tourist facilities and great walks near monasteries like Haghartsin and Goshavank.

■ **Vayots Dzor** (p206)– A region peppered with historic and natural beauty including Noravank church (p207) and Yeghegis village (p209), plus caves, wineries and the relaxing mineral baths at Jermuk (p210).

ITINERARIES

■ **Three Days** - There's lots to do and see around Yerevan: take in live music at a concert or restaurant, and shop for brandy, *oghee* (fruit vodka) and handicrafts. Take short day trips to Garni and Geghard, Khor Virap or a longer one to Lake Sevan and Dilijan.

■ **One Week** - Travel up to Lori to the awesome World Heritage–listed Haghpat and Sanahin churches, stay in Vanadzor or Dilijan, or concentrate on the best of the south – Tatev and Noravank in particular.

■ **Two Weeks** - Take some time around Yeghegnadzor and taste more of Yerevan's cosmopolitanism, organise a village or town homestay, explore more of Dilijan, or head for Sisian and Goris in the south.

■ **One Month** - Allows you to explore more off the beaten track places like Yeghegis, Meghri, Ijevan and Gyumri. Take time for some day hikes, spelunking in Vayots Dzor or climbing on Mt Aragats.

CLIMATE & WHEN TO GO

Most of Armenia has a dry, high-altitude climate except for verdant rainy pockets in Lori, Tavush and Syunik. Spring (March to

---

ARMENIA INDEX

■ Litre of petrol AMD650

■ Litre of bottled water AMD200

■ Bottle of beer AMD230

■ Souvenir T-shirt AMD3000

■ Street treat – *lahmajoon* (lamb and herb pizza) AMD100, *khoravats* (barbecued food) AMD1700

May) has more flowers but autumn (late September to early November) has long, warm days and more stable weather. It's also the time of harvest festivals and delicious fresh produce – Yerevan averages 27°C in both seasons. Summer (June to August) in Yerevan can be 40°C for days at a time, while conditions can be radically different in the north. Lake Sevan has a short summer – late June to September – but is Canadian during winter: -10°C on average. Winter weather lasts until April or May over much of the country. See p312 for details.

CURRENT EVENTS

Despite its limited resources Armenia has become a master at geopolitics. What other country in the world can say it maintains good relations with the United States, Russia and Iran? Recognising Armenia's small but influential role as a moderating force in the region, the US has moved swiftly to forge lasting ties, evinced by its huge new embassy in Yerevan (on 8.9 hectares of land) and incorporation of Armenia into its Millennium Challenge Account, a multi-billion-dollar aid package that rewards developing countries that have met certain requirements, such as press freedom, democracy and government transparency.

Meanwhile, Iran continues to bolster trade ties with Armenia and has signed multi-million-dollar energy and transit deals, including a natural gas pipeline and oil refinery. Russia, the main energy supplier until now, has upped the ante with a deal to build a new nuclear reactor at Metsamor. Russia also maintains a military base near Gyumri and posts its soldiers along Armenia's borders with Turkey and Iran.

While Armenia shoulders up to the big boys of international trade and energy it remains mired in old feuds with its neighbours

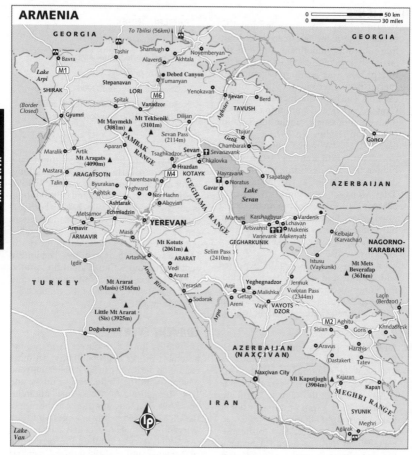

ARMENIA

that make the Montagues and the Capulets seem like bosom buddies.

On the one side stands Turkey and the long-simmering genocide argument. The issue flares up every so often, as it did in 2006 when French law made it a crime to deny the genocide, and again in 2007 when the US House Committee on Foreign Affairs approved a bill to condemn the genocide. More often than not it is the diaspora that pushes this agenda. As the actual events slide into history, modern Armenians still pay the price as diplomatic relations are frozen and the border closed.

Still, free marketeers have found ways around the blockade and manage to import Turkish goods via Georgia.

Recent comments by Turkish Prime Minister Recep Tayyıp Erdoğan that the two sides jointly investigate history hold promise of a thaw. Some Armenians also wonder if a message of good-neighbourly love was cryptically hidden in Eurovision song contest voting. At the 2007 contest Turkey was the only country to give Armenian singer Hayko a maximum score of 12 (who were those judges anyway?).

There is less promise for rapprochement on Armenia's eastern border, where the relationship with Azerbaijan is downright poisonous. Official fighting between the two countries ended in 1994 but the matter still feels closer to war than peace. The status quo – with Armenia officially occupying 16% of

Azerbaijan and negotiations at a standstill – is likely to last for some time.

Closer to home, hot topics routinely surround the booming local economy. With GDP growth rates at around 13% it is growing faster than most markets in Europe – much of the credit has been given to former president Robert Kocharian. The pace of reform shows on the streets of Yerevan, where expensive clothing and cars are everywhere and competition is rife to flash the hottest new designs. Fashion addicts have likewise dispersed themselves into rural areas, where it's not uncommon to see women in stiletto heels and men with pointy-toed leather shoes traipsing through dusty mountain villages.

Economic improvement paved the way for a 60% rise in pensions in 2008, but with per capita income at around US$5700 Armenia still has a long way to go to catch up with Europe. The idea of joining the EU has been thrown around with much interest but given the level of poverty that still exists (around 30%), the high levels of corruption and the shaky democracy, no one is holding their breath.

Other hot topics include Armenia's push to increase its population, by natural means or otherwise. In 2007 parliament passed a dual-nationality bill in hopes of luring diaspora Armenians and foreigners married to Armenians. The Western money that would flood in with the repatriates could be another boost to the economy – Armenia already rakes in around US$5 billion in remittances.

Parliamentary elections in 2007, won by the conservative Republican Party, indicates popular support for the pro-Russian hierarchy and paved the way for Prime Minister Serge Sargsyan to win the presidential election in February 2008. Sargsyan, a former defence minister and war hero in Karabakh, is of the same mould as Kocharian and is likely to build on his predecessor's reforms.

HISTORY
In the Beginning...
Like all countries ancient, Armenia has a murky origin. According to Bible lore Armenians are the descendents of Hayk, great-great-grandson of Noah, whose ark grounded on Mt Ararat after the flood. In recognition of their legendary ancestry, Armenians have since referred to their country as Hayastan, land of the Hayk tribe. Greek records first mention Armenians in the 6th century BC as a tribe living in the area of Lake Van.

The Armenian highlands north of the Fertile Crescent had long been inhabited, and historians believe that local advances in mining, chemical and metallurgical technologies were major contributions to civilisation. With invasion routes open in four directions, the early Armenian kings fought intermittent wars against Persia and the Mediterranean powers. Greek and Roman cultures mixed with Persian angel-worship and Zoroastrianism.

In the 1st century BC the borders of Armenia reached their greatest extent under Tigranes II, whose victories over the Persian Seleucids gave him land from modern Lebanon and Syria to Azerbaijan.

Christianity & the Written Word
The local religious scene in Armenian villages attracted Christian missionaries as early as AD 40, including the apostles Bartholomew and Thaddeus. According to lore, King Trdat III declared Christianity the state religion in AD 301. His moment of epiphany came after being cured of madness by St Gregory the Illuminator, who had spent 12 years imprisoned in a snake-infested pit, now located under Khor Virap Monastery (p176). A version preferred by historians suggests that Trdat was striving to create national unity while fending off Zoroastrian Persia and pagan Rome. Whatever the cause, the church has been a pillar of Armenian identity ever since.

Another pillar of nationhood arrived in 405 with Mesrop Mashtots' revolutionary Armenian alphabet. His original 36 letters were also designed as a number system. Armenian traders found the script indispensable in business. Meanwhile, medieval scholars translated scientific and medical texts from Greek and Latin.

Kingdoms & Conquerors
Roman and Persian political influence gave way to new authority when western Armenia fell to Constantinople in 387 and eastern Armenia to the Sassanids in 428. The Arabs arrived around 645 and pressure slowly mounted from Baghdad to convert to Islam. When the Armenians resisted they were taxed to the point where many left for Roman-ruled territories, joining Armenian communities in a growing diaspora.

ARMENIA

ARARAT: ARMENIA'S HEART OF STONE   *Arpi Armenakian Shively*

Many diasporan Armenians are surprised by the strength of their emotions on seeing Mt Ararat for the first time. 'We grew up seeing only pictures in school textbooks,' says Moses Elmadjian, who was born in Cyprus, 'so when I finally saw the real mountain in my 80s, I was moved to tears.'

Armenians tell many affectionate legends about Mt Ararat. Azadour Guzelian, a retired Armenian-language newspaper editor based in London, has a favourite: 'The night after the Flood waters subsided, Noah went out drinking with his sons, and lost his trousers. According to legend they are still out there, buried under centuries of snow.' Perhaps the first vineyard, reputed to have sprung up here after the Flood, yielded particularly potent grapes.

The mountain's soaring heights and plunging abysses have generated myths and cult worship for thousands of years, and the mystique continues today. In paintings and photographs, on backgammon boards and tea trays wherever Armenian families call home, Ararat's twin peaks are rooted in the national psyche. Canadian-Armenian film-maker Atom Egoyan's 2002 movie, *Ararat*, commemorates the genocide. Armenian-American rock band System of a Down wrote a track, 'Holy Mountain', on the same theme. The mountain has featured in several literary novels, poems, screenplays and even computer battle games: Kurt Vonnegut's novel *Bluebeard* refers to the mountain, and British novelist Julian Barnes weaves plot lines around it in *A History of the World in 10½ Chapters*. Mt Ararat may be the sacred, icy Mt Arreat of PC-based game *Diablo II* and is the site of an epic battle in a video game called *Keio Flying Squadron*.

The words of early-20th-century poet Yeghishe Charents, inscribed on the triumphal arch at one end of Republic Sq, frame a view of Ararat with appropriate sentiment: 'You may look the world over and never find such a mountain…'.

Better conditions emerged in the 9th century when the Caliph approved the resurrection of an Armenian monarch in King Ashot I, the first head of the Bagratuni dynasty. Ani (now in Turkey) served as capital for a stint. Various invaders including the Seljuk Turks and Mongols took turns plundering and at times ruling and splitting Armenia.

By the 17th century Armenians were scattered across the empires of Ottoman Turkey and Persia, with diaspora colonies from India to Poland. The Armenians rarely lived in a unified empire, but stayed in distant mountain provinces where some would thrive while others were depopulated. The seat of the Armenian Church wandered from Echmiadzin to Lake Van and further west for centuries.

The Armenian Question

The Russian victory over the Persian Empire, around 1828, brought the territory of the modern-day Armenian republic under Christian rule, and Armenians began immigrating to the region. The tsarist authorities tried to break the Armenian Church's independence, but conditions were still preferable to those in Ottoman Turkey, where many Armenians still lived. When the latter

pushed for more rights, Sultan Abdulhamid II responded in 1896 by massacring between 80,000 and 300,000 Armenians.

The European powers had talked often about the 'Armenian Question', considering the Armenians a fellow Christian people living within the Ottoman Empire. During WWI some Ottoman Armenians sided with Russia in the hope of establishing their own nation state. A triumvirate of pashas who had wrested control of the Empire viewed these actions as disloyal, and ordered forced marches of all Armenian subjects into the Syrian deserts. What is less certain – and remains contentious to this day – is whether they also ordered pogroms and issued a decree for Armenians to be exterminated. Armenians today claim that there was a specific order to commit genocide; Turks strenuously deny this. What is inescapable is the fact that between 1915 and 1922 around 1.5 million Ottoman Armenians died.

The first independent Armenian republic emerged in 1918, after the November 1917 Russian Revolution saw the departure of Russian troops from the battlefront with Ottoman Turkey. It immediately faced a wave of starving refugees, the 1918 influenza epidemic, and wars with surrounding Turkish,

Azeri and Georgian forces. It fought off the invading Turks in 1918, and left the final demarcation of the frontier to Woodrow Wilson, the US president. Meanwhile, the Turks regrouped under Mustafa Kemal (later Kemal Ataturk) and overran parts of the Caucasus. Wilson's map eventually arrived without troops or any international support, while Ataturk offered Lenin peace in exchange for half of the new Armenian republic. Beset by many other enemies, Lenin agreed.

The Armenian government, led by the Dashnaks, a party of Armenian independence fighters, capitulated to the Bolsheviks in 1921. They surrendered in order to preserve the last provinces of ancient Armenia. The Soviet regime hived off Karabakh and Naxçıvan (Nakhchivan) for Azerbaijan. Forced from their homes, hundreds of thousands of survivors regrouped in the French-held regions of Syria and Lebanon, emigrating en masse to North America and France. Remarkably, the Armenians who stayed began to rebuild with what was left, laying out Yerevan starting in the 1920s. Armenia did well in the late Soviet era, with lots of technological industries and research institutes.

Independence

The debate over the Armenian-majority region of Nagorno-Karabakh inside Azerbaijan brought a new wave of leaders to the fore under Gorbachev's *glasnost* reforms. Armenians voted for independence on 21 September 1991, and Levon Ter-Petrossian, a 40-year-old scholar and leader of the Karabakh Committee, became president. The war with Azerbaijan over Karabakh exploded just as the economy went into freefall. See the Nagorno-Karabakh chapter (p300) for more information on the conflict.

After the war, rumours of coups and assassination attempts prompted Ter-Petrossian to reverse civil rights and throw Dashnak leaders and fighters from the Karabakh War into jail, where some spent three years as political prisoners. Ter-Petrossian was re-elected for another five-year term in 1996 but resigned in 1998, isolated and unpopular.

He was replaced by Robert Kocharian in March 1998, a war hero from southern Karabakh. Kocharian entered the war with one tank and amassed 13 more by the time of the ceasefire. Kocharian quickly moved

to woo back the diaspora, especially the influential Dashnak faction.

By the end of the 1990s the new class of wealthy import barons stood out in shocking contrast to the country's poverty. Anger over this disparity was at least partly responsible for the terrible 1999 massacre in the national assembly, when gunmen, screaming that the barons were drinking the blood of the nation, murdered eight members of parliament and wounded six others. The event sparked a wave of emigration and endless recriminations, but the 1700th anniversary of the founding of the Armenian Church in 2001 marked something of a turning point in the country's fortunes. Memories of the suffering and upheaval since independence linger on, but the rapid economic revival through the 2000s has raised spirits.

PEOPLE
The National Psyche

Visitors are struck by how European Yerevan feels – with cafés, swish clothes, chamber orchestras and churches – but out in the countryside the social attitudes are quite Middle Eastern. The alphabet and language support a deep Christian piety and an intense love of learning and intellectual achievement. Russian poet Osip Mandelstam (1891–1938) said the Armenian language has boots of stone that won't wear out. There is also a sadness to Armenia that underpins the enjoyment of sunshine, music and brandy. Peace with Azerbaijan over Karabakh seems as distant as ever, and the Turkish land border looks no closer to being opened. People feel this suits a small number of import barons to the exclusion of anyone else. Armenians are famously relaxed and unbothered by upheaval; when asked why Armenia hasn't had a postindependence revolution a la Ukraine or Georgia, the answer is all too obvious – after an hour of riveting talk everyone would end up back at their favourite café.

Daily Life

In the clubs and mansions of Nork in Yerevan, the elite text each on cell phones, hang out at the latest new cafés and shop on fashionable Abovyan Poghots. Money comes in from everywhere to keep the country alive – sons in Moscow, daughters in Greece, cousins in Glendale, Toronto and Sydney. Although the national income has climbed back to where it was in the Soviet era, the distribution of wealth is now wildly uneven. Out in the grim factory towns around Lake Sevan, life is a lottery. Jobs are nonexistent, and a whole generation has emigrated to work overseas. The least affected seem to be people from the country, who can usually feed themselves from the land parcelled out to them soon after independence.

Armenian work culture is happily relaxed. People might stay out until midnight, arrive at work the next day at 10am or 10.30am, pop out for an hour or two to pay the bills, and leave work around 6pm. This relaxed attitude to time stretches to appointments – an hour late is no big deal – and to restaurants, where waiters let you linger over coffee or drinks for hours before you ask for the bill.

Population

Accurate population figures are a matter of some debate in Armenia. In 2005 the population was estimated at 3,215,800 people. There were 3.8 million in 1979; another census was held in 1989 but the figures were disrupted by the 1988 earthquake. With the departure of the Azeris and the arrival of Armenians from Azerbaijan pushing the total as high as four million in the early 1990s, it means one million have left since independence, or a quarter of the total. There has been a large exodus from rural areas isolated by the new frontiers, such as Syunik and the Shamshadin region, to Yerevan and abroad.

About one third of the population lives in Yerevan, and more than half in the Ararat Plains within a 60km radius of the capital. Armenians make up 93% of the population, Russians 2%, and Yezidi Kurds, Assyrians and Greeks make up the rest. There is a small

diasporan Armenian community in Yerevan, sometimes called repatriates, different from earlier diasporan generations who arrived after WWII.

Multiculturalism

Over the last 200 years the territory of modern-day Armenia has shifted from encompassing a Muslim majority to an almost monoethnically Armenian population. Indeed, the official motto of modern Armenia is 'One Nation, One Culture'.

In 1828 Armenians made up perhaps 30% of the population, outnumbered by Azeris, Turks and Kurds. Waves of immigration after the Russian conquest pushed this up to about 70% by 1918, when the first republic was declared. More immigrants arrived after WWII, but as recently as 1988 there were Azeri-majority regions on the eastern shore of Lake Sevan and in the corner of Shirak *marz* (region) around Lake Arpi, plus scattered villages across the country. The mutual ethnic cleansing by Armenia and Azerbaijan between 1988 and 1994 removed pretty much all of the 300,000-odd Muslims, and many place names changed from Turkic to Armenian. Other minorities, including Russians and other Soviet nationalities, also departed.

Today non-Armenians make up less than 5% of the total. There are Assyrian Christians in and around Yerevan, members of an Oriental Orthodox Church like the Armenian Church. The half-Assyrian village of Arzni is just north of Yerevan.

The 80,000 or so Yezidi Kurds have their own distinct culture and religious beliefs, following an ancient Gnostic faith, a living link to Zoroastrianism. A company of Yezidi

---

A YEN FOR YAN (OR IAN)

The vast majority of Armenian surnames end in '-ian' or '-yan'. The former is usually western Armenian, the latter eastern, though it's not a set rule. The suffix means 'from' or 'of', either from a town (Marashlian from Marash; Vanetsian from Van), from a parent (Davidian, son of David), from an occupation (Najarian, son of a carpenter; Boyajian, from the Turkish word 'boyaj' for someone who dyes fabrics), or from status or personal traits (Melikyan, son of a king; Sinanian, from a Turkish term for a well-endowed gent). Names with the prefix 'Ter' mean a married priest (Ter Hayr) was an ancestor, eg ex-president Levon Ter-Petrossian. Western Armenian names may spell it 'Der', as in Der-Bedrossian. There are also families with the suffix '-runi', such as Siruni and Artsruni. These families were once aristocrats.

In this chapter we've commonly translated the last three letters of a surname as 'yan', except if that person was western Armenian or if that is the way their name most commonly appears, eg Robert Kocharian and Martiros Sarian.

KIRK KERKORIAN

There's a local joke that if Azerbaijan has oil, Armenia has Kirk Kerkorian (b 1917). The American billionaire casino magnate has channelled upwards of US$180 million through his Lincy Foundation. One of Kerkorian's earlier coups was as boss of MGM studios in the 1970s, when he green-lighted *Midnight Express,* a chilling tale of brutal Turkish justice and prisons written by Oliver Stone. The depiction of Turkey mixed insult (the mostly Greek and Armenian actors spoke an invented gibberish) with a classic story of survival, which is why it still resonates with audiences and Turkey's international image today. Since 2000 the Lincy Foundation has funded the completion of the Sevan–Dilijan tunnel, repaired major roads in Yerevan and across the country, and built apartments to finally house people made homeless by the 1988 earthquake in and around Gyumri, and has also run social programs and business lending schemes. Kerkorian has helped before – during the 1990s when the Turkish-Azeri blockade cut energy supplies, Kerkorian matched diaspora donations dollar for dollar. His money and his faith in Armenia have given diasporan-Armenian relations a huge boost, and single-handedly improved Armenia's economy. In 2005 President Robert Kocharian awarded Kerkorian with the nation's highest honour, the Medal of Fatherland.

---

cavalry fought alongside the Armenians at the battle of Sardarapat in 1918. In the last 100 years most of their villages have been emptied across Turkey and Iraq. Some Kurds, in the Ararat Valley especially, are Christian and becoming assimilated – Kurdish women wearing traditional floral headscarves and bright layers of skirts aren't such a common sight these days. Yerevan is home to the world's oldest Kurdish newspaper, *Rza Taza.* Yezidi herders on the Aragats highlands around Aparan and Talin still graze sheep and goats on the high summer meadows, but these traditions are under threat as the old rangelands are sold up and fenced off.

The Molokans (Milk Drinkers) are a sect of Russian Old Believers split from the Russian Orthodox Church in the 16th century, a bit like Russian Protestants. They're well regarded for their honesty, piety and excellent farm produce. They number about 5000, down from 50,000 20 years ago – many left for Russia and Canada.

Armenian Diaspora

The majority of Armenians live outside historic Armenia, a process that goes back centuries to colonies across Asia and Europe but is mostly due to the 1915–23 genocide.

There are about eight million Armenians living abroad but only 3,205,000 in Armenia and Karabakh. Tbilisi (Tiflis to Armenians) was a 19th-century Armenian cultural capital, and there are somewhere around 300,000 Armenians in Georgia, including a majority in the Samtskhe-Javakheti region ('Javakhk' in Armenian) north of Gyumri. There are big communities in the USA, Russia (especially Moscow), France and other areas of Europe, Lebanon and Syria, plus others in Canada, Australia and South America. Well-known diasporans in these countries include Cher, Andre Agassi, Charles Aznavour and Gary Kasparov.

There is also an old community in Iran, particularly in Esfahan and Tehran. Remarkably, there is still an Armenian community in Turkey. About 60,000 Armenians live in Istanbul. Vakifli, the last Armenian village in Turkey, stands amid orchards on the slopes of Musa Dagh about 40km from Antakya, not far from the Syrian border. The Hemşin are a Muslim mountain people on the Turkish Black Sea coast who speak a distinct Armenian dialect.

Outside Armenia, Russia and Iran, most Armenians speak western Armenian, which differs from eastern Armenian in grammar, slang and the pronunciation of about eight letters out of 38.

RELIGION

Around 90% of the population align themselves with the Armenian Apostolic Church, with smaller numbers of Armenian Catholics, Russian, Greek and Assyrian Orthodox Churches and the neo-Gnostic Yezidis. The Muslim population is minute.

The differences between the Armenian Apostolic Church and the Catholic and Orthodox faiths are subtle but ancient. The first differences arose in AD 451, when the Armenians were too busy fighting the Persians to attend the worldwide church's Council of

---

OLD TIME RELIGION *Arpi Armenakian Shively*

'Armenians are a people who love to cry,' says Ani Pakradouni of Beirut and Yerevan. 'We celebrate five major memorial days a year in church, as well as the death day of each of our loved ones.' The major holidays are Christmas (Epiphany, January 6), Easter in March or April, the Transfiguration of Christ Day on 19 July, the Feast of the Assumption on 16 August, and Holy Cross (Khatchverats) Day on 14 September.

There has been a revival of churchgoing since Armenia regained independence. 'Not only elderly worshippers either,' says Moses Taslakian. 'In fact, I'd say 80% are under 40 years old.' Although sleek newcomers like St Gregory the Illuminator Church in Yerevan are popular, the older churches, many of which have been around for 700 years or more, are particularly loved. 'As comforting as old slippers,' says Londoner Vartan Armen, after his first visit to Armenia.

Most venerable of all is Holy Echmiadzin, founded in AD 301 by Gregory the Illuminator after a dream in which Jesus selected the site. 'You can feel the weight of centuries of devotion around you,' says Ani Pakradouni.

'The sung Mass at Echmiadzin is the most moving experience,' says Movses Tchaparian. 'The Armenian words, icons and candles and even the smell of incense wrap me in an atmosphere of reverence. I truly feel close to God when I stand near the altar.'

Vartan Armen says non-Orthodox worshippers might find the congregation's comings and goings rather distracting. 'At Echmiadzin, everyone stands. There seems to be no rule about when you arrive or leave. People were still squeezing past us halfway through Mass, walking around, lighting candles, talking to friends. Actually, I think there's something charming about it, like being in God's living room.'

Chalcedon. The Armenians disagreed with the authorities in Constantinople over the nature of Christ. The Armenian Church sees the divine and human nature of Jesus Christ combined in one body (Monophysite), while the Greek Orthodox sees each nature as separate. An Arab caliph proclaimed the Armenian Church to be the most senior of the Oriental Orthodox Monophysite Churches in the 7th century, including the Ethiopian, Assyrian and Egyptian Coptic Churches, which explains the Armenian presence in both Egypt and Ethiopia. The presence of the Oriental Orthodox Church in India led to Armenian communities in cities across that country, especially in Madras (Chennai). While the Armenian Church followed neither Peter nor Helena (Rome nor Constantinople), it sometimes steered closer to Rome in the 12th to 18th centuries.

The Mekhitarist fathers, Armenian Jesuits, started the first Armenian printing press on the isle of San Lazzaro in the Venice lagoon in the 17th century. Armenian Catholics make up about 5% of the total Armenian population, and are relatively well represented in Gyumri and Yerevan.

Nearly all Armenians celebrate Christmas on the Epiphany (the baptism of Jesus) on 6 January. Until the 4th century other Christians did as well, until the church in Rome moved the date to 25 December to absorb a popular pagan bacchanal on that date.

The exception is the Armenian Patriarchate of Jerusalem, which follows the original Julian calendar and celebrates Christmas on 19 January.

The church was assimilated into Communist rule by Stalin in the 1930s, and Catholicos Khoren I died in the Gulags in 1938. During WWII the pressure relented a little, and in the Brezhnev years the church began regaining its ancient independence. During the Cold War the diaspora church fractured between the anti-Communist Catholicosate of Sis, based in Antelias, Lebanon, and the Catholicosate of Echmiadzin in Soviet Armenia. The division has been partly reconciled since independence.

ARTS
Literature
Oral folk tales told during long winter nights in villages, such as the *Daredevils of Sassoun* (an epic tale that would give *Lord of the Rings* a run for its money), were the earliest form of Armenian literature. Mesrop Mashtots' creation of the alphabet in AD 405, for the purpose of writing religious texts, set in place the foundation of written stories. The first

words written in the Armenian alphabet were allegedly 'recognise wisdom and advice, heed the words of a genius'.

Classics include St Grigor Narekatsi's *Book of Lamentations* (also just called the *Narek*), a book of simple, practical ways of prayer written when Narekatsi (951–1003) was ill. Mkhitar Gosh (1130–1213) wrote the *Book of Trials* (a code of law) at Goshavank near Dilijan, the first collection of Armenian civil laws.

Medieval Armenian scientists wrote works such as *Useless for the Ignorant,* a work on medicine. The rise of modern Armenian literature began in the 19th century. Khachatur Abovyan's *Wound of Armenia* novelised the shocks, patriotism and hopes of the nation, with a prescient eye to the events to come early in the next century.

The Armenian-American writer William Saroyan (1908–1981) crafted lively short stories on immigrants and Armenians in California.

When Saroyan visited Soviet Armenia he always put an American flag in front of him at public occasions, saying it was a tribute to the country that gave him a life. *The Daring Young Man on the Flying Trapeze & Other Stories,* published in 1934, is probably his best-known collection. Contemporary American-Armenian historians and writers include Richard Hovhanissian and Peter Balakian.

Hardly any translations of Armenian classics are on sale in Yerevan, so try ordering through www.amazon.com, or through specialists such as the bookstore of the New York-based Armenian General Benevolent Fund (www.agbu.org).

Cinema

The ArmFilm studios on the Ashtarak road out of Yerevan once thrived with productions but are now mostly moribund. Sergei Paradjanov (Parajanian) was born in Tbilisi and adopted the Russian -ov suffix to his name. Frequently out of favour with the culture moguls, he still managed to unleash camp-visionary theatrical films including *Colour of Pomegranates, Sayat-Nova, Ashough Gharib* and *Souram Fortress* in the 1960s and 1970s. The reward for his genius was four years' hard labour in a Soviet prison camp. Two more films followed his release from prison but his final masterpiece, *The Confession,* was left unfinished with his own death. While the films may not have seen success in the USSR, he won fans internationally including Fellini and Bertolucci.

Canadian-Armenian director Atom Egoyan has made several films on Armenian themes, including 1993's *Calendar* and 2002's *Ararat,* a film within a film on the genocide. *Armenia* is typical of Egoyan's arthouse leanings, leaving you wondering about how it all fits together more than the subject matter. You could say the interweaving plot structure is intrinsically very Armenian. *Calendar,* another Egoyan arthouse classic, describes the story of a photographer sent to Armenia to shoot Armenian churches for a calendar. The plot, one of lost love, is filled with twists. Much of the dialogue between the characters was improvised.

Music

Armenian religious music's mythically complex harmonies are partly lost, though there are many fine, melancholy choirs of the Armenian liturgy. The great composers

---

RABIZ PARTY

Rabiz is a contraction of the Russian words *'rabochy sskusstvo'* (workers culture). It's entertainment and it's also a lifestyle – the guys in the silk shirts and gold chains driving too fast while smoking and talking on their mobile phones. If you ask a hip student, they'll say that Armenian popular culture is divided between loud, showy, raucous *rabiz* culture on one hand and everything of good taste on the other. *Rabiz* also covers a lot of highly inventive slang. *Rabiz* music is marshrutka-driver (public minivan transport driver) music, a mix of brainless pop and over-the-top tragic ballads (girl has cancer, boy says he'll kill himself before she dies) that strike a sentimental Middle Eastern chord in Armenian hearts. They want music that will make them cry, as well as impassioned love songs and arms-aloft dancing music. This kind of music booms from taxis in Greek, Russian, Turkish and Arabic. The Armenian variety comes from Los Angeles, Beirut and Moscow as well as Yerevan, where it plays in neighbourhood bars, clubs and *khoravats* (barbecued food) joints late into the night.

of the 19th and 20th centuries include Komitas, whose works for choir and orchestra put Armenian music on an international stage, and Armen Tigranyan for his opera *Anush*. Aram Khachaturian is best known for his *Sabre Dance* and the ballet *Spartacus*. Sayat-Nova, oft considered the greatest singer-songwriter in the Caucasus, began his career in the court of Erekle II of Georgia but was exiled for his forbidden love of the king's daughter. The country is still a centre for classical music, with a ballet theatre, an opera company, orchestras for chamber music and symphonies, and an active world of composers and performers.

Folk music is alive and well in town troupes and late-night clubs and *khoravats* palaces. Spend a night at a popular venue like Ashtarak's Ashtaraki Dzor (p174) complex and marvel at the range of talent. The *duduk*, a double-reed instrument made from apricot wood, will become the soundtrack to your journey in Armenia. Its inescapable trill features in traditional music and many modern pop tunes blaring from the speakers of taxi cabs.

For good traditional music try the RealWorld label, which has albums by *duduk* master Djivan Gasparian. Also try Parik Nazarian, Gevorg Dabagian and the album *Minstrels and Folk Songs of Armenia* by Parseghian Records.

Current artists of note include Lilit Pipoyan, a Joni Mitchell–esque singer and songwriter, and Vahan Artsruni, a composer with folk-guitar pickings who also rocks out in Yerevan's small live-rock scene. Arto Tuncboyaciyan's Armenian Navy Band mixes jazz and folk music on the albums *Bzdik Zinvor* (Little Soldier) and *New Apricot*.

There are plenty of emerging young singers, including Hasmik Karapetyan, Armenia's ver-

ARTHUR GRIGORIAN

Singer Arthur Grigorian has enjoyed a long and illustrious career and is now considered to be the 'godfather of Armenian pop music'. His albums include *The Best of the Best* and *Yesterday, Today and...* Arthur is also a peace advocate and vocal supporter of Nagorno-Karabakh, the native land of his father.

What makes a good musician?

A musician should not lie. They must be honest with themselves, God and their fans. They must be willing to bare their souls.

How do you characterise Armenian music?

Armenian pop incorporates much traditional music. It uses traditional instruments like the *duduk, zurna, shiva* and *bulula* and blends classic rhythms and beats that are familiar to all Armenians.

Why does it borrow so much from the traditional?

Armenia is a small country between much larger neighbours. There has always been the threat that we would lose our culture to Russian, Turkish or Iranian invaders. So our defence has been to clutch what remains Armenian to ward off external influences. Even when we adopted pop music from the West it was important to make it uniquely Armenian. Armenians in Turkey and Iran have mixed their music with Turkish and Iranian sounds, which is something we must try to avoid.

Which artists have influenced you?

Among the Western pop artists, I'd say my guru is Stevie Wonder. He is my musical inspiration. In Armenia I appreciate the music of Komitas.

What do you do when you're not making sweet Armenian music?

I love to fly helicopters and airplanes. In my next life I want to be a professional pilot. My friend is a pilot and I occasionally join him in the cockpit. One time he let me fly the entire route from Yerevan to Belfast – the passengers were Armenia's national soccer team!

What is most important for Armenia?

A peaceful solution in Karabakh. Karabakhis are the bravest, smartest people in the world and they deserve a peaceful and prosperous future. There are many external forces that have played a role in Karabakh but it's time for the Karabakhis to determine their own fate. I pray for peace not only in Karabakh but also in Armenia and Azerbaijan.

KOMITAS & SOGHOMIAN TEHLIRIAN

Two figures from the genocide are particularly well remembered by Armenians. Komitas represents the losses. A *vardapet* (monk) of the Armenian church, Komitas travelled through Armenian villages collecting folk songs; he was the first great ethnomusicologist. He also worked on deciphering the mysteries of medieval Armenian liturgical music. His concerts in Europe in the early 1910s were hailed as the arrival of a distinct national musical tradition. His Liturgy remains unfinished. On 24 April 1915 Komitas was in Istanbul when he was rounded up with 250 other Armenian community leaders and intellectuals. He was one of possibly two to survive – his life was literally bought from the Young Turks by a benefactor and he was smuggled to France. But the atrocities he witnessed broke his mind, and he died in an asylum in Paris in 1937 having never again spoken. His ideas for breathing life into the ancient harmonies and chorales were lost with him.

Soghomian Tehlirian represents a different face of the genocide. After losing his family to the killings he ended up in Berlin in the early 1920s, where, on 15 March 1921, he assassinated the man most responsible for the genocide, Mehmet Talaat Pasha. Talaat Pasha was Minister of War in 1915, and founder of the covert Teshkilati Mahsusa (Special Organisation), which among other things recruited psychotic killers from prisons to serve on the deportations. Tehlirian's trial was one of the few public vindications of the genocide. Survivors and witnesses gave testimony on the marches, massacres, tortures and rapes, and Talaat Pasha's prime role. After two days the German jury found Tehlirian not guilty and released him. Other senior Turkish officials were killed in the early 1920s in Operation Nemesis, a secret Dashnak (ARF) plan to execute their own justice. Tehlirian later settled in the US and remains a kind of Armenian icon of revenge.

---

sion of Celine Dion, and Hayko, the Armenian entry to the 2007 Eurovision song contest (he finished eighth).

The diasporan music scene is highly varied – from the Los Angeles metal masters System of a Down, to Cher (Cheryl Sarkissian) and her groundbreaking gowns, to the timeless croonings of Charles Aznavour ('mmm… come closer…eets nice to be like zees'). A concert featuring all three would really be something else.

Architecture

Reconstructions at Erebuni (p156) and the Metsamor Museum (p173) give an impression of the cities of classical Armenia – sprawling palaces with Persian, Hellenic and local influences. Surp Hripsime (AD 618) in Echmiadzin (p173) is a classic of early Christian church architecture, when the halls of basilicas transformed into domed square or cross-shaped churches.

St Gregory the Illuminator built churches on top of pagan temples across historic Armenia. His successors had a flair for placing churches and monasteries above cliffs and on sunlit shelves of land. Saghmosavank (p174) perches on the edge of Kasagh Gorge, pinning down the land and saving it from collapsing into the abyss. Tatev (p216) stands in a similar position on the Vorotan Canyon. Even through the years of the Mongol invasions, stunning monasteries were built at Gandzasar (p306), Goshavank (p192), Haghpat (p201) and Haghartsin (p192).

Armenian architecture has also influenced that of Europe. Crusaders, who had built only square towers, adopted the Armenian method of building round towers on churches and castles. The cross-shaped layout of churches found everywhere is also attributed to Armenian church builders.

Only a few frescoes have survived from the medieval period, with images of varying faintness at Lmbat and other churches near Talin (p175), and at Kobayr (p199) in Lori and the Surp Poghos-Petros Church at Tatev (p216).

Yerevan was rebuked as a hovel of mud houses by visiting Russian tsarist officers at the end of the 19th century, but some fine stone buildings with high walls and arched windows can be found in many old villages and towns such as Meghri, Ashtarak, Malishka and Goris. The tsarist old quarter of Kumayri in Gyumri is the most complete 19th-century urban area in Armenia.

Yerevan is an almost entirely Soviet city with some startling edifices, such as Mother Armenia (p155) and the Cascade (p152). What one writer termed 'random monumentality' describes the impact of Soviet art in Armenia. Silver astronauts, brooding 5m-high eagles,

ARMENIA

and the superheroic muscles of designated national heroes in bronze leap from granite pedestals all over the country.

Visual Arts

There are enough art galleries, artists' studios and house museums to fill several weeks in Yerevan. Miniaturisation and microsculpture is a peculiarly Armenian pursuit, with a number of impressive artists, including Eduard Ter-Ghazaryan of Sisian, whose pieces require a microscope to be appreciated; you can see examples of his work at Sisavan Church (p212).

Martiros Sarian is one of Armenia's most famous painters, and a museum in Yerevan preserves his studio (p153). Suitably enough, a Sarian sculpture in a Yerevan park is the focus of Yerevan's art market, where painters gather to offer a critique of each other's work and sell their paintings (p165). Most of the paintings have religious iconography or capture familiar Armenian landscapes. Yervand Kochar has his own gallery filled with portraits nearby on Moscovyan Poghots (p153).

Yousef Karsh was one of the great portrait photographers, and once achieved a famously defiant photo of Winston Churchill after snatching away his cigar.

The illustrated manuscripts preserved in Yerevan's Matenadaran (p152) and the libraries of Echmiadzin are testament to centuries of monastic endeavour.

The brilliant dyes gleam today from the pages of thousands of manuscripts, prepared with rare dyes and preparations that were state secrets in classical and medieval Armenia. Some highly skilled calligraphers create copies of classic images like the Annunciation, which can be bought in Yerevan (p165).

Theatre & Dance

Theatre runs deep in Armenian culture – a 10th-century fortress at Saimbeyli in Cilicia had three storeys of theatres and two storeys of libraries.

The Hellenic kings of Armenia patronised theatre in the 3rd century BC, and Greek dramas played to King Tigran the Great. There are about a dozen active theatre houses in Yerevan specialising in musical comedy, contemporary plays and drama revivals.

The musical comedies and shows for kids are easy to follow and very professionally done (for booking details see p163).

Armenia has a rich tradition of folk dancing, and chances are you'll stumble across a performance in a public square. Revellers at country weddings might not be so professional, but then it is the real thing. Armenia has a rich diversity of dances and costumes, straight out of a medieval spring festival. There are also dance and ballet companies in Yerevan.

ENVIRONMENT
The Land

Armenia's land is filled with mountain ranges and plateaus with valleys and plains in between, folded and creased into a stunning array of regional environments. Perched on the northeastern edge of the Anatolian Plateau, the country has several peaks above 3000m.

Indeed, only 10% of Armenia lies below 1000m. The country's highest peak, Mt Aragats, is 4090m, though the highest mountain of historic Armenia is Noah's mountain, 5165m Mt Ararat (Masis), in present-day Turkey.

National Parks

About 12% of Armenia is protected by natural and historic reserves, though much of this is Lake Sevan National Park.

In Soviet times the reserves were closed except to scientists. Nowadays all are open, and it's a good idea to leave a tip of around AMD300 per person with the custodian – they don't earn much. The Khosrov Nature Reserve (p176) in the hills beyond Geghard is terrific for hikes, with volcanic 'organ-pipe' cliffs, khatchkars (carved stone crosses) and isolated churches. The Dilijan Nature Reserve protects hornbeam and oak forest, while the woods and canyons of Shikahogh Nature Reserve (p219), south of Kapan, are rarely visited by tourists. The state also protects a number of archaeological sites, including Erebuni (p156), Dvin and Metsamor (p173) around Yerevan, and some rare habitats, such as scrubland near Jrarat south of Echmiadzin, preserving Vordan Karmir beetles, once used to prepare dyes.

Environmental Issues

Parts of the Armenian environment took a terrible beating from Soviet industry. There are stories of driving through the haze around Vanadzor's giant chemical plant when it was in full swing and noticing that your nylon shirt was rotting away. The Metsamor nuclear power station, 30km west of Yerevan, generates 40% of Armenia's energy but does not meet internationally accepted safety standards and will be decommissioned by 2016 at the latest. Plans are being laid to build a new 1000-megawatt plant with Russian aid.

Poverty and the lack of alternative fuels have put pressure on forests. Larger-scale logging of questionable sustainability has occurred in the Lori and Tavush *marz*. The economic recovery might also bring hazards – one mining works apparently restarted with its old exhaust scrubbers already stripped out and sold off.

The air quality in Yerevan suffers from so many vehicles rumbling along past their retirement date and from low-quality fuel. Still, the quality of bird life in Armenia proves that the country has an abundance of healthy wilderness – perhaps as much as 70% of the land surface – from the oak and hornbeam forests of Dilijan and rocky highlands of the Geghama range to the ice fields of Mt Aragats.

Another good-news story is the rising water level of Lake Sevan – conservation efforts have caused the lake level to rise by 2m since 2002.

Environmental awareness is scant. Pipes pour raw sewage into rivers and it's common to see people dumping their garbage into the nearest stream. There is a long way to go to change attitudes but some environmental education programs have begun. The twice-yearly **Sun Child Festival** (www.sunchild.am) gets kids excited about going green.

FOOD & DRINK

Armenian cuisine is a national treasure, a delicate mix of lightly spiced meats, fresh salads, lots of chewy light lavash bread and home-made specialities dating back centuries. It combines elements of the cuisines of all its historic neighbours – Arabic, Russian, Greek and Persian – but remains distinctive. Scientists believe that the first wheat was grown on the southern flanks of historic Armenia, south of Lake Van, while the Romans dubbed the apricot *prunus armeniaca*, or Armenian prune.

A lot of Armenian produce is practically organic by default, and you might notice a difference between industrial-scale Western supermarket chicken and happily free-range Armenian chicken. There is an amusing blog about the joys of Armenian food at http://armenianfood.blogspot.com.

Staples & Specialities

If there's one word for dining, it's *khoravats* (barbecued food). Pork is the favourite, though lamb, beef and sometimes chicken are usually available too. *Ishkhan khoravats* is grilled trout from Lake Sevan. *Siga* is another good grilled-fish dish. Kebabs are also very common.

Broadly speaking, western Armenian cuisine is more similar to Lebanese and Turkish cooking, while eastern Armenian has more Russian and Georgian influences. Besides *khoravats*, staples include dolmas (rice wrapped in vine leaves), soups, vegetable stews and lavash fresh from the oven. Armenians aren't afraid to throw in garlic and salt by the handful to boost the flavour. Hors d'oeuvres include cold salads, salty cheeses and dips such as *jajik* (yogurt with cucumbers and fennel). *Tan abour* is yogurt soup sprinkled with parsley and fennel, much admired for its curative qualities. Pastries appear everywhere, such as Georgian *khachapuri* (cheese pies) and *bourek* (flaky pastry with salty cheese and spinach). Cured meats include *sujukh* or *yeghchik* (dark, cured spicy sausage) and *basturma* (finely cured ham). Desserts include honey-drenched baklava and sweetly crunchy *kedayif* (dessert pastry) though thick chocolate cakes and tortes are popular in the region too.

Drinks

The most popular drink is *soorch* (Armenian coffee), also claimed by Georgians, Greeks and Arabs; a potent, finely ground cup of lusciously rich coffee, with thick sediment at the bottom. It goes well with honeyed pastries such as baklava. Tea is also popular, as are local soft drinks like Hay Cola. There is an interesting array of mineral and table waters, ranging from salty, volcanic Jermuk to lighter Noy and Dilijan waters. Fruit juices are cheap and delicious.

The two main lagers are Kilikia and Kotayk, widely available and quite refreshing on a hot summer afternoon. Kilikia is a typical middle-European lager, very good when fresh. Its main rival, Kotayk, is sold everywhere and is a little more reliable, if bland, while Erebuni has more flavour and is made by the same company. Russian Baltika beer is also sometimes available; Baltika 3 and Baltika 7 are the most common lagers. *Kvas* is a home brew sometimes sold at markets, a lightly alcoholic drink made from rye bread, something like a natural cola or sweet soda.

ARMENIA

FRUIT FANATICS *Arpi Armenakian Shively*

In a nation too often associated with shortages, fruit is enjoyed in abundance in Armenia and woven into the culture. Seventy-eight-year-old Lucine Sherbetjian, originally from western Armenia, croons an undulating folk song from the 1930s with a catchy chorus: 'Oh, Yerevan, with your praiseworthy grapes and the perfume of your peaches.'

'For New Year and our Christmas,' says Houri Taslakian, who lives in Yerevan, 'even the poorest families cover the dining table with dishes of dried fruits and preserves. They are kept full for 15 days so that hospitality never runs out.'

Chocolate and mass-produced sweets are expensive and scarce, so fruit is the basis for several treats. What's top of the chew charts? 'Give me *tetoo lavash*,' says Aline Taslakian from Florida, who summers in Yerevan. 'Paper-thin layers of sour plum puree, they're addictive!' The taste for sweetened fruits extends to liquids: 'In my cousin's house, they serve homemade cherry liqueur to wash down lunch,' says Alice Ekrek, 'and even the kids drink it!'

Grapes and rosy *narinj* peaches are especially prized here, but one fruit reigns supreme. Thanks to plentiful sunshine and an absence of chemicals and pesticides, the flavour of Armenian apricots is regarded as incomparable. Houri Taslakian says Yerevan's annual Golden Apricot Film Festival also pays homage to its finest fruit: 'A basket of apricots is blessed at the opening ceremony.'

Apricots and other fruits also feature in folk medicine. In her book *Armenian Food: Fact, Fiction and Folklore* Irina Petrosian notes several orchard standbys: 'Apricots are regarded as a cure for everything from constipation to heartache. Pomegranate juice is prescribed for diarrhoea and pomegranate rind if you're feeling queasy.'

In Armenia, fruit is an everyday miracle.

The country's national liquor is cognac (around 40% alcohol). There are several other producers, such as Great Valley, but the Yerevan Brandy Company's Ararat label is the real thing, a smooth, intense liquor with a smoky aroma similar to whisky. Armenian *konyak* (cognac) has a huge following in Russia and Ukraine, and even Winston Churchill favoured it over the French stuff, and Stalin used to send him cases of Ararat cognac.

Most red wines are made from the Areni grape, well suited to the hot summers and harsh winters. The one-dollar-a-bottle stuff is what you'd expect, but some of the wines for AMD1500 to AMD5000 are excellent. Frosts and late springs make the Armenian vintage as shaky as the Champagne region. Some reputable Areni makers are Vayots Dzor, Vedi Alco, Getap and Noravank, and new wineries are springing up. White wines are produced from vineyards in Tavush, Lori and Karabakh, and are generally sweet or with extra tannins from the skins.

Where to Eat & Drink

Yerevan's restaurant scene is booming and the quality of the international cuisine continues to improve. Prices are moderate if you are coming from Europe, but pricey if coming from Georgia or Iran. An appetizer, main course and glass of wine in Yerevan will cost AMD4000 to AMD6000 (US$12 to $18), or half that price if you eat somewhere simpler.

Outside Yerevan, the choices can often be limited to *khoravats*, kebabs and sometimes *lahmajo* or *lahmajoon* (spiced-up little minced-lamb pizzas).

Vegans & Vegetarians

There are hundreds of fine meat-free dishes in the Armenian cookbook, but at restaurants the options might only be salad, grilled vegetables, bread and cheese (sorry, vegan comrades). Nuts are sold everywhere – sunflower seeds are a very Middle Eastern obsession. Tomatoes, rice, aubergines, courgettes and a profusion of herbs and spices have created a wealth of vegetarian dishes. Western Armenian cuisine has hummus, tabouleh and other dishes associated with Lebanese cuisine, and there are lots of home-made ratatouilles made from beans, carrots and onions with olive oil. *Kartofel* (pilaf rice) is a buttery mix of dried raisins, apricots and other spices. B&B hosts will do vegetarian meals.

Habits & Customs

Breakfast isn't a big meal here, but for all other mealtimes, Armenians love to sit, drink and eat for hours. Menus are becoming more common, but the custom is to discuss options and prices with the waiter if there's no menu, and often even if there is. Some say it's rude to eat with your left hand, others say that's a Muslim custom and not Armenian.

The drinking culture is highly developed, but it needn't be crippling. As one host said, it's my duty to keep your glass full, it's up to you how you drink it. Women drink wine or brandy rather than vodka. Drunkenness is unacceptable, especially for women. If you want to propose a toast it's polite to ask the permission of the *tamada* (main toastmaker). There's a custom in clinking glasses of holding your glass lower than the next person's, as a sign of deference. This can develop into a game until the glasses are at table level. If you empty a bottle into someone's glass, it obliges them to buy the next bottle – it's polite to put the last drops into your own glass.

Eat Your Words

Armenians often call common foods by Russian, Turkic and even Hindi words.

MENU DECODER

abour – soup
basturma – cured beef or ham
biber – capsicum, pepper
bourek – flaky stuffed pastry
dolma – rice and meat parcels in vine leaves
hats – bread
hav – chicken
hummus – ground chickpea paste with oil
gov – beef
ishkhan – Sevan trout
kebab – ground meat cooked on a skewer
kedayif – crunchy dessert pastry
khamaju – a meat pie similar to *khachapuri*
khash – winter stew of animal parts
khaghogh – grapes
khashlama – lamb stew cooked in beer or wine

khoravats – barbecue, usually pork, lamb or beef, also vegetables and fish, does not include kebab
khoz – pork
kyufta – meatballs mixed with onion and egg
lahmajo (lahmajoon) – minced-lamb minipizza
lavash – thin flat bread
matsoon – yogurt
oghee – fruit vodkas
paneer – cheese
patlijan – aubergine
pomidor – tomato (also *loleek*)
shakar – sugar
siga – river trout
suchush – plum and walnut sweet
sujukh – cured sausage
tabouleh – diced green salad with semolina
tan – yogurt
tsiran – apricot
vochkhar – lamb

YEREVAN Երեվան

☎ 1 / pop 1.1 million

While it's the undeniable cultural, economic and political heart of the nation, Yerevan can at times feel like a city on permanent holiday. All summer long Yerevanites saunter up and down the main boulevards, preening in high fashion and fast cars while occasionally popping into a parkside café to schmooze over a drink or two. It's the most laid-back capital in the Caucasus and it's easy to slide into a torpor for a day or two. The city has some lovely 19th-century Russian edifices in its central core plus rings of parkland and handsome brick squares. Outer areas maintain an air of Soviet sprawl but these are limited by steep hills and gorges. Yerevan's museums and monuments could keep you busy for a few days but the best thing about the place is the people. Expressive black eyebrows, proud noses and classical Greek and Persian profiles appear everywhere, in a street culture

SOME HANDY ADVICE

Drinking fountains are located all over Yerevan and across the country. While these may look tempting, especially on a hot summer day, we suggest avoiding them as the water is not filtered and may contain bacteria such as Giardia. If you are the unfortunate recipient of a Giardia bug go to the nearest chemist for a box of tinidazole (aka Tindamax).

Another piece of advice: do not give money to beggars on the streets of Yerevan. There is an organisation called Orran which supports the homeless and it has done an effective job of taking care of the destitute. Beggars only seem to come out on the street in the tourist season. If you want to give something, it's best to donate directly to **Orran** (☎ 1-53 51 67; www.orran.am).

ARMENIA

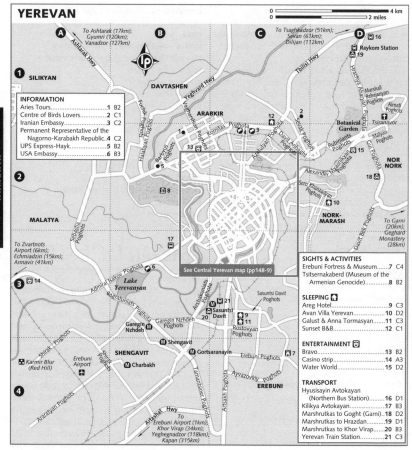

YEREVAN

INFORMATION
Aries Tours.....................................1 B2
Centre of Birds Lovers..................2 C1
Iranian Embassy............................3 C2
Permanent Representative of the
  Nagorno-Karabakh Republic..4 C2
UPS Express-Hayk.........................5 B2
USA Embassy..................................6 B3

SIGHTS & ACTIVITIES
Erebuni Fortress & Museum.......7 C4
Tsitsernakaberd (Museum of the
  Armenian Genocide)..............8 B2

SLEEPING
Areg Hotel......................................9 C3
Avan Villa Yerevan.....................10 D2
Galust & Anna Tormasyan.......11 C3
Sunset B&B..................................12 C1

ENTERTAINMENT
Bravo...13 B2
Casino strip..................................14 A3
Water World.................................15 D2

TRANSPORT
Hyusisayin Avtokayan
  (Northern Bus Station)........16 D1
Kilikya Avtokayan......................17 B3
Marshrutkas to Goght (Garni)..18 D2
Marshrutkas to Hrazdan...........19 D1
Marshrutkas to Khor Virap......20 B3
Yerevan Train Station.............21 C3

See Central Yerevan map (pp148-9)

---

somewhere between Marseilles, village Armenia and old Beirut. Yerevan is a relaxed and safe place where people live at one pace while the traffic goes at another. The cultural life is intense for a city of its size, including dozens of theatres, concert halls, galleries and live music clubs.

At the geographic heart of the country, the city also makes a perfect base to explore other areas. You could even make day trips as far afield as Lake Sevan, Mt Aragats and Vayots Dzor.

HISTORY

Yerevan's history dates back to 782 BC, when the Erebuni fortress was built by King Argishti I of Urartu at the place where the Hrazdan

River widened onto the fertile Ararat Plains. It was a regional capital of Muslim khanates and Persian governors until the Russian annexation in 1828.

The Soviet rebuilding of the tsarist city removed most of its mosques and some of its churches, and hid others away in residential backwaters, but it kept some of the 19th-century buildings on Abovyan Poghots and left the old neighbourhood of Kond more or less alone.

ORIENTATION

Yerevan sits in a valley edged on three sides by hills, with the little Hrazdan River cutting a serpentine gorge west of the city centre. Central streets in the city are laid out on a grid with several ring roads, intersected by the redeveloped Hyusisayin Poghota (Northern Ave). In the centre is Hanrapetutyan Hraparak (Republic Sq), while the Opera House a few blocks north is another focal point. Mesrop Mashtots Poghota (avenue) is one of the city's busiest thoroughfares.

The main bus station is the Kilikya Avtokayan west of town on the Echmiadzin Hwy, which also leads to Zvartnots Airport. Marshrutkas to various parts of the country leave from all over the city centre, with a concentration around the Rossiya Mall on Tigran Mets Poghota.

The main train station is above Sasuntsi Davit metro station. Yerevan's metro has four stations in the city centre with the last stop at Barekamutyun.

INFORMATION
Bookshops
There are quite a few bookshops selling Armenian and Russian publications but stockists of other languages are rare.

Artbridge Bookstore Café (Map pp148-9; ☎ 52 12 39; 20 Abovyan Poghots; ⏰ 8.30am-midnight) Has a small but well-chosen range of titles and a book exchange; see p161 for details.

Macmillan Bookstore (Map pp148-9; ☎ 53 79 82; 9 Gharam Parpetsi Poghots) Has a few English-language novels but mostly sells learning materials, including dictionaries.

Noyan Tapan (Map pp148-9; ☎ 56 81 84; Hanrapetutyan Hraparak) Has a few English novels plus maps and books on Armenia.

Cultural Centres
American Corner (Map pp148-9; ☎ 56 13 83; yer evan@americancorners.am; 2 Amiryan Poghots; ⏰ 9am-5pm Mon-Fri, 10am-4pm Sat) Has a library, internet access and a series of films and lectures.

WI-FI IN YEREVAN
Free wi-fi is available at the departure lounge in Zvartnots airport. You can use wi-fi in the lobby of the Golden Tulip hotel (p159), but you will have to buy something. Pay wi-fi is available at the Tourist Information Centre (p151), the Club (p161), Triumph (p162) and Zodiac (p162). Some of the upscale hotels have a pay wi-fi service for their guests. The Envoy Hostel (p158) charges a reasonable AMD500 per hour.

Emergency
Emergency services ☎ 103
European Medical Centre ambulance ☎ 54 00 03
Fire ☎ 101
Police ☎ 102

Internet Access
There are internet clubs on virtually every city block, varying from cramped basements to places with 20 terminals or more. Many are open very late and cost around AMD300 per hour. Some can be unbearably smoky.

You also need to pay for the megabytes used, so costs rack up every time you click a new page or upload/download something. **Nexus** (☎ 53 33 88; 49 Pushkin Poghots; ⏰ 24 hr) near the Envoy Hostel and **Kino Moskva** (Internet Club; Map pp148-9 ☎ 52 12 70; 18 Abovyan Poghots; ⏰ 9am-10pm) at the Moscow Cinema are both decent options.

Internet Resources
Tour Armenia (www.tacentral.com) and *Armenia Now* magazine (www.armenianow.com) have regular updates of clubs, pubs and restaurants in Yerevan. The website www.armeniadiaspora.com also has some handy information.

YEREVAN IN ONE DAY
Start off with breakfast at a café on Abovyan Poghots with some freshly ground *soorch* (coffee). Take a look around the grand buildings of Hanrapetutyan Hraparak (Republic Sq), and have a browse in the National Gallery. Head up Abovyan and take a look at the Katoghike church. The square around the Opera House has plenty of cafés for lunch dining. The Matenadaran is a fine building with a small but beautiful collection of manuscripts on display, or go up to the Cascade for a grand view over the city, surrounded by flower beds. Then head out to a restaurant for a long dinner of Armenian *khoravats* with salads, desserts and cognac. Check out a club or people-watch from any one of dozens of late-night cafés, around the Opera House and the Ring Park in particular.

ARMENIA

CENTRAL YEREVAN

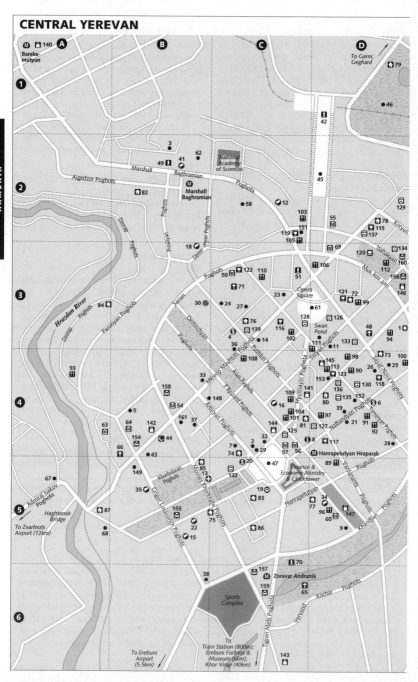

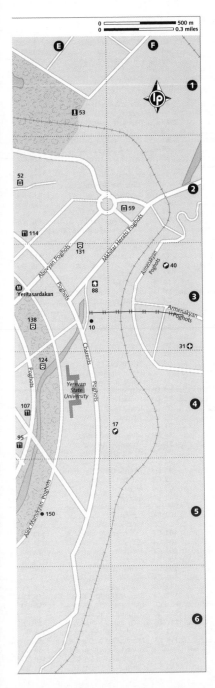

Laundry

There are only a handful of laundromats around town, but all hotels and most B&Bs and homestays can arrange clean laundry. The following places are all full-service and charge by the kilo.

Lavanda (Map pp148-9; ☎ 53 40 31; 56a Pushkin Poghots) Convenient if you are staying at the Envoy hostel.

Selena Service (Map pp148-9; ☎ 53 65 08; 4 Zakyan Poghots) Charges about AMD1500 for a shirt or AMD1000 for trousers or dry-cleaning.

Shahab (Map pp148-9; ☎ 54 31 96; 2 Grigor Lusavorich Poghots).

Media

The main English-language weekly newspaper, *Noyan Tapan,* is available from Noyan Tapan (p147) and Artbridge Bookstore Café (p161) and sometimes from hotels and souvenir shops. Artbridge also has international magazines and newspapers, and these are sometimes available in the lobbies of upscale hotels such as Hotel Avia Trans. The NPAK gallery (p154) puts out the handy *Yerevan Guide* booklet with good listings, tips and reviews; it's also available at hotels and tourist-oriented shops around town.

Medical Services

Yerevan has the best medical facilities in the country, but they're still inadequate by international standards.

4th Yerevan City Polyclinic (Map pp148-9; ☎ 58 03 95; 13 Moskovyan Poghots)

European Medical Centre (Map pp148-9; ☎ 54 00 03; 3/1 Vazgen Sargsyan Poghots)

Nork-Marash Hospital (Map pp148-9; ☎ 65 09 71; 13 Armenakyan Poghots, Nork-Marash)

Pharmacies, marked by the Russian word *apteka,* are common and there's one open late in every neighbourhood. For things like dental emergencies, embassies usually have a list of recommended specialists.

Money

There are moneychangers everywhere in Yerevan and cash machines dispensing drams are becoming quite common. Euros, dollars and roubles can be changed nearly everywhere; the pound and Georgian lari are less commonly traded. **HSBC** (☎ 56 32 39; hsbc@arminco.com; 9 Vazgen Sargsyan Poghots) is the leading international bank and has several branches with cash machines around the city. If you

had to organise a money transfer, this would be an easy place to do it. Travellers cheques are mostly spurned or met with bewildered looks – avoid relying on them if possible or try a bank like HSBC. Handy ATMs that accept Visa and MasterCard include **Anelik Bank** (Map pp148-9; 41 Pushkin Poghots) and **Arexim Bank** (Map pp148-9; 20 Tumanyan Poghots).

Post

The public mail service in Yerevan is slow but fairly reliable. The **Haypost Main Office** (Map pp148-9; Hanrapetutyan Hraparak; ☺ 9am-7pm Mon-Sat) is centrally located. A letter or postcard sent abroad might take one or two weeks, but it gets there. Several local and international companies compete for the parcel business:

FedEx/Transimpex (Map pp148-9; ☎ 54 42 77; tripex@arminco.com; 40 Mesrop Mashtots Poghots)

UPS Express-Hayk (Map p146; ☎ 27 30 90; omae@arminco.com; 1 Kievyan Poghots)

Telephone

Telephone services in Yerevan are reasonable and you usually get through on the first or second attempt. ArmenTel has lost its monopoly so prices will continue to drop on international calls. Internet cafés offer cheap VoIP international calls. Many internet cafes also have **Skype** (www.skype.com) software on their machines.

Tourist Information

Armenia Information (Map pp148-9; ☎ 54 23 03, 54 23 06; www.armeniainfo.am; 3 Nalbandyan Poghots; ☺ 9am-7pm) The best tourist office in the region, with lots of books and brochures, and young staff who are happy to help with virtually anything from nightlife to transport. It keeps lists of homestays and B&Bs in Yerevan and in the provinces. It's just off Hanrapetutyan Hraparak near the metro station of the same name.

Travel Agencies

There are lots of useful travel agencies offering everything from one-day minivan tours to private car tours, from a day to a week anywhere in the country. Some specialise in travel to Iran, Georgia and even Turkey. A selection of recommended agencies:

AdvenTour (Map pp148-9; ☎ 53 96 09; www.armenia explorer.com) Specializes in adventure trips – hiking and mountain biking – plus speciality interests such as photography, bird-watching and archaeology. Call first

as the location is hidden outside the centre but staff will meet you in town.

Ajdahag Mountain Hiking Club (www.ajdahag .narod.ru) Arranges one-day treks up the southern peak of Mt Aragats and Mt Ara, a two-day climb up to Aragats' highest peak, plus hikes in the Geghama Mountains to the petroglyphs on Mt Azhdahak and other peaks.

Aquarius Travel (Map pp148-9; ☎ 53 67 67; www .aquarius.am; 11 Leo Poghots) Arranges Yerevan apartments and homestays, and does tours by car and driver in Yerevan and beyond. Services have received mixed reviews from travellers.

Aries Tours (Map p146; ☎ 22 01 38; www.bedandbreak fast.am; 43 Kyulpenkyan Poghots, Arabkir) Has an excellent B&B network in parts of the country where the local hotels aren't so great, and arranges transport and excursions.

Avarayr (Map pp148-9; ☎ 52 40 42; www.avarayr.am; 1 Pavstos Byuzand Poghots) Avarayr is an adventure-tour company offering treks from three to 12 days (the latter covering much of the country), camping trips for groups, and some unusual cultural and archaeological tours.

Caravan Tours (Map pp148-9; ☎ 56 52 39; www .caravanarmenia.com; 42/1 Teryan Poghots) Arranges apartments, homestays and tours; garners good reports for prompt individual service.

Hyur Service (Map pp148-9; ☎ 56 04 95; www.hyur service.com; 50 Nalbandyan Poghots) Rents apartments and does trips around the country including many day tours from Yerevan.

Levon Travel (Map pp148-9; ☎ 52 52 10; www.levon travel.com; 10 Sayat-Nova Poghota) Good for outbound travel and booking airline tickets.

Menua Tours (Map pp148-9; ☎ 51 20 51; www .menuatours.com; 9 Alek Manukyan Poghots) Does daily tours to sites around the country and is a reliable organiser of apartments, car rental, cell-phone rental and other services.

Sati Tours (Map pp148-9; ☎ 53 10 22; www.satiglobal .com; 21 Mesrop Mashtots Poghota) Highly rated agency with daily excursions to major sites around the country from Yerevan for AMD4600 to AMD12,000 per person, plus accommodation, two- and three-day all-inclusive regional tours, and car and driver hire.

Tatev Travel (Map pp148-9; ☎ 52 44 01; www.tatev .com; 19 Nalbandyan Poghots) Specialises in travel to Iran, including arranging visas. It has daily coaches from Kilikya Avtokayan to Tabriz, Iran, for AMD17,000 one way, and is the local agent for the Iranian Caspian Airlines, which flies Yerevan–Tehran three times a week. Also sells airline tickets and arranges local tours and apartments.

SIGHTS

Yerevan is not 'touristy', and it takes a little exploring to get to know what at first seems like a city of subtle variations on Soviet apartment

ARMENIA

design – the best stuff is hidden indoors, while churches are hidden in courtyards and cul-de-sacs. The oldest surviving part of the inner city is the Kond neighbourhood, between Sarian and Proshyan Poghots, close to the gorge of the Hrazdan. Central Yerevan is small enough to enable you to walk to all the major sites.

We've broken down the sights into two main areas, the northern half of downtown, including Opera Sq and the Cascade, and sights in the southern half of downtown, south of Republic Square.

Opera Square, the Cascade & Moscovyan Poghots

This section includes sights in the northern half of downtown. This leafy area is known for its fashion boutiques, upscale restaurants and outdoor cafés, which seem to cover every patch of available parkland. It also has its share of small museums clustered between the Opera House and the Cascade.

CASCADE

A vast flight of stone steps and flower beds, the **Cascade** (Kaskad; Map pp148–9) leads up to a monument commemorating the 50th anniversary of Soviet Armenia. It completes one end of Tumanyan's north–south axis through the city, in line with Tigran Mets Poghota and the Hyusisayin Poghota (Northern Ave) project. There are five recessed fountains along the Cascade, some with sculpted panels and postmodern *khatchkars*.

The top section of the Cascade was left unfinished when independence arrived, until 2001 when diasporan philanthropist and art collector Gerald L Cafesjian took over the project. Since then the vast concrete structure has been cleaned, the escalators through its core repaired and hundreds of flower beds planted.

Take the escalators up through the belly of the building, which looks like a skyscraper resting on its side, and walk onto the 'roof' to take in the panorama surrounded by flowers. At the top is a rather bleak plaza with the **50th Anniversary of Soviet Armenia Monument** at its centre (though the views are great). The new **Cafesjian Museum** is being integrated into the Cascade to house a vast collection of art and glassware. Cafesjian is spending $30 million to complete the structure and add galleries – final plans include a new arts centre at the top of the Cascade. It's all set to open in the summer of 2009. Fernando Botero's

cheerfully fat sculpture *Cat* stands at the base of the Cascade, the first element of Cafesjian's collection put into place. Botero's *Roman Warrior* has a 'rigid' pose at the top.

OPERA HOUSE

The landmark of the northern part of the city, the **Opera House** (Map pp148-9; Opera House; ☎ 52 79 92; 54 Tumanyan Poghots) is surrounded by parks, cafés, nightclubs and shops. The building has two main halls: the Aram Khachaturian Concert Hall (p164) and the National Academic Opera and Ballet Theatre (p164), thoroughly upgraded in 2003.

Tastes have broadened a bit since Soviet Armenia, and the music scene here goes beyond opera and symphonies to Russian pop, MTV and a night club in the bowels of the Opera House itself. For the same price as a ticket to see *Giselle* (AMD2000 to AMD3000) at the Opera House you can dance to the latest Euro-pop at the Opera Disco, not generally the case elsewhere.

MATENADARAN

Armenia's ancient manuscripts library, the **Matenadaran** (Map pp148-9; ☎ 58 32 92; www.matena daran.am/en; 53 Mesrop Mashtots Poghota; admission AMD500, guide AMD2000; ☑ 10am-4pm Tue-Sat), stands like a cathedral at the top of Yerevan's grandest avenue. It preserves more than 17,000 Armenian manuscripts and 100,000 medieval and modern documents. The first Matenadaran for Armenian texts was built by St Mesrop Mashtots at Vagarshapat (Echmiadzin) in the 5th century.

By the early 19th century only 1800 manuscripts were kept at Echmiadzin, after centuries of invasion, looting and burning. The collection grew in importance after the Armenian genocide in WWI saw the destruction of countless tomes. The current Matenadaran was built in 1959, with a research institute dedicated to preserving and restoring manuscripts attached to it.

At the base of the building there is a statue of Mashtots teaching his alphabet to a disciple, while six other statues of great scholars and writers stand by the door. The outdoor gallery has carved rock tombs and *khatch-kars* brought here from ancient sites around Armenia. Inside, the collection includes Greek and Roman scientific and philosophical works, Iranian and Arabic manuscripts, and the 15th century Homilies of Mush, so heavy that it was ripped in half and carried by two women after the 1915 genocide. The book was not put together until years afterwards – one saviour had emigrated to America. The illuminated works on display show swirls of red and gold combining classical borders with luxuriant flowers and gardens.

Many of the more rare books in the collection are researched behind closed doors and are not on display. The ticket office has a gift shop with a good collection of books and souvenirs.

MARTIROS SARIAN MUSEUM
This museum preserves the studio and some of the works of 20th-century painter Martiros Sarian. Some say the pick of his works adorn galleries in Moscow and Paris. Start your visit to the **museum** (Map pp148-9; ☎ 58 17 62; 3 Sarian Poghots; admission AMD600; ⏰ 10.30am-4.30pm Fri-Tue, 10am-3pm Wed) upstairs with his sombre early works, then watch the colours erupt as he falls in love with Persia and Egypt. His art seems to mature by fusing those colours into a vision of an Oriental Armenia, landscapes of stark mountains, green villages and plunging gorges. Sarian's large studio remains as it was when the artist died in the 1950s.

OTHER SIGHTS
National Folk Art Museum of Armenia (Map pp148-9; ☎ 56 93 83; 64 Abovyan Poghots; admission AMD500; ⏰ 11am-4pm Tue-Sun) Has a large display of Armenia's finest crafts, which reveal the exotic influence of the East in Armenian culture. There's also a nice lace exhibit and some interesting woodcarving.

Museum of Russian Art (Map pp148-9; ☎ 56 03 31; 38 Isahakyan Poghots, admission AMD500; ⏰ 11am-4pm Tue-Sun) A collection of 200 works by 19th-and 20th-century Russian artists, donated by Professor Aram Abrahamian, who had a taste for cheerfully picturesque landscapes. Enter on Tamanyan Poghots.

Yervand Kochar Museum (Map pp148-9; ☎ 52 93 26; 39/12 Mesrop Mashtots Poghota; admission AMD300; ⏰ 11am-5pm Tue-Sun) Features the sculpture and Cubist-style three-dimensional paintings of the brilliant draughtsman and artist.

Churches in the area include the **Zoravar Church** (Map pp148-9; 1694), one of the nicest little secrets in the city, tucked away off Gharam Parpetsi Poghots. The tiny **Katoghike** (Map pp148-9; 13th century) is at the corner of Sayat-Nova Poghota and Abovyan

Poghots. The Soviets were demolishing a later church here in 1936, which exposed the fine inscriptions on the chapel. Amazingly enough for that era, a public outcry let the chapel survive. Fragments from the dismantled church lie around it.

Republic Square, Southern Mashtots & Khandjian Poghots
Sights in this section are grouped in the southern part of downtown. The area around Republic Sq includes government ministries, as well as some of the better hotels and embassies. This section also includes the largely commercial southern part of Mesrop Mashtots Poghota, Haghtanak Bridge and the parkland along Khandjian Poghots.

HANRAPETUTYAN HRAPARAK (REPUBLIC SQUARE)
The former Lenin Sq is surrounded by the city's finest ensemble of buildings, particularly the Armenia Marriott Hotel and the National Art Gallery and State Museum of Armenian History, where Stalinist scale meets Armenian architecture in a huge yellow-and-cream building facing some massive fountains. The statue of Lenin now lies on its back in the museum's courtyard, while the head is apparently stored in the basement. The centre of the square (more of an oval) is now a flat stretch of polished marble. New lights and repaired fountains make Hanrapetutyan Hraparak (Map pp148–9) a focal point on warm afternoons and nights.

STATE MUSEUM OF ARMENIAN HISTORY
This museum spans from Stone Age cave dwellers in the Hrazdan Gorge to the astronomy and metallurgy of 3000 BC Metsamor, the Urartu Empire and the gathering of the Hayk tribes into a nation in the 6th century BC. After that centuries fly past at the **State Museum of Armenian History** (National Museum; Map pp148–9; ☎ 58 38 61; Hanrapetutyan Hraparak; admission AMD800, guide AMD5000; ⏰ 11am-6pm Tue-Sun) through Hellenic Armenia, the arrival of Christianity and long wars against Persia, the Arab conquest and subsequent flowering at Ani, and then the long centuries under Muslim Turkish and Persian rule. There are medieval *khatchkars*, costumes, jewellery, coins, and models of buried settlements and lost churches.

NATIONAL ART GALLERY
Holding the third biggest collection of European masters in the former USSR, many of the works in the **National Art Gallery** (Map pp148-9; ☎ 58 08 12; Hanrapetutyan Hraparak; admission AMD800, guide AMD3500; ☼ 11am-5.30pm Tue-Sun) were appropriated in Europe during WWII. This national treasure includes works by Donatello, Tintoretto, Fragonard, Courbet, Theodore Rousseau, Rodin, Rubens and Jan Van Dyck. There are also many works by Russian painters, and Armenian painters, sculptors and graphic artists including Martiros Sarian, Yervand Kochar and Sedrak Arakelyan. Note that the floors are a little wonky – floor seven is marked floor eight in the elevator, and so forth. If you can talk your way into visiting the roof there are opportunities here for sweeping city views.

YEREVAN BRANDY COMPANY
'The fairyland of the world-famous Armenian brandy', **Yerevan Brandy Company** (Map pp148-9; ☎ 54 00 00; www.ybc.am; Admiral Isakov Poghota; tour & tastings AMD2500; ☼ 10am-5pm Mon-Fri, tours by appointment) runs fun tours with generous tastings from its iconic premises by the Hrazdan River. Other Armenian brandy companies such as Great Valley are neophytes compared to the Yerevan Brandy Company, now part of the French Pernot-Ricard group. The company has cellars of barrels dating back to the 19th century, including one which won't be opened until a Karabakh peace deal appears. Tours take 75 minutes, including tastings, and end at the souvenir shop. It's a pleasant walk across the Haghtanak Bridge or a short taxi ride (AMD500) from the city centre.

BLUE MOSQUE
Of the eight or so working mosques in Yerevan in 1900, the **Blue Mosque** (Map pp148-9; ☎ 42 84 98; 12 Mesrop Mashtots Poghota; ☼ 10am-6pm) is the only one remaining. The **Iran Information & Communication Centre** next door has the key. It's appropriate to wear trousers and a long-sleeved shirt – no bare legs or shoulders. The Soviets turned the mosque into the Yerevan City Museum until it was restored and somewhat 'modernised' by an Iranian religious-government foundation in the 1990s. It lives on as a sign of Armenia's necessarily good relations with Iran.

The mosque was built in 1765 by the Persian Governor Hussein Ali Khan as a place for Friday sermons and features a *medrese* (religious college) built around a garden courtyard, a 24m-high minaret and a brightly tiled turquoise dome.

A seven-hectare fortress was also built during the governor's reign but was destroyed in the 1880s. Today it's the site of the **Yerevan Wine Plant**, just on the city side of the Haghtanak Bridge across from the Metropol Hotel. As you drive from the airport over the Hrazdan River into the city, look at the walls on the left above the river, which are said to be the original walls of this fortress.

SERGEI PARADJANOV MUSEUM
This engaging, eccentric **house museum** (Map pp148-9; ☎ 53 84 73; www.parajanov.com/museum .html; 15/16 Dzoragyugh Poghots; admission AMD700, guide AMD3500; ☼ 10.30am-5pm) of an avant-garde film director and artist (see p139) stands by the Hrazdan Gorge near Surp Sargis. Paradjanov was born in 1924 in Tbilisi but retired to Yerevan after serving prison terms on charges of immorality in the 1970s and 1980s. While some of his international admirers campaigned for his release (with mixed results), his health was affected and he died in 1990. This fine house showcases his colourful, amusing collages and framed found-object sculptures, as well as sketches and designs for his films. There's real wit and flair to his work, and it's well worth visiting even if avant-garde 20th-century film isn't normally your thing. There are postcards and videos of his major films for sale.

MUSEUM OF MODERN ART
Near the corner of Sarian Poghots is the main exhibition centre for contemporary Armenian artists, the **Museum of Modern Art** (Map pp148-9; ☎ 53 53 59; 7 Mesrop Mashtots Poghota; admission AMD800; ☼ 10am-6pm Tue-Sun). It also has an impressive collection of works from the 1970s onwards. The museum is on a narrow lane just off Mashtots. The **Artists' Union** (Map pp148-9; 16 Abovyan Poghots), next to the Golden Tulip – Hotel Yerevan, is another major exhibition space.

NPAK
The Norarar Pordzarakan Arvesti Kentovon (Armenian Centre for Contemporary Experimental Art) is a large, well-appointed **gallery and art complex** (Map pp148-9; ☎ 56 82 25; www.accea.info; 1/3 Pavstos Byuzand Poghots;

admission free; 10am-6pm Mon-Sat) facing the big Vernissage market. Yervand Kochar's 1959 figure *Melancholy* pines at the entrance. Most of the artists in residence are in their 20s, and avant-garde concerts and performances are held in a huge auditorium. Viewed with healthy suspicion by the more conservative arts audience, the next Armenian cultural revolution might start here.

SURP GRIGOR LUSAVORICH CATHEDRAL
Modern Yerevan's first real cathedral (Map pp148–9) was built to celebrate 1700 years of Christianity in Armenia and was consecrated in 2001. This hulking building stands on a small hill where Khandjian Poghots meets Tigran Mets Poghota. It's a bit brutalist in execution, possibly because it hasn't been around for 1000 years and collected age, atmosphere and *khatchkars*. Stairs leading up from Tigran Mets Poghota point straight at the carbuncle of the Kino Rossiya building across the street. There's a statue of Zoravar Andranik at the bottom of the stairs. General Andranik Ozanian led the army that defeated the Turks at Sardarapat in May 1918.

OTHER SIGHTS
The **Museum of the Middle East** (Map pp148-9; ☎ 58 16 51; 1 Aram Poghots; admission AMD300; 11am-4pm Tue-Sat) houses a small but diverse collection of artefacts from Zoroastrian Persia and early regional civilisations from Luristan and Elam. It's at the back of the National Art Gallery, and affords a peek at Lenin's headless statue in a courtyard.

The **State Museum of Wood-Carving** (Map pp148-9; ☎ 53 24 61; 4-2 Paronyan Poghots; admission AMD300; noon-6pm Tue-Sun) is actually an interesting collection of some meticulous pieces, both modern and medieval.

Near the Museum of Wood-Carving, look out for the **Surp Sargis Church** (Map pp148–9; 1853), on Israeliyan Poghots off Mashtots, overlooking the Hrazdan. The Sunday liturgy and choir are particularly good.

Outside the Centre
The following sights lie outside the central core and thus require a fair hike or a short cab or marshrutka ride.

MOTHER ARMENIA
Symbolism abounds in the huge statue of **Mother Armenia** (Mayr Hayastan; Map pp148–9). She looms over the city in line with Mesrop Mashtots Poghota, on a classic Soviet plaza complete with tanks and jets set on pedestals at the eastern end of Haghtanak (Victory) Park. The 23m-high Mother Armenia glares out across the city towards the Turkish border with a massive sword held defensively in front of her. She replaced a Stalin statue in 1967. Two soldiers died when his statue was wrenched off unannounced one night, leading to grim muttering about Stalin still killing from beyond the grave.

Inside the 50m pedestal is a **Military Museum** (Map pp148-9; ☎ 25 14 00; admission free; 10am-5.30pm Tue-Fri, to 3pm Sat & Sun). The interior is based on Surp Hripsime at Echmiadzin, a brave acknowledgment of religion by the architect during Stalin's lifetime. Originally fitted out with displays from WWII (300,000 Armenians died, half of those sent to fight), today most of the space is devoted to the Karabakh War – a Dashnak's paradise which includes a tableau of female soldiers in the Karabakh conflict. All explanations are in Armenian but the dioramas are easily grasped. **Haghtanak Park** (Map pp148–9), next to Mother Armenia, is a mostly overgrown patch of woods. Watch out for children (and sometimes adults) speeding around in miniature cars. There's a quaint amusement park in the park with a Ferris wheel, cafés and outdoor billiards tables.

TSITSERNAKABERD (ARMENIAN GENOCIDE MEMORIAL & MUSEUM)
Commemorating the agony of the 1915–22 genocide of Armenians during the death throes of the Ottoman Empire, the **Museum of the Armenian Genocide** (Map p146; ☎ 39 14 12; Tsitsernakaberd Hill; admission free; 11am-4pm Tue-Sun) and memorial create a moving experience. The museum lies underground in a grey stone hall. Large photographs (many, but not all, with English explanations) tell the story of the genocide simply and baldly. There's no effort to demonise the Ottoman authorities; the facts are allowed to speak for themselves. It starts with the massacres of 1896 and 1909 and the lack of an international response, and then moves on to the murder of Armenian labour conscripts in the Ottoman army in late 1914 and early 1915. The arrest and subsequent murder of community leaders and intellectuals on 24 April 1915 marks the beginning of that nightmare summer. All over Anatolia

ARMENIA

men were arrested, marched out of their towns and murdered at the nearest lonely spot; then came the forced deportations of the remaining women and children and forced marches into the Syrian desert.

A permanent exhibition of paintings of half-dead, naked survivors stands in the hall. The final image is a huge blown-up photograph of an orphanage in Syria after the genocide. Outside there's a magnificent view of Mt Ararat, the symbol of Armenia 40km inside modern Turkish territory.

Nearby there is a *khatchkar* in remembrance of the 1988 Sumqayıt massacre in Azerbaijan, and the graves of early victims of the Karabakh War.

There is a row of trees planted by foreign leaders who recognise the genocide, despite the Turkish government's determination to punish any foreign power that does so. The Turkish denial works on many levels – it never happened, the documents are fake, it wasn't deliberate, the deportations were for their own safety, not that many people died, Turkish people suffered too, it was the fault of the Dashnaks. Considered in full it falls over with inconsistencies, but that doesn't seem to make a difference.

A broad pathway flanked by a 100m-long wall engraved with the names of massacred communities leads to the **memorial**, consisting of a 40m-high spire next to a circle of 12 basalt slabs leaning over to guard an eternal flame. The 12 tilted slabs represent the lost provinces of western Armenia, while the spire has a fine split dividing it into larger and smaller needles, the smaller one representing western Armenia. Some surmise other layers of meanings – the 12 slabs huddle like refugees around a fire on a deportation march, and the spires might be a highly stylised monument to Mt Ararat and its smaller peak, or blades of newborn grass. Set on Tsitsernakaberd Hill (Fortress of Swallows) across the Hrazdan Gorge from central Yerevan, the memorial was built in 1967 after unprecedented demonstrations on 24 April 1965, the 50th anniversary of the genocide. In a rare acknowledgement of public discontent, the Soviets deposed the local Communist Party boss in response and gave permission for the memorial to be built.

A taxi (AMD600 from the city centre) is the easiest way to reach Tsitsernakaberd. If you feel up it you can walk to and from town over the Haghtanak Bridge and past the Hrazdan Stadium.

EREBUNI FORTRESS & MUSEUM

Excavations began at the **Erebuni Fortress** (Map p146) site in 1959 after a farmer found a stone tablet with writing on it in the dirt. Follow Tigran Mets Poghota south past the train station and turn left onto Erebuni Poghots; the site and museum are at the end of the road.

Archaeologists found a large cuneiform slab with the inscriptions of Argishti I, king of Urartu, setting the date the fortress was built at 782 BC. It reads, in part, 'Argishti, the son of Menua, has built this magnificent fortress as a house for Khaldi, the Lord, to the glory of the Biayni countries and to the horror of enemies', which says a bit about the nature of Armenian pride.

The view from the fortress takes in the city and Karmir Blur (Red Hill), where excavations have revealed similar ancient finds. Frescoes in the reconstructed palace wall are replicas. There are huge storerooms for wheat, along with gigantic pitchers for wine and oil, and *tonir* (oven pits). There's also a place for animal sacrifices, and workshops (still buried) for making tools, including arrows for fighting and hunting.

The **Erebuni Museum** (Map p146; ☎ 45 82 07; 38 Erebuni Poghots; admission AMD1000, guide AMD3500; ⏲ 11am-5pm Tue-Sat), at the bottom of the hill, has other cuneiform tablets and jewellery excavated from the site in a striking 1960s Soviet building with huge apricot-coloured *tufa* (volcanic stone) friezes.

To get here from outside the Marriott Hotel, take marshrutka 36, 86 or 76.

WALKING TOUR

This tour can be walked in two stages. Starting at **Marshall Baghramian metro station (1)**, it's a downhill stroll through the heart of the government and embassy district. Walk uphill a bit to the statue of **Marshall Baghramian (2)** below the steps up to the **American University of Armenia (3)**. The marshall was born in Karabakh and led some of the great tank battles of WWII. Next to the statue is the **British Embassy** (4; p221), a good attempt at blending traditional styles with ambassadorial presence. Next along is the **Presidential Palace (5)**, and the **National Assembly** (6; Azgayin Zogov) on a high grassy rise on the right. Opposite stands the **National Academy of**

Sciences (7). Continue on down Baghramian past the Syrian and Chinese embassies. After the Constitutional Court take the first left onto Isahakyan Poghots and another onto the top end of Tamanyan Poghots. A belt of parkland leads to the foot of the Cascade (8; p152), a grand project of steps and gardens leading up to the 50th Anniversary of Soviet Armenia Monument (9). Returning downhill,

---

WALK FACTS

Start Marshall Baghramian metro station
Finish Shuka No 2
Distance 3.6km
Duration 2½ hours

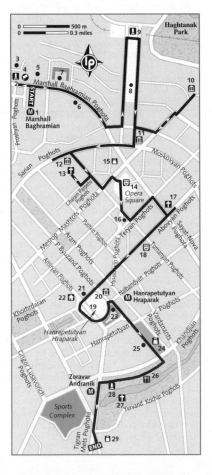

take the first left onto Isahakyan and another left onto Mesrop Mashtots Poghota and climb two blocks to the Matenadaran (10; p152), the repository of Armenia's written and illuminated heritage.

Head back to the base of the Cascade. There are several galleries and museums in the vicinity, including the Yervand Kochar Museum (11; p153). Cross Marshall Baghramian and head along the curve of Sarian Poghots to the Martiros Sarian Museum (12; p153) and its captivating Eastern landscapes. In the courtyards just behind the museum, but accessible only via Gharam Parpetsi Poghots or Pushkin Poghots, is the lovely orange tuff of the Zoravar (13; p153) parish church. It's a short walk along Tumanyan to the Opera House square (14; p152). The area of park around the Martiros Sarian statue across Mashtots by the Opera House holds the painters' branch of the Vernissage Markets (15; p165) on weekends. The Opera House grounds are ringed by some of the city's smartest cafés, clubs and 24-hour bars: a nice place for a rest and a light meal.

Begin stage two at the Northern Avenue project (16), a new development of multistorey buildings starting at Tumanyan Poghots. Head along stylish Sayat-Nova Poghota and turn left on Abovyan. Here stands the gorgeous 12th-century Katoghike (17; p153), a chapel so tiny the congregation stands in the yard. Recent work on the church has expanded it and added lay buildings. Down Abovyan Poghots in the other direction are souvenir shops and the Kino Moskva complex (18; p165). The lower part of the street has some sturdy 19th-century buildings in volcanic hues of orange and black. Abovyan debouches into Hanrapetutyan Hraparak (19; Republic Sq), where the Lenin statue once stood. It now lies headless in a courtyard of the National Art Gallery (20; p154).

Ringing the broad hippodrome-shaped space are the Ministry of Foreign Affairs (21), the Armenia Marriott Hotel (22; p159), the central post and telephone office and the Finance and Economy Ministry (23) with its clock tower. On weekends you can head up Nalbandyan one block on the far side of the National Gallery and take the first right into the main Vernissage Market (24; p165).

The NPAK gallery (25; p154) is next to the Vernissage. After crossing busy Khandjian Poghots continue to the right through the Ring Park with lots of fancy cafés (26; p163)

ARMENIA

to the city's newest landmark, the **Surp Grigor Lusavorich Cathedral (27**; p155). The equestrian statue of **Zoravar Andranik (28)** springs from a pedestal in front of the cathedral. Continuing down Tigran Mets through a bustling hub of shops and marshrutka stands, you can veer onto an extension of Movses Khorenatsi Poghots to **Shuka No 2 (29)**, one of the city's biggest food markets.

COURSES

Lavaryn Dpratoon (☎ 54 29 09, 52 37 78; www.ldt.am; 21a Sayat Nova Poghots) is an Armenian language school for all levels. It's in a building set back from Sayat Nova.

FESTIVALS & EVENTS

Fireworks seem to celebrate a national holiday or commemorate some event or other every fortnight or so. The independence days sometimes see concerts on Hanrapetutyan Hraparak or in the parkland around the Opera House. The major summer event is the **Kenats Festival**, in late September, with concerts, folk dancing and other events. The **Golden Apricot International Film Festival** (www.gaiff.am) is held in July. The HyeFest, in early October, sees the arrival of international theatre groups for a variety of performances.

SLEEPING

Besides the listings below, travel agencies can organise a homestay for around AMD5000 per night or an apartment rental starting from around AMD10,000 per night. You can also check www.armeniainfo.am, which has listings for B&Bs. Prices for midrange and luxury hotels include government taxes. Yerevan is the most expensive city in the region: dorm beds cost AMD5000 to 7000, a budget double is AMD25,000 to 35,000 and a midrange double will set you back AMD35,000 to 55,000. Top-end doubles start at around AMD60,000. See the Armenia Directory (p220) for information on renting an apartment in Yerevan.

Opera Square, the Cascade & Moscovyan Poghots
BUDGET

Envoy Hostel (Map pp148–9; ☎ 53 03 69; www.envoy hostel.am; 54 Pushkin Poghots; dm/s/d inc breakfast AMD7000/18,000/36,000; ⊠ ▣ ⊠) The only bona fide youth hostel in the region, Envoy offers spotless rooms, an English-speaking staff,

non-smoking throughout and a good travellers vibe. It has a perfect location in the city centre, reasonable rates and free city tours each morning. It does get a little loud and crowded when families or big groups turn up and some rooms are boxy and windowless. The breakfast is minimal (bread, tea, jam and cheese) but it has a kitchen for self-caterers. The door is actually on Parpetsi Poghots.

Foreign Students Hostel (Map pp148–9; ☎ 56 00 03; ysugh@xter.net; 52 Mesrop Mashtots Poghota; s/d AMD15,000/23,500) Simple and small rooms are on offer at this university hostel, usually occupied by exchange students and the odd Peace Corps volunteer. There is no reception desk, just go and talk to the administrator in room 106.

Parev Inn (Map pp148–9; ☎ 55 99 85; www.parev.am; 71 11th Aigestan Poghots; s/d incl breakfast AMD22,000/26,000; ⊠) A pleasant guesthouse just up from Mkhitar Heratsi Poghots (near the Nork cable car), run by a Canadian-Armenian couple. Prices are about 25% lower from 1 November to 15 May. The rooms are large and comfortable (if a little bland), with a kitchenette and modern bathrooms. Some rooms are nicer than others so look at a few before settling down. The access road is a little hard to spot – take a sharp right before the CPS petrol station.

Anahit Stepanyan (Map pp148–9; ☎ 52 75 89, 091502 071; 5 Sayat-Nova Poghota Apt 25; per person AMD5000) Among the available guesthouses in Yerevan, this place seems to get the highest praise among backpackers. It consists of two large dorm rooms and a loft. The guest rooms are a little dishevelled and do get crowded but the common area (a living room) is clean and modern. Anahit speaks English.

Gayane Simonyan (Map pp148–9; ☎ 52 75 88, 091737 361; per person AMD5000) There are several homestays in this apartment block; this one is on the floor below Anahit at apartment 22. Gayane's is not as modern or clean as Anahit's, but you'll get a little more privacy. The staircase for Anahit and Gayane is located next to Our Village restaurant.

Anahit Avedisyan (Map pp148–9; ☎ 58 16 17; per person AMD5000) In the same building but one door-entrance east, Anahit lives in apartment 6. She runs a clean, well-maintained flat with two guest rooms, but be prepared for some serious motherly reprimand at the slightest infraction of house rules. The people who run these places all know each other and if one is full you'll be directed to another flat with an available bed.

MIDRANGE

Ani Plaza Hotel (Map pp148-9; ☎ 58 95 00; www.ani hotel.com; 19 Sayat-Nova Poghota; s/d AMD41,000/51,000, deluxe s/d AMD63,000/70,000; ❄) This landmark in the heart of town has been updated to be an upper-midrange hotel. Cheaper rooms have not seen renovation on the same scale as the deluxe rooms, but all are modern and comfortable. Rates include breakfast. At the time of research a fitness centre and an indoor pool were being built.

Republic Square, Southern Mashtots & Khandjian Poghots
MIDRANGE

HY Business Hotel (Map pp148-9; ☎ 56 75 67; www.hybusiness.com; 8 Hanrapetutian Poghots; r AMD25,000, ste AMD45,000-65,000; ❄ 💻) Not a typical hotel, this place is designed for extended stays or families – rooms are large and come with kitchenettes. Internet is AMD2000 per day, breakfast is also AMD2000 per day. It's associated with the American University in Armenia.

Hotel Shirak (Map pp148-9; ☎ 52 99 15; www.shirakhotel.com; 13a Movses Khorenatsi Poghots; s/d AMD25,000/35,000; ❄) A show of Soviet chic glazes the rooms and the lobby of this antiquated hotel. Still, it has a fine downtown location, sunny balconies overlooking a park and a friendly staff. The lack of renovation has at least kept the prices low (and its worth asking for a discount as the price may come down further).

Hotel Erebuni (Map pp148-9; ☎ 58 05 05; www.erebuni hotel.am; 26/1 Nalbandyan Poghots; s/d AMD26,000/32,000, prices 50% lower Nov-Mar; ❄) The Erebuni has seen some refurbishment but it remains a bland post-Soviet experience – you are mainly paying for the central location.

Congress Hotel (Map pp148-9; ☎ 58 00 95; www.congresshotelyerevan.com; 1 Italia Poghots; s/d AMD38,400/52,440; ❄ 💺) Next to a pleasant park and overlooking leafy Italia St, the Congress is notable for its quiet serenity in the city centre. The 128 rooms are clean and modern, although the singles are a little poky. The hotel is best known for its big outdoor swimming pool, accessible by nonguests for a hefty AMD11,000.

Europe Hotel (Map pp148-9; ☎ 54 60 60; www.europehotel.am; 32-38 Hanrapetutyan Poghots; s/d AMD44,000/50,000, ste AMD64,000-80,000; ❄) This quiet hotel in the centre of town has a flair for bright colours in its décor, and a groovy bar and café on the ground floor. The rooms

are a little small but perfectly comfortable. Continental breakfast included.

TOP END

Hotel Avia Trans (Map pp148-9; ☎ 56 72 26; www.aviatrans.am; 4 Abovyan Poghots; s/d/tr/deluxe incl breakfast AMD40,000/50,000/70,000/80,000; ❄) The anonymous looking exterior belies an otherwise pleasant lobby and friendly reception in this central hotel. Wi-fi is available, and the management claims to be building a fitness centre and swimming pool.

Metropol Hotel (Map pp148-9; ☎ 54 37 01; www.metropol.am; 2/2 Mesrop Mashtots Poghota; s/d AMD45,000/55,000, ste AMD65,000; ❄ 💺) With its heavy drapery, maroon colours, renaissance sculptures and gold trim, the Metropol has established itself as the most ostentatious hotel in the city. Facilities include a sauna, a swimming pool and a miniature exercise area. Breakfast is included.

Golden Tulip – Hotel Yerevan (Map pp148-9; ☎ 58 94 00; www.goldentuliphotelyerevan.com; 14 Abovyan Poghots; s/d AMD54,000/64,000, ste from AMD83,000; ❄ 💺) A five-star hotel (by local standards), the Golden Tulip has touches of classical European décor and modern touches like flatpanel TVs and free wi-fi. The piano bar in the lobby is a fine place for a drink, the Rossini Italian restaurant is one of the best in town, and yet its most valued amenity is the fabulous rooftop swimming pool.

Armenia Marriott Hotel (Map pp148-9; ☎ 59 90 00; www.marriott.com; Hanrapetutyan Hraparak; r from AMD60,000; ❄ 💻) With its posh address on Republic Sq, the Marriott stands out as the place to be seen in Yerevan. The hotel includes a ritzy buffet breakfast, a 24-hour gym (one of the best in town), two restaurants (Italian and Middle Eastern) and the popular Meeting Point café at the front. Rooms in the back are quiet and have views of Mt Ararat.

Outside the Centre
BUDGET

Galust & Anna Tormasyan (Map p146; ☎ 45 23 10; 97 Burnazyan Poghots; per person AMD5000; Ⓜ) A couple of blocks from Yerevan train station (and Sasuntsi Davit metro), this two-storey village-style house has four bedrooms. Breakfast costs AMD1000 extra. Rooms with bathrooms are more expensive. Anna Tormasyan speaks basic English and runs a friendly homestay. Guests can use the kitchen and washing machine. The place is about 80m down Burnazyan

ARMENIA

Poghots from the corner with Sasuntsi Davit Poghots (walk over the canal bridge and turn right at the corner with the apartment block). It's on the first corner on the left, with a metal grille gate for the garage.

Sunset B&B (Map p146; ☎ 23 15 16; http://sunsetarm .com; 65 Komitas Poghota, Apt 61; s/d AMD14,000/19,000; 🖳) Sergey and Nune Lalayan are your hosts at this apartment B&B near Haghtanak Park, north of the centre. There are two bedrooms, a kitchen, a living room and internet access. The owners don't live here so you need to call ahead so they can show you the place.

Areg Hotel (Map p146; ☎ 45 62 13; www.areg.am; 80 Burnazyan Poghots; s/d AMD14,700/21,700; Ⓜ) Run by a friendly family, Areg has large, plain rooms with clean bathrooms and satellite TV. It also has a bar and can arrange transport to local sights.

MIDRANGE

Hotel Hrazdan (Map pp148-9; ☎ 53 53 32; www.hotelhrazdan .am; 72 Dzorap Poghots; s/d/ste AMD25,000/40,000/50,000; 🍴 🖳 🏊) A multistorey tower overlooking the Hrazdan Gorge, formerly only for Soviet bigwigs but now privately run and renovated. New rooms are a little plain but light and airy and with nice views.

Hotel Bass (Map pp148-9; ☎ 22 26 38; www.bass. am; 3/1 Aigedzor Poghots; s/d AMD32,000/36,000, ste AMD48,000-56,000; 🍴 🖳 🏊) A friendly boutique hotel in an interesting neighbourhood close to Marshall Baghramian metro station. Large and homey rooms are decked out with TVs, DVD players and free wi-fi for laptop carriers. Sauna and indoor poor are among the amenities. Ask for big discounts in the off-season.

TOP END

Avan Villa Yerevan (Map p146; ☎ 54 27 07; www.tufen kianheritage.com; 16 13th Poghots, Nork; r from AMD45,000; 🍴 🖳) High up in the Nork neighbourhood east of the centre, this is the prime candidate for Armenia's best boutique hotel. Individually designed rooms and furnishings, plus fine food and wine in a handsome stone building overlooking Yerevan.

Golden Palace (Map pp148-9; ☎ 21 99 99; www .goldenpalacehotel.am; Azatutuyan Poghots; r AMD70,000, ste AMD106,000; 🍴 🏊) A strikingly modern hotel, the 66-room Golden Palace is a big glass and steel structure on the edge of Haghtanak Park. Rooms have nice touches like terry-cloth robes and the suites are equipped with a Jacuzzi and

kitchenette. The presidential suite costs a cool AMD800,000 a night – Jacques Chirac stayed here during his 2006 visit.

EATING

Yerevan's dining scene continues to improve with dozens of international offerings, including Japanese, Russian, Georgian, Italian, Lebanese and Greek restaurants. Traditional fare is also thriving; there are plenty of places for carnivores to taste the best lamb, pork and beef *khoravats* Armenia can offer. Street snacks like kebabs wrapped in lavash and pastries and pies are sold from stalls and bakeries in every neighbourhood.

Opera Square, the Cascade & Moscovyan Poghots

RESTAURANTS

Gusto (Map pp148-9; ☎ 58 11 21; 11 Abovyan Poghots; meals AMD2000-3500; ⏱ 8.30am-midnight) Lively, new place for reliable pastas, pizzas and calzones. The scene is a nice mix of singles, families and couples and there is pleasant street-side seating.

Samurai (Map pp148-9; ☎ 58 56 70; 2 Marshall Baghramian Poghota; meals AMD2000-6000; ⏱ 11am-11pm) Atmospheric Japanese restaurant with open seating or recessed tables in small alcoves. Sushi starts from AMD1000 for two pieces all the way up to AMD15,000 for an assorted platter. Chahan (fried rice), ramen, tempura and teriyaki dishes are also available.

Lagonid Bistro-Cafe (Map pp148-9; ☎ 58 49 93; 37 Nalbandyan Poghots; meals AMD2000) A good-value restaurant serving terrific Syrian-Armenian cuisine, including tabouleh (AMD600), hummus (AMD600), and grills and kebabs for around AMD1300. The décor is fairly simple but the food is fresh and tasty.

Karma (Map pp148-9; ☎ 58 92 15; 65 Teryan Poghots; meals AMD2200-3500; ⏱ noon-11pm) North Indian restaurant offering excellent tandoori chicken and vegetarian dishes in beautifully decorated surrounds. It also offers cuisine from elsewhere in Asia, including Chinese, Japanese and Thai dishes.

Our Village (Map pp148-9; ☎ 54 87 00; 5 Sayat-Nova Poghota; meals AMD2300-3000; ⏱ 11am-11pm) A rather fun 'ethnic' Armenian tourist restaurant with excellent home-style cooking and rousing live music, plus sturdy pine tables and a long drinks list. Expect to pay for everything that appears on your table, including the bread.

Old Erivan (Map pp148-9; ☎ 58 88 55; 2 Tumanyan Poghots; meals AMD2500; ⏰ noon-midnight) Part spectacle, part restaurant, this place serves Armenian cuisine amid boisterous minstrels belting out folk music. The atmosphere is cavelike, with lots of antiques and crafts, although the winged centurions are a little over-the-top.

Color of Pomegranates (Map pp148-9; ☎ 58 52 04; 15 Tumanyan Poghots; meals AMD2600-3500; ⏰ noon-11pm) Small, charismatic restaurant decorated with arty relics from Vernissage market. The menu is a mix of European, Armenian and Georgian, with dishes such as *khashiama* (boiled lamb) and beef chops with prunes.

Beijing (Map pp148-9; ☎ 52 78 22; 9 Tumanyan Poghots; dishes AMD2800-4500; ⏰ noon-11.30pm) Finding good Chinese food in the Caucasus is no mean feat, but Beijing pulls it off. It has a smart interior, friendly service and about 300 different dishes.

Bukhara (Map pp148-9; ☎ 52 13 31; 9 Tumanyan Poghots; meals AMD3000-5000; ⏰ 11am-midnight) Yerevan's cosmopolitism continues to expand with this rare Uzbek restaurant. You can enjoy authentic Central Asian *manti* (dumplings – better than the Armenian variety), plus *samsa* (baked meat pastry), *laghman* (noodle dish) and *plov* (a rice dish with meat and fruit) amid traditionally Uzbek décor.

Club (Map pp148-9; ☎ 53 13 61; 40 Tumanyan Poghots; meals AMD3000-5000; ⏰ noon-1am) One of the classiest places in Yerevan, the Club fuses Western Armenian and French cuisine into a fresh and tasty dining experience. It includes a main dining hall, a second drinks-only room with cushions and low tables, and a hidden café in the back where you can enjoy one of the best pizzas in town. Live music is occasionally on offer and there is a separate section for books and handicrafts. Wi-fi is available.

Phoenicia Restaurant (Map pp148-9; ☎ 56 18 94; 3 Tamanyan Poghots; meals AMD6000-10,000; ⏰ noon-1am) A fine upscale restaurant with a refined wine list and an interesting Italian, French and Middle Eastern menu. Expertly prepared steak, shrimp and chicken dishes, plus a few vegetarian options. Beware of unrequested drinks, wine 'top-ups' and other carefully orchestrated rip-off tactics that can send your bill through the roof. The entrance is on Isahakyan Poghots

CAFÉS

Artbridge Bookstore Café (Map pp148-9; ☎ 52 12 39; 20 Abovyan Poghots; sandwiches AMD1200-2000, coffee AMD300-600; ⏰ 8.30am-midnight) This is a comfy, arty café behind a bookstore that sells concert and drama tickets. The food is reasonably priced, the décor is very European and there are even nonsmoking tables. Foodwise, you can't go wrong with the excellent French toast, but the sandwiches and pastas we tried were mediocre for the price.

KHORAVATS: MEAT ON THE GRILL

When dusk descends on Yerevan the smoke begins to rise on Paronyan Poghots (aka 'Barbecue St'). The street is more like a highway and all along its 2km length you'll spot khoravats restaurants in every shape and form, including simple courtyard eateries run by families and large, sophisticated places, especially on Paronyan Poghots, where huge terraces step down into the Hrazdan Gorge.

The cheaper ones, similar to the old days when these house restaurants were rare examples of tolerated private enterprise, are on the upper stretch near in the direction of Marshall Baghramian Poghota. Some have private dining rooms, other have live music and a gregarious atmosphere. If one doesn't suit your mood, just move to the next.

A dinner of tasty grilled pork, lamb and beef wrapped in lavash with salad and onions costs AMD1600 to AMD2000 at the smaller places. Kebab is around AMD600. Many do grilled chicken (AMD1500) as well. Some have home specialities – it helps to go with someone who can recommend a favourite.

Clustered around the corner of Paronyan Poghots and Dzorap ('gorge bank') Poghots are several of the modern variety. Caesar's Palace (Map pp148–9) and Urartu (Map pp148–9) are two of the best and cost a little more (around AMD2300 to AMD5000 per person, not including too many drinks) – if you like a restaurant with a view, it's hard to beat Urartu's perch over the gorge.

Triumph (Map pp148-9; ☎ 56 09 99; 27 Isahakyan Poghots; meals 2000-3000; ☯ 10am-4am) Triumph is a popular place for local youths to preen and promenade. It has a standard range of food and drinks, plus a nice location tucked into a park. Wi-fi is available for a pricey AMD2500 per hour.

Café Central (Map pp148-9; ☎ 58 39 90; 30 Abovyan Poghots; meals AMD2500-3500; ☯ 10am-midnight) With its wood panels, high ceilings, mirrors and art deco air this café feels like a throwback to 1920s. The menu features an extensive range of coffees and cakes plus salads and light meals.

Santa Fe (Map pp148-9; ☎ 56 00 93; Tamanian Park; meals AMD2500-3500; ☯ 9.30am-2am) Very popular place for families as it has an attached playground and kid-friendly menu (fancy a Harry Potter Pasta or Shrek Pizza?), but is sophisticated enough for adults. Very clean toilets are a bonus.

Zodiac (Map pp148-9; ☎ 51 43 10; 105/1 Teryan Poghots; drinks AMD900-1500; ☯ 9am-midnight Mon-Sat, 11am-11pm Sun) Unlike others in this list (which are more like restaurants), Zodiac is a traditional café doling out teas, coffees and pastries. Wi-fi is available for around AMD1000 per hour.

QUICK EATS

Tumanyan Shwarma (Map pp148-9; ☎ 52 07 81; 19 Tumanyan Poghots; shwarma AMD650; ☯ 10am-midnight) One of the most popular shwarma joints in town. The *khoravats* section (AMD1800) is next door.

Time Out (Map pp148-9; ☎ 50 14 83; 1 Hyusisayin Poghota; meals AMD1000-1500; ☯ 10am-midnight) Cafeteria-style place that makes ordering easy: just pick what you want and pay at the counter. Specializes in salads, fruit bowls, juices and light meals.

Republic Square, Southern Mashtots & Khandjian Poghots

RESTAURANTS

City Diner (Map pp148-9; ☎ 54 24 40; 1/3 Byuzand Poghots; dishes AMD1300-2800; ☯ 11am-11pm) Did someone raid a Route 66 souvenir gift shop? This place is wall-to-wall with street signs and license plates in a reaching attempt to create a 1950s American diner. The menu of Philly cheese steaks, bacon burgers and cheese fries is geared towards homesick Americans in dire need of cholesterol. The English-speaking waitstaff provides friendly service.

Shah Pizza (Map pp148-9; ☎ 53 16 73; 34 Meshrop Mashtots Poghots; meals AMD1500-3000; ☯ 10am-midnight) Middle Eastern hookah joint that feels more like Damascus than Armenia. Most of the clientele are Arab businessmen, travellers and expats. It serves, salads, kebabs and of course pizza, as well as flavoured *nargile* (hookah).

Caucasus Tavern (Map pp148-9; ☎ 56 11 77; 82 Hanrapetutyan Poghots; meals AMD1500-3000; ☯ 24 hr) This is one of the more successful 'tourist' restaurants in town. Waiters in Georgian garb dish up cheap drinks such as mulberry *oghee* shots for AMD300, feasts of *khachapuri* pies and main barbeque platters to the sound of live folk music. It claims to be open all night but may close in the wee hours.

Ankyun (Map pp148-9; ☎ 51 33 38; 4 Vardanats Poghots; meals AMD2000-3500; ☯ noon-11pm) With possibly the best Italian food in the city, this place serves great pastas and starters. Try the carpaccio in olive oil or for vegetarians the tomato and mozzarella platter. The steaks are arguably the best in town. The atmosphere is quiet and candlelit, unusual for an Armenian restaurant.

Square One (Map pp148-9; ☎ 56 61 69; 1/3 Abovyan Poghots; meals AMD2500-3500; ☯ 9.30am-2.30am) Turn up at lunchtime any day of the week and you're likely to find this place packed with NGO staffers, diplomats, expat businessmen and local entrepreneurs. The laid-back, congenial atmosphere and English-speaking wait staff are attractive, as is the nonsmoking lounge upstairs. The American-orientated menu features sandwiches, pizzas, pastas, salads, burgers and tasty breakfasts (served all day). There is another branch at the airport.

Restaurant Français (Map pp148-9; ☎ 54 46 44; 30 Arami Poghots; meals AMD3000-4500; ☯ 10am-11am) French bistro aficionados should make their way to this cosy eatery for some fine beef and chicken dishes and tasty appetizers. The menu is written on the chalkboard, and black-and-white scenes of Paris set the mood just right. The building is slated for demolition, so check local listings for the new address.

Dolmama's (Map pp148-9; ☎ 56 89 31; 10 Pushkin Poghots; meals AMD7000-10,000; ☯ 11am-midnight) A small, upmarket restaurant in a homey atmosphere where you'll get personal attention, a lengthy wine list and some interesting local specialities. Try the mountain lamb stew or chicken in wine and walnut sauce, made with the freshest produce available.

CAFÉS

Marco Polo (Map pp148-9; ☎ 54 53 50; 1/3 Abovyan Poghots; pizzas AMD1500; ⓧ 9am-11pm) A popular meeting place, this big, modern café and bar playing cool sounds is at the lower end of Abovyan. It has an extensive list of café snacks (salads, sandwiches, cakes), quite tasty pizzas, and main courses such as grilled lamb with salad for AMD3000. The coffee is good, and you can sit inside on a cold or rainy day.

Sayat Nova (Map pp148-9; ☎ 58 00 33; cnr Sayat-Nova Poghota & Khandjian Poghots; meals AMD2500; ⓧ 10am-2am) A colourful, busy institution combining a bar, a rooftop café, a restaurant and a nightclub. The ground-floor Amazon Restaurant has a tropical Mayan theme straight from Vegas, plus steaks, pizzas and sandwiches. The café helped introduce *nargile* pipes to Yerevan.

DRINKING

Practically all restaurants and cafés serve drinks and are open late, so this is just a selection of specialist drinking spots.

Opera Square, the Cascade & Moscovyan Poghots

Poplovok Jazz Café (Map pp148-9; ☎ 52 23 03; Isahakyan Poghots, btwn Teryan Poghots & Mesrop Mashtots Poghota) A café complex centred on a large pond. Poplovok is the one by the side of the pond, with live jazz most nights. Former president Kocharian is a jazz fan and sometimes drops by. Musicians like Chick Corea have played here.

Cactus (Map pp148-9; ☎ 53 93 93; 42 Mesrop Mashtots Poghota; cocktails AMD2000; ⓧ noon-midnight) An ersatz Mexican restaurant (the basics are there but it lacks the spices; meals AMD3000), best enjoyed for the excellent frozen margaritas.

Pioneer Club (Map pp148-9; ☎ 58 18 19; 2 Marshall Baghramian Poghota; ⓧ 8pm-3am) Part of the active 'exotic' cabaret scene, with a strip club

downstairs but a porn-free bar upstairs, with reasonably priced drinks.

Shamrock (Map pp148-9; ☎ 091788 197; cnr Tumanyan & Sarian Poghots; ⓧ 10am-midnight) Passable Irish pub that attracts locals and the Peace Corps crowd. Sundays tend to be a good gathering night.

Texas (Map pp148-9; ☎ 54 56 03; 19 Tumanyan Poghots; ⓧ 5pm-3am) Sawdust on the floor, wagon wheels, a bull's head, John Wayne posters and the odd wolf pelt set the scene for the Western-style saloon. Yeee-ha.

Lounge Bar Bunker (Map pp148-9; ☎ 56 25 04; 12 Sayat Nova Poghots; ⓧ 6pm-3am) Manhattan-style basement club with a chrome and steel entrance. On weekends a DJ mixes rap and techno, turning the place into a miniclub.

Buddha Lounge (Map pp148-9; ☎ 56 55 00; 50 Mesrop Mashtots Poghots; ⓧ 5pm-3am) Eclectic Asian-themed place in the basement of a building on upper Mashtots. The 22-year-old owner was inspired after visiting the Paris original. Good place to down an exotic drink as you pub crawl across the city.

Pub Ché (Map pp148-9; ☎ 54 76 66; 4 Bayron; ⓧ noon-midnight) The Che Guevara brand name has moved on to Yerevan with this swanky bar. The AMD2700 cocktails are a little pricey, but it's still a fun place to soak in the atmosphere of guns, cigars and Che paraphernalia.

Republic Square, Southern Mashtots & Khandjian Poghots

Cheers (Map pp148-9; ☎ 58 0416; 46 Nalbandyan Poghots; ⓧ 7pm-late) A cheerful, youthful pub popular with tourists, diasporan Armenians and locals. There are good tunes and bright staff with a lethal array of drinks.

ENTERTAINMENT
Theatre, Ballet & Classical Music

Billboards by the Opera House and on Abovyan Poghots advertise upcoming events;

OUTDOOR CAFÉS: LIVIN' THE GOOD LIFE

Café hopping has become something of a citywide obsession. Before, after and sometimes during work locals crowd into the city's outdoor cafes, and there is no shortage. Take your pick from shady spots with umbrellas and café lattes to dimly lit mafia dens serving cakes and cognac. You hardly need this guide to tell you where to go; you'll spot them as you tour the city – just pick one that suits your style. Good places to look include the Cascade area and anywhere around the Opera House. Students tend to gather around the Ring Park near Surp Grigor Lusavorich Cathedral. Most expats prefer the Meeting Point Café in front of the Marriott Hotel (p159). Also look for places on the newly opened Northern Avenue.

the Armenia Information office (p151) and the Artbridge Bookstore Café (p161) can help with tickets and information. Tickets are a steal at just AMD1000 to AMD2000 for most events. The Opera House has a concert hall and a theatre for opera and ballet. Most theatres close during July and August.

Aram Khachaturian Concert Hall (Map pp148-9; Opera House; ☎ 56 06 45; 46 Mesrop Mashtots Poghota)

Arno Babadjanian Concert Hall (Map pp148-9; ☎ 58 28 71; 2 Abovyan Poghots)

Chamber Theatre (Map pp148-9; ☎ 56 63 78; 58 Mesrop Mashtots Poghota)

Hakob Paronyan State Musical Comedy Theatre (Map pp148-9; ☎ 58 01 01; 7 Vazgen Sargsyan Poghots)

Hovhannes Tumanyan Theatre of Marionettes (Map pp148-9; ☎ 56 32 44; 4 Sayat-Nova Poghots)

Hrachia Ghaplanyan Drama Theatre (Map pp148-9; ☎ 52 47 23; 28 Isahakyan Poghots)

Komitas Chamber Music Hall (Map pp148-9; ☎ 52 67 18; Isahakyan Poghots) Near Abovyan Poghots.

National Academic Opera and Ballet Theatre (Map pp148-9; Opera House; ☎ 52 79 92; 54 Tumanyan Poghots)

Discos

The local club scene is well developed, with everything from Manhattan miniclubs to European-style techno caverns. Don't call these places nightclubs, which generally refer to strip clubs.

Aqua (Map pp148-9; Alek Manukyan Poghots; admission AMD1500; ☽ until late Tue-Sun) Sits over the little Getar River in the park in front of the Yerevan State University. This is one of several café-nightspots in this area, lively on weekends.

Astral (Map pp148-9; admission AMD3000; ☽ until late Wed-Sun) Astral is to Yerevan what the Hacienda was to Manchester: ground zero for the dance-music scene. This club is located in a huge underground space next to the Opera House.

Bravo (Map p146; ☎ 27 06 10; 13 Hrachia Kochar Poghots, Arabkir; meals from AMD3000; ☽ until late Tue-Sun) This cheerfully weird complex of theme bar-restaurants with dance floors and live music attracts an older crowd as much for its Japanese and European food as the tropical- and jazz-themed rooms.

Café Atlantic (Map pp148-9; Pushkin Poghots; ☽ 24 hr) This café-bar by the Opera House has pulsing music and a nightclub. It can be a little disconcerting to see children hanging around here until the wee hours.

Club One (Map pp148-9; ☎ 54 64 24; 26a Tumanyan Poghots; admission AMD3000; ☽ until late Wed-Sun) Fairly exclusive club (there is not even a sign) on Tumanyan. Small but clean inside with thumping house music. It tends to absorb a real late-night crowd when other discos are closing so head here around 3am if you are still awake.

Garage Club (Map pp148-9; 54/3 Abovyan Poghots; ☽ until late) Stylish club that blares electronic dance music and hosts 'theme parties'. Can be a bit tight on space.

Kami (Map pp148-9; 18 Abovyan Poghots; ☽ until late) Small lounge and part-time disco with Mondrian art theme and dancing on Friday and Saturday. The rest of the week it hosts live music acts. It's back behind the Syrian sweet shop.

Opera (Map pp148-9; admission AMD2000; ☽ until late Wed-Sun) Disco attracting a slightly older crowd. It's easy to find, right under the Opera House, accessed from the north side.

Relax (Map pp148-9; 105 Teryan, Citadel Business Centre; admission AMD2000; ☽ 10pm-late Wed-Sun) Very popular with the young and wealthy crowd, with quite a few expats and Armenian diasporans thrown into the mix. It has an enormous bar, brings in top-notch DJs and serves decent food as well.

Live Music

Avante Garde Music (Map pp148-9; www.ara.am; 3a Pushkin Poghots; admission AMD2000; ☽ 10pm-late Tue-Sun) Inside a slightly nasty old Russian block, this club hosts jam sessions, jazz and rock bands. Check the schedule on the website. Cover prices vary according to who is performing.

Malkhas Jazz Club (Map pp148-9; ☎ 53 17 78; 52 Pushkin Poghots; cover AMD2000; ☽ 11am-3am) Laid-back club with two levels; a bar upstairs and a lounge in the basement where the bands perform. It also serves excellent food, including steaks, pork chops and pasta, plus a full range of drinks. Owner Levon Malkhasian is considered the father of Armenian jazz – he has a huge library of jazz books and CDs and often closes the club in the daytime so young musicians can rehearse.

Gay & Lesbian Venues

Gay life is fairly low key but moving ahead since the government repealed laws introduced (and enforced) by Stalin – check www .gayarmenia.com. The most popular hangout is **Melines** (Map pp148-9; ☎ 54 46 44; 30 Arami Poghots; ◌ 10pm-3am) a cellar bar located below the French restaurant. The building is slated for demolition but will hopefully relocate. Art Bridge bookstore is another meeting place.

Cinemas

Kino Moskva (Map pp148-9; ☎ 52 12 10; 18 Abovyan Poghots) American blockbusters dubbed into Russian, anyone? Tickets are cheap and there is a bar, an internet club and a nightclub. Nice Soviet-classical balcony.

Kino Nairi (Map pp148-9; ☎ 54 28 29; 50 Mesrop Mashtots Poghota) Sometimes shows movies in English one night a week, and has two slightly alternative late-night bars, the 5th Element (movie theme) and Underground, with cabaret on weekends. Expats enjoy the VIP level that can be rented out for private screenings.

Sport

The local football league has a regular winter season; the national team and top clubs haven't had much luck in European competitions. Basketball is popular among kids, while *nardi* (backgammon) is the elders' game of choice, along with chess.

There are two modern sport and leisure facilities in Yerevan. **Water World** (Map p146; ☎ 63 89 98; 40 Myasnikyan Poghota; admission AMD5000; ◌ noon-8.30pm, nightclub until late Fri & Sat) is a AMD1000 taxi ride towards Sevan. The entry fee covers a range of pools and water rides, plus a beach towel. There are cafés and bars at the complex; it's quite a scene on a hot summer's day with all the kids, jewellery and luxuriant Armenian male body hair. It's open-air and closed in winter, except for penguins perhaps. **Arena Bowling Centre** (Map pp148-9; ☎ 53 61 01; 8 Mesrop Mashtots Poghots; ◌ 9am-9pm Mon-Fri), Yerevan's best bowling hall, is modern and costs, per lane, AMD6000 during the day or AMD12,000 per hour after 6pm.

Casinos

Looking like a Lego version of the Las Vegas Strip, Yerevan's low-rise casino strip (Map p146) stretches from the city limits out towards the airport . It makes for a somewhat surreal entry into Armenia as the neon signs flash past. Despite the novelty of it all, these places rank fairly low on the local entertainment scene and the empty sidewalks are testament to this. It's hardly worth the cab fare to get out here.

SHOPPING

Vernissage market (Map pp148-9; Pavstos Byuzand Poghots) The main weekend flea market caters to locals shopping for car parts and plumbing fixtures as well as tourists rummaging though piles of antiques and old communist medals. It's also a good place to pick up a chess set and intricately carved jewellery boxes among other locally produced handicrafts.

Vernissage art market (Map pp148-9; Mesrop Mashtots Poghota & Sayat-Nova Poghota) Around the Martiros Sarian statue across from Opera Sq, this market deals primarily with paintings; you can turn up some real gems here at negotiable prices. Purchases are made from both dealers and the artists themselves.

Salt Sack (Map pp148-9; ☎ 56 89 31; 3/1 Abovyan Poghots) Better-than-average souvenir and handicrafts shop with some maps and books for sale, and a range of jewellery, pottery, items like woven salt sacks, carpets, dolls and T-shirts.

Made in Armenia Direct (Map pp148-9; ☎ 59 92 93; Hanrapetutyan Hraparak, Marriott Hotel) One of the best selections of crafts and handmade jewellery and religious iconography.

Treasures of Armenia (Map pp148-9; ☎ 52 76 92; 1/1 Abovyan Poghots) Craft gallery run by local designer Nina Hovnanian. Besides unique jewellery, crafts, cushions and clothing there is a tea room where you can break your shopping spree. It's also a fun place just to look at the mind-boggling price tags and wonder, will anyone will buy that US$400 scarf?

Other popular purchases include cognac and carpets. There are lots of cognac stores on the main streets (Mesrop Mashtots Poghota, Sayat-Nova Poghota and Abovyan Poghots).

Tufenkian Carpets (Map pp148-9; ☎ 52 09 11; 21/1 Tumanyan Poghots) is owned by James Tufenkian who made his name in Tibetan carpets and is now working to revive the Armenian carpet-making tradition, which was collectivised and sucked dry during the Soviet era. There are others sold at the main Vernissage market; see p221 for information on customs procedures. Carpets range from US$50 for something basic to US$15,000 for a first-rate hand-woven carpet. Many shops can arrange to ship your carpet home.

Bootleg CDs, games and software are sold everywhere for a pittance. Hayastan market (Map pp148–9), above Barekamutyun metro station, is the closest thing to a department store, but it still has a bootleg feel to it.

ARMENIA

Some others are tucked into underground stores (Map pp148–9) at the Yeritasardakan metro station.

There are two big *shukas* (food markets; Map pp148–9) at 3 Mesrop Mashtots Poghota and at 35 Movses Khorenatsi Poghots, just off Tigran Mets.

GETTING THERE & AWAY

Yerevan can be reached by air from many countries, by road from Georgia and Iran, and by rail from Georgia. If you're travelling to Karabakh, you must come through Yerevan. While there are a couple of arduous bus services to Turkey via Georgia, and flights to Istanbul, the land border is closed. There are no direct routes to Azerbaijan; it's most easily reached via Georgia.

Air

Zvartnots Airport (☎ flight information 187), 11km from Yerevan, is Armenia's major airport. The main terminal looks like a Soviet scale model of the space station in *Star Trek: Deep Space Nine;* hi-tech in conception but low-tech in construction materials. A new US$100 million terminal was opened in 2006 with much fanfare.

The new arrivals hall has a money exchange and booths for ArmenTel and VivaCell if you want to buy a SIM card for your phone. The check-in counters are still in the old terminal, but the departure lounge (with a café and free wi-fi) is in the new terminal. See p319 for details on airlines that serve Zvartnots.

The airport tax when flying out of Zvartnots is AMD10,000, payable when you check in.

Airline Offices

Aeroflot Russian Airlines (Map pp148-9; ☎ 53 21 31; www.aeroflot.ru; 12 Amiryan Poghots)

Air Arabia (Map pp148-9; ☎ 53 45 33; www.airarabia .com; 14 Mesrop Mashtots Poghots)

Air France (Map pp148-9; ☎ 51 22 77; www.airfrance .am; 9 Alek Manukyan Poghots)

Armavia (Map pp148-9; ☎ 56 48 17; www.u8.am; 3 Amiryan Poghots)

Austrian Airlines (Map pp148-9; ☎ 51 22 01; www .aua.com; 9 Alek Manukyan Poghots)

BMI (Map pp148-9; ☎ 52 13 83; www.flybmi.com; 10 Sayat-Nova Poghota)

Caspian Air (Map pp148-9; ☎ 52 44 01; info@tatev .com; c/o Tatev Travel, 19 Nalbandyan Poghots)

CSA Czech Airlines (Map pp148-9; ☎ 52 21 62; www .csa.cz; c/o Visa Concord Travel, 2 Marshall Baghramian Poghota) Near corner with Isahakyan.

Lufthansa (Map pp148-9; ☎ 59 99 22; www.lufthansa .com; Marriott Hotel , Republic Sq)

Syrian Arab Airlines (Map pp148-9; ☎ 53 85 89; c/o Astron Travel, 3 Movses Khorenatsi Poghots)

Bus

Buses are generally cheap and slow old Soviet models, and while they may be half the price of a marshrutka they're often twice as slow as well. Buses mostly serve on village and suburban routes. The main bus station is the **Kilikya Avtokayan** (Map p146; ☎ 54 07 56; 6 Admiral Isakov Poghota), past the Yerevan Brandy Company on the Echmiadzin road, which has international bus services and buses to Gyumri and the towns of the Ararat Plain. The **Hyusisayin Avtokayan** (Map p146; northern bus station; ☎ 62 16 70; Tbilisian Mayrughi) is on the Tbilisi Hwy, 4km from centre, and serves Sevan and Dilijan.

Buses from the Kilikya Avtokayan to as far as Moscow (AMD21,600, about 72 hours, 4am Wednesday and Sunday) and Istanbul (AMD26,300, 41 hours, 1pm Wednesday and Saturday) can take days and are for extreme travellers only. Buses to Batumi (AMD10,000, 14 to 20 hours, 7am Monday and Friday), Tbilisi (AMD3700, about nine hours, 8am and 10am daily) and Tabriz (AMD17,000, 27 hours, 10am daily; book in advance through Tatev Travel, p151) also depart from Kilikya Avtokayan.

Car & Motorcycle

Several agencies rent out cars in Yerevan, including big names like Europcar and Hertz. A three-day rental ranges between AMD56,000 and 176,000 depending on the make and model of your car; you can get anything from a Lada to a Japanese 4WD. It's also possible to hire a driver with the car.

EET (Map pp148-9; ☎ 54 42 05; 15 Tumanyan Poghots)

Hertz (Map pp148-9; ☎ 58 48 18; 7 Abovyan Poghots)

Europcar (Map pp148-9; ☎ 22 94 95; 8 Kievyan Poghots) Also has a desk at Golden Tulip hotel.

Marshrutka

Yerevan is the hub of the national network, and marshrutkas (minivans) leave from spots around the city, from a kerb to a minibus station to one of the main bus stations. For transport all over Armenia they're fast, reasonably efficient and not much more expensive than the buses. The following list is obviously subject to change but it should assist. Ask 'Vor tegh marshrut gnoom eh?' (What is your destination?). Drivers and helpers will often guide foreigners to the right van or put you in the front seat.

Try to arrive about 30 minutes before departure to make sure you get a seat. Marshrutkas almost always leave on time and may even depart a few minutes early.

NATIONAL

Agarak (near Ashtarak) (Grigor Lusavorich Poghots, AMD300, 40 minutes, 9.55am, 11.55am, 1.55pm, 4pm and 5.55pm).

Alaverdi (corner Agatangeghos and Movses Khorenatsi Poghots in front of Rossiya Mall, AMD1700, three hours, 9am, 2pm, 3pm and 4pm).

Armavir (Hoktemberyan) (Kilikya Avtokayan, AMD400, 45 minutes to one hour, every 15 minutes, 7.30am to 9.30pm).

Ashtarak (Grigor Lusavorich Poghots, AMD250, 40 minutes, one or two per hour between 8.40am and 6.40pm).

Dilijan (Hyusisayin Avtokayan, AMD1500, two hours, hourly between 10am and 6pm, plus Ijevan services).

Echmiadzin (Sarian Poghots near corner of Mesrop Mashtots, AMD250, 20 to 30 minutes, every 10 minutes between 8am and 10pm).

Goris Kilikya Avtokayan (AMD2500, 8.50am, 3pm and 5pm); corner Agatangeghos and Movses Khorenatsi Poghots in front of Rossiya Mall (AMD2500, hourly between 7.30am and 3pm).

Gyumri (corner Agatangeghos and Movses Khorenatsi Poghots in front of Rossiya Mall, AMD1200, two hours, every 20 minutes between 7.30am and 8pm).

Goght (for Garni) (GAI Poghots near Mercedes Benz showroom, AMD250, 25 minutes, every 50 minutes between 10am and 9.30pm).

Hrazdan (for Tsaghkadzor) (Raykom Station, AMD400, 40 minutes to one hour, every 30 minutes between 9am and 6pm).

Ijevan (Hyusisayin Avtokayan, AMD1700, 2½ hours, hourly between 10am and 6pm).

Jermuk (Kilikya Avtokayan, AMD1800, two hours, 10am and 3pm).

Kapan (corner Agatangeghos and Movses Khorenatsi Poghots in front of Rossiya Mall, AMD3500, six to eight hours, hourly between 7am and noon).

Khor Virap (Sasuntsi Davit Metro, Sevan Poghots, AMD400, 40 minutes, 11am and 3.30pm).

Meghri (Kilikya Avtokayan, AMD5500, nine to 11 hours, 7am).

Sevan (28 Isahakyan Poghots in front of Drama Theatre, AMD500, 40 minutes, hourly between 9am and 7pm).

Sisian Kilikya Avtokayan (AMD2000, four hours, 8.30am, 10.30am, 12.30pm and 2.30pm); corner Agatangeghos and Movses Khorenatsi Poghots in front of Rossiya Mall (AMD2000, four hours, 9am).

Stepanavan (Kilikya Avtokayan, AMD1500, three hours, 9am, 11am, 2.30pm, 4pm and 5pm).

Vanadzor (corner Agatangeghos and Movses Khorenatsi Poghots in front of Rossiya Mall, AMD1200, two hours, every 20 minutes between 7.30am and 8pm).

Vayk (corner Agatangeghos and Movses Khorenatsi Poghots in front of Rossiya Mall, AMD1000, two hours, hourly between 8am and 7pm).

Yeghegnadzor (corner Agatangeghos and Movses Khorenatsi Poghots in front of Rossiya Mall, AMD1000, two hours, hourly between 8am and 7pm).

INTERNATIONAL

Batumi (Kilikya Avtokayan, AMD12,500, 10 to 15 hours, 7am Tuesday, Thursday and Saturday).

Stepanakert (Kilikya Avtokayan, AMD5000, seven to eight hours, five or so per day between 7am and 2pm).

Tbilisi (Kilikya Avtokayan, AMD6500, six hours, 9am and 11am).

Train

The imposing **Yerevan train station** (Map p146; ☎ information 184; Sasuntsi Davit Hraparak) is off Tigran Mets Poghota south of the city centre, with the Sasuntsi Davit metro station underneath. The booking office is on the ground floor to the right. Information boards are in Armenian and Russian, but some of the staff speak English. The main route loops west and north through Gyumri (3½ hours), on through Vanadzor (8½ hours) and Ayrum near the border (11 hours) and on to Tbilisi (16 hours). There are a couple of local trains to Yeraskh (near the Naxçıvan border) and to Hrazdan.

Trains leave for Tbilisi on even days at 7pm, arriving theoretically at 9.40am, though a couple of hours late is normal. There are also trains every day to Gyumri at 8am and 4.50pm; an open-seating (bench) ticket costs AMD480. There are separate classes for the train to Tbilisi; open seating costs AMD3700, *kupe* (standard) compartments cost AMD5500, while SV (deluxe) compartments cost AMD12,000. Bedding costs AMD1000 in *kupe* compartments but comes free with SV class. The toilets aren't great and the carriages aren't new, but it's a very pretty ride. Book compartments a day ahead, and take food and drinks with you.

ARMENIA

ARMENIA

GETTING AROUND
To/From Zvartnots Airport

Minibuses and buses from Zvartnots (Place of Angels) Airport leave from the car park 300m from the main terminal. Yerevan minibuses 107 and 108 (AMD150, every 20 minutes, 8am to 6pm) run between the airport and Barekamutyun Hraparak (which has the Barekamutyun metro station). Bus 201 goes to the airport down Mesrop Mashtots from the Opera House (AMD150, every 30 minutes, 7.30am to 5.30pm). Alas for public transport users, many flights come and go at night.

The price of a taxi to and from the airport turns on whether you arrange it in advance or chance it with the cowboys outside arrivals. A taxi might cost AMD5000 from the airport, but going from town to the airport you'll probably pay just AMD2000. If you arrive on the last flight you'll have more bargaining power as drivers will be eager to get home. The trip takes about 15 to 20 minutes to central Yerevan.

Public Transport

Yerevan has tonnes of public transport. There are no special passes and you pay as you go – but it's cheap, and it takes you right into the bustle of urban life.

The cheapest are the city minibuses (marshrutkas), renowned here and across the developing world as the worst drivers on the streets. There are hundreds of routes, shown by a number in the front window. They do stop at bus stops, but you can flag one down anywhere on the street. You pay AMD100 when you leave. Ask to stop by saying 'kangnek'. Women travellers should try to sit near the front and next to a female passenger if possible.

There are also buses following numbered routes and trolleybuses running on electricity from overhead cables. Bus and marshrutka tickets cost AMD100 to AMD200.

Bus 32, which goes from Kilikia bus station up Mashtots, past the Opera House and to the northern bus station every 20 minutes or so, is useful.

Best of all there's the clean, safe and efficient **Yerevan metro** (AMD50; ☉ 6.30am-11pm; trains every 5-10 min), which runs roughly north–south through these underground stations – Barekamutyun, Marshall Baghramian, Yeritasardakan, Hanrapetutyan Hraparak,

---

YEREVAN MARSHRUTKAS

11 – Erebuni Museum, Tigran Mets Poghota, Hanrapetutyan Hraparak, Haghtanak Bridge

13 – Kilikya Avtokayan, Haghtanak Bridge, Mesrop Mashtots Poghota, Marshall Baghramian Poghota, Barekamutyun metro

18 – Yerevan train station, Hanrapetutyan Hraparak, Nalbandyan Poghots, Marshall Baghramian Poghota, Ajapniak

43 – Nor Zeytun, Azatutyan Poghots, Haghtanak Park, Yeritasardakan metro, Surp Grigor Lusavorich Cathedral, Gortsaranayin metro

51 – Mesrop Mashtots Poghata, Abovyan Poghots, GAI Mercedes showroom

81 – Avan, Nalbandyan Poghots, Tigran Mets Poghota, Erebuni

101 – Hyusisayin Avtokayan (northern bus station), Tbilisi Hwy, Komitas Poghota

107 – Zvartnots Airport, Echmiadzin-Yerevan Hwy, Sebastia Poghots, Kievyan Poghots, Barekamutyun metro

---

Zoravar Andranik near Surp Grigor Lusavorich Cathedral and Sasuntsi Davit station at the Yerevan train station. The line continues west and south on ground level to stations in the industrial suburbs.

Taxi

Taxis are cheap and plentiful, from well-loved Ladas to late-model Benzes. There are two types – street taxis and telephone or call taxis. Neither type carries meters, so you should set the price before starting off. You'll see numbers for call taxis stencilled on buildings everywhere. Tourist publications such as *Yerevan Guide* carry listings for many companies. A ride within the city centre in a street taxi costs AMD500 anywhere for the first 5km and then an extra AMD100 for every kilometre thereafter.

AROUND YEREVAN

Because Armenia has so much history centred on its capital, it's easy to see many sites on half-day excursions from Yerevan. This section covers the *marz* of Ararat, Kotayk, Armavir and Aragatsotn. You can easily hire a taxi to see many of these places, but it often works out to be cheaper and less hassle to take a day tour with a company like

Hyur Service or Sati (p151). Sample prices include Garni/Geghard for AMD5000 or Khor Virap/Noravank for AMD8000.

GARNI TEMPLE ԳԱՌՆԻ

This comprehensively rebuilt **Heilenic temple** (adult/student AMD1000/250), was dedicated to Helios, the Roman god of the sun. It was built by Armenia's King Trdat I in the 1st century. It became a summer house for Armenian royalty after the Christian conversion.

The area around Garni has been inhabited since Neolithic times, with archaeologists finding Urartian cuneiform inscriptions dating back to the 8th century BC. The high promontory site is protected on three of four sides by a deep valley with rock cliffs, with a wall of massive blocks on the fourth.

The wall featured 14 towers and an entrance graced by an arch. Ruins of the fortress are on the left and right sides as you walk towards the temple from the parking area. The Avan Gorge, carved by the Azat River, lies below.

A **Roman bathhouse**, now partly covered by a modern structure, was built for the royal residence. In the 7th century, a **church** was built nearby. The bathhouse features an intricate **mosaic**, made with 15 colours of natural stones, depicting the goddess of the ocean.

In the ruins of the church next to the temple is a **vishap** (carved dragon stone). This is a marker to show the location of water. Some marks on the middle of the stone are in fact writing from King Argishti from the 8th century BC, which reads 'Argishti, son of Menua, took people and cattle from Garni to Erebuni [the original site of Yerevan] to create a new community'.

From the temple it's possible to reach Havuts Tar Monastery; see below.

In the village of Garni, **Tavern Restaurant & Hotel** (☎ 091357 581; ☾ 11am-10pm) serves *khoravats*. Upstairs, it has clean and comfortable rooms for AM10,000 per night. See also p170 for information on getting to and from Garni.

GEGHARD MONASTERY ԳԵՂԱՐԴ

Named after the holy lance that pierced Christ's side at the crucifixion, Geghard Monastery stands in a steep scenic canyon 9km beyond Garni. The spear itself was once kept here but is now housed in the holy treasury at Echmiadzin (p171).

Legend has it that Geghard Monastery was founded in the 4th century. The most ancient of the **cave churches**, St Gregory's, dates back to the 7th century. Once called Ayrivank (Cave Monastery), Geghard was burned by invading Arabs in 923.

As you approach the monastery, look to the left up the hill for caves that house monastic cells built by monks. Trees here are often dotted with strips of cloth, as are trees on the other side of the monastery near the river. It is said a person can say a prayer or make a wish and tie a strip of cloth to a tree near the monastery to make it come true.

ARMENIA

GARNI TO HAVUTS TAR

Havuts Tar (Chicken Roost) Monastery is a rewarding two-hour hike from the river below Garni. The trailhead is just left of the entrance to Garni Temple. Follow it down to the gorge (continuing down at intersections). Turn left at the bottom of the gorge and after 30 to 40 minutes cross the old stone bridge over the Azat River and pick up the trail on the opposite bank. The trail forks left and leads to a ranger station marking the northern entrance to the Khosrov Nature Reserve. From the guardhouse go left along the narrow trail near the crest for 3km. The kindly old ranger who lives in the shack can point you in the correct direction. The monastery eventually comes into view, with a large *khatchkar* marking the route.

The monastery comprises two parts, an eastern and a western side, constructed between the 11th and 13th centuries. An earthquake in 1679 destroyed much of the complex, but there is still much to explore, including underground chambers and an interesting church with a red and black chequered façade.

Travellers report spectacular hiking from Garni all the way to Lake Sevan. The 50km hike takes four or five days and in summer you'll meet plenty of Yezidi and Armenian shepherds tending their flocks on the slopes of Gora Karaganchal. You'll need to be self sufficient with food, tents, sleeping bags and reliable maps.

ARMENIA

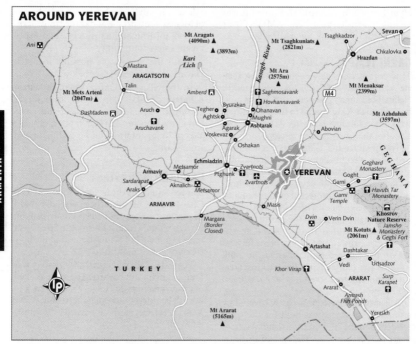

AROUND YEREVAN

Inside the monastery walls, Geghard's two main churches date from the 13th century. The principal structure, **Surp Astvatsatsin** (Holy Mother of God) was built in 1215. The adjoining vestibule, larger than the church itself, with an intricate carved ceiling and nine arches, dates from 1215 to 1225. Outside, above the south door, is a **coat of arms** of the family of the Zakarian prince who built it. The theme is a common Near Eastern one, with the lion symbolising royal might.

On the right-hand side of the vestibule are two entrances to **chapels** hewn from the rock. The left-hand one dates from the 1240s. It contains a basin with spring water believed to be lucky or holy. Splashing some of this water on your body is said to keep your skin youthful.

The right-hand chapel, constructed in 1263, includes the four-column **burial chamber** of Prince Papaq Proshian and his wife, Hruzakan. The family's **coat of arms**, carved in the rock above, features two lions chained together and an eagle.

Outside, steps on the left lead up the hill to a 10m passage into another **church** that has been carved out of the raw rock. The

proportions in this room are nothing short of extraordinary, considering it was carved from the rock around it. The acoustics of the chamber are also quite amazing. In the far corner is an opening looking down on the church below.

On the right-hand side of the church are steps that lead to some interesting **monastic cells** and **khatchkars**. Outside the monastery, next to the stream, is an active *matagh* (sacrifice) site.

Getting There & Away

Marshrutkas to Garni (AMD250, 25 minutes, every 50 minutes from 10am to 9.30pm) depart from GAI Poghots (behind the Mercedes Benz showroom). You can get to the showroom by taking marshrutka 58 or 66 from Berekamutyun metro station or marshrutka 51 from Mesrop Mashtots Poghota`. In Garni the bus leaves you on the main road, a short walk to Garni Temple. The main road continues for 10km to Geghard, but public buses don't go that far. Bus 284 continues to Goght but then it's another 4.5km to Geghard (from where

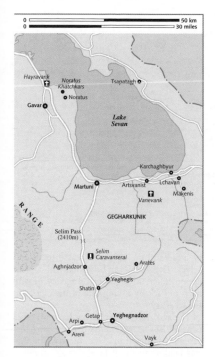

you could walk or hitch a ride the rest of the way). Alternatively, a taxi from Garni to Geghard and back with a one-hour wait is AMD3000.

ZVARTNOTS CATHEDRAL
ԶՎԱՐԹՆՈՑ

Built from 641 to 661, the ruins of the **church** (admission AMD1000; ☼ 10am-5pm) of Surp Grigor Lusavorich (St Gregory the Illuminator) at Zvartnots are different to every other set of ruins in Armenia. Catholicos Nerses II the Builder (building might have been his profession before joining the clergy) sponsored construction of the cathedral. Reputedly one of the most beautiful churches in the world, it housed relics of St Gregory, the first Catholicos of the Armenian Church.

A model of the partially reconstructed church in the Museum of Armenian History (p153) in Yerevan shows it to have been a round creation with a hood-shaped dome 45m high. An earthquake in 930 caused the building to collapse. An arc of finely carved pillars and a massive stone floor are what remains, along with a profusion of decorated stone

fragments. Architecture historians argue over whether the reconstruction in the Armenian History Museum is really true to the church's original design. Either way, the pillars evoke a feeling for a Greek- and Roman-influenced Levantine Christianity similar to many early-Syrian church ruins.

A pool in the centre of the building was used to baptise adults. Around the cathedral are the ruins of the palace of the Catholicos and the wine press and stone tanks of a massive medieval winery. Zvartnots lies in rich farmlands and orchard just south of the Echmiadzin–Yerevan highway, next to the delightfully named village of Ptghunk, 17km from Yerevan and 4km from the centre of Echmiadzin. It's easy to catch public transport either way along the highway.

ECHMIADZIN ԷՋՄԻԱԾԻՆ
☎ 0231 / pop 52,000

Holy Echmiadzin is the Vatican of the Armenian Apostolic Church, the place where Surp Grigor Lusavorich (St Gregory the Illuminator) saw a beam of light fall to the earth in a divine vision, and where he built the first Mayr Tachar (Mother Church of Armenia). For Armenian Christians, Echmiadzin (Descent of the Only Begotten Son of God) has unparalleled importance. Echmiadzin (sometimes spelt Ejmiatsin or Etchmiadzin) was the capital of Armenia from 180 to 340, when Christianity was first adopted by the Armenian nation. The seat of the Catholicos (patriarch of all Armenians) wandered across western Armenia for centuries before returning to the Mayr Tachar in 1441, with substantial rebuilding in the 15th century. The cathedral has sprouted more bell towers over the last 400 years, but the core is much as St Gregory's vision guided him. The Palace of the Catholicos in front of the Mayr Tachar is the home of the present Catholicos, Garegin II, enthroned in November 1999. He is the supreme prelate of the 1700-year-old Armenian Apostolic faith.

Holy See of Echmiadzin
ՄՈՒՐԲ ԷՋՄԻԱԾԻՆ

The main cathedral, **Mayr Tachar**, stands in a quadrangle of hedges and lawn surrounded by 19th-century buildings. By the main entrance at the southern end the large grey **2001 Papal Visit Monument**, built for Pope John Paul II's visit and mass in 2001, stands next to the **Gevorgian Seminary**. The 19th-century **seminary**

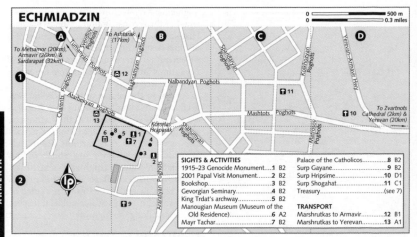

ECHMIADZIN

SIGHTS & ACTIVITIES
1915–23 Genocide Monument....1 B2
2001 Papal Visit Monument.......2 B2
Bookshop.................................3 B2
Gevorgian Seminary...................4 B2
King Trdat's archway.................5 B2
Manougian Museum (Museum of the
   Old Residence)......................6 A2
Mayr Tachar............................7 B2

Palace of the Catholicos..............8 B2
Surp Gayane.............................9 B2
Surp Hripsime.........................10 D1
Surp Shogahat........................11 C1
Treasury.............................(see 7)

TRANSPORT
Marshrutkas to Armavir...........12 B1
Marshrutkas to Yerevan...........13 A1

was closed in 1921 when Echmiadzin was swamped by refugees from the genocide, and it was forbidden to reopen under Soviet rule. The main gate leads past the **bookshop** between buildings holding monastic cells to the central compound. Bearded clergymen in hooded black robes glide along the garden paths around the Mayr Tachar.

The three-tiered bell tower at the entrance of the church is richly carved, and dates from 1648. Inside, the church is modest in scale, about 20m by 20m, but the roof gleams with frescoes. At the centre is an altar at the place where St Gregory saw the divine light strike the ground.

At the rear of the church, through a door on the right of the altar, is the **treasury** (🕐 10am-5pm Tue-Sat, 1.30-5pm Sun). It houses 1700 years of treasure collected by the church, including the Holy Lance (Surp Geghard), the weapon used by a Roman soldier to pierce the side of Christ on his way to Calvary. It's a suitably brutish spearhead set into an ornate gold and silver casing. It was brought to Echmiadzin from Geghard Monastery. There is also an image of the Crucifixion, which, according to tradition, was carved by St John. The treasury has relics of the apostles Thaddeus, Peter and Andrew, some in hand or arm-shaped reliquaries, and fragments of the Holy Cross and Noah's Ark.

A door from the treasury leads under the main body of the church to a pagan shrine with a fire altar, seemingly left in situ in case this whole Christianity thing turned out to be a fad and the old faiths reasserted themselves. The shrine can be visited with a prior appointment through a travel agency, or with a bit of luck by asking one of the clerics in the treasury.

The gardens of Mayr Tachar have a **1915–23 Genocide Monument** and many fine *khatchkars* assembled from around the country. The **archway** leading to the Palace of the Catholicos was built by King Trdat III in the 4th century. The **Manougian Museum (Museum of the Old Residence)** stands next to the palace. It's off-limits to casual visitors but if you have some clout with the Armenian Church it can be visited. Travel agencies in Yerevan can arrange visits to the church's private museum. There are some particularly fine *khatchkars* across the garden from the museum's entrance (some are also near the Papal Visit Monument, see p171), including examples from the recently destroyed cemetery in Julfa's old town in Naxçivan.

Other Churches

The **Surp Gayane** is a short walk past the main gate of the Holy See from the town's main square. St Gayane was the prioress of the 32 virtuous maidens who accompanied St Hripsime to Armenia. The original 6th-century chapel over her grave was rebuilt into a church in 1630. It's a fine orange-toned building with a plain interior and some fine *khatchkars* scattered about.

The 17th-century **Surp Shogahat** rather pales beside the splendour of its neighbours in Echmiadzin, but it's a sturdy stone structure with simple, elegant lines. It was rebuilt on the foundations of a chapel to one of the companions of Hripsime and Gayane.

Surp Hripsime was originally built in 618, replacing an earlier chapel on the site where Hripsime is said to have been killed after she refused to marry King Trdat III, choosing instead to remain true to her faith – she was a pagan who had earlier fled marriage from the Roman emperor Diocletian.

Getting There & Away

Marshrutkas for Yerevan (AMD200, 20 to 30 minutes, 21km, every 10 minutes) leave from Atarbekyan Poghots, two blocks up from the main traffic circle. Transport further west towards Armavir (AMD250, hourly between 11am and 4pm) leaves from Tumanyan Poghots. The minivans leave from Sarian Poghots in Yerevan near the corner with Mesrop Mashtots Poghota.

METSAMOR MUSEUM
ՄԵԾԱՄՈՐ ԹԱՆԳԱՐԱՆ

Besides an internationally renowned nuclear power plant, Metsamor also has intriguing remains of sophisticated early cultures. The **Metsamor Museum** (☎ 0937415 67; admission AMD1000; ⓥ 11am-5pm Tue-Sun), 6km from Metsamor town, displays evidence of thousands of years of civilisation from an early Iron Age settlement excavated nearby. From Echmiadzin take the main road to Armavir, then turn left and travel for 3km to the village of Taronik, then take a right in the village and another left about 500m on. The collection includes gold jewellery from 600 BC and earlier, and an ancient astrological stone.

Outside the museum entrance is a row of **phallus stones**, some measuring 3m high, most brought here from other excavation sites. Dating from pre-Christian times, the stones are fertility symbols created to ask for God's help not only with human fertility, but also for good crops and animal health. Other exhibits require more explanation and an English-speaking guide. Behind the museum, giant stones around the outside of the excavation are part of an ancient **Cyclopean fortress**, yet to be completely excavated.

On the second hill, before descending to the **covered excavation site**, ask someone from the museum to point out the lichen-mottled **astrological stone**, with markings that were part of an early astronomical observatory with similarities to Zorats Karer near Sisian.

SARDARAPAT ՍԱՐԴԱՐԱՊԱՏ

About 10km past the small city of Armavir (Hoktemberyan) in the orchards and farms of the Ararat Plain stands the venerated war memorial site of **Sardarapat**. It was here in May 1918 that the forces of the first Armenian republic under Zoravar (General) Andranik turned back the Turkish invaders and saved the country from a likely annihilation. Built in 1968 with statues of giant bulls, a 35m stone belltower shrine to the fallen, five eagle statues built of tuff and a memorial wall, the site puts an Armenian twist on Soviet war memorials. Nationalist Armenians treat a visit here as a kind of pilgrimage. The nearby **museum** (admission AMD500, guide AMD700; ⓥ 11am-5pm Tue-Sun) has relics from the battle itself in the first hall, as well as exhibits of items from the Neolithic Age up to the Middle Ages. Upstairs there is a treasure trove of carpets, jewellery, ceramics and handicrafts, the sum of which represents the country's best ethnography collection – a celebration of Armenian culture, survival and life.

Getting There & Away

Sardarapat is about 10km southwest of Armavir, signposted near the village of Araks. If time is short it makes sense to combine a visit with one to Echmiadzin or Metsamor. Marshrutkas leave from Yerevan's Kilikya Avtokayan for Armavir (AMD300, 45 minutes to an hour, every 15 minutes, 7.30am to 9.30pm). A taxi from Armavir with two hours at Sardarapat should cost about AMD2000 with bargaining.

ASHTARAK ԱՇՏԱՐԱԿ
☎ 0232 / pop 27,000

Ashtarak is a midsized regional town on the Kasagh Gorge, 22km northwest of Yerevan and somewhat higher at 1100m. Ashtarak is an interesting old town with lots of 19th-century buildings. There's a 16th-century stone bridge below the new bridge, and four churches around town, including the little 7th-century Karmravor church with intricate carvings and a cemetery with *khatchkars* a short way north, and the 6th-century Tsiranavor church on the edge of the gorge. Ashtarak has some very rural neighbourhoods as well, full of fruit

ARMENIA

trees and stacks of hay in late summer. While there is no great need to come to the town itself, it does make a decent transit point for the Kasagh Gorge churches (see below) if you are travelling by local transport.

Kasagh Gorge Churches

Churches from the 6th to the 16th century dot the landscape north and south of Ashtarak along the gorge of the little Kasagh River. Across the gorge from Yerevan on the northern outskirts of Ashtarak is the village of **Mughni**, with the splendid **Surp Gevorg** Church, finished in 1669, featuring striped bands of stone around its central drum and a classic half-folded umbrella cone on top. The village is an easy turn-off from the main highway that runs north to Spitak.

About 4km north of Mughi, along the same highway, is the village of **Ohanavan**. Perched on the edge of the village, overlooking the gorge, is the 7th-century monastery of **Hovhannavank**, famous for producing manuscripts and for its wealth of inscriptions and decorative carvings. It's right on the lip of the gorge, looking as though it pins down the flat volcanic grazing land, preventing it from tumbling into the chasm.

Getting back on the main road north, another 5km north leads to perhaps the prettiest monastery of all, **Saghmosavank**, a cluster of drums and conical domes from the 13th century.

A trail at the bottom of the gorge links Hovannavank and Saghmosavank – you can cover the distance on foot in less than 90 minutes. The trail begins at the new cemetery on the northern part of Ohanavan village. It's unlikely you'll find a taxi at Saghmosavank once you reach the end of the trail. You could arrange to have one from Ashtarak meet you at an appointed time, or just hitch back from the main highway, another 20-minute walk from Saghmosavank. Another option is to take a cab to Saghmosavank, do the walk in reverse and arrange transport back from Havannavank (which is close to Ashtarak).

About 8km southwest of Ashtarak in **Oshakan** is a 19th-century church built over the tomb of St Mesrop Mashtots, the genius who created the Armenian alphabet.

Sleeping & Eating

Ashtaraki Dzor (☎ 3 67 78; Kasagh Gorge, Ashtarak; per person incl breakfast AMD10,000; 🍴) This midrange hotel, built on terraces down the walls of Ashtarak Gorge, is best known for its dining and entertainment. *Khoravats* dinners cost AMD3000, and there's a big dance floor and some pretty good local talent singing and playing. The hotel rooms are modern with satellite TV, though the service is a bit rusty. A fun choice for a weekend out of Yerevan with friends. It's about 4km north of the town centre

Getting There & Away

Ashtarak is on a major road, so public transport is easy. In Yerevan, Ashtarak marshrutkas leave from Grigor Lusavorich Poghots, (AMD250, 40 minutes, every hour from 7.30am to 6.30pm). There are also marshrutkas from here to villages such as Voskevaz and Agarak that go via Ashtarak. A bus travels to Ohanavan around 3pm or whenever it's full. Marshrutkas return to Yerevan from Ashtarak's main *shuka*.

To visit the local sites (eg Hovhannavank and Saghmosvank) by taxi you can save a little money by taking the bus from Yerevan to Ashtarak and then hiring a local taxi at a rate of AMD100 per kilometre.

BYURAKAN & AROUND
ԲՅՈՒՐԱԿԱՆ

The landscape around the village of Byurakan, about 14km west of Ashtarak on the southern slopes of Mt Aragats, includes a couple of astronomical observatories and the impressive remains of the fortress of Amberd, 15km up the mountain. The Surp Hovhannes Church in Byurakan is an interesting early basilica model. Other churches and villages in the vicinity have *khatchkars* and *vishap* scattered about.

The fortress of **Amberd** was constructed on a ridge above the confluence of the little gorges of the Amberd and Arkashen streams. The high stone walls and rounded towers are a rough but effective defence, rebuilt many times but mostly dating from the 11th century. It's easy to see why the site was chosen – at 2300m above sea level, it commands a position above the farms and trade routes of the Ararat Plain. According to local lore, the thick walls of the fortress were never breached – not even by those pesky Mongols. A church stands downhill from the fortress with the ruins of fortified houses and a substantial public bathhouse. A small kiosk here sells drinks and snacks.

The fortress is about a two-hour hike from the scout camp near the very end of Byurakan village. The scenery along the footpath is rewarding. Walk along the Mt Aragats road until you reach the ski house. A sign in Cyrillic and Latin script points ahead – take the left-hand fork anyway. The fortress can be seen from a distance, but you have to walk around a steep valley before reaching it. Although geographically close to Byurakan, the paved road makes a 15km long circuitous route.

The first part of the road heads uphill towards Kari Lich and then branches off to the left 5km before the fortress. As you walk or drive through this landscape look for the large green or white tents owned by Armenian shepherds who graze their flocks here in summer.

The **Tegher Monastery** is about 5km uphill from the village of Aghtsk in the old village of the same name, on the far side of the Amberd Gorge from Byurakan. The church was built by Mamakhatun, the wife of Prince Vache Vahutyan, in 1232.

Sleeping

Byurakan Observatory Hotel (☎ 093 508 681; per person AMD5000) This is an old Soviet establishment on the grounds of the observatory. The hotel itself is a lovely pink tuff building with basic but satisfactory rooms. For an extra AMD1000 you'll get a tour of the observatory at night.

Getting There & Away

There are three buses per day from Yerevan to Byurakan, departing at 10.30am, 12.45pm and 5.30pm from the bus stand on Grigor Lusavorich Poghota in Yerevan (AMD300). If you don't catch one of these there are also a few buses to Agarak, 6km south of Byurakan on the Ashtarak–Gyumri highway. From Agarak you could walk, hitch or hire a taxi. There are very few, if any, taxis in Byurakan itself so if you need a cab to go to Aragats or Amberd its better to take one from Ashtarak. The three buses return to Yerevan at noon, 4pm and 6.30pm.

MT ARAGATS ԱՐԱԳԱԾ ԼԵՐ

Snow covers the top of the highest mountain in modern Armenia almost year-round, so climbing is best in July, August or September. Beware – even in August, clouds can gather in the crater by about 10am, so it's good to start walking as early as possible. It's not unusual for hikers to start on mountain ascents at 5am.

The southernmost of its four peaks (3893m) is easy enough for inexperienced climbers, but the northern peak (4090m) demands greater abilities.

The road from Byurakan winds 27km up to the Cosmic Ray Institute observatory and the waters of Kari Lich. If you have your own sleeping bag, the scientists may be able to find a place for you to sleep (for around AMD2000). Hot water and clean bathrooms are available. Alternatively, there are camping places for those suitably equipped with a tent.

The road ends at the lake, and uphill the route is rocky and strewn with debris. There's no path, but the peaks are visible so you basically slog it uphill. The northern summit can be reached in four to six hours. To get there, walk over the easy pass between the southern and western summits. From the southwest pass, the route descends into the crater where you navigate fields of volcanic stones, then up again to the ridge and northern summit. Alternatively, hike up to the southern summit in just two hours.

Several tour companies can arrange walks up Mt Aragats, including the Ajdahag Mountain Hiking Club (p151) and Avayayr (p151). A two-day trip including guide, transport and camping equipment costs around AMD45,000 per person. **Serzh Hovsepyan** (☎ 35 00 46; serzh_hovsepyan@yahoo.com) is also a recommended guide for climbing the mountain's peaks. Serzh is a member of the Spitak mountain-rescue team.

Getting There & Away

There is no public transport to Kari Lich. Hitchhikers usually take a bus to Byurakan and then try to thumb a lift, which is more likely on weekends. A better idea is to get a group together to climb the mountain and share the costs of a cab from Yerevan, Ashtarak or Byurakan. From Byurakan a cab should cost AMD4500 (one way) after some haggling.

TALIN & AROUND ԹԱԼԻՆ
☎ 2490 / pop 7,600

Talin lies in one of the stonier, more rugged corners of the country, 75km northwest of Yerevan. Many of the surrounding villages were settled by refugees from Van and Kars in historic western Armenia, now part of Turkey, and local folk-dancing troupes preserve

ARMENIA

western Armenian songs and dances. There are also some Yezidi Kurd villages in the vicinity.

Those with an abiding love of Armenian church architecture might want to visit Aruch's 7th-century **Aruchavank Monastery,** midway between Ashtarak and Talin, and the similar 7th-century **Surp Astvatsatsin Church** on the outskirts of Talin itself.

About 5km south of Talin is the interesting 10th-century double fortress of **Dashtadem**, which still shelters flocks of sheep inside its sturdy walls after dark. Follow the highway onto Gyumri to **Mastara** and its very different fortlike church from the 5th century, with rare vestiges of frescoes.

KHOR VIRAP MONASTERY
ԽՈՐ ՎԻՐԱՊ

Khor Virap Monastery, 30km south of Yerevan, is a famous pilgrimage site with an iconic location at the foot of Mt Ararat. You'll see plenty of tempting pictures of the place on postcards and souvenir books long before you get there.

The monastery is on a hillock close to the Araks River, overlooking river pastures, stork nests and vineyards, 4km off the main highway through the village of Pokr Vedi (sometimes also called Khor Virap).

The pagan King Trdat III imprisoned St Gregory the Illuminator (Surp Grigor Lusavorich) in a well (*khor virap* means 'deep well') here for 12 years, where he was secretly fed by Christian women. The king was later cursed by madness (or cursed by sprouting the head of a boar in a more colourful version) and miraculously cured by St Gregory. Historians contend that Trdat may have switched allegiances to tap into the strength of Armenia's growing Christian community in the face of Roman aggression. In any case the king converted to Christianity and St Gregory became the first Catholicos of the Armenian Apostolic Church, and set about building churches on top of pagan temples and teaching the faith.

The ground-level buildings at Khor Virap have been repeatedly rebuilt since at least the 6th century, and the main Surp Astvatsatsin Church dates from the 17th century. Khor Virap is an important pilgrimage site and people often visit for a baptism or after a wedding to perform a *matagh* (sacrifice, often of sheep or chicken), which keeps the priests busy on weekends. It's a shivery experience to climb 60m down into the well. The well is lighted, but you need to wear sturdy shoes to scale the metal ladder. Just outside the monastery walls are some excavations on the site of Artashat, Trdat's capital, founded in the 2nd century BC.

The Armash Fish Ponds, 25km downstream from Khor Virap near the border town of Yeraskh, are home to a great variety of migrating birds in spring and autumn as well as local species.

The ruins of the ancient capital of Dvin are on the edge of the plains near Verin Dvin, about 13km from Artashat.

Getting There & Away
There are two marshrutkas a day to Khor Virap from Yerevan (AMD350, 11am and 3.30pm), and three buses per day (9am, 2pm and 5pm), all from the Sasuntsi Davit metro station. Z

The main highway is 4km away, with lots of public transport to and from Ararat and towns further south. A return-trip by car from Yerevan costs about AMD7000 through a taxi service.

KHOSROV NATURE RESERVE
ԽՈՍՐՈՎԻ ԱՐԳԵԼՈՑ

Khosrov Nature Reserve protects several chunks of rugged hills and wooded slopes in the upper valleys of the Azat, Votankunk and Khosrov Rivers.

The reserve is broken up into four distinct sections – the most popular section is the gorge below Garni and Geghard, which can be explored on foot.

You need a 4WD to reach the other parts of the reserve. The park's main office is in Vedi, 49km from Yerevan. From here 4WD roads climb up past Dashtakar to a bridge across to Urtsadzor, and then up to **Surp Karapet**. It's an isolated spot with a 13th-century church topped by a classic ribbed umbrella cone, more easily reached via the southern highway, at the turn-off about 4km after the hamlet of Tigranashen. The road up to the reserve reaches a pretty camping spot on the Vedi river, then it's a trek on foot into the rugged light forest to the **Jamsho Monastery** and **Geghi Fort**. Companies such as Avarayr (p151) arrange treks and nature tours in the reserve.

NORTHERN ARMENIA

Northern Armenia comprises the *marz* of Shirak, Lori and Tavush – this also includes the rugged bare highlands of Gegarkunik around gorgeous Lake Sevan. The regional landscapes vary from Shirak's open plains to Lori's pine forests and Tavush's lush hornbeam and oak woods around Dilijan. We have listed the sites in the order most visited from Yerevan – most travellers head up to Lake Sevan and then on to Dilijan with a side trip to Ijevan. Travellers usually overnight in Vanadzor before going to Georgia via the Debed Canyon. Stepanavan and Gyumri are also worthy side trips.

LAKE SEVAN ՍԵՎԱՆԱ ԼԻՃ

Perched at 1900m above sea level, the great blue eye of Sevana Lich (Lake Sevan) covers 940 sq km, and is 80km by 30km at its widest. The lake is perfect for escaping Yerevan's summer heat. Its colours and shades change with the weather and by its own mysterious processes, from a dazzling azure to dark blue and a thousand shades in between. The freshwater lake supports a healthy fish population, including the *ishkhan* (prince trout), named for a row of spots like a crown on its head.

When Sevan's outlet, the Hrazdan River, was tapped for hydroelectric plants and irrigation in the 1950s, the lake fell and is now about 20m lower. Other Soviet plans to drain the lake down to one-sixth its size thankfully went nowhere. The retreating waters uncovered forts, houses and artefacts dating back some 2000 years, and made Sevan Island a peninsula.

The exposed land has been designated the Sevan national park, although some of it is disappearing again as conservationists have convinced the government of the need to raise the level of the lake. Since 2002 it has risen by 2m, an environmental achievement that has meant cleaner water and more fish. Much to the consternation of local investors, the rising tide is also starting to flood into some of the beachside resorts.

Tourism is picking up around the lake, but except for a hectic 10 weeks in summer it's

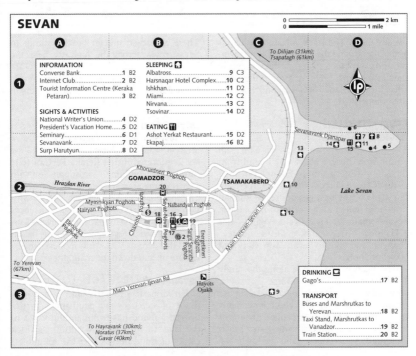

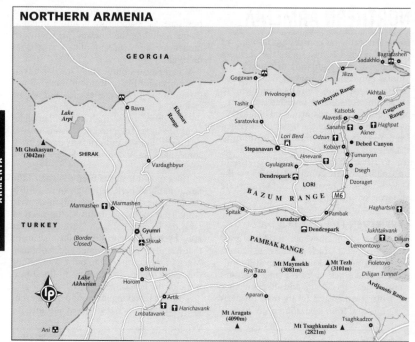

NORTHERN ARMENIA

usually quiet. The stark volcanic highlands and plains around the lake endure a long winter, and except for a string of achievements in medieval church building around the lake's edge, the hinterlands of Gegarkunik *marz* are not often visited.

SEVAN ՍԵՎԱՆ
☎ 0261 / pop 20,000

The bustling little town of Sevan is 6km from Sevan Monastery, a short way inland from the lake's western shores. Founded in 1842 as the Russian village of Elenovka, there are few signs of the past besides some Russian provincial houses at the western end of town. Sevan's main street, Nairian Poghots, has a Haypost office, cafés, a *shuka*, moneychangers and taxis to Sevan Monastery and lakeshore hotels.

The main beach strip is along the sandy south side of the Sevanavank peninsula, crowned by the much-photographed churches on the hill at the end. This beach is suddenly transformed into the Armenian Riviera in the brief hot summers, with bars, beach volleyball, water-skiing and paddleboats.

There are other, quieter beaches closer to Sevan town across the highway near the Hayots Ojakh motel-restaurant. There are fees in summer to use the beaches near Sevan, from AMD2000 to AMD3000 per person depending on the beach.

Information

The **Tourist Information Centre** (☎ 2 02 20; www .sevaninfo.am; 164 Nairyan Poghots; ☺ 9am-noon & 2-5pm Mon-Sat), located in the Keraka Petaran (city Municipality building), can supply you with a map of the area and ideas on activities or accommodation. **Internet Club** (☎ 2 74 83; 1 Kriboidov Poghots; ☺ 10am-9pm) is a couple of blocks south of the City Municipality. **Converse Bank** (☎ 254 52; Nairyan Poghots; ☺ 9.30am-6.30pm) has an ATM that accepts Visa, while moneychangers feature up and down the main drag.

Sevanavank ՍԵՎԱՆԱՎԱՆՔ

Sevan Monastery (Sevanavank) is up a long flight of steps on the peninsula's turtle-backed hill and has commanding views of the lake. In summer and autumn a thick carpet of cloud pushes over the Areguniats

mountains to the north and evaporates at the lake's edge.

The first monument on the steps leading up to the monastery is dedicated to a 20th-century navy captain, commander of the Russian fleet on Lake Sevan. The first church is **Arakelots** (Apostles), followed by **Astvatsatsin** (Holy Mother of God) with a courtyard filled with *khatchkars*. St Mesrop Mashtots had a vision of 12 figures walking across the lake, who showed him the place to found a church. Queen Mariam, wife of Vasak of Syunik, built the churches in 874, and they have recently been restored. In the 19th century the monastery was a place to reform errant monks – there was a strict regime and no women were allowed.

Continue up the hill past the foundations of the **Surp Harutyun Church** to the highest point of the peninsula, with panoramic views. On the far side of the hill are two buildings: one belongs to the **National Writers' Union** (closed to the public), the other is the **president's vacation home**, protected by a high fence. The building on the north side of the peninsula is a new **seminary** for the Armenian Apostolic Church. The students sometimes play football in the

car park near the stairs. There are a couple of souvenir stalls and the Ashot Yerkat restaurant (see p180) too. There's no public transport out here, so arrange for a taxi to wait for you (about AMD2000 with 30 minutes' waiting time from Sevan town).

Sleeping & Eating

Sevan's beach resorts start to fill up – and raise their prices – around late May. Prices may jump by 40% in the high season. The season slows down again in early September. In spring and autumn they remain open with reduced rates and in winter most are shut entirely.

Camping is possible for a fee and there are lots of little *domiks* (housing units made from cargo containers), ministry lodges and guesthouses around the lake that you might unearth if you ask around. Sevan is also close enough to Yerevan for a day trip.

Ishkan (☎ 093359 053; Sevan peninsula; domiks AMD10,000-15,000) Cheap and popular with backpackers, Ishkhan is located conveniently near the parking lot by Sevanavank. It may feel like an Oklahoma trailer park but it should suffice for budget travellers.

Tsovinar (☎ 1-53 05 99, 091601 821; Sevan peninsula; domiks AMD15,000-25,000) A friendly little two-storey lodge about halfway along Sevanavank's main beach. The rooms are small but they have hot water.

Nirvana (☎ 2 21 21; Yerevan Hwy; cottages AMD35,000) Between the Harsnaqar and the peninsula, Nirvana has five-person cottages with hot and cold water and a refrigerator. There's a café-bar here open late and a wide stretch of beach at the front.

Miami (☎ 093570 404; Yerevan Hwy; d AMD20,000, cottages AMD30,000-40,000, villa AMD50,000-70,000) A serene resort with cabins and a main hotel sent around a grassy courtyard with an above-ground splash pool. The scene can get lively with music and dancing.

Albatross (☎ 091485 245; Yerevan Hwy; cottages AMD15,000) About 2.5km southwest of Sevan town, Albatross occupies a quiet stretch of beach with a few colourful *domiks*. Paddleboats and jet skis are available.

Harsnaqar Hotel Complex (☎ 2 00 92; www.harsnaqar hotel.am; fax 2 00 65; Yerevan Hwy; s/d AMD300,000/40,000;) This is the large Holiday Inn–style hotel where the highway meets the lake. It has a waterpark, tennis courts, lawns and a private stretch of beach. It also has an excellent restaurant, with a terrace overlooking the lake.

ARMENIA

Ashot Yerkat Restaurant (☎ 2 50 00; meals AMD2000-3000; ☯ 10am-9pm) You can feast on kebabs, grilled *ishkhan* trout, salads and lavash on the terrace of this restaurant out on the Sevan peninsula. Try the house speciality, 'eat and shut up' – a concoction of sautéed meat and potatoes.

Ekapaj (☎ 2 11 44; Nairyan Poghots; meals AMD1000-2500; ☯ 10am-9pm) A popular and convenient bistro in the middle of town. The usual stuff – kebabs and *khoravats* – is available, plus breakfasts of blintzes and fried eggs.

Gago's (Sayat-Nova Poghots; ☯ 11am-midnight) On the street behind Ekapaj is this friendly café where you can have cold drinks and snacks.

Getting There & Away

By car Yerevan is only 30 to 40 minutes away by freeway. Transport (AMD600, 40 minutes, every hour 9am to 5pm) to Yerevan leaves from the corner of Nairyan Poghots and Sayat-Nova Poghots in the centre of Sevan town.

There's a marshrutka to Vanadzor from the corner of Nairyan and Shinararneri Poghots at 10am (AMD1000) that can drop you in Dilijan. This corner is also a taxi stand. A taxi to Yerevan (67km) costs about AMD7000, to Dilijan AMD3500, to Tsaghkadzor AMD2000, and to Sevanavank with 30 minutes' waiting time about AMD2000. A taxi to one of the hotels around the peninsula costs AMD1000. A four- or five-hour tour of Sevanavank, Hayravank and the *khatchkars* of Noratus should cost around AMD7000.

In summer a train runs from Yerevan to Sevan (AMD200, four hours, 8am), though it's so slow that it could only be considered for the experience.

AROUND LAKE SEVAN

About 30km south of Sevan is the charmingly typical *tufa* **Hayravank Monastery** – 1100 years old, sturdy as the day it was built, and with *khatchkars* in the cemetery attesting to centuries of Armenian life. The promontory it stands on has a fine view of Lake Sevan. Further south is Noratus (sometimes spelt Noraduz), an old village and a fine place to wander around. There's a tall chapel of **Surp Grigor Lusavorich** at one end of town and an ancient *khatchkar*-studded cemetery on the eastern side of the village. Noratus is a good area to find a **beach** on the sunny side of the lake.

The provincial capital of Gegharkunik *marz* is **Gavar** (Kamo), population 30,000, on the cold slopes of the Geghama Mountains west of Lake Sevan. It's a quietly poor town, similar to **Martuni** at the lake's southern end, with a few cafés, a Soviet-era hotel and a feeling that it is just struggling to survive. A newly repaired road heads south through a tunnel under the **Selim Pass** (2410m) from Martuni to Yeghegnadzor in Vayots Dzor. About 20km east of Martuni is the handsome little **Vanevank Church** (903), in a gorge south of the town of Artsvanist. Turn off at Karchagbyur and head up the valley through Lchavan to the centre of Makenis village to find the 10th- to 13th-century churches of **Makenyats Vank**, close to a gorge.

Further on, the road cuts inland to **Vardenis**. One road continues around the eastern side of the lake and another heads towards the mountains and the valuable **Zod gold mines**. A famously rough road used only by fearless truckers and truck-bus hybrids heads on from the mines over the Sodk Pass (2400m) into the wilds of Kelbajar and northern Karabakh.

On the far side of the lake at Tsapatagh is the **Avan Marak Tsapatagh** (☎ 1-54 31 22; www.tufenkianheritage.com; s/d/ste AMD32,700/39,200/65,400; ☒ ☒), a stylish lakeside hotel with a swimming pool – an escape from the bustle of Yerevan. The hotel has sailboats and windsurfers for hire in summer, and the splendid Zanazan restaurant (meals around AMD3500 to AMD6000). By road the shortest route to Yerevan is along Sevan's north shore (140km, two hours).

North of Tsapatagh, Shorja is a poor, desolate village but a logical base for exploring picturesque Artanish peninsula. It's possible to camp at the lakeshore.

Public transport around the lake is sporadic – there are regular marshrutkas and buses from the Hyusisayin Avtokayan (Tbilisian highway) on the northern limits of Yerevan to the main towns (Gavar, Martuni and Vardenis) for around AMD1000. The best way to discover the lakeshore miles of quiet, clean beaches is with your own transport and perhaps camping gear.

In summer, the train from Sevan continues to Shorja on the other side of the lake (AMD430, one hour). There are no toilets on the train. From Shorja you can come back by road to the Dilijan highway (AMD500) and pick up northbound transport, or go all the way back to Yerevan (AMD1000). There is a daily marshrutka from Sevan to Shorja (AMD1000) around 1pm.

(Continued on page 189)

BEST OF GEORGIA, ARMENIA & AZERBAIJAN

Modest in size but grand in stature, Georgia, Armenia and Azerbaijan pack a lot of highlights within their frontiers. Stretching from the steamy Black Sea to the limpid Caspian, these three countries offer excitement and challenges for travellers who have a hankering to explore an oft-forgotten corner where Europe and Asia meet. Here the welcome is spontaneous and effusive, the landscapes and cultures are distinctive and unforgettable, and adventure is never far away.

Georgia

Georgians claim their homeland is the most beautiful country on Earth, and they may not be far wrong. Graceful, cultured Tbilisi takes pride of place, but attractions are spread across the pristine peaks and remote valleys of the Caucasus mountains. And the legendary Georgian hospitality and cuisine will surely be your longest-lasting memory.

① Tbilisi

A maze of narrow streets with distinctive architecture, grand churches and atmospheric cafés, the Old Town (p52) is a must see. From there it's a short walk up to Narikala and Kartlis Deda for panoramic views.

② Svaneti

Wild, remote and unquestionably beautiful, Svaneti (p94) is hard to get to but certainly worth the effort. Set out for great walking around Mestia and the distinctive Svan stone towers.

③ Mt Kazbek

The solemn silhouette of Tsminda Sameba Church (p102) braced by mighty Mt Kazbek is one of the most striking sights in Georgia.

④ Davit Gareja

Contemplate the solitude of a monastic life in the semidesert while you wander the cave chambers, churches and refectories of Davit Gareja (p113).

⑤ Georgian Cuisine

Georgians are nothing if not convivial. Meals are an important part of the day; they are always communal and always lively (p46). Tuck into hearty local specialities and enjoy a sip of local wine.

⑥ Batumi

With its sultry climate and Black Sea ambience, Batumi (p89) is Georgia's summer capital and offers a taste of the tropics in the Caucasus. Head for the beach or savour the *fin-de-siècle* architecture and local Adjaran culture.

⑦ Vardzia

Delve into the depths of the Earth and seek the symbolic heart of Georgia in the cave city of Vardzia (p121), brought to prominence by Queen Tamar in the 12th century.

Armenia

Watching over revered Mt Ararat, Armenia spans rocky highlands while also boasting lush forests and serene, turquoise Lake Sevan. There are remote regions and monasteries to explore, but highlights are as likely to be Yerevan's buzzing arts scene, the Mediterranean mind-set and café culture, or a spontaneous shared meal – and tipple – with locals.

3

4

❶ Yerevan
A city of concert halls, galleries, markets and lively cafés and bars, Yerevan (p145) is the epicentre of Armenian cultural life, yet it retains a small-town ambience.

❷ Vayots Dzor
Armenia's southern province, Vayots Dzor (p206) is peppered with attractions: Noravank monastery and the village of Yeghegis, as well as remote trails suitable for walking or horse riding.

❸ Debed Canyon Monasteries
Climb to the cusp of the Debed Canyon to discover the lofty monasteries of Sanahin and Haghpat (p201). Take in the views across the valley while wandering among gravestones, churches and *khatchkars*.

❹ Echmiadzin
The Holy See of Echmiadzin (p171), with its three-tiered bell tower and interior frescoes in swirls of gold, green and red, is the spiritual centre of Armenia.

❺ Goris
A stop on the ages-old route to Persia, Goris (p213) moves at its own sleepy pace. Wander the tree-lined avenues of this pretty rural town full of 19th-century stone houses.

❻ Dilijan
Nestled amid mountain pastures, Dilijan (p190) is full of quaint gingerbread-style houses and has long been a retreat for artists. Within walking distance are the monasteries of Haghartsin and Goshavank.

Azerbaijan

Diverse in landscape and varied in climate, Azerbaijan has some decidedly un-orthodox attractions, including mud volcanoes and burning rocks. In Azerbaijan the timeless and the contemporary blend to provide countless diversions for hardy travellers: from cosmopolitan Baku and the gritty Caspian shore to Silk Road caravanserais and mountain villages.

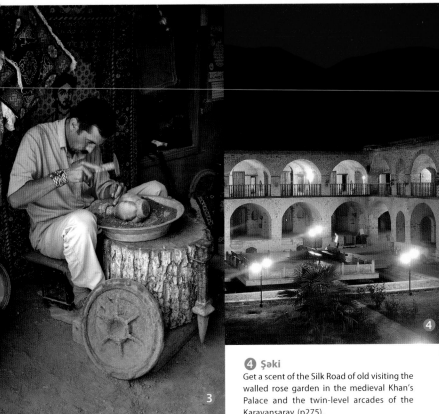

4 Şəki
Get a scent of the Silk Road of old visiting the walled rose garden in the medieval Khan's Palace and the twin-level arcades of the Karavansaray (p275).

1 Old Baku
Mixing tea-house atmosphere with oil-boom optimism, Baku (p236) has a vibe all its own. The heart of the city is the Old City, with its winding alleys, stone mansions, caravanserais and Maiden's Tower.

2 Qobustan
Explore the barren and rocky hills of Qo-bustan (p260) to discover Stone Age petro-glyphs, Roman-era graffiti and – a short distance away – the diminutive, otherworldly mud volcanoes.

3 Lahıc
Ringing with the sound of coppersmiths' hammers and busy with the looms of carpet weavers, Lahıc (p270) is one of Azerbaijan's most enchanting villages, and the surround-ing hillsides are beacons for walkers.

5 Laza & Xınalıq
Two of Azerbaijan's prettiest settlements, Laza (p266) and Xınalıq (p265) are refreshing, mountain-top alternatives to the sun-baked lowlands.

6 Dining in Baku
Restaurants in Baku (p249) offer up Azeri spe-cialities like *shashlyk* and dolma as well as a range of other delectable cuisines – Turkish, Georgian, Ukrainian and Russian.

7 İlisu
Known as Azerbaijan's 'mini-Switzerland', İlisu (p279) is just the spot for a stroll. It makes a great base for hikes to the surround-ing hills and the waterfalls of the nearby nature reserve.

Late-night shopping around Fountain Square, Baku

(Continued from page 180)

TSAGHKADZOR ԾԱՂԿԱՁՈՐ
☎ 0223 / pop 1800

Back when Armenia was part of the USSR Soviet athletes used to come to this tiny village to train for the winter Olympics and other sport competitions. The ski centre is still here and if you happen to be in Armenia in winter Tsaghkadzor (Gorge of Flowers) makes an excellent weekend getaway. The little resort, 57km north of Yerevan, is a virtual ghost town in summer, which is great if you are looking for cut rates on hotels or some crowd-free nature spots.

The main road reaches a central square and veers left up to the House of Writers, or right and around the active Kecharis Monastery. The road straight on from the monastery leads to the cable-car station, while another branches to the left up to the Sport Base. The 6km cable car up Mt Tsaghkuniats runs daily even in summer.

The skiing facilities at the ski resort are basic and a far cry from the Alps but good fun for a day on the slopes.

A single cable-car ride costs AMD1000, and you can hire basic ski equipment, much of it vintage gear from the cable-car station. Better equipment is available from the Hotel Kecharis.

The forests around the base of the mountain provide some nice walks, and in summer there's horse riding from the Tsaghkadzor Sport Base. Horse riding can be organized directly through **Seran Mirzoya** (☎ 093340 058), reached through the Hotel Kecharis.

The **Kecharis Monastery** is a finely carved 11th- to 13th-century complex with *khatch-kars*, a *katoghike* (cathedral), a Surp Grigor Church and a smaller Surp Nishan chapel. It's now the seat of the bishop of Kotayk *marz* and is open daily.

Sleeping & Eating

Many local homes offer homestays for AMD5000 to AMD8000 per person per night. Asking around once you arrive might be leaving it a bit late; see if someone can pass on a recommendation and make contact in advance. There are a couple of cafés open in summer along the main street.

Arminay Akopyan B&B (☎ 5 20 40; 35 Kecharetsu Poghots; per person AMD5000) Clean and friendly guesthouse with hot showers. No English spoken.

Saya Hotel (☎ 5 24 35; Grigor Magistros; r AMD15,000) Increased tourism has seen the recent construction of several hotels on Tsaghkadzor's main square. Saya's clean, quiet rooms offer the best value among them. If it doesn't suit, head across the square to Jupiter or Bagart hotels.

House of Writers (☎ 1-28 10 81; www.writershotel.am; s/d AMD12,000/13,000, apt AMD40,000-50,000; ⬛) This one-time Soviet-ministry hotel has seen significant renovations – the new apartments come with colourful modern furniture and even a fish tank! Unrenovated rooms are at least well-maintained. Follow the main road into town and look for the sign on the left.

Viardo (☎ 5 26 20, 093333 597; 6-person cottages AMD20,000-35,000, 3 meals per day extra AMD4000) A complex with 25 cottages separated by trees. The set-up of each cottage is the same, the difference being that the more expensive ones have been newly renovated. Prices drop 30% outside the summer holidays and ski season. There's a café and a bar here as well. It's on the road to the cable-car station, straight on past the Kecharis Monastery.

Kecharis (☎ 5 20 91; www.kecharishotel.am; Orbeli Poghots; r incl breakfast AMD20,000-30,000; ⬛) A slick, new operation in the centre of town with well-maintained facilities, modern rooms and lots of colourful art adorning the walls. Facilities include a business centre, a sauna and a branch of the popular Jazzve Café. The English-speaking staff can also give tips on local activities or set up horse-riding trips. Prices increase by 30% during the ski season.

Coffee Break (☎ 093-515 234; ☷ 8am-2am) Despite its name, this place features grilled meats and kebabs more than coffee. The wood tables and a stone patio are a fine attempt to blend into the mountain scenery, but the blaring stereo is somewhat less attractive.

Getting There & Away

Tsaghkadzor is only about 40 minutes' drive northeast of Yerevan. There are no direct buses or marshrutkas, but a taxi to Yerevan costs about AMD5500.

There are frequent buses and marshrutkas between Yerevan and Hrazdan, 6km down the valley – a taxi up to Tsaghkadzor from here will cost AMD800. There are only a few taxis in Tsaghkadzor.

ARMENIA

DILIJAN ԴԻԼԻՋԱՆ

☎ 02680 / pop 17,000

It's billed as the 'Switzerland of Armenia' and, although that may be a bit of a stretch, alpine Dilijan is still one of the most pleasant regions in the country.

During Soviet times this was the peaceful retreat for cinematographers, composers, artists and writers to come and be creative; today it's a centre for tourism with a number of fine B&Bs and some renovated old Soviet guesthouses.

There is certainly enough natural beauty to inspire creative thought: the town is surrounded by the lush oak and hornbeam forests and deep mountain soils of the Dilijan Nature Reserve, one of the gentlest landscapes in the country. In summer the villagers herd cattle down from the mountain pastures through the town, and people gather mushrooms and mountain herbs from the rich deciduous forests. Local architecture uses a lot of steep tiled roofs and wooden beams, along with some cute gingerbread-style structures. Even the local Soviet monuments have a touch of flair.

The gorgeous churches of Haghartsin and Goshavank are an easy day trip from Dilijan.

Information & Orientation

The **Dilijan Tourist Office** (Sharambeyan Poghots; ☼ 10.30am-5pm Tue-Sun) is open for business in the tourist enclave on Sharambeyan Poghots, a short walk uphill from the bus turnaround. It can provide lists of local homestays, B&Bs, craftspeople and artists.

Myasnikyan Poghots wriggles up from the main roundabout past the little *shuka* and the Dilijan historic centre to the town centre and out to Shahumian Poghots to the older residential quarters. There's a **Haypost-Armentel** (58 Myasnikyan Poghots) in the town centre. About 200m past the Post Office is the **Internet Café** (☎ 093855 236; per hr AMD400; ☼ 10am-8pm). There are moneychangers on Myasnikyan as well as the **Ardshininvest Bank** (60 Myasnikyan Poghots), next to the Haypost office.

Sights

The **Dilijan Historic Centre** (Sharambeyan Poghots) is a little cobbled street next to Myasnikyan

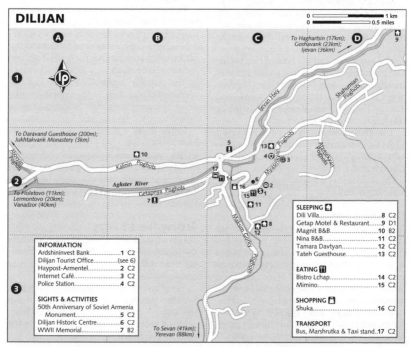

DILIJAN

0 _____ 1 km
0 _____ 0.5 miles

To Haghartsin (17km);
Goshavank (23km);
Ijevan (36km)

To Daravand Guesthouse (200m);
Jukhtakvank Monastery (3km)

To Pioletovo (11km);
Lermontovo (20km);
Vanadzor (40km)

To Sevan (41km);
Yerevan (88km)

INFORMATION
Ardshininvest Bank..................1 C2
Dilijan Tourist Office............(see 6)
Haypost-Armentel....................2 C2
Internet Café..........................3 C2
Police Station..........................4 C2

SIGHTS & ACTIVITIES
50th Anniversary of Soviet Armenia
    Monument.........................5 C2
Dilijan Historic Centre............6 C2
WWII Memorial.....................7 B2

SLEEPING
Dili Villa...............................8 C2
Getap Motel & Restaurant......9 D1
Magnit B&B........................10 B2
Nina B&B...........................11 C2
Tamara Davtyan...................12 C2
Tateh Guesthouse................13 C2

EATING
Bistro Lchap........................14 C2
Mimino...............................15 C2

SHOPPING
Shuka.................................16 C2

TRANSPORT
Bus, Marshrutka & Taxi stand..17 C2

Poghots. This collection of stone and wooden traditional buildings includes shops, a hotel, eateries, souvenir stalls and workshops for local craftspeople. The complex was thoroughly renovated in 2007.

A crownlike monument to the **50th Anniversary of Soviet Armenia** stands near the main roundabout. The **WWII Memorial**, with the huge silver figures of a soldier holding a dying comrade, is on a hillock south of the river.

The ruins of **Jukhtakvank Monastery** are near the Dilijan mineral water plant, 3.2km east along the Vanadzor road and about 3.5km up to the right.

The Surp Grigor Church, built around the 11th century, is missing its dome. The forest setting is a nice place for a picnic. Further on towards Vanadzor the scenery is gorgeous, passing the Russian **Molokan villages** of Fioletovo and Lermontovo.

Sleeping

There are lots of hotels and sanatoriums in and around town, many being snapped up and renovated now that a tunnel cuts travel time to Yerevan to around 90 minutes. The Hotel Lernayin Hayastan was being rebuilt at the time of writing. Some beautifully located resorts, such as the House of Composers, where Khachaturian, Shostakovich and Prokofiev stayed, are still run by government ministries. A local B&B scene is also developing.

Tateh Guesthouse (☎ 25 33, 093890 885; 41 Komisarneri Poghots; per person AMD5000) This large home is run by a young couple. It's not as welcoming as some other places but is central and low-priced. From the main road (just past the internet café), walk down the steps and look for the metal fence with the green trim.

Getap Motel & Restaurant (☎ 56 14, 093460 060; 4.5km along Ijevan Hwy; d/cottages AMD10,000/40,000) Getap means 'riverbank' in Armenian, which sums up the out-of-town location of this motel. There are a couple of spiffy new cottages with enough room for four people, and some rooms in the main building with a basic shared bathroom. The restaurant has little open-sided cabins by the water and serves *khoravats* (including grilled fish) for AMD1500 per person. A taxi to and from Dilijan costs about AMD1000.

Nina B&B (☎ 23 30, 091767 734; 18 Myasnikan Poghots; per person AMD6000) Most backpackers end up at this friendly B&B consisting of three guestrooms. Nina and husband Albert are great cooks and occasionally prepare *khoravats* for guests. It's a very welcoming place and one of the best B&Bs in the country. At the *shuka* turn right and up the short hill (it's well signposted).

Magnit B&B (☎ 093224 725; 86 Kalinin Poghots; per person AMD7000) Huge home with 10 guest rooms, all clean, modern and carefully decorated. It's about 1km from the roundabout on the road to Vanadzor. Breakfast is a pricey AMD2500.

Tamara Davtyan (☎ 56 71, 094573 645, 093573 645; 12 Myasnikyan Poghots; per person AMD10,000) Next door to Dili Villa, this place has set ambitious prices for mediocre accommodation; fortunately, it is open to negotiation. Although it's not a modern home, the family is friendly.

Daravand Guesthouse (☎ 78 57, 094420 965; info@ daravand.com; 46 Abovyan Poghots; s/d without bathroom 9000/14,000, with bathroom AMD10,000/18,000) This character-filled place has well-appointed rooms, a cosy common room and an outdoor deck with gorgeous views. Prices include breakfast, and the food is excellent. Owner Razmik is a diaspora Armenian with an Iranian upbringing and a German education. He can organise day trips to places of interest. The guesthouse is on the road toward Jukhtakvank, 360m off the main Dilijan–Vanadzor road. Look for the red garage and the stairs leading up to the house.

Dili Villa (☎ 70 59; www.dilitours.de; 12a Myasnikyan Poghots; per person incl breakfast AMD13,000) A handsome modern house run by the director of the local art school and his wife (French and English are spoken). There are five rooms and a modern bathroom. Excellent home cooked meals are available, plus lots of fruit and Armenian wines. Owner Ghazar will even paint your portrait upon request! Package tours of the area can be arranged. The guesthouse is 500m past Nina B&B.

Eating

There are a couple of friendly local cafés and restaurants but nothing in the fine-dining bracket.

One of the most popular places around is Getap, the hotel-restaurant on the highway towards Ijevan (see opposite).

Mimino (☎ 41 41; 37 Myasnikyan Poghots; meals AMD1800; ☯ 10am-11pm) A restaurant set slightly off the street near the historical preserve, with Georgian treats such as *khingalee* dumplings and *khachapuri* pies, plus salads.

ARMENIA

Bistro Lchap (☎ 33 80; shwarma AMD800; ⏱ 9am-9pm) Conveniently placed near the bus stop, near the roundabout, this shwarma joint serves to fill up travellers on the move.

Getting There & Around

Buses and marshrutkas to Yerevan leave from the main roundabout by the river. Buses (AMD1000, three hours) leave hourly between 9am and 3pm – some of these are services starting further north from Ijevan or Noyemberyan. Services to Ijevan (AMD500, 45 minutes) run hourly between 9am and noon. Services to Vanadzor (AMD500, 40 minutes) run at 10am, 11am, 2pm and 3pm.

There are taxis at the main roundabout (AMD400 around town). During the day a local bus trundles between the western side of town around Kalinin Poghots up to Shahumian Poghots (AMD100). A taxi to Haghartsin or Goshavank and back costs around AMD5000 or AMD7000 for both combined.

HAGHARTSIN ՀԱՂԱՐԾԻՆ

The handsome **Haghartsin Monastery** (Haghartsin means 'Dance of the Eagles') was built in the 12th century by two brothers, princes of the Bagratuni kingdom. It's hidden away in a lovely forest valley by some massive nut trees. The monastery has three churches, the first for Gregory the Illuminator, the second for the Virgin Mary, named Surp Astvatsatsin (Holy Mother of God) and, the last, a chapel to St Stepanos. An image of the Virgin and Child by the door has distinct Mongolian features – added to convince the next wave of Mongol invaders not to destroy the church. The brothers' family seal can be seen on the back of this church. There are some stunning *khatchkars,* a sundial on the wall of the St Gregory Church, and a refectory (1248) with amazing arching interlocked stone beams. Mass is held in the Surp Astvatsatsin at 11am on Sunday. The monastery is 4km off the main Dilijan–Ijevan road. You can get a lift to the turn-off and easily walk the rest of the way (or possibly hitch there, especially on a weekend when there is more traffic).

From Haghartsin, it's possible to walk on trails over mountain to Dilijan, a 10km hike that requires a little more than three hours. The path is not marked, but with a compass it's fairly easy to find the route. From the monastery, continue on the gravel road down to the river and then up the other bank toward the ridge. A path continues to the right along the tree line with Dilijan eventually coming into view. Note that this route passes precariously close to a military base where shooting exercises are occasionally conducted, so only consider this after consulting with the tourist office in Dilijan.

GOSHAVANK ԳՈՇԱՎԱՆՔ

Goshavank Monastery stands in the mountain village of Gosh, founded in 1188 by the saintly Armenian cleric Mkhitar Gosh, who was buried in a little chapel overlooking the main complex. Goshavank features a main church (Surp Astvatsatsin) and smaller churches to St Gregory and St Gregory the Illuminator. The tower on the *matenadaran* (library) was once taller than the main church. With a school attached, the library is said to have held 15,000 books before it was burned by Timur's army in the 13th century.

Considered one of the principal cultural centres of Armenia in its time, historians believe Goshavank was abandoned at the end of the 14th century. Goshavank then appears to have been reoccupied in the 17th to 19th centuries and restored from 1957 to 1963. The local custodian, Zarik, is a delightful guide and loves to demonstrate the acoustics in the main church with an old prayer. She may also show you a museum filled with artefacts collected from the area.

Zarik's son **Armen Grigoryan** (☎ 094949 001) organises guided hikes to Gosh Lich (Gosh lake; 2.5km away), caves and forgotten forts in the mountain forests. A trek to the little-known remains of Ak Kilise (Turkish for 'White Church') takes about six hours.

Another walk leads 6km to Parz Lich along a marked trail. However, most hikers usually take a taxi to Parz Lich and start the walk there, as it's easier to get transport out from Gosh. There are usually some people at Parz Lich who can show you the trailhead.

Sleeping

Besides the following B&Bs other families in the village have rooms available; ask Zarik and Armen Grigoryan at the monastery for advice. The town also has a small **hotel** (per person AMD10,000), on the main road, 300m before the church. There is usually no-one there, but a caretaker lives in a small home next door.

Osepian B&B (☎ 093942 491; per person AMD7000) This friendly B&B with three rooms is run by

Osepian Artur, the director of the monastery complex. Osepian can spin some yarns about the history of the area.

Gosh's Home (per person AMD7000) A quiet guesthouse in the middle of the village (ask around for directions). Manager Suren Grigorian can help with local logistics and can guide you on local hikes including the one to Parz Lich.

Getting There & Away

Goshavank is 5km off the main Dilijan–Ijevan highway. You can ride on a local bus or marshrutka to the turn-off and walk or hitch the rest of the way. One bus (AMD200) serves the monastery on Tuesday and Friday it goes to Dilijan at 9am and returns from Dilijan at 1pm. On Monday and Wednesday it goes to Ijevan at 9am and returns at noon. A taxi from Dilijan or Ijevan (both 23km away) is the easiest option (about AMD6000 one way).

IJEVAN ԻՋԵՎԱՆ
☎ 0263 / pop 21,000

Surrounded by forested mountains and with the Aghstev River running through its centre, Ijevan is the attractive capital of Tavush *marz*. Ijevan means 'caravanserai' or 'inn' and the town has been on a major east–west route for millennia. The local climate is warmer than Dilijan, and the town is the centre of a wine-growing district with some very acceptable white table wines. The town has some handsome early-20th-century buildings, a big *shuka*, a winery and a little museum. Outside the town there are opportunities for horse riding and hiking.

The local authorities are trying to encourage tourism, though the process has been slow: no one in the tourist office speaks English and most of the dozen or so listed B&Bs seem to only exist on paper. Still, there are some decent cafés in town and a friendly local populace.

Orientation & Information

There are banks on Melibekyan Poghots, the end of which has a distinctive fountain and a couple of cafés. The ACBA Bank next to the fountain has an ATM that accepts Visa.

Buses stop on the main highway close to the fountain; about 100m further is the police station, the Haypost office and the busy *shuka*, with plenty of moneychanging shops and stalls. Various taxis and marshrutkas linger in the vicinity.

The **Ijevan Tourist Information Centre** (☎ 3 32 58; 5a Melikbekyan Poghots; ☉ 10am-7pm Mon-Sat) in the cultural centre–theatre can help you find a guesthouse and may offer some travel suggestions if you can communicate in Russian or Armenian (no English is spoken here). It can provide a town map and a list of B&Bs, most of which are hard to find or no longer function. A couple of doors down from the Tourist Information Centre is an **Internet Club** (☎ 3 19 01; per hr AMD500; ☉ 10am-11pm). **Rouben Simonyan** (☎ 3 24 32) is a local historian who speaks Armenian and Russian and can arrange guides for road trips and hikes to unusual sites in the region.

Sights

The **Ijevan Wine Factory** (☎ 3 42 33; 9 Yerevanyan Poghots; ☉ 9am-6pm Tue & Fri) presses much of the local vintage into dry white and sparkling wines under the Haghartsin, Gayane and Makaravank labels. It offers free tours and tastings with advance notice, and has cellar-door sales. The winery also puts on lunches overlooking the river. It's about 1.5km from the town centre towards Dilijan, just past the little **Ijevan Local Lore Museum** (☎ 3 42 59; 5 Yerevanyan Poghots; admission free, donations appreciated; ☉ 9am-5pm Tue-Sun), with a couple of rooms of ethnographical displays. A short way up the left bank of the Aghstev river from Melikbekyan is a **sculpture park**.

Sleeping

The B&B scene is more than a little dysfunctional. About 10 properties are listed in a brochure at the tourist office; however, none seem to have signs or visible addresses. The B&Bs listed below aren't too hard to locate. The bizarrely named **Hotel Dog** (☎ 3 14 16) next to the sculpture park was being renovated at the time of research and should become the best hotel in town.

Gyulnara Meliksetyan (☎ 3 15 54, 093191 211; 2 Nalbandyan Poghots; per person AMD5000) This B&B is in a big house about 1km north of the centre, with six bedrooms, satellite TV and modern plumbing. Home-cooked dinners cost about AMD1500. To get there, travel north along the main highway from the *shuka* for around 800m, turn left uphill and then take the first right on a dirt track. There are no signs at all, so it's best to take a taxi the first time or call first.

Vardan Vardanyan B&B (☎ 3 36 95; 25 Proschyan Poghots; per person AMD5000) This spacious home is run by the same man who owns the Vardanak Café; he'll probably approach you about accommodation if you eat there. The B&B is on the hill behind the café.

Geghetsik Edilyan Guesthouse (☎ 3 21 95; dm AMD5000, r from AMD10,000) This simple country lodge, off Dilijan road 5km from Ijevan, is run by the gregarious Geghetsik, who speaks Armenian and Russian. It was built as a teachers' college on a hill with views over the Spitak Reservoir. Coming from Ijevan you pass the Spitak Reservoir. Before reaching the railway bridge look for a tunnel under the railway, head uphill 150m and the hotel is on the left. A taxi from Ijevan should cost AMD1000; ask for 'Geghetsiki pansionat'.

Hotel Mosh (☎ 3 56 11, 091452 463; www.hotel-mosh.am; 3 Yerevan Poghots; r with/without bath AMD7000/5000) This eight-room hotel doesn't have much atmosphere, but it's conveniently located on the main road, just past the *shuka*. Hot showers and satellite TV available.

Eating

Vardanak Café (☎ 3 36 95; ⏱ 11am-10pm) Among the three cafés in the centre of town along the main highway, this one, next to the bus station, is the only one that serves hot food. The owner also has a B&B nearby and is keen to assist travellers.

Elit (☎ 091111 300; ⏱ 10am-10pm) This swanky restaurant on the highway serves up *khoravats* in a big banquet hall. It's opposite the winery. It also has guestrooms for AMD10,000.

Getting There & Away

The bus stand is in front of a decrepit hotel, just uphill from the Vardanants Café. There is a little ticket window displaying departure information.

There are marshrutkas to Yerevan (AMD1500, three hours, every hour from 10am to 6pm) that stop in Dilijan 36km down the road. One bus (AMD1000) for Yerevan departs at 9.30am. Dilijan is also served by a bus (AMD300, 9.30am) and a marshrutka (AMD500, 2pm). There is one daily marshrutka to Vanadzor (AMD700, 9.30am). At the time of writing there was no public transport to Georgia, but you could get something to Noyemberyan and change there.

If you are headed that way it's still worth asking about a share taxi to the border or a resumption of bus services.

YENOKAVAN ԵՆՈՔԱՎԱՆ

The rugged mountains around Ijevan hide old roads, forts and churches in their many folds. A fantastic hike to the west of Ijevan can be found along the road leading to the town of **Yenokavan**, which sits by the Sarnajur River. On the southern edge of Yenokavan is a small church perched on a rock overlooking a gorge. Inside the gorge is the 13th-century **Surp Astvatsatsin Church**.

Up the valley from Yenokavan is an interesting new tourist venture run by **Apaga Tour** (☎ 091290 939, 091495 834; www.apaga.info; tigran@artak .net). There are horse stables here, and guided trail rides can be made for AMD3500 per hour or AMD20,000 per day (including meals). Guided hikes are also available if you prefer walking. Apaga also offers accommodation in newly built small cottages for AMD20,000 with three meals; the price also includes a one-hour horse ride.

Down in the river gorge, a separate tourist venture has been set up by a couple of young brothers from Ijevan – **Vahagn and Tatul Tanayan** (☎ 3 14 65, 091365 437). Their camp near the Khachagbyur river is in a beautiful spot they have dubbed 'Peace to the World'. Bring a swimsuit as there are some wonderful bathing pools and cascades nearby. You can stay and eat at the camp for around AMD10,000 (less if you bring your own tent and food). The Tanayans can also show you some caves in the area, some 30m deep. The most interesting is Anapat Cave, which contains unique pre-Christian carvings of faces and human forms.

NORTH OF IJEVAN

North of Ijevan one road turns northwest at Azatamut through the captured Azeri enclaves of Upper and Lower Askipara (now Verin Voskepar and Nerin Voskepar) to Noyemberyan and the Georgian border. Another road turns right just before the border to Berd in Shamshadin district. There are still landmines along this frontier; it's unwise to explore the shattered villages around here.

Just past the turn-off to Noyemberyan there's a road 4km to Achajur village and onwards another 6.5km to the 11th-century **Makaravank** monastery. The beautiful church is set deep in a forest, giving it a very peaceful atmosphere. There are some fine carvings on the exterior and interior of the structures, including ornate altar daises carved with eight-pointed stars, floral motifs, fish, birds and geometrical forms. There is no public transport here, but you may be able to get a lift with locals visiting the site.

Heading on towards Noyemberyan, turn up the valley at Kirants for the epic ride to the **Kirants** monastery – Niva or Villis Jeep only. It's a muddy 14km road hemmed in by forest. After about 10km you can walk up the north bank of the valley about 50m to 100m to find a **medieval stone road** parallel to the new track. The 13th-century Kirants monastery is quite unique, built of brick and decorated with coloured tiles by a Greek-influenced branch of the Armenian Church. The forest setting is very lush, but watch out for ticks in summer.

Other churches in the vicinity include the **Arakelots** monastery, the little **Moro-Dzoro** monastery and **Deghdznuti Vank**, with a rough-hewn chapel from as early as the 4th century, next to a 13th-century church. A guided tour with Rouben Simonyan from Ijevan (p193) or perhaps with someone from Kirants or Acharkut village would be a real advantage.

SHAMSHADIN

The Shamshadin region east of Ijevan is a fertile stretch of woodlands, vineyards and farms carved by three valleys: the Khndzorut, Tavush and Hakhum. With Azerbaijan on two sides and rugged mountains dividing it from the rest of Armenia, it's also quite isolated.

As the crow flies its just 21km from Ijevan to Berd; the mountains in between them, however, have forced the construction of a roundabout road that loops for 67km north and then south. About 44km into the trip you'll spot **Nor Varagavank** up the hillside – the 3km detour is worth the trip to see the ruined monastery. The oldest sections were started in 1198 by David Bagrtuni, son of King Vasak I; a Surp Astvatsatsin Church was added in 1237. The monastery once contained a fragment of the True Cross until it was lost in fighting in 1915.

Berd (population 8000) itself is nothing special but does have a restaurant and a couple of hotels. The **Berd Hotel** (☎ 093930 777; per person AMD5000-10,000) was being renovated at the time of research. Contact Mr Vardgez on the number above. A cheaper place down the road is the **Hotel Raipotreb** (☎ 026721 426; per person AMD2000), which also has a decent restaurant.

The main reason to come to Berd is to hike here along the old road from Ijevan. The 35km road twists and winds through the mountains and past some attractive old villages. The hike takes about 12 hours in total, best spread over two or three days. There are no hotels, but you can ask in the villages for a homestay. Just make yourself known as a tourist as locals are wary of strangers in these parts (you may be mistaken as a wayward Azeri spy or soldier). It's best to have a taxi driver take you the first 5km or so out of Ijevan to get you on the right track. Just make sure they are taking you on the old road that heads east of town rather than the new road going north.

A daily marshrutka (AMD500) leaves from Ijevan to Berd (on the new road) at 9am. It returns from Berd at 2pm. A shared taxi between Berd and Ijevan is AMD1500 per person.

Khoranashat monastery used to be Shamshadin's most visited historic attraction, but these days it's off-limits as it's only a few hundred metres from the border. The villagers of nearby Chinari don't recommend going there – Azeri soldiers nearby are prone to taking pot shots at visitors.

The road from Lake Sevan to the regional centre of Berd is one of the wildest and most beautiful in the country. From Chambarak (Krasnosyelsk) it turns north past the village of Ttujur over the 2286m Getik pass and winds over the summer pastures and through forests along the ridges and flanks of Mt Mrkhuz (2993m).

VANADZOR ՎԱՆԱՁՈՐ
☎ 0322 / pop 170,000

Lining the banks of the Pambak River, Vanadzor, formerly Kirovakan, is a post-industrial Soviet city and administrative centre for the Lori region. The main street, Tigran Mets Poghota, bustles with shops, cafés and the swishest clothes outside Yerevan. The young folk attending the teachers' college add a bit of nightlife to the city. The huge chemical works at the eastern end of town are mostly moribund, but some factories are reopening and some new industries are starting to appear. The city is a useful base for visiting the classic churches of Debed Canyon, with good transport links to other cities.

Orientation

Tigran Mets Poghota has lots of moneychangers' signs as well as a cash machine at the **ACBA Bank** (22 Tigran Mets). The **Converse Bank** (54 Grigor Lusavorich) has an ATM that accepts Visa

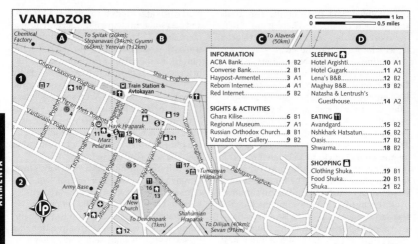

VANADZOR

To Spitak (26km);
Stepanavan (34km); Gyumri (66km); Yerevan (132km)

To Alaverdi (50km)

INFORMATION
ACBA Bank.........................1 B2
Converse Bank...................2 B1
Haypost-Armentel.............3 A1
Reborn Internet................4 A1
Red Internet.....................5 B2

SIGHTS & ACTIVITIES
Ghara Kilise.....................6 B1
Regional Museum.............7 A1
Russian Orthodox Church..8 B1
Vanadzor Art Gallery........9 B2

SLEEPING
Hotel Argishti..................10 A1
Hotel Gugark...................11 A2
Lena's B&B......................12 B2
Maghay B&B....................13 B2
Natasha & Lentrush's
  Guesthouse...................14 A2

EATING
Avandgard......................15 B2
Nshkhark Hatsatun..........16 B2
Oasis..............................17 B2
Shwarma.........................18 B2

SHOPPING
Clothing Shuka................19 B1
Food Shuka.....................20 B1
Shuka.............................21 B1

and MasterCard. There are also internet clubs and internet telephone offices along Tigran Mets, including the **Reborn Internet** (Tigran Mets; per hr AMD300; ⏰ 10am-10pm), near the corner with Batumi, and a post office. Another online option is the **Red Internet** (81 Vardanats Poghots; per hr AMD300; ⏰ 9am-10pm). The train station and the *avtokayan* (bus station) are together at the bottom of Khorenatsi Poghots.

Sights

There's not a whole lot to see, but there are parks and some interesting neighbourhoods to explore. A **regional museum** (☎ 4 17 51; admission AMD500; ⏰ 11am-6pm Mon-Sat) at the western end of Tigran Mets is housed in an unattractive-looking building, diagonally opposite the cinema. At the other end of town the **Vanadzor Art Gallery** (Tumanyan Hraparak; admission AMD200; ⏰ 10am-5pm Tue-Sun) shows off local talent across widely divergent styles of painting and sculpture.

Vanadzor's **shuka** on Myasnikyan Poghots is one of Armenia's busiest regional markets. The old village neighbourhoods of **Dimats** and **Bazum** are east of the town centre, over the Tandzut River. The centre of town has the usual Soviet look, but south along Myasnikyan Poghots there are some elegant stone villas and country houses. There's a little **Russian Orthodox Church**, in the park by the train station, and the Armenian Apostolic church called the **Ghara Kilise** (Black Church), built from suitably black stone and surrounded by an elaborate cemetery. The Armenian church

stands near the lower bridge on Tumanyan Poghots. There's an interesting walk up Abovyan Poghots along the little valley of the Vanadzor River, past boating ponds, tall trees and shuttered sanatoriums to an overgrown **Dendropark** (Forest Reserve).

Sleeping

Hotel Gugark (☎ 4 15 19; Hayk Hraparak; r per person AMD3000-8000) This pre-war Soviet building on Hayk Hraparak has a few scruffy rooms and some renovated ones. It's not the nicest place around, but it's cheap and central, making this a good base for budget travellers.

Natasha & Lentrush's Guesthouse (☎ 4 63 43, 094914 100; 24 Michuryan Poghots; per person AMD7000) A B&B with four rooms in an elegant two-storey villa with a garden. The couple's daughter, Kristine, speaks English. To get there, head up Garegin Nzhdeh Poghots, turn left at the army base and then take the first right after the hospital; No 24 is halfway up the street on the right, distinguished by a large grapevine and a little metal balcony.

Maghay B&B (☎ 4 52 59, 091794 029; marined61@ rambler.ru; 21 Azatamartikneri Poghots; per person AMD7000) Very welcoming B&B with three rooms and a communal bathroom. The family often eats with the guests, which creates a homey atmosphere. To find it, take the lane that goes left of the Nshkhark Hatsatun restaurant; it's at the end of the lane.

Lena's B&B (☎ 2 53 11, 094854 403; 26 Orbeli Poghots; per person AMD7500) Owners Lucine and her mother, Lena, offer a comfortable stay in this pleasant home with three rooms. Lucine speaks English and is switched on to the needs of tourists; she can help organise a trip to the Debed Canyon.

Hotel Argishti (☎ 4 25 56; 1 Batumi Poghots; s/d AMD20,000/25,000) Three blocks from Hayk Hraparak on a quiet street you'll find this decent midrange hotel with high ceilings and a gated rose garden. The furnishings are new and comfortable, and there are some family rooms (for four people) for AMD35,000. It also has a restaurant, a bar and a billiards room.

Eating

Shwarma (28 Tigran Mets Poghota; shwarma AMD400; ⊗ 10am-11pm) Handy fast-food place serving shwarma and cold drinks.

Nshkhark Hatsatun (☎ 4 10 11; 25 Azatamartikneri Poghots; meals AMD1500-2500; ⊗ 11am-10pm) Pizza, cold beer and ice cream are a few of the specialities here, although it can do a good old-fashioned *khoravats* as well. It's a grey stone building with a green and yellow sign in Armenian, standing back from the street, with a park on one side.

Oasis (☎ 4 06 46; 48 Tigran Mets Poghota; meals AMD2000; ⊗ 10.30am-11pm) One of the most popular places in town, Oasis has an extensive menu with most items pictured so you know what you are in for. Many European dishes and some Caucasian regional fare.

Avandgard (☎ 4 07 47; 22 Tigran Mets Poghota; meals AMD1800-2500; ⊗ 10.30am-11pm) Armenian, Georgian and Russian dishes figure prominently at this progressive restaurant with a flashy interior. It serves a nice trout in wine sauce for AMD2200.

Getting There & Around

Vanadzor's *avtokayan* and train station (☎ 2 10 09) are at the bottom of Khorenatsi Poghots. Marshrutkas to Yerevan (AMD1200, two hours, every 20 minutes from 7.30am to 8pm) take a 132km route via Spitak and Aparan to Yerevan. There's also transport to Dilijan (marshrutka or bus AMD500, up to one hour, 10am and 1pm) continuing to Ijevan (AMD1000), Stepanavan (AMD400, 45 minutes, 8.30am, 10am, 1pm, 2.30pm and 4.30pm), Gyumri (AMD800, 9am, 10am, 11am, 1pm and 2pm) and Alaverdi (AMD500, up to one hour, 8am, 10am, 1.30pm, 3pm and 4.30pm). A bus to Tbilisi (AMD3500) departs around 8am.

Trains heading to either Yerevan or Tbilisi will come and go in the middle of the night, making them of little use to travellers. A marshrutka to Tbilisi (AMD3500) leaves at 8.30am.

The churches of the Debed Canyon and Lori Berd can be visited on a day trip by taxi for around AMD6000 to AMD8000 for seven or eight hours, or about AMD5000 to Lori Berd, or you can negotiate with drivers based at the *avtokayan*.

STEPANAVAN & AROUND
ՍՏԵՊԱՆԱՎԱՆ
☎ 0256 / pop 14,000

Stepanavan sits on a plateau above the steep-sided gorge of the Dzoragets River, fabled for its fine summer weather and, less proudly today, as one of the centres of Armenian communism. The area has been a site of settlement for millennia, on fertile fields above the river. The town is quiet, but it's a nice place for a wander (away from the usual monumental Soviet centre) and the locals are friendly.

An early cell of the Bolsheviks led by local lad Stepan Shahumian operated from hideouts and caves before the revolution. Shahumian died in a lonely corner of the Turkmenistan desert with the other 26 'Baku Commissars' in 1918, later sanctified in countless memorials across the region. (The Baku Commissars were Bolshevik leaders in the Caucasus in the early days of the revolution.) A rather dashing Shahumian poses on a pedestal in the main square, Stepan Shahumian Hraparak.

Information

The best information centre outside Yerevan is located here in quiet Stepanavan. Several of the staff at the **Stepanavan Information Centre** (Language and Computer Centre; ☎ 2 21 58; www.stepanavan info.am; 11 Million Poghots) speak English and are happy to answer questions or perhaps arrange a tour for you. They have maps and can organise accommodation at the info centre or elsewhere in town. Check the website for a free downloadable walking tour of the town. **Internet** (per hr AMD400) is available here.

There are banks and shops exchanging money around the main square and the *shuka*. Taxis, buses and marshrutkas leave from the main square.

ARMENIA

Sights

The **Stepan Shahumian Museum** (Stepan Shahumian Hraparak; admission AMD100; ⊙ 11am-7pm) has an art gallery, plus displays on Stepanavan's history, and – excitement, comrades – the life story of the martyred commissar. It's completely built around the Shahumians' home, preserved like a doll house in a giant box.

On the north bank of the Dzoragets about 3km east of Stepanavan is the dramatically sited fortress **Lori Berd** (*berd* means fortress). The road from Stepanavan passes hillocks in the fields, which are actually **Bronze Age tumulus tombs**. The fort sits on a promontory between the gorges of the Dzoragets and Urut Rivers, with huge round towers and massive stone blocks along its exposed side. This was the capital of David Anhogin (949–1049) and later a local power base for the Orbelians and Zakarians, powerful families of Armenian nobles. There is a story that the Mongols captured the fortress after the defenders became distracted by alcohol. There is an ancient cemetery nearby and a 14th-century bridge in the gorge below. A taxi from Stepanavan takes about 15 minutes and costs AMD1000. From the fort it's a good idea to walk back to Stepanavan along a 4.5km trail in the steep-sided gorge. You can reach the trail from the north side of the fort.

The cool and tranquil 35-hectare **Dendropark** (admission free; ⊙ daily May-Oct, Mon-Fri, rest of yr) is a botanical garden near Gyulagarak village, 11km from Stepanavan. Established in the 1930s, it has a vast array of conifers and deciduous trees. The park has been well maintained and the directors welcome visitors. It's especially popular in May when locals with respiratory problems come to inhale the pollen (not recommended for allergy sufferers!). A taxi should cost AMD2500 return. Cross the bridge in Gyulagarak and the park is about 2km away past the 6th-century Tormak Church.

From the Dendropark, the road continues east for 8km to the village of Kurtan. At the gas station in Kurtan veer right, cross the bridge and travel another 7km to **Hnevank** monastery. The monastery stands inside the gorge on the southern side of the canyon, near the confluence of the Gargar and Dzoragets Rivers. It was founded in the 7th century but dates mostly from the 12th century. The monastery was being restored at the time of research and there were plans to build a restaurant on site. From here the road continues to the Vanadzor–Alaverdi highway.

The **Lori Plains** stretch north of Stepanavan to the Georgian border, with a few mixed Armenian-Russian villages such as Saratovka and Privolnoye. The main road passes through the town of Tashir to the minor border post at Gogavan. On the Georgian side a decayed 77km road leads to Tbilisi. Another road (best tackled in summer) climbs to the west over the lonely mountains and meadows of the Khonav range to Shirak *marz* and Gyumri.

Sleeping & Eating

There are three B&Bs on the north side of the river, costing around AMD7000 a night including meals. The hosts know the hospitality business but they may not speak English. Ask at the Stepanavan Information Centre for a recommendation. There's a small hotel being built on the main square.

Anahit Pensionat (☎ 2 25 78; r AMD4000, cottages AMD10,000; ⊠) This Soviet sanatorium is in the forest on the ridge behind town. The cottages have been remodelled and there's a swimming pool (AMD600), a sauna (AMD5000) and some sports facilities. The restaurant here is probably the best in town, and worth visiting even if you're not staying at the hotel.

Information Centre Guesthouse (☎ 2 21 58; stepana vaninfo@gmail.com; 11 Million Poghots; s/d AMD8000/10,000; ⌨) A convenient, low-priced option, the Information Centre has one en suite room with satellite TV and a laundry machine. The entrance is private so you don't need to go through the info centre each time you enter.

Ruzan Marikyan (☎ 2 21 96, 093166 845; info@bedand breakfast.am; 6/6 Left Bank quarter; per person AMD10,000) B&B offering a couple of comfortable bedrooms. The Marikyans are an educated couple (a doctor and an engineer) and although no English is spoken they are very helpful and sincere.

MM Hotel (☎ 2 40 50; 9 Nzdheh Poghots; r AMD15,000, deluxe AMD20,000) New hotel near the Information Centre; rooms come with TV and fridge. Pine floors give the rooms a nice aroma.

Next door to MM Hotel is the similar **Hotel Lori** (☎ 2 23 23) with almost identical prices.

Getting There & Away

Marshrutkas for Yerevan (AMD1500, three hours) leave from the main square at 8am, 10am, 11am, 1pm, 2pm and 3pm. There are four buses a day to Vanadzor (AMD400) at

8.30am, 10.30am, noon and 4pm. A daily bus goes to Tbilisi (AMD3000, 12.30pm). A taxi anywhere in town from the main square costs AMD400.

DEBED CANYON ԴԵԲԵԴԻ ՁՈՐ

This canyon manages to pack in more history and culture than just about anywhere else in the country. Nearly every village along the Debed River has a church, a chapel, an old fort and a sprinkling of *khatchkars* somewhere nearby. Two World Heritage–listed monasteries, Haghpat and Sanahin, justly draw most visitors, but there are plenty more to scramble around. Soviet-era infrastructure is noticeable, however, with electric cables and railway lines running through the canyon, plus an ugly copper mine at Alaverdi. The road through the canyon is also busy, as this is the main artery linking Armenia to Georgia. Tourist facilities include a highly rated Tufenkian Hotel, but there is a dearth of quality budget accommodation; most travellers base themselves in Vanadzor and make day trips.

Sleeping

Hotel Anush (☎ 0322-4 08 08; Vanadzor-Alaverdi Rd; cottage AMD10,000) This stone-clad motel and restaurant is about 12km from Vanadzor, near Pambak village. There are 12 modern rooms with satellite TV and clean bathrooms. The restaurant is a nice place to break for lunch or dinner, and costs about AMD2500 per person.

Avan Dzoraget Hotel (☎ 01-54 31 22; www.tufenkianheritage.com; per person AMD25,000; ☒) A 34-room luxury hotel run by the arty Tufenkian group, near the confluence of the Debed and Dzoraget Rivers, midway between Vanadzor and Alaverdi. Opened in spring 2004, it's by far the best hotel in the region, with a spa, a swimming pool and a restaurant, plus a bar in a Soviet bomb shelter.

Getting There & Away

Buses and marshrutkas travel from Vanadzor to Alaverdi at 8am, 10am, 1.30pm, 3pm and 4.30pm. But once you get to Alaverdi you'll still need transport to visit all the monasteries. Sanahin is fairly easy to reach on your own (using the cable car) and there are regular marshrutkas to Haghpat. But connections to Akhtala and Odzun are rarer, and most independent travellers miss Kobayr because it's poorly signposted. To see the sights quickly and economically it makes more

sense to hire a taxi from Vanadzor. Expect to pay around AMD8000 for the day. If your budget is tight or you prefer to explore the valley at a relaxed pace, hitching and bussing is still an option.

Kobayr ՔՈԲԱՅՐ

Don't blink or you might miss this charmingly ruined 13th-century convent, hidden just off the Vanadzor–Alaverdi highway. The convent lies above the hamlet of Kobayr (also spelt Khober or Kober) – hidden behind trees near the road. Most travellers pass right by having never seen it.

When you spot the signs for Kobayr keep an eye out for the access road that heads up the mountain. Another landmark is the tiny Kobayr train station, a white structure on concrete pillars. Walk over the railway line and find the stone steps that lead into the hamlet. The path continues uphill through the woods (follow the metal pipe); at the metal memorial spring go right and follow the path up the stone steps – in total the climb takes 10 to 15 minutes.

Kobayr is a perfect picturesque ruin, with trees and vines springing from finely carved mossy stones. The main building has lost its roof but has some elegant, partially restored frescoes, and the bell tower is largely intact. At the time of writing locals had begun the process of restoring the monastery – given their painstakingly slow work they are likely to still be there by the time you read this.

Kobayr is about 18km from Alaverdi and 33km from Vanadzor. As it's on the main road you can hop on any passing bus or marshrutka between the two cities.

Alaverdi ԱԼԱՎԵՐԴԻ

☎ 0253 / pop 10,000

The quiet, conservative mining town of Alaverdi is tucked into a bend in the canyon, with rows of apartment blocks and village houses cut into strata by the highway and the railway line. The town is rather poor with few jobs besides those at the half-open copper mine. A cable car (AMD50) climbs the lip of the inner canyon from the mine up to Sadahart and the nearby village of Sanahin. It runs according to work shifts at the mine – 7.45am to 9.45am, 11am to 2pm, 3pm to 7.30pm and 11.15pm to 11.45pm. An ATM is located within the copper mine complex, just past the cable car.

ARMENIA

ARTUR MELKUMIAN

Artur Melkumian, 39, is a construction worker currently helping to rebuild Kobayr Convent. Renovation began in 2006 and is expected to continue until 2011. We asked him about the status of the project.

Is the church being preserved for the sake of history or as an active place of worship?
We are restoring the church so that it can be an active place of worship for the local people. Of course we will also try to build it to the original specifications.

What are the challenges of rebuilding?
We are trying to use traditional methods so we don't use cement. The main challenge has been to understand how the structures were originally built. Scientists and historians have come here to study the original buildings but we still don't understand all the techniques. It's important that we use the same types of plasters and materials to maintain the original look. Also, we're not using modern equipment or cranes so it's really labour intensive to move the materials and stone blocks.

What does the project mean for the community?
We don't have a church in Kobayr so a lot of people are supporting this work. They want to rebuild the community and connect with their traditions.

What does it mean for you personally?
When we were kids we used to come up here and play in the ruins and explore the caves nearby. That was during the Soviet period when no one took care of this place – I saw it graffitied and ruined. We didn't think much of it then because we were just kids. But I understand the importance of it now and it makes me proud to rebuild something I saw neglected for so long. Personally I am not so religious, but after working on this project I have come to appreciate the historical significance of this place. We learn new things about this building every day. We turn over stones and see ancient writing, we dig and find more structures. People in Kobayr live day-by-day and don't think much about history, but this project has taught us a lot about our past.

Tamara's bridge, about 1km down from the bus stand, was built by Queen Tamar of Georgia.

This humpbacked stone bridge was used by road traffic until 25 years ago. There are four kitten-faced lions carved on the stone railing. Legend tells that when a 'real' man finally walks across, the lions will come to life.

SLEEPING & EATING

Formal accommodation is lacking in Alaverdi, but it's possible to stay in local homes in Alaverdi, Sanahin, Odzun and Haghpat if you ask around and have luck on your side. The Flora Restaurant may have some contacts. If you're invited but not asked to pay, discreetly leave AMD5000 behind when you leave.

Flora Restaurant (☎ 2 24 74, 091210 624; Alaverdi; meals AMD2500; ♡ 10am-10pm) To get here, cross Tamara's bridge, climb the stairs on the far side and turn right for a short walk along a road. There are private dining rooms for one to 10 people, clean bathrooms and freshly prepared *khoravats*, kebabs, salads and sometimes dolma.

There are two cafés open in warm weather near Tamara's bridge, good for an ice cream, light snacks and a drink, and stores with pastries around the bus stand.

GETTING THERE & AWAY

The bus and marshrutka stand is a parking bay off the main road – taxis wait here and further up the hill. A bus ticket and information window is located in the back of the lot, next to the Xerox and fax shop. Marshrutkas and buses are available to Stepanavan (AMD700, two hours, 10am, 3.30pm), Vanadzor (AMD500, up to one hour, 8am, 9am, 11.30pm, 1pm) and Yerevan (AMD1700, three hours, 8am, 9am, 12.30pm and 2pm).

There's a bus to the Georgian border (AMD250) at 6pm, or try to jump on a passing marshrutka. The train station is 2km down the valley by the copper mine at Katsotsk. A daily train to Vanadzor leaves at 6pm (AMD200, two hours). A taxi to Haghpat and Akhtala or to Odzun and Kobayr should cost between AMD4000 and AMD5000, or about AMD8000 to all of them.

Odzun ՕՁՈՒՆ

Perched on a broad shelf which terminates at a sheer plunge down to the Debed, Odzun is a substantial settlement of about 6000 with a magnificent 7th-century church in the centre of the village. The unusual monument next to it is a memorial but locals say it has the power to inspire fertility – approach with caution. The sturdy church features magnificent arches outside the main entrance. The custodian turns up sooner or later to unlock the church. There's another church on the edge of the cliff. One kilometre south of Odzun, at the edge of the canyon, is the three-chambered Horomayri monastery, the well-camouflaged remnants of which are visible below the cliff on the right.

Odzun Guesthouse (☎ 094543 673; per person AMD10,000) is 2.5km past Odzun village at the foot of a forested slope. The building is a two-storey 1960s-style motel, with 13 standard rooms and two deluxe rooms with balconies, space and hot water. The place is surrounded by orchard trees and lawns with views over Odzun.

Travellers recommend the more homely and slightly cheaper **Nersisyan Alvard B&B** (☎ 0253-2 50 03; per person AMD8000) located near the upper school.

Buses come here from Alaverdi at 10am, 11am, 2pm and 5pm. A taxi to and from Alaverdi should cost about AMD2000. Odzun is on the road to Stepanavan and a couple of times a day, around 10.15am and 3.45pm, an Alaverdi to Stepanavan bus passes through here.

Sanahin Monastery ՍԱՆԱՀԻՆ

Moss-covered Sanahin is a fascinatingly detailed church and monastery complex, packed with ancient graves, darkened chapels and medieval gallery schools (study halls where pupils sat on benches on either side of a corridor). The inner sanctum of the Surp Astvatsatsin (Holy Mother of God) Church, located in the middle of several buildings, is the oldest structure here, dating back to 928, while its adjoining *gavit* or entrance hall is one of the later buildings, built in 1211. A library was created at Sanahin in 1062, and a medical school flourished in the 12th century. Sanahin means 'older than that one', referring to its younger cousin at Haghpat.

From the cable-car station, walk up to the main square of Sadahart and take a left;

after 900m you reach a T-junction in Sanahin village (separate from Sadahart). Sanahin Monastery is uphill, or follow the sign downhill to the **Mikoyan Museum** (admission AMD200; ☺ 10am-1pm & 2-6pm), a shrine to the Mikoyan brothers Anastas and Artyom. Anastas Mikoyan survived 60 years in the Politburo, outlasting even Stalin, and so deserves a museum. Artyom was the designer of the USSR's first jet fighter in WWII, the MiG. There's an early MiG jet outside the museum (no climbing allowed!). The charming administrator is unstoppable once she starts explaining every photo, medal and uniform on display – a tip of AMD100 or so is a nice gesture after a tour.

SLEEPING

Sadahart is home to the totally decrepit **Hotel Debed** (main square). The hotel was closed at the time of research but some local people have been known to hang around the lobby in order to redirect tourists to their nearby homestays, charging around AMD5000. They may also offer to arrange a taxi for you to see the local sights, but be warned that this service could prove quite expensive. Be sure to research the timetables of onward bus services in advance; although your hosts might claim to know this information, it could be incorrect. Despite their shortcomings these homestays can be a decent place to spend the night.

GETTING THERE & AWAY

The cable car (AMD50) from Alaverdi is a fun way to reach Sadahart, which is a little more than 1km from Sanahin Monastery. There are also marshrutkas and taxis from Alaverdi to Sadahart (AMD800, 5km). You can also inquire about an early-morning bus that travels from Sadahart straight to the Bagratashen–Sadakhlo border. If you are hitching, the turn-off from Alaverdi is 1km south of town at the bridge. Hikers may want to walk from Sanahin to Haghpat, via the village of Akner. The 7km walk takes less than three hours.

Haghpat Monastery ՀԱՂՊԱՏ

This pearl of a monastery perched on the lip of the Debed Canyon has Unesco World Heritage status, along with Sanahin. This place has atmosphere and architectural splendour in abundance and the views around the canyon alone are worth the trip. Founded around 976 by Queen Khosrvanuch, who built Surp Nishan at the centre of the walled complex, it really took off in the 12th century with a magnificent bell tower, library and refectory. An inscription on the *gavit* of Surp Nishan reads in part 'You who enter through its door and prostrate yourself before the Cross, in your prayers remember us and our royal ancestors, who rest at the door of the holy cathedral, in Jesus Christ'. Further around past a cute Surp Astvatsatsin chapel is the freestanding *gavit* built by Abbot Hamazasp in 1257, which has glorious acoustics. Uphill is the bell tower, and off by the wall a stone refectory. *Khatchkars* and study halls surround the central church.

Flora Simonyan B&B (☎ 09479 24 12, 09196 88 16; per person incl breakfast AMD6000) is a basic place with a few rooms, a hot shower and meals. It's next to the parking lot at Haghpat, part of a small snack bar.

Marshrutkas from Alaverdi run at 10am, noon, 1.30pm, 2.30pm, 4.30pm and 5.30pm, costing AMD200. A taxi from Alaverdi to Haghpat and back will cost AMD2000. Alternatively, walk to Sanahin Monastery if you are headed there anyway. It's 7km via Akner village.

Akhtala Monastery ԱԽԹԱԼԱ

Situated at the edge of Akhtala, this 13th-century complex is recommended for its fine decorative carvings and frescoes. A thick wall surrounds it. Historians aren't sure if the church was dedicated to St Gregory (Surp Grigor) or the Apostles (Arakelots). The doors of the church are usually locked and one of the villagers keeps the key; it's just a matter of asking around for it to see the beautiful frescoes in the nave area. If you can't get a key its still possible to peek through a hole in the locked church doors. Surrounding the church are a couple of well-preserved chapels and the ever-present graveyard with some new stones. Akhtala is about 18km northeast (downstream) of Alaverdi. A taxi trip combined with a visit to Haghpat will cost about AMD4000. Without your own car you can hitch to the signposted turn-off, then walk the final 3km up to the church (skirting around the edge of the copper-mine pond), which takes less than one hour.

GYUMRI ԳՅՈՒՄՐԻ
☎ 0312 / pop 120,000

A city of stately Russian architecture, cobbled streets and a bustling market, Gyumri is one of the most attractive towns in the country,

and also one of the most tragic. The 1988 Spitak earthquake levelled large sections of the city and drove most of the survivors away. You can still see devastated buildings around town, as well as historic structures under careful reconstruction.

Twenty years after the quake, life is only beginning to normalise, although locals still seem to talk about it as though it occurred last week. Jobs have returned, permanent housing has replaced most of the cargo container homes and the population has increased two-fold.

The townsfolk of Gyumri have a distinctive accent with hints of western Armenian, and a famously ridiculous sense of humour in tandem with conservative social mores. Other Armenians like to tease Gyumritsis about local delicacies such as *kalla* (cow's head) and the particularly rich stew of *khash* made here in the cold seasons. The winters last longer here than in Yerevan, until April or May.

Few travellers come this way, most people choosing to travel between Yerevan and Tbilisi via Sevan and Dilijan. But if you are on a loop tour of northern Armenia then Gyumri becomes a necessary stop and jumping-off point for several sites including Marmashen and Harichavank. Visitors will be treated to some good-value accommodation, decent restaurants and the remnants of 19th-century Russian colonialism.

History

Gyumri was first settled around 400 BC, possibly by Greek colonists. The town was inhabited periodically until the early 19th century, when the Russians moved in and built a large military garrison. It even received a visit from Tsar Nicolas I who, in 1837, renamed it Alexandropol after his wife. A steady influx of settlers arrived from Russia and the western Armenian cities of Kars and Erzurum. As the third largest city in the Caucasus, after Tbilisi and Baku, Gyumri was an important trading post between the Ottoman Empire and the rest of Asia and Russia. As a transport hub it was a stop on the rail journey from Tbilisi to Tabriz.

In 1920 the Turkish-Armenian war ended here with the signing of the Treaty of Alexandropol, an event that ceased the Turkish advance on Yerevan. In Soviet times the border was shut and Alexandropol became known as Leninakan.

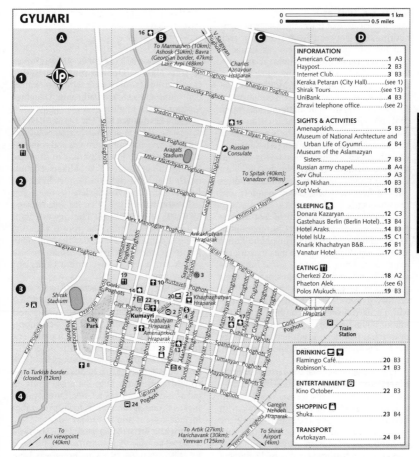

GYUMRI

ARMENIA

The Spitak earthquake on 11 December 1988 put paid to much of Gyumri's historic splendour, as well as the myriad factories established here by the Soviets. Besides levelling large parts of the city and surrounding villages, it killed 50,000 people and made many more homeless. The botched recovery effort would haunt the city for years as successive winters passed without heating or electricity. The early 2000s saw rapid redevelopment and rehousing of the earthquake victims.

Orientation & Information

In downtown Gyumri the centre of the shopping district lies between Haghtanaki Poghota, Azatutyan Hraparak (Freedom Sq) and Khaghaghutyan Hraparak (Peace Sq).

The Haypost office and the Zhravi private telephone office are on little Rizhkov Poghots between the two squares.

Shirak Tours (☎ 3 76 59; www.berlinhotel-gyumri .am; 25 Haghtanaki Poghota) is a useful local tour company run from the Gastehaus Berlin by Alex Ter-Minasyan. He arranges day trips by car to Marmashen for about AMD10,000 and to Harichavank for AMD20,000.

There are several internet cafés and banks along Sayat-Nova and Garegin Nzhdeh Poghots, including the **Internet Club** (☎ 3 27 35; 7 Sayat-Nova Poghots; ☉ 10am-10pm). UniBank has an ATM at Khaghaghutyan Hraparak. You can also use the internet at **American Corner** (☎ 2 21 53; 68 Shirakatsi Poghots; ☉ 9am-5pm Mon-Fri), located next to the City Hall.

ARMENIA

Sights & Activities

The historic core of town, the **Kumayri** neighbourhood, is between Azatutyan Hraparak and the city park. While not as intact as Goris, the buildings of Kumayri are of a finer standard. Gyumri's atmospheric 19th-century Astvatsatsin Church, locally called **Yot Verk** (Seven Wounds), stands on the northern side of the square. The battered and worn roof cones from an earlier incarnation of the church stand outside. On the south side of the square is the **Amenaprkich** (All Saviours) Church, which is being ever so slowly restored to its pre-earthquake glory. Nearby, the *shuka* is something of an attraction with its endless piles of fruit, whirling coffee grinders and rows of cognac bottles.

A couple of blocks north of Yot Verk is the more modest **Surp Nishan** Church, built in 1870 and restored in 2003. The old buildings along Gorki Poghots and by the city park are worth wandering around – some buildings are shells; others have been restored to their prime. On Teryan Poghots there is a 19th-century pyramid-shaped **Russian army chapel** with a peaked silver roof. Continuing over the hill for 500m or so brings you to the **Sev Ghul** or 'black sentry' fort. From here you can see the **Mother Armenia statue** on an adjacent hill, towards the Turkish border.

The **Museum of National Architecture and Urban Life of Gyumri** (☎ 2 36 00; 47 Haghtanaki Poghots; admission AMD1000; ☑ 10am-5pm Tue-Sun) is a substantial building set back from the corner with Teryan Poghots. The 1872 mansion of the Dzitoghtsyans includes fine furniture and authentic décor, plus an art gallery and displays on local history. An attached gallery of sculptures by Sergei Merkurov contains more Lenins and Stalins than you can shake a sickle at. The **Museum of the Aslamazyan Sisters** (☎ 3 01 82; 232 Abovyan Poghots; admission AMD500; ☑ 10am-5pm Mon-Fri) on what was once Kumayri's finest promenade is another house museum with a display of traditional furnishings and more contemporary artworks.

About 30km north of Gyumri, the village of Ashotsk offers a range of activities in both summer and winter, including kayaking, biking and cross-country skiing. **Artur Mikayelyan** (☎ 093352 111, 0235-2 17 58; mika-ski@mail.ru) organises these activities and offers accommodation in his simple home. A weekend of food and lodging costs around AMD15,000. Marshrutkas from Gyumri run to Ashotsk hourly during the day. It's a great way to experience rural Armenia and stay active too.

Sleeping

Donara Kazaryan B&B (☎ 2 42 63; 142 Frunze Poghots; per person AMD6000) Donara runs a homestay from her fine family house, with two chintzy bedrooms and a shared bathroom. Daughter Vartuhi speaks English.

Knarik Khachatryan B&B (☎ 3 48 64, 091453 266; skyngo@list.ru; 31 K Demirtchyan Poghots; per person AMD9000) Large home with four bedrooms and comfortable furnishings. Host Knarik can organize fishing trips in the area. Take Shirkatsi Poghots north, then turn right on Demirtchyan; the B&B is 600m down on the left.

Vanatur Hotel (☎ 3 07 14; 70a Gorki Poghots; r AMD20,000, deluxe AMD30,000) The newest place in town offers comfortable rooms with TV. Deluxe rooms have a Jacuzzi in the bathroom. Prices include breakfast. The restaurant also serves lunch and dinner with a Georgian-inspired menu.

Hotel IsUz (☎ 3 33 99; www.isuz.am; 1/5 Garegin Nzhdeh Poghots; s/d/ste incl breakfast AMD20,000/24,000/30,000; ✷ ▢) This 12-room hotel offers comfortable rooms with minibars, excellent bathrooms and neat decorations including murals. The front desk can arrange transport.

Hotel Araks (☎ 3 58 15; www.arakshotel.am; 31 Gorki Poghots; s/d AMD25,000/30,000; ✷ ▣) High ceilings, frilly drapes and a huge staircase lends an old-world feel to this hotel. Recent renovation makes it one of the best in town. Amenities include a sauna and an indoor pool.

Gastehaus Berlin (Berlin Hotel) (☎ 2 31 48; www.berlinhotel-gyumri.am; 25 Haghtanaki Poghots; s/d incl breakfast AMD27,000/32,000; ✷) This hotel was built as an accommodation wing for a German hospital on the same premises. It seems odd to have doctors and patients always outside, but the hotel itself is welcoming and colourfully decorated. The spacious rooms have comfy beds, satellite TV and minibar. The hotel is home to Shirak Tours, which can help with logistics in the area.

Eating

There are cheap street snacks available from shops and stalls at the *shuka* and a wide range of new and historic restaurants around town. Besides the following the Georgian restaurant in the Vanatur Hotel is recommended, as well as pizza joints at the Hotel IsUz and Hotel Araks.

Polos Mukuch (☎ 3 45 11; 75 Jivani Poghots; meals AMD2500; ☺ 9am-10pm) The latest restaurant to occupy a historic building near the Hotel Araks, Polos Mukuch is popular with family groups and sometimes has entertainment – the menu is in Armenian and has a long list of drinks.

Phaeton Alek (☎ 3 29 88; 47 Haghtanaki Poghota; meals AMD2500-3500; ☺ 10am-7pm) In the cellars of the architecture museum, this spot often hosts groups for an 'ethnic' experience, with old artefacts on the walls and sometimes entertainment as well. Solo diners may not feel so welcome, but the food is hearty and good value.

Cherkezi Zor (Fish Farm; ☎ 3 05 59; meals AMD3000-5000; Bulvarayin Poghots; ☺ 10am-10pm) You'll be guaranteed fresh fish at the appropriately named Fish Farm. Pick what type of fish you want and the chef literally plucks your dinner out of the pool and sets it on the BBQ. It's on the western side of town and a little hard to find. From the stadium, cross the opposite bank and walk north up the canyon for 1.3km. Alternatively, go by taxi.

Drinking & Entertainment

The Flamingo Café and Robinson's occupy the little park in the middle of Khaghaghutyan Hraparak. Both serve drinks and *khoravats* until the last customer staggers away, with a soundtrack of pumping Russian drinking tunes. Of the two, Robinson's is the more interesting, having a jungle setting with tree houses and the like.

Evenings tend to be quiet in Gyumri; you can fill in the time with a film at the **Kino October** (admission AMD700) located on Azatutyan Hraparak.

Getting There & Around

Buses and marshrutkas, including those to Yerevan (AMD1200, two hours, every 20 minutes 7am to 7pm), leave from the *avtokayan* on Tigranyan Poghots. Transport to Vanadzor (AMD800, one hour) leaves almost hourly between 9am and 4.30pm. Marshrutkas travel daily to Tbilisi (AMD5000, 3½ hours, 10.30am).

Vanadzor is on the train line between Yerevan and Tbilisi; there is a train every day in one direction (even days to Tbilisi and odd days back to Yerevan). A seat to Tbilisi is AMD2770 and a cabin berth costs AMD4000; to Yerevan it's AMD480. Train travel is two

to three times slower than road travel; it takes 3½ hours to reach Yerevan and between 10 and 12 hours to reach Tbilisi. Call the station (☎ 2 10 02)to confirm schedules.

There are lots of taxis in Gyumri and cheap marshrutkas all over town. A taxi ride from the *avtokayan* to Garegin Nzhdeh Poghots should cost around AMD500; an urban marshrutka costs AMD100.

Shirak Airport, which is 5km southeast of town, is served by Siberian Airlines (Moscow, Novosibirsk), Ural Airlines (Ekaterinburg), Aeroflot-Don (Sochi, Rostov) and Armavia (Moscow). There are plenty of ticket agencies in town. Flights to Moscow cost around $125 to $140, including the AMD10,000 departure tax, about $25 cheaper on average than from Yerevan. A taxi to the airport is around AMD1500.

MARMASHEN ՄԱՐՄԱՇԵՆ

The monastery at Marmashen is about 10km northwest of Gyumri, just past the village of Varambert in the wide gorge of the Akhuryan River. There are three churches hewn from lovely apricot-coloured tuff clustered together next to an orchard, plus the ruins and foundations of other structures nearby. One of the ruins is of an unusual circular church, recently excavated.

The biggest church, Surp Stepanos, was built between 988 and 1029, with a 13th-century *gavit*. An Italian team led restoration work in the 1960s, so intricately carved old church stones have been incorporated into newer building blocks. Beautiful carved tombs and *khatchkars* dot the land around the churches, and it's a peaceful, rural environment typical of Shirak, with grassy horizons. The caretaker is here 8am to 8pm daily, and he can recite some of the inscriptions on the sides of churches by heart. A return taxi to Gyumri is about AMD3000. Make sure the driver understands that you want to see the monastery and not the nearby village of the same name. There are hourly buses from Gyumri's *avtokayan* to Varambert (AMD120) between 9am and 7pm (look for the bus to Kaps).

HARICHAVANK ՀԱՌԻՃԱՎԱՆՔ

Harichavank monastery is in the sturdy old town of Harich, about 4km from the town of Artik. This complex was the summer residence of the Catholicos of Echmiadzin for a period after 1850 and is surrounded by

19th-century buildings. Harichavank is one of those monasteries where a 7th- or 8th-century chapel has been dramatically expanded with 13th-century *gavits* and domes. There is some beautiful geometric stonework over the main door church and around the dome of the *gavit*.

Inside, the church's caretaker can point out the anteroom/storeroom with a hole in the ceiling leading to a secret upstairs room. During times of invasion, the room was used to house women and children and sometimes even important local officials. A stone would be fitted exactly into the ceiling hole once everyone had climbed to safety.

A direct bus departs Gyumri's *avtokayan* for Harichavank (AMD350, 50 minutes) at 11.30am. If you can't catch it there are marshrutkas and buses to Artik (AMD200, 30 minutes, hourly), from where you can wait around for another marshrutka to Harich or take a taxi from Artik (AMD1800 return). If you have your own vehicle, the monastery is about 15km off the main Yerevan–Gyumri road.

If you are in the area, check out the well-preserved 7th-century church of **Lmbatavank** southwest of Artik; it contains important early frescoes.

ANI VIEWPOINT ԱՆԻ

The southern tip of Shirak *marz* includes the restricted border zone around the viewing point for **Ani**, across the Akhuryan on the Turkish side of the border. You need to pass a Russian-run checkpoint to reach the achingly beautiful view over Ani, the 10th-century capital of Armenia. The ruined city occupies a promontory above the river, an undulating sea of green sprinkled with the bare stones of old churches. The city was captured by the Seljuk Turks in 1064, and abandoned after the Mongol invasions. Its position on the old front line of the Cold War between NATO and the USSR has preserved its isolation. People of Armenian descent can often schmooze their way past, but foreigners usually need to arrange a visit through a travel agency. It's no particular hassle to visit with permission. It's utterly haunting at sunset in late summer or autumn, when the Kurdish herders return to the rough little village outside the city walls. There's a quarry on the Armenian side for the nouveau riche who want buildings

made of Ani tuff. Some of the villagers in the vicinity are descended from genocide survivors, so every year on 24 April there's a tradition of lighting bonfires along the border as a reminder to Turkey. If you only get to see Ani from afar, it's possible to take a virtual tour at www.virtu alani.org.

SPITAK ՍՊԻՏԱԿ

This town is infamously known for being close to the epicentre of the 1988 earthquake. The town was wiped out and 4000 of its residents perished in the 7.2 quake. Housing has since been rebuilt, mainly with donations from overseas. Each housing block bears the distinctive touch of the country that provided the rebuilding costs.

A walk through Spitak cemetery shows the tombstones of those who perished; some of the stones mark whole family graves. The nearby church made of sheet metal was erected shortly after the earthquake as a place to pray for the dead.

A neglected monument to the dead stands on a hill near the town. It's a haunting and forlorn spot that seems not to have been visited in some time, as if the residents of Spitak wish not to be reminded of their grim past.

Spitak is just off the main road between Gyumri and Vanadzor and served by frequent marshrutkas.

VAYOTS DZOR & SYUNIK

Armenia's remote southern regions, between Karabakh to the east and the Azeri enclave of Naxçıvan to the west, are linked to Yerevan by a single, vital highway. Vayots Dzor (Gorge of Woes) centres on the headwaters of the wine-growing Arpa valley. The name comes from a history of ruinous earthquakes across these mountainous valleys and cliffs. It's a great area to explore off-the-beaten-track trails by foot, horse or 4WD Jeep.

In the south, Syunik is full of ancient churches and monasteries, rustic villages making home-made fruit vodkas, forests, high pastures and stunning evidence of much older human cultures in the rocks of Zorats Karer and Ughtasar near Sisian. The 19th-century town of Goris is a great base to

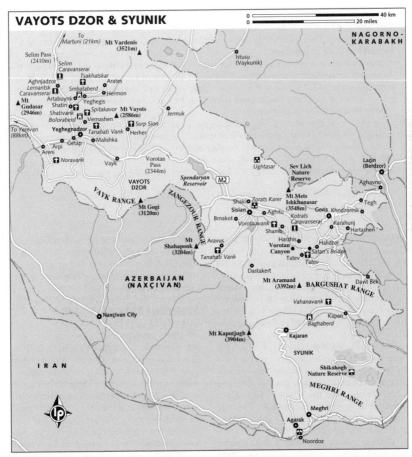

VAYOTS DZOR & SYUNIK

visit Tatev or Karabakh or as a break before the long haul to Iran.

ARENI ԱՐԵՆԻ

Few grape varieties can thrive in Armenia's climatic extremes, but the Areni grape does. Most of the country's vineyards are on the Ararat Plain, but the valleys from the village of Areni up to Yeghegnadzor comprise a quality wine-growing region.

Wineries open for tastings (daily in summer, 10am to 6pm) include **Areni** in the town of Areni, **Ginetas** at Arpi and **Getnatep** on the main highway at Yeghegnadzor. The **Surp Astvatsatsin Church** across the river from Areni sits on a shelf below a cliff. **Getap,** just up the Yeghegis Valley before Yeghegnadzor,

is also a local wine-making centre. **Hotel Noy** (☎ 0872 55 45; Arpi; r AMD7000-18,000;), on the main highway, is a motel-style complex with clean rooms, a bar, a buffet and a swimming pool. The Tufenkian group (www.tufenkian heritage.com) is building a luxury hotel and restaurant at Areni, expected to open in 2008. There are frequent buses and marshrutkas along the main highway.

NORAVANK ՆՈՐԱՎԱՆՔ

This church complex, by the 13th-century architect Momik, is a masterpiece both for its architecture and its dramatic setting. Noravank (New Monastery) was founded by Bishop Hovhannes in 1105, and was last restored in the 1990s. Climb the narrow stone

A SPELUNKER'S DELIGHT

The area around Areni and Arpi is riddled with hundreds of caves, some of which contain a kilometre or more of chambers.

There are some accessible caves in the canyon that leads up to Noravank, including the Trchunneri Karayr (Bird Cave), close to the turn-off and Magili Karandzav, about 1km further into the canyon. Magili is one of the deepest caves in the area and significant as the home of a large colony of fruit bats; Neolithic-era stone tools have also been found here. Unfortunately, vandals have ruined most of the stalactites.

Excellent examples of stalactites and stalagmites can be found at other caves in the area, including the Arjeri, Mozrovi and Jerovank caverns. These caves are not for the inexperienced, so it's best to visit on a guided tour (the caves are also locked to casual visitors). Contact **Amtour** (☎ 10744 266; www.amtour.am) in Yerevan, which organises group tours. When exploring any cave bring a strong flashlight and carry extra batteries. Wear old clothes as you will inevitably get very dirty.

If you take the tour and plan to visit southern Armenia anyway, have the driver leave you in Yeghegnadzor and go from there.

stairs outside **Surp Astvatsatsin** (1339) to get a closer look at its dome. Astvatsatsin is also known as Burtelashen, after its patron, Burtel Orbelian, who is buried here with his family. Historians say the church is reminiscent of towerlike burial structures created in the early years of Christianity. There's a wonderful carving of Christ flanked by Peter and Paul above the door.

The smaller **St Karapet Church** (1227) next to Surp Astvatsatsin is the original shrine built by the miracle-working Bishop Hovhannes. Noravank once treasured a piece of the True Cross stained with the blood of Christ, acquired from a mysterious stranger. The side chapel of St Grigor includes a carved lion-human tombstone dated to 1300.

There are picnic spots and springs around Noravank, as well as an excellent restaurant by the car park. The valley really warms up in the middle of a summer's day, so come early, or late in the afternoon. During medieval summers the monks of Noravank retired to a mountain retreat. The site is at its most spectacular around sunset when the reddish hues of the cliffs are accentuated by the setting sun.

Noravank features on many travel-agency tours from Yerevan, about 90 minutes away by road – many combine a visit with a stop at Khor Virap and a winery. Public transport from Yerevan or Yeghegnadzor takes you as far as the turn-off on the highway, 6km from Noravank. Get out at the Edem restaurant and hitch the rest of the way, a fairly easy process on weekends.

About 4km from the turn-off to Norovank is an unusual cave-café dug out of the side of the cliff. There is no sign, but you'll see the metal grating between the boulders on the right side of the road.

YEGHEGNADZOR & AROUND
ԵՂԵԳՆԱՁՈՐ
☎ 0281 / pop 8200

An overgrown country town built on twisting lanes that wind into the hills, Yeghegnadzor (yeh-*heg*-nadzor) is the peaceful administrative centre of Vayots Dzor. The town is a mainly Soviet-era confection of wide civic spaces and *tufa* apartment blocks. A few small factories (eg a diamond-cutting plant) have opened, but remittances and agriculture provide the biggest incomes. There isn't much to see in the town itself, but it does make a good base to explore the region – you could easily spend three or four days in between trips to Yeghegis village, Noravank, the Ajeri and Arpi caves and the wineries in Areni and Spitakavor.

The town has moneychangers, a **UniBank** (☎ 52 13 43) with an ATM (accepting Visa cards) and the **Arpa Net Internet Café** (☎ 2 21 23; per hr AMD300; ⏰ 9am-9pm) just downhill from the *avtokayan*.

Sights
The **Vyats Dzor Regional Museum** (4 Shahumian; ⏰ 9am-1pm & 2-5pm Mon-Fri, 10am-5pm Sat) in the centre of town describes local history but is frequently closed. A better option is to visit the **Museum of Gladzor University** (☎ 2 37 05; admission

AMD1000; ☽ 9am-5pm Tue-Sun) in the village of Vernashen, 4km uphill from Yeghegnadzor. The museum has displays on monasteries across the country, plus old manuscripts and descriptions of Armenia's various schools and universities. The museum is housed inside a 17th-century church called St Hagop.

The museum marks the end of the village and just past it is a T-junction. The road to the left leads to **Spitakavor** monastery, about 9km along a winding dirt track for vehicles or 5km along a more direct walking path. The road is rough so hiking is a good idea; just bring plenty of bottled water. To find the trail, walk through the village and carry on straight up the western bank of the gorge past a small dam on the river (ignore the vehicle road, which switches back). The 20th-century Armenian fighter Garegin Nzhdeh was buried at Spitakavor in 1983. He fought in the Balkan Wars and, in WWI, went into exile and lobbied the Nazis to restore Armenian territory, before being handed over at the end of the war by the Allies and dying in a Soviet prison. The **Boloraberd fortress** crowns a rocky crest across from the monastery.

Back at the T-junction, the road to the right winds for 6km to Tanahat Monastery. The impressive main **Surp Stepanos Church** was built by the Orbelians. There are significant stone reliefs of animals on the exterior of the church, including the crest of the Orebelians (a bull and a lion) on the tambour. All around the church are ruins that once made up the actual site of Gladzor University.

Another 3.5km along the road leads to the **Monastery of Arkaz**. It is well known for holding a piece of the True Cross under a stone marker in the back of the church. The church sees many visitors during the last two Sundays of October, when locals arrive in droves to sacrifice animals after the harvest.

Sleeping & Eating

Hotel Gladzdor (☎ 2 51 65; main square; per person AMD3000) Just off the main square is this ageing and under-funded Soviet-era hotel with no sign. It has cold bucket baths when water is available and cramped rooms with lumpy beds. It's a bland experience, but there is nothing cheaper if you're on a tight budget.

Gohar's Guest House (☎ 2 33 24; 44 Spandaryan Poghots; s/d incl breakfast AMD8000/15,000) A comfortable homestay with Gohar Gevorgyan, whose house is just past the football field.

It's a good idea to arrange to be picked up. Meals can be prepared on request.

Antione B&B (☎ 093594 544, 093852 542; per person AMD11,000) Antione is a Canadian-Armenian who runs a lovely B&B about 2km uphill from the town centre. It's a modern home with comfortable rooms and a small library of English-language books. Breakfast is available (as it should be at this price). It would be difficult to find the place on your own so call ahead for a pick up.

If you have your own transport there are several riverside restaurants along the main highway that set a good Armenian table for around AMD2000 per person, including kebabs, *khoravats* (including venison, fish and, more controversially, bear-meat *khoravats*), salads and drinks. Open 8am until late outside winter. A popular place for vehicles to stop is **Karitak** (☎ 2 48 06), about 5km west of town on the road to Yeghegnadzor. Edem Café, on the road to Noravank, is another excellent choice; it has live music from 9pm on weekends.

In the various seasons there are roadside stalls selling watermelons, fruit, honey, nuts and homemade wines and conserves.

Getting There & Away

Marshrutkas and buses to nearby villages leave from the *avtokayan* in the centre of town, opposite the Hotel Gladzor. A daily bus to Jermuk (AMD700, 40 minutes) leaves at 2pm. There are marshrutkas to Vayk (AMD200, 20 minutes) twice hourly between 9am and 5pm. Marshrutkas to Yerevan (AMD1200, 90 minutes to two hours, hourly 8am to 6pm) usually leave from the junction with the main highway. Space permitting, you can also flag one down here to go to Goris. As yet there is no public transport to Martuni on the shore of Lake Sevan, but hitching is not too much of a struggle. Taxis can be hired near the *avtokayan* for AMD100 per kilometre. Noravank is about 20km west, while Jermuk is 53km east.

YEGHEGIS & AROUND ԵՂԵԳԻՍ

The beautiful **Yeghegis Valley** is surrounded by towering peaks and contains a rare concentration of churches. This and the surrounding valleys are well worth exploring for a day or two.

To reach the area, turn north off the Yerevan–Goris highway at Getap and after 12km turn right (east) towards Shatin village. The first sight of interest is **Shativank**, a fortified monastery with a church (rebuilt in 1665), a waterworks, a grain-storage silo and two-storey monk and guest quarters. To get there by 4WD Jeep turn right at the end of Shatin towards the river. About 150m past the bridge turn right, then after 500m go left to a cemetery and continue on this track for 7km.

To get there by foot, take the steeper but shorter path from the gorge. To reach the trailhead, take the left fork above the bridge; after 100m take the trail to the right and walk for 45 minutes.

About 2km up from Shatin village, a road branches up the valley to the west towards Artabuynk. About 1km past the village a track goes steeply down to the right towards the stream, which can be crossed by a 4WD vehicle.

From the river it's 6km to the 10th-century **Tsakhatskar monastery**, a crumbling agglomeration of churches and old *khatchkars*. From the stream, continue up the main track, the monastery eventually comes into view on the left.

From the monastery, head back down the way you came and at the fork in the path head left up the slope to **Smbataberd fortress** above Artabuynk. The stretch up to the fort takes about 30 minutes. On the other side of Smbataberd you can look down on the Yeghegis valley.

Yeghegis village is reached by taking the right fork after Shatin (ie away from Artabuynk). The village looks as though it's been inhabited forever; it has a couple of churches, including the very unusual Surp Zorats, where worshippers gathered before an outdoor altar.

It's believed this courtyard was created so that horses and soldiers could be blessed before going off to battle.

Across the river from the village, a metal footbridge leads to an 800-year-old Jewish cemetery – Hebrew letters are clearly visible on some of the grave markers.

The next village up the valley is Hermon, where a rough track north up the valley (on the left) leads to Arates and **Arates Vank**, a monastery with three churches (7th to 13th century). Arates is about 10km beyond Yeghegis.

There is no public transport out here, so the best way to visit is either to hike or hire a taxi (preferably a 4WD).

SELIM CARAVANSERAI
ՍՈՒԼԵՄԱՅԻ ՔԱՐԱՎԱՆԱՏՈՒՆ

Built in 1332, this is the best-preserved caravanserai in Armenia. According to the inscription by the door, this travellers inn for traders and their caravans of pack animals was built by Prince Chesar Orbelian. It was built for the days when the great Silk Road passed from Iran through Goris, the highlands, Yeghegnadzor and Selim Pass on its way to Europe. The inscription also honours the Mongol despot Abu Said II Khan as 'the ruler of the world'. Built on basalt blocks, the building has a central hall for animals divided by two vaulted side aisles with stone mangers.

To reach the caravanserai, head north from the Yerevan–Goris highway at Getap. The site is 30km from the turn-off. It's worth stopping here if you are travelling onwards to Martuni, but it probably doesn't warrant a trip in its own right.

VAYK & AROUND ՎԱՅՔ
☎ 0282 / pop 5400

The rugged hills and valleys around this overgrown village hide lots of artfully positioned churches, monasteries and chapels from the 8th to 12th centuries. Heading 6km up the valley, the first turn-off left leads 10km north to Herher and a cluster of churches at the **Surp Sion monastery** 1km beyond it. There are the ruins of **Kapuyt Berd** (Blue Fortress) and *khatchkars* around Herher as well.

The **Vayk Hotel** in the middle of town is a 19th-century building that was being renovated at the time of research.

You'll find marshrutkas to Yerevan (AMD1400, less than two hours, every two hours 8am to 7pm) from the main road.

JERMUK ՋԵՐՄՈՒԿ
☎ 0287 / pop 7000

This small resort town, 2080m above sea level on the upper Arpa River, was popular in the USSR as a vacation spot for mineral-water treatments and hot springs, some of them very hot. The landscape around Jermuk is very pretty, excellent for walks and hikes.

The spa business gets most of its customers in the July and August holidays, and largely hibernates outside this season. Some of its sanatoriums have immersion pools and treatment areas. The spa attendants take their job seriously – in the old days people would sign up for 18-day courses with medically supervised immersions in Jermuk's waters.

Open to the public is the **Gallery of Waters**, with a façade of archways and a pleasant view. Water runs into stone urns from pipes set in the wall and the temperature of the water is printed next to its pipe. The various waters are said to have different properties, good for curing stomach and liver problems, heart disease and cancer.

The **Armenia Hotel and Health Spa** (9am-5pm) has hot baths, mud treatments, sauna, hydrotherapy rooms and various other treatment rooms. Treatment costs range between AMD600 and AMD2500. Even better, try the Jacuzzi at the Olympia Health Spa across the road.

At the time of research a small ski resort was being built on a hill close to the town. It's not the Alps but should satisfy beginning and intermediate skiers for a half day.

Orientation & Information

The town is entered via a bridge spanning a deep gorge high above the Arpa River; turn left at the end of the bridge, and a few hundred metres along is the taxi and bus stop that serves as a main square of sorts. The Haypost and Telecom offices are here. Just north of the taxi stand is the Armenia Hotel and Gallery of Waters. South of the taxi stand is the short main road with shops and an internet café.

Sleeping

There are lots of informal pensions and spas open in July and August, but options thin out in the winter. Prices below represent low season – in July and August prices can double based on demand.

Hotel Life (2 12 56; Shaumian Poghots; per person AMD5000) On the main street near the shops, this place has four comfortable rooms, each with a divided living room and bedroom, plus en suite facilities. Amenities include TV, VCR (with Hollywood movies dubbed in Russian) and hot showers. This is a real bargain in the low season.

Anush Guest House (2 24 41; Vardanyan Poghots; s/d with half board AMD5000/10,000, deluxe s/d AMD10,000/15000) Partially restored, the old Anush hotel has some excellent deluxe rooms big enough for you and a dozen friends. The standard rooms with separate bath have not been refurbished and are not worth the price. Owner Ashot Margaryan can also arrange

dinners, visits to sanatoriums and transport around the area.

Turis Hotel (2 30 99; Getapnya Poghots; per person incl 3 meals AMD11,000) On a quiet road in the east part of town, the Turis has pleasant and modern rooms in a stately old building. It's 700m east of the main bridge.

Armenia Hotel (2 12 90; 2 Miasnikyan Poghots, s/d incl 3 meals AMD20,000/40,000) Located next to a scenic park and the Water Gallery, the Armenia is the best hotel in town. However, it also doubles as sanatorium so it can be a little creepy to see doctors and patients shuffling about in smocks. The price includes a range of diagnostic treatments – just keep reminding yourself it's all part of the Armenia experience.

Eating

Gandevank Restaurant (2 16 90; meals AMD2500; 10am-midnight) Of the many *khoravats* places we tried around Armenia this one seems to stand out for its succulent grilled meats. The fresh-fruit dessert also deserves a special mention. Coming across the main bridge, turn right (away from the centre); it's about 400m straight ahead in a wood-fronted building.

Besides this place there are a couple of cafés in the centre.

Getting There & Away

Jermuk is 177km from Yerevan, about two hours by the main highway, and then 26km off the main highway on a spur road. In the low season there is one marshrutka to Yerevan each day (AMD2000, 2½ hours) at 7.30am. At 8am there is a bus to Yeghegnadzor (AMD700, one hour) and at 4pm a bus goes to Vayk (AMD500, 30 minutes). More buses and marshrutkas operate in July and August.

SISIAN ՍԻՍԻԱՆ

02830 / pop 18,000

Sisian sits on a high plateau where it snows as late as March or April, and the autumn ends early here too. Long miles of cropland are mown from the Spendaryan Reservoir to Goris after its short growing season, and in September the villages stack up with piles of hay, some taller than their houses. Sisian is a fairly quiet country town with a core of early-20th-century buildings. This land below the mountains of Syunik has been inhabited since forever, back to the ages of Neolithic observatories and animal petroglyphs. Some examples have been gathered in the town's *karadaran*

ARMENIA

(stone museum) park. The site of Sisian itself was inhabited as long ago as 2000 BC.

Sisian is located centrally in the southern end of Armenia and works as a base while heading to or from Yerevan. There's plenty to see and do in and around Sisian, and other regional sites are accessible from here.

Orientation & Information

Sisian is mostly laid out on a grid and is small enough for walking around. The centre of town is on the northern side of the Vorotan River. Marshrutkas leave from the junction on the northern end of the bridge. The main street, Sisakan Poghots, runs parallel to the river, one block inland.

One end of Sisakan has a Soviet memorial cheerfully celebrating the crushing of the Dashnaks in 1920; from here a road swings to the right and up to Sisavan Church.

An internet club is opposite the Hotel Dina. Just past the Dina, the next street left leads to the Basen Hotel. You can change money at stores and kiosks near the main bridge.

Ashot Avagyan (☎ 091584 485; ukhtasar@mail15 .com) is an artist who arranges Jeep trips up the mountains to Ughtasar. Ashot organizes a local arts festival on 11 August that attracts artists and musicians from around the country.

Sights

Originally built in the 6th century, **Sisavan Church** was restored as recently as the 20th century. It combines an elegant square-cross floor with some striking sculptures of royal and ecclesiastical patrons inside and out. Inside there's a display of microsculptures by local artist Eduard Ter-Ghazaryan.

Seen through a microscope, one features 17 images of the cross on a human hair coated with metal.

The road up from town passes a Soviet war memorial with a Karabakh War monument – local men were some of the first to volunteer to join their kin over in the next mountain range when the war began, and paid a heavy price for it.

The **karadaran** park in town one block from Sisakan Poghots gathers together stone carvings from different millennia, with sarcophagi, phallus stones, ram stones and megaliths. You can spot the evolution of the pagan *khatchkars* to rough stone crosses and finally medieval Armenian *khatchkars*.

Facing the park is the **Museum of History** (☎ 33 31; admission AMD500; ☺ 10am-5pm Tue-Sat), with some carpets and ethnographical displays beside maps and historical information, mostly labelled in Armenian with some English. It also has some interesting photos taken after an earthquake levelled the town in 1931.

Sleeping & Eating

Aminhanyan Shavash B&B (☎ 41 42; 9 Tigran Mets Poghots; per person AMD5000) A large house on the outskirts of town managed by English-speaking Gayane. Laundry is available and breakfast is an extra AMD2000. It's 2km from the bus stop on the eastern side of town and difficult to find on your own. A taxi here will cost AMD400.

Hotel Dina (☎ 33 33; 35 Sisakan Poghots; www.dina hotel.am; r with/without bath per person AMD8000/3000, deluxe AMD10,000) A handsome 1930s building with basic shared rooms and nicer double rooms with en suite bathrooms. The receptionist usually won't offer the cheaper rooms unless you ask. Given the low price, quality rooms and central location, this is easily the best deal in town. Breakfast costs AMD2000. The managers speak some English and can help with arranging tours and transport onwards.

Hotel Lalaner (☎ 66 00; www.lalahotel.am; 29 Sisikan Poghots; s/d/deluxe AMD10,000/20,000/25,000) Overlooking the town square, this clean and comfortable hotel has 10 rooms and a restaurant. Deluxe rooms have a Jacuzzi in the bathroom. The hotel also organizes trips to local sights plus activities such as fishing, hiking and camping.

Zorats Qarer B&B (☎ 36 11; info@bedanbreakfast.am; 40 3rd Poghots; per person AMD10,000; 🔌) A modern stone-clad villa at the end of a track about 100m west of Sisavan Church (a 10-minute walk from the centre of town). The four bedrooms are smallish and cosy, with extra bunks for kids. Views of Sisian are spectacular from this spot. It's overpriced compared to the Dina, but the owners are open to negotiation.

Jira Hars (☎ 53 86; Israelyan Poghots; ☺ 10am-10pm) Nestled by the river just next to the bridge, this local *khoravats* joint serves up grilled meat, soups and salads. You can sit inside or in cabanas next to the river. Otherwise, most of the hotels have restaurants, including a good one at the Basen.

Getting There & Away

There are four marshrutkas to Yerevan (AMD2000, four hours, 8am, 9am, noon and 2.30pm) and one to Goris (AMD700, 45 minutes, 8.30am) each day, where the bridge meets Israeilyan Poghots (along the north bank). Taxis wait at this junction too. There's also a bus stop at the turn-off from the Yerevan–Goris road into town, where people often wait for rides.

Local tours can be negotiated directly with the taxi drivers or through one of the hotels. A trip to Shaki Falls or Zorats Karer costs about AMD700 to AMD1000, a ride to Goris AMD5000, and a longer tour to Tatev Monastery and back about AMD9000.

AROUND SISIAN

Two hundred and four upright basalt stones up to 3m high set along sweeping lines and loops, some punctured with sight holes aligned with stars, make up the ancient site of **Zorats Karer**. The site, situated on a rise above the river plains ringed by mountains, is dotted with tombs dated to 3000 BC. Scientist Elma Parsamian argues that the site's elaborate astronomical functions can be shown at the solstices and equinoxes. Lines of stones define an egg-shaped area with a burial tumulus in the centre, with a north arm stretching 170m and a southern alley 160m long. About 70 stones are pierced with finger-sized holes. Along with the 5000-year-old observatory at Metsamor west of Yerevan, it suggests the builders had a deep knowledge of astronomy, including the zodiac and the lunar phases, combined perhaps with worship for stars such as Sirius. Zorats Karer is 3.5km north of Sisian, signposted on the left about 700m before the main highway. The stones are in the fields about 400m from the turn-off.

The **Shaki Waterfall** lies about 4km from Sisian near the village of the same name. About 18m high, it sluices down a wide expanse of stones above the Shaki River. The water is used for Shaki's hydroelectric power station, so the waterfall isn't always 'on'.

About 6km down the Vorotan from Sisian in **Aghitu** (Aghudi) village is a distinctive 7th-century **tower-tomb.** There are dragon stones nearby from the 2nd to 3rd century BC. The road continues as the canyon deepens past Vaghatin to **Vorotnavank**, 12km from Sisian on the south side of the Vorotan, a striking 9th-to 11th-century fortress and church complex built by Queen Shahandukht and her son Sevada. A couple of kilometres down the valley on the other side of the river the road passes Vorotan to the **Shamb hot springs**, where you can warm your toes (you might not want to put much more of your body in the water as it's a little polluted).

The petroglyphs of **Ughtasar** (Pilgrimage Mountain) in the mountains north of Sisian are even older than Zorats Karer. They lie at an altitude of 3300m around a lake on Mt Tsghuk, accessible between June and September, and even then only if it's not a cold summer. Carvings of leaping, dancing animals and hunters adorn rocks and boulders everywhere around the small lake. It's a haunting place surrounded by isolated peaks, and you can only wonder why ancient people would trek to such an inhospitable place to leave their mark on stone. The tracks are steep, rocky and hopeless without a Jeep (Villis) and a guide. Ashot Avagyan (see opposite) helped build the tracks to Ughtasar during the Karabakh War, and can arrange drivers and Villis hire for AMD20,000 per vehicle for a trip of eight to 10 hours – the ascent takes at least three hours.

The ruins of **Tanahati Vank** are 17km southwest of Sisian past the Tolors Reservoir. A university was established here in 1280. Called Karmir (Red) Vank by locals, Tanahat Monastery is on a high promontory by a gorge. The monks here were so pious and ascetic they refused soup, cheese and oil, eating only vegetables, hence the name Tanahat, meaning 'deprived of soup'.

GORIS ԳՈՐԻՍ
☎ 0284 / pop 25,000

The endlessly winding roads that leap through the gorges over the mountains of Syunik come to a major junction at Goris, making this an inevitable stop between Yerevan, Stepanakert and the Iranian border. But it's hardly a place to pass through – Goris is a destination in itself. Boasting fine stone houses with arched windows and balconies on tree-lined avenues, it's a great place for strolling and chatting with locals. The pace of life is slow: there is little commercial or industrial activity, or even tourist kitsch, so it really feels like you've stepped back in time. Goris is known for its variety of homemade fruit *oghee* including the deliciously potent mulberry and Cornelian cherry (*hone*) *oghee* – explore the

ARMENIA

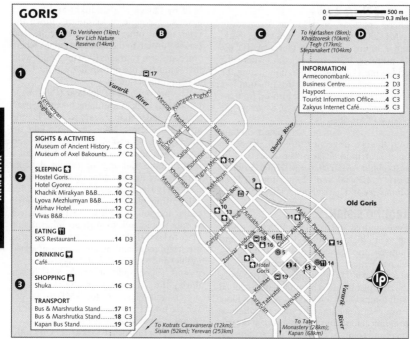

GORIS

0 ————— 500 m
0 ————— 0.3 miles

To Verisheen (1km);
Sev Lich Nature
Reserve (14km)

To Hartashen (8km);
Khndzoresk (10km);
Tegh (17km);
Stepanakert (104km)

Vararik River

Yerevanyan Poghots

Mesrop Mashtots Avangard Poghots

Sherjur River

Old Goris

Syuni Yervand

Safari

Khoyenats

Manukoyan

Pionherner

Tigran Mets

Bakhshyan

Davit Bek

Garegin Nzhdeh Poghots Ankakhutyan

Zoravar Andranik

Mkhitar Poghots

Ghazhi Ashoti Ondan Prelats

Komitas

Surenyan

Suren Tsatevatsi

Narekatsi

Vararik River

Hotel Goris

To Kotrats Caravanserai (12km);
Sisian (52km); Yerevan (253km)

To Tatev
Monastery (28km);
Kapan (68km)

shuka on Syuniki Poghots or ask at a B&B to find some.

There is plenty to see around the town too, including a weird cave city on the other bank of the river and equally bizarre sets of volcanic pillars that spear through the steep grassy slopes above town. Longer day trips can be made to Tatev, the Vorotan Canyon and the caves at Khndzoresk.

There is a fine selection of hotels and B&Bs in town, plus a couple of museums and a busy little *shuka*. It makes a good place to break a long journey between Yerevan and Karabakh – plan on spending a few days to soak it all in.

Orientation & Information

Goris was laid out to a plan by a German architect in the 19th century. The **Tourist Information Office** (☎ 093550 655; 4 Ankakhutyan Poghots; ☟ 10am-5pm Mon-Fri) has a well-informed English-speaking staff and is located just south of the park in the centre of town.

The banks, the **Haypost office** (19 Syuniki Poghots) restaurants and shops are within a few blocks of the main square. The **Zakyus Internet café** (☎ 3 00 27; Gushan Ashoti; per hr AMD250; ☟ 10am-

midnight) just west of the taxi stand is clean and has a good connection. Or try **Business Centre** (☎ 2 30 10; 9 Mesrop Mashtots; per hr AMD250). The **Armeconombank** (☎ 2 42 09; 4 Mesrop Mashtots) has an ATM that accepts MasterCard.

Sights

Locals say the cave shelters and stables of **Old Goris** carved into the hillside on the east side of town were built and inhabited in the 5th century. Several trails lead up over a saddle where there are more volcanic pinnacle clusters to explore. Many of the rooms are linked together, and arched 'shelves' grace some walls. The caves are sometimes used to house cattle – watch your step.

The **Museum of Axel Bakounts** (☎ 2 29 66; 41 Mesrop Mashtots Poghots; admission AMD200; ☟ 10am-5pm Tue-Sun) is a typical Goris villa with stone walls and a veranda looking onto a courtyard. The museum was the home of writer Axel Bakounts (or Bakunts), who died in Stalin's 1937 purges. It features his personal effects and furnishings from the late 19th and early 20th centuries. The friendly director of the museum, Mikaelyan Kajik, may invite you into his office to sample some of the local mulberry vodka.

The **Museum of Ancient History** (Ankakhutyan Poghots; admission free; ☉ 10am-5pm) displays Bronze Age knives, traditional costumes, carpets and other locally found artefacts. The most unique item is a five-sided stone with carved faces that represent the sun, moon, water, earth and sky, believed to date back 4000 years. The museum is dimly lit and everything is labelled in Armenian, but it's still worth a look.

About 2km northwest of the *avtokayan* is the village of **Verisheen**, which houses the ancient St Ripsime Church. The barrel-vaulted structure saw restoration in 2007 and is believed to have been built on top of an old pagan temple. Continuing on the main road northwest you'll spot plenty of cave dwellings by the road.

Sleeping

Hostel Goris (☎ 2 18 86, 093-287 902; jirmar28 @freenet.am; 55 Khorenatsi Poghots; per person AMD7000) This hostel is run by the affable Jirayr Martirosyan, an accomplished artist. There are two rooms, one with three beds and one with a double bed that is suitable for couples. Rooms have TV and are pleasantly decorated. There is running hot water, good coffee and a filling breakfast. The hostel is well signed and right next to the utterly squalid Hotel Goris, which now acts primarily as a shelter for refugees from Karabakh.

Lyova Mezhlumyan B&B (☎ 2 22 98; 7 Makichi Poghots; per person incl breakfast AMD7000; 🖳) A fine stone house close to the Vararik River. It is 200m east of the main square. There's no sign, but the exterior has curved walls reaching in to a recessed door. The large home includes six bedrooms, a large living room and nice bathrooms. Food is fresh and homegrown – the family keeps bees and chickens and grows vegetables. Mrs Mezhlumyan's daughter Nairi speaks English.

Vivas B&B (☎ 2 48 12, 094233 262; www.vivas.am; 65 Syuniki Poghots; dm/d AMD6500/12,000) Another fine B&B, this has both dorm and private rooms. The owners can organise hiking trips in the region.

Hotel Gyorez (☎ 3 00 12; Garegin Nzhdeh Poghots; s/d AMD7000/14,000; 🖳) Clean, functional and somewhat bland hotel that opened in 2007. It's excellent value for solo travellers who want a private room.

Khachik Mirakyan B&B (☎ 2 10 98; 13 Davit Bek Poghots; mirakyanbb@rambler.ru; s/d AMD9500/14,000; 🖳) Situated near the park where Davit Bek meets Syuniki Poghots, Khachik Mirakyan B&B is welcoming and comfortable. There are five bedrooms with private bathrooms, and a great balcony for resting up.

Mirhav Hotel (☎ 2 46 12; 100 Mashrtots Poghots; s/d/tr AMD14,000/19,000/24,000; 🖳) This tastefully designed boutique hotel is probably the best place to stay in southern Armenia. The brick floors, antiques hanging from the walls, wood furnishings and stone façade all blend in Goris' historic character. While providing a rustic atmosphere it maintains modern bathrooms, cable TV and internet. It's run by an Iranian-Armenian named Shahen Zeytourtchian, a retired surgeon who speaks five languages including English.

Eating & Drinking

The best place to eat in Goris is the restaurant at the Mirhav Hotel, which serves a variety of items including rice pilaf and pork chops. It also offers Armenian omelettes, which resemble heated pasta sauce with bread, not unlike *shakshouka* (an Israeli dish). Self-caterers may want to poke around the *shuka*.

SKS restaurant (☎ 2 41 00; Narekatsi Poghots; meals AMD2000; ☉ 10.30am-midnight) If you don't mind loud music this place is fine for dinner, offering the usual array of *khoravats*, kebabs and salads. The clean bathroom is a bonus.

Café (☎ 2 32 78; Tatevatsii Poghots; meals AMD1500-3000; ☉ 9am-1pm) The uninspiring name doesn't quite capture the beauty of this lush

---

PUNCH DRUNK

Oghee (pronounced something like 'orh-ee') are delicious fruit vodkas, sometimes called *vatsun* or *aragh*, made in village orchards everywhere. Around 60% alcohol, *oghee* is made from apples, pears, apricots, pomegranates, grapes, cherries, Cornelian cherries or cornels, mulberries and figs. The best mulberry (*t'te*) and Cornelian cherry (*hone*) *oghee* are intense, lingering liqueurs. Vedi Alco makes some *oghee* commercially, weaker than the village stuff. You won't need to go far to try some; it's a usual accompaniment to a *khoravats* dinner. The drink tastes best in autumn when homes turn into distilleries after the harvest.

garden-cum-café that overlooks Old Goris. It's a popular place for drinks but snacks are also served, including shwarma and boiled crayfish.

Getting There & Away

There are three main stands for onward transport. The old *avtokayan* is on the highway into town (where the highway continues to Yerevan in one direction and Stepanakert in the other direction). From there shared taxis travel to Yerevan for AMD3000. There are marshrutkas to Yerevan (AMD2500, 7.30am, 9am, 10am, noon and 5pm). Transport to Stepanakert (AMD3000) originates in Yerevan – four or five marshrutkas pass here each day; the 12.50pm seems to be a pretty regular service. A taxi to Stepanakert, 104km away, will cost AMD10,000.

Marshrutkas to Kapan (AMD1300, two hours, 9am, noon and 3pm) depart from the corner of Komitas and Syuniki.

Buses for nearby villages, including Tatev (AMD500, 3pm) leave from the *shuka* on Syuniki. A taxi to Kapan costs AMD10,000. A day trip to Tatev costs AMD8000.

AROUND GORIS

There are several historic villages around Goris, many with ancient artificial caves still used as stables. **Khndzoresk**, 10km east of Goris, perches above the ruins of Old Khndzoresk, which was dug into a grassy gorge of soft volcanic sandstone. Whole walls of rock are dotted with caves; you could spend several hours exploring the area.

There are more caves around **Tegh** on the Stepanakert road, and around **Hartashen**, a tough but rewarding 3km on foot from Old Goris or about 8km by road. A smattering of **standing stones** similar to the ones at Zorats Karer is visible from the main road towards Sisian.

Interestingly, there's a village in the gorge below Goris called Karahunj, which means 'stone henge' in Armenian. The substantial remnants of the 12th-century **Kotrats Caravanserai** (built by the Orbelian princes) lie 2km south of the main highway near Harzhis. The **Sev Lich Nature Reserve**, 14km northeast of town on the shoulder of Mt Mets Ishkhanasar, protects a lake (Sev Lich means 'Black Lake') at 2666m. The track up requires a Jeep and a guide.

TATEV ՏԱԹԵՎ
☎ 0824 / pop 300

Built on a fairy-tale natural fortress of rock on the edge of the Vorotan Canyon, Tatev is as jaw-dropping as any of the World Heritage–listed churches in Lori. The views down the gorge reach to the peaks of Karabakh. The road to Tatev turns south of the main highway and reaches the northern edge of the gorge at Halidzor. Near the start of the descent is a gorgeous little cone-roofed stone shelter, at the end of a ridge; it's well worth stopping to look.

At the bottom of the canyon are mineral springs and Satan's Bridge. Legend tells that villagers fleeing to Tatev were blocked by the raging river. Before the invaders attacked, a bridge was magically created by a huge falling rock and the people were saved. The site includes two natural spring pools, so bring a swimsuit. Just past the second pool is a steep slope that leads down to the river. A rope and ladder are on hand to help you down, but it's very dicey and potentially dangerous as you are putting your life in the hands of the rope. A caretaker may be on hand to help you down – if he is not then just forget it. If you do make it safely down the ladder, move to your right to find two limestone caves with rushing water and gorgeous pools. Local authorities are planning to build a staircase down to the caves but until then consider this a very dangerous little trip.

A steep climb up the south side turns left before Tatev village. The great fortified monastery's main church of **Surp Poghos-Petros** (St Paul and St Peter) was built by the bishops of Syunik in the 9th century to house important relics. There are faint signs of **frescoes**, intricate carvings and portraits of the main donors on the northern side. The 11th-century **Surp Grigor Church** nestles next to it, and there's a masterfully miniaturised chapel above the gatehouse. The fortifications, added in the 17th century, have been restored and are full of dining halls, towers and libraries. At the monastery's peak some 600 monks lived and worked at Tatev, and national icon St Grigor Tatevatsi (St Gregory of Tatev, 1346–1409) is buried here.

In the courtyard, look for the 8m octagonal pillar topped by a *khatchkar*. The 9th century monument is said to have predicted seismic activity (or the roar of hooves by approaching armies) by shifting.

Just uphill from the monastery is a café and an **Information Centre** (☎ 0824-9 71 41, 093845 632; sarmen@km.ru; ⊙ 9am-9pm), run by the English-speaking Sarmen Arshakyan. This is the place to ask about hikes in the area or B&Bs where you can spend the night. More information can be found at www.tat ev.org.

The scenery around Tatev is gorgeous and there is plenty of scope for short hikes. One trail leads to **Svarants** (population 100), a hamlet 30 minutes' walk away on the other side of the valley. Another trail heads north to the top of **Petroskhatch mountain**, 4km away from Tatev (the round-trip hike takes under three hours).

Sleeping

There are at least four B&Bs in tiny Tatev, each charging around AMD3000 to AMD5000. They are not signed, but the hamlet is small so just ask around or contact the Information Centre.

Gago B&B (☎ 0824-9 74 48) Has several rooms in a house with a large garden; it's near the school.

Jon & Lena B&B (☎ 0824-9 73 92; zarinev@yahoo.com) In a large house located behind the school. The owner speaks some English.

Getting There & Away

Each day a bus leaves Goris for Tatev (AMD500, 3pm). The bus returns to Goris the next morning at 9am. The other way up here from Goris is by taxi (one way/return AMD5000/8000). There is also a bus from Tatev to Kapan (AMD750) on Tuesday and Sunday at 3pm, and Thursday at 8.30am. The same bus leaves Kapan for Tatev on Tuesday (8am), Thursday (3pm) and Saturday (3pm), from outside the Lernogratz Hotel.

GORIS TO KAPAN

The 68km stomach-churning road from Goris to Kapan dives in and out of the Vorotan Canyon before climbing around the forests and pastures of the Bargushat Range; a total of 49 hairpin turns. Some maps don't show that the road wriggles through occupied Azerbaijan in several places. The removal minefields continues on this border, and there have been injuries and deaths among civilians at villages like Davit Bek as recently as 2007.

The most interesting sight along this route is **Bgheno-Noravank monastery**, which was lost to the world until 1920 when Axel Bakounts stumbled upon it in the forest. The main church dates to 1062 and contains intricately carved biblical reliefs. It's a great camping spot or a logical break for cycle tourists. The turn-off from the highway has a sign directing you towards Bardzravan, a nearby village. After 3.1km, turn off the road to the right and the church is visible after 150m.

Further down the highway, there is a military base (Karmerkar) and a turn-off for the 3km access road to the village of **Davit Bek**. The village is another pleasant stopover and sports a couple of old churches and a pristine river with cascades and swimming holes. From the village there is a pleasant 40-minute walk to a pagan temple. A marshrutka travels from Davit Bek to Kapan (AMD400) each morning at 8.30am, returning at 3pm.

KAPAN ԿԱՊԱՆ
☎ 0285 / pop 45,700

Kapan is Armenia's version of Pittsburgh or Kalgoorlie, a town built for the mining industry that surrounds it. The Russians first started mining here in earnest in the 1850s and the city boomed during the Soviet period, when most of the town's infrastructure was developed. Locals say there's so much unrefined metal beneath the ground that magnetic compasses won't work in some parts of town.

Below the looming peak of Mt Khustup (3210m), Kapan's industrial outskirts and concrete apartment blocks have a harsh appearance, but the town centre, where two rushing rivers meet, has leafy parks and squares. The reopening of the copper-molybdenum mine has kick-started the local economy after a decade of jobless isolation. Australians make up the bulk of the foreign experts, many of whom can be found clutching bottles of beer in the evening at the Hotel Darist. While the local economy moves forward, tourist facilities remain basic, with only a couple of hotels and restaurants and an absence of B&Bs.

Kapan's main church is near the Hotel Lernagordz, and is noted locally for its good acoustics and the priest's fine singing. A **city historical museum** (22 Shahumian; admission free) is worth wandering into if you are killing time in Kapan and need to catch up on your Syunik regional history. Among the thousands of artefacts are 19th-century swords, carpets and kilims.

Karajan lies 33km up the highway from Kapan. The road climbs even further across

ARMENIA

the Tashtun Pass before descending to the Iranian border on the Araks River. Another road heads south from Kapan into the mountainous wilds of the Shikahogh Nature Reserve. This road is being improved and by 2008 should become the primary highway to Meghri.

Orientation & Information

The town centre is a triangle joined by two rivers, with a Davit Bek statue in rippling bronze across the main highway from the confluence. Facing the buildings between the rivers, the Hotel Darist is up the right fork and the Hotel Lernagordz is up on the left. The hulking Marz Petaran (provincial government building), the Haypost building and the Palace of Culture face each other off in the middle of the triangle. There's an **internet café** (per hr AMD300; ☾ 9am-11pm) in the Hotel Lernagordz, and a couple of other, slower places with internet connections among the shops close by. There are banks and shops with cash exchange around the Marz Petaran and around the main *shuka,* across the river from the Hotel Darist. ATMs accepting Visa only can be found at both hotels.

More information is available online at www.kapan.am.

Sleeping & Eating

Hotel Lernagordz (☎ 6 20 86; Davit Bek Hraparak; dm AMD3000, s AMD5000-6500, d 8000-12,000; ⌨) Renovated rooms offer a large TV, a balcony and a hot water shower. Avoid the cheap rooms on the 7th floor, which are filthy and have no water. It ain't the Ritz but it's fine for a night or two, especially for budget travellers.

Hotel Darist (☎ 6 28 62, 6 26 62; 1a Aram Manukyan Poghots; s/d/ste AMD12,000/16,000/25,000) A clean, well-run establishment with renovated rooms and bathrooms – the hotel of choice for Kapan's crew of expat miners. The administrator's office is on the 4th floor. It also has a restaurant on the 1st floor, which serves tasty *khoravats,* salad and bread for AMD2000, and serves drinks until late. The reception is on the 4th floor.

Caravan (☎ 5 49 00, 093304 866; Kajaran hwy; per person AMD12,000) This restaurant and guesthouse is in a pretty valley 8km towards Kajaran. The four rooms are all rather dire for the price, complete with overflowing toilets and lumpy furnishings. The enormous dead spider at the bottom of the dirty pool completed

the picture. On the other hand, the restaurant is fine and one of the best places in the area for a meal. A taxi from Kapan will cost AMD1500; the staff can call a taxi to take you back to town.

The Hotel Darist has the best restaurant in town. Another option is the **Khach Meruk Café** (☾ 9am-midnight), which serves salads and pizzas. It's a pleasant place to hang out if you don't mind loud accordion music. The Caravan Restaurant (see above) is also recommended.

Getting There & Away

There are marshrutkas to Yerevan (AMD5000, six/eight hours in summer/winter, 7am, 8am and noon) from in front of the Hotel Lernagordz. There are three marshrutkas to Goris (AMD1300, 90 minutes to two hours, 9am, noon and 3pm). For Meghri (AMD1000) there is a 2pm bus departing from a stop at the Davit Bek statue. A taxi to Meghri will cost AMD10,000.

AROUND KAPAN

Mt Khustup (3210m) looms high above Kapan. The approach to the peak is via the village of Verin Vachagan, about 3km southwest of Kapan. There are various routes up from here, so ask in the village. It's about 7km to the base of the peak, where a small church has been built. You can get fine views from here; another three hours of hiking is required to reach the peak.

The remains of 9th-century **Vahanavank**, about 7km from Kapan just off the Karajan road, are fairly modest but the epic views across southern Syunik repay the effort of a visit. The monastery was once the religious centre for Syunik's kings. An attempt to restore the monastery in 1978 was later abandoned and what remains is a roofless structure of red limestone.

The ruins of **Baghaberd fortress**, the capital of Syunik until it was sacked by Seljuk Turks in 1170, stands north of the confluence of the Geghri and Voghji Rivers, halfway between Kajaran and Kapan. Once it was the largest historic defence construction in Armenia, but now only its towers and some walls remain. It's a steep scramble up to the fortress walls.

The struggling mining town of Kajaran (population 8000) lies beneath Syunik's highest mountain, 3904m Mt Kaputjugh, 33km west of Kapan. The local hostelry is the **Hotel Ganzasar** (☎ 0285-3 32 04; 2 Lernagordzneri Poghots; per person AMD5000), scraping by on a shoestring with hot water for a couple of hours in luxe rooms. The hotel is on the main square. Between 8am and 9.40pm there are eight marshrutkas (AMD300) between here and Kapan.

The road to the **Shikahogh Nature Reserve**, 45km south of Kapan, climbs up a valley, over a ridge and into the valley of the Tsav River, where at the hamlet of Nerkin Hand there's an ancient grove of massive plane trees. The oak and hornbeam forests either side of the Tsav comprise the nature reserve, though you'll need a Niva or Villis to explore the 100 sq km of gorges and forests.

MEGHRI ՄԵՂՐԻ
☎ 0286 / pop 4500

Strategic Meghri, Armenia's toehold on Iran, is worth exploring for its fine stone houses. The town sits deep in the rocky, lushly irrigated gorge of the Meghri River surrounded by sawtooth peaks. The postindependence borders left Meghri deeply isolated, and the local economy struggles by on remittances, farming and a bit of business from the highway to Iran. The border crossing is at the Araks bridge near Agarak (population 3500), 8km from Meghri, open all day.

The Meghri fortress above the town dates mostly from the 18th century. The brick domes of Surp Hovannes at the Meghri town monastery date from the 17th century. In the centre of the main part of town is the fine St Astvatsatsin Church with a distinctive octagonal dome, built in the 17th century with later frescoes. There's also the Surp Sargis Church across the river in Pokr Tagh, the smaller side of town, with two rows of columns and some delicately restored frescoes.

There are a few Russian soldiers based at Agarak with Armenian troops and officials. Most travellers come this way to cross the border but a few intrepid souls just come for a glimpse of Iran – you can see the ancient village of Noordoz (also spelt Noghdoz or Norduz) across the river, including the minarets of the local mosque. Iranian farmers and shepherds can be seen busily working on the opposite bank. Be very careful about taking pictures in the area – on our visit a Russian border guard checked our camera for sensitive photos.

It's a slow border-crossing (it may close for lunch) but there's no particular hassle. The Armenian side has a bank where you can change money and a few stalls selling cold drinks. There may be one or two taxis, or you could hitch a ride to Meghri.

Sleeping & Eating

There are a handful of B&Bs in Agarak and Meghri, which can be booked through Aries Tours (p151). At the time of research the Hotel Meghri was being refurbished – it's just 50m downhill from the square.

Haer B&B (☎ 4 30 54, 093545 414; info@bedandbreakfast .am; 14 Karakert Poghots; per person AMD5000) Marieta Azatyan runs this B&B with two rooms with double beds in classic provincial style – satin duvet covers, carpets and wood-veneer furniture. The B&B is located 900m from the town square. Walk past the Haypost (VivaCell is another landmark) and follow the road as it curves along the hillside; turn right just after the abandoned stone and brick army fort – it's 50m uphill on the right. The family may invite you for a meal but you may have to pay for it later; ask about food prices to avoid confusion.

Mila Hotel (☎ 4 31 80, 094356267; r per person AMD8000, deluxe 20,000) Three kilometres north of Meghri on the road to Kapan, this small hotel has three basic rooms with shared bath and a better 'deluxe' room with en suite facilities. It's a little overpriced but has a peaceful location and meals are available.

The B&Bs will prepare dinners and lunches with prior notice for about AMD1500. There are no restaurants as such in Agarak or Meghri, but there are a few basic roadside cafés offering *khoravats* for AMD2000.

Getting There & Away

A Yerevan-bound marshrutka (AMD7000, nine hours in summer, 11 hours in winter) departs at 9am from the Hotel Meghri, just off the central square, on Block 2. A bus to Kapan (AMD1000) departs at 7.30am. A taxi to Kapan should cost AMD8000 to AMD10,000 (90 minutes) from Agarak or Meghri. A taxi between Meghri and Agarak costs about AMD2000.

Hitchhiking from Meghri to Kapan is difficult – suspicions run high in this border area and drivers are less prone to pick up strangers. If you're stuck, take a cab to Kajaran and hop on a marshrutka.

On the other side of the border buses are rare or nonexistent, but a taxi to Jolfa (Julfa, Culfa) should cost US$5 to US$8 (40 minutes)

ARMENIA

with bargaining. A shop just outside Iranian immigration exchanges currencies. See p323 for information on buses to Iran, which leave from Yerevan.

ARMENIA DIRECTORY

ACCOMMODATION

Yerevan has a full range of places to stay, from AMD7000-a-night budget options and midrange hotels (AMD25,000 to AMD50,000 for a double room), to good three- and four-star hotels. The new Armenia Marriott Hotel (p159) is the first international-standard hotel in the city. There are a couple of excellent boutique hotels in Yerevan. For upmarket hotels we've included government taxes in the prices.

Across Armenia there is a burgeoning range of budget pensions for around AMD5000 to AMD8000 per person per day. Renting and sharing an apartment is a recommended way to keep costs down (see below).

Outside Yerevan there is a handful of impressive new hotels and some comfortable homestays and B&Bs. Resort areas such as Dilijan, Tsaghkadzor, Jermuk and Lake Sevan have a range of Soviet-era hotels and sanatoriums either recently privatised or owned by government ministries. The websites listed on p222 will inevitably list new places.

Rentals

Renting an apartment is a common practice among visitors to Yerevan. Prices peak between June and October. At the time of writing, AMD10,000 a day got you a single-bedroom apartment with sporadic water supplies a marshrutka ride away from town. Upwards of AMD20,000 a day rented a two- or three-bedroom apartment with a more convenient location. Up to AMD30,000 a day earned a three- or four-bedroom renovated apartment or house. Besides the travel agencies, which frequently arrange apartments (p151), there are some specialists for standard and luxury apartments: www .hyurservice.com, www.visitarm.com and www.realakcern.com.

ACTIVITIES

Armenia is quickly building a reputation among bird-watchers – 346 species have been recorded here, including one-third of Europe's threatened species, and 240 species breed here. The Birds of Armenia Project at the **American University of Armenia** (Map pp148-9; ☎ 27 45 32; www .muhlenberg.edu/depts/biology/boa/book.htm; 40 Marshall Baghramian Poghota, Yerevan) has maps and books on the country's profusion of avian plumage. *A Field Guide to Birds of Armenia* and *Handbook of the Birds of Armenia* are both by Martin S Adamian and D Klem. There's also the **Centre of Bird Lovers** (Map p146; ☎ 24 70 59; adamians@freenet .am; Paruyr Sevak Poghots, Nor Zeytun, Yerevan), which engages in conservation efforts and works with ornithological guides.

Mountain climbing on Mt Aragats is possible in summer, and there are challenging hikes along the Garni Gorge and through the Khosrov Nature Reserve close to Yerevan. Country hikes are made easier by the profusion of piped springs. *Adventure*

THE AYAS NAUTICAL RESEARCH CLUB

One of the best stories about postindependence Armenia concerns a medieval sailing ship in a landlocked country. The Ayas project began back in 1985 when the club's founders became interested in the times of the Cilician Kings, from the 10th to 14th centuries, when Armenian naval vessels and traders plied the eastern Mediterranean from the ports of Ayas and Korykos. Club members discovered old plans of Armenian ships in the British Library. Armenia hasn't had a sea coast since 1375, but they set out to build a sailing ship the old way. After independence, the fuel shortages made the timbers of the Ayas a target for people on the verge of freezing. Club members lived and slept in the boat for several years to protect it. The vessel survived to sail on Lake Sevan in 2002 and in 2004 sailed on the Black Sea all the way to Portsmouth, England. In 2006 the ship continued its journey to St Petersburg, Russia, and along a series of rivers all the way back to the Black Sea where the trip began. The **Ayas Nautical Research Club** (Map pp148-9; ☎ 57 85 10; 1 Charents Poghota, Yerevan) has a substantial library of books on maritime Armenia and its fleets.

Armenia: Hiking and Rock Climbing by Carine Bachmann and Jeffrey Tufenkian will serve you well. It details 22 hiking routes and several rock-climbing spots.

Horse riding is becoming more popular and is a great way to explore out-of-the-way places; a good place to start is Yenokavan Canyon near Ijevan. Sailing and fishing on Lake Sevan on a mild summer's day is idyllic – inquire at the Harsnaqar and Avan Tsapatagh hotels. Underground there are *karst* (limestone) caves in Vayots Dzor, largely unexplored and for experienced climbers only. The cave villages around Goris are an easier challenge.

BOOKS

A glossy little guide with some terrific photos is *Edge of Time: Travelling in Armenia & Karabakh*, which reveals a shining love for the country. *Rediscovering Armenia* by Brady Kiesling and Raffi Kojian details every village and nearly every monument in the country. You can buy it in Yerevan and it's also online (free!) with maps at www.armeniapedia.org. Pictorial books include Jacob Majarian's *Armenia – Pictorial Treasury of an Ancient Land*. Majarian also creates excellent calendars; see www.majart.com.au.

Peter Balakian's justly praised *Black Dog of Fate* deals with suburban Armenian life in the USA and with the silences and agonies of his family's experiences during the genocide. *Visions of Ararat* by Christopher Walker is a collection of writings on Armenia by visitors over the centuries.

The Crossing Place by Philip Marsden is as haunting as travel literature gets, an evocation of the Armenian spirit from the forced marches into Syria through to the old communities of the Middle East and Eastern Europe to a frontier village in the middle of the Karabakh War. Marsden's *The Spirit Wrestlers* explores the Russian dissenter communities in the region, including the Molokans.

Finding translations of writers such as Raffi and Abovyan is best done through specialist bookstores such as the **Sardarabad Bookstore** (www.sardarabad.com) in Los Angeles and the **Armenian General Benevolent Fund bookstore** (www.agbu.org) in New York.

BUSINESS HOURS

Most churches are open 9am to 6pm daily, though in winter you might have to wait a while for the key to appear. Government offices

and international organisations usually work 9am to 5pm weekdays. Fairs and markets open daily. Museums and galleries often close Monday. Shops are usually open 9am to 7pm, or 10am to 10pm. Bank opening hours vary but are usually 9.30am to 5.30pm Monday to Friday and 10.30am to 1.30pm Saturday.

CUSTOMS REGULATIONS

The usual restrictions apply (one carton of cigs, 2L of booze, no guns) and there's no currency declaration to keep. If you plan to take something out of the country considered to be of cultural, historical or national value (eg a rug, a samovar or similar) a certificate is required from the **Ministry of Culture** (Map pp148-9; ☎ 1-52 93 49; 5 Tumanyan Poghots, Yerevan). You'll find it's much easier if the shop you bought the item from arranges the permit for you, or if you can speak Armenian. Otherwise the bureaucracy can be quite baffling.

EMBASSIES & CONSULATES

The following are all in Yerevan:
Canada (Map pp148-9; ☎ 56 79 03; aemin@freenet.am; Marriot Hotel, 1 Amiryan Poghots)
France (Map pp148-9; ☎ 56 11 03; www.ambafrance-am.org; 8 Grigor Lusavorich Poghots)
Georgia (Map pp148-9; ☎ 56 43 57, 58 55 11; geoemb@netsys.am; 42 Aram Poghots)
Germany (Map pp148-9; ☎ 52 32 79; germemb@arminco.com; 29 Charents Poghots)
Greece (Map pp148-9; ☎ 53 00 51; grembarm@arminco.com; 6 Demichyan Poghots)
Iran (Map p146; ☎ 23 49 00; emiranar@arminco.com; 1 Budaghyan Poghots, Arabkir Park)
Italy (Map pp148-9; ☎ 54 23 35; www.ambjevervan.esteri.it; 5 Italia Poghots)
Nagorno-Karabakh (Map p146; ☎ 24 99 28, 52 64 28; www.nkr.am; 17a Zaryan Poghots)
Poland (Map pp148-9; ☎ 54 24 93; polemb@arminco.com; 44/1 Hanrapetutyan Poghots)
Russia (Map pp148-9; ☎ 56 74 27; 13a Grigor Lusavorich Poghots)
Turkmenistan (Map pp148-9; ☎ 65 09 03; serdar@arminco.com; Norki Avginer, House 288/5)
UK (Map pp148-9; ☎ 26 43 01; www.britishembassy.gov.uk; 34 Marshall Baghramian Poghota)
USA (Map p146; ☎ 46 47 00; http://yerevan.usembassy.gov; 1 American Poghota)

Armenia does not have embassies in Australia, Ireland, New Zealand or the Netherlands. Irish travellers should contact the Armenian embassy in the UK. Dutch visitors should contact the Armenian embassy in

Brussels. Australian and New Zealand inquiries should also be addressed to the Armenian embassy in the UK. A full list of Armenian embassies and consulates can be found at www.armeniaforeignministry.com.

FESTIVALS & EVENTS
December to April
Armenia has a full range of festivals, strongly Christian but intimately tied to the seasons, the land and folk traditions. The year ends (and kicks off) with **Navasard** (New Year's). The pre-Christian New Year was on the first day of the month of Navasard (August). The Church fathers moved the date to 31 December, but the name carried over. Households bake cookies and the New Year bread, which contains a coin. Whoever finds it has good fortune coming. **Surp Dzenount** (Christmas) is held on 6 January, the Epiphany (baptism) of Jesus. Hymns and psalms ring out from churches, and water and myrrh are blessed – it's sometimes called water-blessing day. **Trndez** (Purification) occurs 40 days after Christmas (16 February). Bonfires are lit and people leap over them for protection from the evil eye, illness and poisons. Trndez also signals the coming of spring.

Easter Season
Surp Sargis Don (St Sargis Day) falls nine weeks before Easter, between 18 January and 23 February. The handsome warrior saint may appear in the dreams of girls this night, wearing gold armour, to decide their fate – the man she dreams of who gives her water will be her husband. The 40 days of Lent before Easter is a fasting period with holidays such as Shrove-Tide, a good time for public celebrations. **Tsarzardar** (Palm Sunday), one week before Easter, is a proper spring celebration. Trees are brought into churches and hung with fruit. **Zatik** (Easter) falls between mid-March and mid-April, depending on the Church calendar. Households that planted lentil seeds 40 days earlier at the start of Lent lay red-painted eggs on the bed of green shoots on Easter Sunday.

May to November
Hambartsum (Ascension Day) is in May, 40 days after Easter. In the old days young women had the freedom to sing in the fields and socialise on this day. It's also a festival of fate. At midnight, space and time pauses and nature speaks to itself. Witnesses to such a moment will have their dreams fulfilled.

The big summer holiday is the **Vardavar** (Transfiguration), which falls between mid-June and mid-July, when kids and teenagers throw water on everyone they can, and no one takes offence (much). It's hilarious, but not a day for noncolourfast clothing. In pagan times this was the festival of the love goddess Astghik, when her love was spread by sprinkling petals and rose water on the ground. **Astvatsatsin** (Holiday of the Mother of God) in mid-August is when priests bless the grape and fruit harvests. **Khatchverats** (Holy Cross), falling on the Sunday closest to 14 September, is a day for commemorating the dead.

HOLIDAYS
Annual public holidays in Armenia:
New Year's Day 1 January
Christmas Day 6 January
International Women's Day 8 March
Good Friday varies, from mid-March to late April
Motherhood and Beauty Day 7 April
Genocide Memorial Day 24 April
Victory Day 9 May
Republic Day 28 May
Constitution Day 5 July
Independence Day 21 September
Earthquake Memorial Day 7 December

INTERNET RESOURCES
Armenia Diaspora (www.armeniadiaspora.com) Run by the Armenian Foreign Ministry, with news and a very good travel section.
Armenia Guide (www.armeniaguide.com) A strong links website, with connections to the sites listed here and many more.
Armenia Now (www.armenianow.com) A lively, weekly Yerevan-based web magazine with interesting features on life and current events.
Armeniapedia (www.armeniapedia.org) The best resource on everything you ever wanted to know about Armenia.
Blogrel (www.blogrel.com) Ongoing blog that keeps a finger on the pulse of modern Armenia.
PanArmenian.net (www.panarmenian.net) Online community site carrying comprehensive news bulletins on Armenia, Karabakh and regional issues.
Tour Armenia (www.tacentral.com) Another terrific local-culture and tourist-information site.

MAPS
The maps made by Yerevan-based company Collage are the best available, with a full-colour foldout map *Armenia & Mountainous Karabakh*, the nifty, brochure-sized, 26-page

Roads of Armenia and the brilliant *Yerevan Atlas,* with new and old street names, street numbers and lots besides. They cost AMD3000 to AMD6000 from souvenir shops and bookstores in Yerevan. Excellent free maps are available from the Armenia Information office in Yerevan.

MEDIA

The main English-language weekly newspaper is *Noyan Tapan. Armenia Now* (www .armenianow.com) is an online newspaper. Armenian language dailies include *Aravot, Azg* and *Yerkir.*

Hye-FM (91.1 FM) plays a good mix of popular music on international play lists and some local music as well.

The only TV channel with an independent editorial policy, A1, is constantly at odds with government and oft-dragged through the courts. CNN is broadcast over public TV in Yerevan. Big hotels carry satellite TV.

MONEY
Costs

A strong dram means that Armenia is no longer the bargain it once was, but prices are still moderate by European standards. A seat on a minibus to the furthest corner of the country costs AMD5000. A taxi across Yerevan costs AMD500. *Lahmajo (lahma-joon)* cost AMD100, while a hearty meal of *khoravats* with salad, bread and drinks at a country restaurant might cost around AMD1800 per person. Budget accommodation is rarely less than AMD5000. In Yerevan, it's hard to find a private hotel room for less than AMD18,000.

Armenia's currency is the dram. Coins are available in denominations of 10, 20, 50, 100, 200 and 500 drams. Paper currency is available in notes of 1000, 5000, 10,000, 20,000 and 50,000 dram.

Exchanging Money

The best cash currencies are US dollars, euros and Russian roubles, roughly in that order. Georgian lari can also be changed in Yerevan and border towns. Other currencies are hard to change except at a handful of major banks in Yerevan. There are moneychanging signs waving flags and rates at customers everywhere in Yerevan and around *shukas* in all major towns. Virtually any shop can change money legally, and many food stores and

small goods vendors do. Scams seem to be rare, and transactions straightforward.

Travellers cheques are rare in Armenia and not recommended. Bring cash or an ATM or Visa card. Some local ATMs are linked to the Plus system and others to the Maestro system. There are cash machines in prominent locations around Yerevan, including half a dozen HSBC branches. You can withdraw money in US dollars from HSBC machines and sometimes from local bank ATMs as well. All other main cities and even some small towns have ATMs, though you may have to poke around to find one that matches your card. There are Western Union offices all over the country.

Visit www.arca.am/atmsearch.php-en to access a clickable search of every ATM in the country.

Tipping & Bargaining

The usual tipping rule at cafés and restaurants is 10%. Taxi drivers won't complain if you set the price when getting in and stick to it when getting out. Shops have set prices, but *shukas* (markets) and outdoor fruit and vegetable stands are more negotiable. Foreigners might be charged a little extra but might also be laden with extra goods.

POST

National postal service Haypost has offices in every major town. A letter might take anything from two weeks to six weeks to reach North America or Australia, but the service is fairly reliable. If you're sending out something of value you might feel safer with UPS, FedEx or a local courier company in Yerevan (p151).

TELEPHONE

The country code is ☎ 374, while Yerevan's area code is ☎ 1.

It's possible to make calls from central call centres. Give the attendant the phone number, and you'll be directed to a phone booth with a vintage telephone. There's usually a clear line after a couple of attempts.

International calls using either landlines or mobile phones can be expensive. Internet clubs in Yerevan often have VoIP calls at much lower rates (about AMD100 per minute anywhere).

For calls within Armenia, call ☎ 0 + city code + local number; for mobile numbers dial the ☎ 09 prefix first (most people will give you this along with their mobile number), then the number. For international calls, dial ☎ 00 first.

Mobile Phones

Mobile-phone services, operated by ArmenTel and VivaCell, are fairly priced and wide ranging. You can get mobile-phone service just about anywhere in the country these days, unless you are hiking in the backcountry. There is little difference between the two companies, although there seem to be more subscribers to VivaCell (and calling other VivaCell phones is a little cheaper).

TOURIST INFORMATION

The main tourist office is the Armenia Information centre (p151). It has a ton of information, and it's well organised and helpful. Tourist information offices are also located in Dilijan (p190), Goris (p214), Ijevan (p193), Sevan (p178) and Stepanavan (p197).

VISAS

Armenian visas are available at all entry points – 21-day tourist visas cost $30, and three-day transit visas cost $20. The officials might not speak much English, but it's just a matter of filling out a form and paying. A 21-day e-visa from www.armeniaforeignministry.com costs $60 and takes two days to be emailed to you. Print out a copy and have it on hand on arrival and departure. E-visas are only for arrivals at Zvartnots Airport. If you want a longer visa, apply directly to an Armenian embassy. Processing time is usually three to five days and the fee is about $60. You can get up to 120 days, but make sure you ask for this specifically if you want the maximum number of days.

Border Crossings

Armenia's international border posts are as follows:

Agarak Land border with Iran.
Bavra Land border with Georgia.
Gyumri (Shirak Airport) CIS airport.
Guguti-Tashir Land border with Georgia.
Sadakhlo-Bagratashen Land border with Georgia.
Yerevan (Zvartnots Airport) International airport.

Visa Extensions

You can get a visa extension at the Passport and Visa Department of **OVIR** (Map pp148-9; ☎ 53 43 91; 13a Mesrop Mashtots Poghota, room 211; ☻ 2-6pm Mon-Fri). At room 211 you fill in a form and provide a photocopy of the picture page in your passport and return the next day to confirm authorisation of the extension. Once you have confirmation you pay AMD500 for every day you want to extend.

You will be given an account number for you to make the deposit, which can be done at any bank (the ABB across the street will do this for an AMD100 fee). You then go back to room 211 and leave your receipt and passport. You can pick up the extension the following day.

It's possible to avoid the three trips to OVIR by simply overstaying your visa and then paying US$3 per day when you leave. OVIR at Zvartnots is not much of a hassle, and land border guards are similarly happy to accept your money.

For people of Armenian descent and their partners, OVIR issues 10-year residency permits. The process takes about three months and costs around $300.

Visas for Onward Travel
GEORGIA

The **Georgian Embassy** (Map pp148-9; ☎ 1-58 55 11; geoemb@netsys.am; 42 Aram Poghots) provides visas for 60 GEL (US$35). However, these days many Western nationals can enter visa-free and those that need a visa can get one at the border (see p127). Note that visas may not be available at the border for train travellers. The safest bet is to get a visa at the Georgian embassy in Yerevan.

IRAN

The **Iranian Embassy** (Map p146; ☎ 23 49 00; emiranar@arminco.com; 1 Budaghyan Poghots, Arabkir Park) provides visas only after you have received approval from the Iranian Ministry of Foreign Affairs, and for this you'll need to go through a travel agent. The whole process can last two weeks or more. Contact Tatev Travel (p151).

WORK

Wages are very low in most sectors, but there is a ton of NGO and volunteer work going on. NGOs have bloomed everywhere – international relief agencies are well represented, and there are many local and diasporan bodies as well, covering everything from health to the environment to teaching. The website www.armeniadiaspora.com is a good place to start investigating.

Azerbaijan

MICHAEL KOHN

Azerbaijan

Neither Europe nor Asia, Azerbaijan is an incredible tangle of contradictions and contrasts. It's a fascinating nexus of ancient historical empires. Yet it's also a new nation finding its feet as it emerges from a war-torn post-Soviet chrysalis on a petroleum-funded gust of optimism. Surrounded by semi-desert on the oil-rich Caspian Sea, the nation's cosmopolitan capital, Baku, is a dynamic boomtown, where flashy limousines and mushrooming skyscrapers sweep around a picturesque Unesco-listed ancient core. Yet barely three hours' drive away lies an entirely different world: timeless villages clad in lush orchards from which shepherd tracks lead into the soaring high Caucasus mountains. Where Baku is multilingual and go-ahead, the provinces shuffle to the gently paced click of nard (backgammon) on tree-shaded tea-house terraces: women stay home, herds of cattle wander aimlessly across highways, and potbellied bureaucrats scratch their heads in confusion on finding that an outsider has wandered into their territory.

Visiting the country takes creativity and imagination, as the tourist industry is at best 'nascent'. Although there are plenty of rural 'rest-zones' for holidaying city folk, they cater mainly for locals who want to unwind with hefty feasts and family chats, so rarely provide any activities. To reach the most intriguing mountain villages will take initiative if you can't speak at least basic Azeri (or Turkish or Russian). Very few people outside Baku speak English, but the challenge is a great part of the appeal. With a positive attitude, and helped along by Azerbaijanis' deeply ingrained sense of hospitality, any visit is likely to be an enjoyable and highly memorable adventure.

AZERBAIJAN

FAST FACTS

- **Area** 86,600 sq km
- **Capital** Baku (Bakı)
- **Famous for** Oil, saffron, caviar
- **Official Name** Azərbaycan Respublikasi
- **Phrases** *Salam* (hello), *sağol* (thank you)
- **Population** 7,830,000
- **Ubiquitous face** Heydar Əliyev

HIGHLIGHTS

- **Baku** (p236) – With grand stone architecture, a medieval walled city centre and super-stylish dining, Azerbaijan's exciting capital is a dynamic boomtown that changes almost while you watch.
- **Şəki** (p274) – Cupped in beautiful wooded mountains with an 18th-century palace, picturesque old town and unforgettable caravanserai-hotel.
- **Qobustan** (p260) – Explore Stone- and Bronze Age petroglyphs, then move on to a nearby 'family' of wonderfully weird little mud volcanoes.
- **Laza to Xınalıq hike** (p265) – A glorious valley hike linking two of the Caucasus' loveliest mountain settlements.
- **Lahıc** (p270) – Copper beaters' and carpet weavers' workshops line the delightful cobbled main street of this unique Persian-speaking mountain village.

ITINERARIES

- **Three Days** Soak up the atmosphere of bustling Baku and make trips to Qobustan and the Abşeron Peninsula.
- **One Week** Work your way between Tbilisi (Georgia) and Baku via Zaqatala, Şəki and Lahıc or head up from Baku to Quba and explore its mountain hinterland.
- **Two Weeks** Combine the suggestions above and consider adding a trip to the charming south, perhaps en route to Iran.

CLIMATE & WHEN TO GO

The best time to visit lowland Azerbaijan is April to June, when skies are clear and the land is green and full of flowers. October is also lovely in Baku, with warm days and crisp nights, though much of the countryside is parched brown. Summer is unpleasantly hot in low-lying areas, with Baku unpleasantly humid. However, in the higher mountains July is the ideal trekking season, although you might still need a decent jacket at night.

Winters are mild around the Caspian shores but can get strikingly cold inland. You'll need heavy sweaters in Şəki and the mercury can dip below -20°C in Xınalıq or Lahıc, with snow ploughs struggling to keep the roads open. See p312 for climate charts.

CURRENT EVENTS

Azerbaijan's almost deified father-figure, Heydar Əliyev, died in April 2003. A shamelessly dynastic handover then passed power to Əliyev's largely untested son Ilham. Ilham's new role was regularised by an election that he doubtless won, although probably not with the landslide margin that brought protests of irregularities and alleged ballot box stuffing. Pessimistic observers predicted chaos. So far they have been proved very wrong.

The Ilham Əliyev years have been marked by Azerbaijan's dramatic economic recovery, albeit tinged by widespread reports of nepotism, corruption and press-gagging. Helpfully the US$4 billion BTC (Baku–Tbilisi–Ceyhan) oil pipeline began pumping Caspian oil to Turkey just at the time that petroleum prices peaked. While Azerbaijan's oilfields have not proved quite the treasure-troves planners once dreamed of, they have been augmented by very important finds of natural gas. In 2006 GDP rose by a staggering 36.3%. And as money floods into state coffers there has been a building boom, especially in Baku. All across the country, roads are being upgraded, buildings renovated and parks studded with new Heydar Əliyev statues.

However, despite the economic progress many provincial folk look back fondly to the 'fairer days' of the USSR when everyone had work and there was not today's gulf between poor farmers and Mercedes-driving ultrarich biznizmen. Apart from the continued shortage of employment, the overwhelming political issue remains Nagorno-Karabakh. Few Azeris understand why the world isn't rallying to help restore Azerbaijan's territories occupied by Armenians since the early 1990s. Hundreds of thousands of refugees and IDPs (internally displaced persons) remain in makeshift accommodation and although their conditions have improved materially in the last few years, their plight remains very personally felt by all Azeris.

AZERBAIJAN

AZERBAIJAN

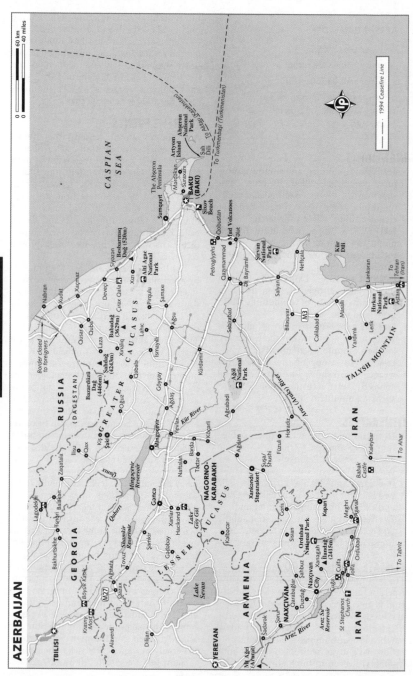

While many older Azeris privately retain fond memories of Armenian neighbours and friends (blaming Russian politics for the war), Armenians are frequently made a scapegoat for any national ill, however unlikely. Fortunately, those advocating a new war to reclaim the lost territories are not a majority. However, the idea is not entirely off the cards should Armenia fail to be 'reasonable' in coming years.

HISTORY

The area of today's Azerbaijan Republic has historically been known variously as Aran, Aghvan, Caucasian Albania and more recently Şirvan. Until the 20th century the ancient term Azerbaijan applied largely, as it still does, to the ethnically fraternal territory centred on Tabriz and Ardabil in Iran. Over the last two millennia it's not just the country's name and rulers that have changed but also its religion, language and even its predominant ethnicity. And having spent most of that time straddling the territories of competing empires, understanding this extraordinary saga really requires getting to grips with Persian, Arab, Turkish and Russian history. No wonder visitors (and even Azeris themselves) get confused. Even if all this seems dry and irrelevant to you, be aware that throughout the Caucasus, ancient history remains a point of day-to-day controversy and is constantly being re-remembered.

Early History

From the 6th century BC (and indeed for much of its later history) proto-Azerbaijan was part of the Persian Empire, with Zoroastrianism developing as the predominant religion. The area emerged around the 4th century BC as the ill-defined state of Aran or Caucasian Albania (no link to the present-day Balkan republic). Around AD 325 Albanians adopted Christianity, building many churches, the ruins of some of which still remain today. The history of the Caucasian Albanians is of great political importance to modern-day Azeris largely for the disputed 'fact' that they weren't Armenian. This, local historians consider, is important in asserting Azerbaijan's moral rights to Nagorno-Karabakh and beyond.

Islam became the major religion following the Arab advance into Albania in the 7th century followed by later waves of Oğuz and Seljuk Turks. For arriving Turkic herderhorsemen, proto-Azerbaijan's grassland plains were much more inviting than the high mountains, so it was here that Turkic ethnicity became concentrated more than elsewhere in the Caucasus. Pockets of original Caucasian Christians lived on in the hills.

The Muslim Era

A classic era of Azeri culture bloomed in the 12th century. The cities of (old) Qəbələ, Bərdə and Naxçivan were thriving. Şamaxı bloomed as the vibrant capital of Şirvan. Gəncə's preeminence was symbolised by the classical 'national' poet Nizami Gəncəvi. However, from the 13th century these cities were pummelled into dust by the Mongols, Timur (Tamerlane) and assorted earthquakes.

It took two centuries and an improving caravan trade to get Şirvan blossoming again. In battle its rulers, the Shirvanshahs, scored a home victory against Arbadil (southern Azerbaijan, now in Iran) in 1462 only to lose in the 1501 rematch. Converted to Shia Islam as a result of that defeat, Şirvan bonded with (south) Azerbaijan, sharing its glory as the Azeri Safavid shahs came to rule the whole Persian Empire.

Greater Azerbaijan thereafter suffered in tussles between Persia and the Ottoman Empires. As Persian power declined in the early 18th century, a collection of autonomous Muslim khanates emerged across Azerbaijan. However, Persia rebounded and several of these khanates united, hoping to preserve their independence. They asked Russia for assistance but got more than they bargained for. The Russian Empire swiftly annexed many northerly khanates. Then Persia's bungled attempts to grab them back ended with the humiliating Gulistan Treaty (1813) in which it lost Şirvan, Karabakh and all navigational rights to the Caspian. A second war was even worse for the Persians, who were forced to additionally sign away the former khanates of Naxçivan, Talysh and Yerevan in the 1828 treaty of Turkmenchay.

The Russian Era

To consolidate their rule over their new Persian conquests the Russians encouraged immigration of Christians, notably non-Orthodox religious sects from Russia, Germans from Würtemburg and Armenians

THE ƏLIYEV DYNASTY

His photos are everywhere. Each town has a new museum and park in his honour. And he is still un-blinkingly referred to as Azerbaijan's 'National Leader' even though he died in 2003, aged 80.

Born in Naxçivan, the ubiquitous Heydar Əliyev (www.heydar-Aliyev.org) worked his way up through the KGB to become the first and only Azeri to be a member of the Politburo, the USSR's supreme body. He ran Azerbaijan in the 1970s as chairman of the Azerbaijan Communist Party. Then after a few years in the wilderness he staged a brilliant political comeback to reinvent himself in 1993 as the free-market president of independent Azerbaijan. While it's easy to retro-spectively criticise his heavy-handed style and lack of concern for free speech, there's no doubt that his personal prestige and immense political savvy was a key factor in halting the bloody war in Karabakh. He also negotiated the huge production-sharing deal with Western conglomerates, which sowed the seeds for the current oil boom.

Given the importance of clan loyalties in Azerbaijan, it was no great surprise that Heydar shoehorned his son Ilham into power before shuffling off to that great Politburo in the sky. While he lacks his father's almost limitless prestige, Ilham's own photos and sayings are steadily multiplying on the nation's billboards. Meanwhile, media attention is increasingly being focused on Ilham's glamorous wife, Mehriban (www.mehriban-Aliyeva.org). As head of the immensely wealthy Heydar Əliyev foundation (www.heydar-Aliyev-foundation.org), she has the enviable job of touring the country, handing out presents and grants, thus ensuring a growing groundswell of popular support. Some even tip her to take over from her husband in the distant future. But don't hold your breath.

from the Ottoman-Turkish Empire. This indi-rectly sowed the seeds of ethnic conflicts that broke out in 1905, 1918 and 1989.

In the 1870s, new uses for petroleum sud-denly turned little Baku into a boomtown and, amazingly, by 1905 it was supplying half the world's oil. Immense wealth was created and a cultural renaissance bloomed. But ap-palling conditions for oil workers created a new, revolutionary underclass, exploited by a young Stalin. The result was a decade of revolutionary chaos that resulted in several horrific inter-ethnic clashes.

Independence & Soviet Reconquest

The Russian revolution of 1917 saw the end of the Tsarist empire. With WWI still undecided, Azerbaijan collapsed into internal conflict. Gəncə democrats declared Azerbaijan the Muslim world's first 'democracy' in 1918, but Baku remained under the control of so-cialist revolutionaries until they were driven out with the help of the invading Turkish army. The Turks rapidly withdrew, leaving the Azerbaijan Democratic Republic (Azərbaycan Xaiq Cümhuriyyəti) independent. It was a forward-thinking secular entity of which Azeris remain intensely proud. However, the republic lasted barely two years. The Bolshevik Red Army invaded in 1920, cre-ating the short lived Transcaucasian Soviet

Socialist Republic in 1922 (along with Georgia and Armenia) as a prelude to the USSR. A series of border changes during this era pro-gressively diminished Azerbaijan's borders in favour of Armenia, and eventually left Naxçivan entirely cut off from the rest of Azerbaijan SSR. The passionate insistence of Azerbaijan's 'father of communism', Nəriman Nərimanov, kept Nagorno-Karabakh within the nation, but for his pains Nərimanov was poisoned (on Stalin's orders) in 1925. His replacement, Mir Jafar Bağirov, unquestion-ingly oversaw Stalin's brutal purges, in which over 100,000 Azeris were shot or sent to con-centration camps, never to return. Following the Khrushchev 'thaw' Bağirov was himself arrested and shot.

During WWII, Hitler made no bones about his priority of grabbing Baku's oil-wealth for energy-poor Germany. Luckily for Baku, the German army became divided and bogged down trying to take Stalingrad on the way. Nonetheless, realisation of Baku's potential vulnerability encouraged Soviet engineers to develop new oilfields in distant Siberia after the war.

Perestroika (restructuring) in the late 1980s was also a time of increasing tension with Armenia. Tit-for-tat ethnic squabbles be-tween Armenians and Azeris over the status of Nagorno-Karabakh bubbled over into virtual ethnic cleansing, as minorities in both republics fled escalating violence. On 20 January 1990, the Red Army made a crassly heavy-handed intervention in Baku, killing dozens of civilians and turning public opinion squarely against Russia. Azerbaijan declared its independence from the Soviet Union in 1991.

Independent Again

Few moments have shocked the nation more than the massacre of Azeri civilians by Armenian forces at Xocalı on 26 February 1992. Public opinion turned against the dithering post-independence president, Ayaz Mütəllibov, who was ousted and replaced in June 1992 by Əbülfəz Elçibəy. He in turn fled a year later in the face of an internal military rebellion. This was come-back time for Parliamentary Chairman Heydar Əliyev, who had been Azerbaijan's communist party chairman in the 1970s and a Politburo member in the 1980s. Shoehorned into the presidency, Əliyev stabilised the fractious country and signed a cease-fire agreement with Armenia and Nagorno-Karabakh in May 1994. However, around 13% of Azerbaijan's territory remained under Armenian occupation, with around 800,000 Azeris left homeless or displaced. Azerbaijan was faced with a tragic impasse. Rehousing the refugees would be seen as an admission of defeat in Karabakh. But renewed conflict would prevent investment and economic recovery. The compromise was to do relatively little, and in the meantime an entire generation of Azeri refugee children have grown up without a proper home or education.

PEOPLE
The National Psyche

The Azeri mindset deftly juggles many apparently contradictory influences: Muslim yet beer-loving, Turkic yet Eurocentric, overwhelmingly hospitable yet plagued by a strong vein of Soviet-era suspicion. A some-

---

DRESS CODE

Unlike neighbouring Iran, there are no legally binding rules on what to wear, and women don't have to cover their hair. However, for men, wearing shorts for anything other than sport or beachwear is considered mildly offensive.

---

what intrusive inquisitiveness towards foreigners contrasts with a resigned acceptance of various societal annoyances such as corruption and a devil-may-care driving style. Azeris have a very strong sense of family and display a total incomprehension at the idea of adults being voluntarily childless. If you're over 30 and haven't procreated be ready for these standard questions: 'How many children do you have? None? Why not? What do you live for?'.

Daily Life

Life revolves around a web of family connections and commitments. Bosses will be totally understanding of any employee who is absent due to a funeral, engagement or wedding of even a very distant cousin. And again the next week.

Finding a job for a relative is considered an obligation rather than nepotism and clan solidarity is often more important than pure politics at upper levels of society. Especially in Baku, women appear very liberated, with their bright make-up and high heels, but in reality Azerbaijan remains very much a male-dominated society.

It's unquestioned that a wife should have food on the table whenever her husband appears. And no local woman would consider drinking tea at one of the *çayxanas*, where many of her male relatives might be happily gossiping and playing nard. The lack of any genuinely free press adds to the extraordinary undercurrents of rumour and misinformation that circulate.

Population

Officially around 90.6% of the population are ethnic Azeris. In reality the percentage is even higher if you discount the ethnic Armenians who inhabit occupied areas in and around Nagorno-Karabakh and thus have had no de facto link with the rest of Azerbaijan since 1994. A significant minority of Lezgins (178,000) live in northern Azerbaijan, notably in Qusar. Many ethnic Russians (now just 1.8%) left after independence, though Baku retains a small, active Russian minority. Some 77,000 Talysh people live in the southern region around Lənkəran speaking their own Iranian dialect. Tiny communities of Avars, Georgians, Udin, Tsakhor and other mountain peoples are dotted along the Caucasian foothills.

NARD, A NATIONAL OBSESSION

Playing nard will hugely enhance your social interaction with Azeris... well at least with Azeri men at a çayxana (teahouse). A variant of backgammon, nard is played on a board divided into four quarters of six slots each. The first aim is to get your 15 counters into the final quarter. Then, when that's achieved, use further dice rolls to remove them from the board. The first player to remove all their pieces wins: the loser buys the next round of tea and jams. Each turn normally allows two moves dictated by rolling two dice. However, rolling a double gets you twice as many moves. Moves are not allowed onto a slot already occupied by an opponent's piece (unlike backgammon where two of an opponent's pieces would be necessary to block a move). Tactical blocking is the main skill of the game because when a player cannot make a legal move he forfeits his turn. If one player has removed all his pieces before the opponent has even reached the fourth quarter, it counts as a double victory.

RELIGION

The nation is religiously very tolerant. Ethnic Azeris predominantly follow Shia Islam. Unlike the Sunni Islam of Turkey or south Asia, Shiism places great emphasis on Imam Ali, considering his descendents as honoured guardians of the message of the Prophet Mohammed. Although this is nominally the same form of Islam as practised in neighbouring Iran, you will see minimal religious fundamentalism in Azerbaijan. Indeed, in the antireligious Soviet days, the idea of being Muslim was more a blurred badge of Azeri nationality than a spiritual faith. Today the nation is effectively relearning Islam from scratch. The result is a fascinating blend of Islamic humanism and open-minded secularism, with elements of pre-Islamic animism and an added soupçon of Zoroastrianism.

As Western-style capitalism seems to be failing to deliver a fairer society, religious adherence is slowly growing. However, relatively few women cover their hair and the Azeris who follow the orucduq (fast) during Ramazan (Ramadan) generally do so for the 'right reasons' (spiritual and physical purification) rather than through any personal compunction. Less pious Azeris use Ramazan as an excuse to cut down on the vodkas rather than to actually stop eating during daylight hours. Restaurants stay open.

Azerbaijan's religious minorities include Sunni Muslims (mostly the ethnic Lezgins) and small groups of Russian Orthodox and Catholics. Official figures give around 2% as Armenian Apostolic, but these folk live in the occupied areas. There's a Georgian Orthodox community around Qax. Nic, near Qəbələ (p273), is the last bastion of the Albanian-Udin church, whose political importance vastly outweighs the size of its tiny congregation. Krasnaya Sloboda near Quba (p263) is a unique mountain-Jewish village and there are small Jewish communities in Baku and Oğuz.

ARTS

Azerbaijan's cultural greats are revered across the country. Their busts adorn Baku's finest buildings, their names are commemorated as streets and their homes are often maintained as shrinelike 'house-museums' (ev-muzeyi), where fans can pay homage.

Cinema

In the Soviet era, Azerbaijan had a decent film industry, with old Baku offering a tailor-made set for many historical epics. The country also has a strong history of animation films. Since independence, movie production has all but stopped, although Ayaz Salayev's The Bat (1995) was awarded the Grand Prix at the International Film Festival in Angers, France. Samil Əliyev's The Accidental Meeting (2002) was also critically acclaimed. The only cinema that regularly shows movies with English subtitles is the Çingis Klubu in Şəki.

Literature

Azerbaijan has a long and distinguished literary tradition. Best known is the Azeri 'Shakespeare', Nizami Gəncəvi (1141–1209), whose ubiquitous statues almost outnumber those of Heydar Əliyev. Nizami wrote in Persian rhyming couplets, but Mehmed bin Suleyman Füzuli (1495–1556) was the first to write extensively in Azeri-Turkish. His sensitive rendition of Nizami's classic 'Leyli and Majnun' influenced many later writers, including poetess Khurshudbanu Natavan

(1830–97), playwright Mirza Fatali Axundov (1812–78) and satirist Mirza Sabir (1862–1911), as well as inspiring Eric Clapton's 'Layla'. Azerbaijan's 20th-century star writer was Səmət Vurğun, whose popularity is particularly pronounced in his native Qazax district. One of the current deputy prime ministers, Elçin Efendiyev, is himself a brilliantly creative playwright.

Music
MUĞAM
Azerbaijan's most significant contribution to world music is *muğam*, recognised since 2003 by Unesco as one of the world's great forms of intangible cultural heritage. Traditionally, a *muğam* master was a wandering vocalist known as an *aşıg*, who made his living by performing at weddings, typically accompanied by players of the plucked tar, bowed *kamança*, and oboe-like *balaban*. To some Western ears *muğam* sounds more like pained wailing than singing, but at its best it's intensely emotional, an almost primal release of the spirit. Listen to Alim Qazimov to get the idea.

Muğam allows a great range of expression and improvisation; traditionally *aşıgs* would compete with each other in contests similar to the bardic competitions of the Celtic world. Such competitions continue today in a more upbeat and light-hearted form known as *meyxana*, whose bantering lyrics and cantering synthesiser accompaniment create a wonderful atmosphere of general mirth.

JAZZ
In Baku, jazz grew popular in the 1950s and '60s and took a distinctive local flavour under Vaqif Mustafazadeh (1940–79), who created a remarkable fusion of American jazz and traditional Azeri *muğam* improvisation. His multitalented daughter Aziza Mustafazadeh (www.azizamustafazadeh.de; b 1969) has continued in her father's footsteps, taking a blend of *muğam* jazz and classical music to a large international audience. She dazzled the crowds at the 2007 Baku International Jazz Festival (http://festival.jazz.az) with an extraordinary performance of 'Shamans', during which she managed to perfectly harmonise with her own echo.

The latest jazz-*muğam* sensations are the Novrasli brothers, including pianist Shahin Novrasli, who returned triumphant from the 2007 Montreux Jazz Festival.

Painting & Sculpture
The emotional roller coaster of independence has inspired a decade of remarkable creativity in Azerbaijani painting, with artists who had been trained within the rigours of strict Soviet technical apprenticeship suddenly allowed a great deal of artistic freedom. Baku galleries are full of inspiring works, though prices are rising rapidly. Collectors are also starting to snap up some of Azerbaijan's brilliant Soviet realist works too, while even felt-tip scribbles by the remarkable neo-impressionist Səttar Bəhlulzadə now cost around US$1000. Although the nation's sculptors have been kept busy recently with neo-Soviet statues of Heydar Əliyev, there are many vastly more imaginative public sculptures, notably by the great Omar Eldarov, whose deeply expressive statue of Hüseyn Cavid dominates Landau Sq.

ENVIRONMENT
The Land
Azerbaijan is enclosed to the north by the mighty Caucasus Mountains that separate it from Dagestan in Russia. To the south the country has a border with Iran running along the Talysh Mountain range. The highest peaks are Şahdağ (4243m) and Bazardüzü (4466m; partly within Russia). The fertile lower slopes of the mountains are clothed in lush pastures and broad-leaved forests that give way to farms and orchards. Only the few 4000m peaks remain snow-capped year-round.

The broad plain of the Kür steppe occupies the centre of the country. This monotonous lowland is intensively irrigated for the cultivation of cotton and grain, but the central Caspian coast south of Baku remains a barren semi-desert. Lush wooded mountains rising to over 3000m occupy the Nagorno-Karabakh region in the west. The 2500m Talysh Mountains in the extreme south are cloaked in subtropical forests, much of which falls within the Hirkan National Park. Azerbaijan has six other national parks and two more are due to be recognised within the life of this book, once the president can get round to opening them.

Perhaps the world's most unexpected nominal 'national park' is Baku's seaside promenade, the Bulvar. There are a further 13 nature reserves, some of which are strictly closed to all visitors.

AZERBAIJAN

Environmental Issues

The Caspian Sea rose so significantly between the 1950s and 1990s that whole stretches of beach and coastal settlement have been submerged. Meanwhile overfishing and pollution led Caspian sturgeon populations to collapse catastrophically, virtually destroying the caviar industry. Much of the damage was done in Soviet days because of intensive, low-tech oil exploitation, excessive use of artificial fertilisers and pesticides and indiscriminate dumping of toxic industrial waste. Worst offenders were the chemical industries of Sumqayıt, which caused a high incidence of still births, birth defects and child mortality. Today, most of those factories have closed. Despite some considerable efforts, massive investment is still needed to decontaminate poisoned lands; some parts of the Abşeron Peninsula look like post-apocalyptic visions dreamed up for a *Mad Max* film.

FOOD & DRINK

Flavours from Turkey, Central Asia, Iran, Russia and the Middle East have converged to form a rich palate of Azeri cuisine. This lacks the unique garlic-walnut fascination of Georgian cookery but has great strengths in fruity sauces, wonderful fresh vegetables and mutton-based soups. The main problem can be getting beyond restaurants' obsession with *shashlyk* (shish kebab).

Staples & Specialities

The cornerstone of Azeri restaurant cuisine is the flame-grilled *shashlyk*. The 'standard' *tikə* kebab consists of meaty chunks, often including a cube of tail-fat which locals consider a special delicacy. *Lülə* kebab is minced lamb with herbs and spices. Both will almost

---

BLESSED BREAD

If you look carefully behind any apartment block you're likely to see bags of bread hanging separate from the domestic trash. That's because bread is considered holy and can't simply be binned, leaving superstitious Azeris with a disposal problem.

Eating bread with someone is considered to seal a bond of friendship, while it's necessary to share sweets or pastries with strangers (or give it to a mosque) when a wish-prayer has been granted.

---

automatically be served with a series of fresh vegetables, fruits, salads, cheese and bread (all costing extra) unless you specify otherwise. Grilled vegetables are often available as a side dish, though vegetarians might be alarmed to find lurking morsels of lamb fat inserted into barbecued aubergines to make them more succulent. Pricier kebab types include *antreqot* (ribs) and *dana bastirma* (marinated beef strips), which are generally leaner.

The classic non-kebab dish is dolma, where various vegetables are stuffed with a mixture of rice and minced lamb, possibly infused with fresh mint, fennel and cinnamon.

Düşbərə is a lightly minted soup containing tiny bean-sized mutton ravioli and typically served with sour cream and garlic. At its best, *düşbərə* is divine, but cheap versions can be bland, despite the vast amount of work required to make them.

Various stews incorporating potato and soft-boiled mutton include *buğlama* (sometimes with cherries), *bozbaş* (with *köfte* meatball) and *piti* (with chickpeas). When eating *piti* don't just dig in. Tear up pieces of bread in a separate bowl and drain off the liquid onto the bread creating a filling 'first course'. Then grind the remaining solids into a mush, not forgetting the fat chunk, which adds an essential part of texture and flavour.

Rare outside southern Azerbaijan, deliciously fruity Talysh cuisine is best known for *ləvəngi* (chicken stuffed with walnuts and herbs), which is recently becoming easier to find in Baku where XVII Əsr restaurant (p250) is a Talysh specialist.

Azeris think of *aş* as their national dish. It's a splendidly fruity variation on *plov* (Central Asian style rice-and-meat) but you'll usually only find it served at major celebrations. Restaurants that offer it usually need a day's notice.

Typical breakfast foods *(səhər yeməkləri)* are bread, butter and cheese, maybe with some honey or sour cream, all washed down with plentiful sweet tea. Egg-meals can be terribly greasy.

QUICK EATS

Azerbaijan's foremost fast food is the döner kebab. Much as in Europe, a large cone of chicken *(tovuq)* or compounded meat *(ət*, essentially mutton) is flamed on a rotating grill then sliced into small morsels that are served with mixed salad in *lavaş* (thin flour tortilla) or *çörək* (bread). Cheap ones (around 70q) typically just use less meat than pricier ones (AZN1.20). Judge the quality by the queue. *Peraşki* are (very greasy) savoury doughnuts. They rarely cost over 10q but are worth avoiding, as the cooking oil is rarely fresh.

Drinks

The national drink is *çay* (tea) usually served in pear-shaped *'armudi'* glasses and sucked through a sugar lump for sweetness, or accompanied by jams and candies. Coffee is a pricey fad in Baku but little seen in the provinces. Azeri *şərab* (wine) is generally rather poor but the *konjak* (brandy) is decent and Xırdalan lager is a very acceptable *piva* (beer). Toasting with *arak* (vodka) remains an important social ritual especially between older men with significant social standing (and bellies) to maintain. However, it is less formalised than in Georgia and less compulsive than in Russia.

Water *(su)* is rarely drinkable from the tap. To save money on bottled water (*qazli* means sparkling, while *qazsiz* means flat), keep an empty bottle handy to fill when passing roadside *bulaği* (springs).

Where to Eat & Drink
SIMPLE EATERIES

The standard cheap eatery is a *yemekxana*, often aimed at providing basic lunches of *piti*, *buğlama*, *çığırtma* or *borş* to workers and small-time bureaucrats (almost always men). Unexotic options like *kotlet* or *sosiska* are also possible. You'll usually pay a little extra for the garnish of *qreçka* or *püre*. Don't expect a menu: simply ask what they've got.

RESTAURANTS

A provincial restoran is slightly more refined than a *yemək xana* but meal choices are often limited to kebabs (from around AZN1.60 a skewer) and accompanying salads, maybe also fish or *tabaka* (flattened whole chicken). For nonkebab food try asking what *qazan-yemeklǝri* (plate foods) are served. Along country lanes many charmingly rustic restorans are tucked into the woodland clearings. They're usually called İstrahǝt Zonası ('rest zone', with attached accommodation) or İstrahǝt Guşasi ('rest corner', without). Reckon on AZN2 to AZN3 per kebab plus around AZN1 to AZN2 per basic garnish.

Baku offers an incredible, ever-changing choice of alternatives, from Mexican to mushy peas via a selection of Georgian, European and oriental alternatives. Prices can approach European levels but 'bizniz lunches' (from noon to 3pm Monday to Friday) are often a good deal.

TURKISH RESTAURANTS

In bigger towns, you'll generally find at least one Türk Restoran (Turkish restaurant). Various precooked meals are displayed in a heated glass-fronted cabinet. Point at what you want and choose a side dish of rice, mashed potato or *vermişel* (macaroni) all for around AZN4 to AZN6.

WEDDING PALACES

By far the most ornate and ostentatious eateries are known as *şadliq sarays* (wedding palaces). Every town has one – often several – but as the name implies these are almost exclusively used for large, prebooked banquets. Getting invited to a wedding offers a brilliant insight into Azeri culture, but bring earplugs to combat superloud music.

Vegetarian & Vegan

Whether Naxçivan melons, Göychay pomegranates, Balakǝn persimmons or Gǝdǝbǝy potatoes, Azerbaijan's fresh fruit and vegetables remain marvellously seasonal and utterly packed with flavour. Perfect-looking but tasteless Western equivalents can't compare to the condensed sunshine of an Azeri tomato. *Çoban*, a green 'shepherd' salad of chopped tomato, cucumber, raw onion, dill and coriander leaves, is served as a preamble to most meals. Most Azeri main meals are squarely based around meat, but if you eat fish there's good *sudak* (pike-perch, available in autumn) or *balıq* (slices of sturgeon best smeared with tangy pomegranate or sour-plum sauce). *Dograma* and *dovga*, both dairy-based soups, are possibilities for non-vegans though hardly a meal in themselves. *Göyǝrti qutab* (spinach-filled pancake-snacks) are sometimes available. Baku's Western, oriental and Georgian restaurants have meat-free options.

Habits & Customs

In Azeri culture, restaurants' roles are social rather than functional, typically serving large groups of Azeris feasting for hours amid vodka toasts. Therefore, you can expect to feel rather out-of-place if eating alone in restaurants beyond expat-savvy Baku.

Eat Your Words
MENU DECODER

aş – fruity plov

bal – honey

borş – borscht, hearty cabbage-based soup

bozbaş – stew-soup usually featuring a meatball formed around a central plum

buğlama – mutton-and-potato stew slow-cooked to condense the flavour and soften the meat. Some chefs booby-trap the dish with sour cherries to give it an appealingly acidic tang

çığırtma – soft omelette often containing chicken and garlic

cız-bız – fried tripe and potato

çörek – bread

dograma – a cold soup made with sour milk, potato, onion and cucumber

dolma – mince-stuffed vegetables. Various dolması include *badımcan* (in aubergine), *bibar* (green pepper), *kələm* (cabbage leaves), *pomidor* (tomato) and *yarpaq* (vine leaves)

dovga – a hot, thick yogurt-based soup

düşbərə – light broth containing tiny dumplings

düyü – rice

gurcu xinqal – Georgian spiced dumplings

kabablar – kebabs. Types include *antreqot* (lamb ribs), *badımcan* (aubergine), *balıq* (fish, usually sturgeon), *dana bastirma* (marinated beef strips), *kartof* (baked potato), *lülə* (minced lamb), *tikə* (lamb chunks, ie 'standard' shashlyk) and *toyuk* (chicken)

kotlet – meat patties

kuftə – köfte

kuku – thick omelette cut into chunks

lahmajun – wafer-thin 'Turkish pizza'. Fill with salad and squeeze on lemon juice

lavaş – very thin bread-sheets

ləvangi – Talysh-style *toyuq* (chicken) or *balıq* (fish) stuffed with a paste of herbs and crushed walnuts

qayğana – scrambled egg

qızıl balıq – salmon

qlazok – fried eggs

qovurma – mutton fried in butter with various fruits

qreçka – boiled buckwheat

qutab – limp pancake turnover half-heartedly filled with *göyarti* (spinach) or *ətlə* (meat)

pendir – cheese

piti – two-part soupy stew

plov – various types of rice pilaf

püre – mashed potato

sosiska – frankfurter

tabaka – pricey, flattened whole chicken

tava-kabab – not a kebab but meat patties cooked into an omelette

xama – sour cream

xaş – heavily garlic-charged soup made from bits of sheep that Westerners prefer to avoid. Wash down with a hair-of-the-dog vodka

xinqal – meaty chunks served with lasagne-like leaves of pasta

yağ – butter

BAKU (BAKI)

☎ 012 / pop 1.85 million

The Azeri capital is the Caucasus' largest and most cosmopolitan city. Few cities in the world are changing as quickly and nowhere else in the Caucasus do East and West blend as seamlessly or as chaotically. Battered Ladas race shiny Mercedes past illuminated stone mansions, shiny glass towers and tatty old Soviet apartment blocks. Pedestrianised tree-lined streets in the elegant centre chatter with teahouses and buzz with expat pubs. Unesco World Heritage status tries to slow the corporate gentrification of the fascinating Old City (İçəri Şəhər) hemmed in by an exotically crenellated arc of medieval fortress wall. Romantic couples defy Islamic stereotypes by canoodling their way around wooded parks and handholding on the Caspian-front bulvar (promenade), whose greens and opal blues make a mockery of Baku's desert-ringed location.

HISTORY

The name Baku might derive from the Persian *bad kube* (city of winds), fitting given the gale-force *xəzri* wind that comes howling in off the Caspian once or twice a month. Or perhaps it comes from the ancient Caucasian word *bak* (sun, or god), hinting at the area's ancient role as a centre for fire worshippers millennia ago. Either way, Baku's first burst of glory came when regional rulers, the Shirvanshahs, moved their capital here following an 1191 earthquake that destroyed their main city Şamaxı (p267). Wrecked by Mongol attacks, then vassal to the Timurids, Baku only returned to brilliance under Shirvanshah Khalilullah I (1417–65), who completed his father's construction of a major palace complex. However, the Şirvan dynasty was ousted in 1501 when Azeri Shah Ismail I (remembered as poet 'Xatai' in Azerbaijan) sacked Baku and then forcibly converted the previously Sunni city to Shia Islam.

When Peter the Great captured the city in 1723, its population was less than 10,000, its growth hamstrung by a lack of trade and drinking water. For the next century Baku changed hands several times between Persia and Russia, before being definitively ceded to the Russians with agreements in 1806, 1813 and 1828.

Oil had been scooped from surface diggings around Baku since at least the 10th century. However, when commercial extraction was deregulated in 1872 the city rapidly became a boomtown. Workers and entrepreneurs arrived from all over the Russian Empire, swelling the population by 1200% in under 30 years.

Baku's thirst was slaked by an ambitious new water-canal bringing potable mountain water all the way from the Russian border, and the city's desert image was softened by parks nurtured using specially imported soil. By 1905 Baku was producing around 50% of the world's petroleum and immensely rich 'oil barons' built luxurious mansions outside the walls of the increasingly irrelevant Old City. Meanwhile, most oil workers lived in appalling conditions, making Baku a hotbed of labour unrest and revolutionary talk. Following a general strike in 1904, the Baku oil workers negotiated Russia's first-ever worker-management contract. But tensions continued to grow.

In the wake of the two Russian revolutions Baku's history became complex and very bloody with a series of brutal massacres between formerly neighbourly Armenian and Azeri communities. When the three south Caucasus nations declared their independence in 1918, Bolshevik-led Baku refused to join Azerbaijan's Democratic Republic. In response Turkish and Azeri troops marched (very slowly) towards Baku. Before they arrived, Baku's leadership was toppled by pro-Russian (but anti-Bolshevik) Mensheviks and a secret British force sailed in from Iran to help them 'defend' the city (well, OK, the oilfields) against the Turks (Britain's WWI enemies). On 20 September 1918, 26 of the former Bolshevik leaders (the '26 Commissars') were rounded up in Baku and shipped across the Caspian to Turkmenistan, where they were taken into the desert and shot. Russia held the British responsible for their deaths and later communist propaganda portrayed the Commissars as great Soviet martyrs, their monuments appearing all across the USSR (there's still one in Baku's Sahil Gardens).

Whatever the reality, Baku's Anglo-Menshevik defence crumbled and the British withdrew ignominiously, their ships slipping away in darkness. However, in the end-game of WWI, the Turks were forced to evacuate too. Less than two years later, on 28 April 1920, the Red Army marched into Baku.

In 1935 the search for oil moved into the shallow coastal waters of the Caspian. A forest of offshore platforms and derricks joined the tangle of wells and pipelines on land. Investment dwindled after WWII and only really resumed in earnest after independence in 1991. Since 1994, however, foreign oil consortia have spent billions exploring these resources and for reasons as much political as economic the world's second-longest oil pipeline, BTC, was built to Ceyhan in Turkey, ensuring that Azeri oil could be exported safely and quickly to the West without transiting Russia or Iran. Especially since BTC went online in 2005, Baku has been booming. As property prices head for London-style highs, the skyline has been transformed by hundreds of new multistorey towers. But get-rich-quick attitudes have meant a shabby disregard for planning standards. Engineers warned that poor construction techniques, corrupt practices and cost-cutting would make many new buildings unsafe, especially given Baku's seismic activity. These fears came horrifyingly true in summer 2007, when a half-finished 16-storey tower collapsed, trapping and killing dozens of people.

More positively, boom money has also paid for the cleaning and attractive lighting of many grand old buildings in the city centre along with the construction of a series of seasonal musical fountains.

ORIENTATION

From the walled Old City (İçəri Şəhər), Neftçilər pr follows the Caspian round to a vast, supremely Soviet edifice called Government House (Dom Soviet) paralleling a seafront park that's universally known as the bulvar.

STREET NAMES

In this book we abbreviate Azeri streets (küçəsi) as küç and avenues/boulevards (prospekti) as pr.

AZERBAIJAN

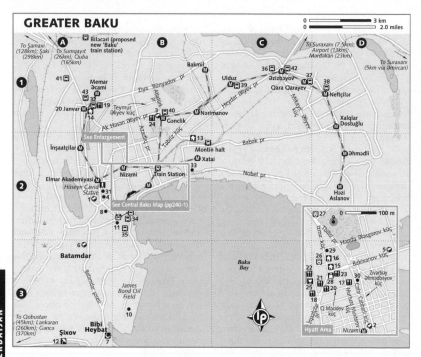

AZERBAIJAN

You'll find most of Baku's charming century-old 'Oil Boom' architecture near a central piazza known as Fountain Square though there are plenty more fountains around town, notably in Heydar Əliyev Park.

The main shopping street, pedestrianised Nizami küç, is still more commonly known by its Soviet-era moniker of Torgovaya (Trade St).

Baku's rich and famous tend to live in the inner suburb of Gənclik, or on the Batamdar ridge overlooking town.

INFORMATION
Bookshops

Akadem-Kitab (Map p242; İstiqlaliyyət küç 51; 10am-2pm & 3-6pm Mon-Fri, to 5pm Sat) Wide range but predominantly in local languages. Next door, Iranian Al Hoda focuses on Farsi literature.

Book Shop of the Presidential Administration (Map pp240-1; N Rəfibəyli küç 29; 10am-2pm & 3-7pm Mon-Fri, to 6pm Sat) Sells an amusing selection of hagiographic literature about both Əliyevs, as well as postcards and several guide-pamphlets that you could have got for free from the tourist information office.

Chiraq Books (Map p242; 4923289; Zərgərpalan küç 4) Baku's friendly English-language bookshop stocks a

decent range of classics, bestsellers, travel guides and locally relevant titles, along with plenty of Christian literature.

Kitab (Map pp240-1-00; Fikrət Əmirov küç 1; 10am-5pm Mon-Sat) The most reliable place to find excellent 1:500,000 topographic maps of Azerbaijan (AZN4). They're rolled up amid other much poorer versions so ask to look at a few. No English spoken.

Qlobus (Map p242; Rəsulzadə küç) Sells intriguing 20-year-old postcards.

Emergency

Operators speak Azeri and Russian but not English.

Ambulance (103)
Fire (101)
Police (102)

Internet Access

Internet cafés are very common, though often hidden away in basements.

Castle VIP (Map pp240-1; Xaqani küç, Molokan Gardens; per hr AZN1; 24hr;) The fastest (if priciest) of three options on the north side of Molokan Gardens. Price drops to 20q per hour after midnight.

C@Z (Map p242; M Əfəndiyev küç; per hr 60q; 10am-2am;) Vast subterranean internet club with Skype-phone options.

Life Internet (Map pp240-1; Azadlıq pr; per hr 40q;) Spacious, with decent connection speeds, above an Azercell dealership.

Virtual (Map pp240-1; Nizami küç; per hr 60q) Central.

Internet Resources

Bakupages (www.bakupages.com) Extensive, but the most interesting features are in Russian.

City Administration (www.bakucity.az/main/index _en.htm)

Window2Baku (www.window2baku.com) Interesting historical photos of the city.

Laundry

Typical charges are AZN2 per kilogram for smalls, AZN2 for shirts and AZN3 for trousers.

Mr Pak (Map pp240-1; 4986365; Azadlıq pr; 8am-8pm Mon-Fri, 10am-7pm Sat & Sun)

Milnaya Opera (Soap Opera; Map p238; 4975767; H Cavid pr 8; per kg with ironing AZN1.90, without AZN1.50; 9am-9pm) Take marshrutka 106 to get here.

Savalan Express (Map pp240-1; 4989339; Səməd Vurğun küç 17; 9am-8pm Mon-Sat)

Left Luggage

At the train station, the most reliable of three **baggage rooms** (Saxlama Kameralari; per day AZN2) is in the tunnel-corridor behind the main ticket-selling concourse.

There's also left luggage in the toilet block behind the main bus station.

Medical Services

Aptek (pharmacies) are generally well stocked and relatively inexpensive. A regularly updated list of emergency medical services appears on the US Embassy's website at http://azerbaijan .usembassy.gov/medical_services.html.

Aptek Həyat (Map pp240-1; 4936161; Bülbül pr 30; 24hr)

HIV tests (4949924) You can organise anonymous tests via this number. No English spoken.

International SOS (German Medical Centre; Map pp240-1; 937354, 934089; www.sosinternational.com; Rəşid Behbudov küç 30; 9am-6pm Mon-Fri, 9am-1pm Sat) Some expat doctors work here, but 15-minute consultations start at US$103.

MediClub (Map pp240-1; 4970911; www.mediclub .az; Üzeyir Hacıbəyov küç 45) Doctors' consultations from AZN24.

Money

ATMs are common throughout Baku. Most accept foreign credit cards and many allow withdrawals in both AZN and US dollars. Exchange facilities don't charge commission and are nearly as ubiquitous. Rates are excellent for US dollars and pretty competitive for euros. For Russian roubles and pounds sterling, rate-splits are poorer (around 4%). Various other currencies (including Georgian lari) can be changed too, though on less favourable terms. Some exchanges open late into the evening while most banks shut by 4pm. The best rates are usually available on 28 May küç at Vurğun Gardens (Map pp240–1).

CENTRAL BAKU

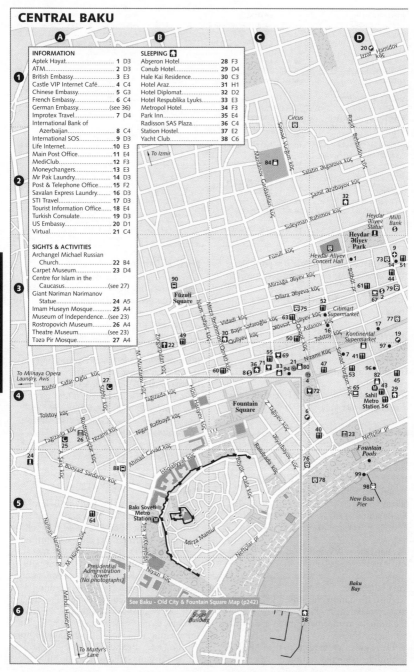

INFORMATION

Aptek Hayat	**1**	D3
ATM	**2**	D3
British Embassy	**3**	E3
Castle VIP Internet Café	**4**	C4
Chinese Embassy	**5**	G3
French Embassy	**6**	C4
German Embassy	(see 36)	
Improtex Travel	**7**	D4
International Bank of Azerbaijan	**8**	C4
International SOS	**9**	D3
Life Internet	**10**	E3
Main Post Office	**11**	E4
MediClub	**12**	F3
Moneychangers	**13**	E3
Mr Pak Laundry	**14**	D3
Post & Telephone Office	**15**	F2
Savalan Express Laundry	**16**	D3
STI Travel	**17**	D3
Tourist Information Office	**18**	E4
Turkish Consulate	**19**	D3
US Embassy	**20**	D1
Virtual	**21**	C4

SIGHTS & ACTIVITIES

Archangel Michael Russian Church	**22**	B4
Carpet Museum	**23**	D4
Centre for Islam in the Caucasus	(see 27)	
Giant Nariman Narimanov Statue	**24**	A5
Imam Huseyn Mosque	**25**	A4
Museum of Independence	(see 23)	
Rostropovich Museum	**26**	A4
Theatre Museum	(see 23)	
Təzə Pir Mosque	**27**	A4

SLEEPING

Abşeron Hotel	**28**	F3
Conub Hotel	**29**	D4
Hale Kai Residence	**30**	C3
Hotel Araz	**31**	H1
Hotel Diplomat	**32**	D2
Hotel Respublika Lyuks	**33**	E3
Metropol Hotel	**34**	F3
Park Inn	**35**	E4
Radisson SAS Plaza	**36**	C4
Station Hostel	**37**	E2
Yacht Club	**38**	C6

AZERBAIJAN

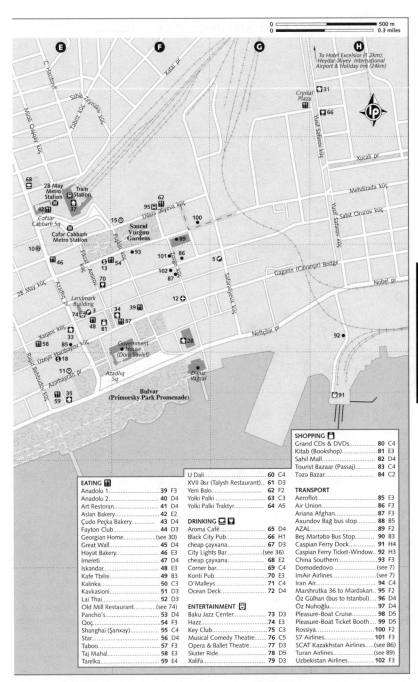

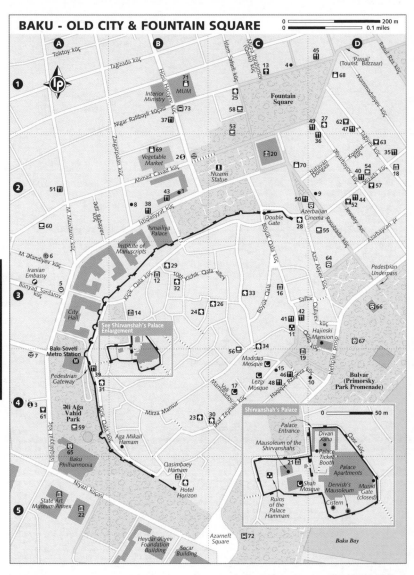

BAKU - OLD CITY & FOUNTAIN SQUARE

Post

Main post office (Map pp240-1; Azərbaycan pr 41; 24hr)
Post office (Map pp240-1; Dilara Əliyeva küç)
Post office (Map p242; İstiqlaliyyat küç 35)

Telephone

New AzEuroTel payphones are pretty rare but when you find one it takes coins or cards and can call international (54q per minute), regional and local numbers. Old payphones are local-only and you'll need a ribbed *jeton* (token), sold from street vendors for 10q.

Look for *jeton var* signs. Post offices have phone-rooms. A small, cheaper **Call Centre** (Map pp240-1; Şeyx Şamil küç 1; 11am-8pm) will charge only 9q per minute to provincial Azeri towns and 27q to most international numbers.

Tourist Information

Tourist Information Office (Map pp240-1; ☎ 5985519; www.tourism.az; Üzeyir Hacibəyov küç 6; ☯ 10am-1pm & 2-6pm Mon-Sat) Gives away a range of glossy pamphlets and a full-colour guidebook.

Travel Agencies

There are foreigner-friendly travel agents. These include:

Improtex Travel (Map pp240-1; ☎ 4989239; www .improtex-travel.com; Səməd Vurğun küç 16) Long-established agency with a huge network of contacts. Services range from visa support and hotel discounting to goat hunting and extreme sports.

SI Travel (Map p238; ☎ 4970800; www.si-travel .com; Hyatt Tower 2, 1033 İzmir küç) Major agency and American Express representatives in Azerbaijan.

Skylife Tours (Map p242; ☎ 4925577; www .skylife-travel.com; Neftçilər pr 97/3) Well-run IATA agent.

STI Travel (Map pp240-1; ☎ 4980880; www.sti.az; Nizami küç 91) A few discounts available for ISIC student card-holders.

DANGERS & ANNOYANCES

The crime rate is very low. Over inquisitive police are more likely to bother you than criminals. Keep at least a photocopy of your passport and visa with you in case of police checks. Avoid photography on the metro, near the Presidential Administration Tower and halfway up the funicular.

SIGHTS

Baku's historic heart is İçəri Şəhər, the Unesco-listed walled Old City. It contains the city's most accessible sights and its quieter back alleys are atmospheric minor attractions in their own right, as are the tree-lined streets of 'oil boom' mansions just beyond.

Maiden's Tower

This tapering 29m **stone tower** (Map p242; adult/student/child AZN2/60q/20q; ☯ 11am-5.30pm Tue-Sun) is Baku's foremost architectural icon. Its century of construction is the subject of much debate, though its present form is 12th century. The Azeri name, Qız Qalası, is usually rendered 'maiden's tower' in English, leading to plenty of patently fictitious fairy-tales. A popular version has a wealthy ruler falling in love with his own daughter. He asks the girl to marry him. Revolted by the thought of incest but unable to disobey her father she stalls, commanding that he build her a tower high enough to survey the full extent of his domain before she decides. When it's finally complete she climbs to the roof and throws herself off.

A better translation of Qız Qalası would be 'virgin tower', alluding to military impenetrability rather than any association with tragic females. Historians agree that it has served as a defensive tower; beyond that some claim it was also a lookout post, a fire beacon, a Zoroastrian tower of silence or even an astronomical observatory. It was certainly an incredibly massive structure for its era, with walls 5m thick at the base and an unusual projecting buttress. Openings on the south side permit light to enter. The eight floors are linked by steps within the walls, except for the ground floor, where a retractable ladder has now been replaced by a modern iron staircase. A deep well descends from a recess in the 2nd-floor chamber. A mysterious doorway on the 3rd floor opens into thin air; its original function (possibly astronomical) remains unknown.

Today, the interior contains an interesting display of old photographs and a souvenir shop, but the highlight is the superb rooftop viewpoint surveying Baku Bay and the Old City.

Palace of the Shirvanshahs

This charming if entirely unfurnished sandstone **palace complex** (Map p242; ☎ 4921073; admission/guided tour AZN2/6; ◷ 10am-6pm) was the seat of northeastern Azerbaijan's ruling dynasty during the Middle Ages. Mostly 15th century in essence, it was painstakingly restored in 2003.

Enter via the main ceremonial courtyard, dominated by a towering (if plain) portal leading into the main **palace apartments**, whose renovation has almost amounted to full-scale rebuilding. A small gateway on the left leads into the courtyard of the **Divan Xanə**, an octagonal, open-sided stone rotunda where the court of Shirvanshah Khalilullah I once assembled.

The western portal is beautifully inscribed with intricate carving and calligraphic inscriptions.

Steps lead down from the ceremonial courtyard to an octagonal water **cistern**,

near which the incredibly sparse **ruins of the Keyqubad Mosque** lead into the so-called **Dervish's Mausoleum**. This empty, pointed-roof structure was the tomb of Seyyid Yəhya Bakuvi, an astronomer, philosopher and mystic at Khalilullah's court. Around the tomb are many carved stone blocks inscribed with Arabic calligraphy, animal figures and human faces. These **Bayıl Stones** were recovered in the 1950s from the 13th-century ruins of Sabayil Qala, a castle that once stood on an island that's now submerged near Baku's southern Bayıl Peninsula.

The next level down lies behind a battlement-topped stone wall. This encloses the small cubic **Shah Mosque** and the **Mausoleum of the Shirvanshahs**, which is largely unadorned within but has some carvings on the portal gateway.

A handful of photographs inside show archaeological finds from the site's 1940s excavations. Another gate leads down to the final terrace and the lumpy **ruins of the Palace Hamam**.

Art Galleries

The **State Art Museum** (Map p242; ☎ 4925789; Niyazi küç 11; admission AZN3; ◷ 10am-5pm Tue-Sun) is housed in two impressive oil-boom mansions. The main building houses a collection of rather staid 19th-century Azeri and Russian art. But there's a much more interesting overview of Azeri modern art in the annexe immediately up the hill. If that's closed, you can still see great modern Azeri art at several commercial mini-galleries with free admission, of which the most imaginative include **Qız Qalası** (Map p242; ☎ 4927481; www.qgallery.net; Qüllə küç 6; ◷ 10.30am-7pm), **Center of Contemporary Art** (Map p242; ☎ 4925906; Qüllə küç 15; ◷ 11am-8pm Tue-Sun) and **Ali Shamsir's Gallery** (Map p242; ☎ 4977136; Kiçik Qala küç 84).

Carpet Museum

Formerly a Lenin Museum, this solidly neo-classical building now houses an interesting **Carpet Museum** (Map pp240-1; ☎ 4932019; Neftçilər pr 123; admission AZN5; ◷ 9.30am-5pm), which charts the history of Azeri carpet making and includes over 1000 rare and beautiful rugs from Azerbaijan, as well as Iran and Dagestan. A guided tour (AZN3 extra) helps to put the designs in context and to explain the significance of their symbols. In the same building are the far less compelling **Theatre**

Museum (☎ 4930229; admission AZN2) and **Museum of Independence** (☎ 4533017; admission AZN2).

Other Museums

Several of Baku's top museums were being very extensively renovated at the time of research but should reopen in 2008 or 2009. These include the **Nizami Museum of Azerbaijan Literature** (Map p242; ☎ 4927403; İstiqlaliyyət küç 53), whose exterior façade has ogive arched niches set with statues of the nation's literary greats. Less impressive from outside but truly stunning within is the **Historical Museum** (Map p242; ☎ 4933648; Z Tağiyev küç 4), housed in the 1896 former home of one of Baku's greatest late-19th-century oil barons.

Baku has many modest 'house museums' commemorating local cultural icons in the homes where they once lived. For foreign visitors a popular choice is the **Rostropovich Museum** (Map pp240-1; ☎ 4920265; Rostropoviçlər küç 19; admission/tour AZN1/3; ☉ 10am-5pm Mon-Sat), given the international fame of the Bakuvian cellist and conductor Mstislav Rostropovich, who lived here as a child. However, it's of very limited interest to nonspecialists and no English is spoken.

Religious Buildings

Several blunt medieval **minarets** rise above the Old City but the intricate stone façade of the **Cümə Mosque** (Map p242) is only a century old. Amid an interesting warren of low-rise old homes that rises up the Yasamal Slopes lies the imposing **Təzə Pir Mosque** (Map pp240-1; ☎ 4923855; Sübhi küç). It was built between 1903 and 1914 but a 2007 renovation has added gilding to its minaret tips and stone cladding to the surrounding buildings, which house the **Centre for Islam in the Caucasus**. Overshadowed by vast new apartment towers is the fine **Imam Huseyn Mosque** (Map pp240-1; Tağizadə küç), featuring some attractive Moorish and Art Nouveau stone-design elements.

Hidden through the Vidadi küç archway off Hüsi Haciyev küç, the modest **Archangel Michael Russian Church** (Map pp240-1; ☎ 4973596; Zərgərpalan küç 38) is the centre of Baku's Orthodox community. It's not geared towards tourists, but you're welcome to admire the icons and colourful ceiling murals.

The sturdy **Armenian Church** (Map pp240-1; Fountain Sq) remains disused for lack of Armenians, a reminder of the brutal cultural divide still caused by the war in Karabakh.

Şahidlər Xiyabani (Martyr's Lane)

High above the city centre's southwest corner lies this sombre **memorial** (Map p238) to Bakuvian victims of the Red Army's 1990 attack. Those martyrs were swiftly joined by many more Azeris who died in the Karabakh conflict. A small memorial to British and Commonwealth troops killed around Baku during WWI has been erected nearby, causing considerable controversy. After all, the British had been sent to prevent the Turkish invasion which most Azeris supported. A small police post above it dissuades vandals.

Even if graves are too maudlin to appeal, Şahidlər Xiyabani has a fine new **Turkish-style mosque** (Map p238) and at the edge of the gardens there's a viewpoint offering some splendid views across the bay and city.

Get here by **funicular** (20q, every 15 minutes) from thesea front, or marshrutka 39T or 177 from behind Bakı Soveti metro.

Nearby is **Faxri Xiyəbani Cemetery** (Map p238; Parlament pr), where Heydar Əliyev's grave is the first place that any dignitary is likely to be taken to on an official visit to Baku.

WALKING TOUR

After climbing the **Maiden's Tower** (1; p243) for some orientating views, wander randomly in the alleyways of **İçəri Şəhər**, making an active attempt to get lost. You're never more than a few minutes' walk from the fortified perimeter wall, and this way you get to absorb some of the atmosphere of the real Old City, small corners of which remain delightfully 'lived-in' despite the encroachment of neohistorical office buildings and multiplying **carpet sellers (2)**. Don't miss the **Palace of the Shirvanshahs (3**; opposite) before exiting into grand İstiqlaliyyət küç, near the splendidly renovated **Baku Philharmonia concert hall (4**; p253). The white tower-block across the road from the **Art Museum (5**; opposite) guarded threateningly by soldiers is the **Presidential Administration (6)**: photography is strictly forbidden, though were it not nobody would think of snapping a picture anyway.

Curving northeast you'll pass the noble, late-19th-century **Baku City Hall (7)** and the **Institute of Manuscripts (8)** which preserves a fine collection of mainly 18th- and 19th-century Korans. Beyond the lovely **Ismailiya Palace (9)** lies the Old City's sturdy, castle-style **Double Gateway (10)**, while on your left is the beautiful façade of the **Nizami Literature**

AZERBAIJAN

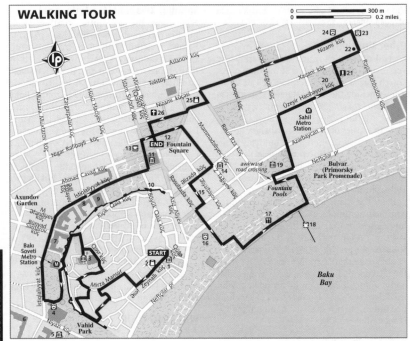

WALKING TOUR

WALK FACTS

Start Maiden's Tower
Finish Fountain Sq
Distance 4km
Time 5 hours

Museum (**11**; p245). Behind that lies **Fountain Sq** (**12**), Baku's pleasantly shady central piazza. It's a great place for people-watching, though the fountains themselves are only switched on during summer evenings. For refreshment consider a shady beer-or tea-terrace or perhaps the trendy **Azza café** (**13**; p253). The surrounding tree-lined streets are full of pubs, restaurants and century-old 'oil-boom' mansions, including one that houses the **Historical Museum** (**14**; p245). Having explored a little, backtrack via the historic if overrenovated **Jewellery Arcade** (**15**) to find the underpass beneath thundering Neftçilər pr. You'll emerge beside the dinky old **Puppet Theatre** (**16**; p253) on the bulvar. Join the smoochy young lovers strolling the seafront promenade or the families enjoying funfair rides. Notice the

open-sided **Mirvari Kafesi** (**17**; Pearl Cafe), whose scallop-shell concrete roof is as archetypally Soviet as the pinafored babushkas who serve here. Nearby is the departure pier for short **pleasure-boat trips** (**18**; adult/child 80q/60q; ☿ summer when calm) into the bay, whose waters glint rainbow colours with the sheen of oil.

Cross back across Neftçilər pr to the colonnaded **Carpet Museum** (**19**; p244) – this can be challenging due to the constant traffic – then stroll through Baku's commercial centre to **Sahil Garden** (**20**). The garden's focus is a now-wordless **memorial** (**21**) to the 26 Commissars, and there are several fine buildings nearby including the statue-encrusted national library, the **Akhundov Kitabxana** (**22**). Around the corner the classically styled **Rəshid Rəşid Behbudov Song Theatre** (**23**) was once Baku's main synagogue (two newer ones still operate).

The city's fine **Opera House** (**24**; p253) welcomes you to Nizami küç, Baku's most cosmopolitan pedestrianised shopping street, whose many fine century-old mansions will lead you back to Fountain Square via the **Passaj Tourist Market** (**25**) and the old **Armenian Church** (**26**; p245).

FESTIVALS & EVENTS

The city's vibrant theatre and concert season runs from mid-September to May, culminating with the world-class **Baku Jazz Festival** (http://festival.jazz.az/). Headline acts have included Herbie Hancock in 2006 and Aziza Mustafazadeh in 2007.

The **Caspian Oil & Gas Show** (www.caspianoil gas.co.uk) in early June is a week-long corporate shindig. While hardly a tourist draw, it brings in delegates from around the world, stretching the availability of top-end hotel rooms. Like other Baku trade fairs (http://cas pianworld.com/en/country_events/aze/) it's held at Baku's soulless **Heydar Əliyev Adina İdman Konsert Kompleksi** (Map p238; Moskva [Tbilisi] pr).

SLEEPING

Within the past five years most of Baku's sleazier accommodation options have been bulldozed, while throughout the city a rash of midrange minihotels is appearing. Prices are comparatively steep, as you might expect in an increasingly oil-rich boomtown. If Baku's hotel prices scare the moneybelt off you, it's possible to sit up all night in one of the 24-hour Internet Klubs. Or take a cross-country night train to anywhere for around AZN4.

Budget

HOTELS & HOSTELS

Station Hostel (Map pp240-1; main train station; dm/s/tw AZN3.60/6/12) By far the cheapest beds in town are within dorms within the ugly, roach-infested concrete tower above the central train station. Sometimes foreigners are refused a place and you're likely to be lodging with an odd collection of petty traders and down-and-outs. There are also a few single and double rooms though these fill very fast. It's all very hit and miss. Enquire (in Russian or Azeri) at the window marked 'İstirahət Otaqlarinin İnzibatçısı' in the station's ticket concourse. Once you've paid you get a slip of paper allowing you to enter the guarded, very creaky lift. Good luck!

1000 Camels Hostel (Map p242; ☎ 4926331, 050 7212995; www.thousandcamels.com; Asəf Zeynallı küç 29/3; dm US$20) Owned by inspiring young Azeri professionals, this small, brilliantly located hostel has just two four-bunk bedrooms off a shared kitchen-cum-sitting room in a typical thick-walled Old City house. The shared bathroom is OK though beds are rather uncomfortable and linen costs AZN1 extra (or use your

sleeping bag). The hostel is through the second door to the left in the tiny, dead-end alley directly west of the Hotel Meridian. A second, vastly less convenient branch is out in the suburbs, near metro Elmar Akademiyasi.

Hotel Araz (Map pp240-1; ☎ 4905063; Yusif Səfərov küç 30; tw/tr from AZN20/30, with bathroom AZN40/60; ❷) Popular with backpackers and Iranian petty traders, the Araz has relatively well-maintained budget rooms, all with air-con, plus two receptionists who can speak OK English. Though clean, the shared facilities were designed with an all-male clientele in mind, so women will cause consternation in the communal shower room. From central Baku take marshrutka 1 from Vurğun Gardens, or 4 from the bulvar.

Cənub Hotel (Map pp240-1; ☎ 5981152; fax 4479488; Azərbaycan pr 31; refurbished/unrefurbished tw with bathroom AZN40/30; ❷) The Cənub's reasonable prices and superbly central location make up for inconsistent hot-water supply and lacklustre service. Refurbished rooms have air-con. Some guests report problems getting in after midnight.

Hotel Velotrek (Map p238; ☎ 4315187-9; Moskva [Tbilisi] pr 3007; per person AZN15) The Velotrek's clean, unfussy rooms with en suite bathroom are relatively new and a bargain when you're travelling alone. However receptionists can be hard to find, the doors lock early and priority goes to visiting sports teams, so you can't necessarily extend your stay. The location is far from central but handy for the main bus station and right beside (if hidden from) 20 Jan metro station. The next-door bicycle club can help long-distance cyclists fix their bikes.

APARTMENTS

Numerous rental agents focus on the expat market but can offer daily rates for short stays. Quality varies but many properties are central and all are likely to have hot water and a kitchenette. English-speaking agents include:

Alla Rakhmanina (☎ 050 3691569; http://travel azerbaijan.land.ru; 1-/2-room apt from US$30/45, 5-night minimum)

Baku Services (☎ 4189661; www.bakuservices.com; from US$78)

Marina Mednikova (☎ 050 4507740; www.bakureal estate.net; from US$40, 3-night minimum)

Midrange

Abşeron Hotel (Map pp240-1; ☎ 4932056; www.hotel -absheron.com; Puşkin küç; 6th, 11th & 13th fl tw/ste AZN65/120, 9th, 12th & 14th fl AZN80/120, 5th, 7th, 8th,

BUSINESS IN BAKU: INTERVIEW WITH AN ANONYMOUS EXPAT BUSINESSMAN

So what's it like doing business in Baku?

You have to have connections here. Even then there's a constant procession of inspectors to check building standards, fire precautions, tax certificate and goodness knows what. Even if you've followed all the rules there's always a 'sweetener' to pay if only to make sure they stamp your papers. So why bother following regulations?! It's a dangerous cycle. Of course, there's money to be made. But don't let anyone know you're doing well. Otherwise the landlord raises your rent to eat up all your profit. Your local business partner forces you out. Or a better-connected local sets up in competition and has his friends send round yet more inspectors to close you down. They can always find something!

Is it getting better?

It was. A lot of great, dynamic young Azeris were getting promoted into higher places. But in the middle ranks there's still a lot of self-serving bureaucrats who think only about skimming off whatever they can. And the sudden flood of oil money means that the good guys seem to have taken their eyes off the ball. If anything things are getting worse. Laws remain opaque and entrepreneurs, local and foreigner, are simply giving up and leaving town.

10th fl AZN120/140; ☒) This vast 1970s concrete monster has finally received a long-overdue renovation and the spacious lobby now looks rather hip. However, while rooms on some floors were entirely rebuilt to approximately Western standards, cheaper options have simply been redecorated and retain lacklustre Soviet bathrooms. Sniff carefully before accepting a room and bring mosquito repellent just in case. The top-floor restaurant isn't lovely but has superb views down onto Government House.

Old City Inn (Map p242; ☎ 4974369; www.oldcityinn .com; 10th Kichik Qala alley 16; s/d/tw US$90/110/120; ☒) With just 12 comfortable (if oddly shaped) rooms, this friendly place has unusually high levels of service, as staff are students of the Western University's tourism courses. The roof offers fabulous 360-degree views if you can manage five flights of stairs.

Yacht Club (Yaxt Klub; Map pp240-1; ☎ 5981895; fax 5981886; s/d/ste US$120/140/210; ☒) This 26-room glass arc is uniquely located on stilts above the Caspian and reached by golf-style electric buggy down a pier. Standards are acceptable, though colours don't always match and not all rooms get sea views. Breakfast included. Booking fee is a whopping 25%.

Azcot Hotel (Map pp240-1; ☎ 4972507; www.azcot hotel.com; N Rəfibəyli 20; d US$129.80-177; ☒) In a superbly central 1885 mansion this friendly hotel uses period settees, large Chinese vases and tasteful art to make corridors feel homely. The comfortable rooms have kettles and minibars. Rates include breakfast and internet access.

Hotel Respublika Lyuks (Map pp240-1; ☎ 5981056; www.hotelrespublika.com; Xaqani küç 24; ste AZN150-320; ☒) This impressive latter-day stone mansion makes no attempt to advertise that it's a hotel, but standards are high, prices fair (by Baku standards) and the suave restaurant offers an incredible lunch deal.

Holiday Inn (Map p258; ☎ 4374949; www.holi dayinn.com; Heydar Əliyev International Airport; d from AZN150; ☒ ☒) With many international flights arriving and departing at antisocial hours, this very comfortable, brand-new hotel offers a stress-free alternative to a 3am taxi ride to/from the city centre. Top-end quality for midrange prices.

our pick Sultan Inn (Map p242; ☎ 4372305; www .sultaninn.com; Böyük Qala küç 20; d AZN150-170; ☒) This luxurious 11-room boutique hotel hits a fine balance between opulent elegance, cosy comfort and trendy modernism. Its perfectly central Old City location is a great plus, with unparalleled views of the Maiden's Tower from the rooftop restaurant.

Metropol Hotel (Map pp240-1; ☎ 4926709; http:// metropolbaku.com; Fikret Əmirov küç 2; s/d from US$171/183; ☒) The Metropol is a boutique hotel that pulls off that 'design-book' trendy feel with primary colours, bold modernist lines and showers that feel like starship transporter booths.

Park Inn (Map pp240-1; ☎ 4906000; www.baku .rezidorparkinn.com; Neftçilər pr; s/d from AZN176/189; ☒) This swish modern business hotel has been very impressively recycled from a once-terrible old Soviet dinosaur. Sea-view rooms cost AZN11 extra. Check out the guests-only top floor where a 'secret' sushi bar will make your credit card wince. Officially the address is Azadlıq 1 but that's misleading as it's not on Azadlıq at all.

Other options include the following:

Altstadt Hotel (Map p242; ☎ 4933492; aae@box.az; Mammadyasov küç 3/2A; d US$50-80; 🛠) Simple eight-room homestay-style guesthouse that's about the cheapest you'll find in the Old City. Minimal English.

Guesthouse Inn (Map p242; ☎ 4371263; ascotinn2@ azdata.net; Harbchilar küç 19-21; d AZN60-75; 🛠) Fairly plain, simple Old City guesthouse. Two rooms lack natural light but top-floor rooms share a view terrace.

Red Roof Old City Guesthouse (Map p242; ☎ 4371263; office@redroofoldcity.az; Sabir küç 12; d AZN85; 🛠) Decent Old City guesthouse with great rooftop views and a little basement pub.

Hale Kai Residence (Map pp240-1; ☎ 5965056; www .hotelhalekai.com; Mirza Ibrahimov küç 18; d AZN90-140; 🛠) Smart, central, American-owned guesthouse with Georgian art and small but pleasant lobby bar. Breakfast included. No lift.

Hotel Balion (Map p242; ☎ 4184329; Əliyarbəyov küç 12; d US$100; 🛠) Rather functional but handy for the nightlife district.

Hotel Kichik Gala 98 (Map p242; ☎ 4371950; www .hotelgef.com/98.html; Kiçik Qala 98; s/d AZN80/100; 🛠) More spacious and slightly more stylish than many of the Old City's mini-hotels.

Marco Polo Icheri-Sheher Hotel (Map p242; ☎ 4925315; www.icherisheher.net; Mammedyasov küç 1/34; d AZN120; 🛠) Cosy, comfortable six-room Old City hotel whose private rooftop offers great views of the Shirvanshah Palace Complex.

Top End

High prices aren't always an assurance of high quality. Some options are shockingly over-priced at walk-in rates but online brokers and travel agencies often offer discounts. Even the best hotels can suffer from a level of service that is friendly and willing but overfamiliar and sometimes incompetent.

Hotel Meridian (Map p242; ☎ 4970809; www .meridianhotel.az; Əsəf Zeynallı küç 39; s/d US$212/224, ste US$271-401; 🛠) Stylish, understated rooms are comfortable and the location behind a neo-antique stone façade at the entrance to the Old City is magnificent. Don't miss the bar and billiard room hidden in a warren of 17th-century subterranean caverns beneath the hotel.

Radisson SAS Plaza (Map pp240-1; ☎ 4982402; http:// baku.radissonsas.com; 14th-17th fl, ISR Plaza; sea view/city view AZN283/330, presidential suite AZN800; 🛠 🛠) Soaring above Fountain Sq, this tower of blue glass and anonymous grey-pink marble offers won-derful city views but the experience is more like renting a luxurious studio than staying in a hotel. Seek out reception in an office in the 17th floor. Guests have free use of the Plaza fitness centre on the ground floor.

Hotel Boutique Palace (Map p242; ☎ 4922288; www .boutique-palace.com; Əziz Əliyev küç 9; d AZN348; 🛠) The unique feature of this somewhat self-indulgent little place is that it's actually built like a limpet onto the ancient old-town wall, as you'll see in the bar. Rooms do have person-ality but aren't enormous and rack rates are shamelessly excessive.

Excelsior Hotel (Map p238; ☎ 4968000; www.excel siorhotelbaku.az; Heydar Əliyev pr 2; d AZN250-350, ste AZN650-2450; 🛠 🛠) The Excelsior appeals to the nouveau super-riche, with a Las Vegas sense of no-expense-spared pseudo-classical grandeur. Rooms are impeccable and the fit-ness centre is superb, but it's a little isolated – 3km east of the centre.

Hyatt Hotels (Map p238; ☎ 4961234; www.baku .hyatt.com; 1033 İzmir küç; d from US$295, ste $390-1062; 🛠 🛠) Together this pair of professionally run international hotels form Baku's most reliable business option. Rooms at the Park Hyatt are somewhat larger but those in the Hyatt Regency have a trendier feel and the Regency's fine 1950s building has a certain Stalinist grandeur. Facilities include three swimming pools, a pair of squash courts and a very extensive gym. Numerous good restau-rants lie nearby.

EATING

Baku is a culinary treat, where good local res-taurants jostle with equally impressive for-eign eateries catering for the sizable expatriate community. Typical restaurant hours here are 11am to 11pm (exceptions are given in the following listings).

Azeri

There's a selection of ultra-cheap if entirely uninspired, male-dominated *yeməkxanalar* around the train station, notably on the south side of Vurğun Gardens. **Qoç** (Map pp240-1; 28 May küç 50; meals AZN1-3; ⏰ 24hr) is typical and opens all hours. **Yeni Bakı** (Map pp240-1; Dilara Əliyeva küç 251; mains AZN1-3; ⏰ 10am-11pm) is less off-putting for women.

Dərviş (Map p242; meals AZN2-5, beer 80q; ⏰ 10am-11.30pm) This friendly and refreshingly unpre-tentious, locals-only place serves simple meals in an ancient stone cavern that's photogenic but prone to overheating.

L'Aparté (Map p242; İstiqlaliyyət küç 51; mains AZN2-7, beers from AZN1.40; 24hr) Open all-hours with a phenomenally wide-ranging menu and surprisingly plush décor given the incredibly modest price range.

Similar great-value equivalents include **Art Restoran** (Map pp240-1; Xaqani küç 51; 24hr) and **Restoran Port** (Map p242; Əliyarbəyov küç; 10am-11pm).

Tarelka (Map pp240-1; off Azərbaycan pr; bizniz lunch AZN3, mains AZN3.50-7) Calm, bright and run by women for women, this narrow little café-resto has décor based around the owner's modest porcelain collection. Food is Russo-Azeri with an AZN10 salad buffet on Sundays.

Pəncərə (Map p238; ☎ 5103700; A Şaiq küç 245; meals AZN4-15, beer from AZN1.80; 10am-1am) The upstairs dining room has a wild-west wooden décor and live piano music. Ground-floor wooden booths emulate the streamside ambience of Azeri rural dining. The menu stretches from local standards to ostrich steaks. Wines from AZN6 a bottle.

Bəh Bəh Club (Map p242; ☎ 4988734; www.bah-bahclub .com; Əliyarbəyov küç 9; mains AZN4.50-10) Kilims on walls, heavy wooden tables and an excellent selection of regional food including *saj* (sizzler-roast) dishes and *fisincan* (Azeri-Iranian walnut-chicken). The live music is low-key.

Fayton Club (Map pp240-1; ☎ 4988101; Rəşid Behbudov küç 17; meals AZN5-20, beers from AZN2) This upmarket yet rustic stone-vaulted basement is decorated with handicrafts, *şəbəkə* (intricately carved, wood-framed, stained-glass windows) and an old cart in an almost-successful attempt to create a feel of 18th-century Azerbaijan. Classic Azeri foods are well made but unless you want the full-blast music show (AZN4 cover), get out before 8pm.

Karvansara Restaurant (Map p242; ☎ 4926668; Böyük Qala küç 11; mains AZN5-15) Choose from two 14th-century caravanserais, one offering atmospherically gloomy private stone cells, the other an intriguing cellar dining room. Prices aren't outrageous but watch out for 'extras'.

XVII Əsr (Map pp240-1; ☎ 4932034; Bəşir Səfəroğlu küç 215; meals AZN7-20) Decorated with old hunting weapons, this cosy mid-market restaurant offers Talysh cuisine that goes well beyond the predictable nut-stuffed *ləvəngi* dishes. Delicious starters (AZN3 to AZN4 per plate) include *XVII əsr qəlyanaltısı* (stuffed dried fruit and walnut-coated chicken balls), *qoz küküsü*

(a patchwork of omelette-like morsels) and *incə salatı* (layered egg-salad with cheese and fruit topping). There's also an AZN7 bizniz lunch.

Muğam Club (Map p242; ☎ 4924085; Həqiqət Rzayeva küç; meals from AZN20, beers from AZN4) A wonderfully atmospheric two-storey caravanserai offers alcove and courtyard dining options accompanied by impressive cabaret shows demonstrating tasters of various Azeri musical and dance styles. The Azeri food is excellent, but prices can be exorbitant (kebabs AZN12!). Often closed for private functions.

Tonqal (Map p238; ☎ 4499198; www.tonqal.com; Ak Həsən Əliyev 82; kebab meals AZN15-25) Ivy-draped carts in overgrown patches of woodland create a delightfully rustic garden atmosphere that's incongruous for the suburban setting. However the only menu is on its website and the many extras can be extremely pricey (plate of fruit AZN20!); plus the only drinking water served is imported.

Many glitzy and relatively overpriced local restaurants feature high-volume Azeri pop music (see Entertainment, p253).

Turkish

Baku's numerous Turkish restaurants serve comparatively inexpensive precooked meals in pleasantly semi-grand arch-vaulted premises. Point at what you fancy from the heated display of precooked meals (AZN4 to AZN6 including side dish) or order pricier made-to-order dishes. Popular choices include **Anadolu 1** (Map pp240-1; ☎ 4980102; www.anadolu.az; Puşkin küç 5), **Anadolu 2** (Map pp240-1; ☎ 4986804; Rəsul Rza küç 3/5), **Star** (Map pp240-1; ☎ 4987625; Bülbül pr 5; 9am-11pm), spacious **Iskəndər** (Map pp240-1; Xaqani küç; 7am-11.30pm) and stylish **Divan** (Map p242; İstiqlaliyyət küç).

Georgian

Apart from the Georgian Home, none of the Georgian places listed here speak English, but who cares with flagons of rustic Georgian house wine at AZN6 per litre?

U Dali (Map pp240-1; ☎ 4949356; Mirzə İbrahimov [Qorki] küç 7; mains AZN4.40-8; 10am-11pm) Misleadingly signed 'Café Napoli', U Dali serves tasty Georgian home-cooking at candlelit basement booths. It's sweetly unsophisticated, the mushroom dishes are excellent.

Similarly priced but less cosy options include **Imereti** (Map pp240-1; Xaqani küç 13) and the very functional **Kavkasioni** (Map pp240-1; Dilara Əliyeva küç) whose double-decker Megruli *khachapuri* (Georgian cheese pie) are superb.

Kafe Tbilisi (Map pp240-1; Hüsü Haciyev küç 80; mains AZN3-5) has a tetchy manager but the prices are very reasonable (if double what the English menu says!). Try the scrumptious eggplant strips topped with walnut paste (40q each).

Georgian Home (Map pp240-1; ☎ 4944385; Mirzə İbrahimov [Qorki] küç 18; mains AZN10-25, beers from AZN3.50) A quantum leap in style, this suave choice makes wonderfully eclectic use of homemade pottery to give the fashionable interior a real sense of personality. Food is excellent but with prices to match. The cheapest bottle of wine costs a thumping AZN35, plus 10% service charge.

Russian & Ukrainian

Yolki Palki (Ёлки Palki; Map pp240-1; ☎ 4942492; Qoqol küç 15; mains AZN3-7) This jolly if cramped log-décor cellar-restaurant fills with whooping live gypsy music many an evening. There's another branch at M Hüseyn küç 88, while the similar **Xutor** (Map p242; ☎ 4372223; M Muxtarov küç 9/3; mains AZN3-6; 11am-11pm) specialises in Ukrainian food. All menus are in Russian.

our pick **Kalinka** (Map pp240-1; ☎ 5962470; Qoqol küç 7; mains AZN3.50-6) Calm and remarkably suave, with soaring high ceiling vaults yet very modestly priced and with a menu in English. The 'black pearls' (stuffed prunes; AZN2) are particularly delicious.

International

You can eat most world cuisines in Baku.

Bibi (Map p238; ☎ 5102632; A Şaiq küç; mains AZN4-10, kebabs AZN2-7; noon-11pm) By far the nicest place in Baku for Persian cuisine, the Bibi offers live but unobtrusive music in its spacious double dining hall with olde-worlde tulip-chandeliers and rush-matting to soften the ceilings. Try the *kəşki badımcan* (eggplant with Iranian whey; AZN4).

Great Wall (Map pp240-1; ☎ 4937672; Üzeyir Hacıbəyov 26; mains AZN5-9, rice AZN1.50) This unpretentious Chinese eatery represents good value.

Asiana (Map p238; ☎ 4368367; Q Məcidov küç; mains AZN6-12, rice from AZN2) Chopsticks balanced on pebbles give a zenlike low-key appeal that's amply complemented by fine Malaysian and Singaporean food.

Mado (Map p238; ☎ 4975544; İnşaatçılar pr 33; nigiri-zushi for 2 AZN3-6, for 6 maki AZN5-13) Designer-hip Japanese restaurant where sushi comes with beautiful ceramic soy sauce jugs and luridly over-pink sushigari. Sadly, the limp *maguro* tastes somewhat bland.

Sunset Café (Map p242; ☎ 4922292; Əziz Əliyev küç 9; sandwiches AZN7-10; noon-11pm Mon-Sat, noon-10.30pm Sun) The ugly plexiglass-fronted building is an eyesore, but the very agreeable cinema-themed interior is perfectly pitched and the generous salads, giant burgers and excellent sandwiches are ever-popular with expats.

Pancho's (Map pp240-1; ☎ 4985700; Xaqani küç 14/16; mains AZN9-15; noon-3pm & 6-11pm) is the most authentic for Mexican food, while **Mexicana** (Map p242; ☎ 4989096; Z Tağıyev küç 17; mains AZN8-11) does a decent AZN9 lunch deal, offering soup, burrito, soft drink and garlic bread.

Mediterranea (Map p242; ☎ 4929866; Həqiqət Rzayeva küç 11; mains AZN7-12, beer from AZN3.20) The garden area is superbly located for summer dining in the shadow of the Maiden's Tower while the sleekly modernised caravanserai-covered courtyard interior is a tempting choice on colder nights. The mostly European main dishes aren't especially memorable but mezze starters are excellent and drinks arrive with complimentary cheese and olives.

Al Fresco (Map p242; ☎ 5981124; Əlizadə küç 9; pastas AZN8-12, mains AZN10-17) Upmarket Mediterranean food in a modern, distinctively feminine, Laura Ashley–style atmosphere, with pastel colours, lacy tones and several round tables.

Scalini's (Map p238; ☎ 5982850; www.scalini.baku.az; Bakıxanov küç 2; pastas AZN9-14, Italian mains from AZN12) Speedy, waistcoated waiters deliver perfect pastas with bucket-loads of parmesan and a selection of home-cooked breads in Baku's most congenial Italian restaurant. The décor is upmarket bistro-style with a relaxed buzz, soaring high ceilings and great movie and Martini posters.

Lai Thai (Map pp240-1; ☎ 050 5785394; Səməd Vurğun küç 21; mains AZN9-18, rice AZN2) The food is lip-smackingly authentic Thai but prices seem steep, given the somewhat unrefined décor.

Shanghai (Şanxay; Map pp240-1; ☎ 4954510; Rəsul Rza küç 31; mains AZN10-12, rice from AZN3; noon-11pm) For good, authentic Chinese food, the Shanghai scores highly despite an un-lovely green-box interior.

Hong Kong (Map p238; ☎ 4369001; İnşaatçılar pr 38; mains AZN9-18, rice from AZN2; noon-11pm) In a fine Stalinist stone corner-block near the Hyatt, pricey oriental food is served in an elegantly modern, mood-lit environment, beneath lamps shaped like abstract squid.

Taboo (Map pp240-1; ☎ 5981761www.taboo-baku.com; ; Üzeyir Hacıbəyov 33; teppanyaki AZN17-45) Flex your credit card for cook-at-the-table teppanyaki or wide-ranging Eurasian delicacies at this 'm'as-tu-vu' palace of low-voltage uberchic.

Maharaja (Map p242; ☎ 4924334; Əlizadə küç 6; mains AZN8-12) is the best of several appealing, upmarket Indian restaurants. Its AZN10 weekday lunch deal is a bargain, with soup, two delicious curries, rice and tea. **Taj Mahal** (Map pp240-1; ☎ 4930049; Xaqani küç 18; mains 7-9, rice AZN1.50, lunch AZN7) also exudes an elegant designer orientalism.

Quick Eats

BAKERIES

Many bakeries offer stand-bars at which to eat snacks (15q to 40q) and cheap if long-stewed cups of tea or cocoa (20q). The Çudo Peçka (Map p238) chain is ubiquitous, and its branch near Hotel Velotrek has seating.

However, the system of pre-paying can be awkward if you don't speak Azeri. **Həyət** (Map pp240-1; Azadlıq pr; ☾ 24hr) is more user-friendly. **Aslan** (Map pp240-1; Cəfaar Cabbarlı Sq), near the metro station, has particularly good Pendirli Xaçəpuri (cheese-filled flaky-pastry squares).

FAST FOOD

Throughout the city you'll find windows selling döner kebabs for around AZN1: **İnter Grand** (Map p242; Z Tağiyev küç 5) is especially popular.

It's fun to visit **McDonald's** (Map pp240-1; Fountain Sq) if only to giggle at spellings such as Biq Mak and Çizburqer.

DRINKING

Bars

As well as those listed there are numerous cheaper lacklustre local places. Many teahouses also serve beer from around 50q.

Corner Bar (Map pp240-1; Rəsul Rza küç; beers from AZN2, snacks AZN2-6; ☾ 3pm-late) The most happening of Baku's many Anglo-Irish-style pubs, the Corner has very competent live music, '33' beer for AZN2 and a decent range of pub grub.

Other reliable expat choices include Finnegans (Map p242) or Adam's (Map p242) for televised sports, plus O'Malleys (Map pp240-1) for its tree-shaded summer terrace.

USSR (Map p242; Z Tağiyev küç; Xırdalan beer AZN2; ☾ 4pm-late) This basement Soviet-nostalgia bar is decidedly downmarket and a little musty, but has some fun photos of politburo stars and a Red Army coat and general's cap that you can don for souvenir photos.

Black City Pub (Map p242; ☎ 4901890; Yusif Səfərov küç 22; Efes beer AZN2) Although it's not worth a special trip, this Germanic wood-interior bar

is a handy choice if you're staying at Hotel Araz. No spoken English, no menu.

Konti Pub (Map pp240-1; ☎ 4989191; Nizami küç 117; snack meals AZN2-8) This medieval-style *bierstübe*-cavern offers the novel concept of letting you pour your own draught beers. Be careful where you sit: some metered taps dispense Xırdalan at AZN3 per litre, others Bavaria at AZN7.20. It's mostly for locals.

Brewery (Map p242; İstiqlaliyyət küç 27; beers AZN2.50, meals AZN8-13) In a spacious, stone-vaulted basement with heavy wooden furniture, Baku's only brew-pub turns out very acceptable dark ales and less successful lagers. Germanic meals and pricey beer snacks are available.

Ocean Deck (Map pp240-1; ☎ 4930223; Molokan Park; small beer from AZN2.50) Plonked in the middle of a duck pond, the terrace of this American café-bar makes a delightful people-watching perch in the summer. However, its small interior is rather lacklustre.

City Lights Bar (Map pp240-1; ISR Plaza, 17th fl, Nizami küç 340; beers from AZN4) This hip, upmarket lounge-bar offers some incredible views of the city from its outdoor terrace.

Teahouses

In Baku, you're likely to pay AZN1 for a pot of tea at one of the open-air male-dominated summer *çayxanas* like those behind the Nizami Cinema, near the train station or a block north of Bibi restaurant in the greater Baku area.

The same tea will cost around AZN2.50 if a 'compulsory' cut-up Snickers bar arrives with your teapot. This will happen at most places on the Bulvar and at the well-located **Kafe Fəvvarələr** (Map pp240-1; Fountain Sq).

It's almost always cheaper to order a beer, which can cost as little as 50q a pint for unpasturised NZS, or AZN1 to AZN2 for a more palatable Xırdalan lager.

A much more upmarket *çay evi* (teahouse) can charge entirely ludicrous sums (AZN6 to AZN20) for a pot of tea with samovar of water and a range of jams and fruit. The best such places tend to be indoors, with comparatively exotic interiors, *qalyan* (hubble-bubble water pipes) to smoke and possibly a belly dancing show, as at **Şarq Əfsanəsi** (Map p242; Eastern Legend; Ahmad Cavad küç 4; tea AZN20, beer AZN5, vodka AZN10; ☾ 3pm-late).

Cafés

Great coffee aromas and hissing cappuccino nozzles entice many a visitor into central

Baku's suave new cafés. Expect to pay around AZN3 for an espresso and at least AZN4 for one of those scrumptious cakes to accompany it.

Azza (Map pp240-1; ☎ 4370111; www.azza.az; İslam Səfərli küç 1A) Three floors of coffee-and-cream minimalism within a historic pavilion right on Fountain Sq. Excellent food including decent pastas (AZN7) is served by self-consciously handsome, slow-motion waiters.

Aroma (Map pp240-1; ☎ 5980707; www.aromacafe .az; Üzeyir Hacıbəyov küç 18; coffees AZN3-6, mains AZN9-24; ☼ noon-11.45pm Mon-Sat, 3-11.45pm Sun) Baku's best combination of comfort, fashionable décor and great coffee. Pod lamps and electro-retro feel downstairs, street-view sofa seats above. It's also a wi-fi hot spot.

Chocolate (Map p242; ☎ 4923526; Böyük Qala St, Old City; coffees AZN2-5; ☼ 11am-midnight) A classy, high-ceilinged café with pseudo-1920s touches, weighted hanging lamps and tasselled tablecloths on small wrought-iron tables. However, macchiatos are far too milky.

Café Mozart (Map p242; ☎ 4981925; Əlizadə küç 2; espresso AZN3; ☼ 9am-11.30pm) With Klimt inside and a super-popular street terrace outside the Mozart remains a long-term favourite for AZN8 Turkish breakfasts, AZN10 lunch buffets or decent steak dinners.

Café Caramel (Map p242; ☎ 4989353; Əlizadə küç 7) Good espressos come with complimentary cookie and glass of chilled drinking water. Small, with modern décor including a bridge-like upper level offering street views down through century-old vaulting.

Public (Map p242; ☎ 4938725; Z Tağiyev küç 17) More comfy sofa seating is hidden away in the back room behind the sparse front bar area. Excellent espressos are comparatively inexpensive (AZN2) and there's an AZN6 lunch deal.

ENTERTAINMENT
Live Music
AZERI

Many top-end restaurants, notably the Muğam Club (see p250), include a cabaret of traditional music and dancing to accompany your meal.

Others, typically in large suburban gardens, offer top Azeri pop stars singing at full blast. Many Westerners consider this more like punishment than entertainment, but if you're interested, a classic venue is **İzmir** (Map p238; ☎ 957373; İzmir küç 5; mains from AZN8, cover AZN30)

where Manana, a sort of local Kylie Minogue, enjoys a bizarre Vegas-style residence.

JAZZ

At its best, Baku's small jazz scene can be one of the most creative anywhere, but quality is variable.

Baku Jazz Center (Map pp240-1; ☎ 4936196; www .jazz.az; Rəşid Behbudov küç 19; cover AZN3; ☼ live music from 9pm) Nightly live performances in a large, somewhat staid dining-room atmosphere.

Karavan Jazz Club (Map p242; ☎ 4971139; Əziz Əliyev küç 4; cover AZN4, beers from AZN2.40; ☼ live music 9-11pm) For years this intimate and brilliantly atmospheric basement club was the heart of Baku's jazz scene, though recently performances have been sporadic and of rather variable quality. Bring mosquito repellent.

Hazz (Map pp240-1; ☎ 5982978; www.hazz.az; Landmark Bldg Lobby, Xaqani küç 45A) Choose from a vast range of designer coffees at this sedately hip businessman's café-cum-wine bar which has low-key live jazz after 8pm.

Belly Dancing

Customers at some restaurants and several upmarket teahouses are subjected to belly-dancing displays of very unreliable quality. Better than most is the show (after 10pm) at the atmospheric, Arabic-themed cellar-restaurant **Xəlifə** (Map pp240-1; ☎ 4989296; Rəşid Behbudov küç 17; mains AZN6-10, beers AZN4, waterpipes AZN12; ☼ 5pm-2am), 'guarded' – in questionable taste – by costumed African 'slaves'.

Theatre & Classical Music

As with all artistic establishments across the ex-Soviet countries, the theatre season runs from mid-September to late May. It's worth seeing a performance at Baku's 1910 **Opera & Ballet Theatre** (Map pp240-1; ☎ 4931651; Nizami küç 95), if only to admire the grand interior. Most productions are lavish and even less exciting repertory performances have the advantage of transcending language barriers.

The brilliant **Philharmonia** (Map p242; ☎ 4972901; İstiqlaliyyət küç 2), originally built as an oil-boom-era casino, has an even grander interior and offers an eclectic (if unpredictable) concert programme.

It's also worth checking the **Musical Comedy Theatre** (Map pp240-1; ☎ 4938837; Azərbaycan pr 8) for operettas, while kids might enjoy marionette shows at the **Puppet Theatre** (Map p242; ☎ 4926425; Neftçilər pr 36).

AZERBAIJAN

Nightclubs

Most of the city-centre basement dives marked 'Disko Klub' are effectively prostitute pick-up spots. However, there are some (partial) exceptions, where groups of revellers will feel comparatively comfortable. **Key Club** (Map pp240-1; Qoqol küç) is relatively professionally run. **X-ite** (Map pp240-1; Bulvar), above the Red Room bar, frequently changes name and format but usually operates as a weekend disco. **Le Chevalier** (Map p238; Grand Hotel Europe, 1025/30 Tbilisi pr; admission AZN5, weekends AZN15, beers from AZN4; 🕙10pm-late Tue-Sun) is the nearest thing to a full-blown nightclub.

Gay & Lesbian Venues

While homosexual acts were decriminalised in 2000, very conservative attitudes still prevail (at least in public) and there is no visible gay and lesbian scene in the city. Discretion is key. Azerbaijan's nascent gay-rights movement has a website at http://mavi-oglan.chat .ru/, but don't hold your breath for any public acceptance or even consciousness of homosexuality in Azerbaijan.

SHOPPING

Also known by its Russian acronym TsUM, Baku's oldest department store is **MUM** (Map pp240-1; Hüsü Haciyev küç) with four floors of stall-shops selling everything from cheap electronics to wedding dresses. The big new Sahil Mall above Sahil metro offers all manner of tacky clocks, tasteless ornaments, shimmery clothes and over-glossy gold. Classier boutiques are found on Rəsul Rza küç, 28th May küç and Atatürk pr.

The **central vegetable market** (Map pp240-1; Ahmad Cavad küç) is loveably dilapidated. For more photogenically piled fruit and illicit caviar (beluga around AZN50 for 113g), head to **Tазə Bazar** (Map pp240-1; Səməd Vurğun küç).

Souvenirs & Carpets

Traditional Azeri hats, copperware and carpets are widely sold though they can generally be obtained more cheaply in the provinces. Nonetheless the Ali Baba-esque shops around Baku's İçəri Şəhər are atmospheric places to nose around and, although prices might not be the most competitive, dealers here will be familiar with the annoying carpet-export procedures. A free tour of the impressive **Azər-İlmə Carpet Factory** (☎ 4659036; www.magicalknots.com; Şəmsi Rəhimov küç) is well worth the 20-minute drive, even if

you don't buy. Take marshrutka 99 from the Bulvar and get off beside Kral Wedding Palace on Ak Həsən Əliyev küç.

The colourful **tourist bazaar** (Passaj; Map pp240-1), along with various souvenir and 'antique' shops, mostly sells tacky rubbish, though the old Soviet-era badges are cheap and fun. **Ziya** (Map p238; İnşaatçilar pr 44; 🕙10am-8pm Mon-Sat) is well stocked, but overpriced, and aimed at Hyatt guests who can't be bothered to shop around.

Discs

In Baku you'll find a vast array of cheap, DVDs (AZN7) and music CDs (AZN3) of dubious legality. **ABC** (Map pp240-1; Fountain Sq) and especially **Grand** (Map pp240-1; Əziz Əliyev küç), with another branch on Nizami küç, offer a surprisingly wide left-field selection of Western music, as well as Azeri and Russian music. Some staff are remarkably knowledgeable.

GETTING THERE & AWAY
Air
INTERNATIONAL FLIGHTS

Baku's Heydar Əliyev International Airport (Map p258) is the busiest in the Caucasus, with flights to/from plenty of European, Russian and Central Asian cities, plus Dubai, Tehran, Tbilisi and Kabul. For more information see p319.

AIRLINE OFFICES
In Central Baku

Aeroflot (Map pp240-1; ☎ 4881167; Üzeyir Hacibəyov küç 25)

Air Union (Map pp240-1; ☎ 4935751; Nizami küç 135)

Ariana Afghan (Map pp240-1; ☎ 5981268; Rixard Zorge küç)

AZAL (Azerbaijan Airlines; Map pp240-1; ☎ 4934004; www.azal.az; 28 May küç 66-68; 🕙8am-8pm)

China Southern (Map pp240-1; ☎ 5981165; www .csair.com/en; 28 May küç 54; 🕙9.30am-6.30pm Mon-Fri, 11am-6pm Sat)

Domodedovo (Map pp240-1; ☎ 4986150; www.akdal .ru/eng; Nizami küç 66)

ImAir Airlines (Map pp240-1; ☎ 5984587, 5982376; Səməd Vurğun küç 16; 🕙9am-6.30pm Mon-Fri, 10am-5.30pm Sat & Sun)

Iran Air (Map pp240-1; ☎ 4985886; 1 Xaqani küç)

Rossiya (Map pp240-1; ☎ 5982931; www.rossiya-air lines.ru/en; 28 May küç 29/11) Formerly Pulkovo Airlines.

S7 (Map pp240-1; ☎ 4983077; www.s7.ru; Zorge küç) Formerly Siberia Airlines.

SCAT (Map pp240-1; ☎ 4935751; www.scat.kz; Nizami küç 135)
Turan Airlines (Map pp240-1; ☎ 4989431; www.turan -air.com; 28 May küç 64-68)
Turkish Airlines (Map pp240-1; ☎ 4975352; Hüsü Haciyev küç 11)
Uzbekistan Airlines (Map pp240-1; ☎ 5983120; www.uzairways.com; Nizami küç 98)

Other

AeroSvit (Map p238; ☎ 4368785; www.aerosvit.com; Hyatt Tower 2, 1033 İzmir küç)
Air Baltic (www.airbaltic.com) Book online.
Austrian Airlines (Map p238; ☎ 4368785; www.aua .com; Caspian Plaza, Cəfər Cabbarli küç)
Lufthansa (Map p238; ☎ 4907050/1; 5th fl, Hyatt Tower 2, 1033 İzmir küç)

DOMESTIC FLIGHTS

Internally, AZAL flies five times daily to Naxçivan (US$100 each way for non-Azeris) and up to thrice weekly to Gəncə (US$50 each way). Domestic tickets are only sold at the often-chaotic 'Naxçivan office' within the **AZAL Building** (Map pp240-1; 28 May küç 66/68; ☺ 8am-8pm) or, for last-minute departures, at the airport (beyond security check!).

Try to book at least a week in advance, especially in summer.

Boat

It's not jazz, not culture, not the great art and not the Abşeron's offbeat curiosities that keep most backpackers hanging around in Baku.

Most are simply waiting for a Caspian ferry. In principle ferries run to Turkmenbashi, Turkmenistan (passenger US$50, several weekly) and Aktau, Kazakhstan (passenger/motorbike/vehicle US$60/137/55-per-metre-length, a few times monthly). But they are primarily rail-cargo ships and don't care a jot about their passengers, and timetables don't exist. Ships leave virtually without warning as soon as the cargo is loaded. Or wait days if there isn't enough.

Be prepared for extreme frustration even once aboard and ask other prospective travellers (often to be found thumb-twiddling at the 1000 Camels Hostel) as to the latest ticket-purchasing procedure: it seems to change all the time. The ticket office (Map pp240–1) is a tiny, sporadically open window on the port access road, around 15 minutes' walk from Government House. Although it won't sell you anything till the night before departure, still go there, put your name on the list and get the mobile phone number of whoever is the duty agent. Then keep calling!

Bus & Marshrutka

A vast new bus station (Map p238; Sumqayıit Şosesi) is under construction 2km north of Şamaxinka. When it opens (probably 2009) most bus services will leave from there. Until then this table will be useful.

AVTOVAĞZAL (MAIN BUS STATION)

The busy **main bus station** (Map p238; Rövşan Cəfərov küç), a short walk east from 20 Janvar

AZERBAIJAN

BUSES DEPARTING BAKU

Destination	Duration (hr)	Cost	Departure point	Notes
Gəncə	6½	AZN5	Avtovağzal	
İsmayıllı	4	AZN4	Şamaxinka	
Lənkəran	5	AZN4	Avtovağzal	
Mərdəkan	1	50q	Vurğun Gardens	bus 36, frequent
Qax	8	AZN7	Avtovağzal	
Qobustan	1	80q	İdman Sarayı	bus 105, regular
Quba	4	AZN3	Şamaxinka Marshrutka	
Qusar	4½	AZN3	Şamaxinka Marshrutka	
Krasny Most (Qırmızı Körpü, Red Bridge)	10	AZN9	Avtovağzal	
Salyan	2	AZN3	Bayil Highway	for Şirvan NP
Şamaxı	2	AZN3	Şamaxinka	
Şəki	6½	AZN6	Avtovağzal	
Sumqayıt direct	1	50q	20 Janvar Metro	very frequent
Sumqayıt via Novxani	1½	80q	Gənclik Metro	bus 998, regular
Tbilisi (Georgia)	12	AZN20	Avtovağzal	9pm, kassa 2

metro station, handles most longer journeys. Departures are commonest in the mornings and late evenings (to arrive early next day).

Between the two main platforms is a row of 16 plastic kiosk-cubes containing money changers, minishops and several *kassa* (ticket booths). Ask the *dispetçer* (first booth) when the next bus is due for your destination and at which *kassa* to buy the ticket; various companies operate the same routes. There's usually no reason to book ahead. If no bus is due to leave take one of the untimetabled, faster (but more cramped) minibuses. These cost slightly more and leave when full from the fringes of the bus station. Touts for shared taxis gather at the eastern exit. That's also where you can jump aboard a southwestbound marshrutka 52 to reach Baku city centre.

Buses supposedly leave most evenings at 10pm for Tehran via Tabriz. Ask **kassa 6** (☎ 4080929) for the latest details. However, it's much more comfortable to do the trip in stages starting with the night train to Astara.

ŞAMAXINKA
The chaotic **Şamaxinka bus station** (Map p238; Moskva [ex-Tbilisi] pr) is 400m north of 20 Janvar metro station. It serves northern towns, plus Şamaxı and İsmayıllı. Marshrutka 57 takes you to the centre.

ISTANBUL BUSES
Several companies, including **Öz Gülhan** (Map pp240-1; ☎ 4188256, Istanbul 0212-5881268) and **Öz Nuhoğlu** (Map pp240-1; ☎ 4447203; Səməd Vurğun 94) run buses to Istanbul (US$60 plus AZN10, 48 hours).

All of them depart at around 3pm on Tuesday, Thursday and Saturday from the respective company offices around Sahil Gardens.

Car
Cars and 4WD self-drive vehicles can be hired through many travel agencies and through

international franchises like **Hertz** (Map p238; ☎ 4978757; Hyatt Regency Hotel; from AZN75) or **Avis** (Map p238; ☎ 4975455; www.avis.az; H Cavid pr 528; from AZN70). Getting a driver adds only around AZN10 per day. To rent more cheaply through **Ayla** (Map p238; ☎ 981415/585; http://ayla.az; Fəzail Bayramov küç 8; from AZN40) you'll need to give an AZN300 deposit. No English is spoken.

It's necessary to get an Azeri-language copy of your licence. Avis can organise this.

Train
Conditions aren't luxurious, but overnight trains give you a sleeping berth, including sheets (handed out once the train is underway), making rail travel preferable to the faster (but less comfortable) buses for longer distances.

You'll need your passport both to buy a ticket and to board the train. Especially for weekend travel it's worth prebooking at least a day or two ahead. Useful overnight trains are shown in the table.

Trains also run regularly to many Russian and Ukrainian cities but at the time of writing the Azerbaijan–Russia border remained closed to foreigners, making such routes impractical for travellers.

Very run-down suburban elektrichky (local trains) serve Sumqayıt and the Abşeron Peninsula towns for a flat 20q fare (paid on board). However, frequency keeps dropping and the system has been threatened with complete closure.

According to press reports the main train station might eventually move way out of town to Biləcəri.

GETTING AROUND
To/From Heydar Əliyev International Airport
The cheapest solution from Baku is to take Mərdəkan-bound marshrutka 36 from Vurğun Gardens to the airport approach road

---

TRAINS DEPARTING BAKU

Destination	Via	Departs	Arrives	Kupe Fare
Balakən	Şəki	10.20pm	10am	AZN4.40
Astara	Lənkəran	11.55pm	9.30am	AZN3.10
Gəncə	Ələt	11.20pm	7.40am	AZN3.20
Ağstafa	Gəncə	9.50pm	7.35am	AZN6.50
Tbilisi	Gəncə	8pm	around noon	AZN26

BAKU BUS STOPS

To use the marshrutkas, learn key stops as they appear on sign boards. 'M xxxx' suggests a stop near xxxx metro station. Other key names to learn:

- **28 May** Loosely interpreted to mean anywhere near the train station (Map pp240–1).
- **Axundov Bağ** (Map pp240–1) A triangular garden close to the Rostropovich Museum.
- **Azneft** (Map p242) The big traffic circle directly southwest of the Old City. Almost all routes marked 'Azneft' or 'Bayil' (a suburb further south) including 4, 88, 99 and 288 will pass the GPO, Carpet Museum and Maiden's Tower.
- **Beş Mərtəbə** (Map pp240–1) Füzuli Sq.
- **Çimərlik** 'Beach', usually implying Şixov.
- **MUM** (Map pp240–1) Handy for western side of Fountain Sq.
- **Təzə Avtovağzal** (Map p238) Main Bus Station, near 20 Janvar metro (will change!).
- **Vurğun Bağ** Anywhere around Vurğun Gardens (Map pp240–1).

(50q, 40 minutes). From there, the terminals are a 1km walk north or 50q by passing shared taxi (if any will stop).

Ironically, you should not take marshrutkas marked 'Aeroport': these don't go to the airport itself but to a vast *yarmarka* (bazaar) from which airport access is painfully difficult.

Taking a cab all the way from Baku shouldn't cost more than AZN15. From the airport drivers ask AZN20, but during daylight it's often possible to pay less by walk-away bargaining if you start outside the domestic terminal.

Public Transport

MARSHRUTKA

A dauntingly vast network of marshrutkas (minibuses) run from virtually anywhere to anywhere else within Baku for just 20q. Pay as you get off.

The main challenge is ascertaining the route number you need before trying to wave one down: few are stationary long enough to decipher their route boards.

Don't be shy asking for help from passers-by and remember to check which direction to head in – the complex one-way system sometimes results in surprises!

Except in a very few central areas where there are fixed *astanovki* (stopping points), the driver can squeal to a halt just about anywhere.

Simply shout *'sakhla'* (stop) or more emphatically *'sakhla burada'* (stop here) to be let out.

METRO

For visitors the Baku metro system is most useful for connecting to the bus station and Velotrek Hotel (20 Janvar metro station) from the Old Town (Bakı Soveti), the Cənub Hotel (Sahil) or Baku train station (28 May). Marshrutkas to many Abşeron towns claim to leave from Əzizbəyov metro station but most currently depart from Gənlik, Nərimanov, Ulduz, Qara Qarayev or Neftçilər metros (depending on destination) since building works have closed the Əzizbəyov bus station.

The flat fare is just 5q per ride. But to use the system you'll need to get a plastic farecard (deposit AZN2) that you charge up with credits (minimum 20).

TAXI

You can flag down a taxi anywhere at almost any time but agree on a price in advance, as metered taxis are a rarity. Very short hops cost AZN2, but most rides start from AZN3.

AROUND BAKU

SUMQAYIT
☎ 018 / pop 280,000

Fans of the truly grim might enjoy Sumqayıt, Azerbaijan's third-largest city. With a wide sand beach it was once projected as a resort town. Instead it became a dystopian industrialist nightmare when much of the Soviet chemical industry was plonked here after WWII. Hauntingly awful acres of rusty

AZERBAIJAN

pipe-workings factory chimneys and are all too visible as you speed past along the Baku–Quba road.

ABŞERON PENINSULA

☎ 012

The Abşeron confounds easy definition. Agricultural land is blanched by salt lakes, sodden with oil-runoff and poisoned by pesticide abuse. Platoons of rusty oil derricks fill horizons with intriguing, abstract sculptures. Yet despite mesmerising ugliness and a traditionally conservative population, the Abşeron still manages to be the seaside playground of Baku's playboy elite. Meanwhile several historic castle towers peep between the dachas, fires that inspired Zoroastrian and Hindu pilgrims still burn, and beneath the cultural surface lie some of Azerbaijan's oddest folk beliefs. It's a perversely fascinating place.

Suraxanı

The unique **Ateşgah Fire Temple** (☎ 4524407; admission/camera/guided tour AZN2/2/6; ☯ 10am-6pm) is one of Azerbaijan's most remarkable sights. It stands on the site of a natural gas vent that was

sacred to Zoroastrians for centuries, though this temple was actually built by 18th-century Indian Shiva devotees. They lived in the surrounding pentagonal caravanserai and performed extreme ascetic practices such as lying on hot coals or carrying unbearably heavy chains. Such eccentric behaviour is depicted by a number of mannequins in the museum section. But the temple's centrepiece is the flaming stone hearth with four stone side flues that also spit dragon breath. At least when the caretaker bothers to turn on the gas. The original natural vent has long been exhausted, so today the flame comes courtesy of Baku's main gas supply.

From Baku take the cruddy old *elektrichka*, marshrutka 84 from Nərimanov metro station or less direct marshrutka 231 from Qara Qarayev metro via the intriguing town of Əmircan. From Mərdəkan take marshrutka 77. All of the above stop near Suraxanı train station. From the south side of the station, walk southeast parallel to the rail tracks for three minutes, then curve right to find the Ateşgah's entrance just beyond. There are some intriguingly decrepit old oilfields nearby.

ABŞERON PENINSULA

Mərdəkan & Şüvəlan

Sprawling **Mərdəkan** sports two sturdy medieval **castle towers** (admission free; ☯ sporadic) hidden away in some vaguely interesting back streets. The pleasant but overpriced **Arboretum** (Mərdəkan Dendrarisi; http://dendrary.in-baku.com; foreigners/locals AZN4/AZN1; ☯ 8am-8pm) has a cactus garden, boating pool, minizoo and fine century-old **oil-boom villa**. Elsewhere, oil baron Zeyalabdin Tağiyev is buried beneath a splendid egg-shaped stone pavilion surrounded by unexplained heaps of architectural fragments. Right behind is **Pir Həsən**, where superstitious locals queue up to have bottles smashed over their heads. Honestly. It's considered a cure for nervousness of spirit. Many more pilgrims visit the **Ziyarətgah** in **Şüvəlan**, 4km further east. That's one of Azerbaijan's most impressive new mosques, replete with beautifully patterned Central Asian–style domes. Most Azeris believe that a wish made here will be granted. And when the wish comes true they return (in droves), offering donations in gratitude.

Marshrutka 36 from Baku's Vurğun Gardens runs to the Ziyarətgah via Mərdəkan, passing within walking distance of all of the sites, though none are easy to find unaided. Marshrutka 77 runs to Suraxanı.

Nardaran

The scene of religious rioting in 2002, Nardaran is the closest that Azerbaijan comes to having a centre of conservative Islam. Women are scarf-clad (if visible at all) and high-walled private houses bear religious slogans in a style reminiscent of workers' banners under communism. The town's spiritual heart is the awesome 1990s **Rehime Khanım Mosque**, built above the grave of the 7th Shiite Imam's sister. A two-minute walk beyond is a modest medieval **castle tower**. Marshrutka 89 from Baku's Qara Qarayev metro terminates at the mosque's gates.

Abşeron Beaches

In summer, fearless local swimmers ignore the peninsula's infamous pollution and crowd the grey-brown beaches of the northern Abşeron coast. The waters do often look temptingly turquoise and there are well-manicured sections of sand near **Mərdəkan** (marshrutka 341 from metro Neftçilər) and on the pay-beaches of **Amburan** (marshrutka 72 from metro Əzizbəyov). Good alternatives lie north of **Novxanı** (marshrutka 998 from metro

---

NEFT DAŞLARI

Built in 1949 Neft Daşları (Oily Rocks) is the world's first and only offshore 'town'. It's constructed entirely on stilts out in the Caspian with some 210km of roads, a cinema, a bakery and even a neat little Heydar Əliyev Park. High-rise Soviet tenement blocks accommodate the rotating population of around 2100 workers, of whom around 300 are women. Although potentially one of Azerbaijan's more intriguing tourist attractions, visiting Neft Daşları remains an invitation-only affair. Even with great contacts, an invitation can take months to arrange at the discretion of Socar, the national oil company. For invitees, access is by 15-minute helicopter hop from southern Artyom Island or six-hour ferry ride from central Baku.

Gənclik) where you'll find the new **AfHotel** (☎ 4483030; www.afhotel.az; s/d AZN100/150; 🔲 🔲), whose **Aquapark** (day-use for nonresidents AZN15; ☯ summer only) is a major complex of swimming pools and waterslides. Nearby are several sets of well-built en suite beach cottages such as **Ləman** (☎ 050 5217188; r AZN60; 🔲) whose prices halve in the low season, making an interesting budget alternative to staying in Baku in winter (if you don't mind an hour's commute).

Artyom Island & Abşeron National Park

If you're looking for a nightmare vision of leaky small-scale oil detritus and rusting old boats set against the contrasting opal brilliance of the Caspian, a classic vantage point is the north tip of Artyom Island. But it's an awfully long way to go for relatively little. Marshrutka 50 from Ulduz metro (AZN1, 80 minutes) terminates in depressing Pirallahı town, from which the nastiest area is 2km north. Police might question your motives for coming here.

The highly unexciting **Abşeron National Park** consists of a few ragged sand dunes and islands down a potholed lane at the Abşeron's windswept south tip. Don't bother.

Yanar Dağ

In the 13th century Marco Polo mentioned numerous natural gas flames spurting spontaneously from the Abşeron Peninsula. Most, as at Suraxanı, burned out when the drilling of oil wells reduced underground pressure. However, **Yanar Dağ** (Fire Mountain; admission free) lives on, making for one of the Abşeron's stranger sights. Locals claim that a natural gas vent on this modest hillock was accidentally ignited by a shepherd's cigarette back in the 1950s. A 10m-long wall of fire has been blazing away ever since. It's best viewed at dawn or dusk. There are plans to gentrify the site but for now the only 'facility' is a semiderelict concrete çayxana offering very pricey tea and jam (AZN8).

Mehdiabad-bound marshrutka 47 from Gənclik metro sometimes continues to Digəh. Yanar Dağ is around 1km beyond. Taxis from Baku want around AZN25 return.

BAKU TO QOBUSTAN

The most popular day trip from Baku takes visitors to the mud volcanoes and petroglyphs around Qobustan, 60km south of the capital (see Map p284). En route is a fascinating collage of beaches, oil workings, dazzling seascapes, spirit-crushing Soviet townships and intriguing semi-deserts plus a dust-billowing cement works thrown in for good measure. At Baku's southern limits lies an incredible 'forest' of 1930s nodding-donkey oil pumps. It has been nicknamed the **James Bond Oil Field** (Map p238) since featuring in the opening scenes of the movie *The World is Not Enough*, but hurry to see it before a long-overdue clean-up operation sanitises the whole area. The scene is best surveyed from near **Bibi Heybət Mosque** (Map p238), which was for centuries the region's holiest shrine. However, the original 13th-century building was demolished by the Soviets in 1934 and today's Ottoman-style structure dates from 1998.

Just beyond is **Şixov Beach** (Map p238), fascinating for photographing bathers gambolling on the 'sand' with a romantic backdrop of giant offshore oil rigs. There are hotels, restaurants and disco-beaches here should you wish to stay a while.

Qobustan

PETROGLYPHS

Behind depressing Qobustan town, barren rocky hill-crags rise from the semi-desert. But it was not always thus. Around 12,000 years ago the Caspian Sea level was some 80m higher. The Caspian foreshores were lush with vegetation and Stone Age hunter-gatherers settled in caves that were then just a short walk

from the waters. The remnants of these caves remain etched with around 6000 fascinating petroglyphs (simple stone engravings). Even if you have no particular interest in ancient doodles, Qobustan's eerie landscape and the hilltop views of oil-workings in the turquoise-blue Caspian are still fascinating.

The **Qobustan Petroglyph Reserve** (☎ 5444208; admission/camera/tour AZN3/2/6; ☒ 10.30am-4.30pm) is run by helpful English-speaking staff and it's well worth paying for a guided tour: deciphering or even spotting the petroglyphs can be pretty tough for the casual visitor. Common themes are livestock, wild animals and human figures, notably shamans. Especially notable is a spindly **reed boat** sailing towards the sunset. Comparing this with similar ancient etchings in Norway led controversial ethnologist Thor Heyerdahl to suggest that Scandinavians might have originated in what is now Azerbaijan.

Seek out the fascinating **tambourine stone**. This resonant rock was played like a primitive musical instrument accompanying a ritual chain-dance (*yallı*) that features in some petroglyphs and was performed to ensure a successful hunt.

The reserve's simple **museum section**, slated for eventual reconstruction, offers some interesting conjecture on daily cave life, setting the scene with mannequins eating and hunting. Tools and weapons found on the site are also displayed.

ROMAN GRAFFITI

Around 2km from the petroglyphs at the bottom of Böyük Dash Mountain, a fenced-in rock sports the easternmost Roman inscription ever discovered. It was chipped out by Julius Maximus, a centurion of the 12th Legion, probably on a reconnaissance mission from Roman Syria during the reign of Emperor Domitian (AD 51–96).

Guides know under which stone the key to the surrounding fence is hidden.

MUD VOLCANOES

On top of otherwise unremarkable Daşgil Hill, some 10km south of Qobustan are an astonishingly weird collection of baby **mud volcanoes** (*palcik vulkanlar*). Here a whole family of 'geologically flatulent' little conical mounds gurgle, ooze, spit and sometimes erupt with thick, cold, grey mud. It's more entertaining than it sounds – even when activity is very modest you get the eerie feeling that the volcanoes are alive. And normally the place is delightfully peaceful, if not completely deserted.

If driving, easiest access is from the Ələt junction, 15km south of Qobustan. Follow 'Şpal Zavodu' signs, but keep straight ahead after crossing the railway. Keep to this unpaved track for 3km then climb the hill to your right.

GETTING THERE & AWAY

Taxis from Baku want at least AZN40 return to see all of the above. Beware that they might not know the mud volcano site. Alternatively, take Ələt-bound bus 105 (80q, one hour) from opposite Baku's İdman Sarayı. Get off before the overpass bridge at the south end of Qobustan town. From here the petroglyphs site is 5km, signposted by a mock rock carving. Savvy local taxi drivers ask a steep AZN10 return to see the petroglyphs reserve and Roman graffiti site, or AZN20 including the mud volcanoes.

ŞIRVAN NATIONAL PARK

Around 100km south of Baku, this **park** (Map p284; Ələt-Salyan highway km33; admission incl guide foreigners/locals AZN4/2; 9am-6pm) is outwardly just a featureless flat plain but it provides Europe's last remaining natural habitat for wild Caucasian antelopes *(ceyran)*. To stand any chance of seeing these loveable creatures you'll need a vehicle. If you don't have your own 4WD it's possible to rent the park's bus (for petrol money) but making necessary arrangements is farcically awkward, as the park has no phone. Salyan- and Lənkəran-bound buses pass the park gates where there's a small reception hut.

NORTHERN AZERBAIJAN

Most of Azerbaijan's scenic highlights lie in the spectacular, snow-capped Caucasus mountains or their luxuriantly forested foothills. Some of these zones are accessible from the delightful Baku–Balakən road (see p267), others from the Quba-Qusar region, where Laza and Xınalıq are Azerbaijan's most magnificently set mountain villages. Both northern and northwestern Azerbaijan offer truly extraordinary contrasts with the semi-desert landscapes around Baku. However, unless

you're prepared to walk for a couple of days across high passes, there's no way to cross between the two.

BAKU TO QUBA

The region's real highlights start beyond Quba. Nonetheless there are some interesting diversions en route, best suited for those with a vehicle. At Giləzi, a newly asphalted side lane runs west towards the gently attractive woodland of the **Altı Agaç National Park** (foreigners/locals AZN4/2). It passes an eye-catching area nicknamed the **Candycane Mountains**, where vivid pink-and-white striped hills are full of little conical fossils.

North of Giləzi the coastal plain narrows. In past times a series of walls and fortresses would have controlled travel along the ancient trade route between Derbent (Dagestan, Russia) and Baku. Today sparse fortress remnants remain on dramatic, spiritually fascinating Beşbarmaq Dağ with a more sizeable castle ruin at Çirax Qala.

Beşbarmaq Dağ

The dull scenery north of Baku gets an unexpectedly abrupt and dramatic boost with the looming silhouette of 520m Beşbarmaq Dağ (Five Finger Mountain). This mystical peak brandishes a rocky fistful of phallic crags atop a super-steep grassy ridge top. It's well worth climbing to the summit, not just for the fabulous Caspian views, but also to observe first hand Azerbaijan's unique take on 'Islam'. Crowds of locals come here seeking good fortune, a child, or the answer to their problems using a mixture of prayer, sacrifice, chanting and very animist kissing of rocks. Everything comes in threes: take three small stones to the top, sip thrice from a cup of holy water, kiss the sacred rock three times then incant your wish…guess how many times. To assist, assorted white-capped holy men lurk in rocky nooks, their pitches marked by a samovar, a few blankets and some photogenically fluttering votive ribbons. Meanwhile a few old crones, snotty children and various hangers-on try to cadge money.

Climbing to the summit from the ridgetop parking area takes around 15 minutes via a wobbly set of metal staircases: start on the southwest side above some tea sheds. Reaching the car park requires a steep 10-minute drive leaving the Quba highway 2km north of a very obvious new stone mosque

AZERBAIJAN

NORTHERN & NORTHWESTERN AZERBAIJAN

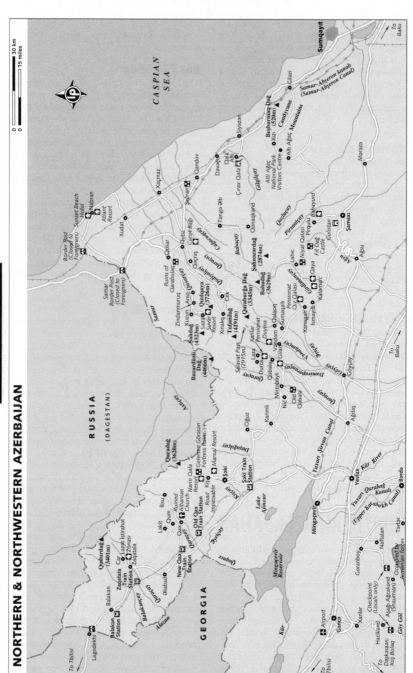

that's amid roadside stalls immediately below the peak. Most Baku–Quba buses make a refreshment stop beside the mosque but although you could walk up Beşbarmaq directly from this point it would take (at least) a very sweaty 90 minutes.

Çirax Qala
☎ 0115

Peeping out from a thickly wooded ridge high above Qala Altı (Under the Castle) sanatorium, this stone keep is very ruinous but nonetheless about the best preserved of Azerbaijan's ancient fortresses.

Originally built by the Sassanid Persians (5th century AD), the surviving tower dates from the 18th century when it was part of the southern defences of the khanate of Quba.

Visiting the castle is most interesting for the sweeping views towards the Caspian and for hikes in the pretty surroundings.

There are rough access roads to Qala Altı sanatorium from Dəvəçi (taxi AZN10/12 one way/return) and from Siyəzən with a bus (80q, 1¼ hours) leaving at noon, returning from Qala Altı at 5pm. A minibus leaves the sanatorium gate at 6.45am for Baku (AZN3, three hours) returning from Baku's Şamaxinka terminal around noon or whenever the driver feels like it.

There are several ways to reach the castle from the sanatorium gates. An unpaved rutted track passes the decaying concrete cube of **Qala Altı Hotel** (no phone; per person AZN4) after 800m, then divides twice. On both occasions take the right-hand fork and you should emerge at the top of a grassy clearing just 15 minutes' woodland stroll from the ruins. You can reach the clearing by Zhiguli (dry weather only, AZN2, 15 minutes) or by horse (sporadically available in summer if you ask around at the sanatorium gates).

Alternatively, on foot you can hike through the forest directly to the castle crag in about 40 minutes, starting opposite the Qala Altı Hotel. The path is fairly easy to spot but has two slightly dangerous slippery scramble sections.

Below the sanatorium are several summer restaurants. Some rent rooms and cottages, including **Zaur** (☎ 050 7197517; d AZN30) and smarter **Göyça** (☎ 050 4518841; d AZN30-40), are 1km beyond.

QUBA
☎ 0169 / pop 55,000

Famous for carpets and apple orchards, the low-key town of Quba sits on a cliff top overlooking the Qudiyalçay River. It was founded in the 18th century as the new capital of local potentate Fatali Khan but rapidly became a quiet provincial backwater once the khanate had been absorbed into the Russian Empire (1806). A fair scattering of modestly historic buildings remain from that period and today Quba's wooded hinterland is becoming a popular spot for Baku weekenders, thanks to its distant horizon of snow-topped mountains and a comparatively cool summer climate.

Information

Eltac Internet (☎ 50555; Qöbələ küç; per hr 40q; ☽ 9am-midnight)

International Bank of Azerbaijan (Fətəli Xan küç) Has an ATM.

Telephone office (☎ 50555; Fətəli Xan küç 59; ☽ 9am-1pm & 2-10pm) International calls 80q per minute.

Tourist Information Office (City office complex, Heydar Əliyev pr) Never seems to be open.

Sights

There's a little **History Museum** (☎ 52554; Ərdəbil küç 93; admission AZN1; ☽ 10am-1pm & 2-5pm Tue-Sat) but the main attraction in Quba is just wandering its orderly grid of quiet leafy streets and admiring the 19th-century Russian houses and distinctive mosques, notably the colourful **Hacı Cəfər Mosque** and the unique, octagonal **Cümə Mosque** with its distinctively pointy metallic dome. Notice also the decrepit century-old **Günbəzli hammam** with its big beehive dome.

Nizami Park is a pleasant tree-shaded retreat overlooking the broad gravel bed of the Qudiyalçay River. A long flight of steps lined with statues of Adonis-like Soviet youth leads down to the old bridge, which links Quba to the town of **Krasnaya Sloboda**, home to a unique Jewish community with two active **synagogues** (☎ 54519).

You can watch Quba's famous carpets being made at **Qadim Quba** (☎ 53270; qadimquba@ box.az; Heydar Əliyev pr 132; ☽ 10.30am-1pm & 2-6pm Mon-Sat), which also has a delightful boutique selling them along with handicrafts and *pax-lava* (alternating layers of chopped nuts and white, stringy, fried pastry, all saturated in a sickly sweet syrup).

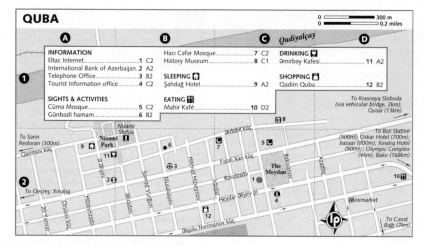

QUBA

0 -------- 300 m
0 -------- 0.2 miles

INFORMATION
Eltac Internet............................1 C2
International Bank of Azerbaijan.2 A2
Telephone Office........................3 B2
Tourist Information office..........4 C2

SIGHTS & ACTIVITIES
Cümə Mosque..........................5 C2
Günbazli hamam......................6 B2

Hacı Cəfər Mosque...................7 C2
History Museum........................8 C1

SLEEPING 🛏
Şahdağ Hotel...........................9 A2

EATING 🍴
Mahir Kafé..............................10 D2

DRINKING 🍷
Əmirbəy Kafesi.......................11 A2

SHOPPING 🛍
Qadim Quba............................12 B2

Sleeping

If nothing suits there are many bungalow resorts along the road to Qəçrəş and others around a little canyon at Təngə Əltı.

Şadağ Hotel (ə Əliyev küç; s/d AZN3/6) This Soviet-era establishment is the only central option. It could have style if it were renovated but for now it's a very basic crash pad with shared 'toilets' and a dribbling tap. If you're lucky.

Xınalıq Hotel (☎ 54445; s/d/tr/q AZN10/7/8/10) Although recently repainted this trader's guesthouse remains basic and dauntingly male-orientated. It's perched above the chaotic market area. The single room has a private bathroom; others share a squat toilet and two downstairs shower booths.

Oskar Hotel (☎ 51516; contact@cannatbagi.com; s/d AZN20/40; summer 🏊) Between the bus station and bazaar, this is not so much a hotel as a set of rooms above a pleasant kebab restaurant. They're cosy and new with en suite hot showers and fresh linen, though the whole place feels slightly jerry-built.

Olympic Complex (☎ 51517; www.gubaolympic.az; Baku Hwy; d/tr/ste AZN50/60/80; 🍴 🏊) The complex's bright airy new rooms are great value with good bathrooms, wood-effect floors and plentiful art prints. Rates include breakfast and use of the superb 50m-long indoor swimming pool. It's 3km east of the bazaar.

Cənət Bağı (Map p262; ☎ 51415; contact@cannatbagi.com; d/ste AZN70/160; summer 🏊) Neat, if less upmarket, than first impressions might suggest, this popular rural complex has two buildings in a woodland clearing 7km south of Quba. Rooms in the old building are slightly more worn but have bigger bathrooms. In the ostentatious three-storey new building, odd-numbered rooms overlook streamside picnic tables. There's an extensive restaurant (kebabs AZN3, beer AZN1.20) and (almost uniquely for Quba) some English is spoken.

Eating & Drinking

Mahir Kafé (Heydar Əliyev pr; snacks 10q-AZN1.50; 🕙 9am-11pm) A very plain place with just two sit-down tables, but serving perhaps the best *lavaş döner* (döner kebab in *lavaş* bread) in all of Azerbaijan (AZN1.20).

Sərin Restoran (Qarimov küç; mains AZN3-7; 🕙 10am-11pm) A selection of inside dining styles and an appealing summertime lawn area make Sərin the nicest place in town. There's no menu but prices are reasonable.

There are several cheap beer-and-tea places around the bazaar area, the Meydan and Nizami park. **Əmirbəy Kafesi** (Əlizadov küç) is typical. Nicer forest kebab places stretch for miles along the Qəçrəş road.

Getting There & Away

Quba's bus station is 2km east of the town centre. For Baku there are painfully rickety buses (AZN1.80, five hours) at 10am, 11.30am and 2pm while the more frequent marshrutkas (AZN3, four hours) and shared taxis (seat/vehicle AZN6/20) depart when full from outside. Marshrutkas/shared taxis cost 40q/AZN1 to Qusar (20 minutes).

Jeeps to Xınalıq depart when completely full from outside Hotel Xınalıq at the back of the bazaar. That's two blocks south, then one east from the bus station. If you get a fair price (AZN8) this is the cheapest way to reach Xınalıq, but the situation is chaotic and very confusing, especially if you don't speak local languages. It's wise to bring a Russian or Azeri-speaking friend to help you negotiate (see right).

Getting Around

By day, marshrutkas marked Otovaqzal–Poliklinika run up Heydar Əliyev pr from the bus station roundabout (20q) returning via Əliqulu Nərimanov küç.

XINALIQ

pop 800 (1700 in summer)

An undisputed highlight of all Azerbaijan, this fabled mountain village speaks directly to the soul. Its timeless stone houses are often wrapped in spooky clouds, giving it a haunted medieval feel.

Then, when the clouds lift, you realise that you're perched on a mountaintop with stunning 360-degree views of the Caucasus. Xınalıq's hardy shepherd folk have their own distinct language (Ketsh) and still live much of their lives on horseback. Nowhere in Azerbaijan offers a more fascinating glimpse of mountain life nor a better opportunity for inspirational hiking.

However, you should hurry to get here. A new road was built in 2006, tourists are starting to discover this gem and already some homes are starting to sprout corrugated metal roofs.

Apart from examining the one-room **museum** (admission 40q; ☙ on request) and gazing at the hypnotic views, Xınalıq's most popular tourist activity is hiking to **ateşgah**, a small ever-burning natural fire-vent. The walk takes about two hours (towards Laza then up a side valley) but finding the site without help is pretty much impossible.

Charming **Xeyraddin Gabbarov** (☎ 050 2259250; www.xinaliq.com) works in Quba but comes from Xınalıq, speaks OK English and for a relatively modest profit can tailor-make a homestay-tour or hiking holiday in Xınalıq.

Note that there are proposals to declare the whole Laza-Xınalıq area as the Şahdağ National Park. If this happens expect to pay an AZN4 entry fee to access the area.

HALT!

Since a new army/customs post was built across the valley from Xınalıq, some travellers have reported soldiers preventing hikers from exploring the nearby valleys including the route to Laza. To avoid problems ask your guide to forewarn the military post before you set off.

Hiking

A delightfully rewarding hike links Xınalıq to Laza (p266) in 10 to 12 hours. Two routes are possible, around the base of Mt Şahdağ or past the fire-vent and over a shoulder of dramatically crag-topped Qızılqaya. A local guide (around AZN30 per day) is particularly important for the latter, as fog can descend suddenly even on an apparently clear day, totally hiding the path. If you have luggage it's also a good idea to hire packhorses (AZN20 to AZN40). In Xınalıqi-Ketsh language *dzhim onongondeh pshii i hadmé ishkeléh Laza guisu* means 'where can I find a horse and guide to take me to Laza?'.

It's also possible and incredibly exhilarating to hike to Vəndam (p273; two days). This requires camping en route, as there are no villages in between. As with any hike, sheepdogs can be vicious.

Sleeping

As yet there's no hotel, but several families can offer informal homestays for around AZN10 to AZN20, including plenty of tea and *ktap* (freshly fried *lavaş*, filled with cheese and green herbs). Such a homestay is likely to be a highlight of the trip. Despite the biting night-time cold, houses are kept cosily warm, their ultrathick walls decorated with richly coloured carpets. Like everything here, finding a place is just a matter of asking around. If you turn up without a guide you'll need at least basic Russian or Azeri. Or try asking in Ketsh *'asir yedemé xinalig'r giyeh yetsindé'* (I would like to stay overnight in Xınalıq).

Getting There & Away

There is no bus to Xınalıq. Shared jeeps (AZN8 per person, 1½ hours) go sporadically from the chaotic bustle outside Hotel Xınalıq in Quba but ascertaining who is leaving when can be very confusing without an Azeri friend to help out. Turning up alone as a foreigner

AZERBAIJAN

can induce a feeding frenzy among the drivers, who will inevitably try to charge more than the going rate. Getting a fair price from a taxi is similarly difficult, with many drivers demanding a ludicrous AZN100 tactically appearing unaware of the road's recent renovation. **Xeyraddin** (www.xinaliq.com) can organise a transfer from Quba by Niva jeep for about AZN40. The route is very dramatic in itself so allow time for several photo stops at various canyons and passes en route.

QUSAR
☎ 0138 / pop 80,000

Pleasant if unremarkable Qusar is Azerbaijan's Lezgin capital. There's a **museum** and impressive new Turkish-style **mosque** but the **ruins of Qarabulaq** offer its only really intriguing sight. Don't expect medieval history. Qarabulaq was a 21st-century holiday retreat, designed with lots of brilliantly idiosyncratic Tolkein-esque twiddles, including concrete knights brandishing flame-throwing weapons. Then in 2005 authorities discovered that the location had been used as the lair for a brutal gang of kidnappers.

The resort was promptly closed down and now creepers are slowly overrunning its eclectic buildings. This adds further to the already bizarre atmosphere. By road, reaching the site requires a 10km loop from central Qusar. Without a car take a city marshrutka towards the trio of river-view restaurants at the western edge of town. Descend an obvious track to the long footbridge and walk the last 1.2km west.

There are a couple of less wacky but still functioning *istrahat zonası* (rural bungalow resort) here too, but most Westerners head straight on to Laza.

AROUND QUSAR
Laza (Qusarçay Laza)
☎ 0138 / pop 150

The soaring mountain valley surrounding Laza is one of the most stunning sights anywhere. Dramatic grass-clad slopes descend from noble Şahdağ (4243m) and craggy Qızılqaya (3726m).

A series of ribbon waterfalls drop over perilous cliff edges and carpets of wildflowers add to the vivid greens throughout late spring and summer. Tiny Laza village is diffuse and its banal houses lack the striking austerity of Xınalıq's dark stone architecture. However a

rocky pinnacle beside the rusty-roofed little mosque adds foreground for photos of the mind-blowing mountain panorama. And the one-day walk to Xınalıq (p265) is a highlight of any trip to Azerbaijan. Laza also makes a great base for climbing Azerbaijan's highest peak, Şahdağ. It's not technically difficult but does involve some ice walking and requires ropes and crampons.

Note: Laza is sometimes called Qusarçay Laza to differentiate it from Qebelinsky Laza (p273). In coming years its slow-paced shepherd life might change radically if, as is planned, a vast new **ski resort** is built 3km to the east along the road to Qusar.

SLEEPING & EATING

The **Azizov family** (☎ 57035) run the village shop and can offer well-kept if simple homestay rooms for around AZN10 to AZN15 per bed. There's a shared shower. **Mevlud Azizov** (☎ 050 6844374) speaks some English and acts as a guide (AZN35/50 per day for hiking/mountaineering).

Suvar Resort (☎ 53671, 57033; www.suvar.az; s/d/ste AZN60/100/150) Occupying a fabulous mountain pasture 2km west of the village, Suvar's bungalow rooms survey one of the finest panoramas in Azerbaijan. Its buildings incorporate rustic design features in well-appointed rooms with decent bathrooms and satellite TV. Prices increase during peak weekends and holidays. The delightful restaurant has stone fireplaces, wood-mosaics and big picture-windows to enjoy the views. Chefs from India can rustle up an amazing range of meals given some warning.

GETTING THERE & AWAY

Qusar–Laza currently takes 1½ bumpy hours by car. However, the road is being asphalted for the ski-resort project so transport details will change. For now, if a vehicle is leaving anyway, locals hitch a ride for AZN3/5 per person in a Zhiguli/Niva. Chartering costs at least AZN20, often double. Suvar charges AZN50 for pick-ups.

There's no bus to Laza (yet). A crushed-full bus to Kuzun (AZN1) departs Qusar at 4.30pm (returning at 7am next day). From Kuzun, Laza is an attractive two-hour hike away: first climb a fairly steep curl of tractor path (for around 20 minutes), then turn right onto the main Laza road. It's not overly taxing but there are a few ambiguous path-turnings and there's nobody to ask en route. Excepting the month of June, it's likely to get dark before you reach Laza so you'd be wise to carry a tent just in case.

Beware of sheepdogs and don't take the more direct Kuzun–Laza route along the riverbank without an experienced guide.

NABRAN

Azeris often recall summers of love in Nabran with a fondness that may lead you to expect a Soviet Ibiza. Don't get carried away. It certainly has the party vibe and people-watchers might find interest observing the tidal wave of Azeri holidaymakers at play in July and August. But with sand like topsoil, the beach is far from idyllic.

Sleeping

Over 30 resorts are extremely spread out along 20km of coast and into the woodlands behind. These range from ragged hut camps and sleazy Soviet sanatoria to po-faced gated complexes for the BMW-driving classes. Booking ahead is essential in summer but out of season you can shop around for real bargains. Unless you find a homestay/apartment in minuscule Nabran village you'll really need a vehicle.

Sunset Beach Hotel (☎ 25375; d AZN50-100, low season AZN30-40; ✿ ✿) Facing the sea, this is one of very few real hotels and is virtually unique in having a restaurant with an English-language menu. Thumping music makes the summer-only swimming pool less than relaxing.

Atlant (☎ 050 3754747; www.atlant-az.net; d Jun/Aug from AZN45/55; ✿ ✿) Set 1km back from the beach, this is Nabran's Butlins, a full-blown holiday camp with comfortably new if functional rooms, a vast range of activities and a big summer swimming pool complex into which someone has sailed a Spanish galleon. Pool use costs AZN6 for nonresidents.

NORTHWESTERN AZERBAIJAN

The spine of this truly charming region is the Balakən–Baku highway, a misnomer for what is mostly a quaint country lane traversing everything from desert to verdant forest. It offers by far the most interesting way to transit between Baku and Tbilisi. In most cases the attractions (timeless villages, ancient Albanian church-ruins and very ruined castle remnants) lie to the north of this road in the thickly wooded foothills of the high Caucasus Mountains. The glorious scenery gets particularly impressive between the towns of İsmayıllı and Şəki, especially in spring, when wildflowers and fields full of poppies add majestic splashes of colour to the woodland foreground. However, while the area is great for admiring the white-tops, if you really want to get among the highest peaks you'd do better to start from Quba (p263) or Qusar (opposite).

Note that by public transport it's easier to travel from west to east. That's because from any town there will be fairly regular Baku-bound marshrutkas, but coming the other way vehicles tend to be full on arrival at any intermediate town.

ŞAMAXI
☎ 0176 / pop 32,000

For centuries, Şamaxı (Shemakha) was one of (northern) Azerbaijan's most prominent cities, an important cultural and trading centre and the royal seat of the Shirvanshahs (9th to 18th centuries). Sadly, earthquakes, fire and invasions have left virtually nothing visible to remind the visitor of Şamaxı's past importance.

In the Soviet era the surrounding hills produced famous wines and cognacs but that industry was decimated by Gorbachev's anti-alcohol campaign and has never fully recovered. These days the town is best seen as a staging point for reaching Pirqulu rather than as a destination in itself.

Orientation & Information

The bus station commands a roundabout on the Baku highway, southeast of the town centre. From here Şirvani küç slopes uphill into town passing the Cümə Mosque, behind the usually closed tourist information booth on the left after 1km. After another kilometre the road starts to curve uphill much more sharply, reaching the centre after around 800m at a colourfully mosaic-muralled theatre. Straight ahead is Nərimanov küç leading towards Pirqulu; to the right Shahriyar küç passes within a block of the Hotel Şamaxı, an Internet Klub and the post office.

Sights

Apart from some historic **tomb towers** across the valley from the ring road, Şamaxı's only real sight is the big, sturdy **Cümə Mosque** (Şirvani küç). The original mosque on this site was supposedly the second oldest in the trans-Caucasus. Excavations of its 10th-century incarnation can be seen in the grounds where a little nodding-donkey pump has nothing to do with oil – it draws water for the con-gregation's ritual ablutions. Today's mosque building was erected in the 19th century, damaged during the civil unrest of 1918 and not restored until recent years. Nonetheless, the powerful, bare stone interior columns exude a feeling of great antiquity and the imam, dressed in fine white gown and mufti hat, is generally very happy for visitors to look around. Shoes should be removed, bags left with the guard and women are expected to cover their hair.

Sleeping

Hotel Şamaxı (per person AZN3-10) This very central, decomposing 10-storey tower block has rooms ranging from nasty to appallingly unkempt. Water comes in fill-it-yourself buckets and toilets haven't flushed in years. Fragments of the former parquet floor lie scattered like an unsolved jigsaw. But the charmingly friendly manager believes the whole place will be el-egantly redeveloped by 2009.

Şamaxı Motel (☎ 050 6822919; Ağsu road; tw from AZN10) Around 500m beyond the western end of the noisy bypass, this busy restaurant aimed at passing motorists and bus passengers has a very mixed bag of rooms at prices that seem to depend mostly on how much staff think you're prepared to pay. Some are full-facility affairs that are remarkably plush with din-ing room and balcony, others just a box with three beds.

Motel Savalan (☎ 055 2543035; Ağsu road; tw/ste AZN10/20) Similar but quieter to the next door Şamaxı Motel, the Savalan's upstairs rooms are somewhat rough with shared bathroom. However, the neatly tiled minisuites are clean and come with hot shower. Being hidden at the back they're somewhat shielded from traffic rumble.

Şamaxı Olympic Complex (☎ 51130; Baku Hwy; tw/ ste AZN50/100; 🏊) These neat new box cottages 400m east of the bus station offer very accept-able motel standard accommodation, and in summer (May to September) guests have free use of the excellent full-sized indoor swim-ming pool. No restaurant though.

Eating

Close to the Hotel Şamaxı there is a well-stocked Arzaq supermarket and several cheap cafés including **Kafe Delfin** (meals 80q-AZN4) which offers spit roast chicken, döner kebabs and various snack foods. There's better dining at the Motels Savalan and Şamaxı, or along the road to Pirqulu if you're prepared to drive. To find the **bazaar** (Rəsulzadə küç) walk towards Pirqulu from Şamaxı's theatre then take the third street to the left.

Getting There & Away

Marshrutkas (AZN3) and shared taxis (AZN4, two hours) to Baku depart from outside the main bus station all day long. Although through-services to Qəbələ, Şəki and Zaqatala pass regularly, they're often full on arrival, making westbound transport somewhat awkward.

AROUND ŞAMAXI

The main draw is relaxing at Pirqulu but with your own vehicle there are many minor curi-osities hidden in the sheepy hills, including a ruined old church at Mədrəsə, ancient *turbe* (tomb-towers) at Kələxana, and a mysteriously timeless atmosphere in old Sündlü village.

Gulistan Castle

Above Xinişli village, 2km west of Şamaxı's bazaar along Rəsulzadə küc, rises a distinc-tive hill, on top of which once stood **Gulistan Castle**, the 12th-century residence of the Shirvanshahs. Remnant stones are pretty minimal but views are sweeping.

Pirqulu

Pirqulu (Pi3rguli) is the kind of place where you'd expect to see the Brontë sisters taking an afternoon constitutional. It commands a windswept hilltop reminiscent of Yorkshire, and makes a decent base for winter sledding or short summer hikes. Pirqulu's one 'sight' is the extensive **Pirqulu Observatory Complex** (☎ 050 4855363; Müşviq; donation appreciated; 🕘 9pm on clear nights Jun-Aug). The biggest of the observatory's domes is an impressively large structure resembling a gigantic nose-less Dalek prototype. The complex was one of the Soviet Union's key space-research centres when it opened in 1966. Since the USSR's collapse, the place has become rather dilapidated, but its main telescope is still in good working condition. Staff speak no English and their attitude to visitors seems to vary unpredictably, from warm welcomes to general gruff rebuffs.

Sometimes you might be shown the collection of meteorites and, on clear summer evenings, there are often star-gazing demonstrations.

SLEEPING & EATING

There are nearly a dozen *istrahət zonası* in and around Pirqulu, most charging from AZN50 for a cottage.

Sometimes discounts are available outside the peak June to mid-September season. All have kebab-burning facilities.

ourpick Babayurd (☎ 050 3900728; d yurt AZN30) Uniquely here you can stay in delightful carpet-draped Uzbek yurt tents, each with twin beds and a tiny shower/squat toilet attached. There's an atmospheric wooden restaurant (kebabs AZN3) arranged in faintly wild-west style around a giant *ocakbaşi* (flued barbecue). The whole complex lies in a beautiful pear orchard. Turn off the Şamaxı–Pirqulu road towards Qizmeydan (just before the end of the asphalt). After 900m turn left then wind round behind the Şəki İstrahət Zonası for 400m.

Magic Life (☎ 050 5200156; d chalets low/high season AZN35/50) This oddly named place might sound like a hippy commune, but it is actually a comparatively modestly priced collection of wooden huts. Although not luxurious, all are equipped with toilet, hot water, TV and fridge. They're hidden in an overgrown thicket of plum and maple trees around 800m beyond the observatory. Animal rights activists might be tempted to rescue the caged wolf and bear that are on sorry display at the Pirqulu Restorani next door.

Fortuna (☎ 050 3715390; 1-/2-room chalets AZN50/60) The Fortuna's main advantage is that it's almost opposite the observatory entrance so it's easy to nip across for an evening's star-gazing. However, the pink-box chalets are small, rather characterless and a little worn, albeit with shower and toilet. They stretch along a ridge in rather regimented fashion towards a restaurant that has attractive views, pool tables and a disco on summer weekends.

Qoşabulaq (☎ 050 4233007; d AZN50) At least five comfortable cottage resorts are spread

over 2km along the Avarği road that turns west 600m north of the observatory. The most appealing of these is comfortable new Qoşabulaq, thanks to sweeping south-facing views from its open balconies. However, cottages are semidetached and share one hot water tank per pair of rooms. The side without the tank is considerably larger. You could take both for AZN100.

GETTING THERE & AWAY

In season, shared taxis run regularly from Şamaxı (AZN2, 40 minutes) but they're pretty infrequent after mid-September. They start outside **Sabir Market grocery** (Nərimanov küç), six blocks north of the theatre in Şamaxi. An 8am minibus (AZN1) and a bus bound for Damirçi via Pirqulu (between 1pm and 2pm) also depart from here.

To get back to Şamaxı, flag down vehicles outside the observatory gates.

One of the observatory workers is usually prepared to double as a taxi driver (AZN12 to Şamaxı) should nothing stop for a while.

İSMAYILLI

☎ 0178 / pop 16,000

The nondescript town of İsmayıllı offers tourists nothing particular to see or do, but serves as a useful transit point for exploring the magnificent mountain country that lies behind.

Almost everything that visitors are likely to need here is on the Şamaxı–Qəbələ road that bypasses the town along its northern edge. This road has three roundabouts. Shared taxis for Baku use the easternmost Çapanay roundabout facing Çaldas petrol. Buses run from here to Lahic (AZN1.40, 1½ hours) at 7am, 11am and 2pm. Some 800m beyond, the next roundabout is the departure point for Baku marshrutkas (AZN4, four hours).

Diagonally right, the road then leads 300m to a third roundabout overlooked by the run-down **Motel Talistan** (☎ 53632; per person from AZN6). The motel's tatty but survivable upstairs rooms share squat toilets and showers. Downstairs rooms (twins AZN20) have just-functioning private bathrooms, which aren't necessary a plus. It's still much better than İsmayıllı's other grim option, the war-torn **Niyal Hotel** (☎ 55109; Heydar Əliyev küç; per person AZN4), 2km south in the town centre.

Some 200m northwest of the Motel Talistan, across a canal, is a tiny internet kiosk-shop. Hidden directly behind that, the very simple but acceptable **Kafe Azerbaijan** (meals AZN2, beer 60q) has tree-shaded open-air tables. Westbound shared taxis and passing buses stop in front for transport towards Qəbələ.

AROUND İSMAYILLI
Qız Qalası
The idyllically situated **Restaurant & Pensionat Qız Qalası** (☎ 050 6136490; small/medium/large cottages AZN50/80/100) offers a delightful accommodation alternative to staying in İsmayıllı. Its bungalows are dotted tastefully through a wonderfully natural woodland, and most are very comfortable, though the cheapest versions are a big step down in quality, with very small bathrooms and are nearer to the throbbing generator.

If you can ford the river (impossible after rain), it's fun to scramble through the glorious mossy birch forests beyond. You could seek out the pitifully fragmentary ruins of the 11th-century **Qız Qalası** castle, though these are just a few waist-high chunks of white-stone wall hidden in the trees.

Taxis from İsmayıllı charge around AZN3 to the *pensionat*. If you can't find a ride back, stroll 4km south down the newly asphalted woodland lane following the Ahohçay River to Xanəgah village then wave down a passing vehicle to İsmayıllı (8km east) or Qəbələ (32km west).

Lahıc
☎ 0178 / pop 1800
With wonderful mountain hikes, horses to rent and a selection of homestays available, the quaint little coppersmith village of Lahıc is a superb place to sample traditional rural life.

And the experience is made richer, as several Lahıcı youths speak English, with more returning from Baku in summer (July to mid-September) to act as guides.

HISTORY
Older villagers speak a dialect that is nearer to Farsi than Azeri and claim that Lahıc is named for the Persian-Caspian town of Lahijun from which their ancestors supposedly emigrated a millennium ago, bringing with them their famous coppersmithing skills.

In its 19th-century heyday, Lahıc boasted around 200 craftsmen, and Lahıc carpets and metalwork fetched high prices in the bazaars of Baghdad. The population was around 15,000 until WWII, when the privations

of war led many to starve or flee across the mountains: the road wasn't built until the 1960s. During 2008 or 2009 the planned introduction of piped water in Lahıc will cause a great improvement in people's lives. However, it will mean the end to the photogenic sight of women filling their *guyum* (traditional copper water vessels) at the village's many springs.

ORIENTATION & INFORMATION
Lahıc starts where the road from İsmayıllı fords the Kişlərçay stream in front of the Cənnət Bağı Guest House. The road then snakes along a cliff top past the İsmayıllı bus stop (150m) and over a small stone bridge to the triangular central square marked by a war memorial (300m). From here the cobbled main street (Hüseynov küç) passes a series of coppersmith workshops before crossing the Lüloçay stream on another bridge after around 700m. The road then continues a similar distance on the far side through a less commercial part of town known as Aracit.

Incredibly, little Lahıc has what is probably Azerbaijan's best-functioning **tourist office** (☎ 77571; www.lahijtur.az; Nizami küç; ⏰ 10am–2pm & 3–7pm Jun–mid-Sep). It organises homestays, guides and horse rentals and sells basic maps (AZN1) and photo CDs (AZN2) to fund its existence. Out of season, the keen English-speaking director **Dadash Əliyev** (☎ 050 6777517) reverts to his role as school teacher, but can still offer assistance. To find the tourist office walk along the main street to the tiny **Internet Klub** (40 Hüseynov küç; per hr AZN1; ⏰ 9am–midnight) and turn right up the narrow alley beyond, climbing steps up to Nizami küç. Then turn right again.

SIGHTS & ACTIVITIES
Lahıc is particularly famous for its **coppersmiths**, whose workshops overflow into narrow, stone-paved Hüseynov küç. On the upper floors of the workshops you can sometimes still find carpet makers at work. As years go by the workshops are increasingly transforming themselves into tourist boutiques but they remain rustic, welcoming places, where craftsmen are happy to be watched and photographed engraving intricate patterns. High global copper prices and growing tourist savvy mean that copperware is not as inexpensive as it used to be, but there are still some relative bargains to be had if you shop around.

The quaint little one-room **Lahıc History Museum** (Nizami küç; donation expected; ☽ 9am-8pm) is housed in a former mosque next door to the tourist office. It displays a typical selection of traditional cooking and farming instruments, ancient weapons and pottery, plus painted portraits of local artists and writers, a disproportionate number for such a tiny place. The **village school** is also open to the curious during the summer, and it's better appointed than most others you're likely to see in Azerbaijan.

One of the joys of Lahıc is hiking up the steep wooded hillsides towards the bare mountaintop sheep meadows (*qaylağ*) where flocks graze in summer and views towards the snow-topped high Caucasus can be magnificent on a clear day. Of the region's (very) ruined fortresses, the most accessible is **Niyal Qalasi**, about 1½ hours' sweaty climb up the Kişcay valley. With a horse and guide you could make a two-day excursion to more impressive **Fit Dağ castle**. The tourist office can offer many more suggestions.

SLEEPING
In Lahıc & Aracit
Camping (for 2 people from AZN5) is possible in the lovely orchard surrounding Cənnət Bağı Guest House, including firewood. You can also pitch a tent in various other village gardens by discussion, or for free in the hills above.

One of the great attractions of Lahıc is sleeping in an archetypal **village home**, away from all car noise. But be aware that, as yet, only the Aracit area has piped water. Be prepared to use long-drop outside toilets and remember that water must be laboriously fetched from the nearest spring.

If a tout doesn't grab you first, it's easy to arrange homestays through the tourist office for AZN8 to AZN15 per bed, or AZN20 to AZN30 with meals.

Year-round options include the **Haciyev Family** (AZN10), whose very simple rooms include one with a colourful antique niche. **Ruslan** (☎ 050 6120553) speaks English and can arrange for you to meet local musicians, but he's only there in summer. Enter via the second garden to the left as you walk towards İsmayıllı from the main square along the cliff-top road.

The tourist officer, **Dadash Əliyev** (☎ 050 6777517; r AZN15) also offers rooms and his house has the luxury of running water.

Cənnət Bağı Guest House (Garden of Paradise; ☎ 77200, 050 5870140; per person AZN15) The charming Ismailov family's homestay is a large, attractive house set in orchards at the entrance to the village. Handily there's almost always an English-speaking Ismailov in residence, who can rustle up guides and horses at relatively short notice. There's no running water (yet) but costs include use of the private 320-year-old *hammam*, which is fun if a little dingy. Breakfast and other meals are available but not included. Double-check food costs, which some readers have found comparatively steep.

Haji Mohammad's Hotel (☎ 77494, 050 5546174; Aracit Sq; tw AZN20) The nearest Lahıc comes to a real hotel, this overgrown new house has a façade of frilly metalwork that doesn't entirely beautify the otherwise quaint Aracit Sq. Unfussy twin rooms lead off large shared sitting rooms and there are two indoor shared toilets and shower rooms. Birds swoop about inside and the place can feel spookily abandoned off-season, but it's certainly peaceful and a great deal.

Around Lahıc
If you want more creature comforts there are two more upmarket rural resorts. Both lie near Qaraqaya, about 6km off the Baku–İsmayıllı road towards Lahıc.

However, both seem a bit overpriced, neither offers the charm of staying in Lahıc itself and neither has air-con – potentially annoying in midsummer, given their lower altitude.

Kalamarc (☎ 050 7302408; chalets AZN80-90) Twelve relatively comfortable pink cottage units with pine interiors are set rather artificially around a grassy clearing with two tear-shaped pools (ornamental rather than swimmable).

Qaya (☎ 050 2158090; tw/ste/cottage AZN80/100/150) The area's only real hotel, Qaya is heavily into white: white marble corridors, whitewashed walls, plump white duvets, new white bathtubs. It's a new four-storey building commanding a lovely woodland clearing. Sadly, the potentially delightful views towards a craggy mountain ravine are wasted, as all the windows face the wrong way and there are no balconies.

EATING
A very simple **yeməkxana** (meals AZN1.50-3; ☽ 10.30am-3.30pm) and **çayxana** (tea 40q; ☽ 7.30am-7.30pm) sit side by side just beyond the main

square where there's also a discordantly modern glass-fronted grocery shop. A **bakery** (Hüseynov küç 75) sells fresh bread (40q).

Girdiman İstirahat Bağı (kebabs AZN2; ☺ variable) Near the school, halfway through the village, the Girdiman's garden has some super glimpses of mountains across the river and its large all-weather dining room stays open year-round.

Yeməkxana Niyal (meals AZN3-6; ☺ May-Oct) In the orchard of Cənnət Bağı, Yeməkxana Niyal serves unexotic kebab meals, salads and pickles at tables that are attractively dotted among the fruit and nut trees.

GETTING THERE & AWAY

Buses to İsmayıllı leave at 8.30am, 12.30pm and 4pm. The drive has some spectacular sections with perilous drops, geological wizardry and a couple of attractive villages en route. Consider paying a taxi at least one way, to allow photo stops (around AZN15 to or from İsmayıllı). Sometimes the road is rendered impassable by landslides but should become more reliable and faster if it's paved in 2008, as mooted.

A direct marshrutka from Lahıc to Baku (AZN6, four hours) departs around 8am from the central square. Ask the driver to save you a seat the night before.

QƏBƏLƏ
☎ 0160 / pop 14,000

Formerly called Qutqaşın, this bustling market town was renamed in 1991 to honour the region's most historic city, though the site of the original 'Old' Qəbələ was actually more than 20km further east (see opposite). Qəbələ town isn't a great attraction but there are attractive picnic spots and streamside restaurants 4km north. Many more appealing villages lie in the surrounding valleys from which you could hike into the high mountains.

Qəbələ's centre is the junction of Heydar Əliyev küç and Qutqaşınlı pr, a point unanimously known as Saat Yanı. That means 'beside the clock', though the clock tower for which it was named has since been replaced by a globe-on-a-stick monument. One block east is the colonnaded 19th-century **mosque** (Heydar Əliyev küç). Around 500m south is the new **Historical Museum** (Tarix Muzeyi; Qutqaşınlı pr; admission 40q; ☺ 10am-6pm Tue-Sun). It displays finds from Old Qəbələ but its most intriguing feature is the fake Stone Age–style swing gate through which one enters. Next door is a typically

grand, wordless **Heydar Əliyev Museum** (Qutqaşınli pr; admission free; ☺ 10am-6pm Tue-Sun).

Sleeping & Eating

Hotel Gilan (Map p262; ☎ 52801; Qutqaşınli pr; s AZN20, small/large ste AZN50/70; 🞣) At the southernmost edge of town, this modern, no-nonsense four-storey box has surprisingly attractive new rooms with great showers. The location, 5km from Saat Yanı, isn't especially handy, though it's only 20q/AZN2 away by shared/private taxi. The hotel food is lacklustre.

Hotel Qəbələ (☎ 52408; info@hotelqebele.com; 28 May küç 31; s/d/ste AZN40/60/80; 🞣) A block north of the mosque, the town's central hotel has been thoroughly renovated and is clean and comfortable. However, rooms lack the panache of Hotel Gilan and the en suite showers don't necessarily run hot. Staff are very obliging and some speak good English. Rear rooms face the mountains. Discounts are possible.

Xanlar Pensionat (Map p262; ☎ 51799; cottage r AZN40-100) Around 5km north of town in attractive mossy woodland off the Laza road, this renowned restaurant is the best of half a dozen miniresorts to offer peaceful rural accommodation. The cheapest cottages are divided into two units, each sleeping two with private shower and toilet and sporting an open-sided dining terrace close to the river. A vast new hotel complex is under construction just beyond.

There are several more hotel-restaurant complexes in Vəndam (opposite).

Getting There & Away

The **bus station** (avtovağzal; Qutqaşınli pr) is 2km south of Saat Yanı (20q by shared taxi). From here marshrutkas leave around twice hourly to Baku (AZN5, five hours) via İsmayıllı and Şamaxı. Buses run to Gəncə at 8am and 8.30am and to Şəki (AZN2, three hours) at 9am and noon.

Shared taxis to İsmayıllı leave sporadically from Saat Yanı. For Vəndam (60q, 20 minutes) they depart from a side lane one short block further east. For Baku, shared taxis start from outside Zərifə Park, 400m east along Heydar Əliyev küç.

AROUND QƏBƏLƏ

Vəndam

☎ 0160 / pop 6000

Around 12km east of Qəbələ, Vəndam is an oversized village around which are dotted a considerable number of comfortable rural getaway-resorts. By far the most appealing (if least accessible) is **Pensionat Duyma** (☎ 91600; tw/ste AZN70/90), a four-storey hotel with utterly lovely views at the trailhead into the high Caucasus. Rooms are neat and comfortable, with pine floors and surrealist paintings on the walls. Mineral water is provided in terracotta flagons. There's an extensive playground complex for kids, an attractive decorative lake and a pair of outdoor summer swimming pools should they ever decide to fill them. Receptionist Ramazan speaks English and might be able to arrange horses.

The resort is a bumpy 5km ride through Vəndam village from the İbragim petrol station where taxi sharks ask a whopping AZN5 for the ride.

HIKING

Vəndam is the easiest starting point for several superb (if somewhat arduous) hikes into the high mountains. The most exciting is a two-day trek that can take you all the way to Xınalıq (p265) across the 2915m **Salavat Pass**. Although shepherds consider this a stroll, you'd be advised to find an experienced guide and pack-horse before attempting it. Weather can rapidly turn nasty and in low visibility the narrow cliff-top paths can be very dangerous. Take plenty of food and a tent.

Drinking water is available at certain points en route, but without a guide you might miss the springs. It's typically easier to find guides in Xınalıq and to do this trek in reverse.

Laza (Qəbəlinsky Laza)

Clinging to the western side of Dəmiraparançay Valley, this photogenic little village offers an alternative to Vəndam as a finishing point for long-distance hikes from Xınalıq. However, you'll have to deal with a humourless army check post and the necessity to ford the mighty Dəmiraparançay – no easy task when the water is high. There's no formal accommodation in Laza and the degraded track from Qəbələ might require a 4WD (around AZN20).

Durca

Racked up a mountain-rimmed amphitheatre of crags, forests and mountain pastures, Durca is a delightful seasonal village where shepherd families spend their summers. It's easier to reach and less sensitive than Laza so more congenial for short day hikes up to the *yaylaq* (high shepherd pastures). The track from Qəbələ is pretty rough but passable by Lada Zhiguli (AZN10 return). Branch left off the Laza road where the asphalt ends.

Old Qəbələ

First mentioned in print in Pliny the Elder's *Natural History* (AD 77), Old Qəbələ was one of the foremost cities of Caucasian Albania, but after several batterings it was finally laid to waste by the Persian invader Nader Shah in the 18th century. It never recovered and the unguarded **site** (admission free) was only rediscovered in 1959.

There's little to see apart from the stumps of two massive brick gate towers at the southern perimeter.

Near the site's northwest entrance, the delightful **Qala Səlbir Kafesi** (☎ 050 3965246; kebabs AZN2) sits in pretty woodland beside a fishpond. The owner is keen to show the extraordinary collection of ancient coins he apparently found while nosing around the ancient site. Incredibly basic rooms are sometimes available at AZN5 per person, but they're a last resort with a tragicomic shared squat toilet outside.

Access is via a narrow lane that heads south for around 9km from the Qəbələ–Şəki road at Mirzəbəyli. There's no public transport but for around AZN20 taxis can take you between Qəbələ and **Oğuz** with side trips to Old Qəbələ and to **Nic**, with its three Albanian churches. Once in Oğuz you could visit a couple more ancient churches and

AZERBAIJAN

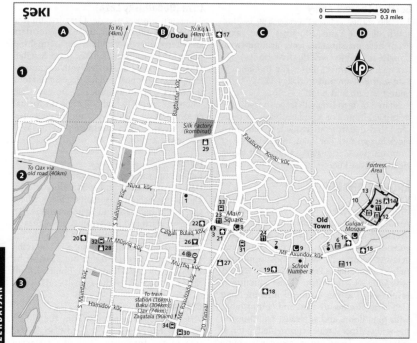

two latter-day synagogues before nipping on a bus to Şǝki (80q, 1¼ hours, six daily, last at 5pm).

ŞƏKI

☎ 0177 / pop 63,000

Snoozing amid green pillows of beautifully forested mountains, Şǝki (Sheki) is one of Azerbaijan's loveliest towns. It has a rich history and is one of the few places in the country where tourism can be described as even vaguely organised. Even so you probably won't see more than a handful of fellow travellers here, even during summer.

History

Historic Şǝki was originally higher up the valley around the site now occupied by Kiş (p278). That town was ruined by floods in 1716 but rebuilt by rebellious Khan Haci Çǝlǝbi, who set up a defiantly independent khanate there in the 1740s. He built a second fortress at Nukha (today's Şǝki). When the original Şǝki was obliterated a second time by more catastrophic floods and mudflows in 1772, Nukha became the new royal capital.

The khanate was ceded to Russia in 1805 but Nukha continued to flourish as a silk-weaving town and an important traders' junction where the caravan route between Baku and Tbilisi met the cross-mountain branch route to Derbent in Dagestan. At its peak there were five working caravanserais here. Nukha was renamed Şǝki in the 1960s.

Orientation & Information

The main square is an attractive park full of teahouses 1.6km north of the bus station. The old town starts around 1km further northeast up MF Axundov küç.

A steep cobbled lane continues 400m up from the Karavansaray to the fortress walls. Within lies the Xan Sarayı (Khan's Palace). Şǝki extends almost all the way to Kiş village, 6.5km north through the suburb of Dodu.

There are several currency exchanges, ATMs and slow Internet Klubs around the main square.

If you can find a space there's much better web-connection at **World.com** (per hr 40q; ☻ 9am-midnight) though demand is heavy. It's within the

Şəki Telkom building through a side entrance marked Abunə Şöbəsi. That's near the **post office** (Rəsulzadə küç; 8am-8pm), which contains a useful **telephone desk** (international calls per min 54q).

An excellent 80-page *Sheki Guidebook* exists, but is hard to find now that the prominently signed Tourist Office is dormant.

Sights

WITHIN THE FORTRESS WALLS

The sturdy stone perimeter wall of Haci Çələbi's Nukha Fortress today encloses an 18th-century palace, several museums and a decent café-restaurant, all set in patches of grass that are kept mown by flocks of sheep.

Xan Sarayı

Şəki's foremost 'sight' is the two-storey **Khan's Palace** (43666; admission/camera/video AZN0.80/2/4; 10am-6pm), which was finished in 1762. It's set in a walled rose garden behind two huge plane trees supposedly planted in 1530. The unique façade is decorated with silvered stalactite vaulting and geometric patterns in dark-blue, turquoise and ochre, magnificently setting off the intricate wood-framed, stained-glass windows known as şəbəkə.

Only one-room deep, the palace's interior is surprisingly petite. However, virtually every square inch is covered with extraordinarily colourful murals. These reach a climax in the central upstairs apartment which vividly features the heroic battles of Haci Çələbi, complete with requisite swords, guns and gory severed heads.

The 'lady's room' to its right (as you face the window) is contrastingly pastoral, decorated with flowers, birds and arabesques. The 'lord's room' to the left has more 'manly' scenes of hunting, mythical beasts, and lions ripping antelopes to pieces.

If you arrive after 6pm or want to see the façade in glorious golden sunset light, the guard might sneak you in for whatever he thinks you're prepared to pay.

Museums

Tour groups are marched dutifully around the **Raşidbey Əfəndiyev Historical-Regional Ethnography Museum** (43702; admission AZN1; 10am-7pm), whose name is more impressive than its exhibits: archaeological oddments, ethnographical artefacts and the usual emotive panels on WWII, Karabakh and the Xocalı massacre.

Across the road is a late-19th-century **Russian church** in unusual cylindrical form, built on the site of a 6th-century Caucasian Albanian original. It now hosts the limited **Museum of National Applied Art** (44901; admission AZN1; 10am-6pm) that displays fairly haphazard collections of Şəki crafts, including metalwork, pottery and embroidery. Hardly worth the money.

More interesting is the **Şəbəkə Workshop** (40932; admission free; 9am-7pm), where local craftsmen (no English) assemble traditional stained-glass windows, slotting together hundreds of hand-carved wooden pieces to create intricate wooden frames without metal fastenings. Small examples are sold as souvenirs.

OLD TOWN

Even if you don't stay here, peep inside the wonderful **Karavansaray** (Karvansara; MF Axundov küç 185), an historic caravanserai with a twin-level

AZERBAIJAN

arcade of sturdy arches enclosing a pretty central courtyard. Stride through the somewhat daunting wooden gateway door and if questioned say you're heading for the restaurant in the garden behind, a lovely place for a cuppa with a slice of Şəki's signature halva (pastry with nuts; opposite).

Immediately downhill is a second, even larger but partially ruined **19th-century caravanserai**. Beyond, Şəki's old town follows a canalised stream down towards the main square passing a pair of **19th-century mosques**, numerous halva shops and a **chess school** with interesting metal reliefs on its outer walls. An appealing maze of red-tiled roofs and shady lanes lies behind.

Did the ethnography museum (p275) make you wonder who the devil was Raşidbey Əfəndiyev? Probably not. But lovers of perversely off-beat attractions can nonetheless admire his spectacles, family portraits and the textbooks he penned at his loveably prosaic **house museum** (Ev muzeyi; ☎ 44258; Əzizbəyov küç; admission 40q; ᗯ 9am-1pm & 2-6pm).

The much more polished **Çingis Klubu** (☎ 47700; MF Axundov küç 91; admission 40q; ᗯ 10am-7pm) celebrates TV journalist and national hero Çingis Mustafayev who died in 1992 filming the Karabakh war. Photos of his life are complemented by a small but very well-chosen gallery of modern Azerbaijani paintings. A basement ethnographic room illustrates typical crafts. There's also an air-conditioned cinema, whose 6pm screenings usually have English subtitles. Most films shown are somewhat more intellectual than typical Azerbaijani movie-house offerings.

Sleeping

HOTELS

Şəki Hotel (☎ 42488; MF Axundov küç 17; d/ste AZN8/30) This nasty nine-storey Soviet wreck looms maliciously above the main square, its concrete almost crumbling as you watch. Just a handful of rooms are functioning off tragically gloomy old corridors. The dowdy suites have at least been renovated and actually have pretty presentable bathrooms. Meanwhile, embarrassed staff may entirely deny the existence of the four surviving 'standard' rooms. These are appallingly decrepit. Have some sedatives ready to deal with the sight of the stained, long-broken toilets. Only for impoverished masochists.

Pensionat Sahil (☎ 45491; S Mumtaz küç; d/q/ste AZN16/30/40; ⊠) The Sahil has simple but perfectly survivable rooms with private bathrooms. It's accessed through tall iron gates beyond the bazaar, then entered round the back through the good-value restaurant-garden. Seek out English-speaking administrator Elbruz Cabbarov.

ourpick Karavansaray Hotel (☎ 44814; reseil_karavan@mail.ru; MF Axundov küç 185; s/d/tr from AZN12/20/24) Staying in this superb converted caravanserai (see p275) is justification enough to visit Şəki. Rooms have wonderful arched brickwork ceilings and while they're certainly not luxurious, all have sitting areas, humorously basic bathrooms and Western loos. There's hot water in the showers but not in the sinks. Prices vary considerably between rooms for no apparent reason, so take the cheapest on offer. Book ahead, especially for single rooms, of which there are only two.

Panorama Inn (☎ 050 6229027; d/tr AZN35/45) Lots of traditional knick-knacks and local fabrics give the seven rooms here a great atmosphere, though all share toilets and the shower block is across the yard – annoying when snows are deep. There are lovely views from the garden-terrace, where breakfast (included) is taken on sunny summer mornings.

Makən Motel (☎ 60372; ME Rəsulzadə küç, Dodu; d AZN40-50) Above a popular local restaurant in Dodu are four new pine-interior rooms with little en suite bathrooms. They're clean but stylistically neutral, except for the carved wooden lamp-holders. Take northbound marshrutka 8.

ourpick Şəki Saray Hotel (☎ 48181; www.shekisaray.az; ME Rəsulzadə küç; d/ste AZN60/200; ⊠) Impeccably chosen neo-oriental touches make this brand-new hotel the most stylish anywhere in provincial Azerbaijan. Staff speak English, standards are tip-top, yet prices are very fair and fall 20% in winter. Thoroughly recommended.

The new Gagarin Hotel and fanciful castle-style Nagorny Resort were under construction in the old town area when we visited. There are several more alternatives around Kiş.

HOMESTAYS

Şəki has a great B&B homestay programme though unfortunately the organiser, **Farhad Azizov** (☎ 050 6126564), doesn't speak English. Call him (in Russian or Azeri) giving your mobile telephone number and explaining where you are (ideally somewhere easily identifiable like the Karavansaray). Within around 20 minutes a taxi should arrive to take you to the chosen house. Give the taxi AZN1, then pay AZN10 per night to the homestay host. Most homestays are very central and delightfully friendly. Breakfast is included but don't expect any spoken English.

Alternatively, homestays can be arranged by English-proficient **İlgar Ağayev** (☎ 055 6238295; ilqaragayev77@yahoo.com) for AZN12. İlgar can also act as an unofficial freelance guide.

Eating
RESTAURANTS
There are numerous very cheap but uninspiring eateries around Təzə Bazaar. Several better restaurants proudly tout their *aş* (fruity *plov*) and piti (two-part stew) but in fact you'll usually need to preorder those dishes.

Çələbi Xan Restoran (main square; mains AZN1-3.50) The interior pine décor is eccentric enough to make you feel you're dining in a cuckoo clock. In summer there's lots of space amid the trees outside and for just AZN1 you can fill up on a hearty borscht and basket of bread.

Şahin Kafesi (mains AZN2-4) Within the fortress walls the café interior is entirely uninspiring but the outside dining booths are quaintly draped in living ivy and the food is way better than you might anticipate. The particularly outstanding vine-leaf mini dolma (AZN2) has a minty tang and arrives in a clay pot.

Şəbəkə Restaurant (Şəki Saray Hotel; mains AZN3-9) If you're craving Western food, this suave jazz-toned hotel-restaurant offers professionally presented dishes at prices that seem expensive in Şəki but would be cheap as chips in Baku. Our penne in pesto sauce (AZN3.20) was perfectly al dente if lacking in pizzazz.

The Karavansaray Hotel (opposite) has two restaurants (mains AZN3 to AZN10, tea AZN1) with a reasonable selection of Azeri favourites. In summer you'll usually dine beneath the sturdy, wooden pavilions in the attractive rose garden.

In winter the catering moves indoors to an atmospheric warren of vaulted chambers, with musicians occasionally cropping up to serenade tour groups.

QUICK EATS
Şəki is famous for its confectionery. Shops all around town flog lurid *nöğul* (sugar-coated beans) and much more palatable *mindal* (hazelnuts in a crisp caramelly coating). But by far the best known offering is Şəki halva – really a misnomer for a kind of *paxlava*.

Drinking
Space Kafe (MF Axundov küç; beer 60q; 🕑 7am-11pm) If you're staying in the Karavansaray Hotel but want to nip out quickly to experience something more 'real', try this little cavern bar in the ninth arched niche to the right of the hotel entrance. Unadorned except for photoposters of waving Əliyevs, the only options are *çay* (tea, 20q) or NZS beer (60q) plus *noxut* (boiled chickpeas) as a bar snack.

Çempion Bar (Xırdalan beer AZN1; 🕑 9am-11pm) This relatively quaint one-room cellar-bar is air-conditioned and comparatively comfortable. It's easy to miss down a narrow stairway beside a barber's shop on 'Tae Kwon Do Alley'.

Buta Bar (Şəki Saray Hotel; beers from AZN2) This chic modern bar is by far the town's most stylish and serves the best coffee in Şəki.

Old Sheki Teahouse (Karavansaray Hotel; 🕑 unpredictable) Fabulously atmospheric, but only serving tea by the samovar accompanied by jams, fruit and confectionery (costing a minimum of AZN6). If you just want a cuppa, head for the Karavansary's garden restaurant (summer only).

Shopping
The expansive Təzə Bazaar sells pottery, metalwork and carpets, as well as masses of fresh fruit, vegetables, meat and cheese. Saffron is a bargain at just 50q a pouch. Get there by southbound minibus 11, 8 or 5.

AZERBAIJAN

ŞƏKI BUSES

Destination	Duration (hr)	Cost	Departures
Balakən	3	AZN2.15	10.10am, 2pm
Qəbələ	2½	AZN2	6.50am, 2pm
Gəncə	3	AZN2.50	8am, 8.30am, 1.30pm
Oğuz	1¼	80q	7.20am, 10.30am, 11.40am, 1.20pm, 3pm, 4pm
Qax	2¼	AZN1.80	7.40am, 10.30am, 1.40pm, 4.10pm
Zaqatala	2½	AZN2	7am, 9am, 11am, 11.40am, 3pm, 4.30pm

Şəki still has a working silk factory *(kombinat)* 50m west of upper Rəsulzadə küç. It doesn't allow tourist visits but opposite the entrance its store, **İpek Magazin** (☎ 42982; ☒ 9am-6pm), sells attractively simple silk scarves from AZN8.

Getting There & Away

There are several useful services from the **bus station** (☎ 44617; Rəsulzadə küç). For Baku via İsmayıllı and Şamaxı, marshrutkas (AZN6, seven hours) depart approximately hourly between 6.30am and 5pm or later, supplemented by big buses around midnight. A shared taxi costs AZN12 per person. Şəki train station is a whopping 17km south of town. A nightly train to Baku departs around 10pm but you can't always count on getting a ticket for same-day departure.

Getting Around

Şəki sprawls over a very large area but there's a usefully extensive network of marshrutkas. The flat fare is 20q.

Bus 22 shuttles past the bus station, passes the southeast corner of the main square and rolls up to the Karavansaray and fortress area. However, it's fairly rare and from the bus station it's best to cross Rəsulzadə küç, turn right then walk one block north to the corner of Hämidov küç. From here frequent marshrutkas 8 and 11 (both starting at Tazə Bazaar) turn left and head for the central square. The 11 continues to the Karavansaray and passes near the Xan Sarayı. The 8 goes on past the Silk Factory and terminates at the Makən Motel in Dodu.

From the train station to town, a single marshrutka (60q) meets incoming trains but fills fast. Taxis cost AZN3. Alternatively, walk 700m east and flag down passing northbound transport from the AzPetrol junction.

AROUND ŞƏKI

Kiş

☎ 0177 / pop 2300

The brilliantly renovated round-towered **Albanian church** (Alban Məbadi; ☎ 98833; foreigner/local/camera/video 80q/40q/AZN2/AZN4; ☒ 9am-8pm Tue-Sun) in Kiş village has been lovingly converted into a very well-presented trilingual museum. It's the best place anywhere to learn about mysterious Caucasian Albania, the Christian nation that once covered most of northern Azerbaijan. In fact the church site goes back well beyond the Christian era and glass-covered grave excavations allow visitors to peer down on the excavated bones of possibly Bronze Age skeletons.

In the delightful cobbled streets around the church you'll find kids playing, old men sporting flat caps, and women fetching water in traditional *guyum*. There are some charming walks up the river valley towards the **Gelersen Görəsən Fortress Ruins**, though surrounding areas are being steadily invaded by new bungalow resorts for vacationing Bakuvians, such as comfortable **Narin Qala İstrahat Zonası** (Map p262; ☎ 45300; pine cottages AZN60-120).

For something much cosier, do a village homestay. Tucked away in orchard gardens just three doors from Kiş church is the delightful **Ilhama's Homestay** (☎ 98417; bed-only/with food AZN5/10). The well-maintained shower and toilet are outside across the lovely orchard garden. Ilhama speaks some English.

Overcrowded day-time marshrutkas 15 and 23 run a few times hourly from Şəki's Tazə Bazaar (20q, 20 minutes).

To find the church get off near the start of the village and walk 800m, looping round and following the signs.

QAX

☎ 0144 / pop 12,000

Most useful as the gateway to İlisu 15km beyond, this pleasant but rather forgotten town is famous for its bottled mineral water and its partly Georgian-speaking population. Travellers are a rarity, with Şəki–Zaqatala buses bypassing the place altogether. The natives are friendly but expect to be stared at.

Qax town has three historic churches, the most celebrated of which is a **ruined Albanian church** perched above the dilapidated A20 road 3km south of town. This road is marked on maps as a direct route to Şəki but is usually impassable further east due to broken bridges.

Friendly and good value, the simple little **Hotel Qax** (Nərimanov küç; per person AZN4) is 10 minutes' walk northeast from the tiny little bus station.

Cranky minibuses to Zaqatala (80q, 1¼ hours) depart roughly hourly. Four daily buses run to Şəki (AZN1.80, two hours) looping past Qax's new train station.

If arriving by train don't get off prematurely at the very isolated old train station 20km further east.

AROUND QAX

Near Qax you'll find the remains of 6th-century Albanian Churches in **Qum** village and in the hills above **Ləkit** but the most popular excursion is to İlisu.

İlisu

☎ 0144 / pop 3400

The small, stone-built village of İlisu is set in the beautiful Qaraçay Valley, nicknamed Qax's 'mini-Switzerland'. Amazingly, it was once the capital of a short-lived 18th-century sultanate. Two modest **castle tower ruins** bear testament and there's an unusual **mosque**. The village is a fascinating place to wander and makes a great base for hikes towards the nearby mountains and waterfalls of the **İlisu Nature Reserve**. Don't go too far, however, as the reserve is a closed zone and the peaks behind form the sensitive Russian border.

Clustered around a 17th-century bridge 3km south of İlisu village are three bungalow resorts, including the cheap but ropey **Ulu Körpu** (☎ 54140; d/tr AZN20/30) and the shamelessly overpriced **Green Park** (Yaşil Park; ☎ 54575; cottage US$150-250; 🍴). Better located and better value is the new **Uludağ İstirahat Mərkəzi** (☎ 93425; per person AZN25; 🍴) at the village's northernmost end. Rooms 35 and 36 have fabulous balcony views.

Minibuses from Qax (50q, 20 minutes) leave at 7.30am, 10.30am, noon, 2pm and 5pm.

ZAQATALA

☎ 0174 / pop 26,000

Azerbaijan's hazelnut capital has a lovely location at the confluence of wide mountain rivers descending steeply from the high Caucasus mountains. It's a pleasantly presented place, with an attractive new **mosque**, a small **Historical Museum** (30 Heydar Əliyev Pr; ⏰ 9am-1pm & 2-6pm) and a pretty little **old town square** featuring some **700-year-old çinar trees**. Hidden close by is the maudlin ruin of a once-fine **Russian Church**. Directly above, Zaqatala's **Russian fortress** (military use, no entry) was built in 1830 and guarded against attacks from the Dagestan-based guerrilla army of Imam Shamil. In more recent times, the fortress imprisoned sailors from the battleship *Potëmkin*, whose famous mutiny at Odessa in 1905 foreshadowed the Russian revolution.

The best web connection is in the rear of the **Hotel Zaqatala** (per hr 60q; ⏰ 9.30am-midnight). **Xalq Bank** (Nizami küç) has an ATM. So does the **IBA** (104 Heydar Əliyev pr), which also changes money.

Sleeping

Hotel Zaqatala (☎ 55709; Heydar Əliyev Pr 92; dm/tw/ste AZN5/15/30) Despite rather rucked corridor carpets, standards are perfectly acceptable in this partly renovated old Soviet hotel. Even the six-bed dorm (men only) has a private bathroom. TV costs AZN5 extra. Choose even-numbered rooms to reduce road noise. Upstairs 'luxe' rooms are planned.

SMU-2 Motel (Göyça; ☎ 52142; tw with private/shared bathroom from AZN14/10; 🍴) This sleepy place has better rooms than you'd expect from the simple exterior and those with bathrooms also have decent air-con. It's hidden behind the Tala roundabout, 1.5km east of the bus station, across the river.

Motel Görüş (☎ 050 3225289; tw & d AZN12) Across the bus station forecourt is a decent, unpretentious restaurant offering three handy if basic rooms. These share a clean bathroom with hot shower, though some of the tiling is broken.

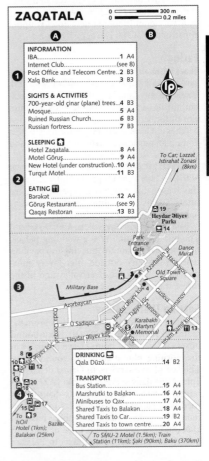

Owner Muxtar is charming but doesn't speak English. A reputedly better motel within the bus station building is usually locked; finding the key-keeper is hard and getting locked out would be a worry.

Turqut Motel (☎ 56229; Imam Şamil küç; tw with private/shared bathroom from AZN30/15) Trios of cheaper non-air-con rooms share one good bathroom, while nicer AZN30 rooms have air-con and tiny new en suite bathrooms. Rooms at AZN50 are bigger but not really better.

IsOil Hotel (☎ 56959; Faiq Əmirov pr 1; ste AZN30-100; 🖳) For now this is Zaqatala's top option and it's relatively stylish (by rural Azeri standards). All rooms come with air-con, sitting area and bathroom. Most have a fridge. Price relates to size, not quality, so the cheapest rooms are a comparative bargain. It's 1km west of the bus station beside the Balakən road.

A very grand-looking new hotel is under construction at 100 Heydar Əliyev pr.

Eating

Qaqaş Restoran (☎ 04427 40626, 055 7445920; Imam Şamil küç; kebabs AZN2, fish AZN2, herb-infused tea AZN1, draught beer 60q) Zaqatala's most intriguing restaurant has a façade of bottle-ends, an interior of timber rooms and a series of wooden perches out back as dining platforms. Up-beat Ukrainian music adds to the reliable food and cheap beer. Recommended.

Bərəkət (☎ 04427 40693; Heydar Əliyev küç 161; meals AZN2-4; 🕙 10am-11pm) Opposite Hotel Zaqatala this reasonably neat yet inexpensive eatery offers Turkish specialities, including fresh-baked *pide* and *lahmajun* (pizzas).

Qala Düzü (Heydar Əliyev Park; tea AZN1; 🕙 summer) The big main building is a wedding palace, not a regular restaurant, but cliff-top pavilion seats in the park outside offer lovely summer views across the river valley and of the forested mountains beyond.

Getting There & Away

Zaqatala's airfield is being upgraded. From the main **bus station** (☎ 050 5028121), Baku-bound buses (AZN7, eight hours) leave regularly in the morning, plus at 2pm and around 11pm. The last of five services to Gəncə departs at 3pm. Nine daily services to Şəki (AZN2, 2½ hours) bypass Qax as the Qax–Şəki direct road is impassable. Marshrutkas to Balakən (60q, 30 minutes) and little bubble-buses to Qax (80q, 1¼ hours) leave once or twice an hour from outside. Shared taxis to Balakən

---

(AZN2, evenings) and into central Zaqatala (20q) depart from across the roundabout.

An overnight train to Baku departs around 8.30pm from the station some 8km southeast of town.

AROUND ZAQATALA

Car

Lost in blossoms and greenery, this is a chocolate-box village of picturesque houses tucked behind mossy dry-stone walls in abundant orchards of chestnut and walnut. The hills above make for delightful hiking, where the thick deciduous forests give way to open, grassy ridges at around 1800m. Amid 3000m-plus peaks beyond, the remote **Zaqatala Nature Reserve** is home to brown bear, wild boar and the endangered Caucasian *tur* (a huge mountain goat).

Near the base of the village, **Ləzzət İstirahət Zonası** (Map p262; ☎ 54455, 050 3834573; s/d cottage AZN30/45) offers 16 stone-and-wattle cottages with old-tiled roofs and functional bathrooms. These are around a grassy clearing focused on a gaudy statue of giant mountain goat. Excellent Georgian, Azeri and Dagestani food is available and the eccentric owner styles himself as the 'King of Zaqatala'. Parking costs 40q.

Shared taxis (50q, 10 minutes) shuttle occasionally up to Car from beside Heydar Əliyev Park in Zaqatala.

BALAKƏN

☎ 0119 / pop 10,000

If you arrive from Georgia via Lagodekhi, then sleepy Balakən will be the first Azeri town you'll see. The town's commercial centre is around the bazaar. However, the town's only sight, a fine 19th-century **mosque**, is 1km further west, two blocks south of the prominent Heydar Bağı gardens.

The imam generally allows visitors to climb the mosque's unique brick **minaret** for a fine view over the town.

If you inexplicably want to spend the night in Balakən, there's a big new hotel under construction, 300m north of the bazaar. Meanwhile, the neat little **AzPetrol Motel** (☎ 52401; Zaqatala rd; dm/tw/d AZN7/20/24; 🏊), 2km east of the bazaar area, is way better than run-down Soviet-era **Balakən Hotel** (☎ 53589; dm/tw from AZN8/16) opposite the mosque. The latter's lobby might be attractively renovated but the stomach-churning en suite bathrooms belong in a horror film.

Getting There & Away

Shared taxis to the Georgian border (AZN1 per seat) depart from MMOil Petrol station on the main roundabout, 200m north of the bazaar. Ponderously slow marshrutkas to Zaqatala (60q, 30 minutes) leave from a small side road off Heydar Əliyev küç, two long blocks west of there. The bus station is 2km east of the main roundabout with a service to Baku (AZN7.20 to AZN8, 8½ hours) at 8.30am and several more between 10pm and midnight. There are also buses to Şəki (AZN2.15, three hours) at 8.20am and to Gəncə (AZN4.10) at 9.30am.

From the train station, 6km out of town, a taxi costs AZN2 to the bazaar, or AZN5 direct to the Georgian border. To Baku the train departs at 7.40pm.

CENTRAL AZERBAIJAN

Azerbaijan's monotonous central plains consist of drearily flat steppe, semi-desert and salt marsh. The scenery gets much more interesting in the beautiful Lesser Caucasus mountains, southwest of Azerbaijan's second city Gəncə, where the originally German village of Xanlar is a minor highlight. However,

---

HOW MUCH?

It's your first day in Azerbaijan. In beginner's Russian you check the taxi price. The driver quotes 'Two' and you agree. But when you later hand him AZN2 he starts shouting and demanding double the fare. This is not a scam. All across the country many people still think in 'Shirvan' (see Money, p297). And two Shirvan is AZN4. So always double-check whether prices quoted are in Manats or Shirvan.

---

the finest areas beyond are in (or sensitively close to) Armenian-occupied Karabakh. The occupation renders huge swathes of central Azerbaijan inaccessible from the rest of the country, including the ancient cultural centre of Şuşa. The ceasefire line is mined and the only access to Nagorno-Karabakh is through Armenia, a trip that's considered illegal trespass under Azerbaijani law. Refugees remain a big political issue and police are often suspicious of foreigners snooping around anywhere much south of the M27 Yevlax–Tbilisi highway.

GƏNCƏ

☎ 022 / pop 300,000

Despite a certain Soviet grandeur, the main touristic reason to come to Azerbaijan's pleasant second city is as a staging post for Xanlar and Göy Göl. Today Gəncə lags very considerably behind the capital in almost all senses. Yet, as it self-indulgently celebrated in 2006, the city has 25 centuries of history behind it and was formerly a much more important cultural centre than Baku.

Most proudly it was home to the national bard Nizami Gəncəvi (1141–1209). However it was levelled by earthquakes and razed by the Mongols in 1231. It rebounded somewhat as capital of one of Azerbaijan's many independent khanates in the late 18th century, before falling into the Russian orbit from 1804. Thereafter, the whole city shifted its centre of gravity to coalesce around the Russian fortress-town of Elizavetpol. From a building that is now the city's agricultural institute, the Azerbaijan Democratic Republic was declared in 1918 and Gəncə served for a few months as the short-lived republic's first capital, until Baku was recaptured from the Bolsheviks.

Information

Several moneychangers north of the Univermaq department store open late.

Internet Klub (Cavadxan küç; per hr 40q) Variable-speed internet.

Kapital Bank (Cavadxan küç) One of several handy ATMs.

MediClub (☎ 569911; www.mediclub.az; Abbaszadə küç 5) Medical help.

Sights

The vast, central Heydar Əliyev (former Lenin) Sq is lined by powerful Stalinist architecture, notably the arcade-fronted **City Hall** and the grand **Hotel Gəncə**. Towards the square's southern

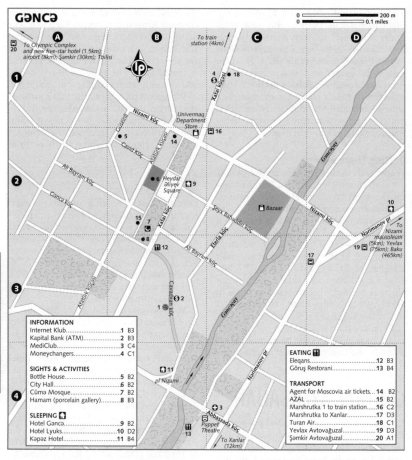

GƏNCƏ

0   200 m
0   0.1 miles

To Olympic Complex
and new five-star hotel (1.5km);
airport (8km); Şəmkir (30km); Tbilisi

To train
station (4km)

Nizami küç

Univermaq
Department
Store

Cavid Küç

Ali Bayram küç

Gəncə küç

Heydər
Əliyev
Square

Şeyx Bahəddin küç

Bazaar

Etefa küç

Ali Bayram küç

Cavadxan küç

pl Nizami

Abbaszadə küç

To Xanlar
(12km)

Puppet
Theatre

Atatürk küçəsi

Xətai küçəsi

Gəncəçay

Nizami küç

Nərimanov pr
To
Nizami
Mausoleum
(5km); Yevlax
(75km); Baku
(465km)

Nərimanov pr

INFORMATION	
Internet Klub	1 B3
Kapital Bank (ATM)	2 B3
MediClub	3 C4
Moneychangers	4 C1

SIGHTS & ACTIVITIES	
Bottle House	5 B2
City Hall	6 B2
Cüma Mosque	7 B2
Hamam (porcelain gallery)	8 B3

SLEEPING	
Hotel Gəncə	9 B2
Hotel Lyuks	10 D2
Kəpəz Hotel	11 B4

EATING	
Eleqans	12 B3
Görüş Restorani	13 B4

TRANSPORT	
Agent for Moscovia air tickets	14 B2
AZAL	15 B2
Marshrutka 1 to train station	16 C2
Marshrutka to Xanlar	17 D3
Turan Air	18 C1
Yevlax Avtovağuzal	19 D3
Şəmkir Avtovağuzal	20 A1

end the old **hammam** now hosts a small, rather
tacky **porcelain gallery** (☎ 565547; admission 20q;
⏱ 5-9pm) near the twin-minareted 1620 **Cüma
Mosque**.

From here you could stroll **Cavadxan küç**,
the city centre's almost-quaint pedestrian
lane, or explore some appealing patches of
wooded parkland that twinkle at night with
(male-dominated) *çayxanas*.

On a quiet residential street, the quirky, ivy-
choked **Bottle House** (Guseinli küç) is a building-
cum-artwork created by İbragim Caffarov
using beer, champagne and water bottles.

East of town is the 1991 **Nizami Mausoleum**
(Baku Hwy; admission free), a space shuttle–shaped
tomb-tower flanked by a series of inspired
sculptures depicting scenes from Nizami's

works. A vast aluminium smelter forms an
incongruous backdrop.

Sleeping

Kəpəz Hotel (☎ 566013; Abbaszadə küç; price negotiable)
Staff assume that anyone who's crazy enough to
check in to this monstrous hulk of decomposing
concrete must also be mad enough to pay whatever they're asked. The ragged room we saw was
barely worth AZN5, certainly not the AZN20
demanded. Don't count on hot water. Only the
6th to 8th floors function and even here *dezhur-
nayas* (floor managers) cackle at guests rather
than helping. Bizarrely lifts work up only!

Hotel Lyuks (☎ 574652; Nərimanov pr 42; d AZN40-
60, ste AZN80-100; ❄) Presentable if fairly bland
modern rooms with cheap ugly curtains and

decent bathrooms. Entrance is hidden at the rear. Handy for the Yevlax bus station.

Hotel Gәncә (☎ 565106; Xatai küç; d/ste AZN50/120; ⊠) This splendid stone-fronted Stalinist edifice remains Gәncә's top choice. Despite a Brezhnevian tendency to underilluminate the grand lobby and corridors, the rooms have been fully upgraded to Western standards. It's wonderfully central.

A large new five-star hotel is under construction opposite the Olympic Complex off Nizami küç near the western edge of town.

Eating

In summer, anyone with a vehicle should consider driving up towards Hacikәnd to dine at one of the pretty woodland eateries en route. In town, the high-ceilinged restaurant at Hotel Gәncә is not as pricey as it looks.

Göruş Restorani (mains AZN2-4; ☾ noon-11pm) Handy for the Kәpәz Hotel, this open-sided riverside eatery has a pretty limited dining choice, but beers cost only 60q.

Eleqans (☎ 568224; Cavadxan küç; mains AZN2.40-5; ☾ 9am-10.30pm) This refreshingly bright Azeri-Turkish restaurant has sturdy wooden furniture, a beer terrace and even a menu(!).

Getting There & Away

Gәncә's airport, 8km northwest of the centre, was rebuilt in 2006. **Turan Air** (☎ 562800; Xatai küç) flies twice weekly to Istanbul (from US$144).

To Moscow-Domodedovo both Turan and **Moskovia** (www.ak3r.ru) fly thrice weekly (US$190). **AZAL** (Atatürk pr; ☾ 9am-6pm) has three scheduled weekly flights to Naxçivan (US$50) and Baku (US$50), though these tend to be cancelled when planes are needed for the busy Naxçivan–Baku run.

Gәncә has two bus stations. The main **Yevlax Avtovağuzal** (Nizami küç) handles most major destinations. The smaller **Şәmkir Avtovağzal** (Nizami küç) serves towns west of Gәncә including Qazax and Krasny Most (Qırmızı Körpü) for the Georgian border (three hours).

Marshrutkas to Xanlar (50q, 25 minutes) leave when full from a point 200m south down Nәrimanov küç.

The train station is 4km north of the centre by marshrutka 1. Several trains run overnight to Baku (from AZN3.10, eight hours), plus one poorly timed daytime 'express' at 4pm (not on Thursdays).

AROUND GӘNCӘ
Xanlar
☎ 230

Founded in the 1830s by German winemakers, the village of Xanlar (Map p262) has an unusually agreeable atmosphere. Although no Germans remain, Germanic key-stone inscriptions appear above picturesque gateways, the old **church** now houses a small museum and several houses on the tree-lined streets are very photogenic. One such hosts the extremely basic **Hotel Koroğlu** (☎ 52274; Heydar Әliyev küç 40; per person AZN5), just five minutes' walk from the marshrutka stand; walk west on Qazimov küç then south down Heydar Әliyev küç.

Göy Göl

The road south from Xanlar winds up through the pretty woodland picnic spots of **Hacikәnd** and onto a ridge with magnificent views of the dramatic Lesser Caucasus range, crowned by the distinctive cleft peak of **Mt Kәpәz**. For now the valley beyond is out of bounds. However it contains one of Azerbaijan's most celebrated beauty spots, the gorgeous, forest-ringed **Göy Göl** (blue lake), which is slated to reopen to tourism as a new national park within the next few years.

TOWARDS GEORGIA

If you're heading to Georgia, by far the most pleasant route is via Şәki and Balakәn. However, there is a shorter route between Gәncә and Tbilisi. This crosses the border at **Krasny Most** (Qırmızı Körpü; Red Bridge),

GӘNCӘ BUSES

Destination	Duration	Cost	Departures (hr)
Baku	6½	AZN6	every half-hour 7.30am-4.30pm plus overnight
Lәnkәran	8	AZN6.20	8am, 9am, 8pm
Qәbәlә	3½	AZN2.80	1.30pm, 2.15pm
Şәki	3	AZN2.50	8.20am, 1.45pm, 4.30pm
Zaqatala	4¼	AZN3.50	8am, 11am, 4pm, 5pm

named for a 17th-century brick bridge in no-man's land. From Gəncə you can make marshrutka hops via **Ağstafa** (where there are three cheap but acceptable minihotels) and **Qazax**.

The latter is full of pretty parks and statues but plagued by suspicious cops, so you might be best advised to simply change marshrutkas at the bazaar and move on. There are several daily buses running to Krasny Most from Baku via Gəncə. Alternatively, you can make hops on very frequent marshrutkas from Gəncə.

SOUTHERN AZERBAIJAN

Southern Azerbaijan's coastal strip is the lush breadbasket of the country, where tea plantations line the roadsides and trees are heavy with citrus fruit. Inland, bucolic forested mountains offer tempting streamside getaways and plenty of hiking potential. The area is home to the hospitable Talysh people, famed for living to great ages. Using the overnight train to Lənkəran, a trip to the

SOUTHERN AZERBAIJAN

south makes an easy escape from Baku or a pleasant stop en route to Iran.

MASALLI & AROUND
☎ 0151

Although less appealing than Lənkəran (opposite), **Masallı** offers an alternative gateway to the pretty Talysh mountains, thanks to the newly upgraded Masallı–Yardımlı road. En route are several woodland café-resorts overlooking attractive **Vilaş Lake** (km10) and at nearby **İstisu**, a recently renovated **hot springs** minisanatorium crowded with slow-moving cure-seekers. Further towards Yardımlı there's an unusual **inflammable river** at Yanardağ (km15) and a seasonal two-level **waterfall** (şəlalə; km27), which is one of Azerbaijan's more impressive. Little **Yardımlı** (km50) has a carpet factory and a pleasant backdrop of grassy hills split by a picturesque chasm, but isn't a major attraction in itself.

Sleeping & Eating
Hotel Masallı (☎ 53231; Heydar Əliyev pr; s/d AZN22/42; 🅿) Should you need to stay in Masallı itself, this Soviet-era building offers a mixed bag of mostly well-upgraded rooms. It's on the main road linking the central bazaar (500m) to the main Baku–Lənkəran highway (1.4km).

Golüstü Park (☎ 050 2206377; Yardımlı rd, km10; r AZN30-70; 🅿) The best value and best located of several places overlooking Vilaş Lake, the well-maintained bungalows and cheaper pine-décor rooms share a good restaurant with wonderful balcony views.

Hotel Daştvənd (☎ 21230; fax 96002; Yardımlı rd, km5; s/d/cottage from AZN40/50/200; 🅿 🅿) The area's only real, modern hotel, the Daştvənd offers good-value, fully equipped rooms and a decent-sized indoor swimming pool with views towards the mountains. It needs to try hard, as its strange location around an artificial pond is back on the agricultural plains before the scenery starts getting interesting.

Yanardağ İstirahət Zonası (☎ 050 3255826; Yardımlı rd, km15; small/large cottage AZN30/40) Hidden in woodlands some way off the road the wooden hut-rooms here aren't especially well built but they're just a short stroll from the flammable river, ideal to see it at night when it's most photogenic. Restaurant attached.

A&E Hotel (☎ 0175 51246; Yardımlı Town; d/tr AZN40/40) Beside the Heydar Əliyev Museum on Yardımlı's main drag, this tiny four-room hotel has attractive pastel-blue rooms with good bathrooms and sailor-striped towels.

Getting There & Away

Shared taxis and marshrutkas for Baku depart occasionally from Masallı's bus station, about 1km south of the bazaar/town centre. However, for both Baku and Lənkəran, it's generally quicker to flag down passing transport on the main road from the eastern end of Heydar Əliyev pr; it's an AZN1 taxi ride from town.

For Yardımlı, a few morning minibuses (AZN2, 1¼ hours) pick up at Masallı's central roundabout. Shared taxis (AZN3) leave from outside Aptek Nur in the nearby central bazaar.

However, to see the sights, consider renting a return taxi for around AZN25 including stops.

LƏNKƏRAN

☎ 0171 / pop 80,000

The biggest town in southern Azerbaijan, sleepy Lənkəran (Lenkoran) is famous for tea and abundant flowers. It has a certain docile charm and sections of seafront have some half-hearted charm, though hiding submerged Soviet detritus.

The town's heart and social centre stretches from beautifully manicured **Dosa Park** to the vaguely quaint train station around which half the town's male population seems to while away their evenings in open-air beer and tea gardens.

Information

Bank Standard (Otel Qala) Changes money; has ATM.
International Bank of Azerbaijan (Dosa Park) ATM.
Lider Internet Klub (Rəsulzadə küç) Speeds are very variable.
Zovq Internet Klub (Etibar Əliyev küç 8)

Sights

The emblem of Lənkəran is a formidable **metal matriarch** bearing a cup of tea in one hand and a sword in the other. This metallic relief is similar in style to Tbilisi's Mother Georgia but on a much smaller scale and increasingly hidden by trees on the eastern wall of the local MUM department store. The town's dominant statues are to local WWII general **Hazi Aslanov**, beside an iconic lighthouse tower, and, of course, to **Heydar Əliyev**, who stands to attention in Dosa (Heydar Əliyev Memorial) Park. Strolling here amid all the fountains, minutely clipped shrubberies and newly mirror-glassed public buildings is especially surreal at dusk in summer, when lugubrious piped music is played from loudspeakers flanking the new, refreshingly air-conditioned **Heydar Əliyev Museum** (admission free; ☉ 8am-1pm & 2-5pm). The main attraction of the nearby **History Museum** (S Axundov küç; admission free; ☉ 10am-1pm & 2-5pm Tue-Sun) is the building itself, a century-old brick mansion built in 'Scooby-Doo gothic' style. It looks great when illuminated at night.

Joseph Stalin was held prisoner in Lənkəran during his early revolutionary days. The sturdy brick-barrel of a **tower** in which he was incarcerated is now under renovation

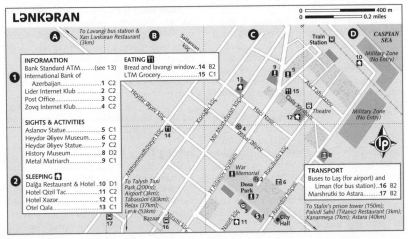

with rumours that it might one day become a tongue-in-cheek Stalin-themed café. Well there's always hope.

Lənkəran's beaches can't be recommended for swimming due to chunks of concrete and ruined building parts that remain submerged since the rising Caspian swept away the former Soviet-era promenade. And part of it is off-limits for military use. Slightly nicer seafront areas (though still not really swimmable) are to be found near the Titanic restaurant (right) and at **Kanarmeşa**, where two vaguely attractive restaurant gardens overlook the waves.

Sleeping

CENTRAL

Dalğa Restaurant & Hotel (☎ 51769, 050 3409203; s/tw/tr AZN20/24/36) Five comfortably modern rooms with good air-con are ranged above the courtyard dining chambers of this comparatively upper-market restaurant. All have decent bathrooms with toothpaste and toiletries provided. The restaurant has an appealing trellis-garden section but bring mosquito repellent.

Hotel Qizil Tac (☎ 51664, 050 6171141; Nəsirli küç 2; tw with private/shared bathroom AZN50/30) There's no real reception or sign for this outwardly plush option just behind Dosa Park. Rooms appear well tended and modern, but the clocks have stopped and sheets arrive in Nescafe bags for you to make your own bed. Toilets lack paper (we were grudgingly given two sheets on request) and night staff disabled the air-conditioning ('it's not that hot tonight'!) – all while persistently requesting beer money.

Hotel Xəzər (☎ 51663; Qala Xiyabanı küç 11; s/tw/tr/q/ste AZN31/52/72/92/86) After years of renovation Lənkəran's most central hotel reopened in 2007. The lobby still gives a certain sense of bygone elegance while rooms are comparatively simple, if comfortable and modern, with decent bathrooms. Manager Anar speaks English.

Otel Qala (☎ 50284; fax 50288; Mirmustafaxan küç 22; s/d/tw/ste AZN41.10/52.20/72.20/122.20) A certain restrained elegance makes the Qala Lənkəran's best hotel with irreproachable modern rooms, monogrammed towels and rugs spread over attractive terracotta floors. English is spoken but the place is often spookily empty, the lift doesn't work and the once-excellent restaurant has reduced its menu to a minimum.

TOWARDS LERIK

Several rural resorts are dotted along the Lerik–Lənkəran road.

Təbəssüm (Map p284; ☎ 0157-56150; Lerik Rd km27; d/tr AZN40/50) Relatively simple but pine-fragrant huts with dining platforms and neat little shower-toilets set in an attractive stream gully.

Relax (Map p284 ☎ 0157 56068; www.relax.com.az/dexen.htm; Lerik rd, km34; d/ste/cottage AZN95/130/140) The two-floor villas and stone-walled bungalows at Relax offer the most luxurious accommodation in the Talysh hills, right down to the monogrammed bathrobes. Activities include minigolf, table tennis, a children's play area and a 5km circuit of mossy-fenced woodland paths, but the pounding disco rather undermines its 'back-to-nature' image.

Eating

For great picnics buy hot bread (isti çörək) and chicken ləvəngi (stuffed with nut paste) from the unmarked window on the corner of H Əliyev küç and Mähəmmədhüseyn küç.

There are several simple eateries and convivial teahouses near the train station and around pedestrianised Qala Xiyabanı küç, where **LTM Grocery** (döner 70q; 🕙 9am-7pm) has a fast-food window.

Xan Lənkəran (☎ 51699; Ləvəngi Bus Station; kebabs AZN2; 🕙 8am-11pm; 🍴) With wooden interior and thatched ceiling, this place is unexpectedly appealing for the location, and offers chicken ləvəngi, as well as cheap beers (50q) should you dare threaten your bladder before a bus trip.

Palıidr Sahil (☎ 055 7508618; Olympic Beach; kebabs AZN2.40) Commonly nicknamed Titanic, the main restaurant building is shaped like a concrete boat sailing towards the beach. Meals include a selection of rice dishes, there's a pleasant garden area, and bungalows (AZN50 to AZN100) are available if you can't face the 3km trip back into town.

With a car, an appealing alternative is to eat at any of the restaurants tucked away off the road to Lerik.

Getting There & Away

Lənkəran's airport is under reconstruction. Laş-bound minibuses pass by.

Ləvəngi bus station (Lənkəran bypass), 3km northwest of the centre, handles long-distance bus services. Baku-bound services leave at least hourly until 6pm, stopping near Masallı en route. There's a Lerik mini-bus at 7.30am.

Local buses depart from around the bazaar. Take Laş buses for the airport, Liman buses for Lәvәngi bus station (20q, last around 4pm). Marshrutkas to Astara (AZN1) leave from Sabir küç, one block north. For Lerik, shared jeeps (AZN3) and charter taxis (AZN10 each way) depart from the **Talysh taxi park** (Koroğlu küç) west of the bazaar. Or flag down passing transport near the airport.

Two trains run to Baku, the seat-only 'express' at 4.59pm (AZN2.80, doesn't run Mondays) and the sleeper at 9.17pm (AZN2.60 *platskart*, AZN3.60 *kupe*, 8½ hours) arriving early next morning. Trains to Astara at 7.23am and 2.23pm (60q, one hour) offer a pleasant way to gaze at the Caspian.

AROUND LƏNKƏRAN
Lerik
☎ 0157 / pop 14,000
The Talysh Mountains are not as high nor as spectacular as the Caucasus but their attractive mix of forest, canyon and sheep-mown uplands makes the area a delightful place to hike, as long as you don't stray too close to the Iranian border. The hub of the mountain region is the overgrown village of Lerik. Even in summer Lerik is refreshingly cool, so remember to bring appropriate clothing. Along the pretty Lәnkәran–Lerik road are many appealing teahouses and rest areas from which to take random strolls in some of Azerbaijan's most appealing mature forests.

Central Lerik is marked by a **bust of Heydar Əliyev** and an eerie **memorial** depicting the faces of the locals who gave their lives in the Karabakh conflict. Several delightful walks are possible by simply striding out of town in any direction. **Gussein Baba's** (☎ 54276; s/d/tr AZN6/10/15) is an unmarked little cafeteria-hotel with perfectly acceptable rooms sharing clean squat toilets and shower right in the middle of town. Find it by going up the hill to the right of the war memorial, passing the tiny **museum** (☉ 10am-1pm & 2-5pm Sun-Fri) and following the pathway immediately to the side of the Lerik Finance Committee (signposted in English).

Several morning minibuses run to Baku via Lәnkәran (AZN7, six hours) from near the Kapital Bank (ATM available) in the valley 1km below and beyond central Lerik.

Hirkan National Park
☎ 0171
In 2004 a vast swathe of dense southern forest was declared the Hirkan National Park. The area is relatively impenetrable, with muddy 4WD tracks and horse trails the only way to get far into the delightful deciduous foliage. The park has a **visitor centre** (☎ 76266; ☉ 9am-1pm & 2-5pm Mon-Sat) on the Lәnkәran–Astara road, where all visitors to the park are supposed to sign in and buy a ticket (local/foreigner AZN2/4 per day) entitling you to the services of a guide on one of 10 *marşrut* (routes). That's great if you're interested in local flora or fancy searching for leopard prints. However, no vehicles are available for hire and without one it's tough to access many of the trails' starting points. One comparatively accessible viewpoint is **Lake Xanbulan**, a modestly pretty woodland-ringed reservoir. Few locals seem to bother paying the park fee to picnic here, and there is no barrier gate, but occasional spot checks do occur.

Deputy Park Director **Haji** (☎ 050 6871009) speaks English and can help arrange AZN10 homestays in nearby Hirkan village. Alternatively, there are reasonably attractive cottages attached to the **Xanbulan Restaurant** (☎ 57190; meals AZN6, bungalow AZN40), 2km off the Lәnkәran–Astara road along the access road to Lake Xanbulan.

ASTARA
☎ 0195 / pop 25,000
Astara has one of Azerbaijan's nicer beaches, but being a border town you'd be unwise to linger too long here and there's little else to do except cross the **border** (☉ 8am-noon & 2-5pm, variable) to Iran. Note that midrange hotels in Azerbaijani Astara are generally better value than the equivalents in Iran's namesake town.

If you're arriving from Iran as a pedestrian you emerge through an oddly unmarked metal doorway into a nest of waiting taxi drivers. Contrary to their assertions, it is very easy to walk to the central square (less than 10 minutes, straight ahead up Heydar Əliyev küç). Close to the square, Kapital Bank has an ATM that accepts international cards and you can change money on the Iranian side.

Sleeping & Eating
There's an unnamed, entirely unappealing crash-pad **hotel** (tw AZN6) right at the pedestrian

border post. Squat toilets and cold tap are shared.

Hotel Xəzər (☎ 53530; Azərbaycan küç; tw AZN10) One short block west of the central square, this clean new place offers bright no-nonsense rooms with shared (but very well-maintained) bathroom.

Hotel Şindan (☎ 34177; fax 34188; H Əliyev pr 11; s/d/ste AZN30/50/70; ☒) Astara's best hotel, this appealing and great-value new midrange option is less than 10 minutes' stroll straight up the main street from the Iranian border crossing. It has immaculate international-standard rooms with marble sinks, good bathrooms and desk-units hiding a minibar. There's a fitness centre (extra fee) and a congenial beer garden.

Getting There & Away

Minibuses to Lənkəran (AZN1, 45 minutes) and night buses to Baku depart from the north end of the central square, two minutes' walk north of Hotel Şindan. A taxi shouldn't cost more than AZN10, including a stop at Yanar Bulağ, though drivers at the border post want twice that amount. Remember to double-check if they're demanding Manats or Shirvans (see Money, p297).

Day buses to Baku depart from a bus stand 2km north of centre. The inconveniently located train station is an AZN3 taxi ride up the coast.

AROUND ASTARA
Yanar Bulağ

If you're in Astara, don't miss the curious **Yanar Bulağ** ('burning spring'), in nearby Ərçivan village. Here, spring water gurgling from a metal stand-pipe is impregnated with methane. Put a lighter to it and it burns, giving a magical little display of the wet and the warm. It's shaded by a modest brick-domed pavilion, right beside the Lənkəran–Astara road, 6km north of central Astara. The water's flammability is secondary to its remedial properties for locals, who collect it by the gallon and seem bemused by visitors' flaming antics.

NAXÇIVAN

This cradle of Azeri culture and history is now a disconnected lozenge of Azerbaijan wedged uncomfortably between hostile Armenia and indifferent Iran. It's kept going

economically thanks to a tiny border with Turkey and numerous subsidised flights from Baku. Historical monuments and intriguing oasis villages are dotted about a fascinating landscape of deserts and melon fields rimmed dramatically by craggy barren mountains.

But visiting requires resourcefulness and imagination. Western visitors are an extreme novelty and even Russian speakers are comparatively rare. While much of the population is extravagantly hospitable, officials beyond Naxçivan City tend to regard lone travellers with a deep suspicion bordering on aggression.

Transiting Naxçivan would make an interesting alternative route when crossing between Turkey and Iran. However, if you're coming from the rest of Azerbaijan you'll need to fly.

HISTORY

Legend claims that Naxçivan was founded by none other than Noah. The biblical ark supposedly crashed through the then-submerged crest of İlandağ (see p293) before landing on nearby Ararat (Mt Ağrı, Turkey), whose twin cones loom powerfully above the western tip of the enclave. In the 12th century Naxçivan was one of three capitals of the Atabey dynasty, which controlled much of western Persia. Throughout medieval times it flourished as an important centre of trade, emerging as an independent khanate in the 18th century. Like many Azeri khanates, Naxçivan was sucked into the Russian Empire following a series of Russo-Persian wars, sealed by the 1828 treaty of Turkmenchay.

When Azerbaijan was briefly independent from 1918 to 1920, it stretched from Baku to Naxçivan. However, in the early Soviet era that followed, Lenin's divide-and-rule policies gave Armenia the province of Zangezour, thus isolating Naxçivan from the rest of Azerbaijan. In 1924 Naxçivan was declared an Autonomous Soviet Socialist Republic.

In January 1990, as the Soviet Union began to crack, Naxçivan became the first part of the Soviet Union to formally declare independence, beating Lithuania by a matter of weeks. It didn't last. Naxçivan soon rejoined the rest of Azerbaijan and remains an integral (if dislocated) part of the nation.

NAXÇIVAN CITY
☎ 0136 / pop 63,200

Occupying a low plateau overlooking the Araz Su Reservoir, this pleasant provincial town offers wide, if distant, panoramas

DON'T MENTION ARMENIA

Given the unconcluded war, it's perfectly understandable that Azeri officials are a little edgy about visitors nosing about in border areas. However, in parts of Naxçivan, many officials treat visitors with quite unguarded hostility. Expressing the merest interest in medieval church sites or any other historical monuments built by the now-vanished Armenian community is likely to land you in hot water. It appears that most such sites have themselves 'disappeared' (see http://forum.openarmenia.com/index.php?showtopic=8751) and some straight-faced officials farcically claim that there 'never were any Armenians here'. Police watch travellers closely, will probably interview your taxi driver and might check your bags for 'pro-Armenian' material. Comically enough, during questioning, a popular technique is to bark at you in Armenian to see if you understand it, as though speaking Armenian was a crime.

towards Iran and Mt Ararat from its soothingly shady parks. Despite a rash of shiny new buildings on its long main streets, the atmosphere is one of sleepy torpor, as the incredible summer heat renders most activities beyond playing nard and drinking tea out of the question.

Information

There are currency exchanges and ATMs throughout the town, notably at the bazaar and the Ticaret Mərkəzi Gənclik. The main post office is under reconstruction. For details of the Iranian and Turkish consulates here, see p295.

Aliheydar Paşayev (☎ 050 5672506; www.natigllc .eu.tp) This urbane and well-connected translator, guide and travel fixer is passionate about Naxçivan, speaks decent English and can miraculously help his guests get aboard seemingly full flights back to Baku.

Bilan Kompüter (Atatürk küç; per hr 60q; ☼ 9.30am-midnight) Decent internet connection.

Sights

MÖMINƏ XATUN

The impressive **Mömina Xatun mausoleum** (☎ 458039; admission free; ☼ 9am-1pm & 2-6pm Tue-Sun) is Naxçivan's icon and one of Azerbaijan's best-known landmarks. It's a glorious, gently leaning 26m brick tower decorated with geometric patterns and Kufic script (a stylised, angular form of Arabic) picked out in turquoise glaze.

Located in the park of the same name, the mausoleum dates from 1186 and entombs the founder of the Atabey dynasty, Shemseddin Eldeniz, along with his beloved wife, for whom the monument is named. The graves themselves were removed to St Petersburg during the 1950s, but the hollow interior features a small exhibition of relevant photos

and drawings, including images of the minaret-gate and historic Cümə mosque that survived beside the mausoleum until the 19th century.

AROUND MÖMINƏ XATUN

Close to Mömina Xatun is a paved, open-air 'museum' of historic **stone rams** and grave markers plus a **promenade** offering views down over the lower town with Mt Ararat visible on an exceptionally clear day. The promenade culminates in a formal garden containing the **Carpet Museum** (☎ 447720; Mömina Xatun Park; admission 50q; ☼ 9am-1pm & 2-6pm Tue-Sun), housed in the re-built palace of Ehsan Khan, Naxçivan's 18th-century monarch. Despite the şəbəkə windows and attractive exterior porches, the building isn't quite as impressive as Şəki's equivalent (p275). Nonetheless the rug displays are well chosen if you want to learn the difference between a kilim and a sumax or palaz, or to recognise the four main styles of Azeri carpet making. The ghoulish centrepiece is a totally non-ironic silk-wool carpet portrait of a young Heydar Əliyev, replete with Soviet medals. Two side rooms relate to the history of the Naxçivan khanate, replicate the khan's cushion-throne and gratuitously add photos of Yerevan (now the Armenian capital) to remind visitors that that was once a Turkic khanate too.

The red-brick **Blue Mosque** (Nizami küç) isn't very blue at all but makes a useful landmark when approaching the Mömina Xatun area by marshrutka.

OTHER SIGHTS

The khans who once ruled from the Carpet Museum were buried in a squat, rather over-restored brick tomb complex with a simple blue-glaze dome. Known simply as the

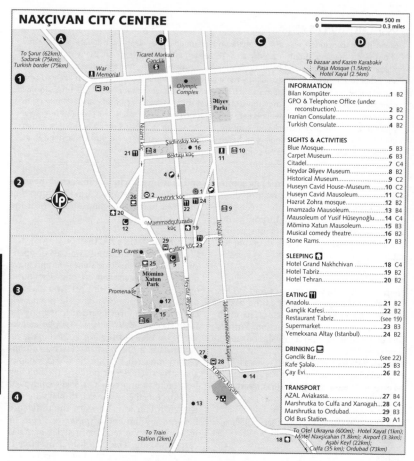

NAXÇIVAN CITY CENTRE

0 ————— 500 m
0 ————— 0.3 miles

INFORMATION
Bilan Kompüter...........................1 B2
GPO & Telephone Office (under
  reconstruction)........................2 B2
Iranian Consulate........................3 C2
Turkish Consulate........................4 B2

SIGHTS & ACTIVITIES
Blue Mosque..............................5 B3
Carpet Museum............................6 B3
Citadel..................................7 C4
Heydər Əliyev Museum.....................8 C2
Historical Museum........................9 C2
Huseyn Cavid House-Museum...............10 C2
Huseyn Cavid Mausoleum..................11 C2
Hazrat Zohra mosque.....................12 B2
İmamzadə Mausoleum......................13 B4
Mausoleum of Yusif Hüseynoğlu..........14 C4
Mömina Xatun Mausoleum..................15 B3
Musical comedy theatre.................16 B2
Stone Rams.............................17 B3

SLEEPING
Hotel Grand Nakhchivan.................18 C4
Hotel Tabriz...........................19 B2
Hotel Tehran...........................20 B2

EATING
Anadolu................................21 B2
Gənclik Kafesi.........................22 B2
Restaurant Tabriz...............(see 19)
Supermarket............................23 B3
Yemekxana Altay (Istanbul).............24 B2

DRINKING
Gənclik Bar.....................(see 22)
Kafe Şəlalə............................25 B3
Çay Evi................................26 B2

TRANSPORT
AZAL Aviakassa.........................27 B4
Marshrutka to Culfa and Xanəgah........28 C4
Marshrutka to Ordubad..................29 B3
Old Bus Station........................30 A1

İmamzadə, it's below a graveyard on what were once the city's **citadel** walls. Access is from the road to the train station (marshrutka 2 from Nizami küç).

Hidden in Naxçivan back streets are a couple of medieval pointed tomb-towers in an octagonal form common throughout eastern Anatolia. The best known is the 1162 **Mausoleum of Yusif Hüseynoğlu**, by the same architect as the Mömina Xatun tower.

The grandly rebuilt **Heydar Əliyev Museum** (admission free; 9am-1pm & 2-5pm Mon-Sat) is a veritable modern palace of shiny marble. It's somewhat more interesting than other such hagiographic shrines elsewhere in Azerbaijan if only because Naxçivan was Heydar's home region. Across the manicured square, Naxçivan's

musical comedy theatre is an archetype of provincial Soviet classicism. Behind lies the striking, if modern, white marble **mausoleum of Hüseyn Cavid** and Cavid's sweet little wooden **house-museum** (452726; admission free; 9am-1pm & 2-6pm), where the writer once lived, long before being infamously deported to Siberia. If you have time to kill, the **Historical Museum** (Dövlat Tarix Muzeyi; 450136; admission AZN1; 9am-1pm & 2-6pm) is attractively presented, if fairly standard.

The town's biggest mosques are modern affairs. Built in pallid yellow brick the **Həzrət Zohra mosque** (İslam Səfərli küç) sports twin, rectilinear minarets and a metal-clad dome looking more like a lagged boiler tank. It's nicknamed the 'Iranian mosque', as it was funded by Naxçivan's southern neighbour.

Not to be outdone, Turks stumped up money to build the impressive **Kazim Karabəkir Paşa Mosque** behind the bazaar. This grandly domed stone edifice has elegant missile-style twin minarets and splendid gilt inscriptions on the white marble doorway. However, if you're coming from Turkey you're likely to have seen dozens of similar structures.

Sleeping

For many years several of Naxçivan's hotels were squarely aimed at weekending Iranian men in search of booze and (relative) sexual openness. However, a recent zero-tolerance crackdown on prostitution has left hotels with very low occupancy, so rates are cheap compared with Baku.

Hotel Tehran (☎ 050 6228285; İslam Səfərli küç 11; s/tw from AZN8/8) Like an Iranian *mosaferkhaneh* (lodging house or cheap hotel), waterless box-rooms are crammed around a very narrow courtyard sharing passably clean squat toilets. Rooms in the rear are windowless but slightly neater, and some singles at AZN12 have simple private bathrooms. The owner seems friendly and speaks passable Russian, but this wouldn't be a place for single women.

Hotel Xayal (☎ 445915; s/d/ste AZN10/20/30; 🔀) Despite some peeling paint, this 1990s suburban building offers by far the best budget deal in Naxçivan. The 12 rooms are large and bright, sporting passable air-conditioning. En suite bathrooms have Western loos, piping-hot showers and clean towels. The challenge is finding it. Take marshrutka 2 or 3 to where either turns 270 degrees at a big Koroğlu statue in a roundabout halfway to the airport. Walk 50m towards the bazaar from there then take the first improbable back lane to the right beside a grotty Soviet apartment block. After the Xayal wedding hall, the hotel is the three-storey pink building through gates to the left. It looks a bit like a grain elevator.

Otel Ukrayna (☎ 455383; Tusi pr; tw with/without air-con AZN28/24, tr AZN30; 🔀) Should the Xayal be full, this ageing peach-coloured establishment would make a passable standby. The large, if slightly shabby, upper-floor air-con rooms have fridges and acceptable bathrooms. However, the ground-floor triple rooms are overpriced (without air-con or bathroom). Corridors are a little gloomy and the faded alpine scenes that cover the landing walls give a maudlin feel to the place. Marshrutkas 2, 3 and airport-bound

6 pass the gates, from which the hotel is set back 100m.

Hotel Grand Nakhchivan (☎ 445930; fax 445932; N Əliyev küç 1; tw/ste AZN50/100; 🔀) Built in 2002, the Grand does indeed look pretty grand from the outside. The tidy modern rooms are quite stylish, and are bigger and brighter than those at the Tabriz. However, hot water can be temperamental, some bathtubs are very stained and the lift has been out of order for years. Don't count on English-speaking assistance.

Hotel Tabriz (Mehmanxanə Təbriz; ☎ 447701; www .tebrizhotel.com; s/d/tr/ste US$50/75/100/150; 🔀) With its shiny blue-glass make-over, liveried doorman and English-speaking receptionists, this 13-storey tower is once again Naxçivan's top accommodation address. Rooms aren't huge but offer full Western-style amenities, including a closable shower-booth in the sparkling-clean bathrooms. The location is brilliantly central, too.

Motel Nəxşicahan (☎ 441441; d AZN70; 🔀) This rather plush stone-clad motel is tucked behind a lonely riverside restaurant-wedding palace whose pleasant willow gardens are the main attraction. Rooms are presentable and vaguely stylish, despite the leopard-print duvets. The location is somewhat awkward, though southbound bus 6 passes by. Breakfast is included but neither English nor Russian are reliably spoken.

Eating

Restaurant Tabriz (13th fl, Hotel Tabriz; ☎ 447701; mains AZN2-8; 🔀) Potentially spectacular views are bizarrely hidden behind opaque lace curtains in what's surely the best restaurant in town, though it's still nothing very fancy. Uniquely there's a menu (partly in English) with pseudo-Western choices including a rather dry, if tasty, meat-chunk spaghetti mapolitan (sic; AZN2), ideally accompanied by a side order of *haydari* (AZN1), a deliciously smoky aubergine 'salad' in garlic-yogurt sauce. Beers (from AZN1.50), wines and spirits are available.

Gənclik Kafesi (Heydar Əliyev pr; dishes AZN1.20-2) Like most decent restaurants in Naxçivan the cavernous Gənclik offers point-and-pick precooked Turkish dishes, though there's also a salad-bar, of sorts. Staff are friendly and women do venture in (usually chaperoned, of course) but there's little atmosphere. Mirrored glass misleadingly makes it appear permanently closed. No alcohol.

AZERBAIJAN

Other slightly cosier but more male-dominated Turkish restaurants include the friendly **Yemekxana Altay** (Istanbul Restaurant; ☎ 451762; Atatürk küç; dishes AZN1-2) and the essentially similar **Anadolu** (Nizami küç; dishes AZN1-2).

Drinking

Local men have a great choice of *çayxanas* to while away those summer days in shady parks. One of the nicest, simply called **Çay Evi** (tea house; per pot tea 60q), sits amid trees that also hide the chess school and philharmonia. For women wanting a teahouse experience without eliciting endless attention the best bet is **Kafe Şəlalə** (per pot tea AZN1), where tables are ranged up an amphitheatre of paved terraces around an artificial waterfall. However, beware that the jams or pickled walnuts that arrive in lieu of sugar will each cost a whopping AZN3 extra.

Naxçivan is one of the driest areas of Azerbaijan in both senses: relatively few restaurants or cafés serve alcohol. However there are several *piva* bars (beer bars) where you can drink refreshingly weak Naxçivan or NZS beers at 60q a pint. There's also a spacious subterranean cavern-bar beneath the **Gənclik Kafesi** (Efes beer AZN1.20); enter from the side. Single women are likely to feel pretty uncomfortable at any of these places but can drink in comparative peace at the Restaurant Tabriz.

Getting There & Away

AIR

AZAL operates at least five flights a day between Baku and Naxçivan (55 minutes) on tatty Tupolev 154s. Additional flights are organised during busy periods but demand can still outstrip supply and it's not unknown to wait a week for a seat to become available, unless you have a well-connected helper. Tickets are only sold from the relevant AZAL *aviakassa* (office) or from booths at the airports. These seem to open and close at whim. Round-trip tickets don't exist.

The one-way foreigner fare (US$100) seems reasonable enough till you realise that locals pay just AZN16. A cheaper Naxçivan–Gəncə flight (US$50) is timetabled thrice weekly. However, at peak times these might be randomly cancelled to provide more planes for the overloaded Baku run. UT Air operates weekly, summer-only flights directly to Moscow.

BUS

Remarkably, six buses a day run from Naxçivan all the way to Istanbul, Turkey (AZN38, 26 hours) via Iğdır (AZN4, five hours). Most start from the airport then pick up passengers at the decrepit old bus station between 8am and 10am. Advance booking is rarely required. Crossing the Azeri–Turkish border the bus takes around 2½ hours, so some Iğdır-bound passengers save an hour by taking shared taxis to the border (around AZN5, including crossing no-man's land). However, this can be confusing and a little daunting if you don't speak local languages.

Naxçivan–Baku buses run at periods of peak demand via Iran but getting the visas (Iranian and Azerbaijan re-entry) will cost vastly more than the fare.

For Ordubad, minibuses (AZN2, 80 minutes) leave roughly hourly in the mornings from beside the Blue Mosque, and then again at 5pm. Shared taxis (AZN3, one hour) are occasionally available.

Marshrutkas for Culfa (AZN1, 40 minutes) and very irregular *raff* (minibuses) to Xanəgah leave from a roadside lay-by just beyond the *aviakassa*.

TRAIN

Naxçivan's railway links to Baku and Moscow haven't worked for well over a decade. The tracks through Armenia and Armenian-occupied territories have been partially torn up so even if peace were to miraculously break out there wouldn't be a rail service ready to run. Two domestic trains from Naxçivan City both depart at 3am and return next morning. One goes to Şəhrur. The other goes to Ordubad (3½ hours) traversing some superb canyon scenery directly north-west of Culfa. However both routes skirt right alongside the sensitive Iranian border so tourists taking any train can expect to be bombarded with questions and might endure a full-scale interrogation.

Getting Around

Taxis charge AZN1 per hop in town, AZN2 at night or to the airport (4km). A pretty comprehensive bus/marshrutka network operates till around 8.30pm but don't expect any service to return the way it came. All cost 20q per trip. Useful route 6 links the bus station to the airport via the Turkish consulate, blue mosque and Koroğlu statue, returning via the bazaar. More frequent route 3 circles from the Olympic Complex round to the bazaar and Xayal Hotel, looping back past the Ukrayna and Grand Nakhchivan hotels to the Culfa bus stand, then side-stepping a block and returning via Inqilab küç. Route 2 does essentially the same thing in reverse albeit transiting the centre on Nizami küç instead of Istiqial and adding a diversion to the train station.

NAXÇIVAN CITY TO ORDUBAD

The drive to Ordubad takes you past some of Naxçivan's most memorable scenery. Several abrupt crags rise powerfully in the middle distance and once you're past Culfa, sections of painted desert sprout lion-paw ridges and red-rock mesas. In between lie just a handful of surreally green oasis villages.

Aşabi Keyf

Contrasting with the thrusting masculinity of Beşbarmaq Dağ (p261), the womblike rocky folds of Aşabi Keyf are decidedly feminine. But both reveal an interestingly animist side to Azeri Islam. A series of overneat restaurant terraces lead up to a cleft cliff that gives something of the feeling of entering Petra (Jordan), albeit on a much smaller scale and without the carvings. Steps lead through the cleft and past a blackened minicave that was once the abode of seven legendary holy men. Quite how they all managed to fit in it is as miraculous as their mythical 309-year sleep. More stairs lead up to somewhat bigger caves, passing a prayer area and two minishrines, one of which displays a tooth - shaped holy rock on a wooden stand. Some devotees puff their way to the top of a metal-ladder stairway to make miniature prayer cairns at the top.

Allow at least half an hour up and back from the car park which is 14km northwest of the Ordubad road. The turning is 8km southeast of Naxçivan City, from which taxis want AZN10 return.

İlandağ

Like a gigantic eroded tombstone, the rocky 2415m peak of İlandağ (Snake Mountain) stands out as the most distinctive natural feature in Naxçivan. It's clearly visible from Naxçivan City almost 30km away. Legend has it that the cleft in the summit was created by the keel of Noah's Ark as the floodwaters abated.

On a separate rocky outcrop above the village of Xanəgah are the remains of the 7th-century Alinca Fortress. A two-hour climb, which involves some steep scrambling, leads through the scant ruins to the summit but you don't need to go all the way up for the magnificent views of İlandağ, which are the main reward.

Culfa
☎ 0136

Unless you're crossing the Iranian border, it's unwise to stop in Culfa. This lacklustre settlement was founded in 1848, 3km southeast of the windswept site of Ancient Jolfa (Cuğa). Ancient Jolfa had been a thriving cultural centre for centuries. However in 1604 Persian Shah Abbas sacked the town and ruthlessly exported its talented Armenian craftsmen to build his glorious new capital at Esfahan. The Armenian quarter of Esfahan is still known as 'New Jolfa'. Today the lumpy remnants of ancient Jolfa include a ruined bridge and the **Gülüstan Türbe**, a beautifully embellished mausoleum stump that features heavily in Azerbaijan's tourist literature. Yet ironically, the easiest way to see this is from across the Araz River on the Iranian side. It's easily visible while driving to beautiful St Stephanos Church. Visiting on the Azeri side, however, or even snooping around Culfa is liable to get you a lengthy interrogation or worse. Culfa's bureaucrats love to pontificate on the area's 'strategic' sensitivity (ie proximity to the Iranian border). But their needlessly paranoid attitude seems to give credence to reports that Cuğa's once-magnificent ancient Armenian cemetery has been desecrated (see http://en.wikipedia.org/wiki/Khachkar_destruction_in_Nakhchivan). Until the 1980s it had featured thousands of fabulous *khatchkars* (medieval headstones).

Ordubad
☎ 0136

Little Ordubad was once the seat of a sultanate but today it lies in a rather forgotten corner of the Zangezur Mountains, trapped between closed Armenian borders and an unbridged stretch of the Araz River. However, this isolation has preserved it as a charming backwater oasis, where houses sit in lush wooded compounds behind timeless mud walls. Minibuses from Naxçivan City terminate outside the town's interesting **museum** (Heydar əliyev pr 18;

AZERBAIJAN

admission free; 9am-1pm & 2-5pm Mon-Fri) housed in an 18th-century domed building that has been used variously as a silk shop, restaurant and *zurkhaneh* ('house of strength' – for the practice of a unique Iranian sport based on sufi philosophy). If you feign ignorance of Russian maybe the museum's superkeen curator won't force you to peruse the books he's written to celebrate Ordubad's 'celebrity' citizens.

Across the road, the **Cümə Mosque** started life as the office of Hatəmbek Ordubadi, the 17th-century vizier of Shah Abbas. It still looks more like a khan's palace than a place of worship. Interesting old photos in the museum show its Soviet-era form, when the arched porches were filled with silver communist statuary and the roof was Russified with a Kremlin-style spire (since removed).

There are several other old **mosques** and attractive alleys to explore but be careful where you point your camera, as virtually any landscape will include a bit of sensitive border and police are quick to smell 'spies'.

The mountains of Ordubad National Park contain many fascinating petroglyphs but getting there is effectively impossible. Ordubad's hotel has closed but the town is easy to visit as a day trip from Naxçivan City. Marshrutkas back (last around 5pm) leave from beside a *çayxana* beautifully shaded by ancient plane trees (*çinar*). For lunch there are a couple of kebab-grill cafés but for a better lunchtime selection head for the very unexotic *yeməkxana* down totally unmarked steps at the rear of the town hall (the new building directly south of the Cümə Mosque).

NAXÇIVAN CITY TO TURKEY

The drive to Turkey is slightly less picturesque than that to Ordubad, but the looming approach of **Mt Ağrı** (Ararat) gives a constantly mesmerising focus when visibility allows. Around 7km out of Naxçivan City a spur road leads up to **Duzdağ** where sanatorium patients come in the evenings to sleep in the asthma-reducing environment of a disused salt mine. It's not open to visitors, but the mountain's candy-striped pink and white contours are very attractive viewed from the road a couple of kilometres later. Around 35km from Naxçivan City, a 5km spur road leads to **Qarabağlar**, where a famous 14th-century tower, crusted with blue glaze-work, entombs a wife of the great Mongol-Persian ruler Hulugu Khan.

The **Sədərək border** (10.30am-2am Azerbaijan time, 8.30am-midnight Turkish time) takes a de facto lunch break around 2pm once most westbound buses have passed through. Turkish visas are available on arrival here for most Western nationalities but oddly not for Brits.

AZERBAIJAN DIRECTORY

ACCOMMODATION

The past five years have seen an astonishing transformation in Azerbaijan's accommodation scene. Many old Soviet hotels have closed or been totally rebuilt, though a few decaying remnants remain as a grimy reminder of the past and as a comparatively cheap boon to budget travellers.

Rural homestays (typically AZN10) are still a relatively new idea but are slowly spreading. Although unevenly spread, there are now many rural resorts known as *istrahət zonası* (rest zones), most offering 'Finnish'-style wooden cottages with en suite bathroom. These are often big enough to sleep a family and typically huddle in woodland clearings and stream sides. The simplest will usually cost just under AZN50 and some flashier resorts can cost up to AZN200, though price isn't always a fair guide to quality.

Several provincial towns have at least one *mehmanxana* (new or rebuilt hotel) that has acceptable lower-midrange value. In Baku there's a vastly wider selection, but finding an en suite room for under AZN60 can be a challenge. Even relatively simple Baku hotels often charge over US$100 a night. Only a few of Baku's numerous new 'boutique' hotels are as stylish as their adverts imply.

BOOKS

Trailblazer's *Azerbaijan with Excursions to Georgia* by Mark Elliott is regarded as a classic handbook to the country. Visitors passing through or just spending a week in Azerbaijan may find its size overwhelming, but the author's zeal for all things Azeri makes it an encyclopaedia as much as a travel guide and it is a must-have among the Baku expat community.

Kurban Said's *Ali and Nino* is a fantastic introduction to the whole Caucasus – the story of a love affair of a young Azeri Muslim and a Georgian Christian princess set in Baku on the eve of WWI, it's a wonderfully atmospheric tale of the city at an age of immense change and modernisation, and an interesting examination of the clash between Europe and Asia on a human scale.

Thomas Goltz's *Azerbaijan Diary* offers a fascinating first-hand insight into the complex politics of the war-torn 1990s but be sure to read Thomas de Waal's *Black Garden* first.

BUSINESS HOURS

As a general guide, offices work 9am to 5pm Monday to Friday, but late starts and long lunches are not uncommon. Most shops operate seven days a week, opening around 10am and closing after 7pm. Bazaars tend to be mainly morning affairs. Restaurants in Baku typically function from 11am to around 11pm but outside Baku opening hours don't necessarily exist and are more dependent on the number of people visiting the establishment.

CUSTOMS REGULATIONS

The once-notorious Azeri customs are relatively professional these days… at least with Westerners. Customs forms are rarely needed, though you should fill one in if you plan to import and later re-export over US$1000 in cash. Taking carpets, artefacts or artworks out of the country is awkward, as you'll need written permission from the Ministry of Culture. The export limit for caviar changes every year. It's currently 200g per person.

DANGERS & ANNOYANCES

Apart from the sometimes-terrifying driving, Azerbaijan is generally a very safe country. You're more likely to encounter hospitality than crime. However, that hospitality is tempered with a certain intrusive inquisitiveness, which can become tiresome. Lone travellers are especially likely to raise questions in local minds. Police in small, out-of-the-way places seem to imagine any outsider to be a potential spy.

EMBASSIES & CONSULATES

Addresses of Azeri embassies abroad are listed in the 'useful information' section of www.tourism.az.

Embassies and consulates, all in Baku unless stated, include:

China (Map pp240-1; ☎ 4974558; Xaqani küç 67; ☽ 10-11.30am Mon & Thu)

France (Map pp240-1; ☎ 4931286; www.ambafrance-az.org; Rasul Rza küç 7)

Georgia (Map p238; ☎ 4974558; Suleyman Dadaşev küç 29, Baku) Marshrutka 177.

Germany (Map pp240-1; ☎ 4654100; www.baku.diplo.de; 10th fl, ISR Plaza)

Iran Consulate (Map p238; ☎ 4980766; www.iranembassy.az; Cəfər Cabbarli küç 44) Consulate (☎ 0136 50343; Atatürk küç 13, Naxçıvan; ☽ 10.30am-noon Mon-Thu)

Kazakhstan (Map p238; ☎ 4656248; Ak Həsən Əliyev [İgilab] küç 82; ☽ 9.30-11.30am Mon-Fri) Walking distance west from Gənclik metro. Visa takes one day.

Russia (Map p238; ☎ 4986016; Bakixanov küç 17; ☽ 10am-1pm Tue & Thu)

Turkey Consular section (Map pp240-1; ☎ 4988133; Xaqani küç 27; ☽ 9.30-11.30am Mon-Fri) Consulate (☎ 0136 57330; Heydar Əliyev pr 17, Naxçıvan)

Turkmenistan Closed in 2001, expected to reopen in 2008.

UK (Map pp240-1; ☎ 4975188/89/90; www.britishembassy.gov.uk/azerbaijan; Landmark Bldg, Xaqani küç 45A) Represents Commonwealth citizens.

USA (Map p238; ☎ 4980335; http://azerbaijan.usembassy.gov; Azadlıq pr 83)

Uzbekistan (Map p238; ☎ 4972549; Badamdar Şosesi, 9th Lane, 437) Take marshrutka 3 from behind Bakı Soveti metro. Infuriatingly the US$75 visa fee must be paid into the central IBA bank, Nizami küç.

FESTIVALS & EVENTS
Religious Festivals

Those holidays that are calculated according to the Islamic lunar calendar occur about 10 or 11 days earlier each Western year. Exact dates must be locally pronounced by Muslim clerics based on moon sightings, but 'predicted' dates are:

Aşura This Shiite holy day commemorates the martyrdom of Imam Hussein, grandson of the Prophet Mohammed, at the AD 680 battle of Karbala. In Iran this solemn occasion is widely marked by processions of men dressed in black flagellating themselves with metal flails. However in Azerbaijan religious fervour is much less marked so only in Muslim hot spots like Nardaran (p259) are you likely to see any such displays. Local Muslim leaders suggest that devotees give blood instead.

Noruz Bayramı (New Year Festival) Marks the return of spring and the start of the New Year, according to the Persian solar calendar. Azerbaijan's biggest celebration, it culminates on the spring equinox (night of 20 to 21 March) but related festivities stretch for a week or more either side of this date. Traditions associated with Noruz Bayramı include spring-cleaning the house, growing wheat and barley sprouts, preparing special rice dishes, and cleansing the spirit by jumping over bonfires on the last Tuesday night before Noruz.

RELIGIOUS FESTIVAL DATES

Year	Aşura	Noruz	Ramazan	Gurban Bayramı
2008	19 Jan	21 Mar	1-29 Sep	8 Dec
2009	10 Jan	21 Mar	21 Aug-19 Sep	27 Nov
2010	1 Jan	21 Mar	11 Aug-8 Sep	16 Nov
2011	22 Dec	21 Mar	1-29 Aug	6 Nov

Ramazan During the Islamic month of Ramazan (Ramadan), many Muslims refrain from eating, drinking and smoking during the hours of daylight. The *orucdaq* (fast) is not very strictly observed throughout Azerbaijan, but many people will fast for at least part of the month.

Ramazan Bayram The day after Ramazan, it is a holiday involving widespread feasting.

Gurban Bayramı (Festival of Sacrifice) Held 11 days before Muslim New Year, commemorates Abraham's test of faith on Mt Moriah, when God ordered him to sacrifice his son Isaac. People visit family and friends, and the head of the household traditionally slaughters a sheep, which forms the basis of a grand feast.

HOLIDAYS

New Year's Day 1 January

Martyrs' Day 20 January (commemorating the massacre of Baku civilians by Soviet troops in 1990); this is not a holiday but a national day of mourning

Xocal Day 26 February (remembering the massacre of Azeris in Xocal in 1992); national day of mourning

International Women's Day 8 March (not a day off but widely celebrated)

Noruz Bayramı 20–21 March

Republic Day 28 May (founding of first Azerbaijan Democratic Republic in 1918)

National Salvation Day 15 June (parliament asked Heydar Əliyev to lead the country in 1993)

Armed Forces Day 26 June (founding of Azerbaijan's army in 1918)

Ramazan Bayram (above)

National Independence Day 18 October (date of Azerbaijan's breakaway from the USSR)

Constitution Day 12 November (framing of constitution in 1995)

National Revival Day 17 November (first anti-Soviet uprising in 1988)

Gurban Bayramı (above)

Solidarity Day 31 December (breaking down of border fences between Azerbaijan and Iran in 1989)

INTERNET RESOURCES

See also Media (right).

Az.az (www.azerbaijan.az) Extensive official site including links to various personal sites of the Əliyevs.

Azerbaijan International (Map p242; ☎ 02 4928701; www.azer.com; İstiqlaliyyət Gəngə 5, Baku) Splendid magazine and website with extremely comprehensive archive of cultural articles and resources.

London Azerbaijan Society (http://karabakh.co.uk) Spells out Azerbaijan's claims to Karabakh. Other more rabidly anti-Armenian sites include www.khojaly.net.

MAPS

The best commercially available map of Azerbaijan is a 1:500,000 topographic sheet (Ümumcoğrafi Məlumat Xəritəsi) sold in better Baku bookshops. It is fairly comprehensive, although not quite all roads are recently updated. More detailed 1:100,000 maps exist but are considered 'secret'. Soviet-era versions available on the web tend to be hopelessly outdated and carrying them could get you into trouble. Any map showing Nagorno-Karabakh as an independent country might also be confiscated by police if found.

While good city maps exist for Baku, for other towns they're virtually impossible to find.

MEDIA

The Azeri press is the least free of the Caucasian countries and has been further pummelled in recent years. Several non-government publications have been closed, sometimes using the ruse of closing their offices for 'safety' reasons. The assassination of leading independent journalist Elmar Huseynov in 2005 hardly helped. Read more on Amnesty International's site http://web.amnesty.org /l ibrary/index/ENGEUR550032007.

ANS (www.anspress.com) and AzerNews (www.azernews.az) offer regular online news reports with English versions more frequently updated than on Day.az (www.tod ay.az).

Magazines

The venerable *Azerbaijan International* (www .azer.com) deals with all things Azeri in detailed themes and maintains magnificent cultural websites. *Azerbaijan Today* (www .azerbaijantoday.az) looks mostly at economic issues through long interview pieces. *InBaku* (http://inbakumagazine.com) is a glossy vanity mag photographing expats at play.

Newspapers

A boon for the large foreign community in Baku is the wide choice of free English-language newspapers available through restaurants and hotels, though most are merely platforms for (useful) advertisements of services and restaurants. Some are written in an impenetrable, propagandist English which is almost comical to decipher. *CBN Extra* (www .cbnextra.com) and *Baku Sun* (www.bakusun .az) combine tabloid headlines with occasional nuggets of serious news.

TV

As part of the nation's ongoing Azerification, once-popular Russian-language channels have been dropped from the terrestrial TV network. However, cable and satellite TV is increasingly available, particularly in better hotels. These offer a vast choice, predominantly Turkish and Russian options but also BBC World, CNN and other Anglophone options.

MONEY
Costs

Baku is in the throes of a major oil boom, meaning that many prices seem inflated and poor value in comparison with those in neighbouring countries. This extends to places where Bakuvians take their weekends ,but out in the more distant provinces prices are contrastingly very inexpensive.

Currency

Azerbaijan's national currency was revalued in 2006 by a factor of 5000. Azerbaijan's new Manat (AZN1) is divided into 100 qəpiq (100q) and is worth somewhere between a US dollar and a euro. Confusingly, many locals still quote prices in old Manat, frequently using the former nicknames 'Shirvan' (10,000 old Manat, ie AZN2) and

Məmməd (1000 old Manat, ie 20q). Especially outside Baku, if someone quotes a price without a unit (eg simply '3'), that's likely to mean three Shirvan, ie AZN6. Contrary to backpacker instincts this is not a scam.

PHOTOGRAPHY & VIDEO

Many Azeri people love to have their photos taken, though it's always polite to ask first. Before snapping other subjects remember that the nation is still in an unfinished war and thus retains a certain sensitivity to the photographing of anything that could be considered strategic. That includes pretty much anywhere near the Armenian border/ceasefire line. Naxçivan is also very sensitive. Don't try to take snaps on the Bakı metro either.

TELEPHONE

Azerbaijan's land-line phone system has been rationalised. Calls now simply require the dialling code and number without the palaver of the old Soviet-era '8-and-wait'. Payphones are increasingly rare. Those antiquated beasts that require *jeton* (tokens) give you an unlimited time for a local call but cannot connect to international, regional or mobile numbers. For that you'll usually need to go to a call centre, typically attached to or within the post office. Standard price calls to most of the world cost 54q per minute.

Mobile Phones

Few locals don't have a mobile phone.

SIM cards can be bought at ubiquitous dealerships and slipped into your own handset. You'll need a photocopy of your passport to buy one. Packages start at AZN5 for the least popular numbers. Azercell is best for rural areas. When calling between phones on the same network, no codes are necessary, just the seven-digit number.

VISAS

Visas are available on arrival in most circumstances at Baku's Heydar Əliyev International Airport but not at land borders.

AZERBAIJAN

MOBILE PHONE PROVIDERS

Provider	Access Code	Nickname	Coverage (% pop)
Azercell (www.azercell.com)	☎ 050	Sim-Sim	99%
BakCell (www.bakcell.com)	☎ 055	Cin	80%
NarMobile (www.narmobile.az)	☎ 070		80%

Border Crossings

Foreigners may enter/exit Azerbaijan at the following points.

Astara Land border with Iran.

Baku port By ferry from Turkmenbashi (Turkmenistan) and Aktau (Kazakhstan).

Böyük Kəsik Railway-only border with Georgia.

Culfa-Jolfa Land border with Iran.

Gəncə International Airport

Heydar Əliyev International Airport For Baku.

Krasny Most (Red Bridge, Qırmızı Körpü, Tsiteli Khidi) Land border with Georgia.

Naxçivan Airport From Moscow.

Postbina (Balakən-Lagodekhi) Land border with Georgia.

Sədərək Land border with Turkey.

Registration

Within three days of arrival, *müveqqəti qeydiyat* (registration) is a legal requirement for those planning to stay longer than a month. Apply at the local police station, bringing copies of your passport and apartment-lease agreement. It can be hard to persuade police to do this procedure and for years the rule has been laxly enforced, however any cops who fancy causing trouble can use this against you and extort hefty fines.

Visas for Onward Travel

Visas for Pakistan are not issued in Baku unless the applicant is a registered resident in Azerbaijan, and there's no Turkmenistan embassy whatsoever. However, visas for China are generally easier to get in Baku than in Central Asia. For Russian, Uzbek and sometimes Kazakh visas you'll first need an invitation letter or tourist voucher (eg from STANtours). For Iran, arrange visa clearance through an agency like Persian Voyages.com at least two weeks before application (in Baku or Naxçivan). Most Westerners can get a Turkish visa at the border but Turkish immigration officers at the crossing from Naxçivan demand that Brits have their visa in advance. See p295 for a list of consulate addresses in Baku and Naxçivan.

Visas in Advance

Applicants need two passport photos, a completed application form and a passport valid for at least one month after travel. Certain embassies demand either a letter of support from a travel agency or a hotel booking confirmation. In these cases, it's usually sufficient to book a midrange or top-end room (no budget hotels are likely to fax confirmation) for your first

> **BORDER NOTES**
>
> ■ Azerbaijan–Russia borders are closed to foreigners.
>
> ■ Azerbaijan–Armenia borders are sealed.
>
> ■ Armenian-occupied areas of Azerbaijan including Nagorno-Karabakh cannot be accessed from the rest of Azerbaijan.

night or two and use the faxed confirmation to receive your visa; you can subsequently simply cancel the booking. Transit visas, usually valid for 72 hours, are issued to those with an onward ticket to a third country in the region.

Single- and double-entry visas are usually issued in five days. Business and multi-entry visas require official invitation letters and referral to Baku, so generally take longer. Visa prices vary by nationality. Typically it's €60 but US citizens pay US$100 and Brits pay US$101. Express processing is not generally an option though it may be possible at the consul's discretion. Fees generally need to be paid into a local bank (often a fair distance away), so don't apply late in the day.

Visas on Arrival

Single-entry 30-day visas are available at Baku airport for the same fees. No Letter of Invitation (LOI) or hotel booking is necessary. There has been discussion about phasing this out so check carefully with your nearest embassy beforehand. Oddly you need to get the entry stamp before going to the visa-application window. Bring two passport photos or you'll have to pay US$20 to a savvy waiting photographer.

Remember that Azerbaijani visas are not issued on arrival at any other arrival points.

WOMEN TRAVELLERS

In Baku local women appear to be very liberated, but it's something of a veneer and in the regions Azeri women tend to be semi-invisible. Western women might be treated as 'honorary men' in social situations, but a woman travelling alone may cause confusion or consternation by sitting down to tea at an all-male *çayxana*. Physical harassment is graciously rare, however stares are common and provincial young Azeri men may think it fair game to snap photos of you on their mobile phones. Getting annoyed rarely helps, as offenders don't imagine they've done anything wrong.

Nagorno-Karabakh
ԼԵՌՆԱԵԻՆ ՂԱՐԱԲԱՂ

Nagorno-Karabakh is an enigma wrapped up inside the Caucasus. It is a 'country' recognised by no-one. It is Armenian culture inside the borders of Azerbaijan. Even the name is something of a mystery, being made up from words of three different languages: *nagorno* means mountainous in Russian, *kara* means black in Turkish and *bakh* means garden in Persian. To confuse things further, the locals refer to their region as Artsakh.

While there exist many questions about Nagorno-Karabakh and its political status, the beauty and cultural richness of this remote mountain landscape are undeniable. Up steep cliffs, wedged into narrow valleys and hidden in remote forests are hundreds of moss-covered churches and monasteries, and while most of them are abandoned, a few are being renovated and reopened.

The war of the early 1990s left deep scars across the landscape, but the people are moving on, rebuilding their country stone by stone. Travel here is still an adventure, involving bad roads, special permits and military-occupied no-go zones, but rapidly improving infrastructure means better hotels, restaurants and facilities in the main tourist areas. Karabakhi hospitality makes wading through the challenges a joy, even in difficult times.

NAGORNO-KARABAKH

FAST FACTS

- **Area** 10,700 sq km
- **Capital** Stepanakert
- **Famous for** Hidden monasteries, mountains, quasi-independence
- **Official name** Lernayin Gharabaghi Hanrapetutyun (Nagorno-Karabakh Republic; NKR), also called Artsakh
- **Phrases** *barev dzez* (hello), *shnorhakalutyun* (thanks)
- **Population** 150,000

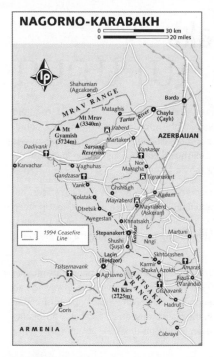

NAGORNO-KARABAKH

Highlights

- **Gandzasar Monastery** (p306) – An extraordinary example of Armenian architecture with rich friezes and magnificent detail.
- **Agdam** (opposite) – Just behind the front line, this large city which was destroyed in the war, is frozen as a dead, melancholy monument.
- **Janapar Trail** (p307) – A 190km-long hiking trail that slashes across the country, leading walkers past old *khatchkars* (carved stone crosses), orchards, forest-topped cliffs and friendly, self-sufficient villages.

History

In this region, names and history are as contested as the land itself. Azeris claim 'Qarabaq' as their cultural heartland, and point to the role of Şuşa (Shushi) in the growth of their literature and language. In Azeri accounts, the Christian inhabitants of Karabakh are descendants of the Christian nation of Albania (unrelated to the present-day state of Albania). Caucasian Albania lost independence after the Arab invasion in the 7th century, and most Albanians converted to Islam, while the remnants of the Albanian Church were usurped by the Armenian Church. Armenians agree that the Albanian Church was officially absorbed into the Armenian Church in the early 19th century, but argue that this was done at Russian prompting to sign off on a 1000-year-old reality. Certainly the locals say they're culturally as Armenian as anyone, with 4000 churches, monasteries and forts on their hills to attest to this.

During the Middle Ages the region was under the control of Persia, with local rule in the hands of five Armenian princes known as Meliks. The Karabakh Khanate, with Panahabad (Shushi) as its capital, passed into Russian hands in 1805. During the 19th century many native Muslims left for Iran while Armenians from Iran emigrated to Karabakh.

Stalin separated Karabakh from Armenia in the 1920s and made it an autonomous region within Azerbaijan. The natural growth of the Azeri population outpaced growth of the Armenian one and Azeri settlers were moved to Armenian villages. By the 1980s the territory's population was down to about 75% Armenian.

Demands to join Armenia grew in 1987–88, until the local assembly voted for independence from Azerbaijan in December 1989, and hostilities commenced. From 1989 to 1994 the area was racked by war, which, in its first stage, pitted the Karabakhtsis against overwhelming Azeri and Soviet forces. Grad antitank missiles fell on Stepanakert from Shushi until 1993, while bands of local men, organised into *fedayeen* (irregular soldier) units, scavenged for weapons and ranged them against the Soviet army. After the fall of the USSR, the war escalated into a heavily armed clash between Armenian troops and *fedayeen* commandos on one side and the Azeri army assisted by Turkish officers on the other. Soon after the Armenian capture of Shushi, the Azeri retreat turned into a rout. Two Azeri governments fell as a result, and Nagorno-Karabakh's entire 50,000-strong Muslim population was forced to flee, joining 150,000 other Azeri refugees from Armenia. A ceasefire was declared in May 1994 and the territorial lines have remained constant since then. The war cost around 30,000 lives.

Since then the territory has struggled on, rebuilding as best it can.

Stepanakert, the self-proclaimed capital, is a town of about 55,000 with a parliament, presidential palace, ministries and a national museum. The local economy includes subsistence farmers and diaspora-funded projects such as the highway to Goris in southern Armenia. The North-South Hwy is currently being built along the spine of the territory, from Martakert in the north down to Karmir Shuka and Hadrut in the south. Tourism is minimal.

Visitors should be aware that because of the region's disputed status, foreign embassy staff can't visit the region. That said, if you stay away from the frontline areas and any military exercises it's no less safe than Armenia. The front line traces along the edge of the hills of Karabakh, where they spread into the plains. The northern frontier is along the Mrav range, with 3724m Mt Gyamish. The occupied territories between Armenia, Karabakh and Iran are mostly empty, with only 25,000 or so settlers rebuilding among the overgrown villages and roofless walls of houses.

International negotiations have repeatedly failed but there are plenty of options on the table. The hope is that at some point an internationally recognised referendum can be held, but this would only be considered legitimate after the return of Azeri refugees who fled the region during the war. Armenia wants the referendum to be held as soon as

WHERE EXACTLY AM I?

According to nearly all international protocols, the territory of Nagorno-Karabakh still legally remains part of Azerbaijan. It is not officially recognised as a sovereign state and we do not regard it as such. It is an independent state only according to the Nagorno-Karabakh Declaration of Independence and can only be visited from Armenia, which controls the territory. To visit you must purchase a Nagorno-Karabakh Republic visa.

possible, while Azerbaijan prefers a timetable of 15 to 20 years. Clearly there are issues to be sorted out.

Bako Sahakyan, Nagorno-Karabakh's president, won his job with an 85% mandate in July 2007 elections. Running on a pro-independence platform, the win was also seen as a referendum for his cause. Despite Sahakyan's lofty title, all political decisions and economic reforms are essentially handed down from Yerevan.

STEPANAKERT ՍՏԵՓԱՆԱԿԵՐՏ
☎ 0471 / pop 55,000

Stepanakert, Karabakh's capital, stands above the Karkar River, surrounded by a typical landscape of forest, pasture and fields backed by craggy mountains. The city is not much different from a typical Armenian town,

NAGORNO-KARABAKH

AGDAM

The travel permit from the Ministry of Foreign Affairs does not include a visit to Agdam, though some travellers do visit this unique place anyway. Karabakh and the occupied land around it have many deserted villages and towns, but no others are quite like this former city of 100,000 people. The city was captured in 1994, sacked and looted. Tall, shattered tower blocks stand in the distance, past a sprawling city centre of one- and two-storey buildings. Shredded playgrounds sprout with shrubs, the streets are cracking open with trees, and ponds fill in bomb craters. The city was picked clean by people from Stepanakert looking for building materials, and by professionals who took out everything from copper wires to bathroom fittings. Besides a few soldiers and scrap-metal hunters, this city is as dead as Pompeii. You could almost forget that the front line between Armenian and Azeri forces stretches north and south at the eastern city limits. Don't venture beyond the mosque (defaced, sadly) at the town centre. You can climb one of the rickety minarets for a 360-degree view of the city. The view one gets from the top is similar to photographs taken of Hiroshima in August 1945.

Agdam remains a sensitive area with a strong military presence and it would be foolish to waltz in by yourself. However, determined travellers have managed to visit by hiring a taxi from Stepanakert. While many go without incident there is no guarantee you won't be arrested. If you travel here bear in mind that cameras are not welcome; even your cab driver may not allow you to take photos.

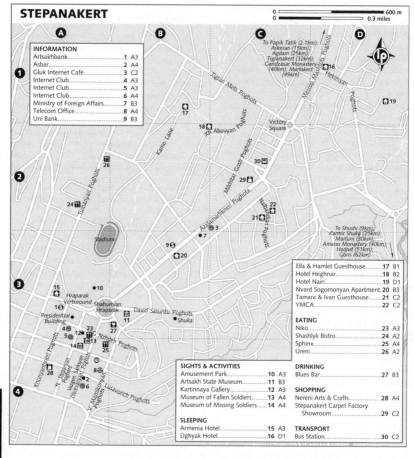

STEPANAKERT

INFORMATION	
Artsakhbank	1 A3
Asbar	2 A4
Gluk Internet Café	3 C2
Internet Club	4 A3
Internet Club	5 A3
Internet Club	6 A4
Ministry of Foreign Affairs	7 B3
Telecom Office	8 A4
Uni Bank	9 B3

To Papik Tatik (2.1km);
Askeran (15km);
Agdam (25km);
Tigranakert (32km);
Gandzasar Monastery
(40km); Martakert
(49km)

To Shushi (9km);
Karmir Shuka (25km);
Martuni (30km);
Amaras Monastery (40km);
Hadrut (51km);
Goris (62km)

SIGHTS & ACTIVITIES	
Amusement Park	10 A3
Artsakh State Museum	11 B3
Kartinnaya Gallery	12 A3
Museum of Fallen Soldiers	13 A4
Museum of Missing Soldiers	14 A4

SLEEPING	
Armenia Hotel	15 A3
Dghyak Hotel	16 D1
Ella & Hamlet Guesthouse	17 B1
Hotel Heghnar	18 B2
Hotel Nairi	19 D1
Nvard Sogomonyan Apartment	20 B3
Tamara & Ivan Guesthouse	21 C2
YMCA	22 C2

EATING	
Niko	23 A3
Shashlyk Bistro	24 A2
Sphinx	25 A4
Ureni	26 A2

DRINKING	
Blues Bar	27 B3

SHOPPING	
Nereni Arts & Crafts	28 A4
Stepanakert Carpet Factory Showroom	29 C2

TRANSPORT	
Bus Station	30 C2

though it does have a bit more vibrancy. There are lively local arts and music scenes, shops on the High Street do brisk business and cafés and restaurants, some surprisingly sleek, are often busy. A good range of accommodation is available. The town maintains a Soviet-era feel despite massive reconstruction since the end of the war – there are more signs in Russian than in Armenian, and much evidence of military and security forces.

Information

There's no official tourist office, but the **Ministry of Foreign Affairs** (☎ 4 14 18; info@mfa. nk.am; 28 Azatamartikneri Poghota; ☼ 9am-1pm & 2-6pm Mon-Fri, noon-4pm Sat) can suggest routes and

places to visit – you have to register there on arrival anyway (see p308).

A detailed map of Nagorno-Karabakh, plus street maps of Stepanakert and Shushi, are produced by Asbar Tourism Agency and available from some gift shops and hotels – we found ours at the Dghyak Hotel.

Uni Bank (13 Azatamartikneri Poghota) has an ATM that accepts Visa. **Artsakhbank** (25 Knunyantsneri Poghots) has an ATM accepting MasterCard. Moneychangers everywhere have rates posted outside shops – rates are much the same as in Armenia.

Stepanakert has at least a dozen **Internet Clubs**, all charging around AMD300 per hour. Most are open 10am to 10pm, with some staying open until midnight. **Gluk Internet Café** (32 Azatamartikneri

Poghota) is reliable or try no-name places at 68 G Nzhdeh Poghots, 23 N Stepanyan Poghots and 16 Vazgen Sarksyan Poghots.

Karabakh Telecom has several phone offices around town (with attached internet cafés). You can also make calls from the main **Telecom Office** (☎ 7 12 75; 30 V Mamikonyan Poghots; ⏰ 8.30am-10pm). Note that neither VivaCell nor ArmanTel prepaid plans will work in Karabakh. Local cell phones work on the Karabakh Telecom network (SIM cards are sold locally).

One recommended local travel agency is **Asbar** (☎ 4 47 58; www.asbar.nk.am; 16a Vazgen Sarksyan Poghots), which handles transportation, apartments, hotels and multilingual guides.

Sights

The **Artsakh State Museum** (☎ 4 36 69; 4 David Sasuntsi Poghots; admission free; ⏰ 9am-5pm Tue-Sun) is rich in local artefacts and contains particularly interesting displays on the Karabakh war, including some of the homemade weapons used in the crushing early days of the fighting. An excellent and free guided tour in English is available on arrival.

The **Museum of Fallen Soldiers** (☎ 5 07 38; btwn N Stepanyan & Vazgen Sarksyan Poghots; admission free; ⏰ 9am-5pm Mon-Sat) honours those men who died in battle during the 1990–94 war with Azerbaijan.

The walls of this stunning museum are lined with photographs of soldiers killed in action and there are displays of weaponry and other memorabilia.

The entrance to the museum is in the back of a pink building that stands on Vazgen Sarksyan Poghots. The door is slightly hidden by cypress trees. Nearby, the **Museum of Missing Soldiers** was closed for renovation at the time of research but should be worth a look.

Kartinnaya Gallery (22 N Stepanyan Poghots; admission free; ⏰ 9am-5pm Mon-Sat) displays the work of local artists and is a good place to tap into the Karabakhi arts community.

For something a little more light-hearted, visit the **amusement park** (⏰ May-Sep) which has rides and live music on warm summer nights.

On the outskirts of the town towards Mayraberd (Askeran) is the **Papik Tatik** monument, which appears on mugs, T-shirts, desk ornaments and more. The tuff statue of a bearded elder and a woman with a veil is named 'We are our mountains', their stony gaze embodying the indomitable local spirit.

Sleeping

There are several homestays in Stepanakert: Asbar (see opposite) may be able to recommend one. If you want a private apartment, contact local journalist **Nvard Sogomonyan** (☎ 5 05 65, 22 16 12; 22 Azatamartikneri Poghota; per night US$25) who has a small place in the city centre, near the Ministry of Foreign Affairs. The apartment is in the northernmost stairwell on the 4th floor.

ourpick Ella & Hamlet Guesthouse (☎ 4 77 38, 25 21 55; 10 Kamo Lane; per person AMD5000) Budget travellers will find a safe haven in this spotless guesthouse. It has five rooms with new furnishings, TV and shared bathroom in a huge villa. There is plenty of privacy and lots of space to spread out. The host family is genuinely courteous and does laundry, although there is no breakfast. It's at the end of narrow Kamo Lane; look for the grey concrete building with the high fence.

Tamara & Ivan Guesthouse (☎ 4 05 97; 21a Nalbandian Poghots; per person AMD5000) This unsigned guesthouse has two spartan guestrooms in a family house. The rooms are bland and boxy and you share the bathroom with the rest of the family. The hosts request payment upfront for the entire stay. It's just past YMCA.

YMCA (Kars Hotel; ☎ 4 71 67; 22 Nalbandian Poghots; s/d AMD7500/10,000, s/d deluxe AMD15,000/20,000) This is certainly not an official YMCA but that is what the sign reads outside the building. To confuse things further the management says the place is actually called Kars Hotel. Rooms are small (the whole building feels a bit cramped) but functional and come with private bathroom.

Hotel Heghnar (☎ 4 86 77, 097266666; www.hegh narhotel.com; 39-41 Kh Abovyan Poghots; s/d/lux AMD18,000/24,000/45,000) Has 12 rooms in two buildings, which can be combined into apartments. It's quite cosy and comfortable with decent beds and big couches, and all the rooms have a balcony. The caretakers speak only Armenian and Russian.

Hotel Nairi (☎ 7 15 03; www.nairi.nk.am; 14a Hekimyan Poghots; s/d AMD18,000/27,000; ❄) This fine establishment has shared bathrooms for the single rooms and en suite bathrooms in its double rooms. The Armenian-Australian owner aims to make Antipodeans feel at home and has painted kangaroos onto walls of the hotel. Meals cost AMD2500, and staff happily arrange transport around the region.

NAGORNO-KARABAKH

AGOB JACK ABOLAKIAN

Agob 'Jack' Abolakian is one of many diaspora Armenians returning to his native land for business opportunities. Jack was born to Armenian refugees, grew up in Syria and later emigrated to Australia, where he became a successful construction baron. His varied background has given him five languages: Armenian, French, Turkish, Arabic and English. Jack opened the first major hotel complex in Stepanakert, the Hotel Nairi, in 1999. We asked him about his decision to invest in an untried market.

When did you first come to Nagorno-Karabakh?

My wife and I visited in 1999 on a holiday. At the time there was only one hotel and it was full so we ended up staying in a private home for four days. The conditions were quite primitive and it made for a very uncomfortable holiday.

And that gave you the idea for the hotel?

Yes, a year later I came back, met with some officials. They thought I was crazy for wanting to build a hotel, but in any case they gave me an abandoned school in hopes I could turn it into a hotel.

How has business been so far?

Better than expected. In 2001 we had all of 400 guests. In 2006 we had more than 6000 guests. It just shows how much has changed in Stepanakert – there is more business, more investment, more life. We're not alone either, there are a dozen new hotels in town and they all do good business.

What has been the most interesting experience in running this business?

A couple of years ago we hosted a group of 45 journalists. Half came from Yerevan and the other half were from Baku. Needless to say this made for some interesting dialogue. I spoke with the Azeri journalists and conveyed my opinion that it's time for peace and reconciliation. They agreed and I felt that their side also wanted to see an end to the conflict. There is a will for peace among the people, but politicians are slow to react.

Do you have any more business plans?

I have many ideas. There are lots of opportunities here, it's a clean slate. I'd like to build a brick factory and we have plans to build 1000 Western-standard homes. We are also looking into agriculture, specifically the export of walnuts – Karabakh walnuts are organically grown and high in quality.

What is the most satisfying aspect of working here?

I am a businessman, so of course it's satisfying when business is good. But it's just as rewarding to know that my investment is helping my homeland. That is something that you can't really put a value on. As a member of the Armenian diaspora, I felt it my duty to help in some way.

Dghyak Hotel (☎ 4 30 24; 1 Hekimyan Poghots; r incl breakfast AMD25,000; ✿) New, thoroughly modern hotel at the northern edge of town. It has 10 rooms, some with air-con, plus an attached art gallery and one of the better restaurants in town.

Armenia Hotel (☎ 5 09 10; Hraparak Veratsnound; s/d/ste AMD25,000/35,000/55,000; ✿) The plushest hotel in town, open since 2007, is right on the main square, near the Presidential Palace and Parliament. Amenities include fitness centre, sauna, cable TV (with BBC news) but there is no internet.

Eating

Besides the following, the restaurants at the Armenia Hotel and the Dghyak Hotel are both recommended for fine dining.

Shashlyk Bistro (☎ 22 21 47; 25 Tumanyan Poghots; kebabs AMD500, khoravats AMD1200; ✽ 10am-midnight) A great option for travellers on the go, this small kebab-bistro is take-out only.

Niko (☎ 4 12 24; 25 Vazgen Sarksyan Poghots; meals AMD3500-5000; ✽ 11am-midnight) Mixed menu of salads, soups and main dishes like beef stroganoff and pizzas. It's in an unmissable streetside patio lit up in the evening with green and purple neon lights.

Ureni (☎ 4 45 44; Tumanyan Poghots; meals AMD3500-5000; ✽ noon-midnight) Garden café popular with the local business community. The menu is a mix of Armenian, Russian and European dishes.

Sphinx (☎ 2 05 33; G Nzhdeh Poghots; meals AMD3500-5000; ✽ 11am-midnight) The most bizarre sight in Stepanakert is the giant Sphinx looming over the door of this restaurant. Plastic palm trees ignited with neon complete the scene. Despite the Egyptian theme, the menu is similar to other places in town, with *khoravats* (barbecued food) and kebabs the prime options.

Drinking

Blues Bar (☎ 5 01 68; Shahumian Hraparak; ⊙ 10am-midnight) Enchanted-forest theme bar with trees and vines emerging from the walls and a ceiling lit with the moon and stars. The back patio is also forested and for once the Latin music adds some variety to the soundtrack. Around the same square there are several other cafés that serve alcohol.

Shopping

Nereni Arts & Crafts (☎ 4 87 11; www.nereni.nk.am; 10 Lusavorich Poghots; ⊙ 10am-7pm) Run by a diaspora Iranian, this shop carries a range of unique handcrafts created by local jewellers and artisans. A similar shop is at the Dghyak Hotel.

The **Stepanakert Carpet Factory Showroom** (☎ 4 07 91; www.hyekeer.com; 31 Azatamartikneri Poghota; ⊙ 9am-5pm Mon-Sat) sells handmade carpets and runners that make great souvenirs. It ships worldwide if you don't want to lug your carpet around the Caucasus.

Getting There & Away

Buses and marshrutkas depart from the **station** (☎ 4 06 61) near Victory Sq on Azatamartikneri Poghota. Possibly in 2008 the station will move to a new facility on the road to Goris. There are three marshrutkas per day to Yerevan (AMD4500, seven to eight hours) leaving at 8am, 9am and 10am. These all pass through Goris (AMD2000, two hours). Later in the day it's possible to find a shared taxi charging similar rates. Chartering a taxi to Goris/Yerevan costs AMD10,000/32,000.

Marshrutkas to Shushi depart on the hour between 8am and 7pm (AMD200, 30 minutes). There are two buses a day to Gandzasar (AMD500, one hour) at 9am and 4pm. There are nine buses a day to Martakert between 8.30am and 4pm (AMD600, 1½ hours). Buses to Martuni (AMD600, one hour) leave at 8.30am, 9am, noon, 1pm and 2pm. Two buses per day go to Karmir Shuka (AMD400, 50 minutes) at 9am and 2.30pm. One bus per day goes to Hadrut (AMD750, two hours) at 9.30am.

Getting Around

There are plenty of marshrutkas (per ride AMD50) that ply the main boulevards of Stepanakert. Numbers 10, 13, 14 and 17 shuttle up and down Azatamartikneri Poghota.

SHUSHI ՇՈՒՇԻ
☎ 0477 / pop 3500

Shushi (Şuşa) stands on a plateau 9km south from Stepanakert, with high walls and views over a wide swathe of central Karabakh. The city was once a centre of Armenian and Azeri art and culture, and during the 19th century it was one of the largest towns in the Caucasus. The city suffered badly during the war and most people left, but recovery is under way.

A fine **medieval wall** protects the eastern ramparts of the town – you'll see it on the left as you approach the town from the highway. The fortress was built in 1750 by Panah Khan. The Azeri army used the town heights to fire barrages of Grad missiles down onto Stepanakert and surrounding villages. It was conquered by a stunning night assault up the cliffs on 8–9 May 1992, a crucial turning point in the conflict.

The scarred centre of town has the restored **Ghazanchetsots Cathedral**, the obvious white church near the Hotel Shoushi. Another church, the 1818 **Kanach Zham** (green church) stands up the hill.

Down the hill, in the older part of town, is a damaged **mosque** that is slowly being restored. The **museum** (☎ 3 19 48), about 350m south of the mosque, is also under renovation. Near the Shushi Municipality building are several old buildings, including a one-time **Russian church** that was later converted into a cinema, as well as the **residence of the Panah Khan**.

Jerderduz, a grazing land for horses, is 1km south of the mosque on the edge of a beautiful gorge. The little red flags sticking out of the field do not denote the location of landmines – these are actually holes on Karabakh's only **golf course** (☎ 3 15 41; 9a Amirian Poghots; per round AMD5000, club rental AMD1600); contact Hrachick Haritiounian. One of the most surreal sights in Karabakh occurs every second morning in summer when an 86-year-old Belgian doctor named John Malcolm comes here to play a round of golf. He welcomes golf partners, but note that only right-handed clubs are available.

Sleeping & Eating

Hotel Shoushi (☎ 3 13 57; www.shoushihotel.com; 3 Amiryan Poghots; s/d incl breakfast AMD17,500/22,500; ❄ ▣) You wouldn't guess there would be a boutique hotel here, but the extremely comfortable Hotel Shoushi stands across from the Ghazanchetsots Cathedral. It has 12 very tasteful, spacious rooms, lots of interesting artwork and a good restaurant. Dinners cost around AMD3000.

Armen B&B (☎ 097240712; shoushi_armen@nk.am; 9 Aram Manoukyan Poghots, Apt 36; per person incl breakfast AMD5000; ▣) Armen Rakedjian, a Frenchman, runs this B&B out of his apartment in upper Shushi. Armen speaks French, English and Armenian and is a mine of information on the area. His building is right next to the corner where the marshrutka terminates. Just ask for 'Armen Français' and someone will show you the way.

Saro's B&B (☎ 097231764; saro62@mail.ru; per person incl breakfast AMD5000) English-speaking owner Sarasar (Saro) Saryan is an enthusiastic host and knows much about Shushi's history. His old home has a garden and large rooms. It's in the lower part of Shushi, but Saro can usually be found at his office in the Municipality.

Homek Restaurant (☎ 097225618; ◷ 10am-11pm) *Khoravats* (barbecued food) place located across from the taxi stand.

Getting There & Away

Marshrutkas between Shushi's main square and the *avtokayan* (bus station) in Stepanakert, 9km downhill, leave every 30 minutes or so during the day (AMD200). By taxi the trip costs about AMD1500.

GANDZASAR MONASTERY

This 13th-century monastery, 40km northwest of Stepanakert, is probably the most important structure in Karabakh. The church of **Surp Hovhannes Mkrtich** (St John the Baptist) is the largest in the grouping, with beautiful friezes around the central drum. There are well-preserved inscriptions and *khatchkars* in the church's *gavit* (antechamber), which is filled with the floor-slab tombs of former bishops and nobles of the region. It is the seat of the Arkepiskopos (Archbishop) of Artsakh.

Vank, the village below Gandzasar, is unlike any other village in Karabakh, thanks to the patronage of native son Levon Hairapetian. The Moscow-based lumber baron has funded large-scale redevelopment of the town, including

a new road from Stepanakert, a school and an enormous hotel that resembles the *Titanic*. The **Eclectic Hotel** (☎ 097267474; per person AMD7000) is great value and has loads of surreal atmosphere, including a totally out-of-place Chinese restaurant run by three chefs from Guangxi province.

A daily bus travels from Stepanakert to Vank (AMD300, one hour) at 9am and 4pm. From the village you need to walk the last 2.5km uphill to Gandzasar, or hire a taxi. The bus returns to Stepanakert straightaway so to get back you'll need to hire a taxi or hitch. A round-trip taxi to Stepanakert is AMD10,000.

On the way back to Stepanakert you can stop by the village of Ghshlagh to the visit the unique **Nikol Duman Memorial Museum** (☎ 071-4 47 58; www .ndumanmuseum.nk.am; ◷ 10am-6pm), which honours the life of the renowned Dashnak leader.

The home, once occupied by Duman himself, is fully restored to its 19th-century condition. Drinks are available and meals are often prepared for groups.

NORTHERN KARABAKH

The road heading northeast of Stepanakert goes 14km to the town and fortress of **Mayraberd (Askeran)**, which has huge medieval walls and towers. Built by Panah Khan in the 18th century, it once stretched 1.5km across the valley. Further north you'll spot abandoned buildings and the odd burned-out tank as you approach Agdam. Signs posted by the Halo Trust indicate that the area has been cleared of landmines. The road branches before Agdam, one road going north to Martakert.

The restored fortress of **Tigranakert** appears on the left side of the road, 32km out of Stepanakert. The key-keeper lives in the little homestead in front. **Martakert** is Karabakh's northern market town and was the scene of fierce battles during the war, changing hands frequently. The **Surp Hovhannes Mkrtich** church in town has been a community reconstruction project. The local **history museum** includes a gallery of photos of men who died in the war.

It is unwise to go further north than Martakert due to the proximity of the front line. Spectacular scenery lies west of the town, including the Sarsang Reservoir, and, downstream on the far bank, the **Jraberd fortress**, with a brilliant defensive position on a gorge within view of the splendidly sited **Yeritsmankants** (Three Youths) monastery – visits to both require permission from the military.

Past the reservoir and up the Tartar River, the road enters dense, lush forests that make for very slow going in wet weather. After about 65km you reach the village of Dadivank and a military checkpoint. **Dadivank monastery** is an overgrown masterpiece with a bell tower, fine *khatchkars* and monastic cells around the main 13th-century Surp Dadi church. Watch out for holes into underground cisterns and chambers as you walk around. The princes of Upper Khachen are buried under the floor of the main church's *gavit*. The road continues up the Tartar River into the Kelbajar region (see right).

SOUTHERN KARABAKH

There are two main routes into southern Karabakh, one towards Martuni and a newly paved stretch of road to Hadrut.

Martuni (population 23,150) is a market town with a few palm trees and a statue of Monte Melkonian, a native of Fresno, California who became a hero in the Karabakh war. From Martuni the road heads south to **Fizuli (Varanda)** which lies mostly in ruins since the 1994 conflict.

The first point of interest on the Hadrut road is the village of **Sarushen**, 26km from Stepanakert, which contains the ruins of Pirumashen Church. The 12th-century relic is near the road but hidden by trees. Next is **Skhtorashen**, about 2km north of Karmir Shuka (Krasni Bazar) and home to a 2000-year-old plane tree so large you could hold a party inside its core.

From the small town of Karmir Shuka you can turn off the main road and visit **Amaras Monastery**, founded by St Gregory the Illuminator and completed by his grandson, Bishop Grigoris. Mesrop Mashtots also founded a school here to educate people in the new alphabet in the 5th century. The current structure is a modest church surrounded by monastic cells. Amaras is 15km from Karmir Shuka. Part of the road is paved, but most is a rough dirt track.

Back on the main road, head 14km south of Karmir Shuka to reach the extraordinary **Azokh cave**, not far from the village of Azokh. Where the paved road ends, continue along the dirt track for about 200m, then hike up the hill to the cave. The cave has six bat-filled chambers connected by tunnels. Remains of ancient humans have been found in the cave, as well as tools and pottery shards. The cave entry is large and stunning, but you'll need a strong torch (flashlight) to view the inner chambers.

About 3km southwest of Azokh is the village of Togh. From the end of the village bear right and continue up a dirt road towards **Gtchavank Monastery**. The monastery is located deep in the forest and it helps to have a local show you the way. This 10th- to 13th-century gem was once the seat of the bishops of Amaras, with a library, intricate *khatchkars* and tremendous views. The monastery has been covered with graffiti, but a cleanup is under way.

If you've come down here via Karmir Shuka and want to take a different route back it's possible to loop back via Fizuli. If time allows, continue to Hadrut, which has a **museum** portraying local history and ethnography.

KELBAJAR ՔԱՐՎԱՃԱՌ

This wild, mountainous region between Armenia and northern Karabakh is ringed by 3000m peaks, with rivers cutting through high gorges and a scattering of villages being resettled by Armenians. Most of the population before the war were Muslim Kurdish farmers and herders – the Bolsheviks toyed with the idea of creating a Red Kurdistan here in the

NAGORNO-KARABAKH ON THE LAM

Dedicated hikers may want to consider crossing Karabakh on foot, taking advantage of a newly marked path that stretches from Hadrut in the south to Kelbajar region in the north. The 190km-long **Janapar Trail** is marked with blue signs that depict a yellow footprint.

Starting from Hadrut, the trail continues to Togh, Gtchavank, the Azokh cave, Karmir Shuka, the Skhtorashen giant plane tree, Avetaranots, Mkhitarashen, Karintak, Shushi, Stepanakert, Aygestan, Ptretsik, Kachaghakaberd, Kolatak, Gandzasar, Vaghuhas and Dadivank. If you have permission to enter Kelbajar, you can follow the trail to the hot springs at Zuar and finally Nor Manashid.

The entire route takes 14 days, so make sure you purchase the 21-day Karabakh visa. There is no need for a tent and you really only need a sleeping-bag liner as there are places to stay in every village and town along the way – just ask around for the local homestay. See www.janapar.org for more details.

1920s. Apart from soldiers, loggers, beekeepers and a few farmers, the region is largely deserted, though some say there are still individual soldiers who lost their minds in the war camped out in the hills. A rough road (jeep only) leads across the Sodk Pass to the Zod gold mines and Vardenis near Lake Sevan.

About 10km west of Dadivank is a military checkpoint. To get past it you'll need permission from the Ministry of Foreign Affairs in Stepanakert. The road northwest of the checkpoint continues for around 50km to Vardenis. This is a rough and remote road to bring petrol and food. The road heading west from the checkpoint leads to **Karvachar**, the biggest town in the region. It's populated with people from the Shahumian district north of Karabakh proper, driven out of Azerbaijan in the early 1990s. Around 8km past the town are a hot spring and geyser.

The southern part of Kelbajar is technically the region of Berdzor (Lachin), which contains the strategic Goris–Stepanakert highway. Close to the checkpoint a sign points to the north up to the **Tsitsernavank Monastery** (Monastery of Swallows), a modest but ancient church, dating back to the 5th century. The road is very bad and you'd need an experienced driver with a 4WD vehicle. The round trip from the checkpoint takes about one hour.

NAGORNO-KARABAKH DIRECTORY
Dangers
Unexploded ordnance (UXO) continues to injure people and livestock and it is unwise to venture into open pasture land anywhere near the front line. Warning signs are prominently displayed in areas close to the main roads. Regarding personal safety, crimes against visitors are almost unheard of; Stepanakert is as safe as Yerevan or any part of Armenia.

Internet Resources
http://shusha.aznet.org Presents the culture and history of Shushi.
www.armeniapedia.org Mostly on Armenia but has excellent reference sections on Karabakh.
www.nkr.am The website of the Nagorno-Karabakh Republic (NKR) Ministry of Foreign Affairs.
www.nkrusa.org Website of the NKR office in Washington, with a list of NKR representatives in 10 or so countries.

Visas
Most people get their visas at the Ministry of Foreign Affairs (p302) in Stepanakert. You

need to fill out a single-page form including every destination you're heading to in Karabakh and attach two photos. A five-day visa is issued on the spot for AMD11,000; a 21-day visa is AMD17,250. Multiple-entry visas valid for up to 90 days are available. Consul staff will ask how you're travelling to Karabakh and where you intend to stay. Note that you will not be permitted to enter Azerbaijan if you have a Karabakh visa on your passport, so if you plan to visit Azerbaijan request that the visa be left outside the passport.

While no checks on your visa are likely to be made while travelling in Nagorno-Karabakh, the papers may be checked on departure at the checkpoint on the Aghavno River between Berdzor and Goris. This is especially true for travellers in a taxi or their own vehicle. Travellers in the back of a marshrutka are usually overlooked, but you should have the visa just in case. There are also checks if you are going into Kelbajar.

Visas are also available in Yerevan at the **Permanent Representative of the Nagorno-Karabakh Republic** (☎ 24 97 05; nkr@arminco.com; www.nkr.am; 17a Zaryan Poghots; ☯ 10am-1pm & 2-5pm Mon-Fri). The visa will be cheaper if you request that it be processed in five days – AMD7000 for a five-day visa and AMD10,000 for a 21-day visa. If you can't be bothered to wait, it's just easier to get a visa in Stepanakert, as you need to register there anyway. Another reason to visit the consulate in Yerevan is to get familiarised with Karabakh – the consulate is very friendly and offers lots of great travel advice and tips on accommodation.

If you are travelling by taxi or private car into Karabakh consider getting the visa in Yerevan – it is by no means necessary, but it may simplify the process when you enter the country.

VISA REGISTRATION
In Stepanakert you must register on arrival (or the next day if it's after hours) at the Ministry of Foreign Affairs (p302). You must restate the places you want to visit, your passport is photocopied and you are issued a registration paper. All this bureaucracy might not happen if you have a 10-year Armenian residency pass. The registration paper might be asked for at the checkpoint on exit. The paper states that you can only travel on the internal roads, which are within the borders of Nagorno-Karabakh, but not including roads around the front line.

Regional Directory

CONTENTS

ACCOMMODATION

The accommodation scene in the Caucasus countries has improved out of sight in the past few years. Genuinely comfortable new midrange hotels are sprouting all around the three countries, a burgeoning network of inexpensive homestays and guesthouses welcomes budget travellers (especially in Georgia and Armenia), and international top-end chains like Hyatt, Hilton and Marriott are setting up shop in all three capitals. Old

BOOK YOUR STAY ONLINE

For more accommodation reviews and recommendations by Lonely Planet authors, check out the online booking service at www.lonelyplanet.com/hotels. You'll find the true, insider lowdown on the best places to stay. Reviews are thorough and independent. Best of all, you can book online.

PRACTICALITIES

- All three countries fall into DVD Region 5 (along with other ex-Soviet countries, Africa and a few Asian countries) and the predominant video format is SECAM.

- Electric power is 220 volts AC, 50Hz. Sockets are designed for European-style plugs with two round pins. Power cuts still happen, but with nothing like the frequency of a few years ago.

- All three countries use the metric system – see the Quick Reference page inside the front cover for conversion from imperial measurements.

Soviet hotels have nearly all closed or been totally rebuilt. The days are gone when your choices were limited to a smelly sanatorium or a crumbling concrete hotel with dodgy plumbing.

Sleeping recommendations in the larger cities in this book are divided into budget, midrange and top-end categories. Midrange means a typical room for two people for the equivalent of between US$50 and US$150 in Tbilisi, US$50 and US$200 in Baku and US$80 to US$200 in Yerevan. Outside the capitals accommodation prices plunge, and while the range of quality accommodation is much smaller, value for money is generally much better. A good midrange room, often in a brand-new hotel, won't cost you more than US$100, and frequently a lot less.

Homestays, guesthouses, B&Bs and pensions in the three countries typically cost between US$15 and US$25 per person, often including a couple of meals, and these are the best option in small towns and rural areas – the hospitality is usually wonderful and it's a chance to get a taste of local life and sample some of the endless variety of Caucasian home recipes. Only occasionally will you have to resort to a dilapidated, dreary Soviet relic for budget accommodation.

Note: the air-conditioning icon, ✵, is used in this book to denote accommodation places that have air-con in at least some (not necessarily all) rooms.

B&Bs, Guesthouses & Homestays

These types of accommodation are people's homes – which could be a city apartment or a village house with a garden and animals – with a few rooms available for guests. In cities you get the occasional upmarket guesthouse with very comfortable, even luxurious, rooms and most of the facilities of a hotel. But most guesthouses, homestays and B&Bs are budget establishments, not luxurious but usually well cared for.

They may have dorm-style accommodation with several beds in each room, or private rooms, or a combination of the two. What most of them offer in common is a friendly welcome, good home-cooked meals and the opportunity to get a feel for local life. Owners are often more than willing, without being intrusive, to dispense local information, help you find guides and rent jeeps, or get the local marshrutka (minivan) driver to pick you up at the door when you leave.

The more popular of them are also very good places to meet other travellers. Bathrooms increasingly feature hot showers and Western-style toilets, though there are still some that don't. All in all, these places provide the perfect accommodation network for budget travellers, though for the moment they are less common in Azerbaijan than in the other two countries.

Camping

There are very few commercial campsites except for a few seaside or lakeside places that open for the summer school holidays. Those that do exist have few facilities besides a basic amenities block with cold water and maybe earth toilets. It's not always safe to camp just anywhere, so if you plan to pitch a tent get good information on local conditions and if you're near a village, ask if it's OK to camp there.

If you can ask permission to camp on someone's land, people are usually happy to oblige.

Hotels

Attractive, modern, midrange hotels – some even meriting the sobriquet 'boutique' – have sprung up all over the region, many of them on a refreshingly small scale with attentive, friendly service. They range from Finnish-style wooden cottages in the woodlands of Azerbaijan to modern Art Nouveau mansions in Batumi. Some older hotels have been attractively renovated. Such places provide well-equipped, comfortable rooms (air-conditioned where necessary) and usually have a decent restaurant and probably a bar and a couple of leisure facilities. Staff are increasingly professional and amiable. The grumpy old Soviet service ethic has pretty much gone the way of Intourist.

The few still-dowdy old Soviet hotels that haven't been renovated provide alternative budget accommodation in some towns. Only a few hotels are still used as housing for refugees.

International-standard top-end hotels from the likes of Radisson, Hyatt and Marriott are generally restricted to the three capitals.

Rental Accommodation

In Yerevan renting an apartment is quite a common practice among visitors as a cost-cutting tactic.

In the peak summer season, around US$60 a day will net you a conveniently located two- or three-bedroom apartment.

Short-term rentals are harder to find in other cities that don't have Yerevan's summer influx from the Armenian diaspora. Some apartments are available in Baku from US$40 a night but you usually need to stay at least a few days.

Sanatoriums

A great many Soviet sanatoriums were built in the days when an entire Ukrainian metallurgical plant would be bussed in for a week of regimented spa treatments, local feasts and compulsory toasts of *druzhba narodov* (friendship of peoples, a central Soviet slogan of unity). Some were run by Soviet ministries as retreats for the upper echelons or for favoured artists and members of the writers, cinematographers and musicians unions.

Almost any kind of mildly health-giving environmental factor could serve as an excuse to build a few sanatoriums – the fresh air of the Black Sea or Caspian coasts, the thick forests of Armenia's Dilijan area, the iron-bearing sand of Ureki, or any kind of mineral-water spring.

Today some sanatoriums lie derelict in forest valleys across the Caucasus. A few soldier on under the ownership of Armenian government ministries or other institutions, but most have been privatised and converted into hotels of varying appeal.

ACTIVITIES

The Caucasus countries, especially Georgia and Armenia, are at last starting to develop their huge potential in the field of activity-based tourism. Tbilisi and Yerevan both have several specialist travel agencies offering trekking, climbing, horse riding and other activities. See the directory at the end of each country chapter for more detail on what's on offer.

Bird-Watching

Armenia and Georgia are increasingly popular as destinations for bird-watching, with their huge range of habitats from alpine peaks to low grasslands. Both countries claim around 350 species, including many that are threatened in Europe but appear in relatively large numbers here.

Hiking & Horse Riding

Walking amid the wonderful hill and mountain scenery is spectacular. Outstanding areas include Svaneti, Tusheti and the Kazbegi region in the Georgian Caucasus, and the Laza, Xınalıq and Lahıc areas in the Azeri Caucasus. An exciting hike of 10 days to two weeks connects Kazbegi to Tusheti via intriguing Khevsureti (p105). Armenia, especially its hilly north, has masses of lovely day trails – through the forested valleys between Haghartsin Monastery and Dilijan, or the mountain forests around Goshavank, or in the Yenokavan Canyon. The Garni Gorge and Khosrov Nature Reserve (p176) offer fairly challenging hikes near Yerevan. Nagorno-Karabakh is best explored on the well-marked, 190km Janapar Trail (p307), which links old monasteries, caves and quaint villages.

A guide is a good idea for some of the more difficult and remote routes. Local guides are available almost everywhere, and good agencies provide them too. Good English-language guidebooks of walking tours are available for both Georgia and Armenia.

Horse riding is popular and easy to arrange in many of the areas that are good for walking. Hikers can take some of the slog out of longer routes by taking a packhorse along.

Mountaineering

The Caucasus presents infinite exciting challenges, with none of the crowds of the Alps. The peaks of Shkhara, Jangha and Kazbek tower above 5000m in the Georgian Caucasus, although the highest peak of the range, Mt Elbrus (5642m) lies entirely within Russia. Kazbek is a classic, not-too-technical climb, and Mt Chaukhi, near Shkhara, is another favourite, with many challenging routes.

The peaks of Bazardüzü (4466m) and Şahdağ (4243m) in northern Azerbaijan have permanent ice near their summits, but in fact offer only moderate climbing routes. Şahdağ is not technically difficult but does require ropes and crampons for ice walking. There is no developed rock climbing in Azerbaijan, but there may be opportunities for adventurous climbers on the remote limestone crags southwest of Quba.

The southernmost of the four peaks of Armenia's highest mountain, Aragats, is easy enough for inexperienced climbers, but its highest, northern peak (4090m) demands greater abilities. *Classic Climbs in the Caucasus* by Friedrich Bender (1992) compiles 80 alpine mountaineering routes, but it's starting to get a bit dated.

Skiing & Snow Sports

There are three ski resorts in the region, with a fourth on the way. The skiing is nothing too challenging but facilities are improving, and skiing here certainly won't bankrupt you.

The best-equipped resort is Gudauri in the Georgian high Caucasus, just a couple of hours' drive from Tbilisi. An added attraction here is heliskiing. Bakuriani (p119) in the Lesser Caucasus is Georgia's 'family skiing' resort and especially popular. Tsaghkadzor (p189), north of Yerevan, was once a training facility for Soviet Olympic squads, and the facilities here are starting to improve. Azerbaijan plans to develop a ski resort at Laza.

The approach road, at least, is already under construction.

Other Activities

Rafting is growing in popularity on Georgian rivers such as the Pshavis Aragvi (p123). Sailing and other coastal water sports are beginning to emerge at Batumi on Georgia's

REGIONAL DIRECTORY

Black Sea coast and at Baku and the Abşeron Peninsula in Azerbaijan – though the oil-derrick-dotted seascape there adds some unusual hazards. Armenia's Lake Sevan has a brief sailing season during the summer.

Armenia's Vayots Dzor region is peppered with karst (limestone) caves, some open to tourists, others largely unexplored and for experienced climbers only.

It's possible for you to ice-skate at places such as Bakuriani (December to March) and Batumi (year-round; p91. But one of the most bizarre sporting experiences the Caucasus region has to offer must be a round of golf at Shushi (p305), in the heart of Nagorno-Karabakh!

BUSINESS HOURS

Working hours tend to be flexible across the region as people pop out to have lunch, pay the bills and do the shopping. Most shops open from around 9am or 10am to 7pm or later. Some stay open on Sundays. Typical office hours are 9am to 5pm Monday to Friday. Museums may open up as late as 11am and most close one day a week, often Monday. Banking hours are typically 9.30am to 5.30pm Monday to Friday, often with a break for lunch. Some banks open Saturday mornings too.

Cafés and restaurants open their own idiosyncratic hours. In the big cities they may stay open from around 9am until the early hours of the next morning. In smaller towns restaurants may only open for lunch and a not-too-late dinner. In Georgia, restaurant hours of noon to midnight are fairly standard.

See the directory at the end of each country chapter for further details on country-specific business hours.

CHILDREN

Family is important in the Caucasus, and children are treasured gifts from God. Local people love meeting children and are very relaxed with them – it's perfectly normal for strangers to strike up a conversation over kids, and for the most part people will be extremely considerate towards travellers with children. However, journeys in sweltering minivans and buses can be trying for children and adults alike, and the delays and minor inconveniences of Caucasus travel can make life difficult at the low-budget level. Disposable nappies are sold in the big cities,

but may be hard to come by elsewhere. Many of the Soviet-era playgrounds have fallen into disrepair, but Georgia at least has a few new very child-friendly attractions such as Tbilisi's Mtatsminda amusement park (p58) and Europark water-slide park (p59), and Batumi's big Ferris wheel (p89) and ice rink (p91). In Yerevan, Haghtanak Park (p155) is a good place to take kids, and there are some professional, non-English but easy-to-follow kids' shows in the city's theatres.

In Baku children like the fairground attractions along the bulvar (seafront promenade). Kids with a taste for the outdoors will enjoy the countryside, where there are lots of cute little farms, picnic spots and short walks.

CLIMATE CHARTS

See also When to Go on p18 for more information.

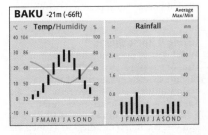

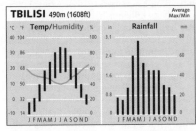

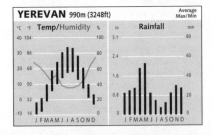

CUSTOMS REGULATIONS

All three countries require you to obtain a certificate from their culture ministry if you want to take out valuable art or artefacts. See the directory at the end of each country chapter for more on this and other customs practices.

DANGERS & ANNOYANCES

Given how troubled their not-so-distant past has been, the Caucasus countries are refreshingly light on dangers and annoyances. Tourists are welcomed, though you may be an object of curiosity and occasionally suspicion in little-visited regions.

Western governments' travel advisory websites (see right) routinely warn of the dangers of pickpocketing and theft, though most travellers encounter no such difficulties. You should obviously take the normal precautions you would when travelling anywhere – don't flash fat wallets or large amounts of cash around, keep a close eye on your belongings in crowded places like markets, bus stations, metro trains and marshrutkas, don't walk alone along dark, empty streets – but in general crime levels against tourists are very low. The epidemic of banditry in Georgia's Svaneti region has been stamped out.

Where you do need to be careful is near politically sensitive regions such as the Nagorno-Karabakh ceasefire line, Abkhazia, South Ossetia, and parts of the official Armenia–Azerbaijan border including the Ijevan–Noyemberyan road. Tensions and conflicts may flare up at any time in or around these areas, so check out the lie of the land before you go. Local police or military are likely to view you with suspicion in these areas, and in little-visited Naxçıvan. Landmines still lie near sections of the Armenia–Azerbaijan border, the Nagorno-Karabakh ceasefire line and in parts of Abkhazia.

Tourists may be questioned in areas of Georgia and Azerbaijan close to the Russian border. Georgia's Pankisi Valley north of Akhmeta, home to some Chechen refugees, has in the past been bombarded by Russia because Chechen rebels were hiding out there, but has been stable for several years. Russian helicopters attacked the upper Kodori Valley in Abkhazia in 2007; the same year a mysterious bomb, which Russia claimed to know nothing about, fell (but didn't explode) near Tsitelubani, close to the border of South Ossetia.

TRAVEL ADVISORY WEBSITES

These government sites have information on potential danger areas and general safety tips:

- **Australia** www.smartraveller.gov.au
- **Canada** www.voyage.gc.ca
- **UK** www.fco.gov.uk
- **USA** travel.state.gov

Away from the ceasefire line and any military exercises, Nagorno-Karabakh is as safe as Armenia. The Kelbajar region between northern Nagorno-Karabakh and Armenia is OK to visit if you have the right permit (see p307), which is easiest if you have an Armenian 10-year residence card.

Corruption is far less of a problem for visitors than it used to be. If you do encounter a sticky-fingered customs officer, it usually pays to stay calm and stand your ground.

Obviously climbing and hiking in the mountains have their potential dangers. Seek local advice, go with company or take a guide, especially if you're heading into isolated areas.

A minor irritant is that locals think it very odd for men to wear shorts, especially in the cities. In the heat of summer you either have to sweat it out or put up with some odd looks and sniggers. For specific advice for women travellers see p317.

DISCOUNT CARDS

An ISIC card entitles you to a surprising number of discounts on entertainment, museums, shops, restaurants, medical and other services and even some places to stay in Tbilisi, Yerevan and Baku. See www.isic.org for details.

EMBASSIES & CONSULATES

It's important to realise what your national embassy can and can't do if you get into trouble. Generally speaking, it won't be much help in emergencies if the trouble you're in is remotely your own fault. Remember that while you are in the Caucasus you are bound by national laws. In genuine emergencies you might be able to get some assistance, but only if other channels have been exhausted; the embassy would expect you to have insurance. If you have all your money and documents stolen, it might assist you with getting a new passport, but a loan for onward travel is out of the question.

Embassies in the three countries encourage visitors to register with them and this is a particularly good idea if you are going off to isolated or sensitive areas. In Nagorno-Karabakh and Abkhazia, you're on your own. Assistance would have to come from Baku and Tbilisi, respectively, which isn't possible. Foreign embassies in Tbilisi, Yerevan and Baku are listed in the directory section of their respective country chapters. Note that some countries may only have one embassy in the region, or none at all. Neither Kazakhstan nor Turkmenistan has an embassy in Georgia, and Turkmenistan's embassy in Baku is not expected to reopen until 2008. Iran has an embassy in all three capitals, plus a consulate in Naxçıvan (Azerbaijan). For Australia, Canada and New Zealand, responsibility for the Caucasian countries is taken by their embassies in Moscow or Ankara. In emergencies, British embassies will usually look after the interests of Commonwealth nationals.

GAY & LESBIAN TRAVELLERS

Homosexuality has been decriminalised in all three countries since 2000, but social acceptance or understanding is minimal and extremely few gays or lesbians openly display their orientation. The three capitals have a small number of gay or gay-friendly bars and meeting places, but beyond that there are few signs of any gay scene. Traditional values and a patriarchal society make homosexuality pretty much taboo. Even in Georgia, generally the most open-minded of the three societies, a Council of Europe–sponsored protolerance public event had to be cancelled in 2007 in the face of virulent antigay opposition, including from the Georgian Orthodox Church, and a participant in a popular TV reality show was expelled after declaring that he was gay.

Gay travellers should be discreet but there's no need for fear – two men or women sharing a bed will often be considered far less scandalous than an unmarried straight couple doing the same. Open displays of affection will draw startled looks pretty much anywhere although, thanks to local custom, nobody will bat an eyelid at two men or two women holding hands or kissing each other on the cheek. Georgia's **Inclusive Foundation** (www.inclusive-foundation.org) is the only public gay organisation in the region.

For those wishing to make contacts in the gay community, the best (and safest) means is the internet – www.gay.com is a good place to start. The International Lesbian and Gay Association has useful information on all three countries at www.ilga-europe.org.

INSURANCE

It is important to be properly insured against theft, loss and medical problems. Health insurance should cover you for visits to private clinics in the capitals, which generally provide the best medical care but can be expensive, and emergency air evacuations – if you do require an operation but can still travel it may be wise to fly to Europe. Check that your policy covers any activities you plan, such as horse riding, climbing, skiing or even short hikes.

INTERNET ACCESS

Almost all towns have internet cafés, charging the equivalent of US$0.50 to US$1.50 per hour, most with reasonable connections. Some of the better hotels in Georgia and Armenia provide wi-fi access in rooms, and there are a few cafés in the three capitals with wi-fi access too. The internet icon, 🖳 , in accommodation listings in this book denotes places to stay where internet-connected computers are available for guests' use – this is often but not always free of charge.

LEGAL MATTERS

The 1990s epidemic of police harassment of foreigners is a thing of the past, but you may be questioned if you visit sensitive areas, such as near the Georgia–Russia or Azerbaijan–Armenia borders or the Nagorno-Karabakh ceasefire line (including Agdam), or Naxçıvan. Outsiders can be viewed with some suspicion in less-visited areas of Azerbaijan.

It's sensible always to carry at least a photocopy of your passport and visa, and the real thing if you are going anywhere where you might be questioned.

Anyone thinking of driving should note that there is a zero limit on blood alcohol for drivers in all three countries. Traffic police are however unlikely to try to extract bribes from foreigners for fabricated or marginal driving offences.

We've heard of difficulties with reporting robberies, both in getting the report made by the police and in getting insurance companies to honour a police report in any of the major languages of the Caucasus. In Azerbaijan the police may be more of a problem than a help in any circumstances.

Drugs are viewed very seriously indeed. Cannabis grows in the region and the seeds are sometimes used as a cooking ingredient, but partaking in any other way carries severe risks. Prisons in the region are dismal, underfunded and very authoritarian.

MAPS

A good regional map such as Freytag & Berndt's *Caucasus* (1:1 million scale) is invaluable for planning. See the Directory section in each country chapter for information on country-specific maps.

MONEY

The easiest way to carry money is with an ATM card, and cash US dollars, euros or Russian roubles as backup. ATMs are plentiful in the cities and can be found in just about every town. They normally accept MasterCard, Visa, Cirrus and Maestro cards and some are able to dispense cash US dollars as well as the local currency (lari in Georgia, drams in Armenia, Manat in Azerbaijan). Visa and MasterCard cash advances are also possible at major banks, and there are Western Union offices in many places in case you need to arrange a money transfer. You can locate nearby Visa ATMs at visa.via .infonow.net/locator/global, and MasterCard ATMs at www.mastercard.com/atmlocator.

Most towns have almost as many money-changing offices as ATMs, and it's entirely legal to change foreign cash into local currency. The greenback is still the most popular foreign currency in the region, now closely followed by the euro. You can't change Azeri Manat in Armenia or Armenian dram in Azerbaijan, but both can be exchanged in Georgia. Georgian lari are exchangeable in both countries. Capital cities and border areas are the easiest places to make these intra-Caucasian transactions.

Travellers cheques are often a real pain to change except at some banks in the three capitals.

You can make purchases with credit cards at the better hotels, restaurants and some shops in the capitals, but less frequently elsewhere.

In this book prices are given in whatever currency they are normally quoted in – usually the local currency but sometimes (chiefly by the more expensive hotels and travel agencies) US dollars or euros.

PHOTOGRAPHY & VIDEO

It's unwise to start pointing your camera anywhere near border areas that might be considered sensitive. This includes pretty much anywhere near the Azerbaijan–Armenia border, the Armenia–Iran border or the Nagorno-Karabakh ceasefire line (including Agdam), and in Naxçıvan. There are also some spots in Baku, including the metro system, where police might bother you if you start waving a camera about (see p243). It is never a good idea to point a camera at military vehicles or army bases.

Extend the usual courtesies when photographing people – people will often happily pose if you ask their permission to snap them, and it's a good way to break the ice.

SOLO TRAVELLERS

Broadly speaking, the biggest irritant for solo male travellers is the drinking culture in all three countries, and for solo women travellers it's unwanted attention from men (p317). You just have to try to steer clear of situations that could become difficult. Popular homestays and guesthouses in Georgia and Armenia are great places for chatting with other travellers as well as enjoying friendly local hospitality, though there are fewer of these in Azerbaijan. Outside the summer months (May to September, especially July and August) there aren't that many travellers going through the Caucasus anyway. If loneliness bites, it's time to hit one of the main cities or take a tour with other people. Except in places that are accustomed to travellers, eating alone in a restaurant may seem odd to local sensibilities, as restaurants more often cater to groups of people. Some places have private dining rooms or booths where solo travellers might feel less awkward.

Learning at least some words in the local language or Russian will help smooth your path with the local people.

TELEPHONE

Antiquated landline telephone systems in all three countries have been or are being updated and now generally provide efficient service. But many local people and businesses now mainly use mobile phones, which offer very reasonable rates for calls and text messages, and provide virtually country-wide coverage. All three countries use the GSM standard, and you can buy SIM cards and prepaid phone cards for your mobile for very little – well worth doing if you are spending more than a few days in any country. A mobile is very useful for checking arrangements, calling ahead to places to stay and so on. Even if you don't speak the local language, you can ask someone else to call for you, using your phone. And people can call you! And, amazingly, sending a text message to another country usually costs as little as texting locally.

Street payphones are now more or less useless (except for some new ones in Baku), but most towns have a telephone centre, often paired with a post office, where you can make national or international calls from booths.

Country codes are: Georgia ☎ 995, Armenia ☎ 374, and Azerbaijan ☎ 994. See the Telephone sections in the individual directory at the end of each country chapter for information on local dialling codes, costs and further useful tips.

TIME

All three countries are four hours ahead of Greenwich Mean Time (GMT+4), making them three hours ahead of most of Western Europe, four hours ahead of the UK, nine hours ahead of New York and 12 hours ahead of the west coast of North America. Armenia and Azerbaijan operate on Daylight Saving Time from the last Sunday in March to the last Sunday in October, putting them five hours head of GMT, and one hour ahead of Georgia, for that period.

TOILETS

Public toilets are rare across the region, and some of the old facilities by churches on pilgrim routes and mosques are positively medieval. At bus stations you may have to pay a nominal fee to the attendant – squat toilets are the norm. There's often a basket for waste paper. If there's any toilet paper it may be grey cardboard-like material, so it's a good idea to carry a supply.

The best places for clean toilets are Western-style restaurants, cafés and bars in the cities. Toilets in restaurants, museums and so on are often marked by stereotypical symbols such as a smoking pipe for men, a high-heeled shoe for women. Some of the more basic homestay and guesthouse accommodation has squat toilets, though Western-style ones are on the increase.

TOURIST INFORMATION

Yerevan has an excellent tourist office (p151), and there are half a dozen generally good ones in other Armenian cities. Georgia is setting up a network of about 20 tourist offices, most of which should be open by the end of 2008. They have access to plenty of information and are mostly very helpful, though still learning their craft.

Azerbaijan has a tourist information office in Baku (p243), with some give-away literature, and an excellent office in Lahıc. Elsewhere, a lot of tourist offices have been built but many of them are open sporadically at best.

There's some good stuff on the internet – see the Internet Resources sections of the directory at the end of each country chapter for recommended sites. The sites of some of the top travel agencies in Tbilisi (p52), Yerevan (p151) and Baku (p243) are helpful too.

TRAVELLERS WITH DISABILITIES

The Caucasus countries have very few facilities to make life easier for travellers with disabilities. Even in the main cities, the cracked and potholed nature of many pavements makes wheelchair use problematic, although the growing number of modern hotels is a positive factor, and the cost of a car and driver/helper isn't extortionate. Some of the best local travel companies (Tbilisi p52, Yerevan p151 and Baku p243) will be able to discuss specific needs.

General information and help for travellers with disabilities is available at websites such as www.accessatlast.com and www.disabledtravels.com.

VISAS

For Georgia, many Western nationals need no visa for visits of up to 90 days (see p127). Those who do need visas can get them at road and air entry points into the country, or from Georgian embassies or consulates.

For Armenia, all visitors need visas and 21-day visas are issued at all entry points. E-visas, for arrivals at Zvartnots Airport only, can be obtained online.

Visas are also necessary for Azerbaijan. Thirty-day visas are available on arrival at Baku airport, but to enter the country elsewhere you need to obtain a visa in advance from an Azeri embassy or consulate.

To visit Nagorno-Karabakh, you need a visa from the Nagorno-Karabakh representative in Yerevan or the Ministry of Foreign Affairs in Stepanakert. Important: you will not be permitted to enter Azerbaijan if you have a Karabakh visa in your passport, so go to Azerbaijan before you get your Nagorno-Karabakh visa, or ask for your Nagorno-Karabakh visa to be left outside the passport.

For more detailed information on all of the above, see the Visas sections in the directory at the end of each country chapter.

If you visit Abkhazia you must get a visa from the Abkhaz Foreign Ministry in Sukhumi – see p86.

WOMEN TRAVELLERS

Among the three countries, women are least restricted in Georgia and more so in Azerbaijan. Women in the Caucasus are generally expected to look after the home in addition to any paid employment they have. While the big cities appear to be open and liberated places, in villages an unmarried local woman seen in public with a man would be expected to be engaged within a fortnight.

Female travellers, especially if travelling alone, will have to ward off some overly friendly males. It's a good idea not to sit next to a strange man on a marshrutka if possible, and to sit near the driver. Eating alone at male-dominated restaurants can be awkward, but some restaurants and cafés offer private dining rooms or discreet vine-covered pavilions and tables. In Azerbaijan most çayxanas (teahouses) and many of the cheap local restaurants known as yeməkxanas are very male-dominated and can be uncomfortable places for women. The same goes for a few of the cheaper lodgings there. Local women do not go into çayxanas.

In mosques and some churches, women should be ready to cover their hair, shoulders and legs. Islam in Azerbaijan is not generally fundamentalist and in most areas women do not cover their hair. Many women in Baku favour lots of make-up and high heels. In the Georgian mountain region of Tusheti women are not permitted to approach the traditional animist shrines known as khati.

Drunkenness is very bad form generally, but for women even being tipsy is frowned upon. However, women aren't expected to drink heavily during toasts – a sip will suffice. Local women smoking in public are often considered to have loose morals; in off-the-beaten-track places women travellers may get some strange looks if they smoke.

Female travellers may be objects of curiosity in more remote regions, and walking alone at night should be avoided if possible.

If you're alone it's unwise to accept an invitation from a man to visit his house or his office unless he's with a female relative; it could be misinterpreted as strong interest on your part.

Transport

CONTENTS

The Caucasus countries are accessible by air, sea and land. Baku (Azerbaijan) has the busiest airport in the region, though Tbilisi (Georgia) and Yerevan (Armenia) both have growing numbers of international flights.

Local politics complicate matters a little on the ground. Georgia's and Azerbaijan's borders with Russia are closed to foreigners (in fact the Georgia–Russia border was closed to everyone at the time of writing), and Armenia's eastern and western borders, with Turkey and Azerbaijan respectively, are sealed. This means the only routes right through the region are from Turkey into Georgia, then south through Armenia to Iran, or east through Azerbaijan to Iran or across the Caspian Sea to Kazakhstan or Turkmenistan. Or vice versa!

THINGS CHANGE...

The information in this chapter is particularly vulnerable to change. Check directly with the airline or a travel agent to make sure you understand how a fare (and ticket you may buy) works and be aware of the security requirements for international travel. Shop carefully. The details given in this chapter should be regarded as pointers and are not a substitute for your own careful, up-to-date research.

Surly, bribe-soliciting immigration officials have become a thing of the past, as travel to and from the wider world has become easier and more common.

GETTING THERE & AWAY

Most visitors fly into the region, but it's also possible to enter by road from Turkey (to Georgia and Azerbaijan) or Iran (to Armenia and Azerbaijan), and by sea from Ukraine or Bulgaria to Georgia, and from Turkmenistan or Kazakhstan to Azerbaijan. Flights, tours and rail tickets can be booked online at www.lonelyplanet.com/travel_services.

ENTRY REQUIREMENTS

Procedures at arrival points are now generally straightforward and quick. It might take a couple of hours to get through the Turkish–Georgian road border at Sarpi on a busy weekend, and the Georgia–Armenia and Georgia–Azerbaijan train borders can involve a halt of up to three or four hours. The cause of the delays is generally customs searches and the officials are not usually all that interested in tourists.

You should have a passport that will remain valid until after you leave any of these countries, and preferably one that will be good for six months from the time you enter any country. (Six months' remaining validity is a minimum requirement if you have to apply for a Georgian visa.)

It's important to note that you will not be permitted to enter Azerbaijan if you have a Nagorno-Karabakh visa in your passport, so if you plan to visit both places, go to Nagorno-Karabakh second, or request that the Nagorno-Karabakh visa be put on a separate piece of paper. Entering secessionist Abkhazia from Russia is considered illegal by Georgia, so any stamps in your passport showing that you have done this might, if you're unlucky, cause you problems if you then try to move into Georgia from Abkhazia. Abkhazian visas, however, are separate documents not stuck into your passport.

Each country has differing visa requirements. Most Western passport holders don't need visas for Georgia (Australians and New Zealanders being among the exceptions) but everybody needs one for Armenia or Azerbaijan. You can obtain a visa on arrival at any Armenian entry point, at most of Georgia's (should you need one) and, for now at least, at Baku airport. You can also get visas from these countries' embassies or consulates before you go, and if you'll be arriving at Yerevan's Zvartnots Airport there's the option of getting your visa by email. See this book's country directories for details of each country's visa requirements.

AIR

A small but growing number of international airlines fly to the three main airports at Tbilisi, Yerevan and Baku. Flight times are around 2½ hours to Moscow, four hours to Europe, five hours to the UK and 12 to 14 hours to the East Coast of North America, not including connections. There are a few direct flights to the Middle East and Central Asia, but very little further afield on to Africa or East Asia. Flying to and from Australasia, you can fly via Dubai or Europe, or even look at a round-the-world ticket. None of the national airlines of the Caucasus are world class, but there are some good European airlines serving all three countries, plus cheaper options via Russia and Ukraine. British Airways is represented by its subsidiary franchise, British Mediterranean Airways.

Airports & Airlines

The region's three main airports are:

Baku Heydar Əliyev International Airport (GYD; ☎ 012-972792; www.airportbaku.com)

Tbilisi Tbilisi Airport (TBS; ☎ 32-433141)

Yerevan Zvartnots Airport (EVN; ☎ 10-53 33 11; www.zvartnots.am)

These airports also have a few international flights:

Batumi (BUS; ☎ 222-75549)
Gəncə (KVD)
Gyumri Shirak Airport (LWN; ☎ 0312-8 58 29)
Naxçıvan (NAJ)

The main airlines of the Caucasus countries – the state-owned AZAL (Azerbaijan Airlines) and the privately owned Airzena Georgian Airways and Armavia – are minor operators in global terms but all provide a range of flights to and from Western Europe, the Middle East and (in Armavia's case) Russia. Their fleets are a mixture of Boeings, Airbuses and CIS-built aircraft such as Tupolevs, Ilyushins and Yaks.

Though standards are improving, maintenance and safety procedures on some airlines flying in and out of the Caucasus countries have not always been up to standard. The British and US governments suggest that travellers fly direct from Western Europe on scheduled international flights.

There have been a couple of serious accidents in recent years. An Armavia Airbus crashed into the Black Sea in 2006, killing all 113 on board; pilot error and bad weather were blamed. An AZAL Antonov-40 crashed into the Caspian Sea in 2005, killing all 23 on board.

The table on p320 shows the main airlines flying into the region and the routes operated.

Tickets

Different deals and offers come and go all the time, but the best advice is to check widely and buy early. There are reliable travel agencies in the major Caucasian cities, some with websites offering specials – see Travel Agencies under Information in the Tbilisi, Yerevan and Baku sections of this book. In researching flights to the Caucasus with a travel agent elsewhere, you may have to suggest possible routes and airlines – and perhaps endure some puzzled looks ('Tbilisi…where is that exactly?'). From more far-flung places like South Africa and New Zealand you should look into a round-the-world ticket with an add-on fare to the Caucasus.

For budget flights to the Caucasus capitals check these websites:

Attitude Travel (www.attitudetravel.com)
Momondo (www.momondo.com)
Skyscanner (www.skyscanner.net)

TRANSPORT

TRANSPORT

AIRLINES FLYING TO GEORGIA, ARMENIA & AZERBAIJAN

Airline	Code	Website	Departure	Arrival
Aeroflot	SU	www.aeroflot.ru	Moscow	Baku, Yerevan
Aeroflot-Don	D9	www.aeroflot-don.ru	Rostov-on-Don, Sochi	Gyumri
AeroSvit	VV	www.aerosvit.com	Kiev	Baku
Air Arabia	G9	www.airarabia.com	Sharjah	Yerevan
Air Baltic	BT	www.airbaltic.com	Riga	Baku, Tbilisi
Air France	AF	www.airfrance.com	Paris	Yerevan
Airzena Georgian Airways	A9	www.georgian-airways.com	Amsterdam, Athens, Dubai, Frankfurt, Kiev, Minsk, Paris, Tel Aviv, Vienna	Tbilisi
Ariana Afghan Airlines	FG	www.flyariana.com	Kabul (planned)	Baku (planned)
Arkia Israel Airlines	IZ	www.arkia.co.il	Tel Aviv	Tbilisi
Armavia	MV	www.u8.am	Aleppo, Amsterdam, Athens, Beirut, Cologne, Dubai, Istanbul, Kiev, Krasnodar, Minvodyi, Moscow, Nizhny, Novgorod, Novosibirsk, Odessa, Paris, Rostov-on-Don, Samara, Simferopol, Sochi, St Petersburg, Stavropol, Voronezh, Volgograd, Yekaterinburg	Yerevan
			Moscow	Gyumri
Austrian Airlines	OS	www.aua.com	Vienna	Baku, Tbilisi
AZAL (Azerbaijan Airlines)	J2	www.azal.az	Aktau, Ankara, Ashgabat, Dubai, Istanbul, Kabul, London, Milan, Minvody, Paris, Tbilisi, Tehran, Tel Aviv	Baku
BelAvia	B2	belavia.by	Minsk	Baku, Tbilisi
BMI	BD	www.flybmi.com	London	Baku, Tbilisi, Yerevan
Caspian Air	CA	www.caspian-air.com	Tehran	Yerevan
China Southern Airlines	CZ	www.flychinasouthern.com	Ürümqi	Baku
CSA Czech Airlines	OK	www.csa.cz	Prague	Yerevan
Domodedovo Airlines	E3	www.akdal.ru	Moscow	Baku, Gəncə, Naxçivan
Donbassaero	7D	www.donbass.aero	Donetsk	Baku, Tbilisi
			Kharkov	Tbilisi
Georgian National Airlines	QB	www.national-avia.com	Almaty, Astana, Dnepropetrovsk, Donetsk, Kharkov, Kiev, Odessa	Tbilisi
ImAir Airlines	IK	www.imair.com	Almaty, Tashkent, Surgut	Baku
Iran Air	IR	www.iranair.com	Tehran	Baku
KMV	KV	www.kmvavia.aero	Minvody	Baku
KrasAir	7B	www.krasair.ru	Krasnoyarsk, Omsk, Samara	Baku
Lufthansa	LH	www.lufthansa.com	Ashgabat, Frankfurt	Baku
			Munich	Tbilisi, Yerevan
Moskovia	3R	www.ak3r.ru	Moscow	Gəncə
Rossiya	FV	www.rossiya-airlines.ru	St Petersburg	Baku
S7 Airlines	S7	www.s7.ru	Moscow	Baku, Gyumri, Yerevan
			Novosibirsk	Baku, Gyumri
SCAT	DV	www.scat.kz	Aktau	Baku, Tbilisi, Yerevan
			Atyrau	Baku
Syrian Arab Airlines	RB	www.syriaair.com	Aleppo	Yerevan
Tbilaviamsheni	L6	www.tam.ge	Donetsk, Kharkov, Kiev, Odessa, Yerevan	Batumi
			Donetsk, Kharkov, Kiev	Tbilisi
Turan Air	3T	www.turan-air.com	Kazan, Novosibirsk, Yekaterinburg, Istanbul, Moscow	Baku
				Gəncə
Turkish Airlines	TK	www.thy.com	Istanbul	Baku, Batumi, Tbilisi
Ukraine International Airlines	PS	www.flyuia.com	Kiev	Tbilisi
Ural Airlines	R6	www.uralairlines.ru	Yekaterinburg	Gyumri
UtAir	UT	www.utair.ru	Moscow, Nizhnevartovsk, Novy Urengoy, Tyumen, Ufa	Baku
Uzbekistan Airlines	HY	www.uzairways.com	Tashkent	Baku

From Asia

There are flights from Aktau, Almaty, Ashgabat (expensive), Astana, Atyrau, Kabul and Tashkent in Central Asia and from Aleppo, Beirut, Dubai, Sharjah and Tel Aviv in the Middle East, but the only direct connection with eastern Asia is China Southern's Ürümqi–Baku route, which has connections with the rest of China. You can connect in Tashkent or Almaty from some other Asian cities. AZAL and Iran Air fly from Tehran to Baku, and Caspian Air from Tehran to Yerevan.

Air Arabia (Sharjah–Yerevan), Syrian Arab Airlines (Aleppo–Yerevan), Arkia (Tel Aviv–Tbilisi) and SCAT (from Aktau to all three Caucasus capitals, with connections from other main Kazakhstan cities) offer some of the best-value flights.

See the table (opposite) for a list of airlines and routes.

Recommended agencies include:
Al Rais Travel (www.alrais.com) In Dubai.
Central Asia Tourism Corporation (www.centralasia tourism.com) In Almaty and other Kazakhstan cities.
Stantours (www.stantours.com) In Almaty.

From Australia & New Zealand

Connections are not great. Look at buying a round-the-world ticket or fly via Europe. The shortest route is via Dubai to Tbilisi, Yerevan or Baku, though this involves changing airlines and it isn't particularly cheap. You may find better fares if you're prepared to connect in Europe using a single airline such as Lufthansa or Austrian.

Good agencies to try in Australia include:
Flight Centre (☎ 13 31 33; www.flightcentre.com)
STA Travel (☎ 134 STA, 134 782; www.statravel .com.au)
Trailfinders (☎ 1300 780 212; www.trailfinders.com.au)
www.travel.com.au

Some recommended New Zealand agencies:
Flight Centre (☎ 0800 243 544; www.flightcentre .com) Offices across New Zealand.
STA Travel (☎ 0800 474 400; www.statravel.co.nz)
www.travel.co.nz

From Europe

You can fly direct to Tbilisi, Yerevan or Baku from Amsterdam, Athens, Cologne, Frankfurt, Istanbul, London, Milan, Munich, Paris, Prague, Riga or Vienna.

Air Baltic, with connections through Riga from many European cities to Tbilisi and Baku, offers some of the lowest fares. Turkish Airlines (via Istanbul) and AeroSvit (to Baku via Kiev) can also be competitive, but it's always worth checking the fares on the major Western European airlines.

In addition to flights to the Caucasus capitals, there's also an Istanbul–Batumi flight on Turkish Airlines. Turkish Airlines' domestic flights to cities in eastern Turkey can take you near Naxçivan or Georgia. See the table (opposite) for a list of airlines and routes.

Recommended agencies include:

FRANCE
Nouvelles Frontières (☎ 08 25 00 07 47; www .nouvelles-frontieres.fr)
OTU Voyages (☎ 01 55 82 32 32; www.otu.fr)
Voyages Wasteels (☎ 01 42 61 69 87; www.wasteels.fr)
Voyageurs du Monde (☎ 08 92 68 8 3 63; www .vdm.com)

GERMANY
Expedia (www.expedia.de)
Just Travel (☎ 089 747 3330; www.justtravel.de)
STA Travel (☎ 069-7430 3292; www.statravel.de)

ITALY
CTS Viaggi (☎ 199-50 11 50; www.cts.it)

NETHERLANDS
Airfair (☎ 070-307 61 10; www.airfair.nl)

SCANDINAVIA
Kilroy Travels (www.kilroytravels.com)

SPAIN
Rumbo (☎ 902-123999; www.rumbo.es)

TURKEY
Orion Tour (☎ 212-232 6300; www.oriontour.com)

UK
Ebookers (☎ 0800-082 3000; www.ebookers.com)
Flight Centre (☎ 0800-5877 0058; www.flightcentre .co.uk)
STA Travel (☎ 08701-630 026; www.statravel.co.uk)
Trailfinders (☎ 0845-058 5858; www.trailfinders.co.uk)
Travelbag (☎ 0800-082 5000; www.travelbag.com)

From Russia & Ukraine

With the land borders closed to foreigners, flying is the only way into the Caucasus countries from Russia. Flights from Russia and

---

CLIMATE CHANGE & TRAVEL

Climate change is a serious threat to the ecosystems that humans rely upon, and air travel is the fastest-growing contributor to the problem. Lonely Planet regards travel, overall, as a global benefit, but believes we all have a responsibility to limit our personal impact on global warming.

Flying & Climate Change

Pretty much every form of motor travel generates CO_2 (the main cause of human-induced climate change) but planes are far and away the worst offenders, not just because of the sheer distances they allow us to travel, but because they release greenhouse gases high into the atmosphere. The statistics are frightening: two people taking a return flight between Europe and the US will contribute as much to climate change as an average household's gas and electricity consumption over a whole year.

Carbon Offset Schemes

Climatecare.org and other websites use 'carbon calculators' that allow jetsetters to offset the greenhouse gases they are responsible for with contributions to energy-saving projects and other climate-friendly initiatives in the developing world – including projects in India, Honduras, Kazakhstan and Uganda.

Lonely Planet, together with Rough Guides and other concerned partners in the travel industry, supports the carbon offset scheme run by climatecare.org. Lonely Planet offsets all of its staff and author travel.

For more information check out our website: lonelyplanet.com.

Ukraine to the Caucasus capitals account for about half of all international flights into the region, although Russia–Georgia flights were suspended at the time of research. Many regional Russian and Ukrainian cities have direct flights to the Caucasus, on a variety of airlines.

You can also fly into the Azerbaijan provincial cities of Gəncə and Naxçivan, and Gyumri in Armenia, from Moscow, and to Gyumri from a few other Russian cities. See the table (p320) for a list of airlines and routes. **Infinity Travel** (☎ 495-234 6555; www.infinity.ru) is a good source of air tickets in Moscow.

From the USA & Canada

So far there are no direct flights between North America and the Caucasus. You need to make a connection in a European city such as Vienna, Amsterdam, London, Frankfurt or Istanbul. Some of the best fares to Tbilisi are available via Vienna on Austrian Airlines, one of the few airlines that flies to both North America and the Caucasus.

Going via Moscow is not a good option because you will probably need a Russian visa.

The cheapest round-trip fares from the eastern US are normally between US$700 and US$900. Flights via Europe take up to 16 hours, not including connection times.

Levon Travel (☎ 800-445 3866; www.levontravel.com) is a specialist in travel to Georgia and Armenia and offers some good fares.

Other recommended agencies:

STA Travel (☎ 800-781 4040; www.statravel.com)
Travel CUTS (☎ 416-979 2406; www.travelcuts.com)

For online bookings:
www.cheaptickets.com
www.economytravel.com
www.expedia.com
www.lowestfare.com
www.orbitz.com
www.travelocity.com

LAND
Border Crossings

For lists of each country's border crossings and the lowdown on visa requirements, see the Visas sections in this book's country directories. Note that Nagorno-Karabakh can only be entered from Armenia.

FROM OTHER COUNTRIES

Land crossings into the region are at Sarpi and Posof–Vale on the Turkey–Georgia border, Agarak (Iran–Armenia), Sədərək (Turkey–Naxçivan, Azerbaijan), Culfa–Jolfa (Iran–Naxçivan, Azerbaijan) and Astara (Iran–Azerbaijan). The crossings from Turkey have heavy truck traffic. For those travelling into Turkey from the Caucasus, most Westerners either need no visa or can obtain it quickly at the border; Turkish immigration officers at the crossing from Naxçivan may however demand that British passport holders (unlike other Europeans) have their Turkish visa in advance.

Turkey's borders with Armenia are closed, and Russia's borders with Georgia and Azerbaijan are closed to third-country travellers. Indeed the Russia–Georgia border was closed to everybody at the time of writing. Borders between Russia and the breakaway Georgian regions of Abkhazia and South Ossetia are open to local travellers (and, it seems, citizens of other CIS countries), but crossing these borders is considered illegal by Georgia. Some travellers who continued on into Georgia after entering South Ossetia or Abkhazia from Russia have been fined or jailed. If you're heading from Russia into Abkhazia, you'll need to have a double-entry Russian visa, as it will be expected that you will be returning to Russia.

GEORGIA–ARMENIA
On the main Tbilisi–Yerevan road the main border crossing is Sadakhlo–Bagratashen, in the east. There's also a railway border point here. Two other road crossings are less frequented: the Guguti–Tashir crossing on the road between Marneuli and Vanadzor, and the Bavra crossing between Ninotsminda and Gyumri.

GEORGIA–AZERBAIJAN
The road border crossings are Krasny Most (Red Bridge) on the main Tbilisi–Gəncə–Baku highway, and Tsodna (Postbina) between Lagodekhi and Balakən in northwest Azerbaijan. The Baku–Gəncə–Tbilisi railway crosses the border at Böyük Kəsik.

Bus, Marshrutka & Taxi
Bus services linking various larger cities cross the Sarpi, Posof–Vale, Agarak, Sədərək and Astara border points, but you can equally well get across all land borders by a sequence of hops by local bus, marshrutka (minibus) and taxi.

IRAN
Daily buses run to Yerevan from Tabriz, Iran (US$52, 14 hours) via the easy-to-cross Agarak border point near Meghri. Tatev Travel (p151) is the Yerevan agent for the Tabriz bus.

There is also a bus service between Tehran and Baku via Tabriz, but it's more enjoyable to do the trip in stages, including the Astara–Baku train.

TURKEY
Several Turkish bus companies run daily buses to Tbilisi from Istanbul (US$40, 27 hours), Trabzon (US$25, 11 hours) and other Turkish cities. **Özlem Ardahan** (☎ in Georgia 899919958) has a daily service via Ankara, Erzurum, Kars and the Posof–Vale border crossing. A Trabzon–Batumi service (US$12, three hours) by **Lüks Karadeniz** (☎ in Batumi 222-33984) runs several times daily. Alternatively, you can travel between these two places by a series of minibus/marshrutka rides with maybe a short taxi trip thrown in – Trabzon–Hopa, Hopa–Sarpi, Sarpi–Batumi. The same goes for the Posof–Vale crossing between Kars (Turkey) and Akhaltsikhe (Georgia).

Companies including **Öz Gülhan** (☎ in Istanbul 212-5881268) and **Öz Nuhoğlu** (☎ in Baku 012-4447203) run buses from Istanbul to Baku (around US$70, 48 hours) three days a week. Six buses a day go to Naxçivan from Istanbul (US$45, 26 hours) via Iğdır (US$5, 5 hours).

Buses from Istanbul to Yerevan (US$100, 41 hours), via Georgia, run twice a week.

Train
The only trains beyond the three republics are from Baku to Russia and Ukraine. With the Azerbaijan–Russia border closed to foreigners, these services are open to Azeris and Russians only.

The railway between Kars in eastern Turkey and Gyumri in Armenia has been closed since 1993. However a new 98km line is to be built between Kars and Akhalkalaki in Georgia (which has a line to Tbilisi), creating a potential rail link between Turkey and all three Caucasus countries. Work was expected to start in 2008, and 2010 has been mentioned as an opening date.

SEA
Georgia
The Ukrainian company **UkrFerry** (www.ukrferry.com) operates two passenger ferries most weeks each way between Poti and Ilyichevsk, near Odessa, Ukraine, and one a week each

TRANSPORT

way between Batumi and Ilyichevsk. The days of the sailings vary and it's not unknown for the two sailings from Poti to go on successive days, followed by a week's wait till the next departure. The website offers schedules, fares and even online reservations, but it can be inaccurate, so double-check schedules in person or by phone.

If you book online, you may find when you get to the port or agency office that no-one knows about it.

You may also find that the local ticket agents in Poti and Batumi won't sell any tickets until the ferry is actually in port, though they'll probably let you put your name on a list.

One-way fares for the 40-hour sail between Ilyichevsk and either Poti or Batumi are between US$150 and US$260 depending on the cabin. The cheapest are usually four-berth cabins or two-berth cabins sharing a bathroom (with shower) with one other cabin. The price includes three meals a day of Soviet-style slop. You can take a motorcycle or car for US$140 and US$375 respectively. UkrFerry also sails between Ilyichevsk and Varna, Bulgaria, and through fares between there and the Georgian ports are available from around US$170.

The Bulgarian company **Intershipping** (www .intershipping.net) operates a weekly passenger-carrying vehicle ferry from Burgas to Poti (per passenger/car €150/300, three days). Returning from Poti to Burgas it calls at Novorossiysk, Russia, though we can't confirm whether Poti–Novorossiysk passages are available.

Note: Georgian visas are not available on arrival by sea at Batumi or Poti, so if you're from a country whose nationals need visas to enter Georgia, you must get one in advance.

At research time there were no other passenger sea services between Georgia and Russia, the Batumi–Poti–Sochi route having been suspended in 2007. You can, however, sail to Sochi from Hopa in Turkey, just 15km from the Georgian border and 30km from Batumi. Information on these sailings is available from the **Batumi ferry terminal** (☎ 222-74912); at research time the hydrofoil *Express Batumi* (☎ in Georgia 893333966) sailed from Hopa at 1pm on Monday, charging US$100 for the seven-hour crossing, while the motor vessel *Michael Svetlov* (☎ 899944504, 893315481) sailed at 4pm Thursday, arriving at 9am next day, for a fare of US$90.

Azerbaijan

Cargo ferries sail from Baku to Turkmenbashi, Turkmenistan (passenger US$50, 12 to 18 hours) several times weekly and to Aktau, Kazakhstan (passenger/motorbike/vehicle per metre length US$60/137/55, 18 hours or more) a few times monthly. When winds are bad these crossings can make people appallingly seasick.

The ships are primarily cargo ships and they have no fixed schedules, leaving whenever they happen to finish loading. The 'ticket office' in Baku (a tiny, sporadically open window) sells nothing until the night before departure, but you should put your name down there and keep calling to check the situation. Baku–Turkmenbashi ferries carry only 11 passengers while Baku–Aktau ferries take 36. Persistence is the key to getting aboard. You have to hand over your passport to buy a ticket, and again when you board the ship, getting it back on arrival at the destination. Your ticket doesn't include a berth but once aboard you can secure one (probably with a hot shower as well as cockroaches) for US$10 or so from the crew. There is a limited canteen on board but this can run out of supplies if there are delays, so you need to carry some of your own. It is not unknown for boats to arrive offshore at Turkmenbashi and then wait days for access to the port (bad news if you have a Turkmenistan visa valid from a fixed date). Delays can also occur getting out of Turkmenbashi port

In Aktau, tickets and information are available from **Tagu** (☎ 3292-513989; cs-kz.narod. ru; Mikrorayon 7, Dom 12).

Remember that Azerbaijan visas are not available on arrival by sea in Baku, so you must obtain one in advance. Travellers arriving at Baku without visas have been refused permission to land. Also note that Turkmenistan embassies may not issue transit visas if you say you are leaving on the ferry, because they know that delays in getting on board a ship can cause travellers to outstay transit visas.

TOURS

Good local agencies such as those listed in this book's Baku, Tbilisi and Yerevan Information sections can provide tours meeting most specifications, and it is often these operators that foreign tour companies use as their partners on the ground in the

Caucasus countries. Recommended foreign-based operators include these:

Erka Reisen (☎ 07257-930 390; www.erkareisen.de) Based in Germany, Erka is a Caucasian travel specialist and offers comprehensive tours of all three countries.

Explore (☎ 1252 760000; www.explore.co.uk) Offers a comprehensive Golden Fleece tour that takes in Georgia and Armenia, with an optional Azerbaijan extension; also a seductive Armenia, Iran and Turkey tour.

Regent Holidays (☎ 0845-277 3317; www.regent-holidays.co.uk) Pioneers of travel to the former Soviet Union, Bristol-based Regent offers tours taking in all three Caucasus countries and an interesting Azerbaijan and Iran option.

Steppes East (☎ 01285 651010; www.steppes east.co.uk) Focusing on bespoke itineraries for individuals, UK company Steppes offers trips to all three Caucasus countries.

GETTING AROUND

AIR

Flights between and within the three countries are few. AZAL flies daily between Baku and Tbilisi, and the small Georgian airline Tbilaviamsheni has three flights a week between Batumi and Yerevan. The only domestic flights are within Azerbaijan: several daily between Baku and Naxçivan, and three a week to Gəncə from both Baku and Naxçivan. Lənkəran airport is due to reopen in 2008. In Georgia, Tbilisi–Mestia and Tbilisi–Batumi flights are often talked about – they may happen some day soon.

BICYCLE

It's rare to see cyclists in Georgia, Armenia and Azerbaijan, probably for three reasons: firstly, the terrain is hilly and the roads are often terrible, so only mountain bikes can cope; secondly, the recklessness of motorists makes cycling pretty hazardous; and thirdly, many local people look down their noses at cyclists – cars are the thing to have! However, some intrepid foreign cyclists do come through here and it looks like a great way to get around Georgia and Armenia, though perhaps less so in Azerbaijan where some truck drivers apparently like to force cyclists off the road for sport.

Take great care on the main roads and bring all your own spare parts.

BUS & MARSHRUTKA

The marshrutka (minivan; short for the Russian *marshrutnoe taxi*) is king of public road transport in Armenia and Georgia, while buses are a bit more common in Azerbaijan. Marshrutkas are 10- to 20-seat minibuses that can pick up and drop off passengers anywhere along their route. There are some reasonably comfortable and modern buses on intercity routes, but most buses in the Caucasus are ageing Soviet-era workhorses with rumbling engines and ripped seats. They are usually cheaper than marshrutkas and have more baggage space, but are quite a lot slower.

It's not necessary (or always possible) to book ahead for buses or marshrutkas, except for a few international services. Arrive at the

SAMPLE BUS & MARSHRUTKA FARES

Bus

From	To	One-way Fare	Duration
Baku	Şamaxı	US$3.50	2hr
Baku	Şəki	US$7	6½hr
Tbilisi	Batumi	US$10	7hr
Yerevan	Batumi	US$30	14hr

Marshrutka

From	To	One-way Fare	Duration
Baku	Quba	US$3.50	4hr
Tbilisi	Batumi	US$10	7hr
Tbilisi	Kutaisi	US$6	4½hr
Yerevan	Batumi	US$35	12hr
Yerevan	Gyumri	US$3.50	2hr
Yerevan	Stepanakert	US$15	7-8hr

TRANSPORT

bus or marshrutka station about 20 or 30 minutes before departure time. Marshrutkas usually have a sign in the front window with the destination in the local language (making them tricky to identify in Georgia and Armenia). To hail one, stick out your arm and wave. If you want to get off, say *gaacharet* (stop) in Georgia, *hosgunkur* in Armenia and *sakhla burada* in Azerbaijan. If boarding a bus at the terminus you sometimes pay at a ticket office, otherwise you pay on board.

In country areas buses and marshrutkas are timed for local markets, arriving in town from a village in the morning and returning in the afternoon, with no public transport out of the village until the next morning. All the produce on board can slow down buses quite considerably on steep stretches and make for awkward seating next to stacks of potato sacks.

Country bus trips can turn into picaresque journeys, involving holding someone's geese on a slow amble through the countryside, stopping to change tyres and to correct tilting suspension.

CAR & MOTORCYCLE

Driving in the Caucasus requires steely nerves and fast reactions, and for this reason most visitors avoid getting behind the wheel. It's easier and cheaper to hire a car and a driver accustomed to the rich and varied local traffic conditions. It's a common practice, and surprisingly economical, to take a taxi for intercity trips. The trip from Tbilisi to Yerevan, for example, costs around US$60, which can be shared between three or four people.

Even main roads can have potholes, and a reasonably smooth-surfaced stretch of road can deteriorate into a cratered track in the space of a few metres. Conditions on major highways are improving, but country roads practically require a jeep (usually a Niva, a Lada jeep). Add to this a lack of signs and road markings, the bravura driving techniques of local road users, and the dangers of unfenced roads and livestock, and the local driving experience leaves a lot to be desired.

Driving is on the right-hand side of the road, or at least it's supposed to be. In reality, vehicles weave all over to overtake and avoid the worst of the potholes. Almost all road signs in Georgia are in Georgian script only; Azerbaijan has a mixture of old Russian Cyrillic signs and newer ones in Latin; and in Armenia signs might be in Russian, Latin or Armenian script. The

police checkpoints you will see are primarily for making checks on commercial vehicles – you should slow down as you pass, but there's no need to stop unless you are flagged down. If you are stopped, hand over your licence and insurance papers, keep smiling and say 'tourist' a lot. Pretend not to speak the language, even if you do, otherwise you will be engaged in an interminable debate. If you have done nothing wrong, don't give in to any demand for bribes – just sit tight, and the policeman will get bored or frustrated and send you on your way. Note that the legal maximum blood-alcohol level for driving in all three countries is zero.

Exploring minor roads and unsurfaced tracks calls for a 4WD, which can be hired, if you're game, from rental agencies in the capitals. (Alternatively, try using an ageing Lada – local people manage to drive these sturdy old workhorses into the most unlikely places! Some travel agencies, hotels and guesthouses can arrange one for you.) It's often easy enough to find a local driver with his own 4WD who will drive you on these roads at a reasonable cost. If you plan to drive yourself in mountain areas, it's safest to travel in a convoy of at least two vehicles. Mountain roads are often blocked or washed away by landslides and flash floods.

Self-drive rental costs from around US$60 to US$100 a day for an ordinary saloon car, to over US$125 per day for a 4WD. Hiring a driver may only add US$15 a day. Note that most rental cars (and foreign vehicles) require 95-octane fuel, which is not as widely available as diesel and low-octane Lada juice – try to find out in advance where 95-octane will be available, and fill up at every opportunity.

Motorcycles are rare birds in Georgia, Armenia and Azerbaijan. The same words of caution apply to them as to cars. You will need to bring spare parts and tools with you.

Bringing Your Own Vehicle

Drivers of cars and riders of motorcycles will need the vehicle's registration papers and liability insurance, and it's best to have an international driving permit as well as your domestic licence.

In addition you may also need a *carnet de passage en douane*, which is effectively a passport for the vehicle and acts as a temporary waiver of import duty. However, drivers taking vehicles into Azerbaijan report having to pay a hefty deposit related to the vehicle's value (€900 for a top-end motorcycle, for example) on entry, which you then get back when you leave. Contact your local automobile association for details about all documentation.

Liability insurance is not available in advance for many out-of-the-way countries, but has to be bought when crossing the border. The cost and quality of such local insurance varies wildly, and you may find in the Caucasus that you are often effectively travelling uninsured.

HITCHING

This is not a common practice, except in rural areas with poor public transport where local people regularly flag down passing vehicles. In such places it is pretty easy to cadge a lift, provided there is any traffic at all. It's good to offer a small amount of petrol money, as local people often do.

Hitching is never perfectly safe anywhere. Solo hitching by men or women is not a good idea – it's best to travel in pairs, preferably with someone of the opposite sex. Refusing rides from drunk drivers is crucial, and in general you can never be too careful.

LOCAL TRANSPORT

All three capitals have cheap and easy-to-use metro systems. Other urban transport comprises a mixture of marshrutkas and buses, with marshrutkas generally quicker and more plentiful. Marshrutkas do stop at bus stops but you can flag one down anywhere on the street.

The problem with both marshrutkas and buses is identifying the one you need, especially in Georgia and Armenia where route boards are in the local alphabet. Try to ascertain before you set out what route number you need. Passers-by and drivers are usually pretty helpful if you're not sure: just say the name of where you want to go, and a nod or shake of the head will give you your answer.

Taxis are plentiful and pretty cheap. Shorter rides of 2km or 3km typically cost US$1.50 to US$2 (US$3 in Baku). It's best to agree on the fare before you get in.

TRAIN

The main railway line in the region runs from Batumi in the west, through Kutaisi, Gori, Tbilisi and Gəncə to Baku, with a branch south from Tbilisi to Yerevan through Vanadzor and Gyumri. Other lines reach towns such as Poti, Zugdidi, Borjomi, Bakuriani, Akhaltsikhe and Akhalkalaki in Georgia, Yeraskh and Hrazdan

SAMPLE KUPE FARES			
From	To	One-way fare	Duration
Baku	Gəncə	US$4	8hr
Baku	Astara	US$3.50	9½hr
Baku	Balakən	US$5	11½hr
Tbilisi	Baku	US$23	14hr
Tbilisi	Batumi	US$13	8hr
Tbilisi	Yerevan	US$14	15hr

in Armenia, and Şəki, Balakən, Lənkəran and Astara in Azerbaijan. In all three countries the national capitals are very much the hubs of the rail networks, and the majority of trains start and end there. Schedule information for trains to and from Tbilisi is given in English on www.info-tbilisi.com.

Trains in the Caucasus are slow and much less frequent than road transport. But they're also very cheap; many intercity trains run overnight so you can save money on a hotel bed. There are four classes of ticket: *spalny vagon* (sleeping car), abbreviated to SV (CB in Cyrillic) or *luks,* is 1st-class, with upholstered berths and only two people to a compartment; *kupe* (compartment), short for *kupeyny,* is 2nd-class, with four to a compartment, harder berths and fold-down upper bunks; *platskartny* or *platskart* (reserved), 3rd-class, has open bunk accommodation, and is more crowded and less comfortable; while *obshchy* (general), 4th-class, is just an unreserved bench seat.

An *elektrichka* is a local service with single-class seating, linking a city and its suburbs or nearby towns, or groups of adjacent towns; often useful for day trips, these can be crowded.

Kupe offers the best compromise between cost and comfort for overnight journeys. Once the train is under way and bedtime approaches, the attendant will dole out sheets for you to make up your own bed. The attendant will also wake you up before arrival and collect the used bed linen. It's best to bring all the food and drink you'll need, though you may be able to nip out during stops and buy overpriced snacks on the platform.

Trains between Georgia and Azerbaijan and Georgia and Armenia may be held up for two or three hours at the borders due to customs searches. Some locals abandon the train and jump into taxis once through immigration.

Health

CONTENTS

Prevention is the key to staying healthy while abroad. A little planning before departure, particularly for pre-existing illnesses, will save trouble later: see your dentist before a long trip; carry a spare pair of contact lenses and glasses; and take your optical prescription with you.

Although some form of medical service is available in nearly all towns, health-care systems in the Caucasus can be very patchy due to underinvestment in hospitals since the fall of communism.

Saying 'thanks' with cash to a nurse or a doctor, even before you are given treatment, is common across the region. The payments are normally shared among medical staff.

There are good international medical services in the three national capitals, but treatment can be expensive. It's crucial to have comprehensive travel insurance with medical evacuation cover, not just a policy that will reimburse you months in the future.

BEFORE YOU GO

Bring medications in their original, clearly labelled containers. A signed and dated letter from your physician describing any medical condition and medications, including generic names, is also a good idea. If carrying syringes or needles, carry a physician's letter documenting their medical necessity.

INSURANCE

If your health insurance doesn't cover you for medical expenses abroad, consider getting extra insurance. Find out in advance if your insurance plan will make payments directly to providers or reimburse you later for overseas health expenditures.

Doctors and nurses in the Caucasus do expect cash payments, but as many of these are unofficial, it's hard to see an insurance company reimbursing you for this, even if you could wangle a receipt.

RECOMMENDED VACCINATIONS

Vaccinations that you are normally advised to have up to date for the Caucasian countries are diphtheria, tetanus, measles, mumps, rubella, polio and typhoid. Further vaccines may be advisable for children or the elderly. Hepatitis A may be recommended for those who are staying for long periods or in areas with poor sanitation. Hepatitis B vaccination may be recommended for people who will be in close contact with the local population, and rabies vaccine for people who will have contact with wild or domestic animals. Malaria is present in southeast Georgia, parts of Armenia's Ararat district, and the rural lowlands of southern Azerbaijan.

Since most vaccines don't produce immunity until at least two weeks after they're given, visit a physician at least six weeks before departure.

ONLINE RESOURCES

There is a wealth of travel-health advice on the internet:

www.mdtravelhealth.com Provides complete travel-health recommendations for every country and is updated daily.

www.nathnac.org The UK's National Travel Health Network and Centre, with good country-by-country travel health information.

www.who.int/ith The World Health Organization publishes a superb book, *International Travel and Health*, which is revised annually and is available free online.

See also Government Websites (opposite).

GOVERNMENT WEBSITES

It's usually a good idea to consult your government's travel-health website before departure, if one is available:

Australia www.smartraveller.gov.au
Canada www.phac-aspc.gc.ca
UK www.dh.gov.uk
USA wwwn.cdc.gov/travel

IN GEORGIA, ARMENIA & AZERBAIJAN

AVAILABILITY & COST OF HEALTH CARE

Medical care may not always be available outside major cities, and medical supplies required in public hospitals may need to be bought from a pharmacy with limited opening hours. Nursing care may be limited; this is something families and friends are expected to provide. In general the best medical care is provided by private clinics in the capital cities, which can be expensive. Your insurance company may be able to help locate the nearest source of medical assistance, or you can ask at your hotel. In an emergency contact your embassy or consulate.

The standards of dental care vary and there is an increased risk of hepatitis B and HIV transmission via poorly sterilised equipment.

Your travel insurance will not usually cover you for anything other than emergency dental treatment.

This is not the place to be stuck without decent medical insurance. EU citizens have the right to free health care in Georgia, Armenia and Azerbaijan under reciprocal arrangements; however, if you visit a typical hospital in the region, it'll be clear who is getting the best deal here.

INFECTIOUS DISEASES
Poliomyelitis

Polio is spread through contaminated food and water. It is one of the vaccines given in childhood and should be boosted every 10 years, either orally (a drop on the tongue), or as an injection.

Rabies

Spread through bites, scratches or licks on broken skin from an infected animal, rabies is always fatal unless treated promptly. Animal handlers should be vaccinated before they go, as should those travelling to remote areas where a reliable source of postbite vaccine is not available within 24 hours. Three injections are needed over the course of a month. If you have not been vaccinated, you will need a course of five injections starting as soon as possible after the injury or within 24 hours. If you have been vaccinated, you will need fewer injections and have more time to seek medical help.

Tick-borne Encephalitis

Spread by tick bites, this is a serious infection of the brain, and vaccination is advised for those in risk areas who are unable to avoid tick bites, such as campers and hikers. Two doses of vaccine will give a year's protection, three doses up to three years.

Tuberculosis

Tuberculosis (TB) is spread through close respiratory contact and occasionally through infected milk or milk products. BCG vaccine is recommended for those likely to be mixing closely with the local population, such as those visiting family or planning on a long stay, and those employed as teachers and health-care workers. TB can be asymptomatic, although symptoms can include a cough, weight loss or fever months or even years after exposure. An X-ray is the best way to confirm if you have TB. BCG gives a moderate degree of protection against TB, but is not available in all countries. As it's a live vaccine it should not be given to pregnant women or immunocompromised individuals.

Typhoid & Hepatitis A

Both these diseases are spread through contaminated food (particularly shellfish) and water. Typhoid can cause septicaemia; hepatitis A causes liver inflammation and jaundice. Neither is usually fatal but recovery can be prolonged. Typhoid vaccine (Typhim Vi, Typherix) gives protection for three years. In some countries, the oral vaccine Vivotif is also available. Hepatitis A vaccine (Avaxim, VAQTA, Havrix) is given as an injection; a single dose will give protection for up to a year, a booster after a year gives 10 years' protection. Hepatitis A and typhoid vaccines (such as Hepatyrix or Viatim) can also be given as a single-dose vaccine.

HEALTH

TRAVELLER'S DIARRHOEA

If you develop diarrhoea, be sure to drink plenty of fluids, preferably in the form of an oral rehydration solution such as Dioralyte. If diarrhoea is bloody, persists for more than 72 hours or is accompanied by fever, shaking, chills or severe abdominal pain, you should seek medical attention.

ENVIRONMENTAL HAZARDS & TREATMENT

Altitude Sickness

Most people feel at least a little unwell if they travel from sea level to 3500m. Headache, fatigue, flu-like symptoms, undue breathlessness on exertion, loss of appetite, nausea, vomiting, minor swelling of the face, feet and hands, dizziness, difficulty sleeping and irregular breathing during sleep are all common complaints. These are symptoms of Acute Mountain Sickness (AMS), which usually develops during the first 24 hours at altitude.

AMS is common at 3500m and likely with rapid ascent to 5000m. Acclimatisation and slow ascent are recommended. Dehydration may worsen symptoms of AMS – drink at least 4L of water a day. A practical way to monitor hydration is by ensuring that urine is clear and plentiful. Avoid tobacco and alcohol. Diamox (acetazolamide) reduces the headache pain caused by AMS and helps the body acclimatise to the lack of oxygen. It is only available on prescription, and those who are allergic to sulphonamide antibiotics may also be allergic to Diamox.

Heatstroke

Heatstroke occurs following excessive fluid loss with inadequate replacement of fluids and salt. Symptoms include headache, dizziness and tiredness. Dehydration is already happening by the time you feel thirsty – aim to drink sufficient water to produce pale, diluted urine. To treat heatstroke, drink water and/or fruit juice, and cool the body with cold water and fans.

Hypothermia

Hypothermia occurs when the body loses heat faster than it can produce it. As ever, proper preparation will reduce the risks of getting it. Even on a hot day in the mountains, the weather can change rapidly so carry waterproof garments, warm layers and a hat, and inform others of your route. Hypothermia starts with shivering, loss of judgment and clumsiness. Unless rewarming occurs, the sufferer deteriorates into apathy, confusion and coma.

Prevent further heat loss by seeking shelter, warm dry clothing, hot sweet drinks and shared bodily warmth.

Insect Bites & Stings

Mosquitoes are found in most parts of the Caucasus, and malaria is present in some areas (see p328). Use a DEET-based insect repellent.

Bees and wasps only cause real problems to those with a severe allergy (anaphylaxis.) If you have a severe allergy to bee or wasp stings, carry an 'epipen' or similar adrenaline injection.

Bed bugs lead to very itchy, lumpy bites. Spraying the mattress with insect killer after changing bedding will get rid of them.

Water

Tap water may not always be safe to drink; it's best to stick to bottled water or boil water for 10 minutes, use water purification tablets, or use a filter.

Do not drink water from rivers or lakes, as this may contain bacteria or viruses that can cause diarrhoea or vomiting. There are many piped springs in farming regions across the Caucasus; many are safe but there's always a slight risk of contamination so follow the above precautions.

TRAVELLING WITH CHILDREN

Make sure the children are up to date with routine vaccinations, and discuss possible travel vaccines well before departure as some vaccines are not suitable for children under one year old.

Be extra wary of contaminated food and water. If your child has vomiting or diarrhoea, lost fluid and salts must be replaced. It may be helpful to take rehydration powders for reconstituting with boiled water.

Children should be encouraged to avoid and mistrust any dogs or other mammals because of the risk of rabies and other diseases.

Any bite, scratch or lick from a warm-blooded, furry animal should immediately be thoroughly cleaned. If there is any possibility that the animal is infected with rabies, immediate medical assistance should be sought.

WOMEN'S HEALTH

Emotional stress, exhaustion and travelling through different time zones can all contribute to an upset in the menstrual pattern. If using oral contraceptives, remember some antibiotics, diarrhoea and vomiting can stop the pill from working and lead to the risk of pregnancy. Time zones, gastrointestinal upsets and antibiotics do not affect injectable contraception.

Tampons are sometimes difficult to find; it's a good idea to bring supplies with you or stock up at big-city pharmacies.

Travelling during pregnancy is usually possible, but there are important things to consider; always consult your doctor before you travel.

The riskiest times to travel are during the first 12 weeks of pregnancy and after 30 weeks.

Language

CONTENTS

Medieval Arab geographers called the Caucasus *jebel al alsine* (mountain of languages). More than 40 different languages are spoken in an area the size of the British Isles. Fortunately, a traveller visiting the south Caucasus should only have to cope with four of these – albeit four different languages belonging to three different language families and written in four different alphabets! However, it would be a pity not to learn at least a little of one or more of the national languages.

RUSSIAN

Russian is widely spoken in all three countries, and few people will ever object to being spoken to in it. More likely, they'll be delighted that a foreigner can communicate with them in any language. If you speak passable Russian, there's no need to try and use the native language (beyond perhaps 'hello' and other basic pleasantries).

For all Caucasian countries, anyone over 35 with even basic secondary education will speak strong Russian. Most young people under 25 will speak little Russian, save those from particularly educated backgrounds. In the three capital cities the penetration of Russian is a lot higher than in the countryside due to the Soviet elite schools that employed (and sometimes still employ) Russian. For a very useful traveller's guide to Russian, get a copy of Lonely Planet's *Russian Phrasebook*.

CONVERSATION & USEFUL PHRASES
Hello.

    Здравствуйте.   *zdrast·*vuy·te
Goodbye.

    До свидания.   da svi·*da·*ni·ya

THE RUSSIAN CYRILLIC ALPHABET

Cyrillic	Roman	Pronunciation
А, а	a	as the 'a' in 'father' (in stressed syllable); as the 'a' in 'ago' (in unstressed syllable)
Б, б	b	as the 'b' in 'but'
В, в	v	as the 'v' in 'van'
Г, г	g	as the 'g' in 'god'
Д, д	d	as the 'd' in 'dog'
Е, е *	e	as the 'ye' in 'yet' (in stressed syllable); as the 'yi' in 'yin' (in unstressed syllable)
Ё, ё **	yo	as the 'yo' in 'yore'
Ж, ж	zh	as the 's' in 'measure'
З, з	z	as the 'z' in 'zoo'
И, и	i	as the 'ee' in 'meet'
Й, й	y	as the 'y' in 'boy'
К, к	k	as the 'k' in 'kind'
Л, л	l	as the 'l' in 'lamp'
М, м	m	as the 'm' in 'mad'
Н, н	n	as the 'n' in 'not'
О, о	o	as the 'o' in 'more' (in stessed syllable); as the 'a' in 'hard' (in unstressed syllable)
П, п	p	as the 'p' in 'pig'
Р, р	r	as the 'r' in 'rub' (rolled)
С, с	s	as the 's' in 'sing'
Т, т	t	as the 't' in 'ten'
У, у	u	as the 'oo' in 'fool'
Ф, ф	f	as the 'f' in 'fan'
Х, х	kh	as the 'ch' in 'Bach'
Ц, ц	ts	as the 'ts' in 'bits'
Ч, ч	ch	as the 'ch' in 'chin'
Ш, ш	sh	as the 'sh' in 'shop'
Щ, щ	shch	as 'sh-ch' in 'fresh chips'
Ъ, ъ	-	hard sign
Ы, ы	y	as the 'i' in 'ill'
Ь, ь	'	soft sign
Э, э	e	as the 'e' in 'end'
Ю, ю	yu	as the 'u' in 'use'
Я, я	ya	as the 'ya' in 'yard' (in stressed syllable); as the 'ye' in 'yearn' (in unstressed syllable)

* Е, е are transliterated *ye* when at the beginning of a word
** Ё, ё are often printed without dots

Yes/No.

    Да/Нет.   da/net
Thank you (very much).

    (Большое) Спасибо. (bal'*sho·*ye) spa·*si·*ba
How are you?

    Как дела?   kak di·*la?

I'm well.
Хорошо. | kha·ra·*sho*
good/OK
хорошо | kha·ra·*sho*
bad
плохо | *plo*·kha
What's your name?
Как вас зовут? | kak vas za·*vut*?
My name is ...
Меня зовут ... | mi·*nya za*·vut ...
Where are you from?
Откуда вы? | at·*ku*·da vy?
I don't speak Russian.
Я не говорю | ya ni ga·va·*ryu*
по-русски. | pa *ru*·ski
I don't understand.
Я не понимаю. | ya ni pa·ni·*ma*·yu
Do you speak English?
Вы говорите | vy ga·va·*ri*·te pa
по-английски? | ang·*liy*·ski?
Could you write it down, please?
Запишите | za·pi·*shi*·te pa·*zhal*·sta
пожалуйста.

EMERGENCIES
Help!
На помощь!/ | na *po*·mashch'!/
Помогите! | pa·ma·*gi*·ti!
I'm sick.
Я болен. | ya *bo*·lin (m)
Я больна. | ya bal'·*na* (f)
I need a doctor.
Мне нужен врач. | mne *nu*·zhin vrach
hospital
больница | bal'·*ni*·tsa
police
милиция | mi·*li*·tsi·ya
Fire!
Пожар! | pa·*zhar*!

NUMBERS
How many? | Сколько? | *skol*'ka?

0 | ноль | nol'
1 | один | a·*din*
2 | два | dva
3 | три | tri
4 | четыре | chi·*ty*·ri
5 | пять | pyat'
6 | шесть | shest'
7 | семь | sem'
8 | восемь | vo·*sim*'
9 | девять | *de*·vit'
10 | десять | *de*·sit'
20 | двадцать | *dva*·tsat'

30 | тридцать | *tri*·tsat'
40 | сорок | *so*·rak
50 | пятьдесят | pyat'di·*syat*
60 | шестьдесят | shest'di·*syat*
70 | семьдесят | sem'di·*syat*
80 | восемьдесят | vo·sim·di·*syat*
90 | девяносто | di·vya·*no*·sta
100 | сто | sto
1000 | тысяча | *ty*·sya·cha

SHOPPING & SERVICES
Do you have ...?
У вас есть ...? | u vas est' ...?
How much is it?
Сколько стоит? | *skol*'ka *sto*·it?
How much is a room?
Сколько стоит | *skol*'·ka *sto*·it *no*·mer?
номер?

money
деньги | *den*'gi
currency exchange
обмен валюты | ab·*men* val·*yu*·ty
shop
магазин | ma·ga·*zin*
bookshop
книжный магазин | *knizh*·nyy ma·ga·*zin*
market
рынок | *ry*·nak
pharmacy
аптека | ap·*te*·ka
hotel
гостиница | gas·*ti*·ni·tsa
square/plaza
площадь (пл.) | *plo*·shchat'
street
улица (ул.) | *u*·li·tsa
toilet
туалет | tua·*let*

TIME & DAYS
Dates are given as day-month-year, with the month usually in Roman numerals. Days of the week are often represented by numbers in timetables; Monday is 1.

When? | Когда? | kag·*da*?
today | сегодня | si·*vod*·nya
tomorrow | завтра | *zaf*·tra
yesterday | вчера | vchi·*ra*

Monday | понедельник | pa·ni·*del*'nik
Tuesday | вторник | *ftor*·nik
Wednesday | среда | sri·*da*
Thursday | четверг | chit·*verk*

Friday	пятница	*pyat*·ni·tsa
Saturday	суббота	su·*bo*·ta
Sunday	воскресенье	vas·kri·*sen*'e

TRANSPORT

If you want to get off a *marshrutka* (minibus), just say *astanavitye pazhalsta*.

Where is ...?
  Где ...?   gde ...?
When does it leave?
  Когда   kag·da at·prav·*lya*·et·sya?
  отправляется?
What town is this?
  Какой этот город?   ka·*koy* e·ta *go*·rat?

airport
  аэропорт   ae·ra·*port*
bus
  автобус   af·*to*·bus
railway station
  железно дорожный   zhi·lez·na·da·*rozh*·nyy
  (ж.д.) вокзал   vag·*zal*
train
  поезд   *poy*·ezt

ARMENIAN

Armenian is an Indo-European language with heavy influences from Persian evident in its vocabulary. There are two main dialects: western and eastern. The latter is the variety you'll encounter in Armenia today.

The Armenian script and alphabet were created by Mesrop Mashtots in the early 5th century for the principal purpose of religious translation. The written language at that time was known as *grabar* (Classical Armenian), and it remained the literary form until modern Armenian literature came to the fore in the 19th century. This newer variety (Modern Standard) was a much more faithful representation of the spoken language. Two letters were added to Mashtots' original alphabet in the 12th century, one to represent changes undergone in the sound system of the language over many centuries, the other to cover the 'f' sound found in loan words.

Armenia has several distinct dialects. The standard eastern Armenian is based on the variety spoken in Ashtarak, close to Yerevan. People from Lori *marz* have a slower, more musical accent, while speakers from

THE ARMENIAN ALPHABET

Armenian	Roman	Pronunciation
Ա ա	a	as in 'hat'
Բ բ	b	as in 'bet'
Գ գ	g	as in 'get'
Դ դ	d	as in 'do'
Ե ե	ye-/-e-	as the 'ye' or 'e' in 'yet'
Զ զ	z	as in 'zoo'
Է է	e	long, as in 'there'
Ը ը	e	neutral vowel; as the 'a' in 'ago'
Թ թ	t	as in 'tip'
Ժ ժ	zh	as the 's' in 'measure'
Ի ի	ee	as in 'meet'
Լ լ	l	as in 'let'
Խ խ	kh	as 'ch' in Scottish 'loch'
Ծ ծ	ts	as in 'bits'
Կ կ	k	as in 'kit'
Հ հ	h	as in 'here'
Ձ ձ	dz	as in 'adze'
Ղ ղ	gh	as French 'r'
Ճ ճ	ch	as in 'each'
Մ մ	m	as in 'met'
Յ յ	y	as in 'yet'
Ն ն	n	as in 'no'
Շ շ	sh	as in 'shoe'
Ո ո	vo-/-o-	as in 'vote'
Չ չ	ch	as in 'chair'
Պ պ	p	as in 'pet'
Ջ ջ	j	as in 'judge'
Ռ ռ	r	a rolled 'r'
Ս ս	s	as in 'sit'
Վ վ	v	as in 'van'
Տ տ	t	as in 'ten'
Ր ր	r	as in 'run'
Ց g	ts	as in 'tsar'
Ու ու	u	as in 'rule'
Փ փ	p	as in 'pit'
Ք ք	k	similar to the 'c' in 'cat'
Օ o	o	long, as in 'wore'
Ֆ ֆ	f	as in 'fit'

The original 36 letters also have a numerical value, meaning any number can be represented using combinations of letters. Ա (**a**) to Թ (**t**) is 1 to 9, Ժ (**zh**) to Ղ (**gh**) is 10 to 90, Ճ (**ch**) to Ջ (**j**) is 100 to 900, and Ռ (**r**) to Ք (**k**) is 1000 to 9000.

Gegarkunik and Karabakh display a particularly strong local accent that can be very difficult for outsiders to understand, and vocabulary that is sometimes even unique to one valley. Armenian has many loan words and phrases borrowed from Russian, Turkish, French and even Hindi.

CONVERSATION & USEFUL PHRASES

Hello.	barev dzez (polite)
	barev (informal)
Good morning.	baree luees
Good evening.	baree yereko
Goodbye.	tsetesutyun (polite)
	hajogh (informal)
See you later.	arayzh'm
Goodbye, good luck.	hajoghutyun
Yes.	ayo (polite)
	ha (informal)
No.	voch (polite)
	che (informal)
Please.	khuntrem
Thank you.	shnorhakal em/
	shnorhakalutyun/merci
	(French, commonly used)
No problem.	problem cheeka
How are you?	vonts ek? (polite)
	vonts es? (informal)
I'm fine, thank you.	lav em shnorhakalutyun
OK/So-so.	vocheench
And you?	eesk' duk?
(very) good	(shat) lav
(very) bad	(shat) vat
I'm tired.	hoknats em
I'm sick.	heevand em
What's your name?	anunut eench eh?
My name is ...	anuns ... e
I'm from ...	yes ... its em
Do you speak English/	khosum es angleren/hayeren?
Armenian?	
A little.	mee keech
I understand.	haskanum em
I don't understand.	chem haskanum
Please speak more	khuntrem em dandagh khosek
slowly.	
I	yes
you	duk (polite, plural)
	du (informal)
I want ...	uzum em ...
I don't want ...	chem uzum ...
I don't know ...	chem eemanum ...

NUMBERS

1	mek
2	yerku
3	yerek
4	chors
5	heeng
6	vets
7	yot
8	ut
9	eenuh
10	tas
20	kuhsan
30	yeresun
40	karasun
50	heesun
60	vatsun
70	yotanasun
80	utsun
90	eeneesun
100	hayrur
200	yerku hayrur
1000	hazar
2000	yerku hazar
1,000,000	mek meelyon

SHOPPING & SERVICES

bank	bank
castle	berd
chemist/pharmacy	deghatun/apteka
church	yegeghetsee
city centre	kentron
closed	pak
currency exchange	dramee bokhanagum
doctor	bjheeshk
guesthouse	panseeonat
hospital	heevandanots
hotel	hyuranots
market	shuka
open	bats
police	vosteegan
post office	post
shop	khanut
stamp	namakaneesh
telephone	herakhos
toilet	zugaran
Do you have a room?	unek senyak?
How much?	eench arjhey?
cheap	ezhan
expensive	tang
good	lav
bad	vat
Where is the toilet?	vortegh e zugarane?

TIME & DATES

When?	yerp?
today	aysor
tomorrow	vaghe
yesterday	yerek
Monday	yerkushaptee
Tuesday	yerekshaptee
Wednesday	chorekshaptee
Thursday	heengshaptee
Friday	urpat
Saturday	shapat
Sunday	keerakee

LANGUAGE

January	*hunvar*
February	*petrvar*
March	*mart*
April	*apreel*
May	*mayees*
June	*hunees*
July	*hulees*
August	*okostos*
September	*september*
October	*hoktember*
November	*noyember*
December	*dektember*

TRANSPORT

When does ... leave?	*yerp jampa gelle ...?*
When does ... arrive?	*yerp gee hasne ...?*
every day	*amen or*
except	*patzee*
cancelled	*hedadzkvadz*
airport	*otanavakayan*
bus	*avtobus*
bus station/stop	*avtokayan/gankar*
car	*mekena*
minibus	*marshrutny/marshrutka*
petrol	*petrol/benzeen*
plane	*eenknateer/otanov*
taxi	*taksee*
ticket	*doms*
Stop!	*ganknee!/getseer!*
Where?	*ur/vortegh?*
here	*aystaeegh*
left	*dzakh*
right	*ach*

AZERI

The Azeri language (known as *azərbaycanca* or *azərbaycan dili* in the language itself) is a member of the Turkic language family, and shares its grammar and much of its vocabulary with Turkish; some knowledge of Turkish is very useful in Azerbaijan.

Azeri was originally written in a modified Arabic script, but this was replaced by a Latin alphabet (similar to the Turkish alphabet) during the country's first period of independence in 1918–20. The Russian Cyrillic alphabet was imposed in 1939 and prevailed during the reign of the Soviets, but in 1991 a modern Azeri Latin alphabet was reintroduced.

THE AZERI ALPHABET

Azeri	Roman	Pronunciation
A a	a	long, as in 'far'
B b	b	as in 'bit'
C c	c	as the 'j' in 'jazz'
Ç ç	ch	as in 'chase'
D d	d	as in 'duck'
E e	e	as in 'bet'
Ə ə	a	short, as in 'apple'
F f	f	as in 'far'
G g	g	like the 'gy' in 'Magyar'
Ğ ğ	gh	a soft growl from the back of throat (like French 'r')
H h	h	as in 'here'
X x	kh	as the 'ch' in Scottish 'loch'
I ı	ı	neutral vowel; as the 'a' in 'ago'
İ i	i	as in 'police'
J j	zh	as the 's' in 'leisure'
K k	k	as in 'kit'
Q q	q	hard 'g' as in 'get'
L l	l	as in 'let'
M m	m	as in 'met'
N n	n	as in 'net'
O o	o	short as in 'got'
Ö ö	er	as in 'her', with no 'r' sound
P p	p	as in 'pet'
R r	r	a rolled 'r'
S s	s	as in 'see'
Ş ş	sh	as in 'shore'
T t	t	as in 'toe'
U u	u	as in 'chute'
Ü ü	ew	as in 'pew'
V v	v	as in 'van'
Y y	y	as in 'yet'
Z z	z	as in 'zoo'

Words in Azeri are usually lightly stressed on the last syllable. Note that in many parts of the country, the hard **k** is pronounced more like a 'ch', so that Bakı sounds like 'ba-chuh' and Şəki becomes 'sha-chee'.

CONVERSATION & USEFUL PHRASES

Hello.	*Salam aleykum.*
Good morning.	*Sabahın xeyir.*
Good evening.	*Axşamın xeyir.*
Good night.	*Gecan xeyra qalsın.*
Goodbye.	*Sağ ol.*
How are you?	*Necasan?*
Yes.	*Bali.* (polite)
	Ha. (informal)
No.	*Xeyr/Yox.*
Please.	*Lutfan.*

Thank you.	Taşakkur ediram.
Thank you very much.	Çox sağ ol.
Excuse me.	Bağışlayın.
Sorry.	Bağışla.
It doesn't matter.	Bir şey deyil.
Cheers! (toasting)	Deyilan sağğvlığa!
Fine! That's great!	Yaxşıdır!
Do you speak English/ French/German?	Siz ingilizca/fransızca/ almanca danışırsınızmı?
I don't speak Azeri.	Mən azərbaycan dili danışmıram.
I don't understand.	Mən anlamıram.
There is.	Var.
There isn't.	Yox.
Where?	Harada?
Who?	Kim?
What?	Na?
Why?	Niya?
How?	Neca?
How much/many?	Na qadar?
cheap	ucuz
expensive	baha
good	yaxşı
bad	pis

NUMBERS

0	sıfr
1	bir
2	iki
3	uç
4	dord
5	beş
6	altı
7	yeddi
8	sakkiz
9	doqquz
10	on
11	on bir
12	on iki
13	on uç
20	iyirmi
30	otuz
40	qirx
50	alli
60	altmış
70	yetmiş
80	saksan
90	doxsan
100	yuz
105	yuz beş
200	iki yuz
349	uç yuz qırx doqquz
1000	min
50000	alli min
1,000,000	bir milyon

SHOPPING & SERVICES

ambulance	tacili yardım maşını
bank	bank
castle	qala
chemist/pharmacy	aptek
church	kilsa
city centre	sahar markazi
closed	bağlı
cold	soyuq
currency exchange	dayişma
doctor	hakim
guest	qonaq
hospital	xastaxana
hot	isti
hotel	mehmanxana
market	bazar
open	açıq
post office	poçt
room	otaq
shop	dukan, mağaza
stamp	marka
telephone	telefon
toilet	tualet

TIME & DATES

When?	Na vaxt?
today	bugun
tomorrow	sabah
yesterday	dunan
Monday	bazar ertasi or birinci
Tuesday	çarşanba axşamı or ikinci
Wednesday	çarşanba/uçuncu
Thursday	cuma axşamı or dorduncu
Friday	cuma/beşinci
Saturday	şanba/altıncı
Sunday	bazar/yeddinci
January	yanvar
February	fevral
March	mart
April	aprel
May	may
June	iyun
July	iyul
August	avqust
September	sentyabr
October	oktyabr
November	noyabr
December	dekabr

TRANSPORT

When does ... leave?	... na zaman qalxir?
When does ... arrive?	... na zaman galir?

every day	*har gun*
except	*başqa*
cancelled	*saxlanılıb*

airport	*hava liman*
avenue	*prospekti*
boat	*gami*
bus	*avtobus*
bus station	*avtovağzal*
bus stop	*avtobus dayanacağı*
car	*maşın, avtomobil*
lane/alley	*xiyabanı*
minibus	*mikroavtobus/marshrutka*
petrol	*benzin*
plane	*tayyara*
port	*liman*
square	*meydanı*
Stop!	*saxla!*
street	*küçəsi*
taxi	*taksi*
ticket	*bilet*
train	*qatar*
train station	*damir yolu stansiyası*

GEORGIAN

Georgian *(kartuli)* belongs to the Kartvelian language family, which is related to the Caucasian languages – it has no linguistic connection to any other known language groups and continues to fascinate linguists. There are three other Kartvelian languages: Svan *(svanuri)*, spoken in the mountains of Svaneti, Mingrelian *(megruli)*, spoken in Samegrelo, and Laz *(zanur-chanuri)*, spoken by the Laz people who live in northeastern Turkey. Georgian is an ancient language with its own cursive script. There are some loan words from other languages which you'll recognise, but generally the vocabulary is very specific to Georgian.

Most Georgians also speak Russian, and aren't reluctant to converse in it. The younger generation is increasingly taking up English as a second or third language, particularly in Tbilisi. However, outside the capital you'll almost certainly need a few phrases of Georgian to help you get around, and any attempt you make to speak the language, however halting, will be greatly appreciated by the Georgians you meet.

Travelling around Georgia without some knowledge of the Georgian alphabet is really hard work. Anyone wanting to make the most of their time should try and learn some of the main letters, if only to identify bus destinations and street names – it's not as daunting as it looks. There are no capital letters, and each of the 33 letters of the modern alphabet has a one-to-one sound relationship.

THE GEORGIAN ALPHABET

Georgian	Roman	Pronunciation
ა	**a**	as in 'father'
ბ	**b**	as in 'bet'
გ	**g**	as in 'go'
დ	**d**	as in 'do'
ე	**e**	as in 'get'
ვ	**v**	as in 'van'
ზ	**z**	as in 'zoo'
თ	**t**	as in 'to'
ი	**i**	as in 'police'
კ	**k**	a 'k' pronounced very far back in the throat
ლ	**l**	as in 'let'
მ	**m**	as in 'met'
ნ	**n**	as in 'net'
ო	**o**	as in 'cot'
პ	**p**	as in 'tip' (with a stop on the outflow of air)
ჟ	**zh**	as the 's' in 'pleasure'
რ	**r**	as in 'rub', but rolled
ს	**s**	as in 'see'
ტ	**t**	as in 'sit' (with a stop on the outflow of air)
უ	**u**	as in 'put'
ფ	**p**	as in 'put'
ქ	**q**	a 'k' pronounced very far back in the throat
ღ	**gh**	as a French 'r'
ყ	**k**	as the 'ck' in 'lick' (with a stop on the outflow of air)
შ	**sh**	as in 'she'
ჩ	**ch**	as in 'chip'
ც	**ts**	as in 'tsar'
ძ	**dz**	as the 'ds' in 'beds'
წ	**ts**	as in 'its' (with a stop on the outflow of air)
ჭ	**ch**	as in 'each' (with a stop on the outflow of air)
ხ	**kh**	as in Scottish 'loch'
ჯ	**j**	as in 'judge'
ჰ	**h**	as in 'here'

Word stress in Georgian is very light and is usually on the first syllable.

CONVERSATION & USEFUL PHRASES

Hello.	*gamarjobat*
Good morning.	*dila mshvidobisa*
Good evening.	*saghamo mshvidobisa*
Good night.	*ghame mshvidobisa*
Goodbye.	*nakhvamdis*
Yes.	*diakh* (polite)
	ki (neutral)
	ho (informal)
No.	*ara*
Please.	*tu sheidzleba*
Thank you.	*madlobt*
Thank you very much.	*didi madloba*
How are you?	*rogora khart?*
Sorry.	*bodishi*
Excuse me.	*ukatsrovad*
It doesn't matter.	*ara ushavs*
Cheers! (toasting)	*gaumarjos!*
Do you speak English?	*inglisuri itsit?*
Do you speak French/ German?	*itsit pranguli/germanuli?*
I don't speak any Georgian.	*ar vitsi kartuli*
I don't understand.	*ar mesmis*
There is.	*aris*
There isn't.	*ar aris*
Where?	*sad?*
When?	*rodis?*
Who?	*vin?*
What?	*ra?*
How?	*rogor?*
Why?	*ratom?*

NUMBERS

1	*erti*
2	*ori*
3	*sami*
4	*otkhi*
5	*khuti*
6	*ekvsi*
7	*shvidi*
8	*rva*
9	*tskhra*
10	*ati*
11	*tertmeti*
12	*tormeti*
13	*tsameti*
14	*totkhmeti*
15	*tkhutmeti*
16	*tekvsmeti*
17	*chvidmeti*
18	*tvrameti*
19	*tskhrameti*
20	*otsi*
21	*otsdaerti*
22	*otsdaori*
30	*otsdaati*
31	*otsdatertmeti*
32	*otsdatormeti*
33	*otsdatsameti*
34	*otsdatotkhmeti*
35	*otsdatkhumeti*
36	*otsdatekvsmeti*
37	*otsdachvidmeti*
38	*otsdatvrameti*
39	*otsdatskhrameti*
40	*ormotsi*
41	*ormotsdaerti*
50	*ormotsdaati*
60	*samotsi*
70	*samotsdaati*
80	*otkhmotsi*
90	*otkhmotsdaati*
100	*asi*
1000	*atasi*

SHOPPING & SERVICES

ambulance	*sastsrapo dakhmarebis mankana*
bank	*banki*
break (eg for lunch)	*tsakhemseba*
castle	*tsikhe*
chemist/pharmacy	*aptiaki*
church	*eklesia*
city centre	*kalakis tsentri*
closed	*daketilia*
doctor	*ekimi*
guest	*stumari*
hospital	*saavadmqopo*
hotel	*sastumro*
market	*bazari/bazroba*
open	*ghiaa*
police	*politsia/militsia*
post office	*posta*
room	*otakhi*
shop	*maghazia*
stamp	*marka*
telephone	*teleponi*
toilet	*tualeti*
How much/many?	*ramdeni?*
good	*kargi*
bad	*tsudi*
cheap	*iapi*
expensive	*dzviri*

TIME & DATES

today	*dghes*
tomorrow	*khval*
day after tomorrow	*zeg*

in 3 days time	*mazeg*
yesterday	*gushin*
day before yesterday	*gushin tsin*
Sunday	*kvira*
Monday	*orshabati*
Tuesday	*samshabati*
Wednesday	*otkhshabati*
Thursday	*khutshabati*
Friday	*paraskevi*
Saturday	*shabati*
January	*ianvari*
February	*tebervali*
March	*marti*
April	*aprili*
May	*maisi*
June	*ivnisi*
July	*ivlisi*
August	*agvisto*
September	*sektemberi*
October	*oktomberi*
November	*noemberi*
December	*dekemberi*

TRANSPORT

When does it leave?	*rodis midis/gadis?*
When does it arrive?	*rodis modis/chamodis?*
every day	*qovel dghe*
except	*garda*
cancelled	*gaukmda*
airport	*aeroporti*
avenue	*gamziri*
boat	*gemi*
bus	*avtobusi/troleibusi*
bus station	*avtosadguri*
bus stop	*gachereba*
car	*mankana*
minibus taxi	*marshrutka*
petrol	*benzini*
plane	*tvitmprinavi*
port	*porti*
road/way	*gza*
square	*moedani*
Stop here!	*gaacheret!*
taxi	*taksi*
ticket	*bileti*
train	*matarebeli*
train station	*(rkinigzis) sadguri*

LANGUAGE

Glossary

You may encounter some of the following words during your time in Georgia (Geo), Armenia (Arm) and Azerbaijan (Az). Some Russian (Rus) and Turkish (Tur) words have been widely adopted in the Caucasus.

abour (Arm) – soup
ajika (Geo) – chilli paste
alaverdi (Geo) – person appointed by the toastmaster at a *supra* to elaborate on the toast
Amenaprkich (Arm) – All Saviours
aptek/apteka/aptiaqi (Az/Rus & Arm/Geo) – pharmacy
Arakelots (Arm) – the Apostles
ARF – Armenian Revolutionary Federation; the Dashnaks
aşig (ashug) (Az) – itinerant musician
Astvatsatsin (Arm) – Holy Mother of God
aviakassa – shop or window selling air tickets
avtokayan/avtovağzal (Arm/Az) – bus station

baklava – honeyed nut pastry
baliq (Az) – fish, usually sturgeon, often grilled
basturma (Arm) – cured beef in ground red pepper
berd (Arm) – fortress
bulvar (Az) – boulevard

caravanserai – historic travellers inn
Catholicos – patriarch of the Armenian or Georgian churches
çay (Az) – tea
çayxana (Az) – teahouse
chacha – powerful homemade liquor
chakapuli (Geo) – lamb and plums in herb sauce
churchkhela (Geo) – string of nuts coated in a sort of caramel made from grape juice and flour
chvishdari (Geo) – Svanetian dish of cheese cooked inside maize bread
CIS – Commonwealth of Independent States; the loose political and economic alliance of most former member republics of the USSR (except the Baltic states)
çörək (Az) – bread

dacha (Rus) – country holiday cottage or bungalow
darbazi (Geo) – traditional home design with the roof tapering up to a central hole
doğrama (Az) – cold soup made with sour milk, potato, onion and cucumber
dolma (Arm, Az) – vine leaves with a rice filling
domik (Rus) – hut or modest bungalow accommodation

dram – Armenian unit of currency
duduk (Arm) – traditional reed instrument; also *tutak* (Az)
dzor (Arm) – gorge

elektrichka (Rus) – local train service linking a city and its suburbs or nearby towns, or groups of adjacent towns
eristavi (Geo) – duke

gavit (Arm) – entrance hall of a church
ghomi (Geo) – maize porridge
glasnost (Rus) – openness

halva (Az) – various sweet pastries, often containing nuts
hraparak (Arm) – square

IDP – internally displaced person
Intourist (Rus) – Soviet-era government tourist organisation
ishkhan (Arm) – trout from Lake Sevan
istirahət zonası (Az) – rural bungalow resort

jeton (Az) – token, eg for old-style payphones
jvari (Geo) – religious cross; spiritual site in mountain regions

kamança (Az) – stringed musical instrument
kartuli – Georgian language
Kartvelebi – Georgian people
kassa (Rus) – cash desk or ticket booth
katoghike (Arm) – cathedral
khachapuri (Geo) – savoury bread or pastry, usually with a cheese filling
khamaju (Arm) – meat pie
khash/khashi (Arm/Geo) – garlic and tripe soup
khashlama (Arm) – lamb or beef stew with potato
khatchkar (Arm) – medieval carved headstone
khevi (Geo) – gorge
khidi (Geo) – bridge
khinkali (Geo) – spicy meat dumpling
khoravats (Arm) – barbecued food
kişi (Az) – men (hence 'K' marks men's toilets)
köfte/kyufta/küftə (Tur/Arm/Az) – minced beef meatballs with onion and spices
körpü (Az) – bridge
kubdari (Geo) – spicy Svanetian meat pie
küçəsi (Az) – street
kupe/kupeyny (Rus) – 2nd-class compartment accommodation on trains
kvas (Rus) – beverage made from fermented rye bread

lahmacun/lahmajoon (Tur/Arm) – small lamb and herb pizzas
lari – Georgian unit of currency
lavash/lavaş (Arm/Az) – thin bread
lәvәngi (Az) – casserole of chicken stuffed with walnuts and herbs
lobio/lobiya/lobya (Geo/Rus/Az) – beans, often with herbs and spices
luks (Rus) – deluxe; used to refer to hotel suites and 1st-class accommodation on trains

Manat – Azerbaijani unit of currency
marani (Geo) – wine cellar
marshrutka (Rus) – public minivan transport
marz (Arm) – region, province
marz petaran (Arm) – provincial government building
matagh (Arm) – animal sacrifice
matenadaran (Arm) – library
matsoni (Geo) – yogurt drink
mayrughi (Arm) – highway
mehmanxana (Az) – hotel
merikipe (Geo) – man who pours wine at a *supra*
meydan (Az) – square
moedani (Geo) – square
most (Rus) – bridge
mtsvadi (Geo) – shish kebab, shashlyk
muğam (Az) – traditional musical style
mushuri (Geo) – working songs
muzhskoy (Rus) – men's toilet

nagorny (Rus) – mountainous
nard/nardi (Az/Arm) – backgammon-like board game

obshchy (Rus) – general-seating class (unreserved) on trains
oghee (Arm) – fruit vodkas; also called *vatsun* or *aragh*
OSCE – Organisation for Security and Co-operation in Europe
OVIR – visa and registration department

paneer/pendir (Arm/Az) – cheese
paxlava (Az) – honeyed nut pastry
perestroika (Rus) – restructuring
pir (Az) – shrine or holy place
piti (Az) – soupy meat stew with chickpeas and saffron
pivo (Rus) – beer
pkhali (Geo) – spinach or beetroot paste with walnuts and garlic
platskart/platskartny (Rus) – open-bunk accommodation on trains
ploshchad (Rus) – square
plov – rice dish
poghota/prospekti (Arm/Az) – avenue
poghots (Arm) – street

qadım (Az) – woman (hence 'Q' marks women's toilets)
qala, qalasi (Az) – castle or fortress

qəpiq – Azerbaijani unit of currency
qucha (Geo) – street
qutab (Az) – stuffed pancake

rabiz (Rus) – Armenian workers' culture, party music
rtveli (Geo) – grape harvest

sagalobeli (Geo) – church songs
sagmiro (Geo) – epic songs
sakhachapure (Geo) – café serving *khachapuri*
sakhinkle (Geo) – café serving *khinkali*
satrap – Persian provincial governor
satrpialo (Geo) – love songs
satsivi (Geo) – cold turkey or chicken in walnut sauce
saxlama kamera (Az) – left luggage room(s)
şəbəkə (Az) – stained-glass windows with intricately carved wooden frames
shashlyk – shish kebab
Shirvan – old Azerbaijani unit of currency, equal to two Manat
shkmeruli (Geo) – chicken in garlic sauce
shuka (Arm) – market
soorch (Arm) – coffee
spalny vagon/SV (Rus) – two-berth sleeping compartment on train
suchush (Arm) – plum and walnut sweet
sulguni (Geo) – smoked cheese from Samegrelo
supra (Geo) – dinner party; literally means 'tablecloth'
supruli (Geo) – songs for the table
surp (Arm) – holy, saint

tabouleh (Arm) – diced green salad with semolina
tamada (Geo) – toastmaster at a *supra*
tan (Arm) – yogurt
tetri – Georgian unit of currency (100 tetri equals one *lari*)
tikə kəbab (Az) – shish kebab; commonly called *shashlyk*
tqemali (Geo) – wild plum, wild plum sauce
tsikhe (Geo) – fortified place
TsUM (Rus) – Tsentralny universalny magazin; central department store; also known as MUM or Univermaq in Azeri
tufa – volcanic stone famous to Armenia
tur – large, endangered Caucasian ibex
tutak (Az) – traditional reed instrument; also *duduk* (Arm)

ulitsa (Rus) – street

vank (Arm) – monastery
virap (Arm) – well
vishap (Arm) – carved dragon stone

xaş (Az) – garlic and tripe soup

yeməkxana (Az) – food house, cheap eatery

zhensky (Rus) – women's toilets

The Authors

JOHN NOBLE
Coordinating Author, Georgia

John, from the UK, first explored the Caucasus region in 1990, when it was still in the USSR and he was writing Lonely Planet's first (and only) guide to that now-defunct country. Arriving in Georgia from Russia was, even then, like taking a big breath of fresh air. Thrilled by the atmosphere of freedom in Georgia and its people's warmth, he has longed to return ever since, a dream that was finally realised when he was asked to cover Georgia for this book. He found Georgia as beautiful, hospitable and unpredictable as ever, and its manifold attractions wonderfully accessible. John has written on many ex-Soviet states for Lonely Planet, but none quite like Georgia.

MICHAEL KOHN
Armenia, Nagorno-Karabakh

Michael's first view of the Caucasus was from the deck of a trans-Caspian ferry, marooned off the coast of Baku after a long and troubled crossing from Turkmenistan in 2006. Intrigued by its politics and intoxicated by its alcohol, Michael returned to the region a year later to update the Armenia and Nagorno-Karabakh chapters of this book. Michael's work in journalism began with a reporting gig in Mongolia in the late '90s, and since then he has been digging up stories and writing travel guides in various former Soviet republics. He has worked on 10 Lonely Planet guides, including *Central Asia* and *Mongolia*. When not on the road he calls northern California home; he can be found virtually at www.michaelkohn.us.

DANIELLE SYSTERMANS
Azerbaijan

Born in Belgium, Dani has spent the last two decades travelling the globe, both modestly for pleasure and more luxuriously in the world of international finance. She first arrived in Baku back in 1995 with an improbable mission: to explain the 'new idea' of credit cards to an audience of sceptical ex-Soviets. Judging from all the ATMs in town these days she was quite successful. Friendships and an unquenchable traveller-curiosity keep bringing her back to the region in a series of visits that have been as stormy as any love affair, and just as compulsive.

LONELY PLANET AUTHORS

Why is our travel information the best in the world? It's simple: our authors are independent, dedicated travellers. They don't research using just the internet or phone, and they don't take freebies in exchange for positive coverage. They travel widely, to all the popular spots and off the beaten track. They personally visit thousands of hotels, restaurants, cafés, bars, galleries, palaces, museums and more – and they take pride in getting all the details right, and telling it how it is. Think you can do it? Find out how at lonelyplanet.com.

Behind the Scenes

THIS BOOK

This 3rd edition of Lonely Planet's *Georgia, Armenia & Azerbaijan* was researched and written by John Noble, Michael Kohn and Danielle Systermans. The 2nd edition was revised by Richard Plunkett and Tom Masters. The 1st edition was written by Neil Wilson, Beth Potter, David Rowson and Keti Japaridze. This guidebook was commissioned in Lonely Planet's London office and was produced by the following:

Commissioning Editor Will Gourlay
Coordinating Editor Penelope Goodes
Coordinating Cartographer Andy Rojas
Coordinating Layout Designer Pablo Gastar
Managing Editor Imogen Bannister
Managing Cartographer Mark Griffiths
Managing Layout Designer Adam McCrow
Assisting Editors Sarah Bailey, David Carroll, Gennifer Ciavarra, Chris Girdler, Anne Mulvaney, Sally O'Brien
Assisting Cartographers Mick Garrett, Tadhgh Knaggs, Joanne Luke, Sam Sayer, Mandy Sierp, Lyndell Stringer
Cover Image Researcher Will Gourlay
Project Manager Glenn van der Knijff
Language Content Coordinator Quentin Frayne

Thanks to Ryan Evans, Justin Flynn, Tony Ghazarian, James Hardy, Abraham Haroutunian, Jim Hsu, Indra Kilfoyle, Yvonne Kirk, Lisa Knights, Chris Lee Ack, Adriana Mammarella, Wayne Murphy, Naomi Parker, Trent Paton, Averil Robertson, Wibowo Rusli, Cara Smith, Celia Wood

THANKS
JOHN NOBLE

Extraspecial thanks to fellow authors Dani Systermans and Michael Kohn and commissioning editor Will Gourlay for their enthusiasm, assistance, professionalism and great work; and to all at Dodo's Homestay, Mark Rowlatt (life and soul of homestays from Mestia to Yerevan) and Ia Tabagari. Thank you also to all the other Georgians, travellers and expats who helped out in so many ways, notably Anthony Schierman and his Megobrebs colleagues, George Kalandadze, Steffen Schülein, Natia Muladze, Lino and Gioia, Tamuna in Mestia, Nick Erkomaishvili, Eka Chvritidze and family, Giga and Maia Zulmatashvili, Bakur Lashkurava, Alan Lansdowne, Pamela Cardwell and Ohad Guetta.

MICHAEL KOHN

Thanks to Will Gourlay for packing me off to Hayastan, and fellow scribes John and Dani for all the heady interemail debate. In Armenia, a special thank you to Raffi Kojian, creator of www.armeniapedia.org, who provided insight on everything from Aragats to Zaur. Big thanks also to Syuzanna Azoyan at the Armenian Tourist Development Agency, and

---

THE LONELY PLANET STORY

Fresh from an epic journey across Europe, Asia and Australia in 1972, Tony and Maureen Wheeler sat at their kitchen table stapling together notes. The first Lonely Planet guidebook, *Across Asia on the Cheap,* was born.

Travellers snapped up the guides. Inspired by their success, the Wheelers began publishing books to Southeast Asia, India and beyond. Demand was prodigious, and the Wheelers expanded the business rapidly to keep up. Over the years, Lonely Planet extended its coverage to every country and into the virtual world via lonelyplanet.com and the Thorn Tree message board.

As Lonely Planet became a globally loved brand, Tony and Maureen received several offers for the company. But it wasn't until 2007 that they found a partner whom they trusted to remain true to the company's principles of travelling widely, treading lightly and giving sustainably. In October of that year, BBC Worldwide acquired a 75% share in the company, pledging to uphold Lonely Planet's commitment to independent travel, trustworthy advice and editorial independence.

Today, Lonely Planet has offices in Melbourne, London and Oakland, with over 500 staff members and 300 authors. Tony and Maureen are still actively involved with Lonely Planet. They're travelling more often than ever, and they're devoting their spare time to charitable projects. And the company is still driven by the philosophy of *Across Asia on the Cheap*: 'All you've got to do is decide to go and the hardest part is over. So go!'

all her wonderful staff, including Artyom and Gohar, and to Alan and Wendy Saffrey for hospitality in Yerevan. I would have been lost most of the time were it not for Armenia's great gang of Peace Corps volunteers. Special thanks to Robert (Sevan), Penny (Kapan), Elizabeth (Gyumri), Gary (Davit Bek), Patti (Yeghegandzor), Colleen (Tatev), Sarah (Kapan), Ben (Jermuk), Anita (Yeghegnadzor), Betty (Sisian), Rudd (Ijevan), Heather (Stepanavan) and Will (Kapan). Thanks also to fellow travellers Elaine (UK) and David (Australia). Best of luck to you all. In Nagorno-Karabakh, thanks to the folks at the Ella and Hamlet Guesthouse and to Armen and Saro, both in Shushi. At home, thanks as always to Baigalmaa.

DANIELLE SYSTERMANS

First and foremost I owe a great debt of gratitude to my husband, Mark, whose abiding love for and interest in Azerbaijan have proved unstoppably infectious. Deepest thanks too to the charming Ibrahimova family who have provided such perfect hospitality, care and insight over many years. And thank you to Will Gourlay and the team at Lonely Planet for sending me on this incredible adventure in the first place. For pure inspiration, I must recognise Fargana and Alim Qasimov, the Novrusli brothers and of course Aziza, whose talent and passion underline all that's great in this fabulous country.

On the road, so many people have helped me that it seems unfair to single out individuals. Thank you all! And thank you to those police who decided against arresting me en route or, at least, let me go without unduly long interrogations.

OUR READERS

Many thanks to the travellers who used the last edition and wrote to us with helpful hints, useful advice and interesting anecdotes:

Anar Abbas, Gurbanali Alakbarov, Peter Arlidge, Kestas Azubalis, Amira Bar, Sandy Bardsley, Jan Bernigeroth, Romesh Bhattacharji, Matthew Boris, David Brower, Andreas Bucher, Niall & Alison Campbell, John Cochrane, Rod Dalmaine, Uwe Danapel, John Deacon, Christopher Deel, Bridgett Dekrout, Eric Delaet, Tim Dellabella, Petr Drbohlav, Carolyn Hardin Engelhardt, George Everest, Éliane Fournier, Elina Galperin, Howard Gethin, Katia Gilaberte, Suzy Gillett, Ann Iren Glimsdal, Irene Grootendorst, Martin Gruner, Nargiz Gurbanova, Johan Dittrich Hallberg, Kristofer Harrison, Ira Hartmann, David Hill, Curran Hughes, Rok Jarc, Erik Jelinek, Jacob Hoejgaard Jensen, Maryam Karim, Mario Kempf, Austin Kilroy, Leylli Knur, Hans Kollmann, Veslemoy Kvalen, Tom De Laat, Anthony Legg, Marie Lepoutre, Bert Leunis, Marius Lifvergren, Kenneth Linka, Natalia Lobanova, Jim Lum, Jorn Lund, Jacob Majarian, Dominik Malysa, Paolo Mari, Anselm Mattes,

SEND US YOUR FEEDBACK

We love to hear from travellers – your comments keep us on our toes and help make our books better. Our well-travelled team reads every word on what you loved or loathed about this book. Although we cannot reply individually to postal submissions, we always guarantee that your feedback goes straight to the appropriate authors, in time for the next edition. Each person who sends us information is thanked in the next edition – and the most useful submissions are rewarded with a free book.

To send us your updates – and find out about Lonely Planet events, newsletters and travel news – visit our award-winning website: **www.lonelyplanet.com/contact**.

Note: we may edit, reproduce and incorporate your comments in Lonely Planet products such as guidebooks, websites and digital products, so let us know if you don't want your comments reproduced or your name acknowledged. For a copy of our privacy policy visit www.lonelyplanet.com/privacy.

Kevin Mccarroll, Christopher Mcdonald, David Meladze, Chinara Mirzayeva, Anita Montvajszki, Annemorin Morin, Marc Mounie, Melissa Mullan, Steve Newcomer, Marc Noguera, Christopher Ossowski, Till Paul, Barry Pell, Simonetta Piergiorgio, Dmitriy Podgorniy, Marek Porzycki, Eddie Racuobian, Patrick Raftis, Eddie Rakoubian, Timothy Reilly, Andoni Rodelgo, Juliana Rodriguez, Anna Rosenquist, Hans Rossel, Uri & Neta Wexler Sal-Man, Micha Scherbaum, Philip Schmidt, Thomas Schmidt, Paul Schmidtberger, Patrik Shirak, Peter Skalkos, Adam Sowan, Karsten Staehr, Anna De Stefano, Karin Steinmetzer, Hein Tolboom, Philippe Tranchant, Toshiyasu Tsuruhara, Ian Underwood, Gail Upperton, Jeannette van Eekelen, Paul Der van Laan, Francisco Vazquez, Jan Vybiral, Jason Weeks, Barbara Weiss, Jonas Wernli, Inger-Anne Becker Wold, Nick Wray, Monika Wucherpfennig, Andrew Young, Taleh Ziyadov.

ACKNOWLEDGMENTS

Many thanks to the following for the use of their content:

Globe on title page ©Mountain High Maps 1993 Digital Wisdom, Inc

Internal photographs: p183 (#3) Paul Carstairs/ Alamy; p186 (#1, #2), p187 (#4) Mark Elliott; p183 (#5) Will Gourlay; p181 Kim Karpeles/Alamy; p184 (#2), p185 (#3) Michael Kohn; p182 (#2), p183 (#4) John Noble; p187 (#3) Gokce Yildirim/Alamy. All other photographs by Lonely Planet Images, or as credited, and by Stephane Victor p182 (#1), p184 (#1), p188; Bill Wassman p185 (#4).

Index

INDEX

000 Map pages
000 Photograph pages

INDEX